THE GREEN GUIDE
France

Lavender fields, Plateau de Valensole © Andreas G. Karelias/Fotolia.com

MICHELIN

THE GREEN GUIDE **FRANCE**

Editor	Clive Hebard
Contributing Writers	Paul Shawcross, Glenn Harper, Terry Marsh
Production Manager	Natasha G. George
Cartography	Alain Baldet, Michèle Cana, Peter Wrenn
Photo Editor	Yoshimi Kanazawa
Proofreader	Janet McCann
Interior Design	Chris Bell
Layout	Michelin Apa Publications Ltd.
	Alison Rayner
Cover Design	Chris Bell, Christelle Le Déan
Cover Layout	Michelin Apa Publications Ltd.

Contact Us

The Green Guide
Michelin Travel and Lifestyle
One Parkway South
Greenville, SC 29615
USA
www.michelintravel.com

Michelin TravelPartner
Hannay House
39 Clarendon Road
Watford, Herts WD17 1JA
UK
✆ 01923 205240
www.ViaMichelin.com
travelpubsales@uk.michelin.com

Special Sales

For information regarding bulk sales,
customized editions and premium sales,
please contact our Customer Service
Departments:
USA   1-800-432-6277
UK   01923 205240
Canada   1-800-361-8236

HOW TO USE THIS GUIDE

PLANNING YOUR TRIP

The blue-tabbed PLANNING YOUR TRIP section at the front of the guide gives you **ideas for your trip** and **practical information** to organise it. You'll find tours, practical information, a host of outdoor activities, a calendar of events, information on shopping, sightseeing, children's activities and more.

INTRODUCTION

The orange-tabbed INTRODUCTION section explores France's **Nature**, geography and geology. The **History** section spans Megalithic culture through the Middle Ages to the present day. The **Art and Culture** section covers architecture, art, literature and music, while **France Today** delves into modern French lifestyle, people and cuisine.

DISCOVERING

The green-tabbed DISCOVERING section features Principal Sights by region, featuring the most interesting local **Sights**, **Walking Tours**, nearby **Excursions**, and detailed **Driving Tours**. Admission prices shown are normally for a single adult.

ADDRESSES

We've selected the best hotels, restaurants, cafés, shops, nightlife and entertainment to fit all budgets. See the Legend on the cover flap for an explanation of the price categories. See the back of the guide for an index of where to find hotels and restaurants.

Sidebars

Throughout the guide you will find blue, orange and green-coloured text boxes with lively anecdotes, detailed history and background information.

😊 A Bit of Advice 😊

Green advice boxes found in this guide contain practical tips and handy information relevant to your visit or to a sight in the Discovering section.

STAR RATINGS★★★

Michelin has given star ratings for more than 100 years. If you're pressed for time, we recommend you visit the ★★★, or ★★ sights first:

★★★ **Highly recommended**

★★ **Recommended**

★ **Interesting**

MAPS

- 🗺 Country map
- 🗺 Principal Sights map
- 🗺 Region maps
- 🗺 Maps for major cities and villages
- 🗺 Local tour maps

All maps in this guide are oriented north, unless otherwise indicated by a directional arrow. The term "Local Map" refers to a map within the chapter or Tourism Region. A complete list of the maps found in the guide appears at the back of this book.

© Taylor Richard/Sime/Photononstop

INTRODUCTION TO FRANCE

France Today   52
21st Century 52
Economy and Government. 52
Food and Drink 53

History   56
Time Line. 56

Art and Culture   66
A Survey of French Art 66

Nature   91
Topography 91

PLANNING YOUR TRIP

When and Where to Go   18
Seasons 18
Climate. 18
Weather Forecast 18
What to See and Do   19
Out and About. 19
Tours 21
Activities for Kids 21
The Islands of France. 22
Shopping. 23
Books 24
Films 25
Calendar of Events   26
Know Before You Go   30
Useful Websites. 30
Tourist Offices Abroad 30
Regional Tourist Offices 31
International Visitors. 32
Entry Requirements. 33
Customs Regulations 33
Health. 33
Accessibility 34
Getting There   34
By Plane 34
By Ship 34
By Coach/Bus. .35
By Car 35
By Train. 35
Getting Around   36
By Train. 36
By Car 36
Where to Stay and Eat   39
Where to Stay. .39
Where to Eat. 41
Useful Words and Phrases   41
Basic Information   44

DISCOVERING FRANCE

Alsace Lorraine Champagne   94
Metz 96
Verdun 99
Champ de Bataille de Verdun 100
Nancy 101
Toul 107
Strasbourg 108
Colmar 118
Riquewihr 122
Mulhouse. 125
Route des Crêtes. 127
Reims 128
Châlons-en-Champagne. 132
Monthermé. 133
Troyes 134
Provins 137

Atlantic Coast   138
Bordeaux 140
Arcachon 146
Angoulême. 147
Cognac. 149
La Rochelle 150
Rochefort. 154
Poitiers 155
Le Puy du Fou 159
Biarritz 160
St-Jean-de-Luz. 164
Dax 165
Pau. 166

Auvergne Rhône Valley   168
Lyon. 170
Vienne. 179
St-Étienne 180

CONTENTS

Le Puy-en-Velay 181
Clermont-Ferrand 185
Le Puy Mary 191
Vichy 193
Moulins 196

Brittany   198
Rennes 199
St-Malo 201
St-Brieuc 204
Lannion 206
St-Pol-de-Léon 207
Brest 209
Quimper 212
Lorient 215
Vannes 218
Belle-Île 222
Nantes 223

Burgundy Jura   226
Dijon 227
Beaune 233
Auxerre 240
Besançon 244
Lons-le-Saunier 248
Bourg-en-Bresse 249

Châteaux of the Loire   252
Angers 253
Saumur 260
Tours 264
Blois 270
Orléans 275

Corsica   278
Ajaccio 279
Bonifacio 282
Bastia 284

Dordogne Berry Limousin   286
Bourges 288
Limoges 293
Périgueux 296
Sarlat-la-Canéda 299
Rocamadour 303
Cahors 306

French Alps   310
Annecy 312
Évian-les-Bains .316
Chamonix-Mont-Blanc 318
Route des Grandes Alpes 321
Courchevel 327
Grenoble 329
Briançon 332
Grand Canyon du Verdon 333

French Riviera   336
Nice 337
Principauté de Monaco 343

Menton 347
Route Napoléon 349
Cannes 352
St-Tropez 356
Toulon 358

Languedoc-Roussillon
Tarn Gorges   360
Montpellier 362
Gorges du Tarn 366
Conques 369
Albi 370
Toulouse 374
Lourdes 381
Carcassonne 387
Narbonne 392
Perpignan 394

Normandy   398
Rouen 399
Le Havre 405
Caen 409
Bayeux 414
Coutances 417
Alençon 420

Northern France and Paris   424
Lille 426
Calais 431
Boulogne-sur-Mer 436
Amiens 438
Arras 443
Paris 445
Château de Versailles 483
St-Germain-en-Laye 488
Compiègne 490
Laon 494
Senlis 495
Château de Chantilly 496
Parc Astérix 497
Disneyland Resort Paris 498
Château de Vaux-le-Vicomte 501
Fontainebleau 502
Chartres 505

Provence   510
Marseille 511
Aix-en-Provence 520
Arles 523
Les Baux-de-Provence 528
Nîmes 530
Avignon 534
Orange 541

Index 544
Maps and Plans 559
Map Legend 560

Welcome to France

There's a perfect side of France for every visitor to discover in this extraordinarily diverse country, from the flat plains of the Pas de Calais in the north to the majestic Alps and Pyrénées mountain ranges in the south; from a sleepy village *pétanque* game to the high fashion and buzzing cultural scene of Paris; splendid châteaux, stunning beaches, world-class skiing, justly famous food and wine – *la Belle France* offers months of memorable travel, wherever and whenever you decide to visit. *Bienvenue!*

ALSACE LORRAINE CHAMPAGNE *(pp94–137)*

Alsace has a very Germanic character and many of its towns and villages reflect this. To the west of the Vosges mountains is Lorraine, which, despite being part of Germany for a while, is more French. Further west is Champagne, well known for its sparkling wine, and to the north, the heavily wooded Ardennes region.

ATLANTIC COAST *(pp138–167)*

The Atlantic Coast region extends from the River Loire in the north to the mighty Pyrénées in the south. It includes most of Aquitaine and Poitou-Charentes – once the territory of the Dukes of Aquitaine – which, for many years, was held by the English.

AUVERGNE RHÔNE VALLEY *(pp168–197)*

The unique volcanic landscape of the Massif Central is at the centre of the Auvergne region and the mountains vary from classic volcanic cones to more eroded rugged shapes. To the east, the land slopes down to the Rhône Valley, where the rivers Rhône and Saône converge on their journey south towards the great city of Lyon and eventually the Mediterranean Sea.

BRITTANY *(pp198–225)*

This rugged Celtic peninsula in the northwest, with its indented coastline and islands battered by the Atlantic, narrow inlets and sandy bays, has a mysterious past, which is reflected in the many prehistoric remains scattered around the region, such as the menhirs at Carnac. The separate identity and culture of the Bretons make this a fascinating part of France.

BURGUNDY JURA *(pp226–251)*

Formerly a great dukedom, Burgundy is placed on the great trade route linking the north with the Mediterranean. Coupled with the proceeds of its viticulture, this led to great wealth which resulted in amazing buildings like the Hôtel-Dieu at Beaune. The Jura in the Franche-Comté Region to the east consists of forested uplands and pasture which produces such culinary delights as Vacherin and Comté cheeses.

CHÂTEAUX OF THE LOIRE *(pp252–277)*

Renowned for its magnificent Renaissance châteaux such as Chambord and Chenonceau, the Loire Valley in the Centre Region is also referred to as the "Garden of France" due to the cultivation of vines, flowers and horticultural crops. The many châteaux actually sit on the banks of the River Loire's tributaries, the Indre and the Cher, and date from the 16C onwards.

CORSICA *(pp278–285)*

Referred to by the ancient Greeks as "Kallisté", meaning "most beautiful", and by the French as *L'Île de Beauté*, this mountainous island certainly lives up to its name. Totally unspoilt, it has both Italian and French influences.

From the gulfs and ruggedness of the west coast to the promontory of the Cap Corse and the cliffs of Bonifacio, this is a truly exceptional place.

DORDOGNE BERRY LIMOUSIN
(pp286–309)

The Dordogne, or the Périgord, is very well known to visitors due to its agreeable climate, its impressive castles and cave systems, not to mention the meandering Dordogne river itself. The Berry and the Limousin to the north, on the other hand, are relatively undiscovered, and provide a great deal of interest, especially at Bourges (in Berry) and Limoges (in Limousin).

FRENCH ALPS *(pp310–335)*

In the southeast of France, stretching from the Mediterranean to Lac Léman (Lake Geneva), the Alps are beloved by winter sports fans, but they also provide dramatic and beautiful mountain landscapes to explore when the snows are confined to the highest peaks. There are National and Regional Parks, which reflect the richness of this environment and allow access to these amazing landscapes.

FRENCH RIVIERA *(pp336–359)*

The Côte d'Azur – or French Riviera – runs along the Mediterranean coastline of southeast France from Menton to Cassis. What started as a popular winter health resort in the late 18C continues to draw thousands of tourists each year. Resort towns here include Cannes, Beaulieu-sur-Mer and St-Tropez. You can't beat its 300 days of sunshine per year and holiday atmosphere.

LANGUEDOC-ROUSSILLON TARN GORGES *(pp360–397)*

Stretching in an arc from the Rhône Delta to the Pyrénées and characterised by vineyards and popular beaches, the Languedoc Roussillon is steeped in history from the Roman era to the medieval. The Gorges du Tarn (Tarn Gorges) to the north are cut into the Grand Causses, from which there are amazing views from the corniche roads.

NORMANDY *(pp398–423)*

Famous for its ciders, cheeses and calvados, the former dukedom of Normandy boasts elegant coastal resorts, while cows, orchards and hedgrows provide rural charm. Rouen's Gothic cathedral and the ruins of the abbey at Jumièges are two of France's most impressive and important historic sights. More recent history is preserved at Caen's Mémorial peace museum and the Normandy Landing Beaches.

NORTHERN FRANCE & PARIS *(pp424–509)*

Extending from the banks of the Seine River to the windy flatlands by the North Sea, this is a region of contrasts. Paris, at the centre of the Île de France, has been the capital since medieval times, and ever since this lively metropolis has played a dominant role in the country's political and cultural life. To the north, Amiens, the cradle of Gothic architecture, and Flanders, with its distinctive Flemish architecture, have much to interest the visitor.

PROVENCE *(pp510–543)*

Centred around the impressive Rhône Delta in the south, this ancient region, blessed with sunshine and occupied successively by Celts, Romans and Franks, retained its independence from the French Crown until the 15C. Fascinating cities such as Nîmes, Marseille, Aix-en-Provence and Arles, and the astonishingly well-preserved Roman remains, such as those at St-Rémy-de-Provence, ensure the ongoing popularity of this region.

Principal Sights

TOULOUSE	★★★	Highly recommended
Autun	★★	Recommended
Giverny	★	Interesting
Montélimar		Other sights described in this guide

Seaside resorts ⌂ , spas ✚ and winter resorts ❄ are classified according to the quality and range of facilities offered.

Shown on this map are the towns and sights in the Discovering France section of the guide, with the additional sights attached to them, as well as principal resorts.

A number of other places, monuments, historical events and natural sites appear in this guide and may be found in the index.

```
0      20      40      60      80     100 km
0    10    20    30    40    60 miles
```

REGIONS

1 Alsace Lorraine, Champagne

2 Atlantic Coast

3 Auvergne, Rhône Valley

4 Brittany

5 Burgundy, Jura

6 Châteaux of the Loire

7 Corsica

8 Dordogne, Berry, Limousin

9 French Alps

10 French Riviera

11 Languedoc Roussillon Tarn Gorges

12 Normandy

13 Northern France and the Paris Region

14 Provence

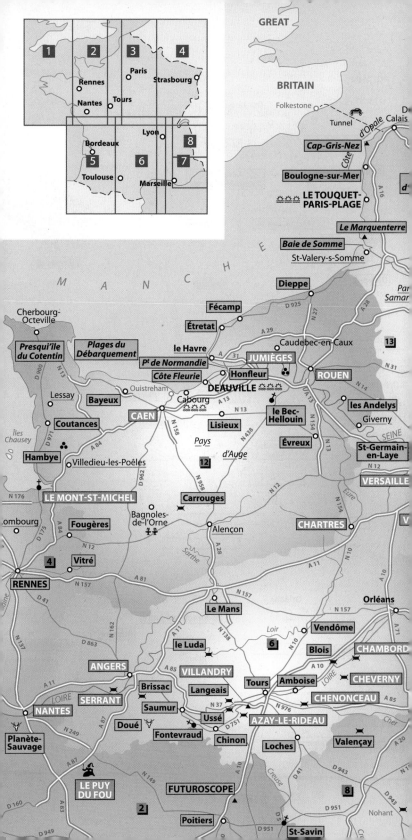

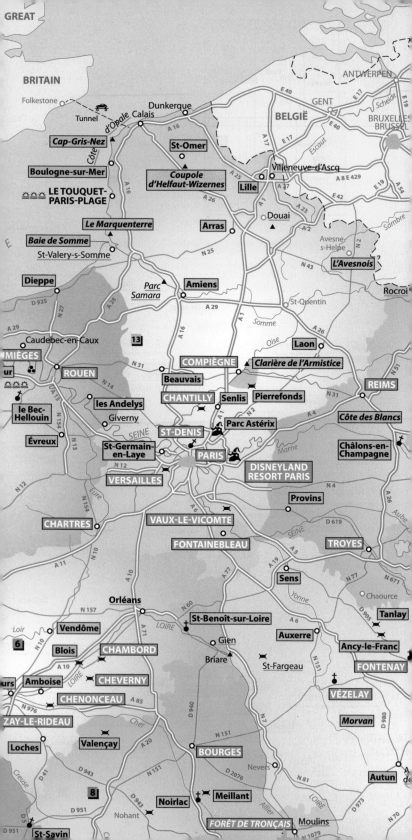

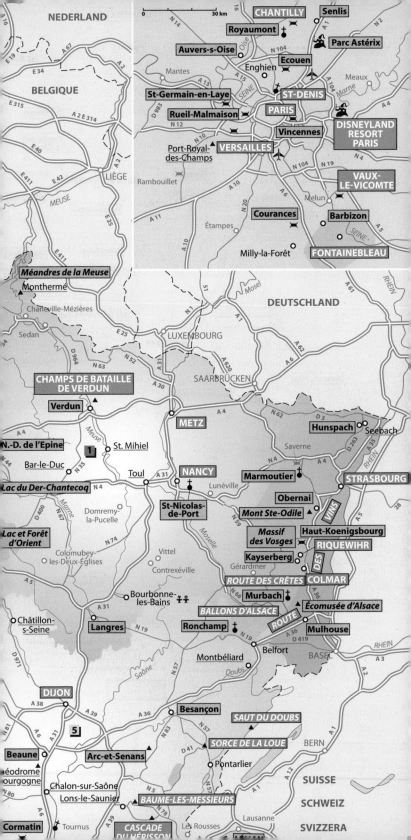

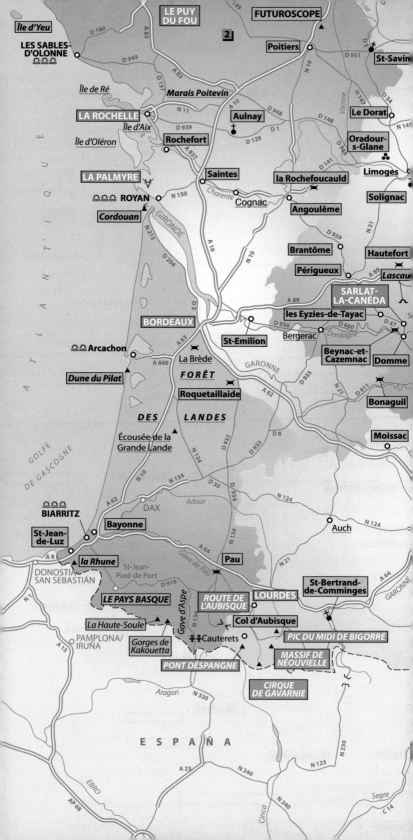

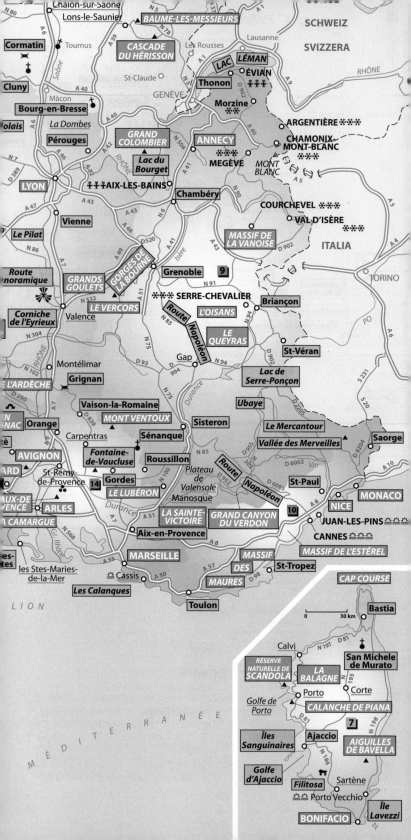

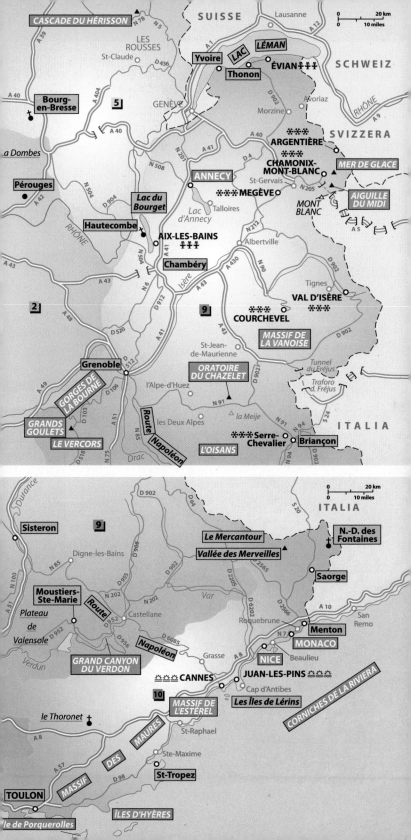

Plage Notre-Dame, Île de Porquerolles, Îles d'Hyères , French Riviera
Taylor Richard/Sime/Photononstop

When and Where to Go

SEASONS

Depending on the reason for your visit, **spring**, **summer** and **autumn** are the best seasons to visit France, each having its own appeal, and there is a region to suit every season. For **winter** sports, the season runs from December to April.

For relaxing out of doors, high summer can be beautiful, but resorts and the principal sightseeing areas are much more crowded.

A better time to travel is May, June or September when French children are at school. Many visitors may prefer the moderate warmth of these early and late summer months to the higher temperatures of July and August, especially in the southern half of the country.

CLIMATE

For an overview of the weather in a specific region of the country, see the **Michelin Green Guide** series, which covers the regions of France. In general the French climate is a moderate one; extremes of either heat or cold are rare for the most part, so that outdoor activity of some kind is almost always possible.

Inland the winters are chilly and darkness comes early, especially in the northern latitudes. As spring turns to summer, the days become long and warm and by June the sun lingers well into the evening. Spring and autumn provide opportunities to explore the outdoors and enjoy the lovely countryside and coastal areas of France. In winter, snowfall throughout much of the interior of the country, as well as in the mountainous regions, permits winter sports, including downhill skiing and snowboarding.

WEATHER FORECAST

For **Météo-France** (national weather bureau, www.meteo.fr) reports in French, ☏3250, then select from the recorded choices (€0.34/min). Information about the weather can be downloaded to mobile phones from http://mobile.meteofrance.com.
♿ See Temperature Chart p48.

For **departmental forecasts** dial ☏08 92 68 02… followed by the number of the *département* you want, e.g. Ain 01; Aisne 02; Allier 03; Ardèche 04, etc.

Mountain weather forecast: ☏3250 (select 4); for information about snow cover and avalanche risk, ☏08 92 68 10 20.

Gordes in autumn, Provence

© Dr. Heinz Linke/iStockphoto.com

What to See and Do

France offers a splendid range of leisure activities from spa treatments and wine tours to outdoor sports and cruises. Below are a few suggestions of ways to enhance your stay.

OUT AND ABOUT

Information and brochures for all sporting, special interest and outdoor facilities may be obtained from **Atout France** (the **French Tourism Development Agency**), Lincoln House, 300 High Holborn, London WC1V 7JH. ✆44 (0)20 7061 6630, or from the local tourist information centres shown within the *Discovering France* section of this guide.

WALKING

Exploring the regions of France on foot is a delightful way of discovering the landscape, and the life and culture of the countryside. Short-, medium- and long-distance footpaths network the whole country. For the nationwide system of long-distance paths, Topo-Guides are published by the **Fédération Française de la Randonnée pédestre**. Some of the guides have been translated into English. They give detailed maps of the paths and offer valuable information to the walker, and are on sale at the Information Centre: 64 r. du Dessous des Berges, 75013 Paris. ✆01 44 89 93 90; www.ffrandonnee. fr, and many bookshops throughout France. A good selection of **English-language guidebooks for walkers** covering many areas of France is available from specialist UK publisher Cicerone Press, 2 Police Square, Milnthorpe, Cumbria LA7 7PY. www. cicerone.co.uk. ✆44 (0)1539 562069.

FISHING

The abundance of rivers, streams and lakes provides anglers with many opportunities to catch salmon, trout, perch, tench or carp. Whatever the site, however, it is necessary to be affiliated to a fishing association and to abide by fishing regulations. Daily fishing permits are available in certain areas. Contact the local tourist office or apply to the local fishing federations or fishing tackle stores. A folding map *Fishing in France (Pêche en France)* is published and distributed by the Conseil Supérieur de la Pêche (134 av. de Malakoff, 75016 Paris. ✆01 45 02 20 20), and is also available from departmental fishing organisations. For information about regulations contact the Tourist Information Centres or the offices of the Water and Forest Authority (*Eaux et Forêts*).

RIVER AND CANAL CRUISING

The extensive network of navigable waterways in France can be explored at leisure. Many tour operators offer touring vacations with motor cruisers. Information on boat hire companies is available from the **Féderation des Industries Nautiques** (✆ 01 44 37 04 00; www.france-nautic.com). Charges usually include boat hire, insurance and technical assistance. Some charter companies also offer bicycles to enable visitors to go shopping and for rides or excursions along the towpath or to neighbouring villages. Visitors usually operate the locks on small canals by themselves; otherwise, it is customary to give a hand to the lock-keeper.

Two publishers produce collections of guides to cruising on French canals. Both series include numerous maps and useful information and are provided with English translations. The publishers are: Grafocarte (125 r. J.-J. Rousseau BP 40, 92132, Issy-les-Moulineaux. ✆01 41 09 19 00) and Guides Vagnon, Les Éditions du Plaisancier (100 av. du Général-Leclerc, 69641 Caluire Cedex. ✆04 78 23 31 14).

SAILING

Many resorts have sailing clubs offering courses. In season it is possible to hire boats with or without crew. Apply to the **Fédération Française de Voile**: 17 r. Henri Bocquillon, 75015 Paris. &01 40 60 37 00; www.ffvoile.net.

CANOEING

A guide is published annually indicating schools and places where canoeing may be practised. Apply to **Fédération Française de Canoe-Kayak** (87 quai de la Marne, 94344 Joinville-le-Pont. &01 45 11 08 50; www.ffck.org).

MOTOR BOATING AND WATER-SKIING

Enquire at local Tourist Information Centres or at resort waterfronts. Anyone who intends to drive a powered boat (6–50hp) within 5 nautical miles of a French harbour must qualify for a sea certificate *(Carte mer)*. Beyond the 5 nautical mile limit an additional sea permit *(Permis mer)* is required. Yachts and boats with engines of less than 6hp are exempt.

SCUBA-DIVING

Apply to the **Fédération Française d'Études et de Sports Sous-Marins** (24 quai de Rive Neuve, 13284 Marseille Cedex 07. &04 91 33 99 31; www.ffessm.fr). The federation publishes *Subaqua*, a bimonthly journal on diving in France.

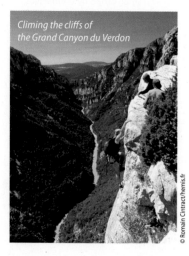
Climing the cliffs of the Grand Canyon du Verdon
© Romain Cintract/hemis.fr

RIDING AND PONY TREKKING

Apply to the **Comité Nationale du Tourisme Équestre, Parc équestre** (41 600 Lamotte. &02 54 94 46 80; www.ffe.com), which publishes an annual handbook covering the whole of France.

GOLF

For location, addresses and telephone numbers of golf courses in France, consult the map *Golfs, les Parcours français,* published by Edition Plein Sud based on **Michelin maps**. You can also contact the **Fédération Française de Golf** (68 r. Anatole France, 92 300 Levallois-Perret. &01 41 49 77 00; www.ffgolf.org).

SKIING

The French Alps is one of the world's major ski and winter sports areas. There is also good skiing in the Pyrenees and the Auvergne.
For all enquiries contact the **Club Alpin Français**, a national federation of 174 local mountain sports associations, based at 24 av. de Laumière, 75019 Paris. &01 53 72 87 00; www.ffcam.fr. Or, for general information, contact **Ski France**, an association of winter sports resorts, for their annual publications *Guide Pratique Hiver/Été* and *Guide des Tarifs* (both free), 61 boulevard Haussmann, 75008 Paris. &01 47 42 23 32.

ROCK CLIMBING

Excursions with qualified instructors are organised by sections of the **Club Alpin Français** and by local guides. Apply to the Tourist Information Centres, or to the **Fédération Française de la Montagne et de l'Escalade** (8–10, quai de la Marne, 75019 Paris. &01 40 18 75 50; www.ffme.fr).

SPAS AND WELL-BEING

Spas have long been part of French life. They are gradually becoming less concerned with medical treatment, and rather more with relaxation, reinvigoration and a modicum of

Château de Valençay and its vineyard, Indre, Centre

S. Sauvignier/MICHELIN

self-indulgent pampering. There are dozens of spas in France, ranging from up-market spa resort hotels to charming small spa villages that have relaxed visitors since the days of the Ancient Romans.

TOURS

The most intimate and revealing way of discovering local France is on foot, but there is an increasing number of tours that are available, some themed, some laissez-faire.

WINE TOURS

In most wine-making regions, wine tours taking in the main vineyards and wineries, or *caves*, are signposted. There are also many local guided tours in wine regions. For information apply to the local Tourist Information Centre.

Buying your own wine directly from the grower can be an adventurous and satisfying holiday occupation. Signs announce farm-gate sales *(vins-vente directe)* or wine tasting and sales *(dégustation vente)*. But it's not the done thing to turn up, slurp your way through numerous glasses of wine, and then buy nothing!

CYCLING HOLIDAYS

A number of UK tour operators organise cycle touring holidays in France, for example Susi Madron's Cycling for Softies (www.cycling-for-softies.co.uk) and Headwater (www.headwater.com).

In France, the cyclists' touring association, **Fédération Française de Cyclotourisme**, organises cycle tours, and provides itineraries detailing distances, difficulty of the routes, and sights to visit. 12 r. Louis Bertrand 94207 Ivry-sur-Seine Cedex. ✆01 56 20 88 88. www.ffct.org.

You can also apply to the **Fédération Française de Cyclisme**, 5 rue de Rome, 93561 Rosny-sous-Bois. ✆01 49 35 69 00. www.ffc.fr. This organisation publishes a guide listing marked mountain-bike tracks.

Lists of local cycle hire shops are available from Tourist Information Centres. Some SNCF railway stations hire out cycles, which can be returned at a different station.

RIDING TOURS

For information about riding holidays, contact the **Comité national de tourisme équestre**, 9 boulevard Macdonald 75019 Paris. ✆01 53 26 15 50, which publishes the annual handbook *Cheval Nature, l'Officiel du tourisme équestre en France,* giving details of selected riding stables and equestrian establishments throughout France.

ACTIVITIES FOR KIDS 👫

In this guide, sights of particular interest to children are indicated with a KIDS symbol (👫). Some attractions may offer discount fees for children.

Golfe de Porto, Corsica

J.-L. Gallo/MICHELINa

Children are welcome everywhere in France; the French are very much family-oriented. It is quite commonplace to see well-behaved children dining in restaurants in the early evening. Moreover, France is a wonderful destination to bring babies, toddlers, in fact, children of all ages. Most attractions, parks, museums and buildings offer reduced rates for children, with very young children often going free.

Useful Websites
A useful source of ideas is **www.france4families.com**, which contains a lot of general information and tips. There are also other useful websites, like **www.takethefamily.com**, which has tips and destination guides, and **www.babygoes2.com**, which contains pages of information to help parents travelling with small children. **www.tinytotsaway.com** allows you to order in advance all the things you would normally pack, from nappies to particular brands of baby food, which they then buy and ship to your hotel/destination, to be there as you arrive.

THE ISLANDS OF FRANCE
See **Michelin Green Guides** to: *Normandy, Brittany, French Atlantic Coast, Provence, French Riviera, and Corse (in French).*

France has an extensive coastline along which are dotted idyllic islands, some as small as a field and others very large – Corsica is three times the size of a small country such as Luxembourg.
The islands are perfect destinations for a change of scenery and pace; their isolation, as well as an air of mystery and charm, adds to the fascination of a way of life shaped by the sea.
The principal islands ranging from north to south and west to east are:

ÎLES DU PONANT
(English Channel–Atlantic Ocean)
◆ **Îles Chausey★:** *65sq km/25sq mi* at high tide attached to **Granville**.
◆ **Île de Bréhat★:** *3sq km/1.2sq mi; 10min* crossing from **Arcouest** near **Paimpol**.
◆ **Île de Batz:** *3sq km/1.2sq mi; 15min* crossing from **Roscoff**.
◆ **Île d'Ouessant★★:** the westernmost island off the Atlantic coast. *15.5sq km/6sq mi, highest point 60m/197ft; 2hr 30min* crossing from **Brest** or *1hr 30min* from **Conquet**.
◆ **Île de Molène:** *0.72sq km/0.27sq mi; 30min* crossing from **Pointe St-Matthieu**.
◆ **Île de Sein:** *0.58sq km/0.19sq mi, highest point 6m/20ft; 1hr* crossing from **Audierne**.

- **Îles de Glénan:** a group of 10 islets, mostly uninhabited, attached to **Fouesnant**.
- **Île de Groix**★: *14.8sq km/5.7sq mi, highest point 49m/160ft; 45min* crossing from **Lorient**.
- **Îles du Golfe de Morbihan**★★: Among the string of islets in the bay, the most noteworthy are **Île-aux-Moines**★, *3.2sq km/1.2sq mi,* and **Île d'Arz**, *3.3sq km/1.25sq mi.*
- **Belle-Île-en-Mer**★★: *84sq km/ 48sq mi; 1hr* crossing from **Quiberon**.
- **Île d'Houat:** *2.9sq km/1sq mi; 1hr* crossing from **Quiberon**.
- **Île d'Hoedic:** *2.09sq km/0.8sq mi; 1hr 30min* crossing from **Quiberon** via **Houat**.
- **Île d'Yeu**★★: *23.3sq km/ 9sq mi;* this island is the furthest from the mainland; *1hr15min* crossing from **Fromentine**.
- **Île d'Aix**★: *1.19sq km/0.5sq mi; 20min* crossing from **Fouras**.
- **Île de Noirmoutier**, **Île de Ré**★ and **Île d'Oléron**★: These are linked to the mainland by a road bridge, and, in the case of Noirmoutier, by the tidal Passage du Goit.

ÎLES DU LEVANT

(Mediterranean Sea)

- **Archipel du Frioul: Île de Pomègues** and **Île Ratonneau** linked by Frioul harbour, **Îlot d'If**★★: *1hr30min* excursion from **Marseille**.
- **Îles des Calanques: Maire, Jarre, Calseraigne, Riou** are great spots for underwater fishing.
- **Île de Bendor**★: *7min* from **Bandol**.
- **Îles d'Hyères**★★★: **Porquerolles**★★★, *12.9sq km/5sq mi, 20min* crossing from Giens; **Port-Cros**★★, *6.35sq km/2.5sq mi, 45min* crossing from **Port-de-Miramar**; Île du Levant, *9sq km/3.8sq mi, 35min* crossing from **Le Lavandou**.
- **Îles de Lérins**★★: **St-Honorat**★★, *0.6sq km/0.2sq mi*; **Ste-Marguerite**★★, *0.27sq km/0.1sq mi, 30min* crossing from **Cannes** or **Juan-les-Pins**.
- **Îles Sanguinaires**★★: *60min* crossing from **Ajaccio**.
- **Îles Lavezzia:** *30min* crossing from **Bonifacio**.

SHOPPING
OPENING HOURS

Ordinary shop hours in towns and villages are typically open Tue–Sat 9am–noon or 12.30pm, 3–7pm. The lunch break is often longer in the South. Food shops may open earlier in the morning, but later in the afternoon, and some, especially bakeries *(pâtisseries)* and grocery

Belle-Île-en-Mer, Brittany

B. Brillion/MICHELIN

stores, open on Sunday morning. In resorts, shops may keep longer hours and stay open all day, all week. Department stores are open Mon–Sat 9am–6.30pm (often with one or more later evenings per week). Hypermarkets are usually open Mon–Sat 9am–10pm.

MARKETS

When travelling around France make sure you have a look around the colourful local markets, an important domestic institution, or the various agricultural fairs which are held regularly throughout the year.

VALUE ADDED TAX

In France a sales tax (*TVA* or VAT) is added to all purchases. For non-EU residents on holiday this tax can be refunded as long as you have bought more than €175 worth of goods at the same time and in the same shop, and have completed the appropriate *Bordereau* form at the shop. The amount permitted may vary, so it is advisable to check first with the VAT-refund counter (*service de détaxe*). Present the *Bordereau* forms to Customs officials on leaving France for processing. Customs Information Centre: ✆08 20 02 44 44 or www.douane.gouv.fr.

WHAT YOU CAN TAKE HOME

There are no limits on the value of goods EU residents may take home from France, provided everything is for personal use. However, in the UK, HM Revenue and Customs attempt to limit the amount of alcohol and tobacco considered reasonable for personal use. These are: 3 200 cigarettes, 200 cigars, 400 cigarillos, 3kg/6.6lb tobacco, 110l/29gal beer, 90l/19.7gal wine, 10l/2gal spirits and 20l/4gal fortified wine. More information is available at **www.hmrc.gov.uk.** Americans are allowed to take home, tax-free, up to US$800 worth of goods, Canadians up to CDN$750, Australians up to AUS$900 and New Zealanders up to NZ$700.

BOOKS

1000 Years of Annoying the French – Stephen Clarke (*Bantam Press, 2010*)
> An idiosyncratic, and occasionally tongue-in-cheek, look at the long-lasting relationship with the French.

Paris Revealed: The Secret Life of a City – Stephen Clarke (*Bantam Press, 2011*)
> The very latest in Stephen Clarke's gentle take on the curiosities of France.

More, More France Please – Helena Frith Powell (*Gibson Square, 2007*).
> Real-life stories about the author and friends in France.

France in the New Century: Portrait of a Changing Society – John Ardagh (*Penguin, 2001*). An acclaimed overview of the political landscape, by one of the most respected commentators on French life.

The French – T Zeldin (*Kodansha Globe, 1996*). A perceptive and entertaining look at the character of this enigmatic nation.

The Man who married a Mountain – Rosemary Bailey (*Bantam Books, 2005*)
> A tale in search of a man, Count Henry Russell, 19C explorer and mountaineer who lived in a cave high in the Pyrenees.

Searching for the New France – J Hollifield and G Ross (*Routledge, 1998*).
> Why France is so anxious about its identity, its role and its future.

Betrayal: France, the Arabs and the Jews – David Pryce-Jones (*Encounter Books, 2008*). How France's relations with the Arab world have led it into trouble.

Horrible Histories: France – Terry Deary (*Scholastic Hippo, 2002*). A comical cartoon summary of French history.

Speak the Culture – France (Thorogood Publishing, 2008).
A general guidebook that shows you where to go in France and what to say when you get there, reasoning that through exploring the people and their lifestyles you will achieve an intimate understanding of France and its people.

Something to Declare – Julian Barnes (Picador, 2002). A collection of essays written over 20 years that attest to Barnes' appreciation of the Land Without Brussels Sprouts.

Exploring Rural France – Andrew Sanger (Passport Books, 1994). Itineraries for off-the-beaten-track tourists.

The Wines and Winelands of France – Geological Journeys – C Pomerol (McCarta Publishing, 1990). What lies behind the extraordinary diversity of the French wine list.

Green Guide to the Wine Regions of France (Michelin, 2010). All you need to explore, visit and taste your way around the country.

1000 Charming Hotels and Guesthouses (Michelin, 2005). An appealing selection of places to stay.

FILMS

Bienvenue Chez les Ch'tis (Welcome to the Sticks) (2008). Although living a comfortable life in Salon-de-Provence, Julie has been feeling depressed for a while. To please her, Philippe Abrams, her post office administrator husband, tries to obtain a transfer to a seaside town, on the French Riviera, at any cost...

Partir (Leaving) (2009). Suzanne is a well-to-do wife and mother in the south of France. Her idle bourgeois lifestyle gets her down and she decides to go back to work as a physiotherapist.

Les Petites Vacances (2006) Grandmother kidnaps the children and takes them on a crazy 'holiday' in the Alps.

French Kiss (1995). Comic romance about a Canadian out to save her marriage plans and the petty crook using her, who travel to Cannes together.

La Haine (1995) . Violence and racism as three youths, one black, one a Jew, one an Arab, get involved in riots in the Paris suburbs.

Le Fabuleux destin d'Amélie Poulain (2001). Touching and lighthearted adventures of the naive Amélie as she looks for love in Paris.

Jean de Florette and *Manon des Sources (1986).* Two peasants in rural Provence outwit the new owner of the neighbouring property. In the second movie, his death is avenged by his daughter Manon.

Être et Avoir (To Be and to Have) (2001). There are still single-classroom schools that bring together, under the same schoolteacher, all the children from the same village, from nursery age to 11. This documentary follows one such rural class over the course of a year.

7 years (2005). Maïté is married to Vincent who has just been sentenced to seven years in prison. The only intimacy left to them lies in the prison's visiting rooms. Twice a week, she picks up his laundry, washes it, irons it, and brings it back.

L'Arnacœur (Heartbreaker) (2010). Alex (Romain Duris) and his sister Mélanie (Julie Ferrier) run a business designed to break up relationships. Taking on a job on the French Riviera, will icy Juliette (Vanessa Paradis) be the client who scuppers the mission?

Calendar of Events

The following selection of events is far from comprehensive; almost every village has a festival at some time during the year. Book accommodation well in advance at festival times, even out of season.

JANUARY
Clermont-Ferrand International Short-Film Festival ℘04 73 91 65 73 www.clermont.filmfest.com

FEBRUARY
Chalon-sur-Saône Carnival, Winter Fur and Pelt Fair ℘03 85 48 08 39
Limoux Traditional carnival every weekend (and Shrove Tuesday). All-night *Blanquette* party follows. ℘04 68 31 11 82 www.limoux.fr
Menton Lemon Festival ℘04 92 41 76 76 www.fete-du-citron.com
Nice Carnival ℘0892 70 74 07 www.nicecarnaval.com
Paris Paris International Agricultural Show www.salon-agriculture.com
Prats-de-Mollo, St-Laurent-de Cerdans, Arles-sur-Tech Traditional carnival ℘04 68 39 70 83 www.pratsdemollolapreste.com
Toulouse *Fête de la Violette* (violet festival) ℘05 62 16 31 31 www.toulouse-tourisme.com
Le Touquet Motorbike race along the beach ℘03 21 06 72 00

MARCH
Clermont-Ferrand *Vidéoformes*: international video and multimedia art festival ℘04 73 17 02 17 www.videoformes.com
Clermont-Ferrand Poetry week ℘04 73 31 72 87 www.auvergne. iufm.fr/poesie.htm
Lyon International Fair ℘04 72 22 33 37 www.foiredelyon.com

MID-MARCH–MID-JULY
Lille Music, art and theatre ℘03 28 52 30 00

LATE MARCH–LATE OCTOBER
Versailles Fountain display with musical performances *(Les Grandes Eaux Musicales)* – every weekend and Bank Holiday ℘01 30 83 78 98

APRIL
Bourges Music Festival ℘02 48 27 28 29
Chartres Students' Pilgrimage ℘02 37 21 51 91 www.chartres-tourisme.com
Chartres Music festival ℘02 22 06 87 87 www.chartres-tourisme.com
Cournon-d'Auvergne Festival for young people: theatre, puppets, dance, music. ℘04 73 69 90 40
Gérardmer Flower Festival ℘03 29 27 27 27
Le Mans 24-hour motorcycle race ℘02 43 40 24 24 www.lemans.org

APRIL–OCTOBER
Parc national des Cévennes Nature festival: themed walks, exhibitions, shows, markets ℘04 66 49 53 01 www.cevennes-parcnational.fr
Chaumont-sur-Loire International Garden Festival ℘02 54 20 99 22

MAY
Aubrac *Fête de la transhumance*: seasonal shepherd's festival held on the weekend nearest to May 25 ℘ 05 65 44 21 15 www.traditionsenaubrac.com
Cannes International Film Festival ℘01 53 59 61 00 www.festival-cannes.com
Évian Classical music ℘04 50 26 85 00
Maguelone Festival of ancient and Baroque music (1st two weeks) ℘04 67 60 69 92

Montauban Music festival
  ℘05 63 63 66 77
Orléans Joan of Arc Festival
  ℘02 38 24 05 05
  www.tourisme-orleans.fr
Orange Music and opera
  ℘02 40 14 58 60
Rouen Joan of Arc Festival
  ℘02 35 08 32 40
Les Saintes-Maries-de-la-Mer
  Gypsy Pilgrimage
  ℘04 90 97 82 55
Touraine The Day of the Loire
  to celebrate the Loire and its
  countryside. ℘02 47 31 42 88
  www.jourdeloire.com

MAY–OCTOBER
Vichy *Une Saison en Eté*: theatre,
  classical music, opera, variety
  shows at the Vichy Opera House
  ℘04 70 30 50 30
  www.ville-vichy.fr

JUNE
Bellac Drama, music ℘05 55 60 87 61
Clermont-Ferrand Medieval Festival
  in Montferrand ℘04 73 23 19 29
  www.montferrandmedieval.org
Le Mans 24-hour car race
  ℘03 43 40 24 24 www.lemans.org
Montpellier International Festival
  of Dance ℘0 800 600 740
  www.montpellierdanse.com
Perpignan Saint-Jean Festa Major
  (with mid-summer bonfires
  around June 21). ℘04 68 66 30 30
  www.perpignantourisme.com
La Rochelle International Regatta
  ℘05 46 41 14 68
Toulouse Rio Loco Festival
  ℘05 61 32 77 28 www.rio-loco.org
Tours *Florilège Vocal*: Choral Festival
  ℘02 47 21 65 26
  www.florilegevocal.com
Vic-le-Comte Celtrad: Celtic music
  festival ℘04 73 69 02 12
Villefranche-sur-Saône
  Midsummer Night: bonfires,
  singers, illuminations
  ℘04 74 65 04 48

MID-JUNE–MID-JULY
Pau Theatre, music and dance
  ℘05 59 27 27 08

MID-JUNE TO MID-OCTOBER
Anjou Anjou Festival in the historical
  sites of Maine-et-Loire
  ℘02 41 88 14 14
  www.festivaldanjou.com
Chaumont-sur-Loire
  International Garden Festival
  ℘02 54 20 99 22
  www.chaumont-jardins.com
Orléans Jazz Festival
  ℘02 38 24 05 05
  www.tourisme-orleans.fr

JUNE–LATE AUGUST
Amboise "At The Court of King
  François" ℘02 47 57 14 47
Toulouse Classical, jazz and rock
  music ℘05 62 27 60 60

JULY
Aix-en-Provence International
  Music Festival ℘0820 922 923
Albi Classical music ℘05 63 49 48 80
Ambert *Festival de Folklore*
  ℘04 73 82 66 34
  www.livradoue-dansaire.com
Auvergne *Thermathlon du Sancy*:
  Fun trek along the Route des
  Villes d'Eaux of the Massif Central
  (mountain biking, walking,
  canoeing, archery)
  ℘04 73 31 20 32
Avignon Theatre Festival
  ℘04 90 27 66 50
Béziers Classical music
  ℘04 67 36 82 30
Cap d'Agde *Fête de la Mer*
  (sea festival; last weekend)
  ℘ 04 67 01 04 04
  www.capdagde.com
Carcassonne Festival of the City:
  Medieval Cité is "set alight" by
  an evening firework display;
  classical music concerts, theatre,
  opera, dance, jazz (July 14)
  ℘04 68 11 59 15
  www.festivaldecarcassonne.com
Carpentras Music and dance
  ℘04 90 60 46 00

Cordes-sur-Ciel *Fête médiévale du Grand Fauconnnier* (historical pageant and entertainments (mid-July) ℘05 63 56 34 63 www.grandfauconnier.com

Forez Concerts of classical music in churches and castles of the region ℘04 73 51 55 67

Frontignan *Festival du Muscat* (mid-month) ℘04 67 18 31 60 www.tourisme-frontignan.com

Gannat International folk music ℘04 70 90 12 67

Juan-les-Pins World Jazz Festival ℘04 97 23 11 10

Lorient Celtic festival ℘02 97 21 24 29

Luz-St-Sauveur *Jazz à Luz* (early July) ℘05 62 92 38 30 www.jazzaluz.com

Montpellier *Festival de Radio-France et de Montpellier Languedoc-Roussillon*: opera, symphonies, chamber music, jazz (2nd fort night) ℘04 67 61 66 81 www.festivalradiofrance montpellier.com

Nantes International Flower Show ℘02 40 47 04 51

Orcines *Open Golf des Volcans*: international golf championship (last week of the month) ℘04 73 62 15 51 www.golfdesvolcans.com

Perpignan *Estivales* (Theatre festival) ℘04 68 66 30 30 www.estivales.com

Quimper Cornouaille Festival ℘02 98 55 53 53

Rennes Theatre, music, dance and poetry ℘02 99 67 11 11

St-Guilhem-le-Désert Musical season at the abbey ℘04 67 96 86 19 www.st-guilhem-le-desert.com

Vollore *Festival des Concerts de Vollore*: Classical music, jazz and *musique tzigane* ℘04 73 51 55 67 http://concertsdevollore.com

JULY AND AUGUST

Sète Festival of St Louis: jousting, fireworks ℘04 67 74 48 44 www.fiestasete.com

St-Bertrand-de-Comminges, St-Just-de-Valcabrère, St-Gaudens, Martres-Tolosane. *Festival du Comminges*, classical music, chamber music ℘05 61 88 32 00 www.festival-du-comminges.com

Vaison-la-Romaine Theatre and dance ℘04 90 36 02 11

MID-JULY–MID-SEPTEMBER

Arles International Photo Festival ℘04 90 96 76 06

St-Rémy-de-Provence Organ music ℘04 90 92 05 22

Sceaux Classical music ℘01 46 60 07 79

AUGUST

Aurillac International Street Theatre Festival. ℘04 71 45 47 45 www.aurillac.net

Allanche Secondhand market: the most important in the Auvergne. ℘04 71 20 48 43

Bayonne Corrida and Street Festival ℘0820 42 64 64

Colmar Alsatian Wine Festival ℘03 89 20 68 92

Béziers Bullfighting Festival ℘04 67 76 13 45 www.languedoc-france.info

Chamonix Mountain Guides Festival ℘04 50 53 00 88

Entrecasteaux Chamber music ℘04 94 72 91 62

Pomarez Running of the Cows ℘05 58 89 30 28

Pont de Salers and other villages International Folklore Festival ℘05 65 46 80 67 www.festival-rouergue.com

Prades Festival Pablo Casals: chamber music ℘04 68 96 33 07

Monteux Fireworks Festival ℘04 90 66 97 52

Montesquieu-Volvestre British Film Festival ℘05 61 90 65 74

St-Pourçain-sur-Sioule Wine and Food Festival ℘04 70 45 32 73 www.tourismesaintpour cinois.com

St-Donat-sur-l'Herbasse
☎04 75 45 10 29 Bach Festival
Sablé-sur-Sarthe Festival of
Baroque music ☎02 43 62 22 22
www.sable-sur-sarthe.fr
Salon-de-Provence Music Festival
☎04 90 56 27 60

SEPTEMBER
Besançon Classical music: Young
Conductors Competition
☎03 81 25 05 85
Deauville American Film Festival
☎02 31 14 14 14
www.festival-deauville.com
Dinan Ramparts Festival (biennial –
next in 2012) ☎02 96 39 75 40
Divonne Chamber music
☎04 50 90 17 70
Lyon Even years: dance; Odd years:
music and modern art
☎04 72 77 69 69
Le Puy-en-Velay *Les Fêtes du Roi de
l'Oiseau* (Festival of the King of the
Birds): all the splendour of a city in
the period of François I; 6 000
people in costume ☎04 71 09
38 41 www.roideloiseau.com

SEPTEMBER–DECEMBER
**Beaujolais, Coteaux du Rhône
and du Forez** Grape Harvest
and Wine Festivals in the wine-
growing regions
Puy-de-Dôme Les Automnales:
theatre and music throughout the
Auvergne ☎04 73 42 23 29
www.puydedome.com

OCTOBER
Lannion Organ and choral music
☎02 96 35 14 14
Montpellier International fair
☎04 67 17 67 17 www.foire-
montpellier.com
Mourjou Chestnut Festival
☎04 71 49 69 34
www.mourjou.com
Perpignan Jazz Festival. ☎04 68
86 08 51 www.jazzebre.com
St-Malo Comics Festival
☎02 99 40 39 63
www.quaidesbulles.com

Sauveterre-de-Rouergue
Chestnut and cider festival
☎05 65 72 02 52

NOVEMBER
Beaune Auction sale of the wines of
the Hospices de Beaune
☎03 80 24 47 00
Belfort Cinema ☎03 84 22 94 44
Le Puy-en-Velay International Hot-
Air Balloon Rally ☎04 71 09 38 41
www.ot-lepuyenvelay.fr

DECEMBER
Marseille Santons Fair
☎04 91 54 91 11
Mont-Ste-Odile Pilgrimage (the
most important in Alsace)
☎03 88 95 80 53
Strasbourg Christmas Market
(Chriskindelsmarik)
☎03 88 52 28 28

DECEMBER 25
Azay-le-Rideau The Imaginary World
of the Château d'Azay-le-Rideau
☎02 47 45 44 40
Blois The Story of Blois
☎02 54 78 72 76
Les-Baux-de-Provence Shepherds'
Midnight Mass and Son et Lumière
in the Loire Valley ☎04 90 97 34 39
Chenonceau The Ladies of
Chenonceau ☎02 47 23 94 45
Cheverny The River Loire down
the ages ☎02 54 42 69 03
Loches The Strange Story of Bélisane
☎02 47 59 07 98
Le Lude Spectacular Historical Events
☎02 43 94 62 20
Valençay Esclarmonde
☎02 54 00 04 42

Know Before You Go

USEFUL WEBSITES

www.ambafrance-uk.org
The **French Embassy**'s website provides basic information (geography, demographics, history), a news digest and business-related information. It offers special pages for children, and pages devoted to culture, language study and travel, and you can reach other selected French sites (regions, cities, ministries) with a hypertext link.

www.franceguide.com
The French Government Tourist Office/Maison de la France site is packed with practical information, advice and tips for those travelling to France, including choosing package tours and even buying a property. The homepage has a number of links to more specific guidance, for American or Canadian travellers for example, or to the FGTO's London pages.

www.francekeys.com
This site has plenty of practical information for visiting France. It covers all the regions, with links to tourist offices and related sites. Very useful for planning all the details of your tour in France!

www.franceway.com
This is an online magazine that focuses on culture and heritage. For each region, there are also suggestions for activities and practical information on where to stay and how to get there.

www.ViaMichelin.com
This site has maps, tourist information, travel features, suggestions on hotels and restaurants, and a route planner for numerous locations in Europe. In addition, you can look up weather forecasts, traffic reports and service station location, particularly useful if you will be driving in France.

www.F-T-S.co.uk
The French Travel Service specialises in organising holidays in France using the rail network. Let FTS organise your travel and hotels anywhere in France.

www.fngi.fr (Tour Guides)
Looking for a professional tour guide? This FNGIC represents and unites licensed tourist guides, while promoting and defending their profession. It is a professional non-profit organisation. It has about 700 members, all of whom passed an examination and received professional accreditation from both the Ministry of Tourism and the Ministry of Culture and Communication. FNGIC, 43, rue Beaubourg, 75003 PARIS. ℘01 44 59 29 15.

TOURIST OFFICES ABROAD

- **Australia & New Zealand**
  Level 13, 25 Bligh Street, 2000 NSW, Sydney, Australia
  61 (0)2 9231 5244
  Fax 61 (0)2 9221 8682
  http://au.franceguide.com
- **Canada**
  1800 av. McGill College, Suite 1010, Montreal, Quebec H3A 3J6
  ℘(514) 288-2026
  Fax (514) 845-4868
  http://ca-en.franceguide.com
- **Republic of Ireland**
  No office ℘+15 60 235 235 (Irish information line);
  http://ie.franceguide.com
- **United Kingdom**
  Lincoln House, 300 High Holborn, London WC1V 7JH
  ℘09068 244 123 (60p/min)
  http://uk.franceguide.com
- **United States**
  Three offices are available, but the quickest way to get a response to any question or request is by phone. http://us.franceguide.com
  New York – 825 Third Avenue, 29th floor (entrance on 50th Street), New York, NY 10022
  ℘France-on-Call Hotline (514) 288 1904

Los Angeles – 9454 Wilshire Blvd, Suite 210, 90212 Beverly Hills, CA ℘310-271-6665
Chicago – Consulate General of France, 205 N Michigan Ave., Suite 3770, 60601 Chicago, Illinois ℘312 327 0290

NATIONAL TOURIST OFFICES

France has a national network of regional and local tourist offices able to provide information useful in planning your trip and answering your questions.

◆ **Fédération Nationale des Comités Régionaux de Tourisme**
17 av. de l'Opéra, 75001 Paris
℘01 47 03 03 10
www.fncrt.com

◆ **Réseau National des Destinations Départementales**
74–76 r. de Bercy, 75012 Paris
℘01 44 11 10 20
www.rn2d.net

◆ **Fédération Nationale des Offices de Tourisme et Syndicats d'Initiative**
11 r. du Faubourg Poissonnière, 75009 Paris www.tourisme.fr

REGIONAL TOURIST OFFICES

Alsace Lorraine Champagne

◆ **Alsace**
20a r. Berthe-Molly, BP 50247, Colmar ℘03 89 24 73 50
www.tourisme-alsace.com

◆ **Lorraine**
Abbaye des Prémontrés, BP 97, 54704 Pont-à-Mousson
℘03 83 80 01 80
www.tourisme-lorraine.fr

◆ **Champagne-Ardenne**
50 av. du Général Patton, 51000 Châlons-en-Champagne
℘03 26 21 85 80
www.tourisme-champagne-ardenne.com

Atlantic Coast

◆ **Aquitaine**
Cité Mondiale, 23 parvis des Chartrons, 33074 Bordeaux Cedex
℘05 56 01 70 00
www.tourisme-aquitaine.fr

◆ **Poitou-Charentes**
8 r. Riffault, BP 56, F-86002 Poitiers Cedex ℘05 49 50 10 50
www.poitou-charentes-vacances.com

Auvergne – Rhône Valley

◆ **Auvergne**
Parc Technologique Clermont-Ferrand La Pardieu, 7 allée Pierre de Fermat, CS 50502, 63178 Aubière Cedex ℘0810 827 828
www.auvergne-tourisme.info

◆ **Rhône-Alpes**
104 rte de Paris, 69260 Charbonnières-les-Bains
℘04 72 59 21 59
www.rhonealpes-tourisme.com

Brittany

◆ **Bretagne**
1 r. Raoul-Ponchon, 35069 Rennes Cedex
℘02 99 28 44 30
www.brittanytourism.com

Burgundy Jura

◆ **Bourgogne**
5 av. Garibaldi, 21006 Dijon Cedex
℘03 80 28 02 80
www.bourgogne-tourisme.com

◆ **Franche-Comté**
La City, 25044 Besançon Cedex
℘03 81 25 08 08
www.franche-comte.org

Chateaux of the Loire

◆ **Centre-Val de Loire**
37 av. de Paris, 45000 Orléans
℘02 38 79 95 00
www.visaloire.com

◆ **Pays de la Loire**
1 pl. de la Galarne, 44202 Nantes Cedex 2
℘02 40 48 24 20
www.enpaysdelaloire.com

Corsica

◆ **Corse**
ATC, 17 bd du Roi-Jérôme, BP 19, 20181 Ajaccio
℘04 95 51 00 00
www.visit-corsica.com

Honfleur, Normandy

© Veni/iStockphoto.com

Dordogne Berry Limousin
◆ **Limousin**
30 cours Gay-Lussac , C.S. 500 95,
87003 Limoges Cedex 1
☎05 55 11 05 90
www.tourismelimousin.com

French Alps
◆ **Rhône-Alpes**
8 r. Paul Montrochet
69002 Lyon ☎04 72 59 21 59
www.rhonealpes-tourisme.com
◆ **Provence-Alpes-Côte d'Azur**
61 la Canebière,
13231 Marseille Cedex 02
☎04 91 56 47 00
www.discover-southoffrance.com

French Riviera
◆ **Riviera-Côte d'Azur**
400 Promenade des Anglais,
BP 3126, 06203 Nice Cedex 3
☎04 93 37 78 78
www.frenchriviera-tourism.com

Languedoc Roussillon
Midi-Pyrénées
◆ **Languedoc-Roussillon**
954 av. Jean Mermoz,
34960 Montpellier Cedex 2
☎04 67 200 220
www.sunfrance.com
◆ **Midi-Pyrénées**
54 bd de l'Embouchure, BP 52
166, 31022 Toulouse Cedex 2
☎05 61 13 55 48
www.tourism.midi-pyrenees.com

Normandy
◆ **Normandie**
14 r. Charles Corbeau, 27000
Evreux ☎02 32 33 79 00
www.normandie-tourisme.fr

Northern France and the Paris Region
◆ **Île-de-France**
11 r. du Faubourg Poissonnière
75009 Paris ☎01 73 00 77 00
www.new-paris-idf.com
◆ **Nord-Pas-de-Calais**
6 pl. Mendès-France,
BP 99,
59028 Lille Cedex
☎03 20 14 57 57
www.crt-nordpasdecalais.fr
◆ **Paris**
**Paris Convention and
Visitors Bureau**, 25 r. des
Pyramides, 75001 Paris
☎0892 683 000 (€0.34/min)
http://en.parisinfo.com
◆ **Picardie**
11 Mail Albert 1er, BP 2616,
80026, Amiens Cedex 1
☎03 22 97 37 37
www.picardietourisme.com

INTERNATIONAL VISITORS
EMBASSIES AND CONSULATES
Australia Embassy
4 r. Jean-Rey, 75015 Paris
☎01 40 59 33 00.
www.france.embassy.gov.au

Canada Embassy
   35 av. Montaigne, 75008 Paris
   ✆01 44 43 29 00
   www.amb-canada.fr

Ireland Embassy
   4 r. Rude, 75116 Paris
   ✆01 44 17 67 00
   www.embassyofireland.fr

New Zealand Embassy
   7ter r. Léonard-de-Vinci,
   75116 Paris
   ✆01 45 00 24 11
   www.nzembassy.com

UK Embassy
   35 r. du Faubourg-St-Honoré,
   75383 Paris Cedex 08
   ✆01 44 51 31 00
   www.ukinfrance.fco.gov.uk/en

UK Consulate
   18bis r. d'Anjou, 75008 Paris
   ✆01 44 51 31 00
   There are also UK Consulates
   in Bordeaux, Lille, Lyon and
   Marseille.

USA Embassy
   2 av. Gabriel, 75008 Paris
   ✆01 43 12 22 22
   http://france.usembassy.gov

USA Consulate
   2 r. St-Florentin, 75001 Paris
   ✆01 43 12 22 22
   There are **American Presence
   Posts** in Bordeaux, Lyon, Rennes
   and Toulouse, and a Virtual
   Presence Post in Lille.

ENTRY REQUIREMENTS

Passport – Nationals of countries
within the European Union entering
France need only a national identity
card (although most airlines require
passports). Nationals of other
countries must be in possession of a
valid national **passport**.

Visa – No **entry visa** is required for
Canadian, US or Australian citizens
travelling as tourists and staying less
than 90 days, except for students
planning to study in France.
If you think you may need a visa,
apply to your local French Consulate.
General passport information is
available by phone toll-free from the
Federal Information Center ✆800-
688-9889. US passport application
forms can be downloaded from
http://travel.state.gov.

CUSTOMS REGULATIONS

The UK Customs website (www.hmrc.
gov.uk) contains information on
allowances, travel safety tips, and to
consult and download documents
and guides.
There are no limits on the amount
of duty and/or tax paid **alcohol and
tobacco** that you can bring back into
the UK as long as they are for your own
use or gifts and are transported by
you. If you are bringing in alcohol or
tobacco goods and UK Customs have
reason to suspect they may be for a
commercial purpose, an officer may
ask you questions and make checks.
There are no customs formalities when
bringing caravans, pleasure-boats and
outboard motors into France for a stay
of less than six months, but a boat's
registration certificate should be
kept on board.

HEALTH

It is advisable to take out
comprehensive travel insurance
cover, as tourists receiving medical
treatment in French hospitals or
clinics have to pay for it themselves.
Nationals of non-EU countries
should check with their insurance
companies about policy limitations.
Remember to keep all receipts.
British and Irish citizens, if they
are not already in possession of an
EHIC (European Health Insurance
Card), should apply for one before
travelling. The card entitles UK
residents to reduced-cost medical
treatment. Apply at UK post offices,
call ✆0845 606 2030, or visit www.
ehic.org.uk. Details of the healthcare
available in France and how to claim

reimbursement are published in the leaflet *Health Advice for Travellers*, available from post offices. All prescription drugs taken into France should be clearly labelled; it is recommended to carry a copy of prescriptions.

ACCESSIBILITY

The sights described in this guide most easily accessible to people of reduced mobility are indicated in the admission times and charges by the symbol &. On French TGV and Corail trains there are wheelchair spaces in 1st-class carriages available to holders of 2nd-class tickets. On Eurostar and Thalys special rates are available for accompanying adults. All airports are equipped to receive physically disabled passengers. **Disabled drivers** may use the EU blue card for parking entitlements. Information about accessibility is available from French disability organizations such as **Association des Paralysés de France** (17 bd Auguste Blanqui, 75013 Paris. ℘01 40 78 69 00; www.apf.asso.fr), who also maintain a nationwide network of branches throughout the country.

The guide **Michelin Camping France** indicates campsites with facilities suitable for the physically disabled.

Getting There

BY PLANE

It is very easy to arrange air travel to either of Paris' two airports (Roissy-Charles-de-Gaulle to the north, and Orly to the south). Contact airline companies and travel agents for details of package tour flights with a rail link-up or Fly-Drive schemes. Visitors arriving in **Paris** who wish to reach the city centre or a train station may use public transportation or reserve space on the **Airport Shuttle** (for Roissy-Charles-de-Gaulle ℘01 45 38 55 72, for Orly ℘01 43 21 06 78). Many airlines, especially on shorter-haul journeys, also operate services to **Nice**, **Lyon** and **Marseille**, as well as other provincial cities, including **Bordeaux**, **Clermont-Ferrand**, **Mulhouse**, **Nantes**, **Toulouse**, **Montpellier**, **Perpignan** and **Nîmes**. Most North American airlines fly to Paris only, but France's regional airports are well connected to both the Parisian airports and to each other. Many have several flights a day to Paris. Many visitors from other European countries arrive on inclusive package-tour flights with a rail or coach link-up, as well as Fly-Drive schemes.

Information, brochures and timetables are available from airlines, tour operators and travel agents.

BY SHIP

There are numerous **cross-Channel services** (passenger and car ferries) from the United Kingdom and Ireland, as well as the rail Shuttle through the Channel Tunnel **(Le Shuttle-Eurotunnel**, ℘08443 35 35 35 (reservations – UK only); ℘0810 63 03 04 (from France); www.eurotunnel.com).

To choose the most suitable route between your port of arrival and your destination use the Michelin Tourist and Motoring Atlas France, Michelin map 726 (which gives travel times and mileages) or Michelin maps from the 1:200 000 series (with the orange cover). For details apply to travel agencies or to:

♦ **Brittany Ferries**
℘0871 244 0744 (in the UK), 825 828 828 (in France), www.brittanyferries.com. Services from Portsmouth, Poole and Plymouth.

♦ **Condor Ferries**
℘01202 207216, www.condorferries.co.uk.

Services from Weymouth, Poole and Portsmouth.

- **LD Lines**
  ☎0844 576 8836, www.ldlines. co.uk. Services from Portsmouth, Dover and Rosslare.
- **Norfolk Line**
  ☎0870 870 5042 (in the UK), 03 28 59 01 01 (in France), www.norfolkline.com. Service between Dover and Dunkerque.
- **P & O Ferries**
  ☎08716 645 645 (UK dialling), or 0825 120 156 (in France), www.poferries.com. Service between Dover and Calais.
- **Seafrance**
  ☎0871 423 7119, www.seafrance.com. Service between Dover and Calais.

Eurotunnel
The fastest way across the English Channel – and you don't see the water. Drive straight onto a rail shuttle that travels through the Channel Tunnel between the M20 near Folkestone (junction 11A) and the A16 near Calais (junction 42). ☎08705 35 35 35 www.eurotunnel.com

BY COACH/BUS
Eurolines, together with National Express, operate regular services between all parts of the UK and towns throughout France. The main UK terminus is Victoria Coach Station, in central London.

- **Eurolines (National Express)**
  Ensign Court, 4 Vicarage Road, Edgbaston, Birmingham, B15 3ES. ☎08705 808080. www.nationalexpress.com/ eurolines.

BY CAR
France has an excellent network of major and minor roads covering long distances, including *autoroutes* – motorways or major highways, often with a toll to pay. Note that when entering the country at a land border, you may already be driving on an *autoroute*. After a short free section, a toll may be payable.

BY TRAIN
All rail services throughout France can be arranged through **Rail Europe** in the UK, online (www.rail europe.co.uk; www.facebook.com/ RailEuropeUK; www.twitter.com/ RailEuropeUK), by telephone ☎0844 848 4070, or call into the **Rail Europe Travel Centre** at 1 Regent Street, London SW1. Rail Europe can also book Eurostar travel.
Eurostar runs from **London** (St Pancras) to **Paris** (Gare du Nord) in under 3hr (up to 20 times daily). In Lille and Paris it links to the high-speed rail network (TGV) which covers most of France.

Gare du Nord, Paris

©Eurostar/Lydia Shalet

Bookings and information ✆08705 186 186 (£3 credit card booking fee applies) in the UK, www.eurostar.com. **Citizens of non-European Economic Area countries** will need to complete a landing card before arriving at Eurostar check-in. These can be found at dedicated desks in front of the check-in area and from Eurostar staff. Once you have filled in the card please hand it to UK immigration staff. **Eurailpass**, **Flexipass**, **Eurailpass Youth**, **EurailDrive Pass** and **Saverpass** are travel passes which may be purchased by residents of countries outside the European Union. In the US, contact your travel agent or **Rail Europe** 2100 Central Ave. Boulder, CO, 80301 ✆1-800-4-EURAIL or **Europrail International** ✆1 888 667 9731.

If you are a **European resident**, you can buy an individual country pass, if you are not a resident of the country where you plan to use it.

Getting Around

BY TRAIN

Rail travel is a pleasure in France, where trains are comfortable, punctual and good value.

A comprehensive rail network, provided by the state's rail operator SNCF, covers almost the entire country. Their sleek, fast TGV trains operate between main towns, with door-to-door journey times that easily rival air travel, especially Paris–Lyon (2 hours) and Paris–Marseille (3 hours). TGVs must always be booked in advance, and all seats are reserved. However, it is often possible to reserve a TGV seat up to just a few minutes before the train departs.

Apart from TGVs, the main city-to-city lines are also served by other comfortable modern trains which do not require advance booking. Away from these major lines, SNCF operates a reliable stopping service within each region, including a variety of smaller trains that reach into rural areas, sometimes supplemented by SNCF's bus services.

Before booking rail tickets, be sure to enquire at the station whether you are entitled to obtain one of the many rail **discount passes**. For example, groups of friends travelling together, or families with a young child, may be eligible. When first starting any journey by train, remember that rail tickets **must be validated** (*composter*) by using the orange automatic date-stamping machines at the platform entrance.

BY CAR

Driving in France should not present much difficulty. For British drivers unaccustomed to driving on the right, extra care will be needed at first, but the rules of the road are otherwise similar to those in other Western countries. Road signs generally use easy-to-understand international visual symbols instead of words.

DOCUMENTS

Driving licence

Travellers from other European Union countries and North America can drive in France with a valid national or home-state driving licence. An **international driving licence** is useful but not obligatory. These can be

Petrol/Gasoline

French service stations dispense *sans plomb 98* (super unleaded 98), *sans plomb 95* (super unleaded 95), *diesel/gazole* (diesel) and GPL (LPG), but it is usually cheaper to fill up at the large hypermarkets on the outskirts of towns.

obtained from motoring organisations, e.g. AA and RAC.

Registration papers

For the vehicle, it is necessary to have the registration papers (logbook) and a nationality plate of an approved size.

Insurance

Certain motoring organisations (AA, RAC) offer accident insurance and breakdown service schemes for members. Check with your current insurance company for coverage while abroad. Because French *autoroutes* are privately owned, your European Breakdown Cover service does not extend to breakdowns on the *autoroute* or its service areas – you must use the emergency telephones, or drive off the *autoroute* before calling your breakdown service.

ENFORCEMENT

Police have wide powers to check documents at any time and to impose heavy on-the-spot fines for almost all driving offences. In the case of more serious offences, especially if alcohol is involved, they may at their own discretion confiscate the vehicle. If paying an on-the-spot fine, you should be given a copy of the officer's report form, a receipt for any money paid, and information on how to proceed if you wish to plead not guilty. In addition to carrying the correct documentation, the driver of a vehicle registered outside France is expected to display a nationality plate of approved size close to the registration plate on the back of the vehicle, unless this already forms part of the registration plate.

INSURANCE

Insurance cover is compulsory, and although an International Motor Insurance Certificate (known in the UK as a green card) is no longer a legal requirement in France for vehicles registered in the UK, it is still the most effective proof of insurance cover and is internationally recognised by the

☺ Speed Limits ☺

- **Toll motorways** (*péage*) 130kph/ 80mph (110kph/68mph when raining)
- **Dual carriage roads** and motorways without tolls 110kph/ 68mph (100kph/62mph when raining)
- **Other roads** 90kph/56mph (80kph/50mph when raining) and in towns 50kph/31mph
- **Outside lane** on motorways during daylight, on level ground and with good visibility: min speed limit of 80kph/50mph

police and other authorities. If you have comprehensive insurance, you may want to check that your insurance cover is unaffected by driving abroad. Some insurers wish to be informed if you intend to take your vehicle abroad. Most British insurance policies give only the minimum third-party cover required while in France – but this amounts to less than it would in the UK. Therefore check with your insurance company before leaving to ensure you are fully covered in the event of an accident.

Ensure you have adequate breakdown cover before arriving in France. UK motoring organisations, for example the **AA** and the **RAC**, offer accident insurance and breakdown service programmes, either on a yearly basis or for temporary periods, for both members and non-members. These offer an emergency phone number in the UK, and a reliable standard of service and workmanship provided locally but approved by the organisation.

Members of the **American Automobile Association** should obtain the free brochure *Offices To Serve You Abroad*. The affiliated organisation for France is the **Automobile Club National** (5 r. Auber, 75009 Paris; ✆01 44 51 53 99).

HIGHWAY CODE

In France the minimum driving age is 18. Traffic drives on the right. All passengers must wear **seat belts**. **Children** under the age of 10 must ride in the back seat.

In the absence of stop signs at intersections, cars must **give way to the right**. Traffic on main roads outside built-up areas (priority indicated by a yellow diamond sign) and on roundabouts has right of way. Vehicles must stop when the lights turn red at road junctions and may filter to the right only when indicated by an amber arrow.

Priorité à Droite

On all two-way roads, traffic drives on the right. The rule of *priorité à droite* also means that priority must be given – in other words, you must give way – to **all vehicles coming from the right, even from minor roads (but not private property), unless signs indicate otherwise**. The principal sign indicating that you have priority over all other roads, even those on the right, is a yellow diamond. In practice, the yellow diamond normally gives priority to traffic on all main roads outside built-up areas.

Traffic within a roundabout (traffic circle) has priority over vehicles entering the roundabout, unless signs indicate otherwise.

Pedestrian priority

Under legislation introduced in 2010, **pedestrians** now always **have priority over cars** when crossing a road. Until recently, they had priority only at specially designated crossings. They need to "show a clear intention to cross" a road – described as "an ostensible step forward or a hand gesture" – and vehicles are required to stop for them. The only exception is where a designated pedestrian crossing is less than 50m away. Drivers who ignore the rules face a fine of €135.

Lights

Full or dipped headlights must be switched on in rain, poor visibility and at night; use sidelights only when the vehicle is stationary. Headlight beams should be adjusted for driving on the right. It is illegal to drive with faulty lights in France, so it is advisable to take a spare set of bulbs with you.

Breakdown

In the case of a **breakdown**, a red warning triangle or hazard warning lights are obligatory.

Alcohol

The regulations on **drinking and driving** are strictly enforced. The maximum permissible blood alcohol content is currently 0.50g/l.

PARKING REGULATIONS

In built-up areas there are zones where parking is either restricted or subject to a charge; tickets should be obtained from nearby ticket machines (*horodateurs* – small change necessary) and displayed inside the windscreen on the driver's side; failure to display may result in a fine, or towing away and impoundment. Other parking areas in town may require you to take a ticket when passing through a barrier. To exit, you must pay the parking fee and insert the paid-up card in another machine which will lift the exit gate.

ROUTE PLANNING

The road network is excellent and includes many motorways. The roads are very busy during the holiday period (particularly weekends in July and August), and to avoid traffic congestion it is advisable to follow the recommended secondary routes (signposted as *itinéraires bis*). The motorway network includes simple rest areas (*aires*) every 10–15km/6–10mi and service areas (*aires de service*), with fuel, restaurant and shopping, about every

40km/25mi. The rest areas are only basically provisioned, often having no more than just toilets. The main service areas are more fully equipped, but vary in size and complexity from perfectly adequate "pit stop" facilities with mini-supermarkets, coffee machines and newspaper kiosks, to extensive complexes often with restaurants and overnight accommodation, too.

For **24hr motorway information** dial ✆01 47 05 90 01.

For **general information** on traffic and *itinéraires bis*, contact Bison Futé; ✆0800 100 200; www.bison-fute. equipement.gouv.fr.

TOLLS

In France, most motorway sections are subject to a toll *(péage)*. You can pay in cash or, increasingly, with a Visa or Mastercard.

CAR RENTAL

There are car rental agencies at airports, railway stations and in all large towns throughout France. European cars have manual transmission; automatic cars are available only if an advance reservation is made.

Drivers must be over 21; between ages 21 and 25, drivers are required to pay an extra daily fee; some companies allow drivers under 23 only if the reservation has been made through a travel agent. It is relatively expensive to hire a car in France. There are many online services that will look for the best prices on car rental around the globe.

Where to Stay and Eat

Hotel and restaurant listings fall within the *Discovering France* section of the guide; they can be found in the *Addresses* sections of the Principal Sights.

To enhance your stay, hotel selections have been chosen for their location, comfort, value for the money, and, in many cases, their charm. Prices indicate the cost of a standard room for two people in peak season.

French cuisine is as varied as it is delicious. We have highlighted an array of eating places primarily for their atmosphere, location and regional delicacies. Prices indicate the average cost of a starter, main dish and dessert for one person. The Legend on the cover flap explains the symbols and abbreviations used in the Addresses sections.

WHERE TO STAY
FINDING A HOTEL

The **Addresses** in this guide describe a number of lodgings arranged by price category. They appear in many of the cities and towns described in the guide. For an even greater selection, use the **Michelin Guide France**, with its famously reliable star-rating system and hundreds of establishments throughout France. The **Michelin Charming Places to Stay** guide contains a selection of 1 000 hotels and guesthouses at reasonable prices. Be sure to book ahead to ensure that you get the accommodation you want, not only in the tourist season but year-round, as many towns fill up during trade fairs, arts festivals etc. Some places require an advance deposit or a reconfirmation. Reconfirming is especially important if you plan to arrive after 6pm.

For further assistance, **Loisirs Accueil** is a booking service that has offices in some French *départements*: 280 bd

St-Germain, 75007 Paris. ☎01 44 11 10 44. www.loisirs-accueil.fr.

The handbook of a respected federation of good-value, family-run hotels (most with restaurants), **Logis et Auberges de France**, is available from the French Tourist Office, as are lists of other kinds of accommodation such as hotel-châteaux, bed-and-breakfasts, etc.

Another resource, which publishes a catalogue for each French *département*, for vacation villas, apartments or chalets, is the **Fédération Nationale des Locations de France Clévacances** (54 bd de l'Embouchure, BP 52166, 31022 Toulouse Cedex 2; ☎05 61 13 55 66; www.clevacances.com).

Relais et Châteaux provides information on booking in luxury hotels with character. For central reservations (UK): ☎00 800 2000 00 02, www.relaischateaux.com.

ECONOMY CHAIN HOTELS

If you need a place to stop en route, these lodgings can be useful, as they are inexpensive (around €40–45 for a double room) and generally located near the main road. While a simple breakfast is available, there may not be a restaurant; rooms are small and functional, with a television and bathroom. All can be booked online.

For reservations
- **Akena:** www.hotels-akena.com
- **Best Hotel:** www.besthotel.fr.
- **SimplyHotelsFrance:** www.sidhole.com
- **Villages Hôtel:** www.villages-hotel.com

The hotels listed below are expensive (from €45), but offer more amenities:

For reservations
- **Campanile, Climat de France, Kyriad** ☎01 64 62 59 70 www.campanile.com
- **Etap** ☎0892 688 900 www.etaphotel.com

- **Ibis** ☎0892 686 686 www.ibishotel.com

RENTING A COTTAGE, BED AND BREAKFAST

The **Maison des Gîtes de France** is an information service on self-catering accommodation in France. Gîtes usually take the form of a cottage or apartment decorated in the local style where visitors can make themselves at home, or bed and breakfast accommodation (Chambres d'hôtes) which consists of a room and breakfast at a reasonable price. Contact the **Gîtes de France** office in Paris (56 r. St-Lazare, 75439 Paris Cedex 09; ☎01 49 70 75 75; www.gites-de-france.fr), which has a good English version. From the site, you can choose and book a gîte, or order catalogues for different regions illustrated with photographs of the properties, as well as specialised catalogues (bed and breakfasts, farm stays, etc.).

If you want to improve your French, then consider the category Chambres d'hôte/Table d'hôte. These are essentially B&B properties, but, being (usually) a little more remote from town centres offer an evening meal. But it's one where you have to join in with the whole family, few of whom would be able to speak English. Regional sites also have information about self-catering cottages in their area, for example www.lagrange-holidays.co.uk and www.loire-valley-holidays.com, on which you can view and book cottages and contact local tourist offices, which may have lists of more properties and local bed and breakfast establishments.

HOSTELS, CAMPING

The international youth hostels movement, International Youth Hostel Federation or Hostelling International, has dozens of hostels in France. There is an online booking service on www.hihostels.com, which you may use to reserve rooms as far as six months in advance. To stay in hostels, you may need a membership card. To obtain an IYHF or HI card (there is no age requirement) contact the IYHF or HI in your own country for information and membership applications (in the UK ✆01629 592700. In the US, there are many HI centres; check the website to find your nearest). There are two main youth hostel associations *(auberges de jeunesse)* in France, the **Ligue Française pour les Auberges de la Jeunesse** (67 r. Vergniaud, 75013 Paris; ✆01 44 16 78 78; www. auberges-de-jeunesse.com) and the **Fédération Unie des Auberges de Jeunesse** (27 r. Pajol, 75018 Paris; ✆01 44 89 87 27; Fax 01 44 89 87 10). There are thousands of officially graded **campsites** with varying standards of facilities throughout the country. The **Michelin Camping France** guide lists a selection of camp-sites. It is wise to reserve in advance.

WHERE TO EAT
FINDING A RESTAURANT
Turn to the Addresses within the *Discovering France* section for descriptions and prices of selected places to eat in the different locations covered in this guide. The Legend on the cover flap explains the symbols and abbreviations used in these Addresses. Use the red-cover **Michelin Guide France**, with its respected star-rating system and hundreds of establishments all over France, for an even greater choice. Restaurants usually serve lunch from noon–2pm and dinner from 7.30–10pm. It is not always easy to find something to eat at other times, except for a simple baguette sandwich in a café, or an ordinary hot dish in a brasserie.

In French restaurants and cafés, the service charge and all taxes are included in the price, so tipping is not necessary. However, it is usual to leave any small change from the bill on the table when leaving.

For a glossary of gastronomic terms and for information on local specialities, ↪see the section entitled Food and Drink in the Introduction.

Useful Words and Phrases

Sights

	Translation
Abbey	Abbaye
Belfry	Beffroi
Bridge	Pont
Castle	Château
Cemetery	Cimetière
Chapel	Chapelle
Church	Église
Cloisters	Cloître
Convent	Couvent
Courtyard	Cour
Fountain	Fontaine
Garden	Jardin
Gateway	Porte
Hall	Halle
House	Maison
Lock (Canal)	Écluse
Market	Marché
Monastery	Monastère
Museum	Musée
Park	Parc
Port/harbour	Port
Quay	Quai
Ramparts	Remparts
Square	Place
Street	Rue
Statue	Statue
Tower	Tour
Town Hall	Mairie
Windmill	Moulin

Natural Sites

	Translation
Abyss	Abîme
Swallow-hole	Aven

Dam	Barrage
Viewpoint	Belvédère
Waterfall	Cascade
Pass	Col
Ledge	Corniche
Coast, Hillside	Côte
Forest	Forêt
Cave	Grotte
Lake	Lac
Beach	Plage
River	Rivière
Stream	Ruisseau
Beacon	Signal
Spring	Source
Valley	Vallée

On the Road

	Translation
Car Park	Parking
Driving Licence	Permis de conduire
East	Est
Garage (For Repairs)	Garage
Left	Gauche
Motorway/Highway	Autoroute
North	Nord
Parking Meter	Horodateur
Petrol/Gas	Essence
Petrol/Gas Station	Station essence
Right	Droite
South	Sud
Toll	Péage
Traffic Lights	Feu tricolore
Tyre	Pneu
West	Ouest
Wheel Clamp	Sabot
Zebra Crossing	Passage clouté

Time

	Translation
Today	Aujourd'hui
Tomorrow	Demain
Yesterday	Hier
Winter	Hiver
Spring	Printemps
Summer	Été
Autumn/Fall	Automne
Week	Semaine
Monday	Lundi

Tuesday	Mardi
Wednesday	Mercredi
Thursday	Jeudi
Friday	Vendredi
Saturday	Samedi
Sunday	Dimanche

Numbers

	Translation
0	zéro
1	un
2	deux
3	trois
4	quatre
5	cinq
6	six
7	sept
8	huit
9	neuf
10	dix
11	onze
12	douze
13	treize
14	quatorze
15	quinze
16	seize
17	dix-sept
18	dix-huit
19	dix-neuf
20	vingt
30	trente
40	quarante
50	cinquante
60	soixante
70	soixante-dix
80	quatre-vingt
90	quatre-vingt-dix
100	cent
1000	mille

Shopping

	Translation
Bank	Banque
Baker's	Boulangerie
Big	Grand
Butcher's	Boucherie
Chemist's	Pharmacie
Closed	Fermé

Cough Mixture	Sirop pour la toux
Cough Sweets	Cachets pour la gorge
Entrance	Entrée
Exit	Sortie
Fishmonger's	Poissonnerie
Grocer's	Épicerie
Newsagent, Bookshop	Librairie
Open	Ouvert
Post Office	Poste
Push	Pousser
Pull	Tirer
Shop	Magasin
Small	Petit
Stamps	Timbres

Food and Drink

	Translation
Beef	Bœuf
Beer	Bière
Butter	Beurre
Bread	Pain
Breakfast	Petit-déjeuner
Cheese	Fromage
Dessert	Dessert
Dinner	Dîner
Fish	Poisson
Fork	Fourchette
Fruit	Fruits
Glass	Verre
Chicken	Poulet
Ice Cream	Glace
Ice Cubes	Glaçons
Ham	Jambon
Knife	Couteau
Lamb	Agneau
Lunch	Déjeuner
Lettuce Salad	Salade
Meat	Viande
Mineral Water	Eau minérale
Mixed Salad	Salade composée
Orange Juice	Jus d'orange
Plate	Assiette
Pork	Porc
Restaurant	Restaurant
Salt	Sel
Spoon	Cuillère
Sugar	Sucre

"Couteau" and "Fourchette"

©Andrew Johnson/iStockphoto.com

Vegetables	Légumes
Water	De L'eau
White/Red Wine	Vin blanc/rouge
Yoghurt	Yaourt

Travel

	Translation
Travel	Voyager
Airport	Aéroport
Credit Card	Carte de crédit
Customs	Douane
Passport	Passeport
Platform	Voie
Railway Station	Gare
Shuttle	Navette
Suitcase	Valise
Train Ticket	Billet de train
Plane Ticket	Billet d'avion
Wallet	Portefeuille

Clothing

	Translation
Coat	Manteau
Jumper	Pull
Raincoat	Imperméable
Shirt	Chemise
Shoes	Chaussures
Socks	Chaussettes
Stockings	Bas
Suit	Costume
Tights	Collants
Trousers	Pantalon

Common Words

	Translation
Goodbye	Au revoir
Hello/Good Morning	Bonjour
How	Comment
Excuse Me	Excusez-moi
Thank You	Merci
Yes/No	Oui/Non
I Am Sorry	Pardon
Why	Pourquoi
When	Quand
Please	S'il vous plaît

USEFUL PHRASES

Do you speak English?
Parlez-vous anglais?
I don't understand
Je ne comprends pas
Talk slowly
Parlez lentement
Where is...?. Où est...?
When does the ... leave?
A quelle heure part...?
When does the ... arrive?
A quelle heure arrive...?
When does the museum open?
A quelle heure ouvre le musée?
What does it cost?
Combien cela coûte?

Where can I buy a newspaper in English?
Où puis-je acheter un journal en anglais?
Where is the nearest petrol/gas station?
Où se trouve la station essence la plus proche?
Where are the toilets?
Où sont les toilettes?
Do you accept credit cards?
Acceptez-vous les cartes de crédit?

USEFUL TO KNOW

On national and departmental roads, there are often roundabouts (traffic circles) just outside the towns, which serve to slow traffic down.
At a French roundabout **(rond point)**, you are likely to see signs pointing to **Centre Ville** (city centre) or to other towns (the French use towns as directional indicators, rather than cardinal points). You are also likely to see a sign for **Toutes Directions** (all directions – this is often the bypass road to avoid going through the town) or **Autres Directions** (other directions – in other words, any place that isn't indicated on one of the other signs on the roundabout!).

Basic Information

BUSINESS HOURS

Offices and other businesses are open Mon–Fri, 9am–noon, 2–6pm. Many also open Saturday mornings. Town and village shops are generally open Tue–Fri; there are local variations. Midday breaks may be much longer in the South. However, in cities, tourist centres or resorts, businesses may keep longer hours or stay open all day, seven days a week, especially if they primarily serve the tourist market.

ELECTRICITY

The electric current is 220 volts/50 Hz. Circular two-pin plugs are the rule.

Adaptors should be bought before you leave home; they are on sale in most airports.

EMERGENCIES

⚑ *See Emergency Numbers box.*
First aid, medical advice and chemists' night-service rotas are available from chemists/drugstores (*pharmacie*, identified by a green cross sign).

EMERGENCY NUMBERS	
Police (*Gendarme*):	☏17
Fire (*Pompiers*):	☏18
Ambulance (*SAMU*):	☏15
European-wide Emergency Number:	☏112

MAIL/POST

Look for the bright yellow *La Poste* signs. Main post offices are generally open Mon–Fri 9am–7pm, Sat 9am–noon. Smaller branches generally open 9am–noon, 2–4pm weekdays. There are often automatic tellers *(guichets automatiques)* inside, which allow you to weigh packages and buy postage and avoid a queue. You may also find that you can change money, make copies, send faxes and make phone calls in a post office.

To post a letter from the street look for the bright yellow postboxes. Stamps are also sold in newsagents and cafés that sell cigarettes *(tabac)*. Stamp collectors should ask for *timbres de collection* in any post office (there is often a *philatélie* counter).

France uses a five-digit postal code that precedes the name of the city or town on the last line of the address. The first two digits indicate the *département* and the last three digits identify the *commune* or local neighbourhood. www.laposte.fr.

MONEY
CURRENCY

There are no restrictions on the amount of currency visitors can take into France. Visitors wishing to export currency in foreign banknotes in excess of the given allocation from France should complete a currency declaration form on arrival.

Coins and notes – The unit of currency in France is the **euro** (€). One euro is divided into 100 cents or *centimes d'euro*. Old franc notes can still be exchanged by the Banque de France until early 2012.

BANKS AND CURRENCY EXCHANGE

Banks are generally open Mon–Fri 9am–5.30pm. Some branches are open for limited transactions on Saturday. Banks limit opening hours on the day before a bank holiday. A passport or other ID may be necessary when cashing cheques in banks. Commission charges vary and hotels usually charge considerably more than banks for cashing cheques, especially for non-residents.

By far the most convenient way of obtaining French currency is the **24hr cash dispenser** or **ATM** (*distributeur automatique de billets* in French), found outside many banks and post offices and easily recognisable by the CB *(Carte Bleue)* logo. Most accept international credit cards (don't forget your PIN) and almost all also give instructions in English.

Note that many ATMs will dispense only up to a certain limit, which may be lower than the daily limit set by your bank. Do not attempt to top up funds the same day (although you can continue to use the card to pay bills in restaurants, for example); this may work with some banks, but at others your card may be declined or, worse, retained. Foreign currency can also be exchanged in major banks, post offices, hotels or private exchange offices found in main cities and near popular tourist attractions.

CREDIT CARDS

Major credit cards (Visa, Mastercard, Eurocard) are widely accepted in shops, hotels, restaurants and petrol stations.

If your card is lost or stolen call the appropriate 24hr hotlines:

- ◆ **American Express**
  ℘ (01) 4777 72 00
- ◆ **Visa**
  ℘ (08) 36 69 08 80
- ◆ **Mastercard**
  ℘ 0800 90 13 87

You should also report any loss or theft to the local police who will issue you with a certificate (useful proof to show the credit card company).

PUBLIC HOLIDAYS

There are 11 public holidays in France. In addition, there are other religious and national festival days, and a number of local saints' days, etc. On all these days, museums and other monuments may be closed or may vary their hours of admission.

PUBLIC HOLIDAYS	
1 January	New Year's Day (*Jour de l'An*)
8 April	Easter Monday (*Pâques*)
1 May	Labour Day
8 May	VE Day
17 May	Ascension Day (*Ascension catholique*)
4 June	Whit Monday
14 July	*Fête* National France's National Day (or Bastille Day)
15 August	Assumption (*Assomption*)
1 November	All Saints' Day (*Toussaint*)
11 November	Armistice Day
25 December	Christmas Day (*Noël*)

SCHOOL HOLIDAYS

French schools close for holidays five times a year. In these periods, all tourist sites and attractions, hotels, restaurants, and roads are busier than usual. These school holidays are one week at the end of October, two weeks at Christmas, two weeks in February, two weeks in spring, and the whole of July and August.

SMOKING REGULATIONS

Since the beginning of 2008, smoking has been forbidden in all public places in France, notably bars, restaurants, railway stations and airports. Ironically, this has created a problem for non-smokers who want to sit outside on a terrace to enjoy the open air, where smoking is not prohibited.

TAX REFUNDS

Non-EU residents are entitled to claim back sales tax (*TVA*) on goods when spending more than €175 at one store on the same day. Ask for your receipts and a form when at the sales desk, and take these and your purchases to the local customs office at the airport before you check in for your flight.

TELEPHONES

The telephone system in France is still operated largely by the former state monopoly France Télécom. They offer an English-language enquiries service on ✆0800 364 775 (within France) or ✆00 33 1 55 78 60 56 (outside France). The French **ringing tone** is a series of long tones; the engaged (busy) tone is a series of short beeps.

To use a **public phone** you need to buy a prepaid phone card (*télécartes*). Some telephone booths accept credit cards (Visa, Mastercard/Eurocard). *Télécartes* (50 or 120 units) can be bought in post offices, cafés that sell cigarettes (*tabac*) and newsagents, and can be used to make calls in France and abroad. Calls can be received at phone boxes where the blue bell sign is shown. The phone will not ring audibly, so keep your eye on the little message screen.

MOBILE/CELL PHONES

While in France, all visitors from other European countries should be able to use their mobile phone just as normal. Visitors from some other countries need to ensure before departure that their phone and service contract are compatible with the European system (GSM).

The three main mobile phone operators in France are SFR, Orange and Bouygues.

- ◆ **Orange**
  www.orange.fr
- ◆ **Bouygues**
  www.bouyguestelecom.fr
- ◆ **SFR**
  www.sfr.fr

Dual- or tri-band mobile phones will work almost anywhere in France, but at international roaming rates. If you are staying for an extended period you might consider renting a mobile phone locally, including Blackberries and iPhones – www.cellhire.fr.

INFORMATION

International Information
UK 📞 00 33 12 44

International Information
USA/Canada 📞 00 33 12 11

International Operator
📞 00 33 12 + country code

Local Directory Assistance 📞 12

INTERNATIONAL DIALLING CODES

Australia	📞 61
Ireland	📞 353
United Kingdom	📞 44
Canada	📞 1
New Zealand	📞 64
United States	📞 1

NATIONAL CALLS

French telephone numbers have 10 digits. Numbers begin with 01 in Paris and the Paris region; 02 in northwest France; 03 in northeast France; 04 in southeast France and Corsica; 05 in southwest France. However, all 10 numbers must be dialled even within the local region.

INTERNATIONAL CALLS

To call France from abroad, dial the country code 33, omit the initial zero of the French number, and dial the remaining 9-digit number. When calling abroad from France dial 00, followed by the country code *(see above)*, followed by the local area code (usually without any initial zero) and the number of your correspondent. To use the personal calling card of a telephone company, follow the card instructions, dialling the access code for the country you are in, e.g.:

◆ **AT&T**
   📞 0800 99-0011
◆ **BT**
   📞 0800 99-0244
◆ **MCI/Verizon**
   📞 0800 99-0019

◆ **Sprint**
   📞 0800 99-0087
◆ **Canada Direct**
   📞 0800 99-0016

Cheap rates with 50 percent extra time are available from private telephones to the UK on weekdays 9.30pm–8am, from 2pm on Saturdays and all day on Sundays and holidays. Cheap rates to the USA and Canada are from 2am–noon all week, and to Australia Mon–Sat 9.30pm–8am and all day Sunday. **Toll-free numbers** in France (also known as *Numéro Verte*) begin with 0800.

For more information about using phones in France, visit **www.orange.fr.**

TIME

France is in the Central European time zone. During the winter months, from 2am on the last Sunday of October to 2am on the last Sunday of March, France is one hour ahead of GMT. From 2am on the last Sunday of March to 2am on the last Sunday of October, it adopts daylight saving time and is two hours ahead of GMT.

WHEN IT IS **NOON IN FRANCE** IT IS	
11am	in London
7pm	in Perth
11am	in Dublin
9pm	in Sydney
6am	in New York
11pm	in Auckland
3am	in Los Angeles

Because the UK changes its clocks to British Summer Time (i.e. daylight saving time) at the same times and on the same dates, France always remains one hour ahead of the UK. In France the 24-hour clock is widely applied.

TEMPERATURE CHART THROUGHOUT FRANCE

	Jan	Feb	Mar	Apr	May	Jun	Jul	Aug	Sep	Oct	Nov	Dec
	9	10	15	17	20	23	25	25	23	18	12	8
Bordeaux	1	2	4	9	12	13	13	13	12	8	4	2
	8	9	11	13	15	18	19	20	18	15	11	9
Brest	4	3	4	7	8	11	12	13	11	8	6	4
	7	8	13	16	19	23	25	25	22	16	11	7
Clermont	-1	-1	2	5	7	11	13	12	10	6	3	0
	5	8	13	16	20	23	26	26	23	16	10	6
Grenoble	-3	-2	2	5	8	12	14	13	11	6	3	-1
	5	6	10	13	17	20	22	22	19	14	9	6
Lille	0	0	2	4	7	10	12	12	10	7	3	1
	12	13	14	17	20	23	26	26	24	20	16	13
Nice	4	4	5	9	12	16	18	16	12	8	5	
	7	7	12	15	19	22	24	24	21	15	10	6
Paris	1	1	3	6	9	12	14	14	11	8	4	2
	12	13	16	18	21	25	28	28	25	20	15	12
Perpignan	3	4	7	9	12	16	19	18	16	12	8	5
	3	5	11	15	19	23	24	25	20	14	8	4
Strasbourg	-2	-1	1	4	6	11	13	13	10	5	2	-1

Maximum temperatures in red; minimum temperatures in black.

TIPPING

Since a service charge is automatically included in the prices of meals and accommodation in France, it is not necessary to tip in restaurants and hotels. However, if the service in a restaurant is especially good or if you have enjoyed a fine meal, an extra tip (this is the *pourboire,* rather than the *service*) will be appreciated. Usually €5–10 is enough, but if the bill is big (a large party or a luxury restaurant), it is not uncommon to leave more. However, in bars and cafés it is not unusual to leave any small change that remains after paying the bill, but this generally should not be more than 5 percent. Taxi drivers do not have to be tipped, but again it is usual to give a small amount, not more than 10 percent. Attendants at public toilets should be given a few cents. Hairdressers are usually tipped 10–15 percent. Tour guides and tour drivers should be tipped according to the amount of service given: from €2–5 would not be unusual.

France's UNESCO World Heritage Sites

World Heritage sites are natural and cultural sites identified by UNESCO following the adoption, during the 1972 General Conference, of the "Convention Concerning the Protection of the World Cultural and Natural Heritage". There are more than 900 sites (700+ cultural, 180 natural and 27 mixed) currently inscribed on the World Heritage List. To be included on the World Heritage List, sites must be of outstanding universal value and meet at least one out of ten selection criteria, divided into six cultural criteria and four natural criteria.

More than 35 sites in France are of such importance internationally that they have been inscribed as World Heritage Sites. This protected cultural heritage includes monuments (buildings, sculptures, archaeological structures, etc) that have unique historical, artistic or scientific features; groups of buildings (such as religious communities, ancient cities); or sites (human settlements, examples of exceptional landscapes, cultural landscapes) which are the combined works of man and nature, and of exceptional beauty.

Some of the sites in France are multiple in nature, for example the numerous Vauban fortifications that appear across much of the country, and the various pilgrimage routes of Santiago de Compostela. Others are more esoteric – the banks of the Seine in Paris, part of the Loire Valley between Sully-sur-Loire and Chalonnes and the Grande Île in Strasbourg. But most focus on one redeeming feature such as the Roman aqueduct at Pont du Gard, Amiens Cathedral and Provins, the town of medieval fairs.

A recent addition to the list for France is the stunningly beautiful episcopal city of Albi in the department of Tarn. And such is the heritage of France that another 35 properties are currently under consideration for inclusion on the World Heritage List, including the Camargue, the Fontainebleau forest, the massif of Mont Blanc, the Carnac stones, the Cévennes and the Grands Causses.

The World Heritage Convention is not only "words on paper", but a vital instrument for firm action in preserving threatened sites and endangered species. By recognising outstanding universal value of sites, governments across the world commit to their preservation and strive to find solutions for their protection.

Albi by the Tarn, Midi-Pyrénées

© Gérard Labriet/Photononstop

Pont Alexandre III at dusk, Paris
©Paul Reid/Dreamstime.com

France Today

21ST CENTURY

France has long enjoyed a strong rural tradition, but today there are far fewer people (only 3.8%) employed in agriculture. Alongside this, France has a very advanced industrial economy (24.3% of the population), but employs the greatest proportion of the population (71.8%, 2010) in the services sector.

LIFESTYLE

For many the concept of the French lifestyle conjures up images of good living with strong emphasis on family values and traditions. And while this remains true for many, there has been a tendency in recent years for busy families to spend less time together and eat less well.

This has led some social commentators to the view that all is not well with French society. That may be the case, but an attempt in 2010 to have the traditional French lunch listed by UNESCO as worthy of cultural World Heritage status shows that the French have not lost their sense of humour.

POPULATION

The total population of France (January 2011) was 65 027 000, an increase of 1.35m over the previous year, and growing at a rate of 0.549%. The estimated birth rate/1 000 population for 2011 is 12.29, a slight but constant decrease that has prevailed throughout much of the 21C. The average age at marriage is just over 30 for men and just under 30 for women, although the rate of marriage is falling with many preferring to cohabit. In 2006, the French government introduced a law raising the age at which a woman can get married from 15 to 18. France continues to have the longest-living citizens in Europe – for men life expectancy is 77 years while for women it is 84.

RELIGION

Freedom of religion is guaranteed by the Constitution, but there is a strict separation of Church and state. The French government does not maintain any records of the statistics of the religion of the inhabitants of France. But since the 1970s, France has become a very secular country with a growing number admitting to being lapsed Christians, agnostic or atheist.

SPORT

Sport has always played an important role in French society, with the most watched sport being football. Both rugby codes (Union and League) are popular, as are athletics, alpine skiing, tennis and, of course, cycling. At lower energy levels, *pétanque* and *boules* are played anywhere there is a small patch of level ground, and are taken very seriously indeed. There is a difference between the two, but only a Frenchman would dare try to explain it!

MEDIA AND INTERNET

Newspapers, both national and local, and magazines are readily available at the many *Maisons de la presse* (newsagents) found in all towns. English-language newspapers are usually only available in larger centres, but are often a day old by the time they arrive on the newsstand.

The internet is now widely available in hotels, fast-food outlets, internet cafés and even the local bar. Most use WiFi connections, for a charge.

ECONOMY AND GOVERNMENT

Economically, France has followed its own path, favouring extensive employee rights, state monopolies, state intervention, heavy subsidies and protectionism. In 2010, France was ranked the fifth- largest economy in the world behind the US, China, Japan and Germany, but just ahead of the UK. France's trade is one of the largest in the world, in 2010 importing and exporting raw materials, cars and electronic products totalling £283bn (€321bn) – exports – and £330bn (€374bn) – imports.

The **government** of France is a semi-Presidential system functioning under a written constitution, and with a parliament of *Deputés* elected every five years and a President also elected every five years. The President has extensive personal powers. At the same time, France is divided into large regions with a high degree of autonomy. Within each region is a multitude of communes, which enjoy a good deal of local self-determination under powerful mayors.

FOOD AND DRINK

France is the land of good food and fine dining, and it has a host of regional specialities. The **Michelin Red Guide: France** lists hundreds of hotels and restaurants throughout the country.

FRENCH CUISINE

Soups

In restaurants, large and small, at least one soup of the day will always be available. The best-known, probably because they are the easiest to make, are cream of asparagus *(velouté d'asperges)*, leek and potato *(soupe de poireaux-pommes de terre)*, onion *(soupe à l'oignon or gratinée)*, *garbure* (a thick soup with cabbage popular in southwestern France) and *cotriade* (Breton fish soup). In rural village bar-restaurants you may be served a dish of raw vegetables *(crudités)* to begin your meal.

Entrées and main courses

In France, the *entrée* is commonly the first dish of a meal (and strictly speaking includes soup). Quite often the first course will be a savoury tart or salad, something light, like *salade niçoise* (tomatoes, anchovies, onions, olives) or *salade lyonnaise* (endive, bacon, croutons, poached eggs), that leads in to the main course. If dining out in a restaurant, especially at lunchtime, do not feel pressured to go for three courses; if all you want is a main dish, just ask for that. France, of course, is renowned for its imaginative and inventive cuisine, and there are many regional dishes that are worth trying, like *aligot* (a dish traditionally made in the Aubrac (Aveyron, Cantal, Lozère) region in the Massif Central), which is a blend of melted Tomme cheese (although others are often substituted, to good effect) and

mashed potatoes, often flavoured with garlic; *cassoulet* (a rich, rib-sticking white haricot bean stew containing meat, usually pork sausages, pork and duck confit. It is slow-cooked and best enjoyed at a leisurely pace with plenty of crusty bread); *tartiflette* (a dish from Savoie, made with potatoes, Reblochon cheese, cream and lardons. It often includes onions); and *ratatouille* (a stewed vegetable dish from Provence, often served as a side dish, but also as a main course in itself served with pasta or bread, perhaps even with rice).

Cheese

The cheese course in French dining comes before the dessert, not after. It is intended to cleanse the palate after the main course, so to better appreciate the flavours of the final course.

Almost every village in France produces its own cheeses, and there is seldom any doubt about origin. General de Gaulle once joked about the difficulties of governing a country with 365 cheeses, one for every day of the year. There are rather more than that these days, but, perhaps surprisingly, fewer than in the UK, which has over 700 cheeses.

Cheese is such a quintessential element of French cuisine that no fewer than 45 of them have been given AOC status *(Appellation d'Origine Contrôlée)*, which effectively controls the production and origin of cheese: 29 cow's milk cheeses; 13 goat's milk; 2 made from sheep's milk and just 1 that is made from mixed milk. That's not *it*, of course; those are just the certified cheeses, where method of production and place of origin are guaranteed. Wander into any town or village market, supermarket or village shop and you will be faced with a bewildering and tasty choice.

But then, when you've found a particular wine that suits your taste, there is nothing nicer than sitting out in the sun with a glass of it and a selection of local cheeses and crusty bread.

Fruit and Desserts

There are innumerable **desserts** to round off a meal. Apart from the baskets of fruit, strawberries and cream, strawberries in red wine, and fruit salads that make use of all the orchard fruits, there are apple, pear and peach compotes, and all manner of cake dishes, such as *tarte Tatin* (a caramelised tart cooked with the filling underneath), walnut cake (*gâteau aux noix*), *far* (a baked custard dessert from Brittany), gingerbread (*pain d'épices*) in the Gâtinais region, *clafoutis* (a blend of milk and eggs mixed with fruit and baked in the oven), and *kougelhopf* from Alsace baked in the form of a ring and served as a dessert or as an afternoon snack. For those with an especially sweet tooth there is crème caramel, baked cream desserts, and soft meringues with custard sauce (*île flottante*) that are found in nearly every region of France.

THE WINES OF FRANCE

The wines of France encompass every variety of taste from sweet whites to the driest, from rich, full-bodied reds to light easy-drinking rosés, from unpretentious, drinkable table wines to the greatest names in the world, including, of course, the very symbol of celebration and delight, champagne.

For wine-lovers, the **Michelin Guide: The Wine Regions of France** offers a comprehensive introduction to French wine-making and features driving itineraries for the 14 main wine regions of the country: Alsace, Beaujolais, Bordelais (Bordeaux wines), Burgundy, Champagne, Cognac, Corse (Corsican wines), Jura, Languedoc-Roussillon, Loire Valley, Provence, Rhône Valley, Savoie-Bugey and the Southwest. Descriptions of over 500 restaurants, hotels and guesthouses are included in this guide to enhance your journey through these regions.

See also the French regional **Michelin Green Guides** for the specific region in which you are interested; for example, the *Green Guide Provence* describes Provençal wines.

The official French wine website, www. wines-france.com, features information about grapes, wine labels, France's wine regions and more.

FOOD GLOSSARY

ail - garlic
aïoli - garlic mayonnaise
aligot - potatoes and Tomme cheese
andouillette - chitterling sausage
anis - aniseed confectionery
asperges - asparagus
bar - sea bass
bergamotes - orange-flavoured, hard-boiled sweets
berlingots - more hard-boiled sweets
bêtises - hard mints
beurre blanc - butter sauce
bouillabaisse - seafood stew
bourride - fish soup
brandade - creamed salt cod
calmar - squid
canard au sang - pressed duck
cassoulet - stew with haricot beans, sausages and pork

Vineyards of Vosne-Romanée, Côte d'Or, Burgundy

cèpes - cèpe mushrooms
charcuterie - smoked, cured or dried meats
choucroute - Sauerkraut
confiseries - confectionery
confits - duck or goose preserved in fat
crêpes - pancakes
crêpes dentelles - thin pancakes
cuisse de grenouilles - frog's legs
daurade, dorade - sea bream
dragées - sugared almonds
encornet - squid
escargots - snails
esturgeons - sturgeon
far - flan with prunes
ficelles Picardes - ham pancakes with mushroom sauce
foie gras - goose liver
fouace - dough cakes
fraises - strawberries
fruits confits - crystallised fruit
galettes - savoury pancakes or waffles
gâteau d'amandes - almond cake
garbure - meat and vegetable stew
gratins - dishes with a crusty topping
jambon - ham
jambon cru - cured ham
lait - milk
lardons - thickly sliced bacon pieces
légumes - vegetables
lotte - monkfish
loup - bass
macarons - macaroons
madeleines - small sponge cakes
magret de canard - breast of duck
marrons glacés - crystallised chestnuts
massepains - marzipan cakes
matelote - eel stew
merlu - hake
meurette - wine sauce
miel - honey
morue - salt cod
mouclade - mussel stew
moules - mussels
moutarde - mustard
noix - nuts
nougat - sugar, honey and nut sweetmeat
nougatine - caramel syrup and almond sweetmeat
oursins - sea urchins
pain d'épice - spiced honey cake

Galette de sarrasin with ham and egg

S. Sauvignier/MICHELIN

pieds de cochon - pigs' trotters
piperade sweet pepper and tomato omelette
poireau - leeks
poisson - fish
poulardes - fatted chickens
poulet - chicken
pralines - caramelised almond confectionery
pruneaux - prunes
quenelles - poached meat or fish dumplings
quenelles de brochet - pike dumplings
quiche (Lorraine) - egg, cream and bacon flan
rillettes - potted pork
rillons - potted chopped pork
rognons - kidneys
saucisson - sausage
seiche - cuttlefish
soupe au pistou - vegetable soup with basil
tartiflette - potatoes, Reblochon cheese, cream and lardons
topinambour - Jerusalem artichoke
touron - soft almond confectionery
tourteau fromager - goat's cheese gateau
tripes - tripe
truffes - truffles
truite - trout
viande - meat
volailles - poultry

History

The great sweep of prehistory has left abundant traces in France, and it is to Frenchmen that much of our knowledge of prehistoric times is due. *See Les EYZIES-DE-TAYAC: Prehistory.*

TIME LINE
ANCIENT TIMES

5000 BC	Megalithic culture flourishes in Brittany (Carnac), then in Corsica, lasting for over 2 500 years.
8C	Celtic tribes from central Europe arrive in Gaul where they build the fortified settlements known as oppidums.
600	Greek traders found a number of cities, including Marseille, Glanum (*see ST-RÉMY-DE-PROVENCE)*, and Aléria in Corsica.
2C	Celtic culture, which had spread as far as Brittany, gives way to both Germanic and Roman influences. The port of Fréjus, on the Mediterranean coast, is founded in 154 by the Romans as a link on the sea route to their possessions in Spain. By the year 122 they have established themselves at Aix, and four years later at Narbonne.
58–52	Julius Caesar's Gallic Wars. He defeats the Veneti in 56 BCE (*see VANVES)*, then himself suffers defeat at the hands of Vercingetorix (*see CLERMONT-FERRAND)* in 52 BCE, though the latter's surrender comes only a few months later.
AD 1C	During the reign of Augustus, Roman rule in Gaul is consolidated and expanded (*see NÎMES)*. Fréjus is converted into a naval base and fortified.

5C	The monasteries set up by St Martin at Ligugé and by St Honorat at Lérins reinforce Christian beliefs and mark the beginning of a wave of such foundations (by St Victor at Marseille, by St Loup at Troyes, by St Maxime at Riez).

THE MEROVINGIANS (418–751)

451	Merovius, king of the Salian Franks (from the Tournai area in present-day Belgium), defeats Attila the Hun (*see CHÂLONS-EN-CHAMPAGNE)*. It is to him that the dynasty owes its name.
476	Fall of the Roman Empire in the West; Gaul occupied by barbarian tribes.
496	Clovis, grandson of Merovius and King of the Franks, is baptised in Reims.
507	Defeat of the Visigoths under Alaric II at Vouillé (*see POITIERS)* by Clovis.
6C	Accompanied by Christian missionaries, settlers from Britain arrive in the Breton peninsulas, displacing the original Celtic inhabitants. But they too are overcome, first by the Franks (in the 9C), then by the Angevins (11C).
732	The Arab armies invading France are defeated at Moussais-la-Bataille (*see POITIERS)* by Charles Martel.

THE CAROLINGIANS (751–986)

751	Pepin the Short has himself elected king by an assembly of magnates and bishops at Soissons, sending the powerless Childeric, last of the Merovingians, to a monastery.
800	Charlemagne is crowned Emperor of the West in Rome.

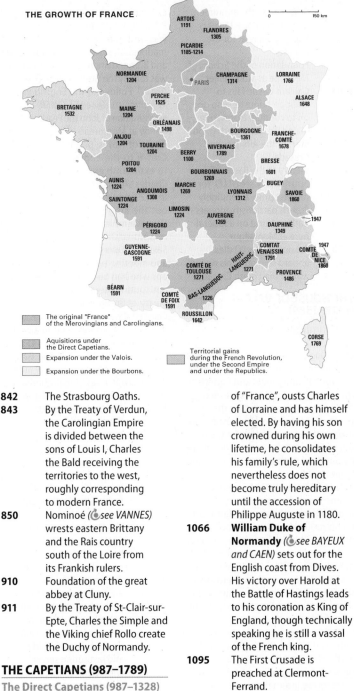

THE GROWTH OF FRANCE

ARTOIS 1191
FLANDRES 1305
PICARDIE 1185-1214
NORMANDIE 1204
CHAMPAGNE 1314
LORRAINE 1766
PARIS
PERCHE 1525
ALSACE 1648
BRETAGNE 1532
MAINE 1204
ORLÉANAIS 1498
BOURGOGNE 1361
FRANCHE-COMTÉ 1678
ANJOU 1204
TOURAINE 1204
BERRY 1100
NIVERNAIS 1789
BRESSE 1601
POITOU 1204
BOURBONNAIS 1269
BUGEY
AUNIS 1224
ANGOUMOIS 1308
MARCHE 1269
LYONNAIS 1312
SAVOIE 1860
SAINTONGE 1224
LIMOSIN 1224
AUVERGNE 1269
1947
PÉRIGORD 1224
DAUPHINÉ 1349
GUYENNE-GASCOGNE 1591
COMTAT VENAISSIN 1791
COMTÉ DE NICE 1860
1947
COMTÉ DE TOULOUSE 1271
HAUT-LANGUEDOC 1271
PROVENCE 1486
BÉARN 1591
COMTÉ DE FOIX 1591
BAS-LANGUEDOC 1226
ROUSSILLON 1642
CORSE 1769

0   150 km

■ The original "France" of the Merovingians and Carolingians.

■ Aquisitions under the Direct Capetians.

□ Expansion under the Valois.

□ Expansion under the Bourbons.

■ Territorial gains during the French Revolution, under the Second Empire and under the Republics.

842	The Strasbourg Oaths.
843	By the Treaty of Verdun, the Carolingian Empire is divided between the sons of Louis I, Charles the Bald receiving the territories to the west, roughly corresponding to modern France.
850	Nominoé (🔊 *see VANNES)* wrests eastern Brittany and the Rais country south of the Loire from its Frankish rulers.
910	Foundation of the great abbey at Cluny.
911	By the Treaty of St-Clair-sur-Epte, Charles the Simple and the Viking chief Rollo create the Duchy of Normandy.

THE CAPETIANS (987–1789)

The Direct Capetians (987–1328)

987	A descendant of Robert the Strong, Hugh Capet, Duke

of "France", ousts Charles of Lorraine and has himself elected. By having his son crowned during his own lifetime, he consolidates his family's rule, which nevertheless does not become truly hereditary until the accession of Philippe Auguste in 1180.

1066	**William Duke of Normandy** (🔊 *see BAYEUX and CAEN)* sets out for the English coast from Dives. His victory over Harold at the Battle of Hastings leads to his coronation as King of England, though technically speaking he is still a vassal of the French king.
1095	The First Crusade is preached at Clermont-Ferrand.
1137	Louis VII weds Eleanor of Aquitaine (🔊 *see*

BORDEAUX); the annulment of their marriage 15 years later is a disaster for the dynasty.

Foundation of the School of Medicine at Montpellier.

1204 Gaillard Castle falls to Philippe Auguste, who goes on to conquer Normandy, Maine, Touraine and Anjou.

1209 Start of the Albigensian Crusade.

1214 Victory at the Battle of Bouvines (☝ *see LILLE)*; for the first time, a genuinely French patriotism appears.

1244 Cathars burnt on a funeral pyre at Montségur.

1270 St Louis (Louis IX) dies aboard ship off Tunis on his way to the Eighth Crusade.

THE HOUSE OF VALOIS (1328–1589)

The Hundred Years' War – 1337–1475

Extending over six reigns, the war was both a political and dynastic struggle between Plantagenets and Capetians over who should rule in France. Accompanied by plague (including the Black Death of 1348) and religious confusion, it was a time of tribulation for the people of France, harassed as they were by bands of outlaws as well as by the English soldiery.

In 1337, Philippe VI of Valois resisted the claims to his throne made by Edward III of England, who was the grandson, on his mother's side, of Philippe le Bel (the Fair). This marked the beginning of the war. Three years after the French defeat at Crécy, Philippe VI purchased the Dauphiné, up to then a territory of the Empire, from its ruler, Humbert II, thereby extending French rule far to the east of the Rhône.

In 1356, King John the Good was defeated by the Black Prince at the Battle of Poitiers (☝ *see POITIERS)*.

Under Charles V, Du Guesclin succeeded in restoring internal order. But at this point in their conflict, both adversaries were beset by problems of their own

caused in England by the minority of Richard II. In France, Charles VI, too, was underage and later affected by madness. The War between Armagnacs and Burgundians began and the Church was torn by the Great Schism (☝ *see AVIGNON)*. Following the English victory at Agincourt (☝ *see ST-OMER)* and the assassination of John the Fearless of Burgundy at Montereau (☝ *see DIJON)*, the Treaty of Troyes, promising the French Crown to the English king, seemed to extinguish any hope of the future Charles VII succeeding.

In 1429, however, after having picked out the king from among the courtiers assembled at Chinon, Joan of Arc recaptured Orléans thereby preventing Salisbury's army from crossing the Loire and meeting up with the English troops who had been stationed in central and southwestern France following the Treaty of Brétigny in 1360. On 17 July Charles VII was crowned in Reims cathedral; in 1436 Paris was freed, followed by Normandy and Guyenne. In 1453, the French victory at Castillon-la-Bataille was the last important clash of arms in the war, which was formally brought to an end by the Treaty of Picquigny.

1515 Accession of François I; Battle of Marignano and the signing of peace in perpetuity with Switzerland.

1520 Meeting of François I and Henry VIII of England at the Field of the Cloth of Gold at Guînes.

1539 The Ordinance of **Villers-Cotterêts**, one of the bases of French law, is promulgated by François I. Among its 192 articles are ones decreeing the keeping of parish registers of births and deaths, as well as law reform outlawing the founding of guilds and instituting secret criminal investigation and the compulsory use of French instead of Latin in legal matters. By this

The Wars of Religion – 1562–98

This is the name given to the 36-year-long crisis marked by complex political as well as religious conflict. During the latter half of the 16C, the French monarchy was in poor shape to withstand the looming hegemony of Spain, with political life in chaos and debt reaching incredible dimensions. The firm stand taken on religion by Spain and Italy on the one hand and by the Protestant countries on the other was missing in the France of Catherine de' Medici's regency, where both parties jostled for favour and a policy of appeasement applied.

The nobility took advantage of the situation, seeking to bolster their power base in the provinces and, under cover of religion, to grasp the reins of government. The Catholic League was formed by the Guise and Montmorency families, supported by Spain and opposed by the Bourbon, Condé and Coligny factions, Huguenots all, with English backing.

Though historians distinguish eight wars separated by periods of peace or relative tranquillity, the troubles were continuous: in the country, endless assassinations, persecutions and general lawlessness; at court, intrigues, volte-faces and pursuit of particular interests. Actual warfare, threatened ever since the Amboise Conspiracy, began at Wassy in 1562, following a massacre of Protestants. The names of Dreux, Nîmes, Chartres, Longjumeau, Jarnac, Montcontour, St-Lô, Valognes, Coutras, Arques and Ivry follow in bloody succession. The Peace of St-Germain in 1570 demonstrated a general desire for reconciliation, but only two years later came the St Bartholomew's Day Massacre in which some 20 000 Huguenots died.

The States General were convened at Blois at the request of the supporters of the League who were opposed to the centralisation of power into royal hands. Fearful of the power enjoyed by Duke Henri of Guise, head of the Catholic League and the kingdom's best military commander, King Henri III had him assassinated in the château at Blois one cold morning in December 1588, only to be cut down himself by a fanatical monk the following year.

This left the succession open for the Huguenot Henry of Navarre, the future Henri IV. By formally adopting the Catholic faith in 1593 and by promulgating the Edict of Nantes in 1598, this able ruler succeeded in rallying all loyal Frenchmen to his standard, putting at least a temporary end to the long-drawn-out crisis.

time provincialism was on the way out, supplanted by a truly national consciousness, the outcome of three centuries of shared ordeals and triumphs.

1541   Calvin's "Institutes of the Christian Religion" is published. In it this native Frenchman, born at Noyon, attempts to stem the fissiparous tendencies of the Reformation and to proclaim its universality. Style, structure and significance combine in this work to make it the first great classic of French literature.

1559   Treaty of Le Cateau-Cambrésis is signed.

1560   The Amboise Conspiracy, harbinger of the looming political and religious crisis.

THE BOURBONS (1589–1789)

Henri IV – 1589–1610

Though his political manœuvrings and his personal conduct did not endear him to everybody, Henri IV put France's affairs on a firm footing once more, attaching the provinces of Bresse and Bugey to the kingdom and setting great architects like Du Cerceau and Métezeau to work on projects in Paris such as the Place des Vosges and the Louvre Gallery, and in La Rochelle and Charleville in the provinces. Important economic reforms were undertaken, and the king's old Huguenot friend, Maximilien de Béthune, Duke of Sully, set the nation's finances in order, dug canals and laid out new roads and port facilities.

In 1600, the landowner Olivier de Serres published his great work on progressive farming technique "The Theatre of Agriculture and Field Husbandry", supporting Sully in his contention that "tilling and stock-keeping are the two breasts from which France feeds".

The king's concern with his people's well-being found expression in his famous statement "a chicken in the pot every Sunday".

1610	Louis XIII becomes king. The country's trade flourishes with the development of inland ports and there are fine planned expansions to a number of towns (Orléans, La Rochelle, Montargis, Langres). The reign is marked by an aristocratic rebellion, as well as by the pioneering work of St Vincent de Paul in social welfare (hospitals, Sisters of Mercy). In the field of ideas, Descartes publishes his "Discourse on Method" (1637), with its reasoning based on systematic questioning ("Cogito, ergo sum"), a starting point for the intellectual revolution which, among other achievements, led to the invention of analytical geometry.
1624	The king's first minister, Richelieu (1585–1642), is successful in his attempts to reduce the power of a Protestantism over-inclined to seek foreign aid (La Rochelle) or to resist the unification of the kingdom (Montauban, Privas). A few

exemplary executions serve to humble the nobility (Montmorency, Cinq-Mars), a process carried further by the demolition of castles. He strengthens France's role in Europe (Thirty Years' War) and, in 1635, founds the Academy (Académie française).

Louis XIV – 1643–1715

The 72 years of the Sun King's reign marked both France and Europe with the force of his personality (*see PARIS and VERSAILLES*). At the time of his accession, the king was only five years old and Anne of Austria confirmed Mazarin in his role as first minister.

Five days later, the French victory at Rocroi (1643) signalled the end of Spanish dominance of Europe's affairs. In 1648, the Peace of Westphalia ended the Thirty Years' War, confirmed France's claim to Alsace (apart from Strasbourg and Mulhouse) and established French as the language of diplomacy.

In 1657, while the king looked on, the two-month siege of Montmédy was brought to a triumphant conclusion by La Ferté and Vauban, thereby putting an end to Spanish rule in the Low Countries. In 1662, the king's first year of personal rule was crowned by the purchase of the port of Dunkerque, a result of the statesman Lionne's diplomacy; the place became a base for smugglers and for privateers like Jean Bart operating in the service of the king.

Anglo-French rivalry for control of the seas (*see BELLE-ÎLE*) now became the main theme of international politics. In 1678, the Treaty of Nijmegen marked the end of the war with Holland, the giving-up of the Franche-Comté and of 12 strongholds in Flanders by Spain, and the reconquest of Alsace. This was a high point in Louis' reign and in French expansion, insured by Vauban's work in fortifying the country's new frontiers. The politics of religion were not always straightforward; for 20 years, the king was in conflict with the pope in what was known as the Affair of the Régale;

in 1685 came the Revocation of the Edict of Nantes with all its dire consequences, and in 1702 the suppression of the camisard revolt. The monarch's later years were clouded by the country's economic exhaustion, though the Battle of Denain in 1712 saved France from invasion by the Austro-Dutch armies and led to the end of the War of the Spanish Succession.

Oriental ventures

In 1664, a century after the voyages of Jean Ango and Jacques Cartier, the French East India Company was revived by Colbert, Louis XIV's great minister of finance. Two years later he authorised it to set up bases both at **Port-Louis** and on waste ground on the far side of the confluence of the Scorff and Blavet rivers. In 1671 the first great merchantman was fitted out for her journey to the East, and the new port was given the name of L'Orient (**Lorient** in 1830). Anglo-French naval rivalry now began in earnest. Over a period of 47 years the Company put a total of 76 ships into use, which, in the course of their long and often dangerous voyages, would bring back cargoes of spices and porcelain (France alone importing over 12 million items of the latter). The initially fabulous profits eventually declined when the Company became a kind of state enterprise under the control of the bank run by the Scots financier Law. In the end, Lorient moved from a commercial role to a naval one.

1715 Louis XV succeeds to the crown at the age of five; the Duke of Orléans is Regent. The reign is marked by indecision, frivolity and corruption; many of France's colonies (Senegal, Québec, the Antilles, possessions in India) are lost. Internally, however, the country prospers, benefiting from a wise economic policy; the standard of living improves and a long period of stability favours agricultural development (introduction

of the potato, artificial extension of grazing lands). Lorraine is absorbed into France in 1766, as is Corsica in 1769.

1774 Louis XVI becomes king. Lafayette takes part in the American War of Independence, brought to an end by the **Treaty of Versailles** in 1783.

The spirit of scientific enquiry leads to rapid technological progress, the growth of industry (textiles, porcelain, steam power) and to endeavours such as Lalande's astronomical experiments and the Montgolfier brothers' balloon flights at Annonay in 1783.

THE FRENCH REVOLUTION (1789–99)

1789 French Revolution begins in Paris.

The Revolution, opening up the continent of Europe to democracy, was the outcome of the long crisis affecting the Ancien Régime.

Hastened along by the teachings of the thinkers of the Enlightenment as much

The Vendée

This is the name given to the Royalist-led but popular uprising in western France in 1793 in reaction to the excesses of the Convention. The *bocage* countryside of much of the area favoured the guerrilla warfare waged by the "Whites" (Catholic royalists) against "Blues" (Republicans), who brought in the Alsatian general Kléber.

In the winter of 1794 thousands of Whites were executed at Nantes, Angers, Fontenay... while the countryside was ravaged by mobile columns of vengeful soldiery (known as the Infernal Columns of General Turreau). Still resistance continued, until finally put to an end by the more conciliatory policies of Hoche.

Attack on the Bastille in 1789 (1845) by unknown artist

©ImageState/Tips Images

as by the inability of a still essentially feudal system to adapt itself to new social realities, the Revolution broke out following disastrous financial mismanagement and the emptying of the coffers of the state.

The main events unfolded in Paris but their repercussions were felt in the provincial cities such as Lyon and Nantes as well as in the countryside.

The year 1789 heralded a number of major historical events for France. The Estates General were renamed the National Assembly, the Bastille was stormed, privileges were abolished (night of 4 July) and the Rights of Man were proclaimed. Two years later, in 1791, the king, fleeing with his family, was arrested in Varennes (22 June) and brought back to Paris, where he was suspended from office on 30 September. The following year the Convention (1792–95) was signed, while in Valmy (20 September) Kellermann and Dumouriez saved France from invasion by forcing the Prussians to retreat; on 22 September France is proclaimed a one and indivisible Republic.

The major landmarks of 1793 were the execution of Louis XVI (21 January), the Vendée revolt, the crushing of the Lyon uprising and the siege of Toulon (July–December). In 1795 France adopted the metric system.

1799	Napoleon overthrows Revolutionary government, puts new constitution in place.

In 1799, Napoleon overthrew the **Directory** (9 November) and declared himself First Consul of the Republic. Finally, in 1801, the Code Napoléon was promulgated throughout the country

THE EMPIRE (1804–15)

1804	On 2 December, Napoleon is crowned Emperor of the French in Notre-Dame by Pope Pius VII. The territorial acquisitions made in the course of the French Revolution now have to be defended against a whole series of coalitions formed by the country's numerous enemies.
1805	Napoleon gives up his plans for invasion of England, abandoning the great camp at Boulogne set up for that purpose. Victory at Trafalgar gives Britain control of the seas, but France's armies win the Battles of Ulm and Austerlitz.
1806	Intended to bring about England's economic ruin,

the Continental Blockade pushes France into further territorial acquisitions.

1808 Some of the best French forces are bogged down in the Peninsular War.

1812 Napoleon invades Russia. The Retreat from Moscow.

1813 The Battle of Leipzig. The whole of Europe lines up against France. Not even Napoleon's military genius can prevent the fall of Paris and the emperor's farewell at Fontainebleau (20 April 1814). Napoleon is exiled to the island of Elba.

THE RESTORATION (1815–30)

1814 Louis XVIII returns from exile in England.

1815 Battle of Waterloo. Napoleon is defeated.

1815 proved a decisive year for France. Following the Hundred Days (20 March– 22 June) – Napoleon's triumphalist journey back to Paris from his exile in Elba – his attempt to re-establish the Empire ended with the victory of the Allies (principally England and Prussia, under the leadership of England's Duke of Wellington) at Waterloo on 18 June. Louis XVIII was once more on the throne, and France was now forced to withdraw into the frontiers of 1792.

Talleyrand's efforts at the Congress of Vienna helped bring France back into the community of European nations. Marshal Ney was executed.

THE JULY MONARCHY (1830–48)

1830 Charles X's "Four Ordinances of St-Cloud" violate the Constitution and lead to the outbreak of revolution. There follow the "Three Glorious Days" (27, 28 and 29 July) and the flight of the Bourbons. Louis-Philippe becomes king.

1837 France's first passenger-carrying railway is opened between Paris and St-Germain-en-Laye.

SECOND REPUBLIC AND SECOND EMPIRE (1848–70)

1848 On 10 December, Louis Napoléon is elected President of the Republic by universal suffrage.

1851 On 2 December, Louis Napoléon dissolves the Legislative Assembly and declares himself president for a 10-year term.

1852 A plebiscite leads to the proclamation of the Second Empire (Napoleon III).

1855 The World Fair is held in Paris.

1860 Savoy and the county of Nice elect to become part of France.

1869 Freedom of the Press is guaranteed.

1870 War declared on Prussia on 19 July. On 2 September, defeat at Sedan spells the end of the Second Empire. Two days later Paris rises and the Republic is proclaimed. But the way to the capital lies open, and soon Paris is under siege.

THE REPUBLIC (1870–THE PRESENT DAY)

1870 Following the disaster at Sedan, the Third Republic is proclaimed on 4 September.

1871 The Paris Commune (21–28 May). By the Treaty of Frankfurt France gives up all of Alsace (with the exception of Belfort) and part of Lorraine.

1881 Jules Ferry secularises primary education, making it free and, later, compulsory.

1884 Trade unions gain formal recognition.

1885   Vaccination in the treatment of rabies (Pasteur). Inauguration of the Eiffel Tower (World Fair).

1894   The Dreyfus Affair divides the country. Forged evidence results in this Jewish General Staff captain being unfairly imprisoned for spying.

1897   Clément Ader's heavier-than-air machine takes to the air at Toulouse.

1904   Entente Cordiale.

1905   Separation of Church and State.

1914   Outbreak of World War I. On 3 August the German armies attack through neutral Belgium but are thrown back in the Battle of the Marne. Four years of trench warfare follow, a bloody climax being reached in 1916–17 around the fortress city of Verdun, where the German offensive is held, at immense cost in lives on both sides. In 1919 the signing of the Treaty of Versailles brings World War I to an end.

1934   France is deeply divided; on 6 February, the National Assembly is attacked by right-wing demonstrators.

Charles de Gaulle on Champs Élysées during the celebration of the Liberation of Paris on 25th August 1944

© Dea Picture Library/age fotostock

Two years later, Léon Blum forms his Popular Front government.

1939   Outbreak of World War II.

1940   France invaded and concedes defeat.

In June 1940, France was overrun by the German army and Marshal Pétain's government requested an armistice. Much of the country was occupied (the north and the whole of the Atlantic seaboard), but the German puppet "French State" with its slogan of "Work, Family, Fatherland" is established at Vichy and collaborates closely with the Nazis. Almost all French Jews were rounded up by the French authorities and deported for extermination. France's honour was saved by General de Gaulle's Free French forces, active in many theatres of the war, and by the courage of the men and women of the Resistance.

1942   Whole country is occupied, and the French fleet scuttles itself at Toulon.

1944   In June the British and American Allies land in Normandy, and in the South of France in August. Paris is liberated.

1945   German surrender signed at Reims on 7 May 1945.

This major conflict (1939–45), which inflamed all continents, is detailed in this guide under the places which it affected most in France.

1947   The Fourth Republic established. Its governments last an average of six months.

1954   Dien Bien Phu falls to the Vietminh. France abandons Indo-China and grants Morocco and Tunisia their independence (1956).

1958   The Algerian crisis leads to the downfall of the Fourth and the establishment of the Fifth Republic under De Gaulle. Civil war is narrowly averted. Nearly all its

French population leaves Algeria, which becomes independent in 1962.

1958 The Fifth Republic established. The European Economic Community (EEC) comes into effect.
The new constitution inspired by General de Gaulle is voted by referendum.

1962 Referendum establishing that the future president of the Republic be elected by universal suffrage.

1967 Franco-British agreement to manufacture Airbus.

1968 The "events of May"; workers join students in mass protests, roughly put down by riot police. The Gaullists triumph in national elections, but it is a hollow victory and De Gaulle, defeated in the referendum of April 1969, retires.

1969 Georges Pompidou is elected president (16 June).

1974 Valéry Giscard d'Estaing is elected president (19 May).

1981 François Mitterrand is elected president (10 May). Inauguration of the TGV line between Paris and Lyon (2hr 40min); Paris–Marseille (1981); and Paris–Bordeaux (1990).

1994 Inauguration of the Channel Tunnel (6 May).

1995 Jacques Chirac is elected president (7 May).

1999 1 January, dubbed "€ Day", marks the beginning of circulation for euro notes and coins.

2002 French franc withdrawn from circulation.

2003 11 000 die in heatwave.

2005 Proposed European Constitution rejected in referendum of French electorate (May). Ethnic minorities rioting in several cities (summer).

2007 Nicolas Sarkozy is elected president of France: and took office on 16 May; the 6th president of the French Fifth Republic, the 23rd president of the French Republic and Co-Prince of Andorra. One of his first "social" acts was to admit singer Barbra Streisand to the Office of Légion d'Honneur.

2009 The leaders of France and Germany appear together at a ceremony in Paris, for the first time since World War I, to commemorate the end of the conflict, saying it is now time to celebrate their countries' reconciliation and friendship.

2010 A German battalion in a French–German military brigade officially takes up arms at a ceremony in eastern France attended by the two countries' defence ministers. This is the first time since World War II that German combat troops are stationed in France.

CONTEMPORARY FRANCE

For most French people the qualities associated with this ancestral land are encapsulated in the traditional **village** – the village where one was born, where one has chosen to live or where one spends one's holidays.

Leaving aside the differences attributed to climatic conditions and building materials, all villages feature common characteristics: the **main street** (Grand'rue) lined with small shops, the **market place**, where local cattle fairs used to be held, and, of course, the **church**, whose chimes continue to herald the fortunes and misfortunes of the community.

Although they see a surge of activity during municipal and trade fairs, French villages are quiet, and peaceful most of the year. Only the traditional **café** and the **boules ground** echo the conversations of the locals idly debating the meaning of life. This strong regionalism has led to frequent conflict with, and hostility to, the central government in Paris. To resolve this long-standing problem, a series of decentralisation reforms was implemented in 1982, creating regional governments with considerable autonomy. **Regional capitals** were established to strike a balance between the capital and the countryside. Despite their long history and local tradition, these regional urban centres tend to be resolutely turned towards the future and illustrate the thriving character of the French regions. However, **Paris** remains the administrative core of the country and a focal point for the whole nation. The seat of political power, and an important centre for world trade, "the City of Lights" is also an exceptional destination for visitors.

This brief description would not be complete without mentioning the **French** themselves. Frequently misunderstood by foreign visitors, often condemned as brusque and unhelpful, they are nonetheless always ready to protect and safeguard their age-old traditions and support a cause in defence of the interests of France and the French way of life. To those who make the effort of going towards them, and who cherish that way of life as they do, the French will always extend a warm, genuine welcome.

Art and Culture

A SURVEY OF FRENCH ART
FROM PREHISTORY TO THE GALLO-ROMAN ERA

Prehistory

While stone and bone tools appeared in the Lower Palaeolithic period, prehistoric art did not make its entrance until the Upper Palaeolithic, (350–100C BCE), and reached its peak in the Magdalenian Period (&see Les EYZIES DE-TAYAC).
The art of engraved wood and ivory objects together with votive statuettes developed alongside the art of wall decoration, which is well illustrated in France by caves in the Dordogne, the Pyrenees, the Ardèche and the Gard. Early artists used pigments with a mineral base for their cave paintings and sometimes took advantage of the natural shape of the rock itself to execute their work in low relief.

The Neolithic revolution (6500 BCE), during which populations began to settle, brought with it the advent of pottery as well as a different use of land and a change in burial practices – some megaliths (dolmens and covered passageways) are ancient burial chambers. Menhirs, a type of megalith found in great numbers in Brittany (Carnac and Locmariaquer), are as yet of unknown origin. The discovery of metal brought prehistoric civilisation into the Bronze Age (2300–1800 BCE) and then into the Iron Age (750–450 BCE). Celtic art showed perfect mastery of metalwork, as in the tombs of Gorge-Meillet, Mailly-le-Camp, Bibracte and Vix, in which the treasures consist of gold torques (necklaces) and other items of jewellery, various coins and bronzeware.

ROMANESQUE PERIOD (11–12C)

In the early 11C, after the disturbances of the year 1000 (decadence of the Carolingian dynasty and struggles between feudal barons), the spiritual influence and power of the Church gave rise to the birth of Romanesque architecture.

Romanesque Architecture

Early Romanesque edifices were characterised by the widespread use of stone vaulting which replaced timber roofs, the use of buttresses and a return to architectural decoration (as in the churches of St-Martin-du-Canigou and St-Bénigne in Dijon). The darkness of the nave was explained by the fact that for structural reasons wide openings could not be cut into the walls supporting the vaulting. The basilica plan with nave

The Gallo-Roman Era and the Early Middle Ages

When the Romans conquered Gaul (2–1C BCE), they introduced the technique of building with stone. In cities, the Empire's administrative centres, the centralised power of Rome favoured a style of architecture that reflected its strength and prestige and imposed its culture. Theatres (Orange and Vienne), temples (the Square House or Maison Carrée in Nîmes), baths, basilicas and triumphal arches were constructed, while the local aristocracy took to building Roman villas with frescoes and mosaics (Vaison-la-Romaine and Grand). The presence of the Romans has had a lasting effect on the shape of France in terms of town-planning, roads, bridges and aqueducts (Pont du Gard). Towards the end of the late Empire, official recognition of the Christian Church in the year 380 prompted the first examples of Christian architecture, among them the baptisteries of Fréjus, Riez and Poitiers.

During the great barbarian invasions of the 5C, figurative art, unknown to Germanic peoples, gave place to abstract (intertwining, circular shapes) and animal motifs. The technique of *cloisonné* gold and silverware (Childeric's treasure) became widespread.

Merovingian art (6–8C), a synthesis of styles, included elements of antique, barbarian and Christian art (the Dunes hypogeum near Poitiers and the crypt in **Jouarre**), out of which evolved medieval art.

The **Carolingian Renaissance** (9C) was marked by a great flowering of illuminated manuscripts and ivory-carving (the Dagulf psalter in the Louvre) and by a deliberate return to imperial, antique art forms (Aix-la-Chapelle and the oratory of Germigny-des-Prés).

The altar in churches of the period is sometimes raised above a vaulted area of the chancel known as the crypt which was originally on the same level as the nave (St-Germain of Auxerre and St-Philibert-de-Grand-Lieu).

and side aisles, sometimes preceded by a porch, predominated in France, although some churches were built to a central plan (the church of Neuvy-St-Sépulcre). Depending on the church, the east end might have been flat or have had apsidal chapels; it was often semicircular with axial chapels (as in the church of Anzy-le-Duc), or may have featured radiating chapels.

More complex designs combined an ambulatory with radiating chapels (the churches of Conques and Cluny).

The first attempts at embellishment led to a revival of sculptural decoration of which the lintel of St-Genis-les-Fontaines Church is one of the earliest examples. Tympana, archivolts, arch shafts and piers were covered with carvings of a religious or profane nature (as in the illustration of the *Romance of Renart* in the church of St-Ursin in Bourges). Interior decoration consisted mainly of frescoes (the churches of St-Savin-sur-Gartempe and Berzé-la-Ville) and carved capitals with the occasional complex theme (as in the chancel capitals in Cluny). The Romanesque decorative style drew largely upon three main models, the Oriental (griffins and imaginary animals) which was spread by the Crusades, the Byzantine (illustrations of Christ in Majesty and a particular style for folds) and the Islamic (stylised foliage and pseudo-Kufic script).

Regional Characteristics

The Romanesque style spread throughout France, affecting some areas earlier than others and developing special stylistic features according to the region. It first appeared in the south and in Burgundy, reaching the east of France at a much later date.

Romanesque architecture in the **Languedoc** owes much to Toulouse's St-Sernin Basilica, whose tall lantern tower pierced by ornamental arcading

Basilique St-Sernin, Toulouse

© Juliane/Fotolia.com

served as a model for many local bell towers. The sculptures on the Miégeville doorway, completed in 1118, have a distinctive style, with highly expressive folds and a lengthening of the figures which is repeated in **Moissac** (◐ *see illustration p70)* and, to a lesser extent, in St-Gilles-du-Gard.

In **Saintonge-Poitou**, the originality of the edifices derives from the great

Ecclesiastical architecture

JOUARRE – Crypte St-Paul (7C)

The crypts of Jouarre Abbey built in the Carollingian period are among the earliest examples of funerary religious architecture popular in the Middle Ages.

Groined vault

Ovolo moulding: egg and dart moulding

Abacus

Capitals generally with Classical orders: Corinthian style capitals enhanced by grooves, ovolo, beads

Recumbent figure

Cenotaph: funerary monument which does not contain remains

Fluting

Shell motif, symbol of immortality

Stone sarcophagus

Porphyry shaft

Torus: raised moulding

Base

R Corbel/MICHELIN

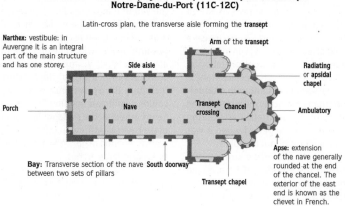

CLERMONT FERRAND (Puy-de-Dôme) – Ground plan of Basilique Notre-Dame-du-Port (11C-12C)

Latin-cross plan, the transverse aisle forming the **transept**

Narthex: vestibule: in Auvergne it is an integral part of the main structure and has one storey.

Arm of the transept

Side aisle

Radiating or **apsidal** chapel

Porch

Nave

Transept crossing **Chancel**

Ambulatory

Bay: Transverse section of the nave between two sets of pillars

South doorway

Transept chapel

Apse: extension of the nave generally rounded at the end of the chancel. The exterior of the east end is known as the chevet in French.

R.Corbel/MICHELIN

height of the aisles which serve to reinforce the walls of the nave and thus lend balance to the barrel vaulting.

The gabled façades, flanked by lantern towers, are covered in ornamental arcading with statue niches and low relief (as in the church of Notre-Dame-la-Grande in Poitiers).

In **Auvergne**, the transept crossing is often covered by a dome, buttressed by high, quadripartite vaulting and supported on diaphragm arches.

This constitutes an oblong mass which juts out above the roof beneath the bell tower. The use of lava, a particularly difficult stone to carve, explains the limited sculptural decoration (as in the churches of St-Nectaire, Notre-Dame-du-Port in **Clermont-Ferrand** and that of **Orcival**, ⓖsee illustrations above and p71). The tympana lintels are gable-shaped.

The development of the Romanesque in **Burgundy** was strongly influenced by the Abbey of Cluny (now destroyed) with its great chancel with radiating chapels, a double transept and the hint of direct lighting in the nave through slender openings at the base of the barrel vaulting.

The churches of Paray-le-Monial and Notre-Dame in La Charité-sur-Loire were built on the Cluniac model.

The basilica of Sainte-Madeleine in Vézelay in the north of the Morvan, with its harmonious, simplified church body and its covering of groined vaults, was

also to influence churches in the region. In the **Rhine** and **Meuse** regions, architectural characteristics from the Carolingian era, with an Ottonian influence, tend to prevail.

This is borne out by double chancels and transepts (as in Verdun) and a central plan and interior elevation like that of the Palatine Chapel in Aachen (as in Ottmarsheim).

Lastly, until a relatively late date the churches in **Normandy** faithfully retained the custom of a timber roof (as in Jumièges and Bayeux). As stone vaulting was introduced decorative ribs gradually came into use (as in St-Étienne in Caen). The monumental size of the edifices and their harmoniously proportioned façades with two towers, are also typical of the Anglo-Norman Romanesque style.

Apart from these regional features some buildings owe their individuality to their function. The **pilgrimage churches**, for instance, had an ambulatory around the chancel, transept aisles and two aisles on either side of the nave to give pilgrims easy access to the relics they wished to venerate.

The main churches of this kind on the way to Santiago de Compostela were St Faith in Conques, St-Sernin in Toulouse, St-Martial in Limoges and St-Martin in Tours (the two latter have since been destroyed).

Romanesque Religious Art

Liturgical items at the time consisted of church plate, manuscripts, precious fabrics and reliquaries. Church treasure would often include a Virgin in Majesty made of polychrome wood or embossed metal decorated with precious stones.

The blossoming of **Limousin enamelware** marked a great milestone in the history of the decorative arts during the Romanesque period when it was exported throughout Europe.

The *champlevé* method consisted of pouring the enamel into a grooved metal surface of gilded copper.

Enamel was used in a number of ways to decorate items ranging from small objects such as crosses, ciboria and reliquaries to monumental works like altars (high altar of **Grandmont** abbey church and items in the Cluny Museum, Paris).

GOTHIC PERIOD (12–15C)

Architecture Transitional Gothic

In about 1140, important architectural innovations in St-Denis Cathedral, such as intersecting ribbed vaulting and pointed arches in the narthex and chancel, heralded the dawn of the Gothic style.

In the late 12C, there were further innovations common to a group of buildings in Île-de-France and in the north of France. They included ogives and mouldings which extended down from the vaulting into bundles of engaged slender columns around the pillars of great arches. Capitals were simplified, became smaller with time and gradually diminished in importance. New concepts of sculptural decorating, including the appearance of statue-columns, affected building façades. In Sens Cathedral, the rectangular layout of the bays called for sexpartite vaulting with alternating major and minor pillars to support large arches.

The major pillars supported three ribs while the minor ones supported a single intermediary rib. Apart from sexpartite vaulting with alternating supports, this early Gothic architecture typical of Sens, Noyon and Laon was also characterised by a four-storey elevation, great arches, tribunes, a triforium and tall bays.

In the years 1180–1200, in Notre-Dame Cathedral in Paris, raised vaults were reinforced by the addition of flying buttresses on the outside of the edifice, while inside, alternating supports disappeared. These new measures gave rise to the emergence of a transitional style which led to Lanceolate Gothic.

Lanceolate Gothic

The Gothic style was at its peak during the reigns of Philippe Auguste (1180–1223) and St Louis (1226–70).

Ecclesiastical architecture

MOISSAC – South doorway of the 12C abbey church

Torus: a large convex moulding separating the covings

Historiated tympanum (decorated with narrative scenes and figures, here Christ in Majesty)

Lintel

Embrasure: arch shafts, splaying sometimes adorned with statues or columns

Scallop motif

Coving: concave moulding

Archivolt: series of mouldings curving round an arch

Medallion

Pier adorned with interlaced lions

Engaged piers supporting the arched mouldings

R.Corbel/MICHELIN

ORCIVAL – Notre-Dame Basilica (12C)

Most of the Romanesque churches of the Auvergne belong to a school which developed in the 11C-12C and is considered one of the most unusual in the history of art in the Western world.

Relieving arch: relieves the weight of the wall above an opening.

Two-storeyed **octagonal bell-tower:** its thrusts are but tressed by the chevet, nave and the arms of the transept.

Twin windows

Transept

Semicircular window

Gable-wall

Window

Modillions: scroll shaped projecting mouldings supporting the cornice.

String-course with billet moulding: ornamental frieze consisting of bands of raised short cylindrical or square blocks placed at regular intervals.

Radiating or **apsidal chapel**

Buttress: external support for a wall, built against it.

Cornice adorned with chequered motif.

Chevet: the east end is the most beautiful and most characteristic of the Auvergne churches owing to the original layout of the various levels.

R.Corbel/MICHELIN

Ecclesiastical architecture

CHARTRES – West front of Cathédrale Notre-Dame (12C-13C)

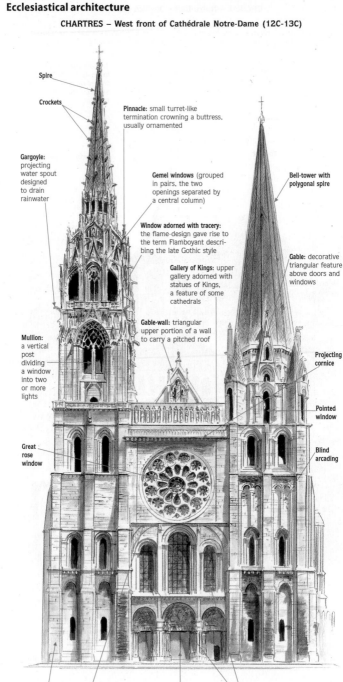

Spire

Crockets

Pinnacle: small turret-like termination crowning a buttress, usually ornamented

Gargoyle: projecting water spout designed to drain rainwater

Gemel windows (grouped in pairs, the two openings separated by a central column)

Bell-tower with polygonal spire

Window adorned with tracery: the flame-design gave rise to the term Flamboyant describing the late Gothic style

Gallery of Kings: upper gallery adorned with statues of Kings, a feature of some cathedrals

Gable: decorative triangular feature above doors and windows

Gable-wall: triangular upper portion of a wall to carry a pitched roof

Mullion: a vertical post dividing a window into two or more lights

Projecting cornice

Pointed window

Great rose window

Blind arcading

Central doorway

String-course: a projecting horizontal band or moulding set in a vertical surface

Buttress

Triplet: three portals or windows often grouped under a relieving arch

R.Corbel/MICHELIN

The rebuilding of **Chartres Cathedral** (1210–30) gave rise to a model for what is known as the Chartres family of cathedrals (Reims, Amiens and Beauvais), which included oblong plan vaulting, a three-storey elevation (without tribunes) and flying buttresses. The chancel with its double ambulatory and the transept arms with side aisles made for a grandiose interior. The upper windows in the nave were divided into two lancets surmounted by a round opening. The façades were subdivided into three horizontal registers, as in the cathedrals of Laon and Amiens. The doorways were set in deep porches with gables while above them was an openwork rose window with stained glass. A gallery of arches ran beneath the bell towers. There are a number of variations of Lanceolate Gothic in France. An example is Notre-Dame Church in Dijon where the ancient section of the sexpartite vaulting has been preserved.

Upper chapel, Sainte-Chapelle, Paris

©Jeff Schultes/Dreamstime.com

Development of the Gothic Style to the 15C

The improvement in vaulting from a technical point of view, in particular the use of relieving arches, meant that the supporting function of walls was reduced and more space could be given over to windows and stone tracery as in St-Urbain's Basilica in Troyes and the Sainte-Chapelle in Paris (1248). This gave rise to the **High Gothic** style in the north of France from the end of the 13C to the late 14C. (Examples include the chancel in Beauvais Cathedral, Évreux Cathedral and the north transept of **Rouen Cathedral**, 🔎*see illustration below.*)

Gothic architecture in the centre and southwest of France developed along unusual lines in the late 13C. Jean Deschamps, master mason of Narbonne Cathedral, designed a massively proportioned building in which the vertical upsweep of the lines was interrupted by wide galleries above the aisles. St Cecilia's Cathedral in Albi diverged completely from Gothic models in the north of France through the use of brick and a buttress system inherited from the Romanesque period. Throughout the 14C, church interiors were filled with

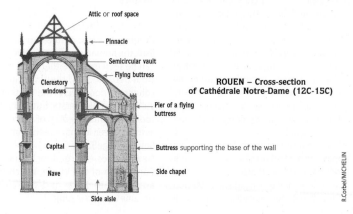

Attic or roof space

Pinnacle

Semicircular vault

Flying buttress

Clerestory windows

Pier of a flying buttress

ROUEN – Cross-section of Cathédrale Notre-Dame (12C-15C)

Capital

Buttress supporting the base of the wall

Nave

Side chapel

Side aisle

R.Corbel/MICHELIN

Ecclesiastical architecture

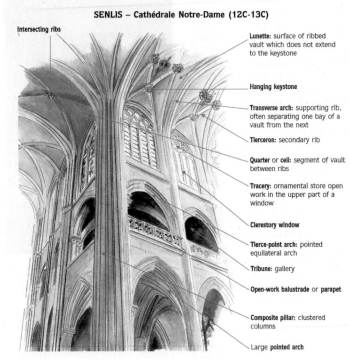

SENLIS – Cathédrale Notre-Dame (12C-13C)

Intersecting ribs

Lunette: surface of ribbed vault which does not extend to the keystone

Hanging keystone

Transverse arch: supporting rib, often separating one bay of a vault from the next

Tierceron: secondary rib

Quarter or **cell:** segment of vault between ribs

Tracery: ornamental store open work in the upper part of a window

Clerestory window

Tierce-point arch: pointed equilateral arch

Tribune: gallery

Open-work balustrade or **parapet**

Composite pillar: clustered columns

Large pointed arch

R.Corbel/MICHELIN

sculptural decoration in the form of rood screens, choir screens and **stalls** (*see illustration p75*), monumental altarpieces and devotional statues.

From the late 14C, development of the main principles of Gothic architecture came to a halt but decorative devices grew apace, giving rise to the elaborate **Flamboyant Gothic** style with its gables, lancet arches, pinnacles and exuberant foliage. This ornamentation, occasionally referred to as Baroque Gothic, also played a part in **civil architecture** (*see illustrations pp80–81*) *in section*). An example is the Great Hall in the Law Courts at Poitiers, carved by Guy de Dammartin in the last 10 years of the 14C. Riom's Sainte-Chapelle, built for the Duke Jean de Berry, is another early example.

Flamboyant Gothic in France left its mark on a good number of public and religious edifices (Palais Jacques Cœur in Bourges and the façade of St-Maclou Church in Rouen) as well as on liturgical

furnishings (the choir screen and rood screen in **Ste-Cécile**'s **Cathedral in Albi**, *see illustration p75*).

Throughout the Gothic period castle architecture remained faithful to feudal models (Angers Castle, the walled city of Cordes and the mountain fortress of Merle Towers) and did not develop further until the beginning of the Renaissance.

Gothic Sculpture

Progress towards naturalism and realism, the humanism of the Gothic style, can be seen in the statuary and sculptural decoration of the time. Statue-columns of doorways in the 12C tended still to be rigidly hieratic but in the 13C took on greater freedom of expression as may be seen in Amiens and Reims (the Smiling Angel).

New themes emerged including the Coronation of the Virgin, which first appeared in 1191, and thereafter became a popular subject.

THANN – Choir stalls in Collégiale St-Thiébaut (14C-early 16C)

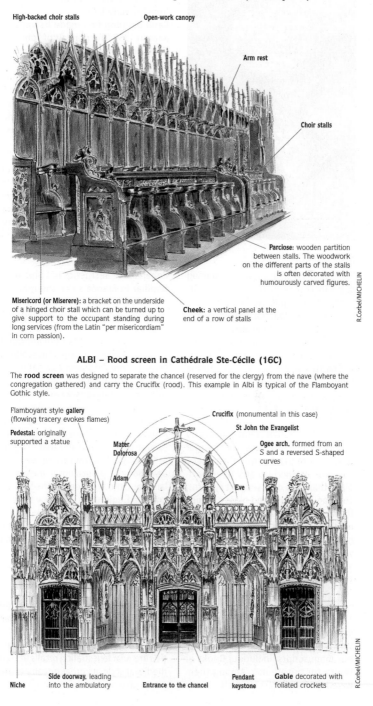

High-backed choir stalls

Open-work canopy

Arm rest

Choir stalls

Parclose: wooden partition between stalls. The woodwork on the different parts of the stalls is often decorated with humourously carved figures.

Misericord (or Miserere): a bracket on the underside of a hinged choir stall which can be turned up to give support to the occupant standing during long services (from the Latin "per misericordiam" in corn passion).

Cheek: a vertical panel at the end of a row of stalls

R.Corbel/MICHELIN

ALBI – Rood screen in Cathédrale Ste-Cécile (16C)

The **rood screen** was designed to separate the chancel (reserved for the clergy) from the nave (where the congregation gathered) and carry the Crucifix (rood). This example in Albi is typical of the Flamboyant Gothic style.

Flamboyant style **gallery** (flowing tracery evokes flames)

Pedestal: originally supported a statue

Crucifix (monumental in this case)

St John the Evangelist

Mater Dolorosa

Adam

Ogee arch, formed from an S and a reversed S-shaped curves

Eve

Niche

Side doorway, leading into the ambulatory

Entrance to the chancel

Pendant keystone

Gable decorated with foliated crockets

R.Corbel/MICHELIN

12–13C stained glass Cathédrale de Chartres

S. Sauvignier/MICHELIN

Stained Glass

The four main areas producing stained glass in France in the 12C were St-Denis, Champagne, the west (Le Mans, Vendôme and Poitiers) and a group of workshops in the Rhine area in eastern France. Master glassworkers developed an intense blue-coloured glass known as Chartres blue which was to become famous. The invention of silver yellow in 1300–10 led to a more translucent enamelled glass with a subtler range of colour.

The combination of stained glass and Gothic architecture gave rise to larger bays – formerly opaque wall space could be opened up and filled with glass, thanks to new support systems. The fragility of stained glass explains the fact that there are very few original medieval windows intact today; many have been replaced by copies or later works. The windows of Chartres, Évreux and the Sainte-Chapelle are precious testimonies to the art.

Illumination and Painting

The art of illumination reached its peak in the 14C when artists freed from university supervision produced sumptuous manuscripts, including Books of Hours, for private use. Among them were Jean Pucelle *(Les Heures de Jeanne d'Évreux)* and the Limbourg brothers *(Les Très Riches Heures du Duc de Berry,* dating from the early 15C).

Easel painting first made its appearance in 1350 (the portrait of John the Good, now in the Louvre, is an example). Italian and more particularly Flemish influences, evident as much in depiction of landscape as in attention to detail, may be seen in works by great 15C artists such as **Jean Fouquet, Enguerrand Quarton** and the **Master of Moulins**.

THE RENAISSANCE

Gothic art persisted in many parts of France until the middle of the 16C. In the Loire region, however, there were signs of a break with medieval traditions as early as the beginning of the century.

Italian Style and Early Renaissance

Renaissance aesthetics in Lombardy, familiar in France since the military campaigns of Charles VIII and Louis XII at the end of the 15C, at first affected only architectural decoration, through the introduction of motifs from antiquity such as pilasters, foliage and scallops (as in the tomb of Solesmes, Château de Gaillon). Little by little, however, feudal, **military and defensive architecture** (see illustrations overleaf) gave way to a more comfortable style of seigniorial residence. The Château de Chenonceau (begun before 1515) and that of Azay-le-Rideau (1518–27) are examples of this development, particularly in their regular layout, the symmetry of the façades and the beginnings of a new type of architectural decoration. However, it was the great royal undertakings of the time that brought about the blossoming of the Renaissance style.

Architecture Under François I (1515–47)

The Façade des Loges (1520–24) in the **Château de Blois** (begun in 1515, see illustration p77) is a free replica of the Vatican loggia in Rome. While the castle's irregular fenestration recalls the old medieval style, its great novelty is the preoccupation with Italianate ornamen-

Civil architecture

BLOIS – Château, François-1ᵉʳ staircase (16C)

The spiral stairway is built inside an octagonal staircase half set into the façade. It opens onto the main courtyard in a series of balconies which form loggias. The king and his court would view all sorts of entertainment from here: the arrival of dignitaries, jousting, hunting or military displays.

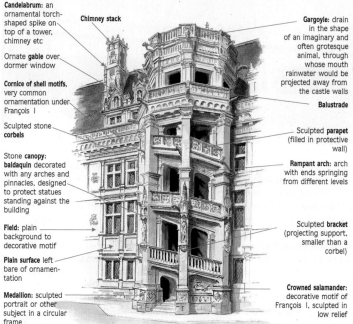

Candelabrum: an ornamental torch-shaped spike on top of a tower, chimney etc

Chimney stack

Gargoyle: drain in the shape of an imaginary and often grotesque animal, through whose mouth rainwater would be projected away from the castle walls

Ornate **gable** over dormer window

Cornice of shell motifs, very common ornamentation under François I

Balustrade

Sculpted stone **corbels**

Sculpted **parapet** (filled in protective wall)

Stone **canopy: baldaquin** decorated with any arches and pinnacles, designed to protect statues standing against the building

Rampant arch: arch with ends springing from different levels

Field: plain background to decorative motif

Sculpted **bracket** (projecting support, smaller than a corbel)

Plain surface left bare of ornamentation

Medallion: sculpted portrait or other subject in a circular frame

Crowned salamander: decorative motif of François I, sculpted in low relief

R.Corbel/MICHELIN

---

tation. During the reign of François I, the **Château de Chambord** (1519–47), which combines French architectural traditions (corner towers, irregular roofs and dormer windows) with innovative elements (symmetrical façades, refined decoration and a monumental internal staircase), served as a model for a good many of the Loire castles including Chaumont, Le Lude and Ussé.

After his defeat at the Battle of Pavia in 1525, François I left his residences in the Loire Valley to turn his attention to those in Île-de-France. In 1527 building began on the Château de Fontainebleau under the supervision of Gilles Le Breton. The interior decoration by artists from the **First School of Fontainebleau** was to have a profound influence on the development of French art.

The Italian artist **Rosso** (1494–1540) introduced a new system of decoration to France that combined stuccowork, wood panelling and allegorical frescoes which drew upon humanistic, philosophical and literary references and were painted in acid colours.

The Mannerist style, characterised by the influence of antique statuary, a lengthening of lines and overabundant ornamentation, became more pronounced after **Primaticcio** (1504–70) arrived at the court in 1532.

The influence of this art could be felt until the end of the century in works by sculptors such as **Pierre Bontemps**, **Jean Goujon** (reliefs on the Fountain of the Innocents in Paris) and **Germain Pilon** (monument for the heart of Henri II in the Louvre), and painters like Jean Cousin the Elder. Court portraitists, on the other hand (**Jean** and **François Clouet** and **Corneille de Lyon**), were more influenced by Flemish traditions.

Place des Vosges, Paris

© Pi Ju Yang/Bigstockphoto.com

Henri IV and Pre-Classicism

After the Wars of Religion (1560–98) new artistic trends revived the arts and heralded the dawn of Classicism. Royal interest in town-planning gave rise to the regular, symmetrical layout of squares (Place des Vosges and Place Dauphine in Paris) and to the harmonisation of the buildings that surrounded them (ground-level arcades and brick and stone façades). These were copied in the provinces (Charleville and Montauban), foreshadowing the royal squares of the 17C, France's *Grand Siècle*.

The Fontainebleau style of adornment continued to develop under the auspices of the **Second School of Fontainebleau**. This was made up of

Military architecture

CARCASSONNE – East gateway of the Château Comtal (12C)

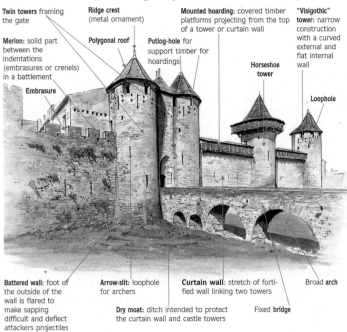

Twin towers framing the gate

Merlon: solid part between the indentations (embrasures or crenels) in a battlement

Embrasure

Ridge crest (metal ornament)

Polygonal roof

Putlog-hole for support timber for hoardings

Mounted hoarding: covered timber platforms projecting from the top of a tower or curtain wall

"Visigothic" tower: narrow construction with a curved external and flat internal wall

Horseshoe tower

Loophole

Battered wall: foot of the outside of the wall is flared to make sapping difficult and deflect attackers projectiles

Arrow-slit: loophole for archers

Dry moat: ditch intended to protect the curtain wall and castle towers

Curtain wall: stretch of fortified wall linking two towers

Fixed **bridge**

Broad **arch**

R.Corbel/MICHELIN

Château de BONAGUIL (13C – early 16C)

Bonaguil Castle, rebuilt from 1483 to 1510 by Béranger de Roquefeuil, is a good example of the improvements made to a defensive stronghold to take account of the development of firearms.

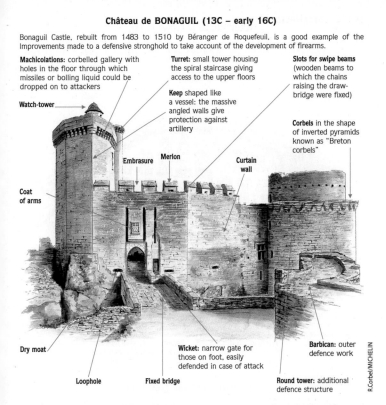

Machicolations: corbelled gallery with holes in the floor through which missiles or boiling liquid could be dropped on to attackers

Turret: small tower housing the spiral staircase giving access to the upper floors

Slots for swipe beams (wooden beams to which the chains raising the draw-bridge were fixed)

Watch-tower

Keep shaped like a vessel: the massive angled walls give protection against artillery

Corbels in the shape of inverted pyramids known as "Breton corbels"

Embrasure **Merlon**

Curtain wall

Coat of arms

Dry moat

Wicket: narrow gate for those on foot, easily defended in case of attack

Barbican: outer defence work

Loophole **Fixed bridge**

Round tower: additional defence structure

R.Corbel/MICHELIN

all the court painters working during the reign of Henri IV and the regency of Marie de' Medici. The style was further shaped by decoration in other royal palaces including the Tuileries, the Louvre and Château-Neuf in St-Germain-en-Laye. **Toussaint Dubreuil** (1561–1602), **Ambroise Dubois** (1542–1614) and **Martin Fréminet** (1567–1619) continued the Mannerism of Fontainebleau (light effects, half-length figures and a lengthening of perspectives) in their works and at the same time sought greater Classicism as well as a revival of themes from contemporary literature (*La Franciade* by Ronsard).

In the late 16C, castle architecture took on a new form with a single main building centred on a projecting section flanked by corner pavilions (Rosny-sur-Seine, and the Château de Gros-Bois). Right-angled wings were done away with and façades were given a brick facing with stone courses.

During the Regency period, the architect Salomon de Brosse (Palais de Justice in Rennes, Palais du Luxembourg in Paris) designed sober, impressive monuments with a clarity of form which contained some of the characteristics of Classical architecture.

16C Decorative Arts

The 16C was a productive period for jewellery-making, in particular for small brooches fastened in the hair or hat and pendants which were used as articles of dress or simply as collectors' items. **Étienne Delaune** (1518–83) was one of the great goldsmiths of the time.

There was rich regional variety in ceramics. Beauvaisis produced famous blue-tinged stoneware. Following the example of Italy, Lyon and Nevers manufactured majolica (glazed and historiated earthenware).

The decorative arts in Saintonge were dominated by **Bernard Palissy**

Military architecture

NEUF-BRISACH (1698-1703)

The polygonal stronghold was developed in the early 16C as firearms became more common in warfare: the cannon mounted on one structure covered the "blind spot" of the neighbouring position. This stronghold was built by Vauban, opposite the formidable Breisach, handed back to the Hapsburgs under the Treaty of Ryswick (1697).

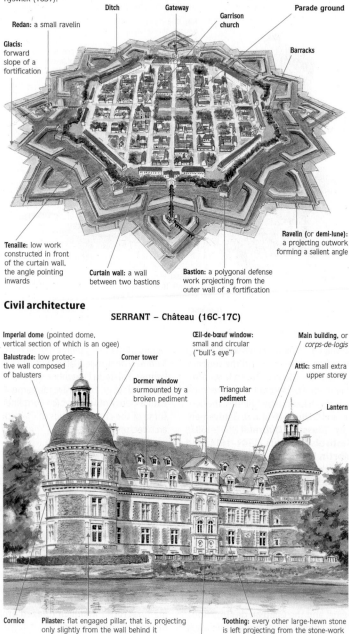

Redan: a small ravelin

Glacis: forward slope of a fortification

Ditch

Gateway

Garrison church

Parade ground

Barracks

Ravelin (or demi-lune): a projecting outwork forming a salient angle

Tenaille: low work constructed in front of the curtain wall, the angle pointing inwards

Curtain wall: a wall between two bastions

Bastion: a polygonal defense work projecting from the outer wall of a fortification

Civil architecture

SERRANT – Château (16C-17C)

Imperial dome (pointed dome, vertical section of which is an ogee)

Balustrade: low protective wall composed of balusters

Corner tower

Dormer window surmounted by a broken pediment

Œil-de-bœuf window: small and circular ("bull's eye")

Triangular pediment

Main building, or *corps-de-logis*

Attic: small extra upper storey

Lantern

Cornice

Pilaster: flat engaged pillar, that is, projecting only slightly from the wall behind it

Avant-corps: part of a building projecting from the rest of the façade for the entire height of the building, roof included

Toothing: every other large-hewn stone is left projecting from the stone-work framing the windows for a more solid and more decorative bond with the adjoining schist walls

R.Corbel/MICHELIN

Civil architecture

BORDEAUX – Palais de la Bourse (18C)

Flaming urn: a characteristic feature in Classical architecture

Triangular pediment with allegorical carving

Œil-de-bœuf: a small, circular window ("bull's-eye")

Trophy: decorative carving of arms grouped around a breast plate or helmet

Dentils: a frieze of small, rectangular blocks

Architrave: the lowest part of the entablature resting directly upon the columns

Ionic capital: capital with a spiral volute

Mullioned window

Cartouche: a panel ornately framed and usually bearing an inscription

Column offset from the wall

Fanlight: upper section of a door or window

Mascaron: ornamental sculpture on keystone or voussoir

Colossal order spanning several storeys

Rusticated stonework: the massive blocks are dressed to a flat surface with chamfered edges

Groove marking the join between dressed stone blocks

R.Corbel/MICHELIN

(c.1510–c.90) who, apart from making a great many plates covered in reptiles, fish and seaweed, all modelled from nature, also decorated the grotto at the Château d'Écouen and that of the Tuileries. Some of his ceramics (nymphs in a country setting) were influenced by engravings from the Fontainebleau School. The technique for painted enamel on copper with permanent colours was developed in Limoges in the 15C during the reign of Louis XI. J C Pénicaud and especially **Léonard Limosin** (1501–75) excelled in the technique, which was favoured in portrait painting by the French court.

FRENCH CLASSICISM IN THE EARLY 17C

Architecture

Three famous architects, **Jacques Lemercier** (c.1585–1654), **François**

Mansart (1598–1666) and **Louis le Vau** (1612–70), played an essential part in drawing up the standards for the French Classical architectural style.

J Lemercier, who built the Château de Rueil, the town of Richelieu and the Église de la Sorbonne in Paris, supported the Italian style which was particularly evident in religious architecture: two-storey façades and projecting central sections with columns and triangular pediments. F Mansart was even more inventive (**Château de Balleroy, Château de Maisons-Laffitte** and the Gaston of Orléans Wing in the Château de Blois). From his time on, castle plans with a central pavilion and projecting section, architectural decoration that accentuated horizontal and vertical lines, and the use of orders (Doric, Ionic and Corinthian), remained constant features of Classical architecture. Le Vau,

*Detail of the Adoration of the Shepherds (c. 1644)
by Georges de la Tour, Musée du Louvre*

©World Illustrated/Photoshot

who began his career before the reign of Louis XIV by designing town houses (Hôtel Lambert in Paris) for the nobility and the upper middle classes, favoured a grandiose style of architecture characteristic of Louis XIV Classicism (Château de Vaux-le-Vicomte).

Painting

The French school of painting blossomed as a result of Simon Vouet's (1590–1649) return to France in 1627 after a long stay in Rome and the foundation of the Royal Academy of Painting and Sculpture in 1648. References to Italian painting, in particular Venetian (richness of colour) and Roman (dynamism of composition), albeit tempered by a concern for order and clarity, are evident in the work of Vouet and that of his pupil **Eustache le Sueur** (1616–55). Painters such as **Poussin** (1595–1665) and **Philippe de Champaigne** (1602–74) produced highly intellectual works that drew upon philosophical, historical and theological themes – all emblematic of French Classicism. Other trends in French painting flourished in the first half of the century.

The realism of the Italian painter Caravaggio influenced the Toulouse school, of which the major artist was **Nicolas Tournier** (1590–post 1660). In Lorraine,

Georges de la Tour (1593–1652) was deeply affected by Caravaggio's style, notably in the use of light and shade and the portrayal of people from humble blackgrounds.

The **Le Nain** brothers, Antoine (c.1588–1648), Louis (c.1593–1648) and Mathieu (c.1607–77), who painted first in Laon and then in Paris, belonged to a trend known as "painters of reality" that favoured genre scenes, drawing more upon the world of the landed upper-middle classes than that of peasant farmers. Their work bore the stamp of Flemish craftsmanship.

Sculpture

Sculpture in the early 17C was influenced by contemporary Italian models. **Jacques Sarrazin** (1588–1660), who studied in Rome, worked in a moderate, Classical mode that derived from antiquity and also drew upon paintings by Poussin (decoration in the Château de Maisons-Laffitte and the tomb of Henri of Bourbon in the Château de Chantilly). François Anguier (Montmorency Mausoleum in the Lycée chapel in Moulins) and his brother Michel (sculptural decoration on the St-Denis gateway in Paris) showed a more Baroque tendency in their treatment of dynamism and the dramatic stances of their sculptures.

VERSAILLES CLASSICISM

During the reign of Louis XIV (1643–1715) the centralisation of authority and the all-powerful Royal Academy gave rise to an official art that reflected the taste and wishes of the sovereign. The Louis XIV style evolved in Versailles and spread throughout France where it was imitated to a lesser degree by the aristocracy in the late 17C.

The style was characterised by references to antiquity and a concern for order and grandeur, whether in architecture, painting or sculpture. French resistance to Baroque, which had but a superficial effect on French architecture, was symbolised by the rejection of Bernini's projects for the Louvre. One of the rare examples of the style is Le Vau's College of Four Nations (today's Institute of France), which consists of a former chapel with a cupola and semicircular flanking buildings.

In Versailles **Louis le Vau** and later **Jules Hardouin-Mansart** (1646–1708) favoured a majestic type of architecture: rectangular buildings set off by projecting central sections with twin pillars, flat roofs and sculptural decoration inspired by antiquity. **Charles le Brun** (1619–90), the leading King's Painter, supervised all the interior decoration (paintings, tapestries, furniture and *objets d'art*), giving the palace remarkable homogeneity. There were dark fabrics and panelling, gilded stuccowork, painted coffered ceilings, and copies of Greco-Roman statues. The decoration became less abundant towards the end of the century.

In 1662, the founding of the **Gobelins**, the "Royal Manufactory for Crown Furniture", stimulated the decorative arts. A team of painters, sculptors, goldsmiths, warp-weavers, marble-cutters and cabinet-makers worked under Charles le Brun, achieving a high degree of technical perfection. Carpets were made at the Savonnerie factory in Chaillot.

The massive furniture of the period was often carved and sometimes gilded. Boulle marquetry, a combination of brass, tortoiseshell and gilded bronze, was one of the most sumptuous of the decorative arts produced at the time.

Versailles park, laid out by **Le Nôtre** (1613–1700), fulfilled all the requirements of French landscape gardening with its emphasis on rigour and clarity. Its geometrically tailored greenery, long axial perspectives, fountains, carefully designed spinneys and allegorical sculptures reflect the ideal of perfect order and control over nature.

Sculptures were placed throughout the gardens. Many of the works were by the two major sculptors of the time, **François Girardon** (1628–1715) and **Antoine Coysevox** (1640–1720), who drew upon mythology from antiquity. The work of **Pierre Puget** (1620–94), another important sculptor, was far

Orangery, Versailles

© Timehacker/Dreamstime.com

83

more tortured and Baroque – an unusual style for the late 17C.

FRENCH ROCAILLE (1715–50)

The 18C style in France grew from a reaction against the grandeur of the Louis XIV style, which was considered ill-adapted to the luxurious life and pleasures of the aristocracy and the upper-middle classes during the regency of Philippe of Orléans (1715–23) and the reign of Louis XV (1723–74). Rocaille was an 18C Rococo style or ornamentation based on rock and shell motifs.

Architecture

Rocaille architecture, at least on the outside, remained faithful to some of the principles of Classical composition – plain buildings with symmetrical façades and projecting central sections crowned by a triangular pediment – but the use of Classical orders became less rigid and systematic. The most representative examples of this new type of architecture were town houses such as the Hôtel de Soubise by **Delamair** and Hôtel Matignon by **Courtonne**, both in Paris.

The majestic formal apartments of the previous century gave way to smaller, more intimate rooms such as boudoirs and studies. Inside, woodwork, often white and gold, covered the walls from top to bottom (Hôtel de Lassay in Paris and the Clock Room or Cabinet de la Pendule in Versailles). The repertoire of ornamentation included intertwining plant motifs, curved lines, shells and other natural objects. Paintings of landscapes and country scenes were inserted in the woodwork above doors or in the corners of ceilings. **Verberckt**, who worked in Versailles for Louis XV, was an exceptionally skilled interior decorator.

Painting

The generation of painters working at the turn of the century was influenced by Flemish art. Artists such as **Desportes** (1661–1743), **Largillière** (1656–1746) and **Rigaud** (1659–1743) painted sumptuously decorative still lifes and formal portraits. Secular themes including scenes of gallantry *(fêtes galantes)* and fashionable society life became popular. **Watteau** (1684–1721), **Boucher** (1703–70), **Natoire** (1700–77) and **Fragonard** (1732–1806) reflected the taste of the day in their elegant genre scenes, some with mythological overtones, of pastoral life and the game of love.

Religious painting was not neglected in spite of these trends. Charles de la Fosse (1636–1716), one of Le Brun's pupils, Antoine Coypel (1661–1722) and especially **Restout** (1692–1768) adapted it to the less stoical ideals of the 18C by stripping it of too strong a dogmatism. There was a revival in portraiture during the 18C. **Nattier** (1685–1766), official painter of Louis XV's daughters, produced likenesses in mythological guise or half-length portraits which were far less pompous than the usual court picture. The pastellist **Quentin de la Tour** (1704–88) excelled in portraying his subjects' individual temperament and psychology rather than their social rank by concentrating more on faces than dress and accessories.

The lesser genres (still lifes and landscapes), scorned by the Academy but favoured by the middle classes for the decoration of their homes, blossomed considerably at the time. **Chardin** (1699–1779) painted simple still lifes in muted tones and Flemish-inspired scenes of everyday life, giving them a realistic, picturesque quality.

Sculpture

Baroque influence swept through sculpture in the first half of the century. The **Adam** brothers (Neptune Basin at Versailles), **Coustou** (1677–1746) (Horses of Marly) and **Slodtz** (1705–64) introduced the style's expressiveness into their work to lend movement and feeling. The main characteristics of Baroque art were flowing garments, attention to detail and figures shown in action.

In contrast, the contemporary work of **Bouchardon** (1698–1762), who trained in Rome and was therefore influenced by antique sculpture, tended to be

Panthéon, Paris

Ph. Gajic/MICHELIN

more Classical (Fountain in the Rue de Grenelle in Paris).

Decorative Arts

The rise of fashionable society brought with it a great need for luxury furniture that matched the style of woodwork inside elegant homes. New types of furniture were created: after commodes (chests of drawers) came writing desks – upright or inclined, escritoires, chiffoniers and countless small tables. For the comforts of conversation there were wing-chairs and deep easy chairs. There were also *voyeuses* or conversation chairs (special seats in gaming houses placed behind players to allow spectators to watch) and all manner of sofas and seats on which to recline (couches, lounging-chairs, divans and settees). Curved lines were favoured, as were rare and precious materials like exotic woods and lacquered panelling often set off by floral marquetry and finely chased gilded bronze. Among the great rocaille cabinet-makers were Cressent, Joubert and Migeon, while the principal seat carpenters of the time were Foliot, Sené and Cresson.

The **Vincennes Porcelain Factory** moved to **Sèvres** in 1756 and produced luxury items of which some were decorated in deep blue known as Sèvres blue. Gilt ornamentation was theoreti-cally used only for royal services. Rocaille gold and silver plate was adorned with reed motifs, crested waves, scroll-work and shells often arranged in asymmetrical patterns. **Thomas Germain** (1673–1748), one of the most prestigious names in the trade, supplied the princely tables of the time.

NEOCLASSICAL REACTION

The middle of the century brought a reaction against rocaille on moral and aesthetic grounds. The style was considered to be too florid and frivolous, the result of decadence in both morals and the arts. Classical models from antiquity and the 17C were then deemed the only recourse to revive proper artistic creation.

Architecture

The new style of architecture that emerged was more austere and tended towards the monumental. Sculptural decoration on façades grew more restrained and the Doric order became widespread (Église St-Philippe-du-Roule by J F Chardin in Paris). Some buildings, like the Église Ste-Geneviève (the present-day Panthéon) in Paris by **G Soufflot** (1713–80), were direct copies of antique models. Louis XVI commissioned men like **Victor Louis** (1731–1802) who designed the Bordeaux theatre,

A T Brongniart (1739–1813) and **J F Bélanger** (1744–1818) for most of the great architectural undertakings of the time. The philosophical influence of the Enlightenment led to a keen interest in the architecture of functional, public buildings such as the Royal Salt-works in Arc-et-Senans by **Claude-Nicolas Ledoux** (1736–1806).

Sculpture

Sculptors distanced themselves from rocaille extravagance by striving towards a natural portrayal of anatomy. **E M Falconet** (1716–91), **P Julien** (1731–1804) and **G C Allegrain** (1710–95) drew upon Greco-Roman models for their greatly admired sculptures of female bathers. **J A Houdon** (1741–1828), one of the greatest sculptors of the late 18C, made busts of his French and foreign contemporaries (Voltaire, Buffon and Madame Adélaïde for the first, and Benjamin Franklin and George Washington for the second) which constituted a veritable portrait gallery.

The busts, executed in an extremely realistic manner, many without wigs or articles of dress to detract from the faces, were the culmination of modelled portraiture in France. Houdon also sculpted tombs and mythological statues. **J B Pigalle** (1714–85) maintained the style of sculpture predominant at the beginning of the century that the Neoclassical reaction had not managed to stifle entirely (mausoleum of the Marshal de Saxe in the Église St-Thomas in Strasbourg).

Painting

In the 1760s, attempts by the Royal Academy to restore a style of painting known as the grand manner encouraged the emergence of new themes such as antique history, civic heroism and 17C tragedies. These were adopted by painters like **J L David** (1748–1825), **J B M Pierre** (1714–89) and **J F P Peyron** (1744–1814). The style drew upon low-reliefs and statuary from antiquity and followed the principles of composition used by painters like Poussin and other 17C masters.

Works by **J M Vien** (1716–1809) and **J B Greuze** (1725–1805) showed a less austere approach to painting, with more room for sensibility and emotion, which heralded the romanticism that was to blossom after the Revolution.

Decorative Arts

Louis XVI furniture kept some of the characteristics inherited from the beginning of the century such as the use of precious materials and chased gilt bronze ornamentation, but curves and sinuous shapes gave way to straight lines. As far as decoration was concerned, while the floral motifs and ribbons of the past were maintained, ovoli friezes, Greek fretwork and fasces were willingly introduced. **René Dubois** (1738–99) and **Louis Delanois** (1731–92) initiated the Greek style derived from antique furniture seen in friezes at Herculaneum and Pompeii. Prestigious artists of the genre included Oeben and Riesener, while Carlin, followed by Beneman and Levasseur, specialised in furniture adorned with plaques of painted porcelain. At the end of the century new decorative motifs, including lyres, ears of corn, wickerwork baskets and hot-air balloons, were imported from England. The technique of hard-paste porcelain that was introduced into France at the beginning of the 1770s took the lead over soft-paste porcelain in the factory at Sèvres. Figurines of **biscuit** porcelain (white, fired, unglazed pottery) shaped on models by Fragonard, Boucher and other artists, became very popular.

The iconoclasm that prevailed during the **Revolution** marked a break in the history of French art. The Louvre opened in 1793, paving the way for many more museums in France.

19C

Art During the First Empire

After his investiture in 1804, Napoleon favoured the emergence of an official style of art by commissioning palace decoration (Tuileries, destroyed in 1870, and Fontainebleau) and paintings that related the great events of the Empire. The artists to benefit from the Emperor's patronage were men like J L David and his pupils **A J Gros** (1771-1835) and **A L Girodet-Trioson** (1767-1824).

Paintings of the time took on new themes derived from the romanticism in contemporary literature, orientalism and an interest in the medieval. National historic anecdotes were painted by artists who, like the troubadours, praised heroic deeds and fine sentiment.

Artistic development in the realm of architecture was less innovative. Napoleon commissioned large edifices commemorating the glory of the *Grande Armée* including the Carrousel Arch, the column in Place Vendôme and the Temple de la Madeleine (now a church). The official architects **Percier** (1764–1838) and **Fontaine** (1762–1853) were responsible for the overall supervision of the undertakings, setting models not only for buildings but also for decoration at official ceremonies and guidelines for the decorative arts.

Ambitious town-planning projects like the reconstruction of Lyon were also completed under the Empire.

Former royal palaces were refurnished. The style of First Empire furniture derived from the Neoclassical with massive, quadrangular, commodes and jewel-cases made of mahogany with gilt bronze plating and antique decorative motifs. **Desmalter** (1770–1841) was the main cabinet-maker of the imperial court. The sculptors **Chaudet** (1763–1810) and **Cartellier** (1757–1831) supplied models for furniture ornamentation in the Neoclassical style which also inspired their statues. After the Egyptian Campaign, motifs such as sphinxes and lotuses began to appear in the decorative arts.

Restoration and the July Monarchy

Two major trends affected French art between 1815 and 1848. The first was the gradual disappearance of the Neoclassical style which, however, still influenced church building (Notre-Dame-de-Lorette and St-Vincent-de-Paul in Paris); and the second was the birth of historicism, a style that fostered regard for the architecture of the past, particularly of the medieval period (Église Notre-Dame in Boulogne-sur-Mer and Marseille Cathedral by Léon Vaudoyer). The trend was furthered by the founding of the *Monuments Historiques* (a body set up for the classification and preservation of the national heritage) in 1830 and the enthusiasm of **Viollet-le-Duc** (1814–79).

The Second Empire

On the accession of Napoleon III the arts in general were affected by a spirit of **eclecticism**. The Louvre, completed by Percier's disciple Visconti (1791–1853) and **H Lefuel** (1810–80), and the Paris Opera by **Garnier** (1825–98) were among the greatest undertakings of the century. References to architectural styles of the past (16C, 17C and 18C) were present everywhere. Nevertheless, the introduction of new materials such as glass and cast iron (the Gare du Nord by Hittorff and the Église St-Augustin by V Baltard) showed the influence of technological progress and a new rational approach to building.

Baron Haussmann (1809–91), Prefect of the *département* of the Seine, laid down the principles for a public works programme that was to modernise the capital. Prefect C M Vaïsse carried out a similar plan in Lyon.

The Valpinçon Bather (1808) by Jean Auguste Dominique Ingres, Musée du Louvre

©World Illustrated/Photoshot

Academicism reigned over the **painting** of the time. **Cabanel** (1823–83), **Bouguereau** (1825–1905) and the portraitist **Winterhalter** (1805–73) drew their inspiration just as easily from antique statuary as from works by 16C Venetian masters or Rococo ornamentation.

However, **Courbet** (1819-77), **Daumier** (1808–79) and **Millet** (1814–75) formed an avant-garde group that fostered realism in painting with subjects from town and country life.

Ingres (1780–1867) who represented the Classical trend, and **Delacroix** (1798–1863), the great romantic painter of the century, were both at the height of their powers. Great architectural projects stimulated the production of **sculpture. Carpeaux** (1827–75), responsible for the high-relief of Dance on the façade of the Paris Opera, transcended the eclecticism of his time by developing a very personal style that was reminiscent of, and not simply a copy of, Flemish, Renaissance and 18C art. Dubois (1829–1905), Frémiet (1824–1910) and Guillaume (1822–1905) were more academic in their approach.

A taste for pastiche prevailed in the decorative arts.

The shapes and ornamental motifs of the Renaissance, the 16C and 18C were reproduced on furniture and *objets d'art*. The advent of **industrialisation** affected certain fields. The goldsmith Christofle (1805–63) and the bronze-founder Barbedienne (1810–92) made luxury items for the imperial court as well as mass-produced articles for new clients among the rich upper-middle classes.

Late 19C Artistic Trends

Architecture during the Third Republic was mainly marked by edifices built for Universal Exhibitions held in Paris (the former Palais du Trocadéro, the Eiffel Tower, the Grand-Palais and the Pont Alexandre-III). The pompous style of the buildings with their exotic ornamentation derived from the trend for eclecticism.

In the 1890s, **Art Nouveau** architects, influenced by trends in England and Belgium, distanced themselves from the official style of the day. They harmonised decoration on façades with that inside their buildings and designed their creations as a whole – stained glass, tiles, furniture and wallpaper. Decoration included plant motifs, stylised flowers, Japanese influences and asymmetrical patterns. **Guimard** (1867–1942) was the main proponent of the style in France (Castel Béranger in Paris and entrances to the capital's metro stations).

La Gare Saint-Lazare (1877) by Claude Monet, Musée d'Orsay

The decorative arts followed the Art Nouveau movement with works by the cabinet-maker **Majorelle** (1859–1929) and the glass and ceramics artist **Gallé** (1846–1904) in Nancy.

In the field of painting, the **Impressionists** began exhibiting their work outside official salons in 1874. **Monet** (1840–1926), **Renoir** (1841–1919) and **Pissarro** (1830–1903) breathed new life into the technique and themes of landscape painting by working out of doors, studying the play of light in nature and introducing new subjects drawn from contemporary life. **Manet** (1832–83) and **Degas** (1834–1917) joined the group temporarily.

Between 1885 and 1890, Neo-Impressionists like **G Seurat** (1859–91) and **Signac** (1863–1935) brought the Pointillist (painting with small dots) technique known as divisionism to a climax. The Dutch painter **Van Gogh** (1853–90) settled in France in 1886. His technique of using pure and expressionist colours with broad, swirling brushstrokes coupled with his belief that expression of emotional experience should override impressions of the external world were to have a great influence on early 20C painters. **Cézanne** (1839–1906) and **Gauguin** (1848–1903), who were influenced by primitive and Japanese art, partly dispensed with Impressionism to give more importance to volume. In 1886, seeking new inspiration, Gauguin moved to Pont-Aven, a small town east of Concarneau in Brittany that had often been visited by the painter Corot in the 1860s. Fellow artists **Émile Bernard** and **Paul Sérusier** formed the Pont-Aven School that favoured synthesist theories and symbolic subjects which paved the way for the **Nabis**.

Among the Nabis were artists like **Denis** (1870–1943), **Bonnard** (1867–1947) and **Vuillard** (1868–1940) who advocated the importance of colour over shape and meaning. Sculpture at the end of the century was dominated by the genius of **Rodin** (1840–1917). His expressionistic, tormented, symbolic work stood free from formal academic conventions and was not always understood in his time.

20C

Avant-Garde Movements

At the beginning of the 20C, proponents of the avant-garde reacted against the many trends of the 19C including the restrictions laid down by official art, academicism in painting and Art Nouveau in architecture.

The **De Stijl** movement was characterised in architecture by simple, geometric buildings adorned with sober low-reliefs. One of its most magnificent examples was the Théâtre des Champs-Élysées by the Perret brothers with sculptural decoration by **Bourdelle** (1861–1929). In the field of sculpture, the artists **Maillol** (1861–1944), **Bartholomé** (1848–1928) and **J Bernard** (1866–1931) opposed Rodin's aesthetic concepts and produced a very different type of art by simplifying their figures, in some cases to the point of schematic representation. **Fauvism** was the great novelty at the Autumn Salon of painting in 1905.

A Derain (1880–1964), **A Marquet** (1875–1947) and **M de Vlaminck** (1876–1958) broke up their subject matter through the vivid and arbitrary use of colour, a technique which was to pave the way for non-figurative painting. After an early period with the Fauvist movement, **Matisse** (1869–1904) went his own way, developing a personal style based on the exploration of colour.

A further major avant-garde movement in painting followed on from **Cézanne**'s structural analysis in which he broke up his subject matter into specific shapes. The trend was taken up by artists like **Braque** (1882–1963) and **Picasso** (1881–1973), whose exploration led to **Cubism**, a new perception of reality based not on what the eye saw but on an analytical approach to objects, depicting them as a series of planes, usually in a restricted colour range. The style dominated their work from 1907 to 1914.

Members of the *Section d'Or* (golden section) Cubist group like **A Gleizes**, **J Metzinger** and **F Léger** (his early works) were less revolutionary and more figurative. The main contribution to French Cubism in the field of sculpture came from **Henri Laurens**, who was influenced by Braque. **Surrealism** breathed new life into the art world in the 1920s and 1930s. It was a subversive art form that created an irrational, dreamlike, fantasy universe.

For the first time chance and promptings from the subconscious were integrated into the creative process. **Duchamp** (1887–1968), **Masson** (1896–1997), **Picabia** (1879–1953) and **Magritte** (1898–1967) all formed part of the movement.

Artistic Creation Since 1945

Abstract art began to affect the field of painting after World War II. **Herbin** defined it as the triumph of mind over matter. In 1949 he published Non-figurative, Non-objective Art (L'Art non figuratif non objectif) and greatly influenced young artists of the **geometric abstract** art movement. All his works from the 1950s onwards have been one-dimensional patterns of letters and simple geometric shapes painted in pure colours.

The **lyrical abstract** artists focused on the study of colour and texture. **Riopelle** applied his paint with a knife while **Mathieu** applied it directly from the tube. **Soulages**, who was influenced by art from the Far East, produced meditative, expressive work in shades of black. **Nicolas de Stael**'s art constituted a link between abstract and figurative in that his abstract compositions were the result of observations of real objects which could sometimes be distinguished in the final work.

In the 1960s, **New Realism** (Nouveau Réalisme), a form of pop art, with **Pierre Restany** as its leading theoretician, attempted to express the reality of daily life. Industrial items, the symbols of modern society, were broken up (by the artist **Arman**) and assembled (by **César**) or trapped in glass.

Yves Klein (1928–62) took his adherence to New Realism a step further in his Monochromes by trying to capture the universal essence of objects. He rejected formal and traditional values, as did **Dubuffet** (1901–85) who, in 1968, wrote a pamphlet entitled Asphyxiating Culture (Asphyxiante culture), which made a stand for permanent revolution. Dubuffet's later art consisted of puzzles of coloured or black and white units.

Since the 1960s, the problems posed by town-planning have led to a re-evaluation of the relationship between architecture and sculpture and an attempt to reconcile the two arts.

The **Support-Surface** movement (**Claude Viallet**, **Pagès** and **Daniel Dezeuze**) of the 1970s reduced painting to its pure material state by focusing on the way the paint was applied. Paintings were removed from their stretchers and cut up, suspended and folded.

The 1980s saw the return of Figuration in manifold ways. References to tradition are evident in the work of artists like **Gérard Garouste, Remi Blanchard, François Boisrond, Robert Combas** and **Jean-Charles Blais**. The great vitality of contemporary art can be seen in the extremely wide variety of styles and trends favoured by artists today. Many modern artists still focus on the horrors of war, notably **Boltanski**, and his wife, **Annette Messager**, who portrays issues of identity and feminism.

The photographer, installation and conceptual artist **Sophie Calle**'s work is distinguished by its use of arbitrary sets of constraints, and evokes the French literary movement of the 1960s.

The death of sculptor **Louise Bourgeois** in May 2010 marked the end of an extraordinarily long career, in which she produced work (first in France, then New York) during most of the 20C avant-garde artistic movements. Exploring themes of femininity, sexuality and isolation, her most famous pieces include the monumental spider bronzes Maman.

Nature

TOPOGRAPHY

France has a fortunate location in the European continent – not detached from it like the British Isles, nor projecting away like Iberia or Greece, nor set deep in its interior like the countries of Central Europe, yet in touch with the resources and the life of the whole of Western Europe and the seas around it, Atlantic, Channel, Mediterranean and North Sea.

There are four main river systems: in the east is the valley of the Rhône, (813km/505mi), which together with its tributary the Saône (480km/298mi) links the Paris basin with the Mediterranean; in the north, the Seine (776km/482mi) drains into the English Channel; in the west, the longest of all, the Loire (1010km/630mi), rises in central France and flows into the Atlantic, as does its southern cousin the Garonne (575km/357mi) which rises in the Pyrénées and drains into the Gironde estuary. Within this unified and robust framework there flourishes a geographical identity which is unmistakably French yet of an unrivalled local richness and variety.

GEOLOGICAL HISTORY

It has been said that the whole of Earth's history – the building of the planet – can be traced within the confines of France. The country's complex geological history starts in the Primary Era (600 million years ago), when the Hercynian folding was responsible for the raising up of the great mountain ranges which were the ancestors of today's Massif Central, Armorican Peninsula, Vosges and Ardennes.

In Secondary Era times (beginning 200 million years ago), the Paris region, Aquitaine, the Rhône and Loire valleys and the southern part of the Massif Central all lay under the sea which gradually filled them with sedimentary deposits.

New mountain ranges reared up in the Tertiary Era (beginning 60 million years ago): the Alps, Pyrénées, the Jura and Corsica. The shock-waves of this violent mountain-building were felt far afield, particularly in the Massif Central where great volcanoes erupted.

The Quaternary Era (2 million years ago) saw an alternation of warm and cold periods; glaciers advanced and retreated and rivers swelled and shrank, sculpting much of the land surface into its present forms.

CLIMATE AND RELIEF

In climatic terms too, France gathers into herself each of the contrasting patterns of the continent as a whole; Atlantic, Continental and Mediterranean influences are all present (in northern and western France, central and eastern parts of the country, and the south, respectively), contributing decisively to the formation of soils and their mantle of vegetation as well as to the processes which have shaped the geological foundation into the patterns of today's relief.

Climate change is impacting on France as elsewhere, affecting winter sports (50 percent decrease in snow in the French Prealps, for example), inducing an upward migration of alpine plants, a higher incidence of heat waves, forest fires and droughts, such as that of 2003, and an advance of fruit tree flowering. In Alsace, the number of days with a mean daily temperature above 10°C has increased from 170 to 210 since 1970.

The north of the country is largely composed of great sedimentary basins, scarp (côtes) and vale country, drained by slow-flowing rivers like the Seine and the Loire. At the extremities of these lowlands are rugged areas formed of Primary rocks, the much-eroded granites of Brittany and the gneisses and schists of the Ardennes, and the higher massifs of the Vosges and the centre. Beyond lie the fertile plains of Aquitaine and Languedoc while the corridor carved by the Rhône and Saône links the north and south of the country. Finally come the "young" mountains of the Jura, Alps and Pyrénées; their high peaks and ranges, while forming fine natural frontiers, are by no means impermeable to political, commercial and cultural currents.

Lac d'Annecy - a view of Duingt and the Massif des Bauges, French Alps
© Pierre Jacques/hemis.fr

DISCOVERING FRANCE

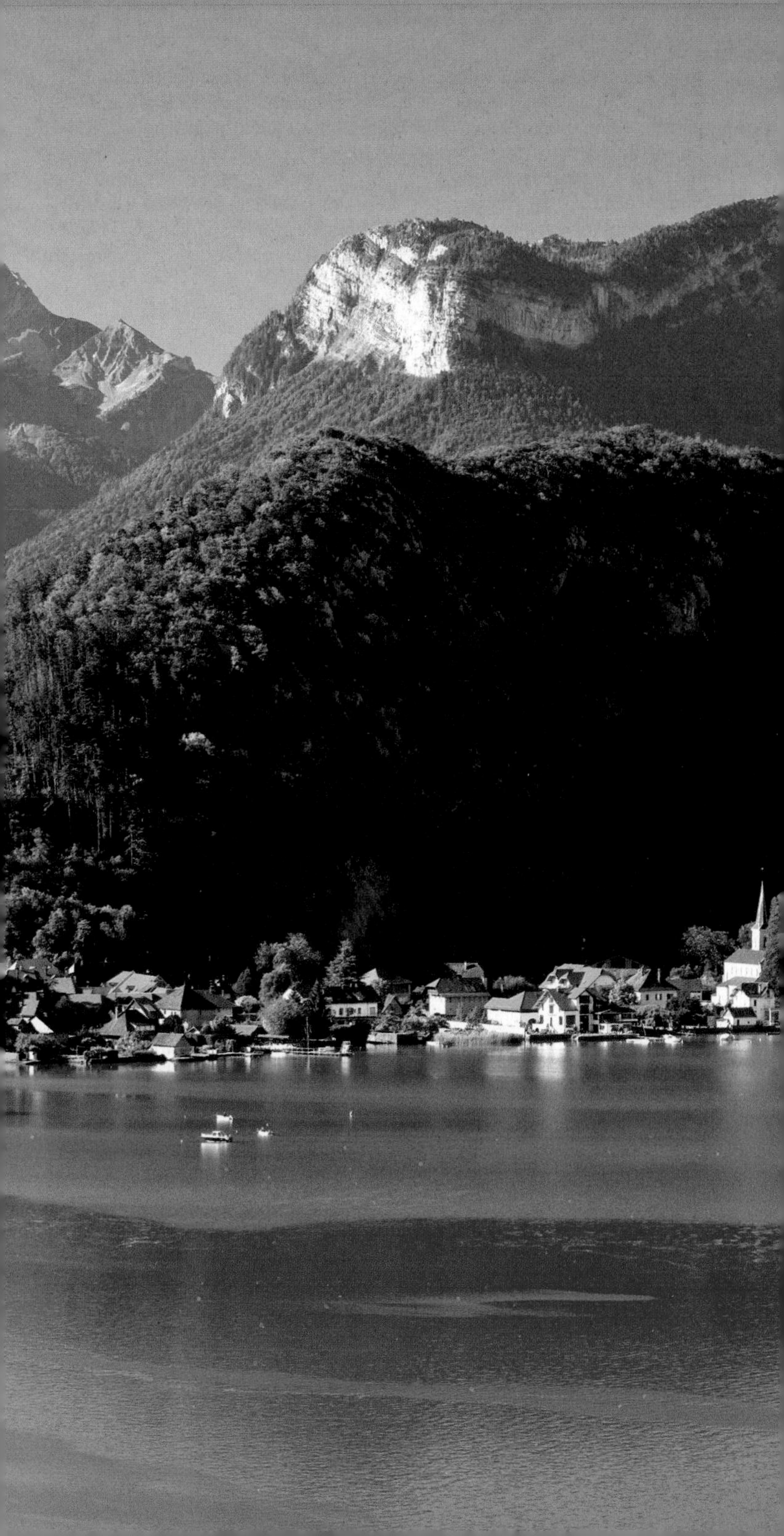

ALSACE LORRAINE CHAMPAGNE

Alsace forms France's window onto Central Europe. Its capital, Strasbourg, was part of the Holy Roman Empire. Together with the other towns and villages along this left bank of the Rhine, it has a picturesqueness of decidedly Germanic character. **Lorraine** owes its name to ancient Lotharingia, central of the three kingdoms into which Charlemagne's inheritance was divided. The presence of coal, iron-ore and salt led to the development of heavy industry. The **Champagne** region to the west is renowned for its sparkling wine, and the **Ardennes** to the north is one of Europe's most extensive areas of forest, with fine stands of oak, beech and conifers.

Highlights

1 UNESCO World Heritage Site Place Stanislas, **Nancy** (p101)

2 La Petite France, **Strasbourg** (p113)

3 Grünewald's masterpiece, The Issenheim Altarpiece, **Colmar** (p118)

4 Gothic Cathédrale Notre-Dame, **Reims** (p128)

5 Old timber-framed houses, Vieux Troyes at **Troyes** (p134)

has influenced everything from the food to the music to their livelihoods. In 1900, 86.8 percent of those living in Alsace-Lorraine spoke German. Today, most residents speak German, French and Alsatian, a dialect which is a combination of the two languages. Alsace has become a symbol of the transnational European economy. For the past 30 years, regional development has centred around this theme. Strasbourg, seat of the Council of Europe, was one of the first "Eurocities" on the continent.

Geography – The Rhine forms a frontier between Alsace and Germany, flowing through a broad rift valley defined by the Black Forest and the Vosges uplands. Further west in Lorraine, a series of limestone escarpments is pierced by major rivers flowing northwest.

Around Reims, steep slopes carry vineyards, and beyond stretches one of France's most productive agricultural regions. To the north, the Ardennes stretches into Belgium and merges with the German Eifel.

History – Alsace and Lorraine have long been fought over by France and Germany. Part of the Germanic Holy Roman Empire until 1648, the territory has changed hands four times since 1871. Champagne has been part of France since the 14C and the Ardennes has seen many battles, from the Franco-Prussian War to World War II.

Alsace, Lorraine and Champagne have diverse populations with people who celebrate many traditions and heritages. At some point over the years, both France and Germany have claimed the people of Alsace as their own, and that

Riquewihr

R.Mattès/MICHELIN

Economy – Alsace produces many varieties of wine. Together with Lorraine it is also one of the most important industrial areas of France. Lorraine depends heavily on timber production and dairy produce, while retaining an important metal sector. Farms in Lorraine are France's leading producers of rape seed, used for making cooking and salad oil; the flowering plants make bright yellow fields. Champagne's economy is mainly agriculture, while the Ardennes depends heavily on timber, tourism and its agricultural industries.

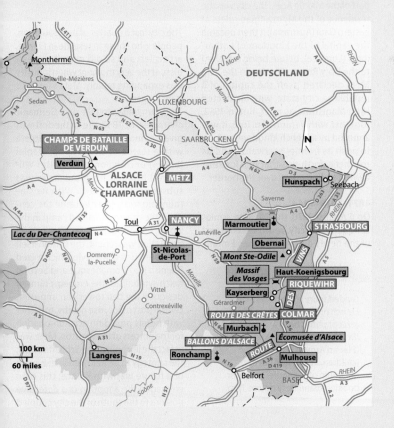

Metz★★★

Lorraine

From the limestone escarpment of the Côtes de Moselle high above Metz, the Lorraine plateau can be seen stretching away eastwards towards the German frontier. The city itself lies at the meeting point of the Moselle with the Seille, a strategic site whose importance was appreciated by the Romans; it was here that their great highways leading from the Channel coast to the Rhine and from Trier to Italy were linked, their course marked today by Metz' busy shopping street, Rue Serpenoise.

▶ **Population:** 124 961
◔ **Michelin Map:** 307 I 4
▤ **Info:** Place d'Armes. ℘03 87 55 53 76. http://tourisme.mairie-metz.fr.
◗ **Location:** Metz is a major junction at the heart of Lorraine, and lies due S of Luxembourg, 50km/31mi from the German border and 160km/100mi NW of Strasbourg.
℗ **Parking:** 13 car parks with 7 000 parking spaces, most underground. Much of the centre is traffic free.
◔ **Timing:** Metz is a large city, and exploring it will take time. Allow at least a full day to visit the historic heart of the city.

A BIT OF HISTORY

In the 4C, as a response to the threat posed by the Germanic tribes to the east, fortifications were built. In the early part of the Middle Ages, the city was the residence of the Merovingian rulers of Eastern Gaul (Austrasia); it then became the capital of the kingdom of Lotharingia (Lorraine), before being attached to the Holy Roman Empire. In the 12C, Metz declared itself the capital of a republican city-state, with an elected High Magistrate as ruler. But in 1552, together with Verdun and Toul, it was annexed by a French kingdom seeking to push its frontier eastwards, and its role henceforth was that of a fortress-town standing guard over the border.

1871–1918–1944

On 6 August 1870, the Prussian armies conquered the city, which became part of the newly declared German Empire.

The city lost a quarter of its population, people who chose to resettle in France; artists left and so did many businessmen, at the very moment when industry was expanding rapidly. Metz's loss was Nancy's gain.

The town began to take on a Germanic character. In 1898 the cathedral was given a neo-Gothic portal, complete with a statue of the Prophet Daniel looking uncommonly like Kaiser Wilhelm II (though his moustache was subsequently clipped). With its surrounding forts, Metz became the centre of the greatest fortified camp in the world. From 1902–08 the area around the station was rebuilt; the station itself was constructed in a style which mixed Rhenish neo-Romanesque and Second Reich symbolism (the emperor himself designed the bell tower); an imposing central post office rose nearby, together with hotels providing accommodation for the officers of the garrison. Metz was in fact the linchpin of the Schlieffen Plan, the strategy to be followed in the event of a future war with France; this plan envisaged the adoption of a defensive posture to the south of the city coupled

---

☺ Guided Tours ☺

Guided tours around Metz (1h, in French only) are available Mon–Sat (except public hols) at 3pm (St Etienne cathedral) and 4pm (Place d'Armes). ◉€5/person (children, 12–18, half price). Minimum of 4 people, and prior booking mandatory before 1pm.

with a vast turning movement to the northwest, which would sweep through Belgium and then descend on Paris. In 1914 this plan all but succeeded; the German armies marched steadily forward for six weeks, coming within 50km/30mi of Paris, only to be thrown back by Marshal Joffre at the Miracle of the Marne. In the inter-war period, the ring of forts around Metz was incorporated into the Maginot Line.

Their defensive strength was such that the Allied armies took two and a half months to eject their German occupants in the autumn of 1944.

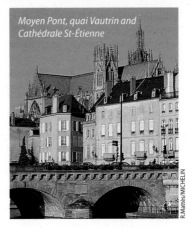

Moyen Pont, quai Vautrin and Cathédrale St-Étienne

R.Mattès/MICHELIN

SIGHTS

Cathédrale St-Étienne★★★

The cathedral grew out of the joining together around 1240 of two churches which up to then had been separated by an alleyway. The 13C and 14C interior recalls the Gothic style of Champagne; its relative narrowness combines with the modest height of the aisles to exaggerate the loftiness of the nave which does in fact reach 41.77m/137ft. The late Gothic chancel, crossing and transepts were completed at the beginning of the 16C.

The cathedral is known as "God's Lantern" (Lanterne du Bon Dieu) due to its stained-glass windows **(verrières★★★)**. The rose window of the west front is 14C work, the lower part of the north transept window 15C, and the upper part of this window together with the glass of the south transept and the chancel, 16C. Contemporary glass can be seen beneath the towers and above all in the north ambulatory and on the southwest side of the north transept (the *Earthly Paradise* by Chagall).

Musées de Metz Métropole-La Cour d'Or ★★

2 rue du Haut Poirier. ⏱*Open Mon–Fri (except Tue) 9am–5pm, Sat–Sun 10am–5pm.* ⏱*Closed 1 Jan, Good Fri, 1 and 8 May, 14 Jul, 1 and 11 Nov, and 25 and 26 Dec (24 and 31 Dec afternoons).* ⎈*€4.60 (no charge first Sun in the month).* ☎*03 87 20 13 20. http:// musees.metzmetropole.fr.*

The museums are housed in the buildings of a former Carmelite convent (17C), a 15C tithe barn (Grenier de Chèvrement) and several link rooms and extensions. In the basements are the remains of ancient baths.

The complex uses the latest display techniques to present a fascinating survey of times past.

Section archéologique★★★

On display in the archaeological section are artefacts found in Metz and the surrounding area. The finds attest to the importance of the town, which was in turn Gaulish, a major crossroads in Gallo-Roman times, and a cultural centre under the Carolingian kings. The **Grenier de Chèvrement**★ is a fine building (1457) used to store cereals given over as tithes.

Centre Pompidou-Metz

1 parvis des Droits de l'Homme. ⏱*Open daily (except Tue) Mon, Wed 11am–6pm, Thu, Fri 11am–8pm, Sat, 10am–8pm, Sun 10am-6pm.* ⏱*1 May.* ⎈*€7 (Exhibitions).* ☎*03 87 15 39 39. www.centrepompidou-metz.fr.*

This is the first so-called "decentralised" branch of Paris's famous Centre Pompidou to open outside Paris.

It exhibits artworks of the 20C and 21C to further its mission of promoting art in Europe. The building, with exhibits spread across three galleries, has a 77m/253ft-high spire. The exhibitions, most taken from the Musée National d'Art Moderne in Paris, are all temporary to allow for the continuing evolution of artistic styles that prove ripe for presentation.

Surrounded by pleasant green space, there is a café, restaurant for more formal dining, cinema, and activities for young children and teenagers.

ADDITIONAL SIGHTS
Porte des Allemands★
This massive fortress, which formed part of the town walls running along the Moselle and the dual-carriageway ring road south and east of Metz, straddles the River Seille.

Place St-Louis★
Situated in the heart of the old town, the rectangular place St-Louis is lined on one side with buttressed arcaded buildings dating from the 14C, 15C and 16C that once housed the money-changers' shops. At the end, on the corner of rue de la Tête-d'Or, note the three golden Roman heads protruding from the wall, which gave the street its name.

ADDRESSES

🛏 STAY

🍽 **Chambre d'hôte Bigare** – *23 r. Principale – 57530 Ars-Laquenexy, 9km/ 5.6mi E of Metz, Château-Salins direction then D 999. ℘03 87 38 13 88. 2rms.* If the bustle of city life doesn't suit you, a short journey will bring you to this friendly local village house. Simple rooms and reasonable prices.

🍽 **Hôtel de la Cathédrale** – *25 pl. de la Chambre. ℘03 87 75 00 02. www.hotelcathedrale-metz.fr. 20rms. ⌸€11.* A charming hotel situated in a lovely 17C house, completely restored. The attractive rooms have cast-iron or cane beds, old parquet flooring and furniture, some of which is oriental. Most rooms face the cathedral, just opposite.

🍴 EAT

🍽 **La Gargouille** – *29 pl. de Chambre. ℘03 87 36 65 77. www.lagargouille.com. Closed Mon lunch, Tue eve and Wed.* Don't be fooled by the ordinary façade of this restaurant located down from the cathedral: behind it lies a sumptuous interior with velvet-covered seats, cosy little booths and 1900-style décor typical of the Nancy School, all making for a warm ambience. The food is exceedingly refined: carpaccio de fois gras au sel de Guérande, or joue de bœuf sauce vigneronne.

🍽 **La Robe des Champs** – *14 en Nouvelle rue. ℘03 87 36 32 19.* You can't miss the yellow façade and Provençal-style terrace of this pleasant bistro in a pedestrian town-centre street. Potatoes, as the name infers ("in its jacket"), take pride of place in this friendly, unpretentious establishment.

🍽 **Restaurant du Fort** – *Allée du Fort – 57070 St-Julien-lès-Metz, 8km/5mi NE of Metz, Bouzonville direction on D3, then a minor road. ℘03 87 75 71 16. Closed Sun eve and Wed. Booking advisable at weekends.* At the end of a forest track you will be amazed to discover this 1870 fort, evidence of the Moselle's turbulent history. Part of it has been restored to create a restaurant offering Lorraine cuisine.

🍽 **Restaurant du Pont-St-Marcel** – *1 r. du Pont-St-Marcel. ℘03 87 30 12 29.* A 17C restaurant not far from St Étienne's cathedral, standing on piles beside a branch of the Moselle. Inside, an amusing contemporary fresco depicts a 17C fairground scene, complete with acrobats and theatre. The staff wear costumes to serve the local cuisine.

🍽 **L'Écluse** – *45 pl. de la Chambre. ℘03 87 75 42 38. Closed Sat noon and Sun and Mon eves.* Refined modern style, with art on display, and well-prepared contemporary dishes.

🍽 **Maire** – *1 r. du Pont-des-Morts. ℘03 87 32 43 12. www.restaurant-maire. com. Closed Wed lunch and Tue.* There is a superb view of the Moselle from this town-centre restaurant. Enjoy the chef's carefully prepared dishes, whether in the salmon-pink dining room with its pale wood furniture or on the terrace.

Verdun★★

Lorraine

This ancient stronghold occupies a strategic position on the Meuse. The Upper Town with its cathedral and citadel is poised on an outcrop overlooking the river.

- ▶ **Population:** 20 255
- **Michelin Map:** 307 D 4
- **Info:** Place de la Nation. ☎03 29 86 14 18. www.verdun-tourisme.com.
- ▶ **Location:** Roughly mid-way between Metz (80km/50mi to the east) and Reims (120km/75mi to the west).

A BIT OF HISTORY

The Gauls were the first to build a fortress here on the left bank of the Meuse. They were followed by the Romans, but Verdun entered the mainstream of history with the signing of the **Treaty of Verdun** in 843.

By its terms, Charlemagne's realm was divided up among his grandsons, contrary to their father's wish for its preservation as a single unit.

The emperor, Lothair, received the central zone (Northern Italy, Provence, the Rhineland and the Low Countries); Louis, the Germanic countries, and Charles the Bald, Gaul. The repercussions have been felt throughout the centuries, and the treaty has been referred to as "the most significant in all the continent's history", partly because Louis was dissatisfied with his portion and launched what might be considered the first of all Franco-German wars in 858 following the death of Lothair.

The town was besieged in 1870 at the start of the Franco-Prussian War, then occupied for three years. In World War I, Verdun was the scene of some of the bloodiest fighting of the Western Front, in a battle that lasted 18 months (*see CHAMP DE BATAILLE DE VERDUN*).

SIGHT
Ville Haute★

The seat of a bishop, the fortified upper town rises in stages from the banks of the river. The city's historic buildings include **Cathédrale Notre-Dame★**, laid out like the great Romanesque basilicas of the Rhineland, and the Bishop's Palace **(Palais épiscopal★)**, constructed by Robert de Cotte in the 18C.

ADDITIONAL SIGHT

Citadelle Souterraine (Underground Citadel) – self-guided vehicle travels 7km/4.3mi of tunnels equipped to fulfil the needs of the army.

Palais épiscopal

R. Mattes/MICHELIN

Champ de Bataille de
Verdun★★★
Lorraine

The name of Verdun is forever linked to the decisive struggle on which turned the outcome of the First World War (1914–18). The gaze of the world was fixed for a year-and-a-half on the violence endured by both sides, in a battle which inspired the utmost steadfastness and courage.

A BIT OF HISTORY

At the outbreak of war in August 1914, Verdun lay a mere 40km/25mi from the Franco-German frontier. The 21 February 1916 dawned bright but cold. A devastating bombardment preceded the Germans' frontal assault on the French lines. Within four days Douaumont Fort had fallen.

This was the moment at which General Pétain took effective charge of the battle; by the time of his replacement in April 1917, it was clear that the German attempt to break the staying-power of the French army had failed. Verdun, the

Info: Place de la Nation, Verdun. ℰ03 29 86 14 18. www.verdun-tourisme.com.

Location: The battlefields are 10km/6.2mi NE of Verdun.

hinge of the whole Western Front, could not be taken.

A series of battles raged throughout March and April in the Argonne, around Les Éparges; and, closer to Verdun, on Hill 304 and the other eminence known chillingly as the Mort-Homme (Dead Man's Hill). On 11 July, the final German offensive ground to a halt in front of the Souville fort, a mere 5km/3mi from the city. The French counter-offensive began in October 1916. By 20 August 1917, the Hell of Verdun, which had cost the lives of over 700 000 men, was over.

☺ Guided Tours ☺

The *Circuit Découverte* is a bus tour (in French only) of the battlefields (*2–6pm, from Tourist Office.* ☞*€27*).

Douaumont Ossuary and the graves, Verdun battlefield

© philippe montembaut/Fotolia.com

Nancy★★★

Lorraine

Capital of the industrial area of Lorraine, Nancy is sited on the low-lying land between the River Meurthe and the Moselle Heights (Côtes de Moselle).

A BIT OF HISTORY

The city was founded in the 11C, but its history begins in the 15C when the Dukes of Lorraine asserted their independence. In the 17C, the new town (*Ville neuve*) was planned on a regular pattern by the artist **Claude Lorrain** (1600–82). Louis XIV 's architect Mansart designed the town hall (**Palais du Governement★**) in 1699. Ever since the Treaty of Munster in 1648, the Duchy of Lorraine had been in a precarious situation; an independent enclave in French territory, it still formed part of the Holy Roman Empire. Though French in language and culture, its people were proud of their independence.

In 1738, following the War of the Polish Succession, Duke François I, son of Leopold and husband of Maria-Theresa of Austria, found himself having to cede Lorraine in exchange for Tuscany. In his place, Louis XV appointed, as ruler for life, his own father-in-law Stanislas Leszczynski, and by 1766 the Duchy had been painlessly incorporated into the French kingdom, a notable success for Cardinal Fleury's foreign policy. Stanislas was a man of peace, fond of his daughter the Queen of France, a lover of good living and of the opposite sex, and a passionate builder.

- **Population:** 108 172
- **Michelin Map:** 307 I 6
- **Info:** 14 pl. Stanislas. ℘03 83 35 22 41. www.ot-nancy.fr.
- **Location:** Nancy lies 56km/35mi due S of Metz.
- **Don't Miss:** Place Stanislas.
- **Timing:** Discover Nancy using *Les Taxis de Nancy* on one of three guided routes that feature multi-language commentary (Mon–Sat €28; Sun €35 per person).

He set out to join together the old quarter of Nancy with the "New Town" by means of a set-piece of civic design in honour of his son-in-law. The great project was completed between 1752 and 1755.

WALKING TOURS

1 LORRAINE'S CAPITAL CITY
Place Stanislas★★★

Place Stanislas was added to the UNESCO World Heritage list in 1983. In charge of the work were the architect Emmanuel Héré (1705–63) and Jean **Lamour**, a metal-worker of genius. Héré designed the Hôtel de Ville and the flanking buildings with their fine façades. To the north the square is defined by two further buildings, similar in general treatment, though with only one storey. The whole forms a space of exceptional elegance and clarity of structure. Further enclosure is achieved

PRACTICAL INFORMATION

Guided tours – Nancy, City of Art, organises 1hr30 guided tours (French only): €7. Audioguides are also available: €6. *Enquire at tourist office or buy online.*

Tourist train – May–Sept: 40min tour of the historic town by miniature train. Departs from place de la Carrière, daily at 10am, 11am, 2pm, 3pm, 4pm. €6 (6–14 years €4). *℘03 89 73 74 24. www.petit-train.com.*

City pass – This pass from the tourism office gives entry to six museums in the area. €10.

Weekends in Nancy – Hotel stays of two nights and more are rewarded by a welcome gift and reductions on visits to the town. Ask at the tourist office for details.

Place Stanislas – gilded railings and the statue of Stanislas

by Jean Lamour's brilliant ironwork. Perfectly integrated into the architectural concept, his **gilded railings** with their crests and floral decoration are of inimitable gracefulness.

Louis XV's statue in its centre was destroyed during the Revolution; in 1831 a statue of Stanislas replaced it and the square was renamed after him.

Hôtel de ville

The town hall was erected between 1752 and 1755. The pediment is decorated with the coat of arms of Stanislas Leszczynski: Polish eagle, Lithuanian knight, Leszczynski buffalo.

Arc de Triomphe★

This deep triumphal arch, built between 1754 and 1756 to honour Louis XV, is modelled on Septimus Severus' arch in Rome.

On the right-hand park side, there is a monument dedicated to Héré, on the left a monument dedicated to Callot.

Place de la Carrière★

This elongated square dates from the time of the dukes of Lorraine; originally used for cavalry drills, it was remodelled by Héré and is now lined with beautiful 18C mansions. Fountains decorate the corners and at each end there are railings and lanterns by Lamour.

Palais du Gouverneur★

Facing the Arc de Triomphe across place du Général-de-Gaulle and place de la Carrière, this edifice is the former residence of the governors of Lorraine.

▶ *Turn right to enter the park.*

La Pépinière

👥 This fine open space includes a terrace, an English garden, a rose garden and a zoo.

▶ *Take the exit for rue Ste-Catherine.*

Muséum-aquarium de Nancy

🕙*Open daily 10am–noon, 2–6pm.*
🕙*1 Jan, 1 May and 25 Dec.* 🎫*€4 (children €2).* 📞*03 83 32 99 97. www.man.uhp-nancy.fr.*
👥On the ground floor is the **tropical aquarium**★ which comprises 70 ponds full of numerous species of fish; the first floor has over 10 000 stuffed animals.

Place d'Alliance

Designed by Héré, the square is lined with 18C mansions and adorned with a fountain by Cyfflé, commemorating the alliance signed by Louis XV and Maria-Theresa of Austria in 1756.

▶ *Take rue Bailey, then turn right onto rue St-Georges.*

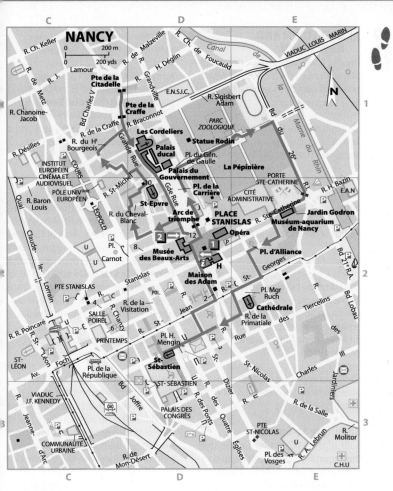

Cathédrale

This 18C edifice features superb railings inside the chapels. The Virgin and Child in the apse was carved in the 17C. The sacristy houses the **treasury** containing the ring, the chalice, the paten, the comb and the evangelistary of St Gauzelin, who was bishop of Toul during the first half of the 10C.

◐ *Rue Montesquieu leads to rue Primatiale, which you follow to the right. Walk along the central market and continue until place Henri-Mengin.*

Église St-Sébastien

This masterpiece by architect Jenesson was consecrated in 1732; it has a striking concave Baroque **façade**★. Inside, the three naves are surmounted by unusual flattened vaulting resting on massive Ionic columns. The chancel has retained some elegant woodwork. The side altars are the work of Vallin (École de Nancy).

◐ *Retrace your steps and take a left onto rue St-Dizier, right onto rue St-Georges and then left onto rue des Dominicains.*

Maison des Adam

57 rue des Dominicains. This is the elegant home of the Adam family, who were renowned sculptors in the 18C and decorated the house themselves.

◐ *Return to Place Stanislas.*

② OLD TOWN AND NEW TOWN

The Old Town is the historic heart of the city, centred on place St-Epvre. When it extended outside its original gates, the New Town was born.

▷ *Begin at place Vaudémont and take Grande-Rue. Turn left onto rue Callot and continue to rue de la Monnaie.*

The Hôtel de la Monnaie at No 1 was built by Boffrand. This road leads to place de La-Fayette, a square adorned with a statue of Joan of Arc by Frémiet (a replica of the statue is in Paris).

▷ *Turn right on rue de la Source.*

The **Hôtel de Lillebonne** (*No 12*), with its fine Renaissance staircase, houses the American library. Next door at No 10, note the unusual doorway of the Hôtel du Marquis de Ville, decorated with a bearded head.

▷ *Take a right onto rue du Cheval-Blanc and then left onto rue de la Charité.*

Basilique St-Epvre

Built in the 19C, in neo-Gothic style, this imposing church is dedicated to a 6C bishop of Toul. Its elegant west front is preceded by a monumental staircase (a gift from the emperor of Austria).

▷ *Take rue Mgr-Trouillet off place St-Epvre and continue on this road, which crosses rue St-Michel.*

The Renaissance **Hôtel d'Haussonville** is at No 9, with its outside galleries and Neptune fountain.

▷ *Continue on the road which becomes rue des Loups.*

The Hôtel des Loups (No 1), again by Boffrand, and the Renaissance doorway of Hôtel de Gellenoncourt (No 4) are particularly worth noting.

▷ *At the end of rue des Loups, turn right onto rue du Haut-Bourgeois.*

Admire the Hôtel de Fontenoy (No 6), designed by Boffrand at the beginning of the 18C, and the **Hôtel Ferrari**★ (No 29), also by Boffrand, with emblazoned balcony, monumental staircase and a Neptune fountain in the courtyard.

▷ *Turn left towards the gate.*

Porte de la Craffe★

This gate, which formed part of the 14C fortifications, is decorated with the thistle of Nancy and the cross of Lorraine (19C). The gate was used as a prison until the Revolution. To the north stands the **Porte de la Citadelle** which used to secure the old town. This Renaissance gate is decorated with low-relief sculptures and trophies by Florent Drouin.

▷ *Retrace your steps and then take the Grande-Rue.*

Palais ducal★★

Dating from the second half of the 13C, the palace was in ruins when René II had it rebuilt after his victory over Charles the Bold of Burgundy. In the 16C, Duke Antoine had the Porterie (gateway) completed, together with the Galerie des Cerfs (Deer Gallery). In 1850 the palace was skilfully restored – the northern part was entirely rebuilt. The plain façade overlooking Grande-Rue enhances the elegant and rich decoration of the **Porterie**★★.

ADDITIONAL SIGHTS
Musée de l'École de Nancy★★

36-38 rue du Sergent Blandan. ⏰*Open Wed–Sun 10am–6pm.* ⬤€6. ⏰*Closed 1 Jan, 1 May, 14 Jul, 1 Nov, 25 Dec.* ✆*03 83 40 14 86. www.ecole-de-nancy.com.* Housed in an opulent residence dating from the turn of the 20C, this museum offers a remarkable insight into the renewal movement in the field of decorative arts that took place in Nancy between 1885 and 1914 and became known as the **École de Nancy**.

Musée des Beaux-Arts★★

3, pl. Stanislas. ♿🕐*Open daily except Tue 10am–6pm.* 🕐*Closed 1 Jan, 1 May, 14 Jul, 1 Nov, 25 Dec.* 👁€6.
📞*03 83 85 30 72.*

The impressively refurbished Museum of Fine Arts, housed in one of the pavilions on place Stanislas, contains rich collections of European art from the 14C to the present day which are not arranged chronologically – to great advantage.
The Modern Art collection, housed in the contemporary extension, is essentially represented by Manet, Monet, Henri Edmond Cross, Modigliani, Juan Gris, Georg Grosz, Picasso, and a few early 20C artists from Lorraine. Sculptures include works by Rodin, Duchamp-Villon, Lipchitz, and César.

Musée Lorrain★★★

64 Grande-Rue in the Palais ducal. 🕐*Open daily except Tue 10am–12.30pm, 2–6pm.* 🕐*Closed 1 Jan, 1 May, 14 Jul, 1 Nov, 25 Dec.* 👁€4.
📞*03 83 32 18 74.*

The museum contains a wealth of exceptional documents illustrating the history of Lorraine, its artistic production and its folklore, displayed on three floors.
The pavilion at the bottom of the garden houses an **archaeological gallery** concerned with prehistory, the Celtic period, and Gallo-Roman and Frankish times.

Église des Cordeliers★

🕐*Open daily except Mon 10am–12.30pm, 2–6pm.* 🕐*Closed 1 Jan, 1 May, 14 Jul, 1 Nov, 25 Dec.* 👁€4.
📞*03 83 32 18 74.*

The now-restored 15C Franciscan convent and adjacent church were erected on the initiative of Duke René II.
The **church★** has only one nave, as is usual for the church of a mendicant order. A chapel on the left-hand side contains the **recumbent figure of Philippa of Gelderland★★**, René II's second wife, carved in fine limestone, one of the finest works of Ligier Richier. Against the south wall (near the high altar), note the funeral recess of **René II's funeral monument★**, carved by

Mansuy Gauvain in 1509. The effigy of Cardinal de Vaudémont (d 1587) is the work of Florent Drouin. The latter is also the author of a remarkable Last Supper, a low-relief sculpture after the famous painting by Leonardo da Vinci.
Built from 1607 onwards, the **Chapelle ducale★** was modelled on the Medici Chapel in Florence. The cloisters and some rooms of the former monastery are restored and now house a rich **Musée d'Arts et Traditions populaires**.

Jardin botanique du Montet★

100 r. du Jardin Botanique.
♿🕐*Gardens open Mon–Fri 10am–noon, 2–5pm, Sat 2–5pm, Sun and public holidays 2–6pm (5pm Oct–Mar); Greenhouses open: 2–5pm, Sun and public holidays 2–6pm (5pm Oct–Mar).* 🕐*Closed 1 Jan, 25 Dec and 1st Tue of the month (greenhouses).* 👁€4 greenhouses (gardens: no charge). 📞*03 83 41 47 47. www.cjbn.uhp-nancy.fr.*

The botanical gardens contain some 15 thematic collections (Alpine, ornamental, medicinal plants, an arboretum etc), and 6 500 species grow in the hot houses: orchids, and insect-eating and succulent plants.

Église Notre-Dame-de-Bon-Secours★

Avenue de Strasbourg.
Built in 1738 for Stanislas by Emmanuel Héré, on the site of René II's chapel commemorating his victory over Charles the Bold (1476), this church is a well-known place of pilgrimage.
The richly decorated interior includes carved confessionals in Louis XV style, railings by Jean Lamour and a splendid Rocaille pulpit.
The chancel contains **Stanislas' tomb★** and the monument carved by Vassé for the heart of Marie Leszczynska, Louis XV's wife, on the right-hand side and, on the left, the **mausoleum of Catherine Opalinsk★★**, Stanislas' wife.

ADDRESSES

🛏 STAY

Portes d'Or – *21 r. Stanislas. ℰ03 83 35 42 34. www.hotel-lesportesdor.com. 20 rooms. ⧠€6–9.* The main advantage of this hotel is its proximity to place Stanislas. The pastel-coloured rooms are not very large but have modern furniture and are reasonably well equipped.

Maison d'hôte Myon – *7 r. Mably. ℰ03 83 46 56 56. www.maisondemyon.com. 5 rooms.* An entirely restored 18C hotel transformed into a *maison d'hôte* in the heart of Nancy near the Place Stanislas.

Hôtel Crystal – *5 r. Chanzy. ℰ03 83 17 54 00. 58 rooms. ⧠ €11.50.* This hotel near the station is a good place to stay in Nancy. Its modern, spacious rooms have been nicely arranged and decorated and feel welcoming.

🍴 EAT

Grand Café Foy – *1 pl. Stanislas. ℰ03 83 32 21 44. Closed Sun eve, Tue eve and Wed.* Climb the lovely stone staircase to reach this first-floor restaurant above the café-brasserie of the same name in place Stanislas.

Les Pissenlits – *25 bis r. des Ponts. ℰ03 83 37 43 97. www.les-pissenlits.com. Closed Sun and Mon.* There's always a crowd in this bistro near the market. The atmosphere is relaxed, the cuisine innovative and diverse.

Le V Four – *10 r. St-Michel. ℰ03 83 32 49 48. Closed Sat lunch, Sun eve and Mon.* It may be small, but this restaurant in the heart of the old city is popular among the locals.

Le Gastrolâtre – *1 pl. Vaudémont. ℰ03 83 35 51 94. Closed Mon lunch, Thu eve and Sun.* This popular bistro just behind place Stanislas is run with a master's hand by a media boss. Its mouth-watering menu and characterful cuisine combine local flavours with those from the south of France.

Grenier à Sel – *28 r. Gustave-Simon. ℰ03 83 32 31 98. www.legrenier asel.eu. Closed Sun and Mon.* This restaurant is in a little-frequented street on the first floor of one of the oldest houses in town. In the large country-style dining room you can enjoy food with a modern flair.

🍷 NIGHTLIFE

L'Arquebuse – *13 r. Héré. ℰ03 83 32 11 99. www.larq.fr.* A high-class bar with refined décor and a wide choice of cocktails with atmospheric music and disco, attracting a mixed clientele of smart students and businessmen. The place to go after 2am.

L'Échanson – *9 r. de la Primatiale. ℰ03 83 35 51 58. Closed Sun, Mon.* A pleasant little wine merchant that also serves as the local bistro. A dozen or so wines are available by the glass, accompanied by a savoury snack.

Nouveau Vertigo – *29 r. de la Visitation ℰ03 83 32 71 97. Tue–Thu 11am–2am, Fri 11am–4am, Sat 4pm–5am. Closed Mon–Sun.* The centre-piece of Nancy cultural life, this bar doubles up as a restaurant and venue for café-theatre evenings and concerts. Beer and cocktails.

🎭 ENTERTAINMENT

Get hold of a programme!
The magazine *Spectacles à Nancy* will keep you informed. *www.spectacles-publications.com.*

Nancy Jazz Pulsations *100 Grande Rue. ℰ03 83 35 40 86. www.nancyjazz pulsations.com.* Ten days of non-stop jazz at various venues across the city. Jazz heaven!

Concerts and Stage Performances
The Opéra de Nancy et de Lorraine, Ballet de Nancy, Théâtre de la Manufacture, Centre dramatique national Nancy-Lorraine, Association de musique ancienne de Nancy, Ensemble Poirel, Orchestre symphonique et lyrique de Nancy, Association Lorraine de musique de chambre, Gradus Ad Musicam and La Psalette de Lorraine all put on numerous concerts and shows throughout the year.

Gastronomie en Musique –
Ask the tourist office about these summer evening musical performances (*Thu–Sun in different areas of the city*).

Toul★

Lorraine

On the banks of the river Moselle, the handsome fortified town occupies a strategic position at the intersection of highways and waterways.

- **Population:** 16 395
- **Michelin Map:** 307 G 6
- **Info:** Parvis de la Cathédrale. ℘03 83 64 11 69. www.ot-toul.fr.
- **Location:** Toul lies on a wide loop in the Moselle river, 22km/14mi W of Nancy, and 75km/47mi to the E of Saint-Dizier.

A BIT OF HISTORY

Together with Metz and Verdun, the city was one of the three Imperial Bishoprics which were annexed by Henri II in 1552 and were finally recognised as belonging to the French Crown by the Peace of Westphalia in 1648.

Vauban built new ramparts round the city in 1700 (the Porte de Metz is all that remains today), which were subsequently improved at intervals so that on the eve of World War I Toul was acknowledged as one of the best-defended strongholds in Europe.

SIGHTS

Cathédrale St-Étienne★★

Built from 1221 to 1496, cathedral has a very simple elevation. The highly pointed arches of the first five bays of the nave are in the High Gothic style of the 14C. The west front (**façade★★**), almost overloaded with architectural ornament, lost its statuary at the time of the French Revolution. The **cloisters★**, adorned with fine gargoyles, are among the most extensive in France.

Musée d'Art et d'Histoire★

25 rue Gouvion Saint Cyr. ◷*Open daily (except Tue): Apr–Oct 10am–noon, 2–6pm; Nov-Mar 2–6pm.* ◷*Closed 1 Jan, Easter, 1 May, 25 Dec.* ◉€3. ℘03 83 64 13 38. www.art-of-the-day.info. Housed in the Hôtel-Dieu, there are numerous collections tracing the history of Toul. There are 28 themed rooms which cover everything from the prehistoric period through the Middle Ages to recent history.

Église St-Gengoult★

This former Collegiate church, erected in the 13C and 15C, is a fine example of Champagne Gothic architecture.

The West front has an elegant doorway dating from the 15C. The Cloister★★ dates from the 16C and the outside decoration of the galleries is in Renaissance style.

Fortified town of Toul

©Guido Alberto Rossi/Tips Images

Strasbourg★★★

Alsace

This important modern city, with a busy river port and renowned university, is not just the lively capital of Alsace. It is also where the Council of Europe and European Parliament are located.

At the same time, the Grande Île, the historic centre around the cathedral, has been listed as a UNESCO World Heritage Site since 1988.

A BIT OF HISTORY

Strasbourg's name comes from the German meaning "City of the roads", and the place is indeed a meeting point for the highways, railways and waterways linking the Mediterranean with the Rhineland, Central Europe, the North Sea and the Baltic via the Belfort Gap and the Swabian Basin.

On 14 February 842, the **Strasbourg Oaths** were sworn by two of the sons of Louis the Pious (son of Charlemagne). Brothers Charles and Louis undertook to be loyal to one another in their attempt to frustrate the ambitions of their elder brother Lothair. Protocol demanded that each declare the oath in a language comprehensible to his brother's entourage; thus it was that the text read out by Louis the German is considered to be the oldest such document in a Romance language, the first written example of the language which has evolved into modern French. Strasbourg remained a **free city** within the Holy Roman Empire even after the virtual incorporation of the rest of Alsace into France by the Peace of Westphalia in 1648, but eventually submitted to annexation by Louis XIV in 1681.

On 24 April 1792, Frédéric de Dietrich, Strasbourg's first constitutional mayor, threw a farewell celebration for the volunteers of the Army of the Rhine. The conversation turned to the need for a marching song to match the troops' enthusiasm. Rouget de Lisle was asked to compose "something worth singing"; by morning he had finished, and

▶ **Population:** 276 194

Michelin Map: 315 K 5

Info: 17 pl. de la Cathédrale. www.otstrasbourg.fr. There is also a satellite office at the TGV station.

Location: On the banks of the river Ill, Strasbourg is less than 8km/5mi W of the Rhine, and 150km/95mi E of Nancy.

Don't Miss: Notre-Dame Cathedral and the Musée de l'Œuvre Notre-Dame. For a relaxing time and to see chimney nesting storks visit the parc de l'Orangerie.

Timing: Allow at least a full day to explore the Grande Île and Petite France, preferably more.

Parking: Parking areas around the outskirts of Strasbourg allow you to leave your car and travel into the town centre by tram. City-centre parking is not easy for visitors.

sang his "marching song for the Army of the Rhine". Not long after, it was adopted by the Federates of Marseille, and ever since has been known as the **Marseillaise**.

In 1870, Strasbourg was seized by Germany after a long siege. It continued to grow, under the influence of Prussian culture. It became French at the 1918 Armistice, but was again taken by Germany from 1940 to 1944.

Two parts of the old city evoke the delightful spectacle of a bygone Alsace of timber-framed houses with the whole array of traditional features, wooden galleries, loggias on brackets, windows with tiny panes of coloured glass, as well as the overhanging upper storeys, which continued to be built here after 1681 even though they had been banned in France proper.

PRACTICAL INFORMATION

PARK & RIDE – Eight car parks situated on the outskirts of town are at the disposal of visitors *(from ⌦€2.70 to ⌦€3; tram ticket offered)* who are invited to take a tramway into town. The car parks are indicated by a square panel with the letters P+R on a violet background.

TRAMWAYS – *CTS. ℰ03 88 77 70 70.* 4 lines link many tourist sights in and around Strasbourg. *Lines A, B and C operate Mon–Sun 4.30am–0.30am; line D operates Mon–Sat 7am–7pm except during the summer school holidays.*

BUSES – *CTS. ℰ03 88 77 70 70.* 26 bus routes crisscross the Strasbourg conurbation; in addition, 11 intercity buses link the city with the most beautiful Alsatian villages.

TICKETS: A **Unipass** *(⌦€1.20)* is a single-journey ticket valid for an hour on the bus and tram network; A **Tourpass** *(⌦€3.10)* is valid for 24 hours for an unlimited number of journeys. A **Familipass** *(⌦€4.20)* is valid for 24 hours for an unlimited number of journeys, for a family of 2 to 5 persons travelling together *(minimum: 1 adult and 1 child).*

Strasbourg Pass – Issued by the tourist office, this pass allows free or half-price admission to 10 sights and monuments. *Valid for 3 days, it is on sale in the tourist office information centres (place de la Cathédrale, place de la Gare and Pont de l'Europe) and in some hotels. ⌦€11.90.*

Guided tours – The town organises guided tours (1hr 30min) by approved guides. *⌦€6.80. Enquire at the tourist office.*

Audio-guided tours – The itinerary, meant to last 1hr 30min, enables visitors to discover the cathedral, the old town and the Petite France at their own speed. A leaflet is given with the Walkman *(deposit: €30).* 24-hour hiring cost: *⌦€6. Apply at the tourist office.*

Mini-train – *Apr to Oct.* Departure place du Château, next to the cathedral, every half-hour or every hour depending on time of year. *⌦€4.80. ℰ03 88 77 70 03. Guided tour of the old town (50min) with a stop at Barrage Vauban.*

Boat trips on the Ill – ♿Guided trips (1hr 10min) along the River Ill *(departure from the Palais Rohan pier)* taking in the Petite France, past Barrage Vauban, then the Faux Rempart moat as far as Palais de l'Europe. *Apr–Oct: 1hr 10min, departure every half-hour 9.30am–9pm; Nov–Dec and Jan–Mar: 4 departures a day 10.30am, 1pm, 2.30pm and 4.30pm. ⌦€7 (children ⌦€3.50).*

SIGHTS
Cathédrale Notre-Dame★★★
1 r. Rohan. ◷Open daily 7–11.20am, 12.35–7pm; no visits during services. ℰ03 88 21 43 34. www.cathedrale-strasbourg.fr.

In 1176, the cathedral was rebuilt in red Vosges sandstone on a site above flood-level but nevertheless using bundles of oak piles as a foundation (these were recently reinforced with concrete). Externally, this is still a Romanesque building as far as choir, transept and lantern-tower are concerned. The famous Gothic **spire★★★** (*⌦€3*) is an architectural masterpiece, its vertical-ity emphasised by its forward position immediately over the west front. An unmistakable landmark, visible over much of the Alsace plain, it rises to a height of 142m/466ft. The openwork octagon supporting it was erected between 1399 and 1419 by a Swabian architect and given an extra 7m/23ft in height during the course of construction for reasons of prestige. Its final stage was designed and built between 1420 and 1439 by a Cologne architect, using techniques from the previous century; it is particularly notable for the projecting structures carrying the external stair-cases.

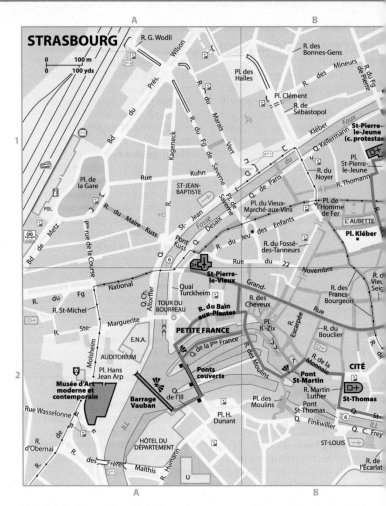

The High Gothic west front (**façade**★★★) was the work of Erwin von Steinbach. It is decorated with a wealth of sculpture (statues and low-reliefs of many different periods), especially in the central portal (**portail central**) with its double gable and delicate lancets masking part of the rose window. The three lower levels of the tympanum have particularly fine 13C work, including depictions of the Entry into Jerusalem, scenes of the Passion and Resurrection, and the Death of Judas; in the arching can be seen the Creation, the story of Abraham, the Apostles, the Evangelists and the Martyrs.

In the south doorway (**portail Sud**) is a famous portrayal of the Seducer about to succeed in tempting the most daring of the Foolish Virgins (she is undoing her dress). The statues of the Church and Synagogue (copies) on the south side of the cathedral are equally celebrated. Inside, the nave elevation is a straightforward example of the High Gothic style of the 14C, with an openwork triforium and wide aisles lit by elegant window-openings.

In the south transept is the 13C Angel pillar (**pilier des Anges**★★) or Last Judgement (**du Jugement dernier**); its delicate statuary, on three levels, raises Gothic art to a peak of perfection. **Stained-glass windows**★★★ from the 12C, 13C and 14C are remarkable. The **astronomical clock**★ (clock chimes at

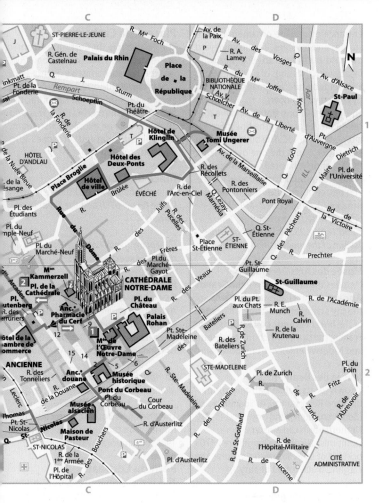

12.30pm) nearby, dating from 1838, con-tinues to draw crowds with its automata ringing out the quarter-hours (the figure of Death has the privilege of sounding the hours) and the crowd of figures brought out to mark midday (12.30pm).

Musée de l'Œuvre Notre-Dame★★

3 pl. du Château. Ⓘ*Open Tue–Fri noon–6pm, Sat–Sun 10am–6pm.* Ⓘ*Closed 1 Jan, Good Fri, 1 May, 1 and 11 Nov, 25 Dec.* €6 *(no charge 1st Sun of the month).* 🖉*03 88 52 50 00.* *www.musees-strasbourg.org.* Housed in a number of old dwellings just to the south, this museum greatly enhances the visitor's appreciation of

the cathedral. Its great treasure is the famous **Tête de Christ**★★ from Wissem-bourg in northern Alsace.

In addition, there is the oldest stained glass in existence and, above all, many of the cathedral's original statues, includ-ing the Church and the Synagogue, the Wise and Foolish Virgins. The architect's drawings of the west front and the spire are here too.

Palais Rohan★

2 pl. du Château. 🖉*03 88 88 50 50.* *www.musees-strasbourg.org.* Residence of the Prince-Bishops of Strasbourg, the palace was built between 1732 and 1742, a fine building in the Classical manner, with a curving entrance colonnade ornamented with statues and trophies, a main courtyard defined by balustraded galleries, a façade with dressings of pale limestone, a fine entablature, and mansard roofs lit by bull's-eye windows.

The Prince-Bishops' state rooms are considered to be among the finest French interiors of the 18C. The building's most elegant façade is the one overlooking the River Ill; it has tall Corinthian columns, a dome and a balustraded terrace. The palace also houses several **museums**★★ (&⊙*open Wed–Mon 10am–6pm; ⊙closed 1 Jan, Good Fri, 1 May, 1 and 11 Nov, 25 Dec. ☞€6, no charge 1st Sun of the month).*

Musée des Arts Décoratifs★★

Includes the State Apartments **(Grands Appartements)** and tells the story of the city's crafts and craftsmen. It has one of the finest **ceramic collections**★★ in France, particularly rich in Strasbourg and Niderwiller faience and porcelain.

Musée des Beaux-Arts★

Known for its Italian paintings (Primitives and Renaissance), its Spanish works (Zurbaran, Murillo and Goya) and 15–17C Netherlandish Old Masters.

Don't miss Nicolas de Largillière's 1703 portrait of *La Belle Strasbourgeoise*, the elegant, black-robed beauty.

Musée Archéologique★★

Covers the period between the Quaternary era and the end of the first millennium AD. There are displays on prehistory, extinct animals, ceramics, and on Roman and Merovingian times.

☙WALKING TOURS

1 OLD TOWN★★★

Allow at least one day

The old town nestles round the cathedral, on the island formed by the river Ill. This is the World Heritage Site, and a place to explore leisurely.

Place de la Cathédrale★

The **Pharmacie du Cerf** on the corner of rue Mercière, which dates from 1268, was the oldest chemist's in France until it closed in 2000.

On the north side of the cathedral, the **Maison Kammerzell**★ (1589), restored 1954 and now an excellent restaurant, has splendid carved frescoes and wooden sculptures.

Place du Château

Here are the Musée de l'Œuvre Notre-Dame (*☞see p111)* and the **Palais Rohan**★.

▷ *Follow rue de Rohan then turn right onto rue des Cordiers.*

Place du Marché-aux-Cochons-de-Lait★

A charming square lined with old houses including a 16C house with wooden galleries. The adjacent place de la Grande-Boucherie looks typically Alsatian.

▷ *Turn left onto rue du Vieux-Marché-aux-Poissons.*

The **Ancienne Douane** (former customs house) is on the right; it was rebuilt in 1965 for temporary exhibitions.

Pont du Corbeau

This is the former "execution" bridge from which those condemned for infanticides and patricides, tied up in sacks, were plunged into the water.

▷ *A carriage entrance at No 1 quai des Bateliers leads to the Cour du Corbeau.*

Cour du Corbeau★

Once a fashionable inn, which welcomed illustrious guests, such as Turenne, King Johann-Casimir of Poland, Frederick the Great and Emperor Joseph II, the picturesque courtyard dates from the 14C.

Quai St-Nicolas

The embankment is lined with some fine old houses; three are now the Musée Alsacien *(23–25 quai St-Nicolas;* ⊙*open*

La Petite France

R. Mattes/MICHELIN

Mon, Wed–Fri 12pm–6pm; ∞€6; ℘03 88 52 50 01). Louis Pasteur lived at No 18.

▶ *Cross the Pont St-Nicolas and take quai St-Thomas.*

Église St-Thomas
This five-naved church, rebuilt at the end of the 12C, became a Lutheran cathedral in 1529. It contains the 18C mausoleum of the **Maréchal de Saxe**★★ sculpted by Pigalle.

▶ *Walk along rue de la Monnaie to the Pont St-Martin.*

The bridge offers a fine **view**★ of the tanners' district. The river divides into four branches (watermills, dams and locks can still be seen).

▶ *Walk along rue des Moulins then follow the edge of the island.*

La Petite France★★
Once the fishermen's, tanners' and millers' district, this is today one of the most interesting and best-preserved areas of the old town.
Quai de la Petite France runs alongside the canal, offering a charming **scene**★ particularly at dusk of the old houses reflected in the water, notably in the **Rue du Bain-aux-Plantes**★★.

Ponts Couverts★
This is the name given to three successive bridges spanning the River Ill; each guarded by a massive square tower, remaining from the 14C fortifications. The bridges once had wooden roofs.

▶ *Turn right just before the last tower and walk along quai de l'Ill.*

Barrage Vauban
60 steps to Panoramic terrace.
◷*Open daily 9am–7pm. ∞No charge. ℘03 88 60 90 90.*
There's a striking **view**★★ of the Ponts Couverts, la Petite France and the cathedral from the terrace of the casemate bridge (part of Vauban's fortifications).

▶ *Go back over the Ponts Couverts.*

Rue du Bain-aux-Plantes★★
The street is lined with timber-framed corbelled houses dating from the Alsatian Renaissance (16–17C). Note, the tanners' house (Gerwerstub, No 42), from 1572, and Nos 31, 33, 27 and 25 (1651).

▶ *Return to Grand'Rue.*

Église St-Pierre-le-Vieux
This church consists of two adjacent churches: one Catholic and the other Protestant. The north transept of the

Catholic church (rebuilt in 1866) contains 16C carved-wood panels by Veit Wagner, depicting scenes from the Life of St Peter and St Valerus.

▷ *Return to the cathedral by Grand Rue, lined with 16–17C houses.*

② OLD TOWN VIA PLACE BROGLIE

▷ *Start in front of the cathedral, follow rue Mercière and turn right.*

On **place Gutenberg** stand the Renaissance **Hôtel de la Chambre de Commerce** and Gutenberg's statue by David d'Angers. No 52 rue du Vieux-Marché-aux-Poissons is the birthplace of Jean Arp (1887–1966), a sculptor, painter, poet and major protagonist of modern art.

▷ *Take the busy rue des Grands-Arcades.*

Place Kléber
On the north side is an 18C building called "l'Aubette" because the garrison came here at dawn *(aube)* to get their orders. In the centre is a statue of Strasbourg native **Jean-Baptiste Kléber** (1753–1800), a brilliant general of the Revolutionary period, who is buried beneath it. Reliefs depict his victories at Altenkirchen and Heliopolis.

Église St-Pierre-le-Jeune
◷*Open Palm Sunday–1 Nov Mon 1–6pm, Tue–Sat 10.30am–6pm, Sun 2.30–6pm.* ✆*03 88 32 41 61.*
Three successive churches have stood on this site. All that remains of the first church is a tomb with five funeral recesses, believed to date from the end of the Roman occupation (4C AD); the lovely restored cloisters belonged to the church built in 1031.
The present Protestant church (13C, restored 1900) contains a fine Gothic **rood screen** decorated with paintings from 1620.

▷ *Walk along quai Schoepfin.*

Place Broglie
This square was laid out in the 18C. On the south side is the **town hall**★ built by Massol, former residence of the counts of Hanau-Lichtenberg. At the eastern end are the municipal theatre (1820) and the **Hôtel de Klinglin** (1736).

Rue du Dôme and adjacent streets
The old aristocratic district adjoining place Broglie has guarded several 18C mansions, particularly rue Brûlée: the **Hôtel des Deux-Ponts** (1754) at No 13, the bishop's residence at No 16, and at No 9 the town hall's side entrance.

ADDITIONAL SIGHTS
Musée d'Art Moderne et Contemporain★★
1 place Hans-Jean-Arp. ♿◷*Open Tue–Fri noon–7pm (Thu 9pm), Sat–Sun 10am–6pm.* ◷*Closed Mon, and 1 Jan, Good Friday, 1 May, 1 & 11 Nov, 25 Dec.* ⊜€7. ✆*03 88 23 31 31. www.musees-strasbourg.org.*
Standing on the bank of the River Ill, this modern building was designed by Adrien Fainsilber, the architect of the Cité des Sciences et de l'Industrie at La Villette in Paris. The display covers the diverse artistic strands, which have left their stamp on the history of modern art. Several rooms are devoted to **Jean Arp** and his wife Sophie Taeuber-Arp, who, in collaboration with Theo Van Doesburg, made a series of stained-glass panels re-creating the constructivist interiors (1926–28) of l'Aubette on place Kléber. As a reaction against World War I, the Dadaists signed derisory, even absurd, works (Janco, Schwitters). Following in their footsteps, the Surrealists Brauner, Ernst and Arp tried to introduce the world of dreams into their works.

Capital of Europe
Palais de l'Europe★
Allée Spach, av de l'Europe. ♿☞ *Guided tour (1hr) by reservation. Service des visites, Conseil de l'Europe, 67075 Strasbourg Cedex.* ✆*03 88 41 20 29.*
The palace houses the **European Council**, including the council of min-

View of Obernai from the vineyards in autumn

© Walter Bibikow/age fotostock

isters, the parliamentary assembly and the international secretariat. The buildings, inaugurated in 1977 were designed by the French architect Henri Bernard. The palace contains 1 350 offices, meeting rooms, a library and the largest parliamentary amphitheatre in Europe. Opposite, the **Parc de l'Orangerie**★ was laid out by Le Nôtre in 1692 and remodelled in 1804 for Empress Josephine's stay. It includes a lake, a waterfall and a zoo; storks are a familiar sight everywhere.

Palais des Droits de l'Homme

Nearby, on the banks of the river Ill, stands the futuristic new Palais des Droits de l'Homme, designed by Richard Rogers, which houses the European Court of Human Rights.

EXCURSION
Wine Villages

Some of the most picturesque villages in Alsace are a short drive from the city. **Saverne**★ The town at the entrance to the Vosges uplands has **old houses**★ and a splendid red sandstone **château**★ with a monumental Louis XVI **façade**★★ giving onto the park.

Église de Marmoutier★★ This 12C former abbey church has a fine **west front**★★ in the red sandstone of the region, in Romanesque style incorporating Carolingian and Rhineland influences.

Hunspach★★

Hunspach is in the extreme NE of France, close to the Rhine and the German border. Carefully preserved and free from incongruous modern additions, it is one of Alsace's most charming villages. Flowers fill the streets of timber-framed houses with projecting roofs and bull's-eye windows (a Baroque feature). Many of the buildings are old farmhouses, with yards opening off the street; orchards, vines and long-handled pumps complete the picturesque scene. Nearby **Seebach**★ *(5km/3mi NE by D 249)* is a wonderful example of the flower-decked Alsatian village with its half-timbered houses adorned with awnings and gardens.

Obernai★★

Obernai is north of Colmar on the main highway to Strasbourg. Sited where the lower, vine-covered slopes of Mont Ste-Odile meet the plain, its ruined walls eloquent of its ancient independence and its narrow, winding streets lined with high-gabled houses, the little town of Obernai seems to represent the very essence of Alsace.

With its cheerfully coloured timber-framed buildings, the picturesque **Place du Marché**★★ is Obernai's centrepiece, graced by a fountain with a statue of St Odile. Its Town Hall (**Hôtel de Ville**★, 15-16C) has a fine oriel window, a 16C

Corn Hall (**Ancienne Halle aux blés**★) with a stork's nest above its doorway, and the Chapel Tower (**Tour de la Chapelle**★), a 13C bell tower.
There are many **old houses**★ in the streets around place du Marché. In rue des Pèlerins, note the three-storey stone house dating from the 13C.

ADDRESSES

🛏 STAY

Couvent du Franciscain – *18 r. du Fg-de-Pierre.* ☎*03 88 32 93 93. www.hotel-franciscain.com. Closed last week Jul, 1st week Aug. 43rms.* ☐ *€9.50.* At the end of a cul-de-sac you will find these two joined buildings. We recommend the rooms in the new wing. A good option within walking distance of the old city.

Hôtel Pax – *24 r. du Fg-National* ☎*03 88 32 14 54. www.paxhotel.com. Closed 23 Dec–4 Jan. 106rms.* ☐ *€9. Restaurant* ☐☐. A family hotel in a busy street on the edge of the city's old district. Its plain rooms are well kept, and its restaurant serves regional dishes.

EtC Hôtel – *7 r. de la Chaine.* ☎*03 88 32 66 60. www.hoteldesfrancsbourgeois.com. 35rms.* ☐*€8.50.* Situated in a peaceful area beside the cathedral and la Petite France in the heart of the old city.

Aux Trois Roses – *7 r. Zürich.* ☎*03 88 36 56 95. www.hotel3roses-strasbourg.com. 32rms. €8.50.* Cosy duvets and pine furniture add to the welcoming feel of the quiet guest rooms in this elegant building on the banks of the Ill. Fitness area with sauna and jacuzzi.

Hôtel de l'Ill – *8 r. des Bateliers.* ☎*03 88 36 20 01. www.hotel-ill.com. 27rms. €7.50.* Renovated hotel with family atmosphere. The rooms of differing sizes are impeccably clean, while the old-fashioned breakfast room has a cuckoo clock.

Le Kléber – *29 pl. Kléber.* ☎*03 88 32 09 53. http://hotel-kleber.com. 30rms.* ☐*€8.50.* "Meringue", "Strawberry" and "Cinnamon" are just a few of the names of the rooms in this comfortable hotel. Contemporary, colourful décor with a sweet-and-savoury theme.

Des Princes – *33 r. Geiler.* ☎*03 88 61 55 19. www.hotel-princes.com. Closed 25 Jul–25 Aug, Jan 2-10. 43rms.* ☐ *€13.* A welcoming hotel in a quiet residential neighbourhood. Guest rooms with classic furnishings and large bathrooms. Breakfast served to a backdrop of bucolic frescoes.

Hôtel Cardinal de Rohan – *17 r. Maroquin.* ☎*03 88 32 85 11. www.hotel-rohan.com. 36rms.* ☐ *€13.* Named after the nearby palais de Rohan, this little hotel is on a pedestrian street near the cathedral. Its quiet, pleasant rooms are furnished in Louis XV, Louis XVI or rustic style; those on the south side have air conditioning.

Gutenberg – *31 r. des Serruriers.* ☎*03 88 75 76 67. www.hotel-gutenberg.com. 42rms.* ☐ *€10.* This building dating back to 1745 is now a hotel with an eclectic mix of spacious guest rooms.

🍴 EAT

Pommes de Terre et Cie – *4 r. de l'Écurie.* ☎*03 88 22 36 82. www.pommes-de-terre-cie.com. Booking advisable.* If you want a change from *choucroute*, this friendly restaurant specialises in jacket potatoes accompanied by meat, fish or cheese. Local produce.

Flam's – *29 r. des Frères.* ☎*03 88 36 36 90. www.flams.fr. Booking advisable at weekends.* This half-timbered house very close to the cathedral houses a restaurant specialising in *flammekueches*. 15C painted ceiling.

Pfifferbriader – *6 pl. du Marché-aux-Cochons-de-Lait.* ☎*03 88 32 15 43. Closed Sun.* Feel at home in this low-beamed dining room, with windows decorated with wine-making scenes. Tasty regional dishes including *käsekneffles, choucroute* and *bäeckehoffe* are served along with classic French cuisine. Good choice of regional wines.

Le Pigeon – *23 r. des Tonneliers.* ☎*03 88 23 31 30.* This typical *winstub* owes its name to two pigeons sculpted on the façade of one of the oldest houses in Strasbourg..Traditional Alsatian cooking.

La Taverne du Sommelier – *Ruelle de la Bruche (Krutenau disdict).* ☎*03 88 24 14 10. Booking essential.* The type of little restaurant it's always a pleasure to discover. The décor is perfect to set off the intimate atmosphere. The menu follows the seasons, while the wine list features wines from the Languedoc and the Rhône Valley.

Petit Ours – *3 r. de l'Écurie (quartier des Tonneliers).* ✆*03 88 32 13 21. Booking advisable.* Great little restaurant decorated with Tuscany-inspired colours. Light floods through the bay windows of one room, and the cellar is also very pleasant. Each dish (mostly fish) is characterised by a particular herb or spice.

Au Renard Prêchant – *34 r. de Zürich.* ✆*03 88 35 62 87. Closed lunchtime on Sat, Sun and public holidays.* A 16C chapel in a pedestrianised street, which takes its name from the murals decorating its walls telling the story of the preaching fox. Rustic dining room, pretty terrace in summer, and reasonable fixed-price lunches.

L'Ami Schutz – *1 Ponts Couverts.* ✆*03 88 32 76 98. www.ami-schutz.com. Closed Christmas Holidays.* Between the Meanders of the Ill, typical cosy *winstub* with wood panelling (the smaller dining room has greater charm). Terrace beneath the lime trees.

Au Pont du Corbeau – *21 quai St-Nicolas.* ✆*03 88 35 60 68. Closed Sun lunch and Sat except Dec.* A renowned restaurant on the banks of the Ill, next to the Alsatian Folk Art Museum. Regionally inspired menu that focuses on local specialities.

La Vignette – *29 rue Mélanie at La Robertsau.* ✆*03 88 31 38 10.* An earthenware stove and old photos of the neighbourhood adorn the dining room of this café-restaurant. Appetising, market-inspired cuisine.

Ancienne Douane – *6 r. de la Douane.* ✆*03 88 15 78 78. www.anciennedouane.fr.* This building, on the banks of the River Ill, dating from 1358 has had a variety of uses but is now a charming restaurant in the centre of the old city.

Tire Bouchon – *1 Ponts Couverts.* ✆*03 88 32 76 98. www.letirebouchon.fr.* Charming restaurant located near the cathedral in a typical narrow Alsatian street, with an extensive wine cellar and offering traditional cuisine.

Aux Armes de Strasbourg – *9 pl. Gutenberg.* ✆*03 88 32 85 62.* An oasis of peace in the famous place Gutenberg in the old town.

L'Épicerie – *6 r. de Vieux Seigle.* ✆*03 88 32 52 41. www.lepicerie-strasbourg.com. Closed 22 Dec–7 Jan, holidays.* Nostalgic atmosphere with a 1960s ambience.

S'Burjerstuewel - Chez Yvonne – *10 r. Sanglier.* ✆*03 88 32 84 15. www.chez-yvonne.net. Closed Christmas holidays.* This *winstub* is one of the city's institutions, evidenced by the photos and dedications of its famous guests. Regional cuisine.

Le Clou – *3 r. du Chaudron.* ✆*03 88 32 11 67. www.le-clou.com. Closed Wed lunchtime, Sun and holidays.* This small wine bar in a little street near the cathedral is eternally popular, with its typical décor, friendly atmosphere and good Alsace cooking.

Fleur de Sel – *22 quai des Batelliers.* ✆*03 88 36 01 54.* Opened in 2005 on the south bank of the Ill across the Pont Ste Madeleine. Traditional Alsatian and French cuisine.

Buerehiesel – *in the Parc de l'Orangerie.* ✆*03 88 45 56 65. www.buerehiesel.fr. Closed 2 Aug–24 Aug, 30 Dec–21 Jan, Sun and Mon.* Famous chef Antine Westermann has handed over to his son Eric in the kitchens, but this remains one of Alsace's gastronomic temples. The setting is a beautiful half-timbered farmhouse.

🍷 ON THE TOWN

Au Brasseur – *22 r. des Veaux.* ✆*03 88 36 12 13. Daily 11.30am–1am.* This micro-brasserie proposes a wide variety of beers brewed on the premises. Locals also come here to dine and for jazz, rock and blues concerts at weekends.

Bar à Champagne – *5 r. des Moulins.* ✆*03 88 76 43 43. www.regent-hotels.com. 5pm–2am.* This is the hotel bar of the luxurious Regent Petite France, which was a mill for 800 years. No effort has been spared to ensure that you spend a relaxing evening here: the fine contemporary décor, the riverside terrace, discreet background jazz, a good choice of cocktails and the best champagnes.

Colmar★★★

Alsace

The capital of Upper Alsace is situated at the point where the Munster valley widens out into the broad plain of the Rhine. Since the 13C the town has prospered on the proceeds of the wine trade and boasts fine monuments. More recently, industries have spread along the Logelbach Canal.

A BIT OF HISTORY

In 1834 **Frédéric Bartholdi** was born here, the patriotic sculptor responsible for many striking works, including New York's Statue of Liberty.

Between 1871 and 1918 Alsace and Lorraine were part of Germany. A particular irritant to authority was the Colmar writer and caricaturist Jean-Jacques Waltz (1872–1951), known as "Hansi", who was imprisoned at the outbreak of war in 1914, but escaped to enlist in the French army. In early February 1945, the French army under General de Lattre de Tassigny launched an attack on Colmar to eliminate German resistance. On 1 February the German lines north of Colmar were overrun by American troops, who stood aside to let the French 5th armoured division of General Schlesser enter Colmar.

SIGHTS

Musée Unterlinden★★★

1 r. d'Unterlinden. ⏱*Open May–Oct daily 9am–6pm; Nov–Apr Wed–Mon 9am–noon, 2–5pm.* ⏱*Closed 1 Jan, 1 May, 1 Nov, 25 Dec.* 🎟€8. ✆03 89 20 15 50. www.musee-unterlinden.com.

The museum, situated on place d'Unterlinden through which flows the Logelbach canal, is housed in a former 13C monastery. The ground floor is devoted to religious art and presents

> ### 🎭 Guided Tours 🎭
>
> Tours *(1hr15min)* of the old town for individuals are organised from Jul–Sept. ✆*03 89 20 68 92.* 🎟*€4*

▸ **Population:** 68 010
⏱ **Michelin Map:** 315 I 8
🛈 **Info:** 4 r. des Hunterlinden. ✆03 89 20 68 92. www.ot-colmar.fr.
▶ **Location:** Colmar is located 71km/44mi SSW of Strasbourg, 40km/25mi N of Mulhouse.
⬡ **Don't Miss:** The Old Town; Retable d'Issenheim, the 16C masterpiece of Matthias Grünewald on display at the Musée Unterlinden; Colmar by Night – The town's most beautiful buildings are lit up at night; a Boat Trip.
👪 **Kids:** Musée Animé du Jouet et des Petits Trains.

rich collections of paintings and sculpture dating from the late Middle Ages and the Renaissance.

👪 Musée Animé du Jouet et des Petits Trains

40 r. Vauban. ⏱*Open Jan and Jun daily (except Tue) 10am–noon, 2–6pm; Jul–Aug and Dec, daily, 10am–6pm; Sep daily 10am–noon, 2–6pm; Oct–Nov daily (except Tue) 10am–noon, 2–6pm.* 🎟*€4.50, child €3.50.* ✆*03 89 41 93 10. www.museejouet.com.*

Housed in a former cinema, collections include numerous railway engines, trains, and dolls in many different materials.

Retable d'Issenheim★★★

In the chapel.

In 1512 **Matthias Grünewald** was called to Issenheim 22km/14mi south of Colmar to paint the **Issenheim altarpiece** for the chapel of the Antonite convent. This extraordinary work should be seen, not as a collection of separate masterpieces, but as an integrated whole, conceived and executed as a programme whose logic, while still puzzling to the specialist of today, probably lies in the convent superior's particular vision of the meaning of suffering. Everything contributes to the overall effect, not only the choice of themes and their relationship to one another, but also the pose and expression of the figures, the symbolic meaning of the various themes, animals and monsters, and even the use of colour.

Ville Ancienne★★

The heart of the old town comprises the Place de l'Ancienne Douane, Rue des Marchands and Rue Mercière (Haberdasher Street).

There are many picturesque old houses, with corner turrets, oriel windows and half-timbering, and balconies adorned with flowers. Particularly striking are the **Maison Pfister**★★, with frescoes and medallions and a pyramidal roof, and the Old Customs House, **Ancienne Douane**★, of 1480, with a timber gallery and canted staircase tower.

Petite Venise★(Little Venice)

From place d'Unterlinden, follow rue des Tanneurs along the canal.

The **quartier des tanneurs** (tanners' district), renovated in 1974, is named after the inhabitants who used the river to tan and wash hides (a practice discontinued in the 19C). Timber-framed houses were narrow but high, creating lofts to dry the skins.

Cross the River Lauch to enter the **Krutenau district**★, once a fortified outlying area; this district's market gardeners once used flat-bottomed boats, similar to Venetian gondolas.

Turn right along quai de la Poisonnerie. Cross the next bridge to the corner of rue des Écoles and rue du Vigneron, to see Batholdi's **Fontaine du Vigneron,** a celebration of Alsatian wines.

Continue along quai de la Poissonnerie then **rue de la Poissonnerie**★, lined with picturesque fishermen's cottages. It runs into rue de Turenne, formerly rue de Krutenau, the old vegetable market. Take rue de a Herse then turn right onto a narrow street leading to the river.

Stroll along the bank to **Pont St-Pierre**. From the bridge, there is a lovely **view**★ of Petite Venise.

Below the bridge, **boat trips** (⌚*Apr–Sept 30min trips 10am–7pm; Oct and Mar Sat–Sun 10am–noon, 1–6pm; ⬭€5.50 (children under 10 no charge); ℘03 89 41 01 94*) are available to explore the district further.

Turn right onto rue du Manege leading to place des Six-Montagmes-Noires. Batholdi's **Fontaine Roesselmann** stands on the square; it is dedicated to the town's hero.

Walk towards the bridge on the right: the river, lined with willow trees, flows between two rows of old houses.

Continue along rue St-Jean. On the left is the rather Venetian **Maison des Chevaliers de St-Jean** (1608).

Colourful houses of the old town

A little farther is the lovely place du Marché-aux-Fruits with its Renaissance style **Maison Kern**, the pink sandstone **Tribunal civil**★ and the Ancienne Douane.

EXCURSIONS
Kaysersberg★★
▶ *12km/7.4mi NW of Colmar.*
🛈 *39 r. Gén de Gaulle.* 🌮*03 89 78 11 11. www.ville-kaysersberg.fr.* 🅿 *The village is completely pedestrianised, with car parks on its south, west and east approaches.*

Kaysersberg is a typically pretty Alsace village; its flower-bedecked streets have many old houses, several dating from the 16C, and behind the pretty little town rise the serried ranks of vines on the slopes of the Vosges hills.

Kaysersberg was a Roman town known as *Caesaris Mons* (the Emperor's Mountain), due to its strategic position along one of the most important routes linking ancient Gaul with the Rhine Valley.

The great doctor, theologian and pioneer of Third World aid, Albert Schweitzer (1875–1965), was born at 126 Rue du Général de Gaulle (next to the **Musée Albert-Schweitzer**; �🕐 *open May–Oct daily 9am–noon, 2–6pm;* ⊛*€2*) which contains memorabilia.

Château du Haut-Kœnigsbourg★★
▶ *The castle is roughly 21km/13mi N of Colmar. It is reached on a steep, winding access road in the hills between Sélestat and Ribeauvillé.*

♿🕐*Open Jan, Feb, Nov, Dec 9.30am–noon, 1–4.30pm; Mar, Oct 9.30am–5pm; Apr, May, Sept 9.15am–5.15pm; Jun–Aug 9.15am–6pm.* 🕐*Closed 1 Jan, 1 May, 25 Dec.* ⊛*€8, no charge 1st Sun in the month (Nov–Mar).* 🌮*03 88 82 50 60. www.haut-koenigsbourg.fr.*

This vast, mock-medieval edifice in pink sandstone overlooks the Alsace plain from its lofty rock rising through the treetops of the Vosges forest.

The castle, which was first mentioned in 1147, was built by the Hohenstaufens

on a promontory overlooking the Alsace plain, at an altitude of 700m/2 297ft.

In 1479 it passed to the Habsburgs who had it rebuilt with a modern system of defence. Sadly this did not prevent the Swedes taking and sacking the castle 150 years later.

For the next 200 years it was an imposing ruin, until in 1899 it was offered for sale by the town of Sélestat.

The present building is the outcome of an almost complete reconstruction in neo-feudal style carried out on the orders of Emperor William II between 1900 and 1908 during the period when Alsace and Lorraine had been reincorporated into Germany.

ADDRESSES

🏠 STAY

🛏 **Chambre d'hôte Les Framboises** – *128 r. des Trois-Épis, 68230 Katzenthal, 5km/ 3mi NW of Colmar, Kaysersberg direction then D10.* 🌮*03 89 27 48 85. 4rms.* Head for the open countryside and this village among the vines. The proprietor distils his own *marc* (grape brandy) from Gewürztraminer and provides accommodation in wood-panelled attic rooms. Don't miss the puppet show in the mornings!

🛏 **Colbert** – *2 r. des Trois-Épis.* 🌮*03 89 41 31 05. 50rms.* 🛏*€6.* This functional hotel near the station provides a comfortable place to stay. The rooms are well equipped with new bedding, effective soundproofing and air conditioning, and some have a balcony. Bar and disco for those in search of nightlife.

🛏🛏 **Hôtel Au Moulin** – *Rte d'Herrlisheim – 68127 Ste-Croix-en-Plaine, 10km/6.2mi S of Colmar on A35 and D1.* 🌮*03 89 49 31 20. www.aumoulin.net. Closed 5 Nov–31 Mar. 14rms.* 🛏*€9–10.* This old mill deep in the country is perfect for those seeking peace and quiet. Its spacious rooms are all the same but nicely arranged. A small museum of old local objects has been created in a neighbouring building.

🛏🛏 **Hôtel Turenne** – *10 rte de Bâle.* 🌮*03 89 21 58 58. www.turenne.com. 83rms.* 🛏*€8.50.* On the edge of the old town, this hotel occupies a pleasing building with a pink and yellow façade. Its rooms have been nicely renovated and are well soundproofed. A few small but neat and reasonably priced single rooms are available.

⊜⊜⊜ **Hôtel le Colombier** – *7 r. de Turenne. ✆03 89 23 96 00. www.hotel-le-colombier.fr. 24rms. ⌑€12.* This lovely 15C house in old Colmar combines old stone and contemporary décor by retaining elements from its past, such as the superb Renaissance staircase. Contemporary furniture, modern paintings and carefully arranged rooms.

¶/ EAT

⊜ **Le Caveau St-Pierre** – *24 r. de la Herse (Little Venice). ✆03 89 41 99 33. Closed Mon. Booking advisable.* A pretty wooden footbridge across the Lauch leads to this 17C house, which offers a little slice of paradise with its rustic, local-style décor and a terrace over the water. Local cuisine.

⊜ **La Maison Rouge** – *9 r. des Écoles. ✆03 89 23 53 22.* The somewhat ordinary façade hides a delightful rustic interior. Regional and home-made cooking take pride of place.

⊜ **Schwendi Bier-U-Wistub** – *23–25 Grand'Rue. ✆03 89 23 66 26.* You will instantly warm to this charming winstub with its ideal location in the heart of old Colmar. The principally wooden décor and the cooking, which is good quality and served in generous portions, are a tribute to Alsace. Huge terrace to be enjoyed in summer.

⊜ **Winstub La Krutenau** – *1 r. de la Poissonnerie. ✆03 89 41 18 80. Closed Sun and Mon out of season .* At this *winstub* beside the River Lauch you can go boating in Little Venice and eat a *flammekueche* on the flower-decked terrace beside the canal in summer. A fun way, with no obligations, to learn about this lovely part of Colmar – recommended.

⊜⊜ **Caveau Chez Bacchus** – *2 Grand'Rue, Katzenthal, 5km/3mi NW of Colmar, Kaysersberg direction, then D10. ✆03 89 27 32 25. Closed at varying times; call in advance.* There's a friendly atmosphere in this wine bar dating from 1789 in a wine-making village. Massive exposed beams and helpings of Alsatian cuisine to match

– guaranteed to satisfy the healthiest of appetites. Automated puppets entertain the children with a lively show.

⊜⊜ **Winstub Brenner** – *1 r. de Turenne. ✆03 89 41 42 33. Closed at varying times; call in advance.* The terrace by the Lauch in Little Venice is very popular on fine days. Not surprising, as the setting is ideal and the food, though simple, is served in generous portions.

☺ NIGHTLIFE

Théâtre de la Manufacture – *6 rte d'Ingersheim. ✆03 89 24 31 78. Performances Mon–Wed and Fri 8.30pm, Thu 7pm, Sat 6pm.* Contemporary theatre, music, dance. **Alsation Folk Evenings** – *pl. de l'Ancienne Douane. Mid-May–mid-Sept Tue 8.30pm.* **Théâtre Municipal** – *3 r. Unterlinden. ✆03 89 20 29 01/02.* Classic plays, comedy and opera.

⭢ SHOPPING

Domaine viticole de la Ville de Colmar. *2 r. Stauffen. ✆03 89 79 11 87. www.domaineviticolecolmar.com.* Founded in 1895, this estate grows seven *cépages* and boasts a host of *grands crus* in addition to sparkling wines. Wide range of wines, brandies and liquors on sale.

Caveau Robert-Karcher – *11 r. de l'Ours. ✆03 89 41 14 42. www.vins-karcher.com.* The vineyards of this family business are northwest of Colmar, but the cellar, dating from 1602, is in the town centre.

Fortwenger – *32 r. des Marchands. ✆03 89 41 06 93. www.fortwenger.fr.* It was in Gertwiller in 1768 that Charles Fortwenger founded his gingerbread factory, but this Colmar shop sells a wide range of delicious sweet products.

Maison des Vins d'Alsace – *Civa, 12 ave de la Foire-aux-Vins, BP1217. ✆03 89 20 16 20. www.vinsalsace.com.* Five local organisations concerned with Alsace wines are based in this centre. Visitors can study a map showing all the wine-making villages and *grands crus*, learn about wine making and see a film.

Riquewihr★★★
Alsace

Situated along the Route des Vins, the tiny, beautiful village of Riquewihr is surrounded by medieval walls. It prides itself on its fine Riesling; the vintners' houses in its picturesque streets were designed with the production of wine in mind. The town looks pretty much the same today as it did in the 16C.

🐾 WALKING TOUR

▶ *Go through the archway of the town hall and follow rue du Général-de-Gaulle straight ahead. On the left the Cour du Château leads to the Château.*

Château des Ducs de Wurtemberg

Completed in 1540, the castle has kept its mullioned windows, its gable decorated with antlers and its stair turret. It houses the **Musée de la Communication en Alsace**.
A small open-air museum of architectural remains and the 1790 Altar of Freedom can be seen in front of the east side.

▶ *Continue along rue du Général-de-Gaulle.*

No 12, known as the **Maison Irion** (1606) has a corner oriel; opposite, there is a 16C well. Next door, the **Maison Jung-Selig** (1561) has a carved timber frame.

- ▶ **Population:** 1 302
- 🚗 **Michelin Map:** 315 H 8
- ℹ **Info:** 2 r. de la 1re Armée. ℘03 89 73 23 23. www.ribeauville-riquewihr. com or http://riquewihr. reseaudescommunes.fr/ communes.
- ▶ **Location:** Riquewihr is on the Rhine border with Germany, in eastern France, nuzzled in the Vosges mountains, 16km/10mi NW of Colmar.
- 🅿 **Parking:** Use the parking facilities on the outside of the town: place des Charpentiers; rue de la Piscine; rocade Nord.
- 🕐 **Timing:** Allow 2hr and time to try a glass of the region's famous Riesling.

Maison Liebrich★ (Cour des cigognes)

A well dating from 1603 and a huge wine press from 1817 stand in the picturesque courtyard of this 16C house, surrounded by balustraded wooden galleries (added in the 17C).
Opposite stands the **Maison Behrel** adorned with a lovely oriel (1514) surmounted by openwork added in 1709.

▶ *Take the first turn on the right and follow rue Kilian. Maison Brauer at the end of the street has a fine doorway (1618). Continue along rue des Trois-Églises.*

Driving the Route des Vins

The well-signposted 180km/112mi itinerary, known as the Route des Vins (Wine Road), winds its way along the foothills of the Vosges from Marlenheim to Thann, the northern and southern gateways to Alsace where there are information centres about Alsatian vineyards and wines. The first driving tour from Marlenheim to Châtenois *(68km/42mi)* takes in the pretty villages of Wangen and Itterswiller. From Châtenois to Colmar *(54km/34mi)*, the road passes the WWII cemetery near Bergheim and Hunawihr, famous for Alsacian storks. A final stretch between Colmar and Thann *(59km/37mi)* will take you to the birthplace of Alsacian vine-growing, Wettolsheim, and Pfffenheim, which has a 13C church.

ROUTE DES VINS

Vineyard

Wine-growing town

0   5 miles   10 km

Place des Trois-Églises

The square is framed by two former churches, St-Érard and Notre-Dame, converted into dwellings, and a 19C Protestant church.

◐ *Return to rue du Général-de-Gaulle.*

Maison Preiss-Zimmer★

The house that belonged to the wine-growers' guild stands in the last but one of a succession of picturesque court-yards. Further on, on the right, stands the former **tithe court** of the lords of Ribeaupierre. On place de la Sinn, which marks the end of rue du Général-de-Gaulle, is the pretty 1580 **Fontaine Sinnbrunnen**.

Rue et cour des Juifs

Narrow rue des Juifs leads to the picturesque Cour des Juifs, the old ghetto, from which a narrow passageway and wooden stairs lead to the ramparts and the **Musée de la Tour des Voleurs**.

Dolder★

Built in 1291, this gate was reinforced during the 15C and 16C.

▷ *Go through the gate to the Obertor.*

Obertor (upper gate)

Note the portcullis and the place where the former drawbridge was fixed. On the left, you can see a section of the ramparts and a defence tower.

▷ *Return through Dolder and along rue du Général-de-Gaulle then turn right onto rue du Cerf.*

Maison Kiener★

No 2. The house built in 1574 has a pediment with an inscription and a bas-relief depicting Death getting hold of the founder of the house. Opposite, the **Auberge du Cerf** dates from 1566.

▷ *Continue along rue du Cerf then turn left onto rue Latérale.*

Rue Latérale

Lovely houses on this street include the **Maison du marchand Tobie Berger** at No 6, which has a 16C oriel and a Renaissance doorway in the courtyard.

▷ *Turn right onto rue de la 1re-Armée.*

Maison du Bouton d'Or

No 16. The house goes back to 1566. An alleyway, just round the corner, leads to another tithe court, known as the Cour de Strasbourg and dating from 1597.

▷ *Retrace your steps then continue past the Maison du Bouton d'Or along rue Dinzheim to rue de la Couronne.*

Maison Dissler★

No 6. With its scrolled gables and loggia, this stone house (1610) is an interesting example of Renaissance style.

ADDITIONAL SIGHTS

Musée du Dolder

Access by staircase to left of the Porte du Dolder. ◷*Open Jul–Aug daily, 1.45–6.30pm. Apr–Jun and Sep–Oct Sat–Sun and holidays 1.45–6.30pm* ◷*Closed 1 Nov to Easter.* ⊛€2.50.

The museum houses mementoes, prints, weapons, tools and furniture, associated with local history.

Maison Hansi

◷*Open May-Dec daily 10.30am–6pm, Jan weekends 2–6pm, Feb–Apr Tue–Sun 2–6pm.* ◷*Closed 1 Jan, 25 Dec.* ⊛€2. ℘*03 89 47 97 00.*

This museum contains watercolours, prints and decorated ceramics by the Colmar artist and cartoonist, JJ Waltz, known as Hans, whose brother was a chemist in Riquewihr.

ADDRESSES

⌂ STAY

▱ **Chambre d'hôte Gérard Schmitt** – *3 chemin des Vignes.* ℘*03 89 47 89 72. Closed Jan–Mar. 2rms.* A house with a garden in the higher part of the village, on the edge of a vineyard. The wood-panelled rooms have sloping ceilings. High standard of cleanliness and reasonable prices.

▱▱▱ **Hôtel L'Oriel** – *3 r. des Écuries-Seigneuriales.* ℘*03 89 49 03 13. www.hotel-oriel.com. 22rms.* ⊠*€11.50.* This 16C hotel is easily recognised by its wrought-iron sign. The lack of straight lines in the building, combined with simple décor and old Alsatian furniture and exposed beams, creates a romantic atmosphere.

⌾ EAT

▱ **Auberge St-Alexis** – *68240 St-Alexis 6km/4mi W of Riquewihr on minor road and path.* ℘*03 89 73 90 38. Closed Fri.* It's worth venturing into the forest along a dirt track to this former 17C hermitage.

▱▱▱ **Le Sarment d'Or** – *4 r. du Cerf.* ℘*03 89 86 02 86. www.riquewihr-sarment-dor.com. Closed Sun eve, Tue lunch and Mon.* Pale wood panelling, copper light fittings, fireplace and huge beams create a lovely warm atmosphere in this restaurant. The cooking is traditional and uses seasonal ingredients.

Mulhouse★★

Alsace

Mulhouse became a free Imperial city as early as the end of the 13C, and in the 16C formed part of the *Decapolis,* the league of ten towns of Alsace.

A BIT OF HISTORY

A historic manufacturing and trading centre, the city's independent spirit led it into an association with the cantons of Switzerland. In 1524, the Republic's government adopted the principles of the Reformation and a little later on adhered to Calvinism. Theatrical performances were banned and inns had to close by 10pm. However, the spirit of the new religion spurred on industrial development and prompted social and cultural initiatives. It joined France voluntarily in 1798. Mulhouse was already long established as a textile centre, when, in 1746, three of its citizens, J-J Schmaltzer, the painter J-H Dollfus and the merchant S Koechlin together founded the first mill producing calico cotton fabrics. Production advanced by leaps and bounds. In 1812 the Dollfus and Mieg mill was the first to install steam power.

SIGHTS

Hôtel de Ville★★

Since 1558, the City Hall has symbolised Mulhouse's civic and political liberties. It is a unique example in France of a building of the Rhineland Renaissance by a Basle architect; the exterior is decorated solely by artists from Konstanz. It was remodelled in 1698. It is this later decoration which has been restored to its former glory. The coats of arms of the Swiss cantons painted on the main façade on either side of the covered double flight of steps recall the historical link with Switzerland.

♣♣ Musée de l'Automobile – Collection Schlumpf ★★★

15 r. de l'épée. ♿ⓒ*Open 1–2 Jan, 5 Feb –3 Apr and 5 Nov–Dec daily 10am–5pm; 3 Jan–4 Feb Mon–Fri 1–5pm, Sat–Sun 10am–5pm; 4 Apr–Oct 10am–6pm.*

▶ **Population:** 113 477
♿ **Michelin Map:** 315 i 10
Info: 2 rue Wilson. ✆03 89 35 48 42. www.mulhouse.fr.
● **Location:** 40km/25mi S of Colmar, this large city lies at the meeting point of France, Germany and Switzerland.
☺ **Don't Miss:** Find time for the fascinating textile museum, where beautiful fabrics with historic designs are on sale.
♣♣ **Kids:** Those who love cars – old and new – will enjoy the Musée de l'Automobile.

ⓒ*Closed 25 Dec.* ⚬€10.50; child €8.20. ✆03 89 33 23 23. www.collection-schlumpf.com.

The splendid, definitive collection of 500 vehicles was lovingly built up by the mill-owning Schlumpf brothers. The collection vividly evokes the history of the motor car from the steam-powered Jacquot (1878) to the latest models. Most are in working order; several had famous owners – Charlie Chaplin's Rolls-Royce is here.

♣♣ Musée français du Chemin de fer★★★

2 r. Alfred de Glehn. ⓒ*Open 1–2 Jan, 5 Feb–3 Apr, and Nov–Dec 10am–5pm; 3 Jan–4 Feb Mon–Fri 10am–2pm, Sat–Sun 10am–5pm; Apr–Oct 10am–6pm.* ⚬*€10 (7–12 yr-olds €7.60); combined ticket with Musée national de l'Automobile €17.50.* ✆03 89 42 83 33. www.citedutrain.com.

The French Railways (SNCF) collection, splendidly displayed, illustrates the evolution of railways from their origins until today. The main hall includes footbridges offering a view inside carriages, pits making it possible to walk beneath engines, and drivers' cabins.

The panorama of steam engines that spans more than 100 years includes famous engines such as the Saint-Pierre, built of teak, which ran between Paris and Rouen from 1844 onwards, the very fast Crampton (1852) which reached speeds of around 120kph/75mph, and the 232 U1 (1949), the last operating steam engine.

The museum also boasts the drawing-room carriage of Napoleon III's aides-de-camp (1856) decorated by Viollet-le-Duc, and the French president's carriage (1925) decorated by Lalique and fitted with a solid-silver washbasin. In striking contrast, the bottom of the range includes one of the fourth-class carriages of the Alsace-Lorraine line.

Musée de l'Impression sur étoffes★

&⊙*Open daily except Mon, 10am–noon, 2–6pm.* ⊙*Closed 1 Jan, 1 May, 25 Dec.* ⊕€7. ℘*03 89 46 83 00. www.musee-impression.com.*

The Museum of Printed Fabric is housed in a former industrial building, which once belonged to the Société Industrielle de Mulhouse.

The Museum of Printed Fabric (created in 1857) illustrates the birth and development of the industry from 1746 onwards: engraving and printing techniques are explained, and impressive machines used throughout the ages are employed for regular demonstrations. There are displays of original 18C shawls with oriental motifs.

This museum and its lovely shop are a must for anyone interested in fashion, interior design and the decorative arts.

ADDITIONAL SIGHTS

Musée Historique★★
⁂ **Électropolis**★ *(55 r. du Pâturage)* – history of electric power.
Parc Zoologique et Botanique★★
(51 r. jardin zoologique)
Musée du Papier-peint★
(La Commanderie, 28 r. Zuber, Rixheim, 6km/3.7mi east of Mulhouse) – all about wallpaper.

EXCURSION
Ecomusée d'Alsace★★

◗ *68190 Ungersheim, about 16km/ 10mi NW of Mulhouse.* ⊙*Check website for opening times and prices.* ℘*03 89 62 43 00. www.ecomusee-alsace.fr.*

An open-air museum founded in 1984 to preserve local heritage comprises some 60 old buildings dotted over an area of 25ha/50 acres. The old buildings dating from the 15–19C, which were saved from demolition and carefully dismantled and re-erected to create a village setting, are fine examples of rural habitats from the various regions of Alsace. The museum, which is constantly evolving, also includes industrial structures; next door to the museum are the restored buildings of a potassium mine which was worked from 1911–1930.

Walk around the half-timbered buildings grouped by region (Sundgau, Reid, Kochersberg, Bas-Rhin) and complete with courtyards and gardens, to appreciate the development of building techniques and the varied architecture of farm buildings according to the regions and periods.

Specific buildings such as a fortified structure, a chapel, a school and a washhouse evoke community life in a traditional Alsatian village. Old plant varieties are grown in a typical field which also serves for farming demonstrations.

An area devoted to funfairs includes a rare merry-go-round (1909). Many local people act as volunteers and help with various entertainment features which really bring the trades of yesteryear to life. Visitors will discover the age-old crafts of carpenters, blacksmiths, clog makers, potters, coopers, coalmen and masons as well as the evolution of living conditions, including reconstructed interiors complete with kitchens, alcoves and "stube", the living area with its terracotta stove.

You may purchase souvenirs, crafts and local delicacies on site; there is also a hotel, bakery and restaurants. A wide range of events, depending on the season, are organised, including boat trips, theme days and guided tours of the potash mines by train.

Route des Crêtes★★★

Alsace

In World War I, the French and German armies confronted each other along the old frontier between the two countries formed by the crest-line of the Vosges. Hugging the ridge is the strategic north–south road planned by French military engineers to serve the front; today it forms a fine scenic route, the Vosges Scenic Road, running for 63km/39mi from the Bonhomme Pass (Col du Bonhomme) in the north to Thann in the south. It offers the visitor a splendid introduction to the varied landscapes of these uplands, which include the sweeping pasturelands of the summits, an array of lakes, and the broad valleys of the Fisch and the Thur.

EXCURSIONS
Col du Bonhomme
949m/3 114ft high, this is the pass linking the provinces of Alsace and Lorraine.

Col de la Schlucht
1 139m/3 737ft. This is the steepest but also one of the busiest of the routes through the Vosges. The eastern slopes are subject to intense erosion because of the gradient of the torrential rivers; at a distance of only 9km/5.6mi from the pass, the town of **Munster**★ lies 877m/ 2 877ft below, while Colmar, 26km/16mi away, is 1 065m/3 494ft lower.

Hohneck★★★
1 362m/4 469ft.
Rising near the central point of the range, this is one of the most visited of the Vosges summits. From the top there are superb **views**★★★; to the east, the **Munster Valley**★★ plunges steeply down towards the broad expanses of the Alsace plain, while to the west is the Lorraine plateau, cut into by the valley of the Vologne.

> - **Michelin Map:** 315 G 8, F 8, F 9 and G 9
> - **Location:** The route starts 30km/18.6mi W of Colmar and heads S to Thann.
> - **Don't Miss:** The panoramas between Le Hohneck and the Grand Ballon.

Grand Ballon★★★
1 424m/4 672ft. The Grand Ballon forms the highest point of the Vosges.
From the top *(30min round-trip on foot)* the magnificent **panorama**★★★ extends over the southern part of the range, whose physiognomy can be fully appreciated. The eastern and western slopes are quite unlike each other; the drop to the Alsace plain is abrupt, while to the west the land falls away gently to the Lorraine plateau. Glacial action in the Quaternary era is responsible for many features like the massive rounded humps of the summits *(ballons)*, and the morainic lakes in the blocked valleys. Above the tree line, the forest clothing the hillsides gives way to the short grass of the wide upland grazing grounds known as the Hautes-Chaumes.

Vieil-Armand★★
The war memorial *(monument national)* marks one of the most bitterly contested battlefields of World War I.

View from the summit of Hohneck

© Yves Talensac/Photononstop

Reims★★★

Champagne-Ardenne

The ancient university town on the banks of the River Vesle is famous for its magnificent and important cathedral, where French kings were traditionally crowned.
It has a wealth of other architectural masterpieces. Reims is also (along with Epernay) the capital of champagne's wine industry. Most of the great champagne houses' cellars are open to the public.

▶ **Population:** 185 541
⌚ **Michelin Map:** 306 G 7
ℹ **Info:** 2 r. Guillaume de Machault. ✆0892 701 351. www.reims-tourisme.com.
◗ **Location:** Reims is 143km/89mi NE of Paris on the A 4 *autoroute*, and 275km/171mi from Calais on the A 26, which skirts the town. Take any turning for Centre Ville.

A BIT OF HISTORY

Under the Romans, Reims was the capital of the province which was to become Belgium. It was at Reims, in 496, that Clovis, King of the Franks, was baptised by St Remigius (St Rémi). This was a political event of some significance, since it made the ambitious 35-year-old warrior the only Christian ruler in the chaotic times following the collapse of the Roman Empire. It was he who halted the advance of the Visigoths at Poitiers, subsequently pushing them back, first to Toulouse, then all the way into Spain. With him, the source of political authority in Gaul passed from Provence to the north.

At the time of the Carolingians, a feeling for beauty became evident at Reims; ancient texts were carefully copied, manuscripts illuminated, ivory carved and masterpieces of the goldsmith's art created. The period produced Charlemagne's Talisman (now in the Bishops' Palace) as well as the Épernay Gospel. In 816, Louis I the Pious had himself crowned here, as Charlemagne had done at Rome 16 years before. It was from this point that the dynasty acquired a sort of religious character, though it was not until the crowning of Louis VIII, 400 years later, that the city became the recognised place for coronations, with a ceremonial ever more elaborate and charged with symbolism. By the time of Charles X, 25 kings had been crowned here. The most moving coronation was that of Charles VII on 17 July 1429, which took place in the middle of the Hundred Years' War in the presence of Joan of Arc; the Maid of Orléans had given Frenchmen the first

Champagne

Though covering only 2 percent of the total area planted with vines in France, this northernmost of the country's wine-growing regions is perhaps its most prestigious. The product was known in Roman times, when it was a still wine. It was Dom Pérignon (1638–1715), cellar-master of Hautvillers Abbey (Abbaye de Hautevilliers), who had the idea of making it sparkle by means of double fermentation, a process carried out today by the use of cane sugar and yeasts. The vines are spread over an area totalling 30 000ha/74 000 acres, on the lower slopes of the chalk escarpment of the Côte de l'Île-de-France for preference. The most renowned vineyards are the Montagne de Reims (robust, full-bodied wines), the valley of the Marne (fruity wines with plenty of bouquet) and the Côte des Blancs (fresh and elegant wines). Champagne is a blended, branded wine, the prestige of the great labels dependent on the expertise of the master-blenders. Some 215 million bottles are produced in an average year, with over 75 million of them for export.

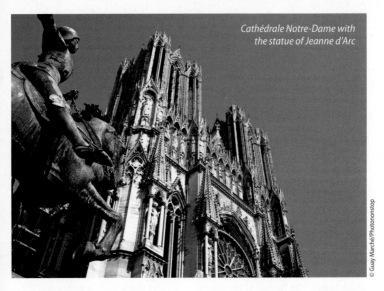

Cathédrale Notre-Dame with the statue of Jeanne d'Arc

inklings of national identity, and had persuaded the king to make his way to Reims, even though this involved him in crossing the hostile Burgundian territory of Philippe le Bon (the Good).

On 7 May 1945, in a modern technical college near the station, the document was signed which marked the surrender of Germany. Confirmed the day after in Berlin, this brought to an end World War II in Europe.

SIGHTS
Cathédrale Notre-Dame★★★

Place Cardinal Luçon. ○*Open daily 7.30am–7.30pm; no visits during services.* ○*Guided multilingual tours on request.*

The present building was begun in 1211. It is one of the great cathedrals of France, built in the Lanceolate Gothic style pioneered at Chartres, but with more sophisticated ornamentation, especialy in its window tracery. The west front has wonderfully soaring lines and superb 13C sculpture, whose masterpiece is the world-famous Smiling Angel (in a splay of the north portal).

Inside is one of the greatest achievements of the Gothic, the west end of the nave, best seen towards the end of the afternoon when the sun lights up the two rose windows.

Reims was occupied by the German army from 3–12 September 1914, and for four years remained in the battle zone. By the end of the war, out of a total of 14 130 houses, only 60 remained habitable. The cathedral, one of the country's most precious buildings in terms of both artistic and historic value, was in ruins. The artillery bombardments of 19 September 1914 and April 1917 had been particularly destructive. The skilful restoration has largely been financed by the Rockefeller Foundation.

Palais du Tau★★

2 pl. du Cardinal-Luçon. ○*Open early May–early Sept Tue–Sun 9.30am–6.30pm; rest of the year 9.30am–2.30pm, 2–5.30pm.* ○*Closed 1 Jan, 1 May, 1 and 11 Nov, 25 Dec.* ○*Guided tours (1hr15min) of the palace available (in French); reserve 1 week in advance; guided tours (2hr30min) of palace and cathedral; reserve 2 weeks in advance.* ○*€7.* ○*03 26 47 81 79. http://palais-tau.monuments-nationaux.fr.*

Dating from 1690, the former palace of the bishops of Reims was built by Mansart and Robert de Cotte. In it is housed some of the cathedral's original statuary and tapestries, among them two huge 15C Arras tapestries depicting scenes from the life of Clovis.

The treasury has many objects of outstanding interest, such as the 9C Talisman of Charlemagne, the 11C cut-glass Holy Thorn reliquary, the 12C coronation chalice, the St Ursula reliquary with its cornelian casket, the Holy Ampulla reliquary, and a collar of the Order of the Holy Ghost.

Basilique St-Rémi★★

Place Chanoine Ladame. ⏰*Open daily 8am–7pm. Son-et-Lumière shows Jul– Sept Sat 9.30pm.* ✆*No charge.* ✆*Guided tours on request.*

Dating from 1007, this is the city's most venerable church, though restorations have left little that is Romanesque and less that is Carolingian. The west front was rebuilt during a major restoration in 1170; it is remarkable for its Romanesque south tower. The façade of the south transept with its statue of St Michael was reconstructed in the 14C and 15C. The sombre interior **(intérieur★★★)** is remarkable for its length (122m/400ft) in proportion to its width (26m/85ft). The oldest part of the church is the 11C transept. In the 12C, the choir was rebuilt in the Early Gothic manner and the whole nave given Gothic vaulting.

ADDRESSES

🏠 STAY

🛏 **Ardenn Hôtel** – *6 r. Caqué.* ✆*03 26 47 42 38. www.ardennhotel.fr. Closed Dec–early Jan. 14rms.* ⌑*€5.50.* This hotel, behind an attractive brick façade in a quiet little town-centre street, has tastefully decorated rooms and smiling service.

🛏🛏 **Crystal** – *86 pl. Drouet-d'Erlon.* ✆*03 26 88 44 44. www.hotel-crystal.fr. 31rms.* ⌑*€9.* A haven of greenery right in the centre of town is the main attraction of this 1920s house. The renovated bedrooms all have excellent bedding. Breakfast is served in a delightful flowered courtyard garden in summer.

🛏🛏 **Hôtel La Cathédrale** – *20 r. Libergier.* ✆*03 26 47 28 46. 14rms.* ⌑*€7.* This smart, welcoming hotel stands in a street leading to the cathedral and has small, bright and cheerful rooms with comfortable beds,

while the breakfast room is decorated with old engravings.

🛏🛏 **Hôtel Continental** – *93 pl. Drouet-d'Erlon.* ✆*03 26 40 39 35. www.grandhotel continental.com. Closed 21 Dec–7 Jan. 50rms.* ⌑*€14.* The attractive façade of this central hotel adorns one of the city's liveliest squares. The rooms, in varying styles, are reached by a splendid staircase. Elegant Belle Epoque sitting rooms.

🛏🛏 **Grand Hôtel du Nord** – *75 pl. Drouet-d'Erlon.* ✆*03 26 47 39 03. www.hotel-nord-reims.com. Closed Christmas period. 50rms.* ⌑*€9.* Recently renovated rooms with all mod-cons in a 1920s building set in a pedestrians-only square. The rooms facing the back are quieter. Many restaurants nearby.

🛏🛏🛏 **Hôtel Porte Mars** – *2 pl. de la République.* ✆*03 26 40 28 35. www.hotel portemars.com. 24rms.* ⌑*€12.* Drink tea in the cosy sitting room, or enjoy a drink in the sophisticated bar. A delicious breakfast is served in the attractive glass-roofed dining room decorated with photographs and old mirrors. The comfortable, well sound-proofed rooms all have a personal touch.

🍴/ EAT

🍽🍽 **Brasserie Le Boulingrin** – *48 r. Mars.* ✆*03 26 40 96 22. www.boulingrin.fr. Closed Sun.* This Art Deco-style restaurant dating from 1925 has become an institution in Reims life. The owner is much in evidence, overseeing the operations and creating a congenial atmosphere. The menu is inventive and the prices reasonable.

🍽🍽 **Café du Palais** – *14 pl. Myron-Herrick.* ✆*03 26 47 52 54. www.cafedupalais.fr. Closed Mon eve and Sun.* This lively café near the cathedral was founded in 1930. With its original glass roof and a warm red décor, it serves generous portions of salad and other daily dishes, which are much appreciated, as are the home-made pastries. You can also enjoy a reasonably priced glass of champagne.

🍽🍽 **Da Nello** – *39 r. Cérès.* ✆*03 26 47 33 25.* A Mediterranean welcome awaits you at this Italian restaurant where the tables look onto the kitchen and the pizzas are baked in the oven in the centre of the room. Fresh pasta, grilled dishes and daily specials according to what the market has to offer… and all served with an authentic Italian accent.

⊜⊜ **La Table Anna** – *6 r. Gambetta.*
☏03 26 89 12 12. Closed Mon. Champagne
takes pride of place in the window of this
establishment next door to the music
conservatory. Some of the paintings
adorning the walls are the work of the
owner. Traditional dishes are renewed
with the seasons.

⊜⊜ **La Vigneraie** – *14 r. de Thillois.*
☏03 26 88 67 27. www.vigneraie.com.
A celebrated gastronomic halt in the
centre of Reims, La Vigneraie boasts
a fantastic collection of carafes. Tasty
classical menu and fine wine list.
Excellent value for money; all is calm,
luxurious elegance and courtesy, just
steps from the cathedral.

⊜⊜⊜ **Au Petit Comptoir** – *17 r. de Mars.*
☏03 26 40 58 58. Closed Sun, Mon. This
imposing restaurant with its wooden
terrace is right behind the town hall.
Inside the black-and-white décor and
studied lighting lend a cosy atmosphere.
Traditional cooking and spit-roast dishes.

🎭 NIGHTLIFE

Place Drouet-d'Erlon – This square is the
prime starting point for anyone wanting
to go out on the town. There is something
for everyone, whether you are looking
for a bar, pub, restaurant, tearoom or
brasserie.

La Chaise au Plafond – *190 ave d'Épernay.*
☏03 26 06 09 61. Founded in 1910, this bar
and tobacconist's is famous for the chair
that has remained stuck to the ceiling
ever since a shell hit the establishment on
12 September 1914. Terrace in summer.
Selection of 150 cigars (Cuban, Honduran
or from Santo Domingo).

CHOCOLATIERS

Deléans – *20 r. Cérès. ☏03 26 47 56 35.*
Closed Aug. Cocoa-based specialities have
been made here in the old-fashioned way
since 1874. Try Néluskos (chocolate-coated
cherries in cognac), and *petits bouchons
de champagne*, enclosed in a giant
champagne cork made of chocolate.

Fossier – *25 cours JB Langlet. ☏03 26 47
59 84.* Founded in 1756, the biscuit- and
chocolate-maker Fossier creates the
ultimate in Reims confectionery.
Pay a visit to the shop and factory and
learn how to *piouler* (stir) your glass of
champagne correctly!

La Petite Friande – *15 cours JB Langlet.*
☏03 26 47 50 44. For over 170 years, the
establishment has prided itself on being
the specialists in authentic *bouchons
de champagne*, made with *marc de
champagne*. Another of their delicious
creations is *bulles à la vieille fine de la Marne*.

CALENDAR

Fêtes Johanniques – *2nd weekend in
June.* 2 000 walk-ons in period costume
accompany Joan of Arc and Charles VII
during a massive street festival.

Flâneries musicales d'été – *Jun–Jul.* Over
150 street concerts throughout the town,
including shows by major international
stars in some of the town's most
prestigious and unlikely venues.

CHAMPAGNE HOUSES

Several of the world's most renowned
champagne-makers have their cellars in
Reims, and offer guided tours, tastings
and discount purchases.

Mumm *34 r. du Champ-de-Mars.
www.mumm.com*

Piper-Heidsieck *51 bd Henry-Vasnier.
www.piper-heidsieck.com*

Pommery *5 pl. du Gén.-Gouraud.
www.pommery.com.*

Ruinart *4 r. des Crayères.
www.ruinart.com.*

Taittinger *9 pl. St-Nicaise.
www.taittinger.fr.*

Veuve Clicquot-Ponsardin
*1 pl. des Droits-de-l'Homme.
www.veuve-clicquot.fr.*

Châlons-en-Champagne★★

Champagne-Ardenne

Its centre traversed by the River Marne and two canals, the Mau and the Nau, Châlons, formerly known as Châlons-sur-Marne, is a dignified and attractive commercial town with some fine buildings.

> ▶ **Population:** 47 567
> ⓖ **Michelin Map:** 306 I 9
> 🛈 **Info:** 3 quai des Arts. ✆03 26 65 17 89. www.chalons-tourisme.com.
> ◐ **Location:** 46km/29mi SE of Reims, and 32km/20mi E of Épernay.

A BIT OF HISTORY

The valley of the Aube to the southwest of the town was the setting in 451 for the series of battles known as the Catalaunian Fields **(Champs catalauniques)**.

Having given up his intention of sacking Paris, then known as Lutetia, because of the intervention of St Genevieve, Attila the Hun was engaged here by the Roman army under Aetius; after fierce fighting, he quit the battlefield and fled eastwards.

During the Wars of Religion, the town remained loyal to the King who declared it to be the "main town of the Champagne region" and in 1589 it became the seat of an annexe of the Paris Parliament. Châlons was the birthplace in 1749 of Nicolas Appert, a pioneer of the food industry and the inventor of a system of preserving food by sterilisation.

SIGHTS

Cathédrale St-Étienne★★

✆05 61 03 03 03. ◐Open Feb–Dec, call for opening hours. ⓐAdmission charge. The present building was begun around 1235 in the Lanceolate Gothic style invented 40 years previously at Chartres, though there is little evidence of stylistic development having taken place.

The cathedral is famous for its stained glass (**vitraux**), Renaissance as well as medieval. The 13C glass includes the tall windows in the choir, the north transept (with the wonderful hues of green characteristic of the region), and the first bay on the north side (the Tanners' window – note the hanging skins). The finest windows, however, are those of Renaissance date, in the side chapels of the south aisle, showing scenes from the Creation, the earthly Paradise, the Passion, the Life of Christ and the Lives of the Saints.

Église Notre-Dame-en-Vaux★

◐Open daily 10am–noon, 2–6pm, Sun 2.30–6pm. ✆03 26 65 63 17. This typical early Gothic church with a characteristic four-tier elevation has a particularly noteworthy ambulatory, inspired by the one at St-Rémi in Reims, together with the stained glass in the windows of the north aisle, again showing superb skill in the use of green. To the left of the church, the **Musée du Cloître de Notre-Dame-en-Vaux**★★ (◐ open daily except Tue: Apr–Sept 10am–noon, 2–6pm; Oct–Mar 10am–noon, 2–5pm (Sat, Sun 6pm). ◐closed 1 Jan, 1 May, 1 and 11 Nov, 25 Dec. ✆03 26 64 03 87) houses **sculptures**★★ from the old Romanesque cloisters, a rare example of the most accomplished medieval architecture.

EXCURSION

Bar-le-Duc★

◐Bar-le-Duc (pop. 16 950) sits halfway between Strasbourg and Paris. 🛈 7 r. Jeanne-d'Arc. ✆03 29 79 11 13. www.barleduc.fr. This old capital of the Duchy of Bar is divided into two sections. The historic Ville Haute rests on a plateau, while the industrial Ville Basse is laid out along the River Ornain and the Rhine-Marne canal. The upper town is a beautiful ensemble of grand and aristocratic 16–18C houses, especially notable in the triangular Place St-Pierre.

Monthermé★

Champagne-Ardenne

Monthermé has a spectacular site★ just downstream from the meeting point of the Semoy with the Meuse, and makes a good starting point for walks or cycle rides into the Ardennes.

▶ **Population:** 2 579
◉ **Michelin Map:** 306 K 3
▯ **Info:** pl. J.-B. Clément.
  ℘03 24 54 46 73.
  www.montherme.fr.
▷ **Location:** The little town is close to Charleville-Mézières, 104km/65mi to the NE of Reims, not far from the Belgian border.

EXCURSION

La Meuse Ardennaise★★ (The Meuse Gorge through the Ardennes)

▷ *72km/45mi.*

One of Europe's great rivers, 950km/590mi in length, the Meuse rises on the Langres uplands. It flows between the escarpment of the Côte des Bars and the dip-slope of the Côte de la Meuse, before penetrating the high plateau of the Ardennes in a deep gorge. Its meanders here mark the course it traced out in Tertiary times; since then, the plateau has been uplifted, but the river has succeeded in entrenching itself in the landscape.

From Charleville-Mézières to Givet there is a succession of single meanders (Monthermé, Fumay, Chooz), double (Revin) and even triple ones (Charleville). The valley has long formed a corridor of human activity, with its water, rail and road communications, and with a skilled workforce producing engineering products and domestic appliances. Monthermé has long been a centre of trade union activity, with considerable conflict between workers and employers.

Downstream from Monthermé the most interesting sites are: the **Roches de Laifour**★ and the **Dames de Meuse**★ opposite one another; **Revin**, where the old town and the industrial area each occupy their own peninsula; **Fumay**, with its old quarter, once famous for its quarries producing violet slate, and **Givet**, sited at the exit from a side valley originally fortified by Charles V and strengthened by Vauban.

EXCURSION

Rocroi★

▷ *Rocroi stands close to the Belgian border.* ▯ *Place d'Armes.* ℘*03 24 54 20 06. www.otrocroi.com.*

First laid out in the 16C in a clearing in the Ardennes forest, Rocroi is a typical Renaissance fortified town. After the principality of Sedan had been incorporated into France in 1642, the death of Richelieu and the ill health of Louis XIII made a long period of uncertain rule by a regent seem likely. The prospect whetted the expansionist appetites of Philip IV of Spain, for whom the capture of Rocroi would open the way to Paris via the valleys of the Aisne and the Marne. On 19 May 1643, three days after the death of Louis XIII, a bold manoeuvre by the Duke d'Enghien, the future Grand Condé, routed the redoubtable Spanish infantry. This, the first French victory over the Spaniards for more than a century, reverberated around Europe. Mazarin was now able to implement Richelieu's foreign policy. After his involvement in the disturbances known as the Fronde, Condé went over to the Spaniards, and, in 1658, was responsible for capturing Rocroi for them. But in the following year, the Treaty of the Pyrenees gave the fortress town back to France and Condé to his king.

Ramparts

The ramparts of Rocroi were improved by Vauban. With their glacis, bastions, demi-lunes and deep defensive ditches they are a fine example of the great engineer's mastery of his art.

Troyes★★★
Champagne-Ardenne

The lively centre of this distinguished old trading town is a charming collection of picturesque half-timbered houses, many beautifully restored.

A BIT OF HISTORY

Today Troyes shares with Reims the distinction of being one of the capitals of the province of Champagne, though historically the city looks southeast towards Burgundy rather than northwards to the Ardennes. The town developed in the Seine valley on the great trade route between Italy and the cities of Flanders. It had a considerable Jewish population, among them the influential scholar Rashi (1050–1105).

In the Middle Ages the town hosted two huge annual fairs, each lasting three months, and attracting merchants and craftsmen from all over Europe. But by the end of the 14C, the pattern of commercial exchanges had changed, and these gatherings fell into decline.

Troyes has long been France's most important centre of hosiery manufacture, an industry introduced at the beginning of the 16C. The city's wealth enabled it to overcome the great fire of 1524; houses and churches were rebuilt in a style showing both the Italianate influence of artists who came from Fontainebleau around 1540, as well as the persistence of medieval traditions.

SIGHTS
Le Vieux Troyes★★

The outline of the old part of the city bears a curious resemblance to a champagne cork, with the area around the cathedral forming the head.

The majority of the old houses are timber-framed. The most elegant infill is the characteristic local chequer-board pattern made from brick, slate or chalk rather than the cob or daub commonly employed. The best examples of such houses are in Rue Champeaux, Ruelle des Chats, Rue de Vauluisant and the Cour du Mortier d'Or.

▶ **Population:** 63 155
♿ **Michelin Map:** 313 E 4
ℹ **Info:** 16 bd Carnot (by the station) ✆03 25 82 62 70, and r. Mignard (pedestrian zone, opposite Saint Jean church). ✆03 25 73 36 88 www.ot-troyes.fr.
▶ **Location:** 125km/78mi S of Reims by *autoroute*, and 176km/110mi SE of Paris in the cradle formed by the A 5 and A 26 *autoroutes*.
🅿 **Parking:** If you are visiting the old town, park the car behind the town hall (place Alexandre-Israël) or along boulevard Gambetta.
🔍 **Don't Miss:** For shopping bargains, visit the big factory outlet malls on the edge of town.
🕐 **Timing:** Allow half a day or more to enjoy Vieux Troyes.

😊 Guided Tours 😊

Guided tours, including audio-tours, can be booked all year round at the tourist office, who also sell the useful **Pass'Troyes** (€12). *Ask at the tourist office.*

Maison de l'Outil et de la Pensée ouvrière★★

7 r. de la Trinité. ⏱*Open daily 10am–6pm (Oct–Mar daily except Tue).* ⏱*Closed 1 Jan and 25 Dec.* 👝€6.50. ✆03 25 73 28 26. www.maison-de-l-outil.com.
Housed in the Hôtel du Mauroy, it is a fine architectural setting for the fascinating range of objects displayed. The dignity of labour is celebrated here in the subtle diversity of forms as much as in the individual character and highly specialised function of each object.

Église Ste-Madeleine

This church is Troyes' oldest place of worship. Much rebuilt in the 16C, it is famous for the rood screen (**jubé**★★);

this has scalloped arches with no intermediate supports, fine glass (**verrières★**), as well as a statue of **Sainte Marthe★** of striking gravity.

Musée de Vauluisant★

4 r. Vauluisant. ○*Open May–Sept: Wed 2–7pm, Thu–Fri 10am–1pm, 2–7pm, Sat–Sun 11am–1pm, 2–7pm; Oct–Apr: Wed–Thu 2–5pm, Fri–Sun 10am–noon, 2–5pm.* ○*Closed Mon-Tue.* ⊛*€3 (no charge 1st Sun in the month).* ☏*03 25 73 05 85.*

The fine 16C Renaissance **Hôtel de Vauluisant★** contains a museum of **local art** and a **museum of hosiery** with exhibits depicting the industry's evolution, including historic looms and other machinery.

Cathédrale St-Pierre et St-Paul★★

The cathedral was begun in 1208 and continued until the 17C, enabling the regional Gothic style to be traced over the whole period of its evolution. The building has remarkable proportions, exceptionally rich decoration and a beautiful nave. The stained-glass windows (**vitraux★★**) of the cathedral cover a total area of 1 500sq m/16 000sq ft. One of the supreme achievements of this art form, they transform the building into a cage of glass.

Musée d'Art Moderne★★

14 Place Saint-Pierre. ♿○*Open May–Sept: Tue–Fri 10am–1pm, 2–7pm, Sat–Sun 11am–7pm; Oct–Apr: Tue–Fri 10am–noon, 2–5pm, Sat–Sun 11am–6pm.* ○*Closed public holidays.* ⊛*€5 (no charge 1st Sun in the month).* ☏*03 25 76 26 80.*

This is the collection built up since 1939 by Pierre and Denise Lévy, noted hosiery manufacturers. It comprises thousands of items dating from 1850–1950, many of them donated to the State and now on display in the former Bishops' Palace.

Particularly well represented here are the **Fauves**, who, together with Braque, Dufy, Matisse and Van Dongen, "made colour roar". Derain too, one of the first

Maison du Boulanger and Tourelle de l'Orfèvre, Le Vieux Troyes

B. Brillon/MICHELIN

to appreciate the art of Africa, is very much present, as is Maurice Marinot, a local artist and glass-maker.

ADDITIONAL SIGHTS

Basilique St-Urbain★ – 13C Gothic architecture.

Église St-Pantaléon★ – Collection of religious statuary.

Musée St-Loup (*1 r. Chrestien de Troyes*)– Fine art and **archaeology★**.

Pharmacie Musée★ de l'Hôtel-Dieu (*Quai des Comtes de Champagne Troyes*) – Rich collection of 18C earthenware.

ADDRESSES

🛏 STAY

🛏 **Les Comtes de Champagne** – *56 r. de la Monnaie.* ☏*03 25 73 11 70. 36rms.* ☲ *€7.* It is said that the four 12C houses which make up this hotel used to belong to the counts of Champagne who minted their coins here. Renovated rooms; those with kitchen facilities could be ideal for families.

🛏 **Motel Savinien** – *87 r. Fontaine, at Ste-Savinien, 3km/1.8mi W of city centre.* ☏*03 25 79 24 90. www.motelsavinien.om. Closed Sun and Mon. 49rms.* ☲ *€10.* This conveniently placed motel by the ring road on the west of the city centre is a large, quiet, well-maintained 1970s building. Rooms are practical, regularly updated. Traditional cuisine served on the terrace.

⛵/EAT

😋 **Aux Crieurs de Vin** – *4–6 pl. Jean-Jaurès.* 𝄐*03 25 40 01 01. Closed Sun and Mon.* Wine connoisseurs will appreciate this establishment, which is part wine and spirits shop, part atmospheric pre-1940s-style bistro.

😋 **Bistro DuPont** – *5 pl. Charles-de-Gaulle, 10150 Pont-Ste-Marie, 3km/1.8mi NE of Troyes on N 77.* 𝄐*03 25 80 90 99. Closed Sun eve and Mon.* Flowers and smiles from the staff provide a fine welcome. In a simple but carefully planned setting, the cheap and cheerful dishes suit the style of the bistro.

😋 **Le Bistroquet** – *Pl. Langevin.* 𝄐*03 25 73 65 65. Closed Sun except lunch from Sept–Jun.* This restaurant is situated in the centre of the pedestrianised part of Troyes, and is reminiscent of a Parisian brasserie. The large dining room is attractively lit by a decorated glass ceiling, and has leather seats, indoor plants and a lively atmosphere.

🛒 SHOPPING

Specialities – *Andouillettes* (chitterling sausages): grilled, unaccompanied or drizzled with olive oil flavoured with *fines herbes* and garlic. Other specialities include Chaource cheese, cider or champagne *choucroute.*

Market – Daily market in the Place St-Remy halls. The main market is held on Saturdays. There is another in the Chartreux area on Wed and on Sun morning. Country market every 3rd Wed on Boulevard Jules-Guesde.

Jean-Pierre-Ozérée – *Halles de l'Hôtel-de-Ville.* 𝄐*03 25 73 72 25.* Maturing of cheeses, including Chaource, Mussy and Langres. A useful alternative if you don't have time to go to the production site yourself.

Le Palais du Chocolat – *2 r. de la Monnaie.* 𝄐*03 25 73 35 73. www.pascal-caffet.com. Closed Sun afternoon.* An emporium of chocolate, as well as ice cream, sorbets and pastries.

Marques Avenue – *114 bd de Dijon,* 𝄐*03 25 82 00 72. Closed Sun.* With 120 boutiques, Marques Avenue is the biggest centre for discount fashion stores in Europe. Here you will find all the big brand names, French and foreign.

Marques City – *Pont-Ste-Marie. www.marquescity.com. Closed Sun.* Stores offering almost 200 labels at discount prices, ranging across sportswear, formal wear and quality accessories. Three restaurants on site.

McArthur Glen – *Voie des Bois - 10150 Pont-Ste-Marie.* 𝄐*03 25 70 47 10. Closed Sun and 1 May.* Opened in 1995, the village includes 84 end-of-line shops along an outside covered gallery.

🎭 NIGHTLIFE

Le Bougnat des Pouilles – *29 r. Paillot-de-Montabert.* 𝄐*03 25 73 59 85.* The high-quality vintages in this wine bar are sought out by the young proprietor himself, from among the smaller producers in the region.

Le Tricasse – *16 r. Paillot-de-Montabert.* 𝄐*03 25 73 14 80. Closed Sun.* This most famous of Troyes' nightspots is in a smart area and offers a glorious mix of music, from jazz to salsa to house.

Le Chihuahua – *8 r. Charbonnet.* 𝄐*03 25 73 33 53.* This fashionable cellar bar also has dancing.

La Chope – *64 ave du Gén.-de-Gaulle.* 𝄐*03 25 73 11 99.* Wide selection of beers, whiskies and cocktails.

La Cocktaileraie – *56 r. Jaillant-Deschainets, BP 4102.* 𝄐*03 25 73 77 04.* A hundred or so cocktails are on offer, around 45 whiskies and many prestigious champagnes.

🎭 ENTERTAINMENT

Théâtre de Champagne – *r. Louis-Mary.* 𝄐*03 25 76 27 60 / 61. Closed Jul–Aug.* Opera, comedy, art-house theatre, variety shows.

Théâtre de la Madeleine – *r. Jules-Lebocey.* 𝄐*03 25 43 32 10. Performances Mon–Sat 10am–12.30pm, 2–6pm.* Arthouse theatre, comedy, variety shows.

Provins★★

Champagne-Ardenne

The ancient fortified city of Provins sits atop a ridge overlooking the Seine valley and the Champagne chalklands, roughly equidistant from both Paris and Troyes.

The town has a famous outline (once painted by Turner), dominated by a tower (Tour de César) and the dome of Église St-Quiriace. Provins' role as an important centre of commerce was confirmed in the 12C when it became one of the two capitals of the County of Champagne.

Its annual fairs were renowned, part of a round of such events which also took place at Lagny, Bar-sur-Aube and Troyes. For a number of years in the 13C, Edmund of Lancaster was Lord of Provins, at a time when the place was known for its roses, in those days a rare flower.

He incorporated a red rose into his emblem; a century-and-a-half later it was this flower which triumphed over the white rose of York in the Wars of the Roses.

VISIT

Ville Haute★★

Still protected to north and west by its 12C and 13C walls★★, its most splendid feature is the **Tour de César★★**, a massive 12C keep with an additional rampart built by the English in the Hundred Years' War as an artillery emplacement. There is also a 13C tithe barn (*Grange aux Dîmes*), which belonged to the canons of St-Quiriace. Also of note is the group of **statues★★** at the Église St-Ayoul.

EXCURSION

Église de St-Loup-de-Naud★

▶ *11km/6.8mi SW.*

The church belonged to a Benedictine priory of the Archbishopric of Sens, and was one of the first in the area to be vaulted in stone.

Erected in the 11C and 12C, it demonstrates the gradual evolution of the Romanesque into early Gothic. The choir dates from the 11C, as does the

▶ **Population:** 12 627
- **Michelin Map:** 312 I 4
- **Info:** Chemin de Villecran. ℰ 0 64 60 26 26. www.provins.net.
- **Location:** 70km/44mi NW of Troyes, and 93km/58mi SE of Paris, Provins is easily reached by road or rail from the capital.
- **Don't Miss:** A relaxing stroll around the upper town.

early Romanesque cradle-vault next to it. The dome over the crossing, the barely projecting transepts and the first two bays of the nave were built at the beginning of the 12C.

Finally, around 1160, the last two bays of the nave were completed; they are square in plan and have alternating pillars and twin columns on the model of Sens Cathedral. The well-preserved **doorway★★**, under the main porch, shows similarities with the Royal Doorway (*Portail royal*) of Chartres Cathedral; Christ in Majesty surrounded by symbols of the Evangelists on the tympanum, apostles in arched niches on the lintel, statue-columns in the splays, and figures in between the arch mouldings.

Tour de César

S.Sauvignier/MICHELIN

ATLANTIC COAST

The Atlantic Coast region of France stretches from the estuary of the Loire in the north to the mighty natural frontier of the Pyrénées to the south. It is bounded on the west by the apparently endless Atlantic coastline and to the east by the lush countryside of the Limousin, the Périgord and Gascony. It encompasses some of the modern region of the Pays de Loire, the whole of Poitou-Charentes and the western half of the Aquitaine.

Highlights

1 **Église Monolithe**, a church hollowed out of rock at **St Émilion** (p144)

2 Medieval towers of the **Vieux Port** at **La Rochelle** (p151)

3 1C Roman arena at **Saintes** (p155)

4 Science-based leisure park near Poitiers: **Futuroscope** (p158)

5 History theme park based round a castle, **Le Puy de Fou** (p159)

Geography – With the exception of the Pyrénées in the south, the region consists for the most part of a flat coastal plain, rising gently to the more undulating countryside in the east. In the north there are great marshy tracts like the Marais Poitevin and dunes bordering sandy beaches. To the south is the Gironde, the name given to the broad estuary of the Garonne, and the Atlantic coast south of here runs in a straight line almost to Spain, interrupted only by the Bay of Arcachon. Behind the vast sandy beaches rise the highest sand dunes in Europe while inland is the Landes, an immense wooded area planted with with pine trees.

History – In Classical times the Roman province of Aquitania included all the Atlantic Coast region. Following the collapse of the Roman Empire, it came under the control of Visigoths and then Franks. During the medieval period the region passed to the English Crown as part of Eleanor of Aquitaine's dowry, and not until the end of the Hundred Years' War did it revert to France. During the Revolution there was less support here for the new Republic than in other areas of France.

Economy – The Poitou Charentes region is mainly agricultural and cereal production is very important, as are cattle rearing and dairy farming. Cognac is produced in the area around the town of the same name and exported worldwide. The area around Bordeaux is renowned for its fine wines, and the produce of the famous châteaux are much sought-after. The Landes area produces vast quantities of timber and is the largest maritime pine forest in Europe.

Vieux Port, La Rochelle

S. Sauvignier/MICHELIN

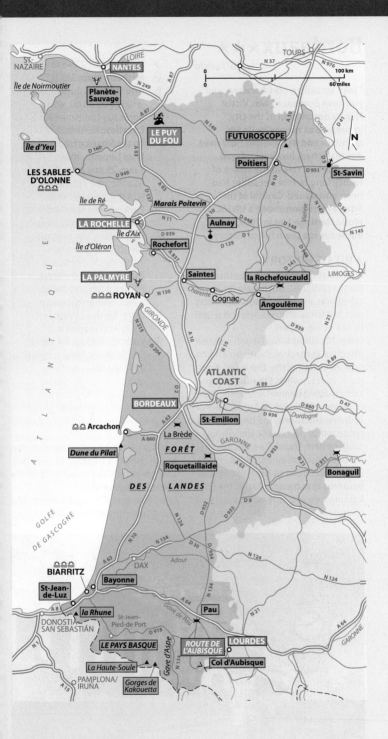

ST-NAZAIRE

LOIRE

TOURS

N 37

N 976

NANTES

N 249

A 87

0   100 km
0   60 miles

N

Île de Noirmoutier

Planète-Sauvage

A 87

LE PUY DU FOU

N 149

Creuse

A 41

FUTUROSCOPE

Île d'Yeu

D 160

A 83

Poitiers

N 10

D 951

St-Savin

LES SABLES-D'OLONNE

D 949

A 83

D 137

Île de Ré

Marais Poitevin

N 11

A 10

Aulnay

D 948

Vienne

N 147

D 54

D 145

LA ROCHELLE

Île d'Aix

D 939

D 129

D 1

D 148

Île d'Oléron

Rochefort

A 837

D 141

D 948

LIMOGES

LA PALMYRE

Saintes

Charente

la Rochefoucauld

ROYAN

N 150

Cognac

Angoulême

GIRONDE

N 215

A 10

N 10

D 939

N 21

D 204

D 2

ATLANTIC COAST

A 89

A 89

BORDEAUX

A 63

St-Emilion

D 936

Dordogne

D 660

D 47

Arcachon

A 660

La Brède

GARONNE

Dune du Pilat

FORÊT

Roquetaillade

A 62

D 933

N 21

D 911

Bonaguil

DES

LANDES

D 8

D 932

N 124

D 933

N 10

N 134

D 30

Adour

N 124

N 124

BIARRITZ

A 63

DAX

D 934

N 21

GARONNE

St-Jean-de-Luz

Bayonne

A 64

A 64

A 8

la Rhune

Gave de Pau

Pau

DONOSTIA/SAN SEBASTIÁN

St-Jean-Pied-de-Port

D 918

LE PAYS BASQUE

ROUTE DE L'AUBISQUE

LOURDES

PAMPLONA/IRUÑA

N 1

A 15

La Haute-Soule

Gorges de Kakouetta

Gave d'Aspe

Col d'Aubisque

N 134

A T L A N T I Q U E

GOLFE DE GASCOGNE

Bordeaux★★★

Gironde

"Take Versailles, add Antwerp, and you have Bordeaux" was Victor Hugo's description of the city, impressed as he was by its 18C grandeur and its splendid tidal river. Bordeaux had, however, played an important role in the affairs of France long before Versailles had been envisioned. Capital of the Aquitaine region, made a UNESCO World Heritage Site in 2007, Bordeaux is a town full of history.

A BIT OF HISTORY

A large settlement even before the Roman conquest, **Burdigala** (as it was called) was always an important trading port, but frequently attacked and seized by sea-going raiders.

From 7C, Good King Dagobert took effective control of the town and its region, creating the Duchy of Aquitaine. In 1152, when **Eleanor of Aquitaine** married Henry Plantagenet, Duke of Normandy, Count of Anjou, ruler of Touraine and Maine, the bride's dowry consisted of practically the whole of southwestern France. Two months later her new husband inherited the English Crown, becoming Henry II of England. Bordeaux thus became part of the English kingdom, and so remained for three centuries.

▶ **Population:** 239 642

◔ **Michelin Map:** 335 H 5

▣ **Info:** 12 cours du 30-Juillet. ℘05 56 00 66 00. www. bordeaux-tourisme.com.

◑ **Location:** Bordeaux is on the S bank of the River Gironde, about 48km/29.8mi from the Atlantic, and 216km/157mi N of the Spanish border.

🅿 **Parking:** There are car parks alongside the river.

◉ **Don't Miss:** The extensive collection of paintings in the Musée des Beaux-Arts. Of course, there are Bordeaux's world-famous wines. Take an excursion to the Bordeaux Vineyards – you won't regret it.

👥 **Kids:** Workshops for kids at Cap Sciences; films, a sound and light show and fun questionnaire at Planète Bordeaux in Beychac to learn all about wine.

It was the English demand for wine that began the city's tradition of seafaring, and promoted the expansion of the Bordeaux **vineyards**.

Even during the Hundred Years' War claret continued to flow north to Eng-

Tram in front of the Grand Théâtre, Place de la Comédie

© Gérard Labriet/Photononstop

land. In 1453, Bordeaux and Guyenne (Old English for Aquitaine) were won back for France in the final battle of the Hundred Years' War.

The French Crown appointed **Intendants** to rebuild and govern Bordeaux as a well-planned city to replace the tangle of medieval streets. In the course of the 18C they succeeded in transforming Bordeaux, giving it the Classical face it wears today, with grandiose set-pieces of urban design: the quaysides, the Place de la Bourse, the great avenues, the Town Hall (Hôtel de Ville) and the Grand Théâtre.

During the French Revolution, the Bordeaux *députés* formed the group known as the **Girondins**. Accused of conspiring against the Revolution, 22 of them were tried in May 1793 and executed.

In the 18C, goods from the Caribbean added to the huge volume of trade, further stimulating the development of this great port lying 98km/61mi inland.

SIGHTS
VIEUX BORDEAUX
The old town has undergone extensive restoration in an effort to return the ancient ochre stonework of its 18C buildings to its original splendour. The restored buildings include those along the **quayside** following the bend of the Garonne for 1km/0.5mi.

Grand-Théâtre★★
pl. de la Comédie. ✆*05 56 00 85 95. www.opera-bordeaux.com.*
This theatre is one of the finest in France. Its architect was Victor Louis (1731–1802), a proponent of the Louis XVI style; here he succeeded in creating a combined theatre and concert hall which recalls antiquity not only in its sheer scale but also in its restrained use of decoration.

Place du Parlement★
A good example of the urban planning carried out in the reign of Louis XV, the square has a number of houses with ground-floor arcades, transom windows and decorative masks. The harmony and unity of the square is emphasised by the balcony running the whole length of the façades.

Quartier des Chartrons★
This old neighbourhood, behind the quayside devoted to the wine trade and ships' chandlers, became fashionable in the 18C when the city's great families built their town houses here.
Some of the streets (Rue Notre-Dame, Cours de la Martinique, Cours Xavier Arnozan) have many fine dwellings with Classical façades, attics, wrought-iron balconies (balconsa) and transom windows with entablatures.

Esplanade des Quinconces
The sheer size of this esplanade is impressive. It was laid out on the site of the old Château de la Trompette during the Restoration (early 19C).

Monument aux Girondins
pl. des Quincones.
It consists of a column topped by Liberty casting off her chains and two bronze **fountains**★ symbolising the Triumph of the Republic (facing the Grand Théâtre) and the Triumph of Concord.

ADDITIONAL SIGHTS
Place de la Bourse★★
Named after the Stock Exchange (La Bourse), this magnificent square was formerly called place Royale and was the work of the father-and-son architects Jacques Jules (1667–1742) and Jacques-Ange (1698–1782) Gabriel.
On the northern side is the Stock Exchange itself. On the southern side is the former Hôtel des Fermes (tax assessors), housing the **National Customs Museum**.

Basilique St-Michel★
pl. Canteloup et Meynard.
🕐*Open Mon–Sat 8.30am–6pm, Sun 8am–noon.* ✆*05 56 94 30 50.*
The construction of St Michael's Basilica began in 1350, and lasted for two centuries, during which time the original design was much modified. The side chapels were added after 1475. The generous dimensions of the restored

basilica are impressive. Inside, the two-storey elevation is emphasised by high arcades, topped with tall clerestory windows, and wide side aisles. The lines of the flattened east end are barely affected by the three small chapels.

The modern stained-glass windows, behind the high altar, are by Max Ingrand. The organ loft and pulpit date from the 18C. The latter, mahogany with marble panels, is surmounted by a statue of St Michael slaying the dragon.

Cathédrale St-André★

pl. Pey Berland. &Ⓛ*Organ concerts Jul–Aug Tue 6.30pm.* ⌒*No charge.* ℘*05 56 52 68 10.*

This cathedral, dedicated to St Andrew, is the most impressive of all the religious buildings in Bordeaux. The 11–12C nave was altered in the 13C and again in the 15C. The Gothic chancel and the transept were rebuilt in the 14C and 15C. Later, when the roof of the nave threatened to collapse, the building was strengthened by buttresses and flying buttresses.

Porte Royale★ – This 13C entrance to the right of the north doorway is renowned for its sculptures, inspired by the outstanding statuary adorning religious buildings in Île-de-France (the region surrounding Paris, where Gothic architecture originated). Most remarkable are the Twelve Apostles in the entrance bay and, on the tympanum, the fine Gothic *Last Judgement.*

East End – The exterior is distinguished by its fine proportions and by its elevation: the two-tiered flying buttresses soar over the side aisles. Between the supports separating the axial chapel from the one on the left, note the statues of St Thomas, patron saint of architects, holding his square, and Mary Magdalene, in 15C costume, with her jar of sweet-smelling ointment.

South Transept Doorway – This entrance to the cathedral is below a pediment pierced by an oculus and three rose windows. The upper part, embellished with trefoil arcades, also boasts an elegant rose window set within a square. The west front, destroyed in the 18C and then rebuilt, remains unadorned.

Interior – The impressive nave features late Gothic upper parts, resting on 12C bases. Note the lierne and tierceron vaulting over the first three bays. The pulpit, fashioned from mahogany and coloured marble, is 18C. The different height of the **chancel**★, also Gothic, contrasts with the nave and is accentuated by the slenderness of the tall arches, above which a blind triforium is illuminated by Flamboyant clerestory windows. An ambulatory with side chapels encircles the chancel.

Against the fourth pillar to the right of the chancel, there is a charming early 16C sculpture group depicting St Anne and the Virgin. The axial chapel closes off the 17C choir stalls. Opposite, a fine 17C door of carved wood separates the chancel from the nave.

On the inner face of the west front is the **Renaissance organ loft**. Below it two bas-relief sculptures trace the development of Renaissance sculpture.

Musée des Beaux-Arts★★

20 cours d'Albret. &Ⓛ*Open Wed–Mon 11am–6pm.* Ⓛ*Closed public holidays.* ⌒*No charge, except for temporary exhibitions:* €*5.* ℘*05 56 10 20 56.*

The Fine Arts Museum bordering the gardens of City Hall displays a fine collection of 15–20C paintings in the north and south galleries. The **south wing** houses paintings from the Italian Renaissance. The **north wing** is given over to modern and contemporary works. A final room is dedicated to more contemporary works.

Musée d'Aquitaine★★

20 cours Pasteur. &Ⓛ*Open Tue–Sun 11am–6pm.* Ⓛ*Closed public holidays.* ⌒*No charge (temporary exhibitions:* €*5).* ℘*05 56 01 51 00.*

This regional museum, housed in the former Literature and Science Faculty and laid out on two levels, traces the life of Aquitaine Man from prehistoric times to the present day.

Collections in the **prehistory section** contain precious relics of arts and crafts practised by the hunters of the Stone Age. In the **Gallo-Roman section**, aspects of day-to-day religious and economic life in the Aquitaine provincial capital are illustrated through ceramics, glassware, mosaics, fragments of cornices and bas-relief sculptures.

Bordeaux's golden age (18C) saw the development of grandiose urban projects and the building of splendid mansions which were luxuriously furnished. Several displays focus on country life and farming in former times. The accent is always placed on the natural resources of Aquitaine, which embraces the rural landscape of Béarn, the Landes (moors) of Gascony, the Gironde and its vineyards, and of course Arcachon and its oyster farming.

Musée d'Art contemporain (CAPC)★

7 r. Ferrère. ⚐🕐*Open Tue–Sun 11am–6pm (Wed 8pm).* 🕐*Closed public holidays.* ✎*No charge (temporary exhibitions: 5€).* ✆*05 56 00 81 50.*

The former **Lainé warehouse**★★, built in 1824 for storing goods imported from the French colonies, has been successfully remodelled into a Museum of Contemporary Art. It houses the collections of the Centre d'Arts Plastiques Contemporains de Bordeaux (CAPC), which are particularly strong on works from the 1960s and 1970s.

The museum also functions as a cultural centre with conferences and debates, guided tours on a particular artist or aspect of contemporary art, children's workshops and film projections.

Vinorama

10 cours du Médoc. 🕐*Open Jul–Aug Tue–Sun 2–6pm; Sept–Jun Mon–Fri 2–6pm (last admission 45min before closing time).* ✎*€5.40.* ✆*05 56 39 53 02. http://cugnac.perso.cegetel.net.*

Thirteen tableaux with costumed figures recount the history, production and commercialisation of Bordeaux wines from antiquity to the present day.

The tour ends with a wine-tasting session including a vintage wine from 1850, a modern wine, and wine drunk in Roman times with the addition of honey and spices.

👥 Croiseur Colbert★★

Facing 60 quai des Chartrons. 🕐*Open Apr–May, Sept, Mon–Fri 10am–6pm, Sat–Sun 10am–7pm; Jun–Aug, daily 10am–6pm; Oct–Mar, Sun 1–6pm.* 🕐*Closed 1 Jan, 25 Dec.* ✎*€8 (child €5.50).* ✆*05 56 44 96 11. http://colbert. croiseur.free.fr. The tour of the ship consists of three signposted circuits.*

⚐*The last two include steep steps and are not recommended for the less agile.*

The **Colbert** has been berthed in Port de la Lune since 1993, casting its imposing triangular silhouette onto the waters of the Garonne. This anti-aircraft warship was launched in 1959 and carried out its first mission in Toulon as the Mediterranean Squadron's flagship.

She was then converted into a missile-launcher and served during the 1970s in the Atlantic Squadron in Brest. The exhibits vary according to the circuit chosen – weapons' room (Masurca and Exocet systems), the engine room, the control rooms, the two officers' quarters, the crew's galley, a medical centre, including an operating room and dentist, post office and many other facilities designed for daily life on board a warship in the second half of the 20C. The cabins belonging to the different members of the crew can also be viewed, including the Admiral's cabin with its chimney piece, where famous guests such as Général de Gaulle were entertained.

EXCURSIONS
The Bordeaux Vineyards★

The Bordeaux wine region, which extends over approximately 135 000 ha/ 333 585 acres in the Gironde *département,* is the largest producer of quality wines in the world.

The areas to the north produce red wines: Médoc on the west bank of the Gironde with Bourg on the east bank, and St-Émilion and Pomerol north of the Dordogne. The remaining area produces white wines: Entre-Deux-Mers between the Dordogne and the Garonne, and Graves and Sauternes to the south.

Haut Médoc

It boasts the most prestigious "châteaux" with a wine-making tradition dating back to the reign of Louis XIV. Some of the châteaux and the famous cellars are open to visitors, in particular Château Margaux, **Château Mouton-Rothschild**★ and Château Lafite.

St-Émilion★★

The region is famous for its full-bodied and fragrant red wines produced under the strict control of the Jurade, a guild founded in the Middle Ages which was reconvened in 1948. *See ST-ÉMILION.*

Sauternes

The vineyards on the slopes of the lower valley of the Ciron produce renowned sweet white wines, in particular Château Yquem.

Château de Roquetaillade★★

The château is S of Langon on the River Garonne, on the edge of the Landes region. Guided tours (1hr) Jul–Aug, daily 11am–5pm; Sept–Oct 3pm, 4pm; Nov–Easter Sun, public holidays and school holidays 3pm, 4pm; Easter–Jun 3pm, 4pm. Closed 25 Dec. €8. 05 56 76 14 16. http://chateau-roquetaillade.free.fr.

This imposing medieval castle, built in 1306, is part of a compound made up of two forts dating from the 12C and the 14C within a single walled enclosure. Six enormous round towers, crenellated and pierced with arrow slits, frame a rectangular main structure. In the courtyard stands a powerful square keep and its turret. There are also vast vaulted rooms and monumental chimneys.

St-Émilion★★

The town is 10km/6.2mi E of Libourne. It has to be explored on foot, so wear comfortable shoes suitable for steep cobbled lanes. Place du Marché is the focal point. Le Doyenné, Place des Créneaux. 05 57 55 28 28. www.saint-emilion-tourisme.com. Guided tours available.

St-Émilion offers both simple and sophisticated attractions to art-lovers and gourmets alike.

The town is divided into two hill sites, with the Royal Castle and Deanery (Doyenné) symbolising the age-old rivalry between the civil and religious authorities.

Its sun-baked, pantile-roofed stone houses nestle in an **amphitheatre**★★ on the slope of a limestone plateau. Apart from its wines, the town is known for its strange underground church.

Château de La Brède★

The castle lies S of Bordeaux, along the A 62, exit 1.1. Avenue du Château, 33650 La Brède. Guided tours (30min) end Feb–18 Dec 9am–noon (group tours), 2–5.30pm (hours may extend according to season). €7. 05 56 20 20 49. www.chateaula brede.com.

In the peaceful countryside of the Graves area along the Garonne River, this **château**, protected by its moat, still keeps its aristocratic 15C appearance. It was the birthplace of **Charles Montesquieu** (1689–1755), Baron de la Brède – a magistrate of Bordeaux.

ADDRESSES

STAY

Hôtel Acanthe – *12 r. St-Rémi.* 05 56 81 66 58. www.acanthe-hotel-bordeaux.com. 20rms. €6.10. A central location and very reasonable prices are strong points of this recently renovated hotel. The bright rooms are big enough and well sound-proofed.

Hôtel Notre-Dame – *36 r. Notre-Dame.* 05 56 52 88 24. www.hotelnotre dame.com. 21rms. €6. An unpretentious little family hotel in an 18C house just behind the Quai des Chatrons. Rooms small but well kept.

Hôtel Opéra – *35 r. de l'Esprit-des-Lois.* 05 56 81 41 27. 27rms. €6. Near the Grand Théâtre et the Allées de Tourny, here's a modest little family hotel.

Hôtel Continental – *10 r. Montesquieu.* 05 56 52 66 00. www.hotel-le-continental.com. 50rms. €8.50. In the old city, here's a venerable 18C mansion with a fine staircase in the hall.

⊜⊜ **Hôtel Presse** – *6–8 r. de la Porte-Dijeaux.* ℘*05 56 48 53 88. www.hotel delapresse.com. 27rms.* ⊑ *€12.* In the pedestrian shopping quarter of the old city, this is a nice little hotel despite the rather difficult access by automobile.

⫠ EAT

⊜ **Chez Mémère** – *11 r. de la Devise.* ℘*05 56 81 88 20.* Under the vaulted ceiling of this 16C workshop, discover the flavour and ambience of a fine meal Chez Mémère (At granny's).

⊜ **Lou Magret** – *62 r. St-Rémi.* ℘*05 56 44 77 94. Closed Sun and public holidays.* If overwhelmed by the choice of restaurants in this street, try this pleasant establishment whose speciality is *canard de Chalosse*, duck served grilled or with a delicious sauce.

⊜ **La Table du Pain** – *6 pl. du Parlement.* ℘*05 56 81 01 00.* A wide selection of sandwiches, toasts and salads is offered at this restaurant with stone walls, old shelves and waxed pine furnishings.

⊜⊜ **Le Bistro du Musée** – *37 pl. Pey-Berland.* ℘*05 56 52 99 69. Closed Sun.* This bistro with a pretty green wood entrance makes a promising impression from the start. Southwest cuisine and a fine Bordeaux wine menu.

⫛ ENTERTAINMENT

L'Onyx – *11 r. Fernand-Philippart, Quartier St-Pierre.* ℘*05 56 44 26 12. www.theatre-onyx.net.* The city's oldest café-theatre, L'Onyx is an essential stop for local culture.

La Boîte à Jouer – *50 r. Lombard.* ℘*05 56 50 37 37. Performances 8.30pm. Closed Jul–Sept.* This theatre has two small rooms (60 and 45 seats) where lesser regional, national or international troupes specialised in contemporary or musical theatre perform.

Opéra de Bordeaux-Grand-Théâtre – *pl. de la Comédie.* ℘*05 56 00 85 95. www.opera-bordeaux.com.* The Grand Théâtre de Bordeaux is one of the most handsome of France. Symphonies, operas and ballets are performed here under excellent acoustic conditions.

Théâtre Fémina – *20 r. de Grassi.* ℘*05 56 79 06 69.* With 1100 seats, this handsome edifice sets the stage for plays, comedies, operettas, dance and concerts.

⫐ SHOPPING

Librairie Mollat – *15 r. Vital-Carles.* ℘*05 56 56 40 40. www.mollat.com.* France's first independent bookshop is still a veritable regional institution.

Baillardran Canelés – *Galerie des Grands-Hommes.* ℘*05 56 79 05 89.* Located in the Grands-Hommes market, this boutique makes delicious *canelés*, the small brown Bordelais cakes.

Confiserie Cadio-Badie – *26 allées de Tourny.* ℘*05 56 44 24 22. Closed 2 weeks in Aug, Sun and public holidays except Christmas and Easter.* You can't help but be charmed by the old-fashioned style of this appealing boutique founded in 1826. Their truffes and Armagnac-flavoured *bouchons bordelais* are worth a special trip.

Chocolaterie Saunion *56 cours Georges-Clemenceau.* ℘*05 56 48 05 75. Closed Sun and Mon morning, public holidays except Christmas, New Year and Easter.* One of the most illustrious chocolate confectioners of Bordeaux – a must.

Conseil Interprofessionnel des Vins de Bordeaux – *1 cours du XXX Juillet.* ℘*05 56 00 22 66. www.vins-bordeaux.fr. Closed weekends and public holidays.* This is where you'll find ample information about Bordeaux wines and vineyards. Several different wine cellars are found around this centre.

Darricau – *7 pl. Gambetta.* ℘*05 56 44 21 49. www.darricau.com.* Since the turn of the 20C, this *chocolatier* pampers the city with the irresistible *pavé Gambetta* (praline with raisins soaked in wine), Bordeaux bottle-shaped chocolates (*confits de sauterne* or *de médoc*), la *cadichonne* (crunchy vanilla) and *niniches* (soft caramel with dark chocolate).

Arcachon★★

Gironde

A century and a half ago, the site of Arcachon was no more than a pinewood. Today, it is one of the most popular resorts on the French Atlantic.

A BIT OF HISTORY

Arcachon was born when a couple of speculators, the **Pereire brothers**, laid a railway line to the coast in 1852.

The resort quickly grew and was popular for both winter and summer holidays. It is divided into "seasons" – a winter resort (**ville d'hiver**★), with fine villas among the pines; a summer resort (**ville d'été**), with the seafront and attractive **Boulevard de la Mer**★; and the fashionable autumn and spring districts (**ville d'automne** and **ville de printemps**) with opulent houses near Pereire park.

SIGHTS
Bassin★ (Bay)

Bordered by the resorts of Arcachon, Andernos and the wooded dunes of the Cap Ferret peninsula, this vast airy bay, with Bird Island (Île aux Oiseaux) at its centre, extends over an area of 250sq km/96.5sq mi, four-fifths of which is exposed at low tide.

With its great stretches of oyster beds totalling 18sq km/7sq mi in all, Arcachon is one of the main oyster-farming areas. Drive along the waterfront, or take a

▶ **Population:** 12 084
Michelin Map: 335 D 6-7
Info: Esplanade Georges Pompidou.
℘05 57 52 97 97. www.arcachon.com.
Location: The resort fronts the vast Bassin d'Arcachon inlet, 64km/40mi SW of Bordeaux.

trip in a pinasse, one of the traditional boats used by the oyster farmers (*many excursions available from Thiers and Eyrac landing stages (Arcachon) and other landing stages around the Bassin. ℘05 57 72 28 28. www.bateliers-arcachon.com*).

Dune du Pilat★★

7.5km/4.5mi S.

This hill of sand, the highest (114m/374ft) and longest (2 800m/3 062yd) in Europe, drops on its landward side almost sheer to the pine woodland.

Its summit offers a thrilling view along the long, straight sands of the 230km/143mi **Côte d'Argent** (Silver Coast) with its splendid Atlantic rollers. Every year the ocean deposits another 15cu m/529.7cu ft of sand per m of coastline, continually building up the dune which in 1774 swallowed up the church at Soulac. The **panorama**★★ of ocean and forest is especially lovely at dusk.

Dune du Pilat

F. Mousis/MICHELIN

Angoulême★★
Charentes

Angoulême has a walled historic Upper Town, which rises high above a more industrial modern Lower Town; narrow streets lace through the lofty Upper Town, lined with beautiful old buildings, and the ramparts give immense views. Angoulême is France's "Cartoon Capital", and everywhere you'll see the influence of its celebrated *Festival international de la bande dessinée*, devoted to the art of the strip cartoon.

A BIT OF HISTORY

Famous residents: Angoulême boasts two famous **literary characters**: Jean-Louis Guez de Balzac (1597–1654), one of the original members of the Académie Française; and Honoré Balzac (1799–1850), a novelist and playwright who made Angoulême his home.

In 1806, 77-year-old **General Resnier** launched himself from the city's northern ramparts in a **flying-machine** of his own invention. The general suffered a broken leg, and a plan for the invasion of England by this method was shelved.

Bande Dessinée (strip cartoon, often known simply as BD) is an important entertainment for adults and kids alike in France. Angoulême's cartoon festival owes its origins to an exhibition in 1972, "Dix Millions d'images".

In 1974, a regular *Salon de la bande dessinée* was started, which attracted many top cartoonists. In 1996, it became the popular international festival held in January each year.

VISIT
Cathédrale St-Pierre★
18 r. Fénelon, Angoulême.
Extensively destroyed by the Calvinists, the cathedral was restored in 1634 and again from 1866 onwards.
The early 12C statuary of the west front (**façade**★★) is mostly intact; more elaborate than the other façades typical of the region around Angoulême, its

▶ **Population:** 46 069
Michelin Map: 324 K-L-M 5-6
Info: 7 bis r. du Chat. ℘05 45 95 16 84. www.angouleme-tourisme.com.
Location: Angoulême is 115km/71mi S of Poitiers and 43km/27mi E of Cognac.
Kids: In this cartoon-crazy city, there are brilliant graffiti and *trompe l'œil* everywhere. The tourist office has a map of some of the best, or find their locations online at www.toutenbd.com/murs_peints.

themes include the Ascension and the Last Judgement. Particularly noteworthy among the 70 statues and low-reliefs are the superb Christ in Majesty surrounded by the Evangelists, the medallions of saints and a battle scene inspired by *La Chanson de Roland (Song of Roland)*.

Centre National de la Bande Dessinée et de l'Image – strip-cartoon centre
121 r. de Bordeaux. Open Jul–Aug: Tue–Fri 10am–7pm, Sat–Sun and public holidays 2–7pm; Sept–Jun: Tue–Fri 10am–6pm, Sat–Sun and public holidays 2–6pm. Closed 1 Jan, 1 May, 25 Dec. €6.50 (children €4). ℘05 45 38 65 65. www.cnbdi.fr.
This seriously wacky cartoon centre houses a museum, temporary exhibitions and a library, all of which are well worth visiting.

FRAC Poitou-Charentes
63 bd Besson Bey. Open Tue–Sat 2–7pm. No charge. ℘05 45 92 87 01.
Housed in a new centre designed by Jean-Marie Mandon, this is the regional centre of the Poitou-Charentes Contemporary Art Collection, with a collection of recent artistic works from around the world.

Musée du Papier "Le Nil"

134 r. de Bordeaux. &⟳*Open Jul–Aug: Tue–Fri noon–6.30pm, Sat–Sun 1–6.30pm; Sept–Jun: Tue–Fri 10am–noon, 2–6pm, Sat–Sun 2–6pm.* ⟳*Closed public holidays.* ⊷*No charge.* 𝄢*05 45 92 73 43. www.angouleme.fr/museep.*

The former Bardou-Le-Nil paper mill, which specialised in the production of cigarette papers, operated here on the banks of the River Charente until 1970. The building has since been converted into a museum devoted to the paper industry, which brought wealth and prosperity to the region.

EXCURSION
Château de La Rochefoucauld★★

▶ *The château and village are in the Charente, NE of Angoulême.* 🯄*1 r. des Tanneurs.* 𝄢*05 45 63 07 42. www.chateau-la-rochefoucauld.com.*

This elegant Renaissance château, reminiscent of the Loire, stands outside a picturesque village of the same name.

The property is the seat of a noble family, which gave the name François to all its first-born sons and which produced many a very distinguished soldier, statesman, artist and churchman. **François VI** (1613–80) established his reputation as the greatest of France's maxim-writers. In his younger days, he had been a brave soldier but a somewhat inept plotter; he had been imprisoned by Richelieu, fought on the wrong side in the Fronde and was almost blinded by a blast from a harquebus (the first gun fired from the shoulder). With a perception of the world sharpened by an understandable pessimism, he produced the *Maxims* for which he is famous, for example: "Hypocrisy is the tribute vice pays to virtue", and "We are all brave enough to bear other people's misfortunes."

The first fortification here was a wooden structure built by Foucauld, the youngest brother of the Viscount of Limoges, in 980 and named Foucauld's Rock.

During the following century a stone keep with a surrounding wall was constructed and the medieval works were completed by five towers, later raised in height to demonstrate the power of the Rochefoucauld family.

In 1520 François II de la Rochefoucauld and his wife Anne de Polignac transformed the severe fortress into a sophisticated Renaissance residence, albeit retaining the medieval towers, with a chapel, a terrace and 16C façades. They also added galeries and a staircase based on a design by Leonardo da Vinci which had been given to Anne by King François I.

Château de La Rochefoucauld

©Tom Dautlich/iStockphoto.com

Cognac★

Charente

For many years Cognac was a river port on the calm waters of the Charente, exporting salt and, from the 11C, wine.

In 1570, it was one of the four strongholds conceded to the Protestants under the Treaty of St-Germain. Place Francois I, a busy square with an ornamental fountain, links the old part of Cognac, on the slope above the river Charente, with the sprawling modern town.

▶ **Population:** 19 715
◔ **Michelin Map:** 324 I 5
▤ **Info:** 16 r. du 14-juillet.
　℘05 45 82 10 71.
　www.tourism-cognac.com.
◖ **Location:** Cognac is 43km/
　27mi W of Angoulême.
☺ **Don't Miss:** A visit to one
　of the distilleries.

A BIT OF HISTORY

Early in the 17C local vintners started to distil wines that travelled badly, in order to help turnover, reduce excise dues and facilitate storage.

The taste for the product spread to Holland, Scandinavia and Britain, whose long association with brandy is reflected in some of the great names of Cognac, Hine, Martell, Hennessy. A century later it was realised that ageing improved the quality of the spirit.

SIGHTS

Quartier Ancien

The Grande-Rue has a fine half-timbered example dating from the 15C, the Rue Saulnier a number of 16C houses with rusticated stonework and elaborate doorways and windows, while in the Rue de l'Île d'Or is the Hôtel de l'Échevinage (House of the Magistrates), distinguished by its corner niches. The château was rebuilt by John the Good in 1450.

Les Chais

☙ *Guided tours (45min–1hr30min).*
The cellars and storerooms spread out along the riverside quays, near the port and in the suburbs, house the casks in which the slow alchemy between spirit and oak occurs.

Hennessy

1 quai Hennessy. ♿☙*Guided tours Mar–mid Apr, Oct–Dec, Mon–Fri 10–11am, 2–4.30pm; May–Sept daily 10–* 11.30am, 2–5pm. ⏱*Closed 1 May, 25 Dec.* ℘05 45 35 72 68. www.hennessy.com.

The business was founded in 1765 by a captain of Irish origin serving in Louis XV's Irish Brigade. His descendants still head the company today. A Cooperage Museum **(Musée de la Tonnellerie)** is devoted to the manufacture of brandy casks.

Rémy Martin

Domaine de Merpins, rte de Pons. There is a vast array of visiting options; check the website for details. ℘05 45 35 76 66. www.remy.com.

The distillery, founded in 1724, creates its cognac exclusively from the prestigious Grande Champagne and Petite Champagne vintages.

Cognac Production

The production of cognac is the result of a two-stage distillation process, using the special still of the region. The 90 000ha/220 000 acres of vineyards yield a white wine which is light, flowery and quite acid; it takes nine litres of it to make one of brandy. It is then kept in barrels made of porous oak from the Limoges district for at least two and a half years, during which time the brandy absorbs tannin and resins from the wood, and oxygen from the atmosphere, to which it loses 2½ percent of its volume per annum – the "angels' portion", equivalent to 2 million bottles a year!

Martell

pl. Edouard-Martell. Guided tours (1hr) Apr–Oct Mon–Fri 10am–5pm, Sat–Sun and public holidays noon–5pm. Closed Sun in Oct. €7.50. 05 45 36 33 33. www.martell.com.

Founded in 1715, this is the oldest of the famous cognac distilleries. Three rooms of the founder's residence have been restored and convey the working environment of an entrepreneur in the early 18C.

Other cognac houses with cellars open to visitors include **Camus**, **Otard** and **Prince Hubert de Polignac**.

Musée d'Art et d'Histoire

48 bd Denfert-Rochereau. Open Jul–Aug: daily (except Tue) 10am– 6.30pm; May–Jun, Sept: Mon–Fri (except Tue), 11am–1pm, 2–6pm, Sat–Sun 1–6pm; Oct–Apr: daily (except Tue) 2–5.30pm. Closed 1 Jan, 1 Nov, 25 Dec. €4.80. 05 45 32 07 25. www.musees-cognac.fr.

This municipal museum is housed in Hôtel Dupuy d'Angeac, in the grounds of the town hall.

The displays cover the history and civilisation of the Cognac area from the earliest times to the present through maps, plans, prints and photographs; headdresses, bonnets and traditional costumes; glasswork from the collection of Claude Bouiher (who invented a bottle-moulding machine in 1897); fine glazed earthenware; and fossils (mainly shellfish) found in the region's Secondary limestone formations.

A section devoted to archaeology contains prehistoric stone artefacts such as ceramics and a Neolithic dugout canoe, pottery, statuettes and bracelets from the Gallo-Roman period.

The first display in the **basement** is a documentary illustration of the history of brandy. The **first floor** houses paintings, sculpture, furniture and *objets d'art*, both French and foreign, from the 15C to the 19C.

La Rochelle★★★

Charente-Maritime

This lively port is much frequented by artists and tourists. It owes its origin to the fort built in the 11C during the centuries of English rule.

A BIT OF HISTORY

La Rochelle was one of the first places in France where the Reformation took hold. After the St Bartholomew's Day Massacre (1572), La Rochelle became one of the main centres of Protestant resistance.

The religious freedoms secured by the Edict of Nantes in 1598 brought several years of peace. By 1627, however, the town's continued adherence to Protestantism had become intolerable to Richelieu, not least because of its English connection. Richelieu personally directed a siege of La Rochelle that took 15 months to starve the town into submission. 23 000 citizens perished.

▶ **Population:** 78 424
Michelin Map: 324 D 3
Info: 2 quai Georges Simenon, Le Gabut. 05 46 41 14 68. www.holidays-la-rochelle.co.uk.
Location: On the west coast of France, 62km/ 39mi SW of Niort. The town centre lies around the Vieux Port.
Timing: Allow half a day to explore the old port area, but use La Rochelle as a base from which to visit Île de Ré, and the coastline down to Rochefort.
Kids: Aquarium (quai Louis Prunier; www.aquarium-larochelle.com); Musée des Automates (www.musees larochelle.com).

The 5 000 who survived were spared, though a number of their leaders, including the mayor, Jean Guiton, were banished for a period of several months. La Rochelle contributed more than its share to the opening up of the world beyond Europe; in the 15C, it was from here that the first colonists embarked for Canada and Jean de Béthencourt sailed to discover the Canary Islands; in the 16C, La Rochelle's fishing fleet operated in the rich fishing grounds off Newfoundland.

Other explorers to set out from here were René-Robert Cavelier, Sieur de La Salle, who sailed down the Mississippi to the Gulf of Mexico in 1681–2, and René Caillié, the first European to get back from Timbuktu alive.

La Rochelle's shipowners profited from international trade, and above all with the West Indies, where they owned vast plantations; they drew wealth, too, from the triangular trade involving selling cloth to Africa, transporting African slaves to the Americas, and bringing American products to Europe.

VISIT
Vieux Port★★
The old port was originally laid out by Eleanor of Aquitaine; its entrance is guarded by two towers, probably built by the English in the 14C and once forming part of the town's ring of fortifications.

La Tour St Nicolas★ (open daily; closed 1 Jan, 1 May and 25 Dec; €4.60, or €10 ticket combined with the Tour de la Chaine and Tour de la Lanterne; 05 46 34 11 81)
Situated to the east has rested on its foundation of oak piles for six centuries; 42m/137.8ft high and with immensely thick walls, it is a fortress in its own right.

Vieux Ville ★★
The 18C **Porte de la Grosse-Horloge★** leads into the Old Town.
As well as timber-framed medieval houses and fine Renaissance residences, there are substantial 18C stone townhouses adorned with astonishing gargoyles.

The splendid **Hôtel de Ville★**, built in Tuscan style, has a courtyard **façade★** of 1606, with an arcaded gallery.

ADDITIONAL SIGHTS
Museum d'Histoire Naturelle★★ (28 r. Albert 1er)
Musée du Nouveau-Monde★
Musée des Beaux-Arts (10 r. Fleuriau)
Musée d'Orbigny-Bernon★ (2 r. Saint-Côme) – local history, ceramics
Tour de la Lanterne★ (esplanade St Jean d'Acre)
Musée des Automates★ (r. La Désirée) – automatic figures in lifelike set-pieces
Parc Charruyer★ (av. Maurice Demas).

EXCURSIONS
Île de Ré★
The island, which is also known as White Island and has been linked to the mainland by a viaduct since 1988, is a popular resort. Part of the salt marshes to the north has been set aside as a bird sanctuary.

Marais Poitevin★
 The region lies N and NE of La Rochelle.
The vast Poitou marshlands occupy what was once a wide bay, the Golfe du Poitou. It is now a conservation area. Under clear, luminous skies, its meadows are bordered by slender poplar and willow. The boats of the marshlanders glide on a network of waterways.

Les Sables-d'Olonne
 Les Sables-d'Olonne stretches between a small port and an immense beach of fine sand running for more than 3km/2mi at the foot of the Remblai (an embankment-promenade).
 1 promenade Joffre, Les Sables-d'Olonne. 02 51 96 85 85. www.ot-lessablesdolonne.fr.
 There are a number of car parks along the seafront, as well as in the town centre.
Les Sables-d'Olonne is an important seaside resort on the Côte de la Lumière, built on the sands of what was once an offshore bar. Port Olona is the starting

point for the round-the-world yacht race held every four years, known as the "Vendée Globe" – a tough challenge for single-handed sailing boats with no ports of call allowed and no help on the way (www.vendeeglobe.org).

Le Remblai★

This embankment was built in the 18C to protect the town from the incursions of the sea. Today the fine promenade along its top is bordered by shops, hotels, cafés and luxury apartment blocks with splendid views of the beach and the bay. At the western extremity of Le Remblai is the municipal swimming pool and one of the casinos. Behind the modern blocks, the narrow streets of the old town beckon.

La Corniche

This southerly prolongation of Le Remblai leads to the new residential district of La Rudelière. After 3km/2mi the clifftop route arrives at **Le Puits d'Enfer** (Hell's Well) – a narrow and impressive cleft in the rock, where the sea foams and thrashes.

♞♟ Parc Zoologique

rte du Tour de France. ♿🕐Open daily 7 Feb–3 Apr and 1–24 Oct 1.30–6.30pm; 4 Apr–30 Sept 9.30am–7pm. ✆€13 (child €8). ☎02 51 95 14 10. www.zoo-des-sables.com.
In this pleasantly laid out "green belt" environment, visitors can observe a variety of wildlife including camels, llamas, kangaroos, monkeys and rare birds.

Royan☖☖☖

▶ Royan is located on the Atlantic Coast, 35km/22mi SW of Saintes.
🏛Palais des Congrès, Royan. ☎05 46 23 00 00. www.royan-tourisme.com.
🅿There are a number of car parks along the seafront, as well as in the town centre.
The town of Royan, capital of the Côte de Beauté, was rebuilt after the bombardments that flattened it in 1945. Today it has once more found the popularity and prosperity that characterised it at the end of the 19C. Royan is ideally

located on a headland at the entrance to the Gironde. At the western end of the seafront is the port. This comprises a dock for trawlers and the sardine boats, a marina for yachts and cruisers, and a tidal basin with the jetty from which the ferry to Pointe de Grave leaves.
Boat trips are organised in summer, especially out to Cordouan lighthouse.
Beaches of fine sand curve enticingly at the inner end of the town's four bays indenting the coastline. The largest cove is warm and sheltered from the wind. Apart from the natural beauty of the area and a particularly mild climate, Royan also benefits from a seaweed-cure centre and numerous other attractions, hence its popularity.

Église Notre-Dame★

1 r. de Foncillon. ☎05 46 23 99 77. www.notre-dame-royan.com.
The church (reinforced concrete coated with resin to protect it from wind erosion) was built between 1955 and 1958 to plans by architects Guillaume Gillet and Jean-Albert Hébrard.

♞♟ Les Jardins du Monde★

5 av. des Fleurs-de-la-Paix. ♿🕐Open daily Jul–Aug 10am–8pm; Feb–Jun and Sept–Dec 10am–6pm (last entry 1hr before closing). ✆€9 (child €6). ☎05 46 38 89 11.
On the banks of the marais de Pousseau, in an area which has been drained since the war, this 7.5ha/18.5-acre floral garden, open since 2002, is enshrined within a high metallic structure and three large steel sails. The vast semicircular entrance is followed by a large tropical greenhouse which shelters a beautiful **collection of orchids**★.
The atmosphere changes completely as you reach the bonsai pavilion where you can admire rare specimens, which are sometimes more than centuries old. Then, in the open air, the gardens offer various styles: the Japanese Zen garden, the Louisiana forest, the marsh house, the labyrinth of mist (bamboo forest).
☺The park can partly be visited by electrical boat: a 20min tour will enable you to cross the marsh canals and give

you access to the swamp and the bamboo forest. You will also find a shop, a restaurant and activities for children.

👥 Zoo de la Palmyre ★★★

▶*The zoo is situated in the middle of the Forêt de La Palmyre, 15km/9mi NW of Royan.*

♿🕐*Open daily Apr–Sept 9am–7pm; Oct–Mar 9am–6pm; Sea lion and parrot shows Apr–Oct.* 🎫*€14 (child €10).* 📞*08 92 68 18 48. www.zoo-palmyre.fr.*

This attractive 14ha/33-acre zoo is one of the most visited in France. Every year 250t of fodder, 180t of fruit and vegetables, 70t of straw, 50t of meat, 20t of fish, 30t of mixed food and 10t of grain support the animals. The zoo breeds species threatened with extinction (such as elephants and cheetahs); the lion cub nursery brings pleasure to young and old alike.

In order to avoid missing something, it is advisable to follow the marked 4km/2.5mi trail. All along the way, panels explain the habits and characteristics of the various species.

More than 1 600 animals from every corner of the globe are scattered throughout the pine forest with its numerous lakes and hills, in areas similar to their natural habitat.

Animals demonstrate their amazing agility, with performing wild birds, such as parrots and cockatoos, riding bicycles, driving cars and roller-skating.

ADDRESSES

🛏 STAY

😐🛏🛏🛏 **Hôtel les Brises** – *chemin digue Richelieu (av. P.-Vincent).* 📞*05 46 43 89 37. www.hotellesbrises.com. 48rms.* 🍽 *€12.* This 1960s hotel is well situated and has lovely views.

😐🛏🛏🛏 **Hôtel Champlain** – *30 r. Rambaud.* 📞*05 46 41 23 99. www.hotel champlain.com. 36rms.* 🍽 *€12.* On a busy street near the historic district, this 16C convent features a discreet, pleasant garden – a marvellous place to unwind after a busy day in town.

😐🛏🛏🛏 **Hôtel de la Monnaie** – *3 r. de la Monnaie.* 📞*05 46 50 65 65. 35rms. www.hotel-monnaie.com.* 🍽 *€13.* Right behind the Tour de la Lanterne, this splendid 17C mansion, where coins used to be made, is an agreeable address.

🍴 EAT

😐🛏 **André** – *pl. de la Chaîne.* 📞*05 46 41 28 24.* A visit to La Rochelle is not complete without a meal at André! On the old docks, facing the Tour de la Chaîne, this enormous restaurant comprises a dozen bistro-style dining rooms where customers sit elbow to elbow to feast on seafood.

😐🛏 **Le Boute-en-Train** – *7 r. des Bonnes-Femmes.* 📞*05 46 41 73 74. Closed Sun, Mon.* Near the markets, this charming restaurant serves a variety of quiches and food fresh from the marketplace.

😐🛏 **À Côté de chez Fred** – *32–34 r. St-Nicolas. Closed Sun, Mon.* 📞*05 46 41 65 76. Reservations recommended.* This little restaurant gets its provisions from its neighbour and sister… the fishmonger.

😐🛏 **Le Mistral** *10 pl. Coureauleurs, in the Le Gabut district.* 📞*05 46 41 24 42. Closed Sun.* This wood-clad house is located a stone's throw from the tourist office.

😐🛏 **Le Petit Rochelais** – *25 r. St-Jean-du-Pérot. Closed Sun.* 📞*05 46 41 28 43.* An inviting atmosphere complements the traditional French cuisine.

🍷 BARS / 🍴 CAFÉS

Café de la Paix – *54 r. Chaudrier.* 📞*05 46 41 39 79.* Behind its carved wood façade, this big café was a hospital in 1709, a theatre during the Revolution and since 1900 a café popular with visiting artists such as Colette.

Cave de la Guignette – *8 r. St-Nicolas.* 📞*05 46 41 05 75.* Try the house speciality, *Guignette*, an aperitif made of wine and fruit.

Rochefort★★

Charente-Maritime

Rochefort takes pride in an illustrious maritime past. There is still something exotic in the air around the Arsenal, where great expeditions were masterminded.

A BIT OF HISTORY

In 1665, Colbert chose a site 22km/13.7mi up the River Charente and commissioned Vauban to extend the defences of the existing fort. Though the place had few natural advantages as a port, the presence of easily fortifiable islands and promontories facilitated the task.

Seven years later, the work, which included a harbour for the navy, was complete, and by 1690 Rochefort rivalled the naval bases of Toulon and Brest. The increasing draught of modern vessels led to the harbour's obsolescence and it closed in 1926.

VISIT

Rochefort's history has left many richly ornamented houses; the former rope-walk (**corderie★★**), 374m/1 200ft long; the great timber hall built by naval carpenters (now a covered market and conference centre); and the Sun Gateway *(Porte du Soleil)*, which formed the entrance to Colbert's **Arsenal**. Admirers of the writer Pierre Loti (1850–1923), a native of Rochefort and lover of the exotic, should pause at the **Maison de Pierre Loti★** *(🐾 guided tours (45min); 🎟€7.65)*, now a museum evocative of his travels.

Corderie Royale

©alexandre neumann/Bigstockphoto.com

▶ **Population:** 26 455
🧭 **Michelin Map:** 324 E 4
Info: Avenue Sadi-Carnot.
🕿 05 46 99 08 60.
www.paysrochefortais-tourisme.com.
▶ **Location:** Rochefort is 38km/23.5mi SE of La Rochelle.
🖐 **Don't Miss:** The Arsenal district.

ADDITIONAL SIGHTS

Musée de l'Ancienne Ecole de Médecine Navale★
(25 r. de l'Admiral Meyer)
Musée d'Art et d'Histoire★
(63 av. Charles de Gaulle).

EXCURSIONS

Aulnay★★

▶ *The village of Aulnay sits 58km/36mi inland from Rochefort.*
🛈 *290 av. de l'Église.* 🕿 *05 46 33 14 44.*
Originally in the province of Poitiers, Aulnay was apportioned to Saintonge when France was divided into *départements* by the Constituent Assembly on 22 December 1789.

It is known for its 12C Romanesque **Église St-Pierre★★** on rue Haute de l'Église which stands among the cypresses of its ancient burial ground with its Gothic Hosanna Cross. It was built between 1140 and 1170 at a time when Eleanor of Aquitaine ruled southwestern France as queen first to Louis VII, then to Henry II of England.

Its structure, notably its tribuneless triple nave, is essentially in the Romanesque style typical of the Poitou area, while its sculpture is characteristic of Saintonge.

Saintes★★

▶ *Saintes is mid-way between Cognac and Royan, 45km/28mi from Rochefort.*
🛈 *62 cours National.* 🕿 *05 46 74 23 82.*
www.ot-saintes.fr.
With its plane trees, white houses and red-tiled roofs, Saintes has a curiously Mediterranean feel. This pleasant

regional capital on the River Charente has a rich cultural and historical heritage. Saintes was already a regional capital in Roman times, with a bridge over the Charente aligned on today's r. Victor-Hugo.

In the Middle Ages, the town was an important stop on the pilgrims' route to Santiago de Compostela.

Two great religious establishments developed on its outskirts: St-Eutrope on the west bank of the river, the Abbey for Women *(Abbaye aux Dames)* on the east bank. The historic core of the town has been restored and pedestrianised.

The Arena and the Arch of Germanicus★

The arch was built in AD 19 at a point on the east bank of the Charente where the roads from Poitiers and Limoges converged on the Roman bridge.

An archaeological museum houses objects saved when the ruins of the Roman city were demolished. To the

---

Pierre Loti

The author Pierre Loti (real name Julien Viaud) was born in Rochefort at No 141 of the street that now bears his nom-de-plume. Loti, a much-travelled naval officer, accomplished sportsman and something of a dandy with a distinguished bearing, was also a novelist of great sensitivity and an exceptional storyteller. Inspired by his voyages to exotic destinations, he wrote *Pêcheur d'Islande* (Iceland Fisherman), *Aziyadé, Ramuntcho* and *Madame Chrysanthème*, books that were instrumental in his acceptance as a member of the élite Académie Française at the young age of 41.

---

west, on the slopes of the west bank of the river, is an amphitheatre **(arènes★)**, one of the oldest (1C AD) in the Roman world.

Poitiers★★

Vienne

Key events in France's history have occurred in and around this city and the medieval districts in its heart have much of interest to sightseers.

A BIT OF HISTORY

Poitiers was established in Gallo-Roman times on the promontory overlooking a bend in the River Clain, a site which commanded the "Gate of Poitou", the almost imperceptible rise in the land some 30km/18.6mi south, which divides the Paris Basin from Aquitaine. It was here in 732 that Charles Martel (688–741) won a great victory against invading Arab forces at **Moussais-la-Bataille** on the banks of the Clain, thereby saving Europe from Islamic rule.

Poitiers was under English domination twice: in the 12C and the 14C. On 19 September 1356, a famous episode in the Hundred Years' War took place at **Nouaillé-Maupertuis** on the steep

- ▶ **Population:** 91 965
- ⏲ **Michelin Map:** 322 H-I 5
- 🛈 **Info:** 45 pl. Charles-de-Gaulle. ☏05 49 41 21 24. www.ot-poitiers.fr.
- ◔ **Location:** The city is 102km/64mi S of Tours. The old town centre sits on a promontory almost surrounded by the rivers Boivre and Clain.
- 👪 **Kids:** 12km/7.4mi from Poitiers, the science-themed leisure park Futuroscope is a must.

---

banks of the River Miosson. Jean II le Bon (the Good) was fighting with the French forces, who were defeated. The French king surrendered and was taken to London, where he remained in comfortable exile. The result was the signing four years later of the Treaty of Brétigny under which the French agreed to give

Poitiers to the English. In 1372, Bertrand du Guesclin retook the town, presenting it to the king's representative, Duke Jean de Berry, brother of Charles V.

In 1418, the fleeing Charles VII set up his court and parliament here, and four years later he was proclaimed king. In March 1429, in the Gothic Great Hall (**Grande Salle**★) of Poitiers' recently rebuilt Law Courts (**Palais de Justice**), Joan of Arc was subjected to a humiliating investigation by an ecclesiastical commission.

In the 16C the city played host to Rabelais, then Calvin and the writers of the Pléiade. In 1569, the place was besieged for seven weeks by a Protestant army under Coligny. In the 18C, under the rule of the centrally appointed governors known as Intendants, Poitiers became a tranquil provincial capital.

SIGHTS
Baptistère St-Jean★
r. Jean Jaurés. Open varying hours, call ahead. 05 49 41 21 24.

This is one of France's most venerable Christian buildings. It goes back to the 4C, when St Hilary was elected Bishop of Poitiers, 27 years after the Edict of Constantine. Hilary played a leading role in the conversion of Gaul.

The narthex and baptistery proper have the characteristic architecture of 4C Gaul. The narthex was restored in the 10C and is polygonal in form; there are panels of Roman brickwork under its windows, and beneath the gables are strange pilasters with capitals carved in low relief.

Inside are marble columns and arcades with richly decorated capitals. Right up until the 17C, the octagonal pool was the city's sole place of baptism, originally by total immersion.

Église St-Hilaire-le-Grand★★
r. du Doyenne.

This great Romanesque edifice was built in 1049; it was an important staging-post on the pilgrimage route to Santiago de Compostela and in architectural terms is Poitiers' most interesting church.

In 1100, it was given stone vaults to replace the original wooden roof, which had been destroyed by fire.

The distance it was possible to span in stone was naturally shorter than in timber, and the designer thus had to reduce the width of the nave and increase the number of aisles; he set up a double row of columns linked ingeniously with the original walls and carrying a series of domes.

Église Notre-Dame-la-Grande★★
pl. Charles-de-Gaulle.

The church is a good example of the local version of the Romanesque style as it had developed around 1140. Its harmonious appearance is due to the great height of its rib-vaulted aisles. It has a splendid 12C west **front**★★★, richly decorated with sculpture. Six round columns hold up the choir vault, which was painted in the 12C with a fresco depicting the Virgin in Majesty and Christ in Glory.

Palais de Justice
pl. Alphonse-Petit. Open Mon–Fri 8.45am–noon, 1.45–5.30pm. Closed public holidays. No charge. 05 49 50 22 00.

The **Grande Salle**★ of Poitiers' recently rebuilt Law Courts was where Joan of Arc was questioned about her visions and her instructions from God.

The vast hall, scene of solemn audiences, great trials and the sessions of the Provincial Estates, was built under the Plantagenets and restored by Jean de Berry.

ADDITIONAL SIGHTS
Cathédrale Saint-Pierre★
r. de la Cathédrale. Open daily summer 8am–7pm, winter 8am–6pm. 05 49 41 21 24.

St Peter's Cathedral was begun at the end of the 12C and almost completed by the end of the 14C – the date of its consecration; it is striking for its huge dimensions.

Exterior – The wide west front, with its rose window and three 13C doorways, is flanked by two asymmetric towers. That on the left *(northern)* side, supported by a series of engaged colonnettes, retains an octagonal storey topped by a balustrade.

The tympana of the doorways are carved with fascinating sculptures, among them the *Crowning of the Virgin (to the left)*; the dead hurrying from their graves and the heavenly elect separated from the damned delivered to Leviathan *(in the centre)*; the teaching of St Thomas, patron of stone-carvers, the miraculous building of a mystical palace for the King of India *(to the right)*.

Note on the way around the massive strength of the buttresses and the absence of flying buttresses. At the far end of the building the dizzy height (49m/161ft) of the flat **east end** can be appreciated – especially as this is emphasised by a falling away of the land.

Interior – On entering, visitors are struck by the sheer power of the architecture: the wide shell of the cathedral is divided into three aisles of almost equal height, and the impression of a perspective soaring away towards the east is accentuated by a progressive narrowing of the aisles and a lowering of the central vault from the chancel onwards. Twenty-four domed rib vaults – a Plantagenet influence – crown the eight spans of each of the three aisles. Despite its flat exterior, the east end is hollowed out enough to form three apsidal chapels. A cornice embellished with historiated modillions supports a narrow gallery running around the walls above a series of blind arcades.

Among the stained-glass windows at the far east end is a late 12C representation of the *Crucifixion* showing a radiant Christ flanked by the Virgin and St John. Above and below this are: the Apostles, with their faces raised towards a *Christ in Glory*, set in a mandorla; the *Crucifixion of St Peter* and the *Beheading of St Paul*. The **choir stalls**★, dating from the 13C, are said to be the oldest in France. The carved corner-pieces represent the Virgin and Child, angels carrying crowns and the architect at work.

The 18C organ, built by François-Henri Clicquot (1732–90), member of a celebrated dynasty of organ-makers working in Reims and Paris in the 17C and 18C, is located on the inner side of the west front, within a beautiful shell-shaped loft with basket-handled arching.

Musée Ste-Croix★★

3 bis r. Jean Jaures. ○*Open Oct–May: Tue–Fri 10am–noon, 1.15-5pm, Sat–Sun 2–6pm; Jun–Sept: Tue 10am–noon, 1.15–8pm, Wed–Fri 10am–noon, 1.15–6pm, Sat-Sun 10am–noon, 2–6pm.* ○*Closed public holidays.* ◎€4. ℘05 49 41 07 53. www.musees-poitiers.org.

The museum is housed in a modern building standing on the site of the former Holy Cross Abbey (Abbaye Ste-Croix).

Archaeology – *Basement: access down a staircase at the far end of the first hall.* The collections here concentrate on the Poitou of prehistory to medieval times. The chronology of the Palaeolithic Era is set out, with displays of flint implements, tools and other items discovered during digs (fragments of a bronze roasting spit from the 7C BC, an ingot of pure copper, objects buried c 700 BC). A number of Gallo-Roman finds are presented against a backdrop of the remains of antique walls: inscriptions, fragments of columns, bas-relief sculptures and statues, among them the head of a man and a famous **Minerva** in white marble (1C AD) unearthed in Poitiers. Fine funerary stones from Civaux, including Man as a Child, are also on show.

The rest of the collections are displayed in a number of rooms on several different levels linked by stairways or steps.

Painting – The staircase at the end of the archaeology gallery leads to a fine series of paintings from Abbaye Ste-Croix by the Dutch painter Nicolas Van der Maes depicting the 17C *Mysteries of the Life of Christ*.

Other paintings include works from the **late 18C:** the local artist J A Pajou *(Oedipus cursing Polynices)*, and Géricault's circle *(Masculine Anatomy)*. The **19C** is represented by Alfred de Curzon, a local painter *(The Convent Garden)*,

Octave Penguilly-l'Haridan (*The Parade of Pierrot*), Charles Le Brun (*Portrait of Germaine Pichot*) and Léopold Burthe (*Ophelia*). A number of works by **Orientalists** are grouped together, they include: *Jewish Fête in Tangier* by Alfred Dehodencq, *Fantasia* by Eugène Fromentin and *A Street in Constantinople* by André Brouillet.

Église Ste-Radegonde★

1 r. Ste-Croix. ◷*Open daily 8.30am–6pm, religious festivals 8.30am–7pm.* ℘*05 49 41 21 24.*

This former collegiate church was founded around AD 552 by Radegund with the idea that it would eventually become the last resting place of her nuns from Holy Cross Abbey. The church is characterised by a Romanesque apse and a belfry-porch which stand at opposite ends of a nave in the style known as Angevin Gothic.

EXCURSIONS
🎢 Futuroscope★★

◔ *The Park is on the northern outskirts of Poitiers.* ◷*Open throughout the year, but check website for exact details.* ◉*€36 (child €27).* ⬛ *Futuroscope Destination, BP 3030, 86130 Jaunay-Clan.* ℘*05 49 49 11 12. www.futuroscope.com/eng.*

This vast, science-oriented leisure park offers a range of exciting shows, games and entertainments based on the theme of the screen image. There are restaurants, shops, and "experiences" such as "fly me to the moon" and "the future is wild".

Numerous attractions include **Lac enchanté** and its **Théâtre Alphanumérique** which present hi-tech productions. **Kinémax, Omnimax, Solido, Showscan** and **Imax 3D** show films using 3D films, hemispherical cinema, etc.). **Images-Studio★★★**, a vast glass structure, shows what goes on behind the scenes.

St-Savin★★

◔ *The abbey is on the west bank of the River Gartemps, 42km/26mi E of Poitiers.*

⬛*Place Peyramale, Lourdes.* ℘*05 62 42 7 40. www.lourdes-infotourisme.com.*

St-Savin lies among the pasturelands of the eastern border of the old province of Poitou, an area of sandy clay soils known as Les Brandes. Its former abbey church still draws visitors in spite of the depredations of the centuries.

L'Abbatiale★★

1 pl. du Castet. ◷*Open all day. Use discretion in visiting during religious services.* ☞*Guided tours (1hr15min plus 30min for the film); call in advance.* ◷*Closed Jan, 11 Nov, 25 and 31 Dec.* ◉*€6.* ℘*05 62 97 02 23.*

The abbey church was mostly built in the space of 50 years, between 1040 and 1090. The fame of St-Savin rests on its Romanesque **murals★★★**, the finest in the whole of France. They seem to have been painted around 1100 by a single team of artists over a period of only three to four years.

ADDRESSES

🛏 STAY

🍽 **Chambre d'hôte Château de Vaumoret** – *r. du Breuil Mingot. 10km/6.2mi NE of Poitiers. Take the D3 towards La Roche-Posay, then the D 18 to Sèvres-Anxaumont.* ℘ *05 49 61 32 11. 3rms.* Although only a short distance from Poitiers, this B&B is surrounded by peaceful countryside. Housed in a delightful 17C château, this is the perfect place to unwind.

🍽 **Hôtel Gibautel** – *rte de Nouaillé.* ℘*05 49 46 16 16. 36rms.* This modern hotel situated opposite a clinic on the outskirts of Poitiers has small, modern and well-equipped rooms.

🍽 **Hôtel Château de Périgny** – *Périgny, 86190 Vouillé. 17km/12mi NW of Poitiers via the N 149 and a secondary road.* ℘*05 49 51 80 43. 39rms.* Right in the middle of a park, this 15C château is a haven of peace and tranquillity. The rooms are furnished in period or modern style; those in the annexe are a little more basic. Attractive patio-terrace. Contemporary cuisine.

♀/EAT

ST-BENOÎT

🍽️🍽️🍽️ **Le Chalet de Venise** – *6 r. du square (le bourg). ℘05 49 88 45 07.* This charming restaurant is situated just outside Poitiers in the village of St-Benoît.

🍽️🍽️🍽️ **L'Orée des Bois** – *13 r. Naintré. ℘05 49 57 11 44. http://oreedesbois. objectis.net. Closed Sun (Nov–Apr) and Mon.* This building, covered in Virginia creeper, is a restful place for a meal away from the bustle of the city centre. There are two country-style dining rooms, one with a fireplace. Traditional local fare.

POITIERS

🍽️🍽️ **Les Bons Enfants** – *11 bis r. Cloche-Perse. ℘ 05 49 41 49 82. Closed Sun eve and Mon.* Amidst the many schools of this neighbourhood, this little restaurant with a green façade boasts a large painting of a group of late 19C schoolchildren. The restaurant specialises in regional cuisine.

🍽️🍽️ **Maxime** – *4 r. St-Nicholas. ℘05 49 41 09 55. Closed Sat (except eve Nov–Feb) and Sun.* Situated near the Musée de Chièvres in a quiet street in the city centre, this restaurant serves traditional French cuisine. Attractive mix of red and yellow hues in the contemporary-style dining room.

🍽️🍽️🍽️ **Poitevin** – *76 r. Carnot. ℘05 49 88 35 04. Closed Sun eve.* The accent is on traditional regional cuisine in this busy restaurant which is popular with locals. Sample specialities such as *mouclade charentaise* or *farci poitevin* in one of four comfortable contemporary-style dining rooms.

MARKET

The main food market takes place *(Mon–Sat)* in the market hall near Église Notre-Dame-la-Grande. There is an excellent choice of fruit and vegetables, fish, meat, cheese and bread.

Le Puy du Fou★★★

Vendeé

This huge theme park, based around a real château and its grounds, takes visitors on an adventure through 2 000 years of Vendean history. On summer evenings its château sparkles under the lights of a famous *Son et Lumière*; by day the museum, Écomusée de la Vendée★★, evokes the past of the Vendée region, while various attractions along a trail (Grand Parcours★★) lure visitors into the 12ha/29.6 acres of grounds. Puy du Fou is Latin for "beech hill".

VISIT

👥 Grand Parc★★

🕐 *Opening times vary, call ahead. ℘02 51 64 11 11. 🎫Admission fees vary during the year.*

Puy du Fou is a multi-attraction theme park offering ongoing entertainment throughout the day and amazing spectacles in the evening. Even if all you do is follow the paths around lakes

♿	**Michelin Map:** 316 K 6
🅸	**Info:** 30 r. Georges Clemenceau, BP 25, 85 590 Les Epesses. ℘0820 09 10 10. www.puydufou.com.
▶	**Location:** 122km/76mi NW of Poitiers, near Cholet.
🕐	**Timing:** There is a hotel and restaurant on the site, ideal for an unhurried visit including the evening show.

and through lovely woodland, visiting the medieval villages and the animal parks, the day will fly by. It is likely that the original **castle**, built in the 15C and 16C, was never completed; it was in any case partly destroyed during the Wars of the Vendée.

There remains a fine late Renaissance pavilion at the end of the courtyard, preceded by a peristyle with engaged Ionic columns. This now serves as an entrance. The left wing of the château is built over a long gallery.

Cinéscénie

©Puy du fou®

Cinéscénie★★★

🕐 *Show lasts 1hr 45min. Fri and Sat 10pm, but check ahead. Reservations necessary.* 📞*02 51 64 11 11.*

The terrace below the rear façade of the château, together with the ornamental lake below it, makes an agreeable background for the spectacular *"Cinéscénie"* in which "Jacques Maupillier, peasant of the Vendée" directs a company of 700 actors and 50 horsemen in a dazzling show.

The history of the Vendée is relived with the help of an impressive array of special effects, fountains, fireworks, laser and other lighting displays.

Biarritz★★★
Pyrénées-Atlantiques

With its splendid beaches of fine sand and high-quality facilities, golf courses and luxury hotels, this Basque Coast resort enjoys an international reputation. Biarritz is Europe's surfing capital and teems with thousands of visitors coming to ride the waves year-round.

A BIT OF HISTORY

Over a century ago, Biarritz was a place of no particular distinction, its beaches attracting people from nearby Bayonne. Fame came suddenly, with the visits of Empress Eugénie and Napoleon III, followed by many of the illustrious names of the period. Queen Victoria was here in 1889, and after 1906 Biarritz became a favourite of Edward VII.

Now enhanced by modernisation, Biarritz continues to offer pleasures which

- ▶ **Population:** 26 929
- **Michelin Map:** 324 C-D 2
- **Info:** 1 Square d'Ixelles. 📞05 59 22 37 00. www.biarritz.fr.
- ▶ **Location:** Biarritz lies on the Atlantic coast, 32km/20mi N of the Spanish border.
- **Don't Miss:** The view of La Perspective, a promenade overlooking Plage des Basques, is one of the highlights of Biarritz.
- **Kids:** Musée de la Mer.

never pall; its beaches, promenades and gardens to either side of the rocky promontory of the Plateau de l'Atalaye remain as attractive as ever. The orientation of the beaches also produces rollers that attract surfers.

VISIT
Promenades
Pleasantly shaded and landscaped streets lead from the main beach (*Grande Plage*) to the Virgin's Rock (**Rocher de la Vierge★**).

To the south is the viewpoint (Perspective de la Côte des Basques) offering an uninterrupted **view★★** towards the mountain peaks of the Basque Country.

👥 Musée de la Mer
Plateau de l'Atalaye, Biarritz. 🕐*Open Jul–Aug: 9.30am–midnight; rest of the year 9.30am–7pm.* 🕐*Closed Mon in Nov–Mar.* 👁8€ *(child €5.50).* 𝄐*05 59 22 33 34. www.museedelamer.com.*

A remarkable aquarium, set on **Rocher de la Vierge★**, this place also has an outdoor pool on the top floor with seals that perform for curious visitors! A great place for all the family.

EXCURSIONS
Bayonne★★
Biarritz, Anglet and Bayonne merge to form a single urban area of which Bayonne, with its busy quaysides and old streets, is the commercial centre. Its harbour on the estuary of the Adour handles maize, sulphur and chemical products. The picturesque Rue du Pont-Neuf is flanked by arcades and tall houses.

Musée Bonnat★★
5 r. Jacques, Laffitte, Bayonne. ♿🕐*Open Nov–Apr Wed–Mon 10am–12.30pm, 2–6pm; May–Oct Wed–Mon 10am–6.30pm.* 🕐*Closed public holidays.* 👁€5.50. 𝄐*05 59 59 08 52. www.museebonnat.bayonne.fr.*

This beautiful building houses works by the artist and collector, Léon Bonnat, as well as artwork and sculptures by artists including Degas and Rubens.

Musée Basque★★
37 quai des Corsaires, Bayonne. 🕐*Open Jul–Aug 10am–6.30pm; rest of the year Tue–Sun 10am–6.30pm, 2–6pm, Wed 6.30–9.30pm.* 🕐*Closed public holidays.* 👁€5.50. 𝄐*05 59 59 08 98. www.musee-basque.com.*

One of the finest regional ethnographic museums in France and probably the best on Basque ethnography. Exhibits cover agriculture, seafaring and *pelota* – a ball game.

Cathédrale Sainte-Marie de Bayonne★
r. Notre-Dame. 🕐*Open 7am–12.30pm, 3–7pm.* 𝄐*05 59 59 17 82. http://moulian.free.fr.*

Set in the historic quarter of Bayonne, this Gothic-style building was built in 13–17C. The present cathedral replaced a Romanesque one destroyed by fire in 1258 and again in 1310. Admire the **cloisters★**.

Grande Plage, Biarritz

Y. Kanazawa/MICHELIN

Route Impériale des Cimes★

◗ *Bayonne to Hasparren 25km/15.5mi.*
This section of Napoleon I's scenic highway was part of an overall project to link Bayonne with St-Jean-Pied-de-Port for strategic reasons. It follows a highly sinuous alignment and affords fine **views**★ of the Basque coast and countryside.

Bidart⌂

◗ *6km/3.7mi S.*
The small resort of Bidart, halfway between Biarritz and St-Jean-de-Luz, is built at the highest point on the Basque coastline, on the edge of a cliff.
From Chapelle Ste-Madeleine *(accessible from r. de la Madeleine)*, the clifftop **view**★ looks over the Jaizkibel (a promontory closing off the Fontarabia natural harbour), the Trois Couronnes and La Rhune.
The charming **place centrale** is framed by the church, the pelota *(jai alai)* fronton and the town hall. Local pelota matches and competitions are always watched by enthusiastic crowds. **Rue de la Grande-Plage** and **promenade de la Mer** lead steeply down to the beach.

ADDRESSES

☜ STAY

◛◛ **Hôtel Atalaye** – *6 r. des Goëlands, Plateau de l'Atalaye.* ✆*05 59 24 06 76. www.hotelatalaye.com.* ⌁*€6.50. 24rms. Closed 15 Nov–18 Dec.* This imposing villa owes its name to the superb Atalaye plateau overlooking the Atlantic Ocean. The rooms with a sea view are especially attractive. Free parking nearby (Oct–mid-Jun).

◛◛ **Hôtel Gardenia** – *19 av. Carnot.* ✆*05 59 24 10 46. www.hotel-gardenia.com. 19rms.* ⌁*€7. Closed Dec–Feb.* This central hotel with a pink façade has all the charm of a private home. Its quiet, attractive rooms are regularly redecorated.

◛◛◛ **Hôtel Maïtagaria** – *34 av. Carnot.* ✆*05 59 24 26 65. www.hotel-maitagaria. com. 16rms.* ⌁*€8.50.* A warm, friendly reception in this little hotel near the garden, just 500m/550yd from the beach.

The rooms, of varying sizes, are bright and functional. Small, flower-filled garden at the back.

◛◛◛ **Le Petit Hôtel** – *11 r. Gardères.* ✆*05 59 24 87 00. www.petithotel-biarritz.com. 12rms.* ⌁*€6. Closed fortnight in Nov and Feb.* This appealing hotel is ideally located for exploring the town or spending time on the beach. Its soundproofed rooms have been renovated in tones of blue or yellow; all have internet access.

◛◛◛◛ **Brit Hotel Marbella** – *11 r. du Port Vieux.* ✆*05 59 24 04 06. www.hotel-marbella.fr. 29rms.* ⌁*€10. Restaurant*◛◛◛. A five-minute walk from the beaches and la Rocher de la Vierge in the old harbour district, this hotel offers bright rooms with a sea view, and air conditioning. The hotel restaurant serves Basque and Spanish cuisine within a rustic ambience.

☍/EAT

◛◛ **La Goélette** – *4 r. du Port-Vieux.* ✆*05 59 24 84 65.* Take a break from shopping and treat yourself to a meal in this pleasant restaurant. Cuisine with an accent on fish and salads.

◛◛ **Le Clos Basque** – *12 r. Louis-Barthou.* ✆*05 59 24 24 96. Closed a fortnight in Feb and Jun, Sun eve (Sept–Jun), Mon.* Excellent local cuisine and a warm, friendly atmosphere mean that there's rarely a spare table in this popular restaurant.

◛◛ **La Pizzeria des Arceaux** – *20 av. Édouard VII.* ✆*05 59 24 11 47. www. la-pizzeria-des-arceaux.com. Closed Mon, Tue lunch.* This lively pizzeria just a stone's throw from the city hall is particularly popular with a young, trendy crowd.

◛◛◛◛ **Chez Albert** – *r. du Port Vieux.* ✆*05 59 24 43 84. www.chezalbert.fr. Closed Wed (Sept–Jun).* Situated close to the church of Saint Eugénie, this busy fish and seafood restaurant affords fine views over the fishing port.

◛◛◛◛ **Plaisir des Mets** – *5 r. Centre.* ✆*05 59 24 34 66. Closed Tue eve, Wed–Thu.* This attractive small restaurant is situated near the market hall, just a short stroll from the sea. The modern cuisine highlights seasonal and regional produce. Light, modern décor.

🍷 BARS AND CAFÉS

L'Impérial (Hôtel du Palais) –
*1 av. de l'Impératrice. ☎05 59 41 64 00.
www.hotel-du-palais.com.* "La Villa
Eugénie", the scene of Napoleon III's love
affair with the Empress Eugénie, became
the majestic Hôtel du Palais in 1893. E
njoy a glass of champagne and savour
the atmosphere in the hotel's elegant bar,
the Impérial, where a pianist makes the
ambience complete from 7.30–11pm
every evening.

Le Caveau – *4 r. Gambetta. ☎05 59 24 16
17. http://lecaveau-biarritz.com.* One of the
trendiest bar-discotheques in the region,
Le Caveau is popular with locals and
visitors, as well as the inevitable stars on
holiday. *The* place to be seen in Biarritz.

La Santa Maria – *esplanade du Port-Vieux.
☎05 59 24 53 11.* The splendid view of the
Rocher de la Vierge and the Port Vieux
beach is one of the attractions of this little
bar perched on a rock. A terrace, a few
stools and a bar counter in a cave make
this a pleasant, unpretentious spot where
you can sample tapas while listening to
the little orchestra.

🎭 ENTERTAINMENT

Gare du Midi – *21 bis av. du Mar.-Foch.
☎05 59 22 44 66. www.entractes-
organisations.com. Tickets available
from the tourist office.* The city's main
theatre, with a seating capacity of
1 400, puts on a range of plays, music
concerts and ballets. It is also the home of
the Biarritz ballet company.

Casino Barrière de Biarritz –
*1 av. Édouard-VII. ☎05 59 22 77 77.
www.lucienbarriere.com.* Located on the
Grande Plage, this enormous casino has a
table games room (roulette, blackjack) and
180 slot machines as well as Le Café de
la Plage brasserie, Le Baccara restaurant,
Le Flamingo discotheque, a show room
(theatre, dance) and a ballroom.

🛍 SHOPPING

Cazaux et fils – *10 r. Broquedis.
☎05 59 22 36 03.* The Cazaux family has
been involved in making ceramic pottery
since the 18C. Jean-Marie Cazaux is happy
to talk about his profession, describing it as
"austere and solitary".

Fabrique de chistéras Gonzalez –
*6 allée des Liserons, Anglet. ☎05 59 03
85 04.* Founded in 1887, the Gonzalez
company produces hand-made *cestas*
(wicker scoops that extend from the
protective pelota glove). In one hour you
will learn everything about the history and
manufacture of pelotas and *cestas*.

Chocolats Henriet – *pl. Clemenceau.
☎05 59 24 24 15.* Established after WWII,
Henriet is the local guiding light in
chocolates and confectionery, featuring
calichous (Échiré butter and fresh cream
caramels) and *rochers de Biarritz* (bitter
chocolate, orange rinds and almonds).

Maison Arostéguy – *5 av. Victor Hugo.
☎05 59 24 00 52. www.epicerie-fine.net.*
Founded in 1875, this famous Biarritz
grocery store (formerly the "Epicerie du
Progrès") has kept its original walls,
shelves and façade.

🏃 SPORT AND LEISURE

Hippodrome des Fleurs – *av. du Lac
Marion. ☎05 59 41 27 34. www.hippodrome-
biarritz.com.* Horse races have been held
in this trotter's hippodrome on July and
August evenings for over fifty years.

Piscine municipale – *bd du Gén.-de-
Gaulle. ☎05 59 22 52 52.* Located on the
shore, this municipal complex features
heated sea-water pools as well as a jacuzzi,
hammam and sauna.

Thermes Marins – *80 r. de Madrid. ☎05
59 23 01 22. www.biarritz-thalasso.com.*
This spa features a leisure pool and jacuzzi
and offers various treatments, such as
affusion or underwater showers, seaweed
treatment booths, massages and sea-air
bath booths.

St-Jean-de-Luz★★

Pyrénées-Atlantiques

A popular beach resort and harbour town at the mouth of the river Nivelle, St-Jean-de-Luz is one of the principal centres of the French Basque country.

▶ **Population:** 14 322
  Michelin Map: 342 C 2
  Info: Bd. Victor Hugo.
    & 05 59 26 03 16.
    www.saint-jean-de-luz.com.
◗ **Location:** The town is on the Atlantic seafront just S of Biarritz, close to the Spanish border. The centre is on the right bank of the Nivelle.
◉ **Don't Miss:** The port area.

A BIT OF HISTORY

The main event to occur in the town was the marriage of Louis XIV of France to the infanta of Spain, Maria-Theresa. The wedding was initially held up by the king's passion for Marie Mancini, but in the end was solemnised here, on 9 June 1660.

SIGHTS

The Port and Barre district

This is the original St-Jean-de-Luz. As early as the 11C, its sailors were hunting whale off Labrador. By the 15C, their quarry had changed to the abundant cod of the great fishing grounds off Newfoundland.

The part of the town known as **La Barre** was where the ship-owners lived; its growth was intimately linked to the fortunes of its fleet. The 16C and 17C brought good times, though the place was burned down by the Spaniards in 1558, then ravaged by high tides in 1749 and 1785.

Église St-Jean Baptiste★★

r. Gambetta.

Work on enlarging the church, begun in 1649, had still not been completed when the royal wedding took place here in 1660. It is the finest church in the French Basque country, with a resplendent 17C gilded altarpiece **(retable★)** attributed to Martin de Bidache, a painted wooden ceiling and oak-built galleries on several levels.

EXCURSIONS

Corniche basque★★

◗ *14km/8.7mi S, then extending S to Hendaye.*

The Socoa cliff **(Falaise de Socoa★)**, an unusual example of coastal relief,

is best seen at low tide. Following the submersion of the former coastline by the waters released by the melting of the Quaternary glaciers, the beds of highly laminated schists were attacked by wave action.

La Rhune ★★

◗ *14km/8.7mi SE, then as far as Sare.*

Towards the end of the 6C, the Basques were probably pushed northwards by the Visigoths. Those of their number who settled in the plains of Aquitaine intermarried with local people, eventually becoming the Gascons.

Those who remained in the mountains, however, kept their independence and their enigmatic language, thus guaranteeing their very distinct identity.

The mountain called La Rhune ("good grazing" in Basque) is one of the symbols of the Basque country; its **summit** *(accessible by rack-and-pinion railway)* rises to a height of 905m/2 969ft, offering a wonderful **panorama★★★** of the Bay of Biscay, the Landes and the ancient provinces of Labourd, Navarre and Guipuzcoa.

At the foot of the mountain lie the villages of **Ascain★** and **Sare★**, both with many characteristically Basque features. The houses are timber-framed; the white rendering of the walls makes a pleasant contrast to the reddish-brown colour usually applied to the timber, while the cemeteries adjoining the churches have the typical discoidal tombstones arranged in a circle.

Dax ♈♈♈

Landes

Spa Dax, the most popular spa in France, is reputed for its hot mud treatments. The maceration of silt from the River Adour in water from the hot springs encourages the development of vegetable and mineral algae. The town, built on the edge of the Landes pine forest, is an enjoyable place to visit, with riverside walks and colourful public gardens.

A BIT OF HISTORY

A lake village, with houses on stilts, once stood on the site where Dax is built today. However, alluvia from the Adour gradually silted up the lake and the village developed on dry land. The hot springs received favours and prospered after Emperor Augustus brought his daughter Julia here to treat her rheumatism.

After celebration of the marriage between Louis XIV and Maria Teresa in St-Jean-de-Luz, the couple stopped at Dax on their way home to Paris. The townsfolk set up a triumphal arch at the entrance to the town depicting a dolphin emerging from the water, and an inscription in Latin, was a pun on the words dolphin and *dauphin* (identical in French) in the hopes that the couple's stay in Dax would bear fruit.

▶ **Population:** 21 491
🕐 **Michelin Map:** 335: E-12
ℹ **Info:** 11 cours Foch, Dax. ✆05 58 56 86 86. www.dax-tourisme.com.
▶ **Location:** Between Mont-de-Marsan and Bayonne, Dax lies 35km/22mi NE of Capbreton and 21km/13mi N of Peyrehorade.
🅿 **Parking:** There are car parks near the cathedral and along the banks of the Adour. Some of the streets in the town centre are pedestrianised.
👓 **Don't Miss:** The Fontaine Chaude and the town's parks and gardens; the duck and goose market *(marché au gras),* held every Saturday morning in the market hall.
🕐 **Timing:** If you enjoy a festival atmosphere, then August is the best time to visit Dax. This is when the town holds its annual *féria*, a week-long festival.
👪 **Kids:** Musée de l'Aviation Légère de l'Armée de Terre.

Fountain Chaude

S. Sauvignier/MICHELIN

TOWN CENTRE
Fontaine Chaude
pl. de la Fontaine Chaude.
The hot spring at the centre of town is the main attraction in Dax.

Its thermal waters have been tapped since Roman times, gush forth at a temperature of 64°C/147°F into a huge basin surrounded by arcades. Nearby in place Thiers is the statue of **Borda**, an 18C marine engineer born in Dax.

Banks of the Adour
There are several **riverside walks**. Upstream from the bridge, on the south side, is **Parc Théodore-Denis**, where Gallo-Roman ramparts provide a shady walk under a row of plane trees.

Downstream is **Jardin de la Potinière**, leading down into the heart of the thermal district, while just beyond is the *Trou des Pauvres* or paupers' hole, once a public bath.

Musée de Borda
Chapelle des Carmes, 11 bis r. des Carmes. ◷*Open Tue–Sun 2–6pm.* ◷*Closed public holidays.* ⊜*€3 (no charge first Sun of month).* ☏*05 58 74 12 91.*
The museum contains collections of Gallo-Roman and medieval archaeology (statuettes and 1C bronzes discovered in Dax), 18–20C paintings of the world of bullfighting, and Dutch landscapes.

🔼 Musée de l'Aviation Légère de l'Armée de Terre (ALAT)
Dax Aerodrome, 58 av. de l'aérodrome (Take the D 6 southwest towards Peyrehorade, then the D 106 and turn right). ♿◷*Open Mar–Nov Mon–Fri 2–5.45pm (Jul–Aug Mon–Sat).* ⊜*€5 (child €1.80).* ☏*05 58 74 66 19. www.museehelico-alat.com.*
The museum houses an historical gallery with collections of documents, memorabilia, uniforms, etc. A hangar contains more than 30 well-preserved aeroplanes and helicopters.

Pau★★
Pyrénées-Atlantiques

Overlooking the Gave de Pau torrent, the town has guarded an important route to Spain since Roman times. Since 1450 it has been the capital of the Béarn country, in touch with both the lowlands and the high mountains of this ancient southwestern province of France.

A BIT OF HISTORY
The Béarn and its people
The province has an attractively varied landscape of hills, vineyards, orchards and pasture. Houses are large, with steep slate roofs.

Gaston IV Fébus (1331–91), an authoritarian ruler who surrounded himself with men of letters, was the first to fortify Pau. **Jean II d'Albret** acquired the Foix country through his marriage to Catherine de Foix in 1484, but was obliged to abandon southern Navarre to the king of Spain. In 1527, his son Henri

▸ **Population:** 85 804
🜚 **Michelin Map:** 342 J 3
▤ **Info:** Place Royale. ☏ 05 59 27 27 08. www.pau-pyrenees.com.
◖ **Location:** Pau lies between Biarritz (121km/76mi to the W) and Toulouse (194km/121mi to the E).
🅿 **Parking:** Try the Place Clemenceau or Place de Verdun in the city centre.

II married Marguerite d'Angoulême, the sister of François I: it was she who brought the art of the Renaissance to the castle and, fired with Reformation zeal, made the place one of the intellectual centres of Europe.

Their daughter, **Jeanne d'Albret**, married Antoine de Bourbon, a descendant of Louis IX; this enabled her own son Henry of Navarre (the future Henri IV) to garner the inheritance of the House

Château de Pau

©Emmanuelle Bonzami/Bigstockphoto.com

of Valois on the extinction of the line, thereby "incorporating France into Gascony by way of the Béarn" (Henri IV).

SIGHT
Boulevard des Pyrénées★★

From this splendid panoramic avenue running along a high ridge between the château and the park, there is a famous **view**★★★ over the valley to the Pyrénéan foothills, and, in clear weather, far beyond, to the Pic du Midi de Bigorre and the Pic d'Anie.

ADDITIONAL SIGHTS
Château★★

2 r. du Château. ⟶Guided tours (50min) daily: Jan–mid-Jun, mid-Sept–Dec 9.30-11.45am, 2–5pm; mid-Jun–mid Sep t9.30am-12.15pm, 1.30–5.45pm. ⟳Closed 1 Jan, 1 May, 25 Dec. ⟨€6. ℘05 59 82 38 00. www.musee-chateau-pau.fr.

The castle, built by Gaston Fébus in the 14C on a spur overlooking the river, has lost its military aspect despite the square, brick keep, which still towers over it.

Transformed into a Renaissance palace by Marguerite d'Angoulême, the building was completely restored in the 19C in the time of Louis-Philippe and Napoleon III.

Musée des Beaux-Arts★

1 r. Mathieu Lalanne. ⟳Open Mon, Wed–Fri 10am–noon, 2–6pm, Sat–Sun 10am–12.30pm, 2–6pm. ⟳Closed 1 Jan, 1 May, 25 Dec. ⟨€4. ℘05 59 27 33 02.

In the Fine Arts Museum old masters are exhibited next to local, little-known artists in tasteful thematic displays of old and contemporary works.

EXCURSIONS
La Haute Soule★★

▶ *The region is in the high Pyrénées near the Spanish border.*

One of the original seven Basque provinces, the Upper Soule has retained the dances and folk traditions most characteristic of the region. This is ideal country for forest walks (and cross-country skiing) in rough terrain. The pastureland here is the summer home of many flocks of sheep. **Forêt des Arbailles★★** and **Fôret d'Iraty★** are extensive beech forests covering the higher reaches.

Col d'Aubisque★★★

▶ *The Aubisque Pass lies in the Pyrénées region, SW of Lourdes.*

The main east–west axis of the Pyrénées is interrupted by a number of high north–south passes. The Col du Tourmalet is the highest (2 114m/6 936ft), while the magnificent Col d'Aubisque (1 709m/5 608ft), which separates the Béarn from the Bigorre country, is by far the most spectacular.

AUVERGNE RHÔNE VALLEY

The Auvergne forms the core of the Massif Central. It is a volcanic landscape unique in France, with mountains, lakes and rivers in deep gorges where the great variety of relief makes for fine upland walking country, while the towns and villages of sombre granite have their own allure heightened by the presence of some of France's finest Romanesque churches. To the east an escarpment leads down to the sun-drenched Rhône Valley with its mighty river charging down to the Mediterranean, which could not be in greater contrast to the verdant, rugged uplands of the Auvergne.

Highlights

1 The view from **La Colline de Fourvière** in Lyon (p173)
2 The huge Statue of the Virgin Mary at **Puy-en-Velay** (p181)
3 Walk up **Puy Mary** (p191)
4 Viaduc de Garabit at **St-Flour** (p192)
5 Le Quartier Thermal at **Vichy** (p193)

Geography – The volcanoes of the Auvergne vary from the classic cones of the Monts Dômes to the rugged shapes of the much-eroded Monts Dore. Mainly agricultural, the grazing grounds of the higher land complement the rich alluvial soils of the lower ground. The volcanic activity has created an array of lakes and other water bodies; at Aydat a lava flow has blocked a valley trapping its waters, while the same effect has been produced at Chambon by a volcano erupting into the valley itself. Elsewhere the hollows produced by a series of volcanic explosions have filled with water while elsewhere lakes have formed inside a crater. Further east the valley of the Rhône, and its tributary the Saône, seem to divide the ancient uplands to the west from the younger, folded rocks of the Alps to the east. This natural ruggedness has impeded accessibility from the rest of France, and bred generations of people who are proud and austere, whose way of life rests on a vibrant agrarian economy.

View of Vieux Lyon

R. Mattes/MICHELIN

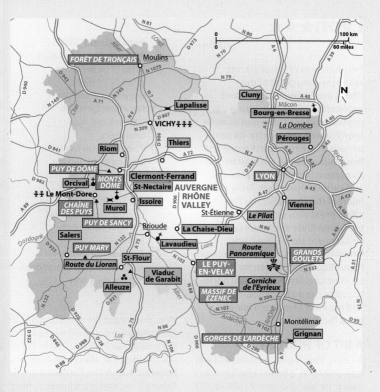

History – The Auvergne was named after the Arveni, whose King, Vincingetorix, had the distinction of defeating Julius Caesar. The victory was short-lived, however, and the region was in turn ruled by Romans, Visigoths and Franks before becoming a Duchy and, later, a Province. The Rhône Valley, long and wide, has served as a communications corridor of great importance for centuries, linking northwestern Europe to the Mediterranean. For this reason the Romans founded Lyon, and the châteaux perched on spurs high above the river provide further evidence of its importance. Today, is it very much a crucible of differing cultures, and an area at the leading edge of industrial progress.

Economy – In Auvergne, this is based mainly on tourism, charcuterie, cheese and the Michelin tyre plants around Clermont-Ferrand. In the Rhône valley the area around the great city of Lyon is marked by centuries of industrial activity. Industry came to the area in the 16C with the introduction of silk production around Lyon. Coalfields later enabled the expansion of industry, but once the seams ran out, energy supply was derived from hydroelectric installations upstream and downstream of Lyon, and, since the 1970s, by nuclear power plants along the Rhône valley.

The taming of the Rhône means 2 000t barges can reach the city. However, the improved waterway carries only a fraction of the total traffic using its corridor; it is supplemented by the A 6 motorway, two national highways, a main-line railway on each bank, and gas and oil pipelines. A series of canals provides a total of 330km/205mi of navigable waterway between Lyon and the sea. Increasingly, the area's economy today is bolstered by tourism, both urban and rural.

The region is dominated and influenced by Lyon, the second-largest city in France, with a lively cultural life, fine architecture and heritage, and with a long-held reputation for good food.

Lyon★★★

Rhône

Two millennia of history, a site at the meeting point of the Rhône and Saône corridors and an exceptionally enterprising population have combined to make Lyon France's second city. Its past periods of greatness, in Roman and Renaissance times, are matched by its present industrial, commercial and cultural dynamism. Truly the heart of the city, la Presqu'île offers great views of the quays of the Saône River and Vieux Lyon. Department stores, boutiques, cinemas and bars line rue de la République, well known for its 19C architecture. Stretching from north to south, rue du Président-Herriot and rue Paul-Chenavard are also good for shopping.

▶ **Population:** 1 348 832
Michelin Map: 327 H-I 5
Info: 19 pl. Bellecour. ℘04 72 77 69 69. www.lyon-france.com.
Location: Lyon lies 100km/62mi W of Chambéry.
Parking: Lyon has many underground parking garages.
Don't Miss: The Renaissance old quarter, Vieux Lyon, on the right bank of the Saône.
Timing: You can spend anything from an afternoon to a few days here.

A BIT OF HISTORY

A Celtic, then Gallic, settlement, Lyon was chosen as a base camp by Julius Caesar for his conquest of Gaul. Under Augustus it became the capital of the Roman Empire's "Three Gauls" (Aquitaine, Belgium and the province around Lyon), complementing the older province centred on Narbonne.

Agrippa was responsible for choosing Lyon as the hub of the road system, constructed originally in pursuit of political ends. It was here that the great route coming north from Arles met the other highways from Saintes, Orléans and Rouen, from Geneva and Aosta, and from Chalon with its links to Amiens, Trier and Basle.

The manufacture of pottery became established here as early as the 1C AD, only to move later to La Graufesenque on the Tarn (*see MILLAU).* The Amphitheatre of the Three Gauls on the hill, Colline de la Croix-Rousse, was joined by the Temple of Rome and of Augustus and by the Federal Sanctuary where the noisy annual assembly of the 60 tribes of Gaul was held under Roman supervision. Christianity reached Lyon via Vienne by the middle of the 2C, brought by sol-diers, traders and Greek missionaries. In 177, there were riots on the occasion of the annual assembly, and Saints Pothinus and Blandina, along with 48 others, became the city's first Christian martyrs. Twenty years later, Saint Irenaeus, head of the Church in Lyon, was to meet the same fate.

According to St Gregory of Tours, the Gospel was reintroduced to Lyon around 250 by Roman missionaries, and, under Constantine, Christianity is supposed to have flourished here as in the other cities of the Empire.

The era of invention – Lyon played a leading role in science and technology at this time. Among its eminent citizens should be noted the following:

Marie-Joseph Jaquard who built a power-loom in 1804; **André Ampère,** inventor of the galvanometer, electromagnetism and electrodynamics; **Barthélemy Thimonnier**, who invented the sewing machine in 1829; **Jean-Baptiste Guimet**, who, in 1834, succeeded in making the dye ultramarine; the **Lumière brothers** (Auguste and Louis), the creators of cinematography; **Hector Guimard**, one of the founders of Art Nouveau in architecture, the designer of the entrances to the metro stations of Paris.

GETTING AROUND

Maps – In addition to the maps included in this guide, Michelin town plans 30 and 31 and Michelin map 110 (the surroundings of Lyon) will be useful.

Access – By road via motorways **A 6, A 7, A 42** and **A 43**. The city also boasts a regular 2hr link with Paris by TGV. Perrache and La Part-Dieu stations are close to the town centre by métro. There are flights to and from most major cities via Lyon-St-Exupéry airport, linked to the town centre by a shuttle service.

Parking – There are several underground car parks strategically placed for easy access to the town centre. Some of these are architectural gems, the most spectacular being the Parc Célestins by Buren, whose columns adorn the Jardins du Palais-Royal in central Paris.

Public transport – The underground train/subway (métro) is the most convenient mode of public transport, and is especially well adapted to the needs of tourists. The best-value ticket to buy is the **1-day Ticket-liberté**, for unlimited travel on the Lyon urban transport network (métro, bus, funicular railway, trolley-bus). Details from TCL (Transports en Commun Lyonnais) kiosks and *www.tcl.fr*.

Cultural Pass: You can buy a 1-, 2- or 3-day **Lyon City Card** which will gain you admission to museums, sights and transport, as well as reductions in theatres, on shopping, etc. Adult prices range between 1 day (€21), 2 days (€31) and 3 days (€41).

TOURING THE TOWN

Planning your visit – If you have only **one day** to spend in Lyon, then you must devote the morning to Old Lyon (on foot), to the Fourvière terrace and the Roman theatres (use the funicular), but you will not have time to visit the museums; the afternoon should be spent touring Presqu'île with its Fabric Museum, and either visiting the Fine Arts Museum or taking an enjoyable walk around the Gros Caillou, on the slopes of the Croix-Rousse.

Two days will enable you to get better acquainted with Fourvière and the various museums and to stroll along the River Saône on the first day. The second day should be devoted to touring Presqu'île and to visiting its museums; you should even have time to take a stroll in the Croix-Rousse district.

Organised tours – Lyon, which is listed as a "Town of Art and History" by the French government, offers discovery tours conducted by guide-lecturers approved by the Ministry of Culture and Communication. Information at the tourist office or on *www.vpah.culture.fr*. The Lyon tourist office offers tours of the city on foot, or by bus, boat, taxi or even helicopter.

Lecture tours are available around Old Lyon, Croix-Rousse and the Tony Garnier district.

Bateaux-mouches river trips – *13 bis quai Rambaud.* ℘*04 78 42 96 81. www.naviginter.fr*. These unique long-boats enable visitors to discover a different face of Lyon, seen from its four river banks: one trip explores the confluence of the Saône and Rhône; the other follows the Saône up to and round the Île-Barbe.

SHOPPING

Markets – The **Marché de la Création, quai Romain-Rolland**, and the **Marché de l'Artisanat, quai Fulchiron**, are held on Sunday mornings. These are no run-of-the-mill craft markets, as the workmanship is outstanding. Used-book sellers line the quai de la Pêcherie every afternoon. There are regional products and small taverns at the Halles de Lyon, 102 cours Lafayette. For food, head for the quai Saint-Antoine, where food markets with producers from all over the region set up stall and sell their produce.

There is also a Farmers' Market twice a week in the place Carnot, in front of the Gare Perrache.

Jardin Botanique

© Jakezc/Fotolia.com

Lyon, City of Light

With the famous Festival of Lights held here on 8 December, when the city twinkles with the light of thousands of candles, Lyon was already predisposed to investing generously in street lighting, and it has done just that in the shape of a project called "Plan Lumière", which places the emphasis on public safety and the highlighting of the city's architectural heritage. Over 100 monuments and locations have been selected for inclusion in a comprehensive and homogeneous system of illumination which gives them a whole new dimension. Fourvière Basilica stands out like a lighthouse on the top of its hill; the opera house takes on a futuristic appearance with its huge glass superstructure glowing red; squares such as place des Terreaux or place de la Bourse and the banks of the Saône and the Rhône are lit up by subtle lighting in a variety of colours in warm or cold tones depending on the location. The Part-Dieu district with the distinctive Crédit Lyonnais tower soaring up from it, the Port St-Jean, the Hôtel-Dieu and many more of the city's famous monuments feature in this huge light show which weaves an atmosphere of fairy tale and magic. Along with the various events put on in the evenings, this invitation to explore "Lyon by night" proves irresistible.

Such is the drama and the skill of the artists, that many of the sites that feature in the Fêtes des Lumières need to be revisited to fully appreciate the magic of it all. During the four days, visitors are free to stroll around the "City of Light", appreciating a life-size art show at the cutting edge of technology. It is a breathtaking experience, and rightly praised and renowned.

A guide to the "Plan Lumière" is available from the tourist office. www.lyon.fr.

Place Bellecour

© Jakezc/Fotolia.com

SIGHTS
La Colline de Fourvière
(Fourvière Hill)

The name of the hill is derived from the old forum *(Forum vetus)* which was still here in the reign of King Louis I in the 9C. Its site is now occupied by the pilgrimage chapel (with its Black Virgin) next to the basilica of 1870. Roman Lyon had numerous public buildings, including the imperial palace (the Capitol) giving onto the forum, a theatre and an odeon (both rebuilt) on the slope of the hill, baths, a circus building and several temples, as well as the amphitheatre on the east bank of the river.

The terrace to the north of the basilica forms a splendid **viewpoint**★ overlooking the confluence of the Rhône and Saône and encompassing the hills and Dauphiné plain over which the great city has spread.

Musée gallo-romain de Fourvière★★

17 r. Cléberg. &⌚*Open Tue–Sun 10am–6pm.* ⌚*Closed 1 Jan, 1 May, 1 Nov, 25 Dec.* ⌧€7. ☎*04 72 38 49 30. www.musees-gallo-romains.com.*

The most striking exhibit is perhaps formed by the Claudian Tables (**Table Claudienne**★★★) of bronze, discovered in 1528. They record the speech made by Claudius in AD 48 which gave the citizens of Gaul the right to become senators. It is possible to compare this ponderous "official" version with the more witty and revealing transcription made by Tacitus.

Le Vieux Lyon (Old Lyon)★★★

The medieval and Renaissance quarter of Lyon, the precursor of today's city, extends along the west bank of the Saône at the foot of the Fourvière hill. Of interest in the old town are the many passages or alleyways known as "traboules" – from the Latin trans ambulare meaning "walking through".

The passageways run perpendicular to the streets and link the buildings by means of corridors with vaulted or coffered ceilings leading to inner courtyards.

Primatiale St-Jean★

Begun in 1192, today's church was preceded by a number of sanctuaries, including an early Christian baptistery, remains of which are on the north side of the building. The cathedral was enlarged during the reigns of Philippe Auguste and St Louis, beginning with the Romanesque east end. The 280 medallions adorning the west front were begun in 1310; in their wealth of detail and great variety they are comparable with those of Rouen Cathedral or the chapel of the Papal Palace at Avignon, though the juxtaposition of the sacred, profane and grotesque is sometimes disconcerting.

Inside, the chancel (**chœur**★★), together with the apse, is the oldest part of the church. The apse, with its fluted pilasters below a blind arcade and a frieze of palm-leaves, is typical of Romanesque architecture of the Rhône valley. It is lit by a 13C stained-glass axial window with a fine medallion depicting the Redemption. There is a 14C astronomical clock (**horloge astronomique**★) with original ironwork.

Quartier St-Jean★★

Lyon was incorporated into the French kingdom at the beginning of the 14C. In the Middle Ages it was a border town facing the Dauphiné, Savoy, and the Holy Roman Empire. Charles VII made it a trading centre of European importance when he founded the twice-yearly fair in 1419. Louis XI introduced the weaving of raw silk imported from the Levant and from Italy, but local opposition led the only silk-mill to transfer its operations to Tours. Forty-four years later, Louis doubled the number of fairs; long-distance trade was encouraged and patterns of commercial activity developed which were far in advance of the time; accommodation at inns and hostels was improved, and clearing houses were set up, forerunners of the great bank founded in the 16C.

Trade flourished, and with it came a period of great prosperity for the city, its merchants, bankers and high officials. Lyon seethed with activity and ideas; its streets were lined with elegant Flamboyant Gothic façades with asymmetrical window patterns; behind them, down narrow alleys, lay courtyards like the ones at 11 and 58 rue St-Jean. More numerous are houses of Renaissance date, decorated with Italianate motifs such as (polygonal turrets, superimposed galleries, basket-handle arches and corner signs like the figure of the ox at the junction of rue du Bœuf – Hôtel Paterin (4 r. de la Juiverie), sculpted in the 16C by John of Bologna.

The **Hôtel de Gadagne**★ houses the **Musée historique de Lyon**★ *(1 pl. du Petit Collège; www.museegadagne.com)* and the **Musée international de la Marionnette**★ *(as for the Musée historique de Lyon)*, the latter created by Laurent Mourget (1769–1844), whose **Guignol** is the very embodiment of the spirit of the Lyon populace.

With the development of the characteristic forms of the French Renaissance come superimposed orders, as in the Hôtel Bullioud *(8 r. de la Juiverie)* with its gallery and corner pavilions by the local architect **Philibert Delorme**.

Printing had been invented in Korea in 1403, then again at Mainz in 1447, and made its first appearance on the banks of the Saône in 1485. The world of the transcriber or of the illuminator would never be the same again. The spread of books transformed Europe with its diffusion of learning, in literature, science and technology and accounts of voyages. The Reformation, born from widespread reading of the Bible, came about some 50 years after the invention of the printing press.

This was also the age of Louise Labé, known as la "Belle Cordière" (Ropemaker's wife), whose salon became a centre for literature and the arts; among those writing was the Lyon poet Maurice Scève.

By 1548 there were almost 400 printers working in the city, including Sébastien Gryphe, Guillaume Rouille and Étienne Dolet, the publisher of Marot and of Rabelais; the latter served as a doctor at the Pont-du-Rhône hospital for three years, carrying on a correspondence with Erasmus and Du Bellay. It was Du Bellay who published **Rabelais**' *Pantagruel* in 1532 and Gargantua in 1534 to coincide with the Lyon fairs.

Musée de l'Imprimerie★★

13 r. de la Poulaillerie. ♿🕐*Open Wed-Sun 9.30am-noon, 2-6pm.* ✏*5€.* 📞*04 78 37 65 98. www.imprimerie.lyon.fr.*
The museum traces the evolution of printing from its very beginnings in Lyon, from the first wood engravings to the discovery of typography and to photocomposition.

La Presqu'île (Lyon's Peninsula)

The modern centre of the city is sited on a long tongue of alluvial material brought down by the Rhône. The formation of the "Peninsula" has shifted the junction of the two rivers 4km/2.5mi southwards since Roman times.

The area was first of all a military encampment, then its proximity to the two rivers made it a favourable place for trading and warehousing. Finally it became the very core of the city; its development along Classical lines begun under Henri IV and Louis XIII was continued in the 18C and 19C, until the urban area spread outwards to the modern suburbs and beyond. The great city's character comes across not only in the busy Rue de la République, with its fine 19C façades and elegant shops, but also in the pleasantly shaded Place de la République, with its trees and fountains.

Place Bellecour

Planned by Henri IV in 1609, the project could not be started until 50 years later, when the city had finally succeeded in purchasing the land.

The designer was Robert de Cotte, who arranged the avenues of trees on the south side of the square in such a way as to disguise its irregular shape. The buildings lining the square were razed during the Terror in retribution for the city's resistance to the Convention. "Lyon is no more," it was triumphantly proclaimed at the time, but the square was rebuilt in the 19C.

Hôtel-Dieu

1 pl. de l'Hôpital.

The plans for this, one of the kingdom's most important buildings, were drawn up by Soufflot in 1740. It marks a significant stage in the evolution of French architecture with its long façade facing the Rhône, its projecting central section with Ionic columns and its dome rising from a square base and crowned with a square lantern.

The way in which the transoms of the windows are decorated with linen motifs evokes its function as a hospital. A balustrade relieves the great length of the main façade and disguises the low roofs.

Place des Terreaux

This is sited where the Saône flowed into the Rhône in Roman times. The older inhabitants of the city are particularly fond of the square with its **fountain**★, which has four eager horses representing rivers bounding oceanwards.

The town hall dates from the reign of Louis XIII, although its façade was rebuilt by Robert de Cotte after a fire and is typically 18C, with a dome and a rounded tympanum supported by atlantes.

Musée des Beaux-Arts★★

20 pl. des Terreaux. &⊙*Open Wed–Sun 10am–6pm (Fri 10.30am–6pm).* ⊙*Closed public holidays.* ∞€7–12. ✆04 72 10 17 40. www.mba-lyon.fr.

The museum presents a remarkable survey of art through the centuries throughout the world. Its collections are organised into five separate departments: painting, sculpture, art objects, antiquities and graphic art.

The highlights of the selection of European painting include 35 **Impressionist** works, **The Ascension**★ by Perugino, an imposing *St Francis* by Zurbarán, and *The Adoration of the Magi* by Rubens.

Also illustrated is the evolution of French painting from the 17C (Philippe de Champaigne) to the 19C (*Femme au perroquet* by Delacroix) and 20C (*Corbeille de Fruit* by Chagall).

There is a very fine collection of ancient art: temple doors from Mehamoud (Egyptian section); and a remarkable kore (statue of a young girl) from the Acropolis (Ancient Greece).

Musée des Tissus et Musée des Arts Décoratifs★★★

34 r. de la Charité. &⊙*Tue–Sun 10am–5.30pm.* ⊙*Closed public holidays, Easter, Whitsun.* ∞€7. ✆04 78 38 42 00. www.musee-des-tissus.com.

Apart from its exhibits devoted to very early examples of the weaver's art, the collection consists mostly of Lyon silk from the 17C onwards, by masters such as Philippe de Lasalle.

There are Louis XV lampas and embroidered satins, embroidery and cut velvets of the Empire and Restoration periods. On the slopes of the hill, Colline de la Croix-Rousse, is a network of covered passageways called *traboules*, once used to protect the precious sheets of silk. They proved useful during the French Revolution, too, and were much used by the Resistance in World War II.

ADDITIONAL SIGHTS

Musée des Hospices Civils

1 place de l'Hôpital. ⊙*Closed for restoration.* ✆04 72 41 30 42.

This museum is housed in the 17C building of the Hôtel-Dieu extended by Soufflot in the 18C.

It contains an important collection of old ceramics used in pharmacies, a considerable amount of furniture including fine chests of drawers, objects made of pewter and *objets d'art*, in particular a bust by Coustou. Also on display are instrument cases once used by dentists, surgeons and doctors.

Basilique St-Martin-d'Ainay

This church, consecrated by Pope Pascal II in 1107, has undergone major alterations. The porch-belfry is topped by a pyramid roof, surrounded by unusual corner acroteria which give it its characteristic outline.

Note the animal frieze beneath the cornice between the second and third levels, and the decoration of inlaid bricks.

Centre d'Histoire de la Résistance et de la Déportation★

14 av. Berthelot.
🕐*Open Wed–Fri 9am–5.30pm, Sat–Sun, 6pm.* 🕐*Closed Christmas public holidays except 8 May.* ∞€4.
📞*04 78 72 23 11. www.chrd.lyon.fr.*
The museum is partially located in buildings that from 1882 to the early 1970s were the Military Medical School and which, from 1942 to 1944, housed the headquarters of the Gestapo in this region.

Opéra de Lyon

On the south side of the square, opposite the Hôtel de Ville, stands the new Lyon opera house, the result of a successful modernisation scheme.

The façade of the old building has been preserved and the eight muses of the pediment appear to hold up the immense and splendid glass semi-cylindrical roof, the design of the architect Jean Nouvel.

With a capacity of 1 300 seats, The Opéra includes an orchestra (60 musicians), a ballet (30 dancers), a choir (26 singers) and a solid expertise. With Ivan Fischer holding the baton, l'Opéra National de Lyon is an international-class company. A 200-seat amphitheatre is the stage for a more varied programme, including classical, jazz and world music.

The building takes on a particularly impressive appearance during the evening illuminations, which floodlight it in predominantly red tones, throwing its architectural contours into sharp relief.

Musée d'Art Contemporain★

Cité Internationale – 81 Quai Charles-de-Gaulle. 🕐*Open daily except Mon, Tue noon–7pm.* ♿ ∞€6. 🕐*Closed 1 May, 25 Dec.* 📞*04 72 69 17 17. www.mac-lyon.com.*
This new cultural focus is built around the atrium of the old market hall. Its modern structure allows for great flexibility of display and for works of art to be exhibited to their best advantage. The museum collection is very varied.

👥 Planétarium de Vaulx-en-Velin

11km/7mi E of Villeurbanne.
🕐*Open daily Oct-Jul, hours vary according to events.* 🕐*Closed 1st Mon of each month.* ∞€6.50 (children €4).
📞*04 78 79 50 12.*
www.planetariumvv.com.
As a prelude to the show, a scientific display reveals the secrets of the heavens. The 15m/49ft hemispherical screen surrounds you, and captivates young and old alike.

👥 Grand Aquarium de Lyon★

7 rue S.-Déchant. 🕐*Open Wed–Sun 11am–7pm (Jul–Aug 10am–7pm).*
🕐*Closed 1 Jan, 25 Dec.* ∞1€4 (children €10).* 📞*04 72 66 65 66.*
www.aquariumlyon.fr.
This new, rather unobtrusive building on the banks of the Saône offers you a journey to the different rivers and oceans of the world: impressive fish reign supreme in rivers of temperate climates; nearby, sharks swim round a wreck inside a huge pool on two levels; a myriad of small brightly coloured fish of all shapes feel quite at home in tropical waters.

EXCURSIONS
Pérouges★★

▶ *25km/15.5mi NE of Lyon.*
🛈*Entrance of the Cité.* 📞*04 74 46 70 84.*
Tightly contained within the ramparts, the tortuous streets and ancient houses of the old town (pop 1 103) have formed the perfect setting for many a period film including *The Three Musketeers* and *Monsieur Vincent.*

Cité ancienne★★

On its hilltop site dominating the Ain valley, this fortified town was originally founded by settlers who came from Perugia in central Italy long before Caesar's invasion of Gaul. It was virtually rebuilt in its entirety after the war of 1468 with Savoy.

The older buildings are timber-framed with projecting upper storeys. The modest artisans' houses contrast with those of the richer townsfolk and gentry, which have mullioned windows and basket-handle arches.

The Upper Gate **(Porte d'en Haut★)** is the principal entrance to the town; the main square, the **Place de la Halle★★★**, has a splendid old hostelry and the **Musée du Vieux-Pérouges**, which contains many local artefacts, a restored weaver's workshop and a medieval garden with medicinal herbs.

La Dombes★

▶ *The Dombes plateau is situated between Lyon and Bourg-en-Bresse and is bordered by the River Ain and the Saône.* ⓘ *3 Place de l'Hôtel de Ville , 01330 Villars les Dombes.* ℘*04 74 98 06 29. www.villars-les-dombes.com.*

The Dombes plateau owes its unusual appearance and its charm to the presence of over 1 000 lakes dotted across its entire area. Here and there are low hills, formed by moraines, which were transformed in the Middle Ages into veritable earth fortresses surrounded by moats. Rural housing in the Dombes region is built mainly of cob *(pisé)*, whereas the castles and outer walls are built of rough red bricks known as *carrons* (terracotta).

The region's history, too, is somewhat out of the ordinary. Dombes was raised to the rank of a principality by François I following the confiscation of the property belonging to the Constable of Bourbon in 1523. A sovereign Parliament sat in Trévoux, its main town, and continued to sit until the mid-18C.

A Bit of Geography

The impermeable soil encouraged local people very early on in their history to turn their fields into lakes enclosed by mud dikes. The Grand Étang de Birieux, one of the most extensive of the lakes, but now subdivided, dates from the 14C. In the 16C, Dombes boasted almost 2 000 lakes, many filled with stagnant water, which led to an unhealthy climate. Most of the lakes are intermittent, one being emptied to fill another: they are filled with water and stocked with fish for a period of six or seven years, then drained and for one year turned over to agriculture.

A Bird's Paradise

The ♟**Parc des Oiseaux★** bird sanctuary (*1km/0.6mi south of Villars-les-Dombes on N 83;* ♿⏰*open daily Mar, Oct–Nov 10am–5.30pm, Apr–Jun, Sept 9.30am–7pm, Jul–Aug 9.30am–8pm;* ⏰*closed Dec–Feb;* ✆*from €13 (children 6–14 years, €10);* ℘*04 74 98 05 54; www.parcdesoiseaux. com*) close to the Dombes Nature Reserve, lies along one of the main migration routes in Europe. Over 2 000 birds from five continents live in the park. At the entrance, the "Birds' House" provides a warm, humid atmosphere for a wonderful selection of brightly

Spoonbill
J. Damase/MICHELIN

coloured exotic birds. Enjoy a walk round the park along the footpaths running round the lakes, which are the breeding ground for large birds such as common and night heron as well as rarer species in giant aviaries. Besides the spectacular Vallée des Rapaces, the Volière du Pantanal and the Cité des Perroquets are also fascinating. The park is engaged in several conservation programmes aimed at endangered species. These are explained to children through various activities in the Maison des Enfants.

ADDRESSES

🛏STAY

🛏🛏 **Hôtel St-Paul** – *6 r. Lainerie. ℘04 78 28 13 29. 20 rms. ⌁7€.* A small Renaissance hotel at the centre of Vieux-Lyon.

🛏🛏🛏 **Maisons d'Hôtes du Greillon** – *12 montée du Greillont. ℘06 08 22 26 33. www.legreillon.com. 5rms.* Away from the noise of the city, this 18C house has a terrace and garden, unique for hotels in the centre of the city.

🛏🛏🛏 **Hotel des Artistes** – *8 r. G-André. ℘04 78 42 04 88. www.hotel-des-artistes.fr. 45rms. ⌁€12.* The proximity of the theatre, and the fact that many artists have stayed at the hotel, have influenced its decoration.

🛏 **Hôtel B&B** – *93 cours Gambetta. ℘08 92 707 534. www.hotel-bb.com. 114 rms. ⌁€6.* A chain hotel offering a central location, with spacious and comfortable rooms and king-size beds.

🛏🛏🛏 **Hôtel Ariana** – *163 cours Émile-Zola, 69100 Villeurbanne. ℘04 78 85 32 33. www.ariana-hotel.fr. 102 rms. ⌁ €11–13.* This is a practical address for those who wish to stay amid the 1930s high-rises of Villeurbanne.

🍴EAT

🍽 **Le Vieux Lyon** – *44 r. St-Jean. ℘04 78 42 48 89. Closed Sun evening.* Local epicureans are all familiar with this tavern, in operation since 1947, where good humour and hospitality reign.

🍽🍽 **Restaurant de Fourvière** – *9 pl. de Fourvière. ℘04 78 25 21 15. www.la tassee.fr.* Perfectly situated, this restaurant enjoys a superb panorama.

🍽🍽 **Lolo Quoi** – *42 r. Mercière. ℘04 72 77 60 90.* In this pedestrian street, those in the know go to Lolo.

🍽🍽 **Brunet** – *23 r. Claudia. ℘04 78 37 44 31. Closed Sun–Mon and Tue lunch. Reservations recommended.* An authentic Lyon *bouchon* (tavern), with elbow-to-elbow tables, and tasty little dishes enhanced by an enticing selection of wines by the carafe.

🍽🍽 **Le Mercière** – *56 r. Mercière. ℘04 78 37 67 35. www.le-merciere.com.*

Reservations recommended. Located in a passageway giving onto one of the most popular restaurant streets in town, this old house serves traditional cuisine.

🍽🍽 **La Table d'Hippolyte** – *22 r. Hippolyte-Flandrin. ℘04 78 27 75 59. Closed Sat lunch, Sun–Mon.* The ideal setting for a candlelit supper.

🍽🍽 **Maison Villemanzy** – *25 montée St-Sébastien. ℘04 72 98 21 21. www.maison-villemanzy.com. Closed Sun, and Mon lunch.* Perched on the slopes of Croix-Rousse, this restaurant offers a superb terrace view over the city.

🍽🍽 **Le St-Florent** – *106 cours Gambetta. ℘04 78 72 32 68. Closed Sat and Mon lunches, Sun and public holidays.* The place to appreciate *poulet-de-Bresse*.

🍽🍽 **L'Orangerie de Sébastien** – *Domaine de Lacroix-Laval, 69280 Marcy-l'Étoile. ℘04 78 87 45 95. www.orangerie desebastien.fr. Closed Sun evening, Mon and Tue.* The orangery is part of a 17C château, and serves dishes of the day on a beautiful terrace.

🎭THEATRE AND ENTERTAINMENT

Le Guignol de Lyon – *Compagnie des Zonzons, 2 r. Louis-Carrand. ℘04 78 28 92 57. www.guignol-lyon.com. Reservations essential.* Children's performances combine burlesque and fantasy. The shows for adults are more malicious.

Auditorium-Orchestre national de Lyon – *149 r. Garibaldi. ℘04 78 95 95 95. www.auditoriumlyon.com.* The Auditorium regularly hosts l'Orchestre National de Lyon.

Maison de la Danse – *8 av. Jean-Mermoz. ℘04 72 78 18 10. www.maisondeladanse. com.* From flamenco and tap dancing to ballet and the traditional dances of East and West.

Opéra National de Lyon – *1 pl. de la Comédie. ℘0826 305 325. www.opera-lyon.org.*

Halle Tony-Garnier – *20 pl. Antonin-Perrin. ℘04 72 76 85 85. www.halle-tony-garnier.com.* This huge metallic structure presents a remarkable diversity of events from circus to Lionel Richie and Johnny Hallyday.

Vienne★★

Isère

Vienne is favoured with a sunny **site**★ on the east bank of the Rhône. The town overlooks the bend formed by the river as it makes its way through the crystalline rocks marking the last outcrops of the Massif Central.

A BIT OF HISTORY

Vienne came under Roman rule 60 years before Caesar's conquest of Gaul. In the 3C and 4C, the city was the centre of the vast province known as the Viennoise stretching from Lake Geneva to the mouth of the Rhône. Great public buildings were erected at the foot of Mount Pipet, opposite **St-Romain-en-Gal**, the Gallo-Roman city **(cité gallo-romaine★)** with its houses and shops. In the 5C, Vienne became the capital of the Burgundians, who ruled over the east bank of the Rhône before being chased away by the Franks in 532. Ruled subsequently by its archbishops, the city became the object of the rivalry between the Kingdom of France and the Holy Roman Empire, until its final incorporation into France at the same time as the Dauphiné, in 1349.

SIGHTS

Temple d'Auguste et de Livie★★

pl. Charles de Gaulle.

This Classical temple was first built in the reign of Emperor Augustus shortly before the beginning of the Christian era; it seems likely that it was then reconstructed about 50 years later.

At the time it would have dominated the Forum to the east. It has been well preserved through successive re-use as a public building of various kinds (church, Jacobin club, tribunal, museum, library), and subsequently through its restoration by Prosper Mérimée in 1850.

The 16 Corinthian columns rise from a podium rather than directly from the ground in the Greek manner. In the pediment are traces of a bronze inscription to the glory of Augustus and Livia.

▶ **Population:** 30 448
Michelin Map: 333 C 4
Info: Cours Brillier. 𝒫04 74 53 80 30. www.vienne-tourisme.com.
Location: Vienne lies 38km/24mi S of Lyon.
Timing: Half a day will suffice, but stay longer to appreciate the place.

Temple d'Auguste et de Livie

J. Damase/MICHELIN

Cathédrale St-Maurice ★★

pl. Saint Maurice. ⏰*Open daily 10am–6pm.* ☞*No charge.* 𝒫*04 74 53 80 30. www.cathedraledevienne.com.*
Built from the 12–16C, the cathedral combines Romanesque and Gothic elements. Only 35 years after its completion, the cathedral suffered mutilation during the Wars of Religion.

It underwent extensive restoration in the 19C, but much remains to be admired, including the fine Renaissance window in the south aisle, the 13C low-relief between the sixth and seventh chapels in the north aisle depicting Herod and the Magi, and the rare 11C Bishop's Throne *(in the apse behind the high altar)*.

ADDITIONAL SIGHTS

Théâtre romain★ *(r. du Cirque)*
Église et Cloître St-André-le-Bas★ *(pl.du Jeu de Paume)*
Musée Lapidaire St-Pierre★ *(pl. Saint-Pierre)*

St-Étienne★

Rhône-Alpes

St-Étienne lies close to the Massif du Pilat, Grangent lake and the Forez plain. The town is located at the centre of a coal basin which supplied over 500 million tonnes of coal until the mines were closed in the 1980s. Since then St-Étienne has adopted a new image: the façades of its buildings have been cleaned, its gardens and parks renovated. The busiest area lies along a north–south axis: place Jean-Jaurès to place de l'Hôtel-de-Ville. The 15C and 16C main church of St-Étienne, popularly known as the "Grand'Église", remains dear to the hearts of the local people.

▶ **Population:** 175 940
Michelin Map: 327 F 7
Info: 16 av. de la Libération. 42000 St-Étienne. ☎04 77 49 39 00. www.tourisme-st-etienne.com.
Location: 62km/39mi SW of Lyon.
Parking: The centre of St-Étienne is a difficult place to drive and park. The tram is the best way to get around. A one-day pass is available from the tourist office.
Don't Miss: The Museum of Modern Art's superb collection of photographs and the Old Town.
Kids: Go stargazing at the Planetarium.

VISITS

Musée du Vieux St-Étienne★

⊙*Open daily except Sun, Mon and public hols, 2.30–6pm.* ⊛€3. ☎04 77 25 74 32. www.vieux-saint-etienne.com.
An 18C toll-marker from the old Outre-Furan district signals the entrance to the Hôtel de Villeneuve (18C). The City Museum inside is arranged on the first floor, in a series of rooms with fine moulded and coffered ceilings.

Musée d'Art Moderne★★

▶*4.5km/3mi from the city centre. Leave St-Étienne N via rue Bergson towards La Terrasse and follow signs to the Musée d'Art Moderne.*
⊙*Open daily except Tue 10am–6pm.*
⊙*Closed 1 Jan, 1 May, 14 Jul, 15 Aug, 1 Nov, 25 Dec.* ⊛€5. ☎04 77 79 52 52. www.mam-st-etienne.fr.
The Museum of Modern Art of St-Étienne Métropole houses one of the largest collections of art from the 20C and 21C in France. The building was designed by the architect Didier Guichard in 1987 and offers a wide and luminous exhibition space.
The Collection includes works from many different movements such as Cubism, Surrealism, Neo-expressionism, Pop Art, New Realism and Minimal Art. The Collection also contains about 2 300 photographs which depict the history of photography and is one of the largest single collections of photographs held in France.

Musée d'Art et d'Industrie★★

⊙*Open daily except Tue 10am–6pm, Mon 10am–12.30pm and 1.30–6pm (last admission 30min before closing).*
⊙*Closed 1 Jan, 1 May, 14 Jul, 15 Aug, 1 Nov and 25 Dec.* ⊛€5. ☎04 77 49 73 00. www.saint-etienne.fr.
This Art and Industry Museum, located in the former Palais des Arts, is a real repository of local and regional know-how relating to tool-making and the evolution of equipment and machinery from the 16C up to the present day.

Planetarium★

Espace Fauriel, 28 rue P.-et-D.-Ponchardier. ⊙*Open: call or check website for times of shows and visits.*
⊙*Closed Sept, 1 Jan, 1 May, 25 Dec.* ⊛€6.60 (children €5.50). ☎04 77 33 43 01. www.astronef.fr.
Crowned by a hemispherical dome, this planetarium is fitted with highly sophisticated equipment which enhances its shows about the universe.

Le Puy-en-Velay★★★

Haute-Loire

The town occupies one of the most amazing sites in France, its most striking landmark being the huge **statue of the Virgin Mary** atop a tall column of volcanic rock. Le Puy has been famous for pilgrimages since Bishop Gotescalk made one of the first pilgrimages to Santiago de Compostela from here in 962.

> ▶ **Population:** 20 046
> ♿ **Michelin Map:** 331 F 3
> ▤ **Info:** Place du Clauzel. ℰ04 71 09 38 41. www.ot-lepuyenvelay.fr
> ▶ **Location:** Le Puy-en-Velay lies 75km/46.5mi SW of St-Étienne, and 126km/79mi SE of Clermont-Ferrand.
> ⊚ **Don't Miss:** The fantastic views from the upper rim of the basin, especially during sunset, or the lively Saturday market at Place du Breuil.

VISIT

Rocher Corneille

This is an outlier of the volcano of which the Rocher St-Michel was the vent. It is topped by a 16m/52ft statue of Notre-Dame of France made in 1860 from more than two hundred melted-down cannons captured at the Siege of Sebastopol during the Crimean War. Reached by a steep path, the terrace at the foot of the statue offers the best viewpoint over the extraordinary **site**★★★ of Le Puy.

La Cité Épiscopale (Cathedral Quarter)★★★

The city's growth dates from the 11C, when it took over the urban functions of nearby St-Paulien and when it formed an important destination on the pilgrimage road to Santiago de Compostela in Spain. The cathedral's fortifications are evidence of the bishops' quarrels with the local lords over sovereignty and taxes raised from the pilgrims.

In the centre of the old town, the area around the cathedral has a sombre air, with its buildings of granite and lava, narrow arcaded entranceways, mullioned windows, heavy iron grilles and paving stones.

Chapelle St-Michel-d'Aiguilhe and Rocher Corneille

J.Damase/MICHELIN

Lace

Lace-making was widespread in the area around Le Puy as early as the 17C, though its high point was reached in the 19C, in part due to the efforts of Théodore Falcon (1804–56), who encouraged high standards in both design and quality. Before World War I, bobbin lace and needlepoint lace were equally popular, but after 1919, the former (also known as pillow lace) became dominant, with threads of linen, silk and wool used to form patterns of great variety and delicacy.

Cathédrale Notre-Dame★★★

Guided tours available; contact the tourist office. ✆04 71 09 38 41. www.cathedraledupuy.org.

The first building to occupy the site was a Roman temple. This was followed around 430 by a sanctuary dedicated to the Virgin Mary, built at the same time as Santa Maria Maggiore in Rome. Rebuilding and extension took place from the 10C on, and in the 19C major restoration was carried out.

The lofty west front rises from its monumental steps to dominate the Rue des Taules. The windows in the third storey mark the extension to the nave which took place at the end of the 12C and which is supported on massive arcading. The overall impression is a highly ornamental one, due to the pierced or blind Romanesque arches, the use of polychrome granite and basalt stonework, the mosaics in the gables and the columns with carved lava capitals.

The steps continue to rise, giving a good view of the carved doors of the Golden Doorway (Porte Dorée) with, on the left, a depiction of the Nativity, and on the right, Christ's Passion. In the 10C and 11C, the apse was rebuilt and the transepts and first two bays of the nave erected.

At the beginning of the 12C the two adjacent bays were built and vaulted with splendid domes. The two last bays were added at the end of the 12C.

Dating from the 11C and 12C, the cathedral **Cloisters**★★ have polychrome mosaics, an allegorical Romanesque frieze at the base of the roof, a fine 12C wrought-iron **grille**★ and, in the Reliquary Chapel (Chapelle des Reliques), a celebrated Renaissance fresco depicting the Liberal Arts. It also qualifies as one of the starting points of the pilgrim route to Santiago de Compostela.

Religious Art Treasury★★

The Treasury, displayed in the former Velay State Room above the Chapel of Relics, contains a large number of works of art, including an 11C silk cope, a 13C engraved enamel reliquary, a polychrome-stone 15C Nursing Virgin, a magnificent 16C embroidered cloak for the Black Virgin, and a piece of 15C parchment showing the Genesis of the World to the Resurrection.

Chapelle St-Michel-d'Aiguilhe★★

🕐*Open daily: Feb–mid-Mar 2–5pm; mid-Mar–Apr and Oct–mid-Nov 9.30am–noon, 2–5.30pm; May–Jul 9am–6.30pm; Jul–Aug 9am–6.45pm; Sept 9am–6.30pm.* 🕐*Closed 1 Jan and 25 Dec.* ✆€3. ✆04 71 09 50 03. www.rochersaintmichel.fr.

268 steps lead to the chapel perched on its 82m/270ft lava pinnacle. Arabesques and polychrome mosaics of Byzantine inspiration decorate the chapel doorway. Inside, the complex vaulting gives some indication of the difficulties the 11C architect had to overcome in transforming the original Carolingian sanctuary; one of his contributions was the addition of a gallery to the narthex. Note two capitals reused in the smaller gallery, the 10C murals in the apse depicting the heavenly kingdom, and a Romanesque Christ-reliquary carved in wood.

ADDITIONAL SIGHT
Musée Crozatier

🕐*Open subject to renovation until 2012, but partially reopened in 2009; call for opening hours and admission charges.* ✆04 71 06 62 40.

The museum collections are housed in an imposing building (1865) erected at the bottom of the Henri Vinay garden, which includes, among other monuments, the beautiful portal from Vorey Priory.

EXCURSIONS
Château de Polignac
◆ *5km/3mi NW.*
www.ot-lepuyenvelay fr.
There is a striking view of this medieval fortress from the N 102 main road. Its defences were so strong that its lords were known as the "Kings of the Mountain". From the 17C to the 19C, their descendants held prominent positions in political and diplomatic life.

Lac du Bouchet★
◆ *21km/13mi SW.*
The clear waters of the lake, surrounded by coniferous woodland, occupy the almost perfectly circular crater of an ancient volcano. Around it stretch the extensive Devès uplands, formed by a series of fissure-eruptions and overlying the even older granite foundation of the landscape.

Massif Du Ézenc★★★
◆ *The area lies SE of Le Puy-en-Velay.*
These dramatic volcanic uplands in the southern part of the Velay region form the watershed between Atlantic and Mediterranean. They lie at the centre of a belt of igneous rocks cutting across the axis of the Cévennes.

☛WALKS
Mont Mézenc
▮ *2hr-round trip on foot from the Croix de Boutières pass.*
Two great lava flows extend downwards from the twin summits of the mountain, from which a vast **panorama**★★★ extends over the Velay. Quite close at hand can be seen the village of Les Estables.

Gerbier de Jonc★★
▮ *1hr30min round-trip on foot.*
Screes of bright phonolite clatter under the feet of the many who clamber to the summit of this lava pinnacle, from which there is a fine **view**★★.

Cascade du Ray-Pic★★
◆ *11km/6.8mi S of the Gerbier de Jonc.*
▮*1hr30min round-trip on foot.*
In a harsh setting formed by a succession of lava flows, the Bourges torrent drops in a series of falls. In the bed of the stream, dark basalt contrasts with lighter granite.

Lac d'Issarlès★
◆ *20km/12.4mi E of the Gerbier de Jonc.*
This pretty, rounded lake with its blue waters occupies the crater of an extinct volcano, 138m/450ft deep.

La Chaise-Dieu★★
◆ *The village (pop 778) is 40km/25mi from Le Puy.* ℘*04 71 00 06 06.*
www.abbaye-chaise-dieu.com.
Set amid lush green countryside and rolling hills between Le Puy and Thiers, the ornate abbey comes as a magnificent surprise.

Église abbatiale de St-Robert★★
◷*Open year-round; hours vary, so call ahead.* ◷*Closed Mon in Dec and Feb (except school holidays), 25 Dec, 1 Jan.* ⊜*€4.* ☛*Guided tours available.*
Over 1 000m/3 280ft up on the high granite plateau of Livradois, **La Chaise-Dieu Abbey**, from the latin *Casa Dei* or House of God, was already a famous monastery in the 11C. Founded in 1043 by St Robert, it had a thriving community of about 300 monks at the time of his death in 1067. In the 12C its importance was second only to that of Cluny and by the 13C it had 300 dependent congregations. The abbey's decline set in after 1518, when abbots were henceforth appointed by the king, with fiscal, rather than religious, considerations taking first place.
The granite west front with its twin towers (the spires have disappeared) speaks strongly of the abbey's former grandeur and austerity. Within, the structure is of a noble simplicity, a single-storeyed elevation. The **Monks' chancel**★★ was built from 1344 to 1352 by Pope Clement VI (the former monk Pierre Roger who

went on to become the fourth Avignon Pontiff), who is buried here in the Choir. The 14 Flemish **tapestries**★★★ (1500–18), of wool, linen and silk, came from Arras and Brussels. The tapestries are hung over the richly carved 15C **stalls**★★, 144 in number. In the **Dance macabre (Dance of Death)**★ figures of the mighty are shown next to their likeness in death.

A great organ was installed at the west end in 1683 and enlarged in 1726; the organ-case **(buffet★)** is elaborately sculpted and contrasts with the spirit prevailing in the choir's architecture. Note also the Gothic **cloisters**★.

Brioude★

The town is mid-way along the road from Clermont-Ferrand to Le Puy-en-Velay.

Le Doyenné, Pl. Lafayette.
04 71 74 97 49. www.ot-brioude.fr.

Brioude (pop 6 820) is a bustling market town overlooking the lush plain of the River Allier. Allow half a day to fully explore the St Julien Basilica and the rest of the town.

Basilique St-Julien★★

pl. Grégoire-de-Tours. Open daily 9am–noon, 2–5pm. Guided tours available. No charge. 04 71 74 94 59. http://en.ot-brioude.fr/basilica.html.

This vast Romanesque church was built at the spot where, according to tradition, Julian, a centurion of a Roman legion based at Vienne, was martyred in 304. For many years it attracted throngs of pilgrims on the road which, beyond Le Puy, passed through Langogne and Villefort, at the time the only route between the Auvergne and Languedoc. Work on the present building began with the narthex in 1060, and was completed in 1180 with the construction of the choir and east end. The nave was raised in height and given a ribvault in 1259.

The east end **(chevet★★)** is one of the final examples of Romanesque architecture in the Auvergne. Its five slate-roofed radiating chapels have richly decorated cornices and capitals, above which runs a band of mosaic masonry. The south porch **(porche★)** has kept its typical Auvergne five-sided lintel, its wrought-iron strap-hinges and two fine bronze knockers.

The warm colouring of the interior is due to the combination of sandstones and basalts of red, pink and brown hue. The nave is paved with cobblestones laid in the 16C and only recently exposed again.

The presence locally of both sandstones and marble was a distinct advantage to the four, possibly even six, masons' workshops responsible for the decoration of the church during the 12C and 13C. The capitals **(chapiteaux★★)** are exceptional; note particularly (in the south aisle near the entrance) an armed knight, perhaps a participant involved in the First Crusade (which had been preached at Clermont-Ferrand), together with a usurer (the sculptor's social comment on this curse of the Middle Ages). Further up the south aisle are two 14C works, the Virgin Birth and Our Lord as a Leper.

There are murals too, though not, unfortunately, very well preserved, but covering an area of around 140sq m/ 1 507sq ft.

There are two outstanding subjects: the figure of St Michael in the first bay of the nave; and the composition in the gallery of the narthex (south room): Christ in Glory, the Chosen and the Damned, the Virtues and the Vices and 100 angels, and, on the timber wall, a stunning 13C Fall of Satan.

Lavaudieu★

10km/6.2mi SE of Brioude

The 11C Benedictine priory, attached to the great abbey at La Chaise-Dieu, has charming cloisters **(cloître★)** with timber-built galleries and 14C **frescoes**★ in the chapel and refectory.

Clermont-Ferrand★★

Puy-de-Dôme

The site★★ of Clermont is unique; the old town, including the cathedral, is built on a volcano, whose black lava makes for an unusual townscape. To the north are the plateaux of Chanturgue and Les Côtes, once the site of a Gallic oppidum, and an example of the phenomenon known as relief inversion, which has protected them from erosion and left them standing out from the surrounding country. To the west are the summits of the Puys, the mountain range that gives Clermont its incomparable setting, best viewed from the Place de la Poterne with its pretty fountain (**Fontaine d'Amboise★**) of 1515.

A BIT OF HISTORY

Clermont was the great oppidum of the Arverni (the Celts who gave their name to the Auvergne). Here in the spring of 52 BC, Julius Caesar and his legions were roundly defeated at the battle of Gergovie by the forces of the Gallic chieftain **Vercingétorix**, whose spirited equestrian statue by Bartholdi stands at one end of Clermont's Place de Jaude. Caesar soon returned, this time winning

- ▶ **Population:** 142 407
- ⚲ **Michelin Map:** 326 E-G 7-10
- **Info:** Pl. de la Victoire. ℰ04 73 98 65 00. www.clermont-fd.com.
- ▶ **Location:** 126km/79mi NW of Le Puy-en-Velay.
- ⏱ **Timing:** Allow at least half a day to explore the centre. Start at the place de Jaude, the focal point for anything that's going on.

☺ Guided Tours ☺

The tourist office organises various walking tours around Clermont, the Port Walk or the Montferrand Walk. Ask at the tourist office for the *Parcours dans la ville* brochure.

a decisive battle at Alésia (modern Alise Ste-Reine), and captured Vercingétorix who was taken to Rome where he was paraded in triumph and ritually strangled after being imprisoned for six years in the Tullianum in Rome.

It was at Clermont on 28 November 1095 that Pope Urban II launched **the First Crusade**. Clermont was also the town of the remarkable writer, mathematician, thinker and inventor **Blaise Pascal** ("The heart has its reasons that reason

The Capital of the Motor Tyre

Two men, Aristide Barbier and Édouard Daubrée came together around 1830 to make agricultural machinery as well as gunshot, and rubber belts and tubes. In 1889, their factory was taken over by brothers **André** and **Édouard Michelin**, the grandsons of Barbier. Building on their tradition of applying scientific method to the work of

industry, the company has subsequently flourished through study of clients' needs, scrupulous observation of reality and previous experience. This process has led from the detachable bicycle tyre of 1891, the car tyre of 1895, the low-pressure "Confort" tyre of 1923, the "Metalic" of 1937, the radial tyre of 1946 (designated "X" in 1949), to the Michelin Energy tyre (1990s). This "green" tyre technology – based on reduced rolling resistance – enables fuel savings.

knows not" – Blaise Pascal 1623–62). Among other things, at 19 he invented an adding machine (*on display in Musée du Ranquet*).

SIGHTS
Basilique Notre-Dame du Port★★

5 r. Saint-Laurent. ℘*04 73 91 32 94.*
See Introduction: Art – Architecture.
This is the finest of the larger Romanesque churches of the Lower Auvergne, unforgettable in its beautiful simplicity. It was built around 1150 over a crypt of the 11C. Inside, the raised chancel (**chœur★★★**), admirably proportioned, is divided from the ambulatory by eight slender columns; their capitals (**chapiteaux★★**), together with those of the wall of the ambulatory, are among the finest in Auvergne.

Cathédrale Notre-Dame-de-l'Assomption★★

The stained-glass medallions (**vitraux★★**) of the 12–15C are copies of those in the Sainte-Chapelle in Paris. The **Treasury★** displays 12–19C collections of gold, silver and enamel ware.

L'Aventure Michelin

32 r. du Clos Four, Cataroux industrial site, N of the city. *Open daily except Mon Sept–Jun 10am-6pm; Jul–Aug 10am–7pm.* €8. ℘*04 73 98 60 60. www.aventure-michelin.com. To make the most of your visit, book online.*
An exhibition space, opened in March 2009 and spanning two floors, displays the workings of Michelin, past, present and future. Visitors learn about the history of Michelin tyres, the Michelin Man (Bibendum), and can admire a replica of the Bréguet XIV aeroplane built by Michelin during World War I.

ADDITIONAL SIGHTS
Old Montferrand★★

Montferrand was founded by the counts of Auvergne who built a fortress on a rise that is now the site of place Marcel-Sembat, in order to counter the authority of the bishop, who was also Lord of Clermont. In the early 13C the town was rebuilt on the orders of a powerful woman named Countess Brayère and was turned into a bastide, a fortified hilltop town laid out to a strictly symmetrical geometric pattern.

Montferrand was a commercial centre at the junction of several roads and, in the 15C, the wealthy middle classes began to commission townhouses. The narrow plots of land made available by Countess Brayère's town plan, however, forced the architects to design houses that were deep rather than wide.

The proximity of Clermont caused rivalry and jealousy between the two towns. Montferrand eventually went into decline. In 1962 work was undertaken to renovate the old Montferrand, a project involving some 80 old townhouses and mansions.

Place de la Rodade

This square was once known as place de Belregard because of the view over the Puys range. In the centre stands the Four Seasons fountain made of lava stone.

▶ *Enter the old town of Montferrand via rue de la Rodade.*

Hôtel Regin

This 15C and 16C townhouse belonged to a family of magistrates and is typical of the mansions built in Montferrand.

Hôtel Doyac

Late 15C mansion built for Jean de Doyac, Royal Bailiff of Montferrand and Minister to Louis XI. Huge, imposing Gothic doorway.

Hôtel du Bailliage

Bailiwick House is the former Consuls' Residence. Its gargoyles and vaulted rooms are of interest.
After rue de la Rodade widens, a set of timbered houses with corbelling comes into view on the left in the renovated district. Their rounded doorways are set out on high landings that show the original level of the roadway.

▶ *Turn back; go right on r. Marmillat.*

Hôtel de la Porte
In the courtyard of this mansion, also known as the Architect's House, there is a staircase turret decorated with a Renaissance sculpture from 1577.

▷ *Turn right onto rue de la Cerisière.*

Hôtel de la Faye des Forges
A glass door protects a delightful inner door with a carved tympanum decorated with lions. The house opposite has a double timber gallery, an unusual feature in Montferrand.

▷ *Turn left along rue des Cordeliers onto rue Waldeck-Rousseau.*

Rue Waldeck-Rousseau runs along the inside of the old ramparts, high above the road laid out along the moat which was once liable to flooding by the Tiretaine.

▷ *Turn right onto Rue du Temple, back to Rue des Cordeliers.*

Rue des Cordeliers
Note the Renaissance ground floor flanked by pilasters and the delightful little inner courtyard.

Carrefour des Taules
This is the central junction in the old town. Its name is a reminder that this was a butchers' market.

Maison de l'Apothicaire
1 rue des Cordeliers.
The old Apothecary's House dates from the 15C and has two timbered upper storeys. At the top of the house, the brackets on either side of the gable are decorated with an apothecary and the patient awaiting his operation.

▷ *Turn left onto rue du Séminaire.*

Halle aux Toiles
The old cloth market has a long balcony supporting a fine row of four basket-handled arches and corresponding side doors.

Hôtel d'Étienne Pradal
The ground floor of this mansion has superb semicircular and basket-handled arches. Its "Montferrand roughcast" and cornerstones made of lava stone are typical of the town's architecture.

Musée d'Art Roger-Quilliot★★
🕐*Open daily except Mon 10am–6pm.*
🕐*Closed 1 Jan, 1 May, 1 Nov, 25 Dec.*
&.◉€5, no charge 1st Sunday of the month. ✆04 73 16 11 30.
A change of use – The history of these premises reflects the history of Montferrand and Clermont, each in turn the seat of official bodies. The museum stands on the site of the Palais Vieux above the town walls. It was the seat of the royal bailiwick of the Cour des Aides of the Auvergne, the Limousin and the Marches; the monumental gateway built in the early 17C in front of the courtyard that precedes the chapel is all that remains of this building.
When Montferrand and Clermont were combined, the Cour des Aides moved to Clermont and the Ursuline Order of nuns took over and reconstructed the buildings. The site was turned into a seminary after the Revolution, then into a military hospital from 1914 to 1918, and into barracks for riot police and *gendarmerie*, before being transformed into a museum.
The buildings and their surroundings are a reflection of Montferrand. They constitute the old "Gateway of the Rising Sun" and open the historic centre of the town to its suburbs.

Musée Bargoin★
45 r. Ballainvilliers. 🕐*Open daily except Mon 10am–noon, 1–5pm (Sun, public holidays 2–7pm).* 🕐*Closed 1 Jan, 1 May, 1 Nov, 25 Dec.* ◉€4.50, no charge 1st Sunday of the month. ✆04 73 91 37 31.
This museum houses a sizeable **prehistoric and Gallo-Roman archaeological collection**★ on the ground and basement floors, comprising artefacts discovered locally, particularly during recent excavations in the city of Clermont itself.

The Gallo-Roman period is the best represented, with a marvellous collection of statuettes of animals, men, women and children in white terracotta, pottery from Lezoux with fine examples dating from the 2C, and vestiges of the great temple of Mercury built on the summit of the Puy-de-Dôme at the beginning of the Imperial era.

The **Carpet Museum** includes over 80 carpets from the Middle and Far East: Turkey, the Caucasus, Iran, Afghanistan, Turkestan, Tibet, China etc.

Royat

1km W of Clermont-Ferrand.
1 av. Auguste-Rouzaud, 63130 ROYAT.
04 73 29 74 70. www.ot-royat.com
Royat is a large, elegant thermal spa terraced on the slopes of the Tiretaine valley. The Tiretaine flows from the granite plateau at the base of the Dômes mountain range; until it leaves Royat, it is a torrent. The bottom of its bed was filled with lava from the Petit Puy de Dôme, and the waters then cut gorges in it.

The **waters** of Royat were exploited by the Romans, who built public baths here. Although the baths met with mixed success until the mid-19C, they have enjoyed popularity and fame ever since. A hydropathic establishment was built, and the visit here by Empress Eugénie in 1862 launched Royat as a spa.

Parc Thermal

This spa garden, completed by the new English-style park through which flows the Tiretaine, contains the hydropathic establishment and the casino.

The remains of the **Gallo-Roman public baths** can be seen. One of the pools had mosaic-covered arches and marble-covered walls. Terracotta pipes brought the water into the pool in small, semicircular cascades.

Grotte des Laveuses

The "Washerwomen's Cave" is on the banks of the Tiretaine. Several springs gush from the volcanic walls before flowing into the Tiretaine.

Église St-Léger★

Built in the 11C, this fortified building deviates significantly from the churches of the Auvergne, for it more resembles the churches of Provence. The bell tower is 19C.

EXCURSIONS

Issoire★★

37km/23mi S of Clermont-Ferrand.
Pl. du Général de Gaulle. 63500 Issoire. 04 73 89 15 90. www.sejours-issoire.com.

This old Auvergne town is situated at the point where the Pavin valley meets the flatter fertile country of the southern Limagne. In 1540 the town became a notable centre of Protestantism. More recently it has acquired an industrial character, with important engineering works. But there is still an agreeable, provincial ambience about the place that rewards even the shortest break.

Abbatiale St-Austremoine d'Issoire★★

Guided tours (1hr30min) available. 04 73 89 15 90.
Built around 1135, this is the largest Romanesque church in the Auvergne. It was extensively restored in the 19C (west front, roof, bell tower, many of the capitals, the polychrome interior decoration).

The east end (**chevet★★**) is a fine example of Auvergne Romanesque, generously and harmoniously proportioned and rich in detail. Inside, an impression of strength and solidity, characteristic of these Auvergne churches, is given by the four great arches at the crossing and by the ambulatory with its ribbed vault. The influence of the Mozac School of sculpture is clearly seen in the capitals (**chapiteaux★** – c. 1140) carved from the local volcanic rock; particularly fine are those showing the Last Supper and Christ washing the feet of the disciples. In the narthex is a 15C mural of the **Last Judgement★**, a favourite subject of the time, here treated with great verve and a degree of satire.

Puy de Dôme with Puy de Pariou in the foreground

© Gérard Labriet/Photononstop

Le Puy de Dôme★★★

At 1 465m/4 806ft, this mountain is the highest of the peaks in the volcanic landscape known as the Puys. The Gauls erected a sanctuary to their god Lug here, and the Romans built a temple to Mercury. In 1648, Pascal conducted an experiment here proving Torricelli's theory about atmospheric weight, taking readings of the height of a column of mercury while his brother-in-law simultaneously did the same in Clermont-Ferrand; the difference was a decisive 8.4cm/3.3in.

From the summit there is a vast **panorama**★★★ over the city of Clermont-Ferrand, the Grande Limagne basin and the Puys themselves. The Puys, or the Monts Dômes as they are sometimes known, extend over an area 30km/18.6mi long and 5km/3mi wide; in it, there are a total of 112 extinct volcanoes, all more than 50 000 years old.

Orcival★★

▶ *26km/16mi SW of Clermont-Ferrand.*
▮ *Le Bourg.* ℘*04 73 65 89 77.*
www.terresdomes-sancy.com
Many houses in this tiny Auvergne village still have their original roof coverings of tiles cut from the phonolitic lavas of the nearby Roche Tuilière, the core of an ancient volcano. Founded by the monks of La Chaise-Dieu in the 12C, Orcival had become an important

parish by the middle of the 13C and has been a centre of pilgrimage since that time. More recently it has been the home town of the ex-president of France (1974–81), Valéry Giscard d'Estaing.

Basilique Notre-Dame★★

🕓*Open year-round.* ☜*Guided tours available; ask at the tourist office. Illustration –* 👁*See Introduction: Art and Culture.*
Completed around 1130, this basilica is a fine example of the Auvergne Romanesque, with a many-tiered apse, powerful buttresses and massive arches. Inside, the majestic crossing is lit by 14 windows, while both chancel and crypt, the latter with a spacious ambulatory, are masterpieces of their kind.

Le Puy de Sancy★★★

▶ *48km/30mi SW of Clermont-Ferrand. Sancy station sits 4km/2.5mi along D 983. Take the cable-car ride (3min), then 20min on foot to the summit.*
The Puy de Sancy, the highest peak in central France, rises to 1 885m/6 184ft from the set of extinct volcanoes called the Mont Dore massif, one of the most picturesque areas in the Auvergne.

Panorama★★★

1hr30min to the summit and back on foot by a rough path from the top station of the cable railway.

With the heights of the Mont Dore massif in the foreground, the immense views extend northeastwards over the Puys and to the Cantal massif in the south. The hedged fields of the valley bottoms give way, at1 100–1 400m (3 600-4 600ft), to a forest of beech, spruce and fir, while the landscape as a whole is enhanced by the presence of volcanic lakes.

On the eastern slope of the massifies the pretty mountain village of Basse-en-Chandesse★, made of lava, with picturesque **streets** and houses, a barbican, and a little **church**★ with sturdy columns and rough capitals.

Église de St-Nectaire★★

Les Grands Thermes, St-Nectaire. ✆*04 73 88 50 86. www.ville-saint-nectaire.fr. The church dominates St-Nectaire-le-Haut. The lower village, St-Nectaire-le-Bas, is a thermal spa, spreading along a green valley. Pl. de l'Eglise.* ○*Open daily Apr–Oct 9am–7pm; Nov–Mar 10am–12.30pm, 2–6pm.* ✆*Guided tours available on request.* ✆ *04 73 88 50 67.*

This little Romanesque church enjoys a spectacular location on the eastern slopes of the Monts Dore. Built around 1160 as a dependency of the great Chaise-Dieu monastery, it suffered much damage during the French Revolution, and underwent major restoration in 1875. The church has a number of notable features, including a massive **narthex**. The 103 **capitals**★★ (most are 12C) are justly famous. The treasury (**trésor**★★ – north transept) houses a statue of Notre-Dame-du-Mont-Cornadore (a Virgin in Majesty of the 12C), **a reliquary bust of St Baudime**★★, a 12C Limoges masterpiece, as well as a reliquary arm of St Nectaire in repoussé silver and a pair of Limoges book-plates of about 1170.

Château de Murol★★

▶ *6km/3.7mi E of Église de St-Nectaire.*

The ruined castle rises from a basalt platform formed by a lava flow from the Tartaret volcano. The site with its polygonal keep was fortified as early as the 12C because of its strategic position

between Auvergne and Cantal. At the end of the 14C, it became one of the main seigneurial residences of the province; Guillaume de Murol was responsible for those features which still distinguish the stronghold today (internal courtyard, main tower, and north and east walls) and which serve to remind us both of the medieval obsession with security and of the fiercely guarded independence of the Auvergnat nobility. A century later, the castle was brought into line with Renaissance tastes. However, the Wars of Religion led to the place being modernised in a military sense, with the building of bastions and watch towers, as well as an outer wall rising directly from the cliff, all reinforcing the site's natural defensive ability to withstand bombardment or sapping. Now no longer impregnable, the fortress was spared Richelieu's demolition programme, but fell into ruin in the 19C.

LES MONTS DORE★★

The Monts Dore consist of three major volcanoes: the Puy de Sancy (○*see PUY DE SANCY*), the Puy de l'Aiguiller and the Banne d'Ordanche, which together with their secondary cones form a region characterised by rugged mountains whose steep, grassy upper slopes provide summer pasture for cattle.

Traditionally these animals produced the famous St Nectaire cheese, although nowadays beef cattle are also fattened here before they are taken to the autumn markets.

The Monts Dore are very popular with those seeking outdoor pursuits, and walking, paragliding, canoeing and sailing can all be found here. During the winter there are also plenty of skiing opportunities.

The mighty River Dordogne rises on the Puy de Sancy, beginning as two separate streams, the Dore and the Dogne, and plunges down its slopes before becoming the meandering giant which flows through the verdant countryside of the Corrèze, the Lot and the Aquitaine region to the west where it finally reaches the Gironde estuary north of Bordeaux.

Le Puy Mary★★★
Cantal

At 1 787m/5 863ft, Puy Mary is one of the main peaks of the once immense Cantal volcano, which had a circumference of 60km/37mi and a cone rising to 3 000m/10 000ft. It is also the most visited natural reserve of the Auvergne region and has to be managed very sensitively. As a consequence, the local authoriies have implemented "Operation Grand Site: Puy Mary – Volcan du Cantal".

⚲ **Michelin Map:** 330 E 4
▶ **Location:** These peaks are NE from the town of Aurillac. The summit is reached by a steep but paved path from Pas-de-Peyrol – 1hr round-trip on foot.

The basaltic lava (unlike the trachytes of Mont Dore) yields rich herbage which is grazed by the reddish Salers cattle, which in their turn yield the milk for the famous Cantal cheese.

GEOGRAPHY

Sharp ridges divide the country up into a series of amphitheatres, in each of which the same set of activities is carefully staged. Meadows and cropland fill the valley bottoms around villages, though in areas less exposed to the sun there are birchwoods, grown for fuel.

On the middle slopes are beeches, used for a range of purposes, and recently planted conifers. Higher still come the upland pastures, dotted with stone-built huts used until lately as summer dwellings by shepherds or for cheese-making. Known as burons, they are planted round with ash trees, a useful source of fodder in times of drought.

VISIT
Panorama★★★

Glacial action has decapitated the volcano and worn it down. The view from the top takes in a landscape punctuated by the remains of volcanic vents and lava flows which seem to have only just cooled. The **Pas-de-Peyrol★★** too affords fine views.

ACTIVITIES

The authorities are determined that any development in the area should be compatible with the concept of sustainable tourism. While a large range of sport and leisure facilities is offered to suit all tastes and interests,

Ridge along Le Puy Mary

J. Damase/MICHELIN

they are closely monitored and must fit in with the long-term plans for the site. *For further details see: www.puymary.fr.*

Mountain biking – This is ideal territory to explore on two wheels and if you do not have your own machine then mountain bike rental and even guided tours can be obtained.

Horse riding – If you prefer four legs then various circuits both on horseback and even by donkey are available.

Other activities – Walking, hang-gliding, canyoning, cross-country skiing, fishing, rock climbing and white-water sports.

ADDITIONAL SIGHTS
Salers★★

In the heart of the Cantal region, the village is 43km/26.7mi north of Aurillac. *Pl. Tyssandier d'Escous. 04 71 40 70 68. www.pays-de-salers.com.*

High up among the vast grazing-grounds of the volcanic Cantal uplands, Salers, one of the "Most Beautiful Villages of France", has long been a market centre and staging-post for travellers. The tiny town has a maze of tortuous streets leading to the main square.

The **Grande-Place★★** is something of a stage-set, overlooked by the corner-towers and turrets of the grandiose 16C lava-built **houses** of the local notables. The Renaissance **Ancien Bailliage** has typically Auvergnat window-mouldings and angle-towers, while the **Hôtel de la Ronade** has a five-storey Gothic turret.

The church (**église★**) has a 12C porch and, inside, a fine 15C polychrome sculpture of the **Entombment★**.

Salers is also the name of a locally produced tasty farmhouse AOC cheese made from unpasteurised cow's milk.

St-Flour★★

St-Flour is 63km/39mi SE of Riom along the A 72/E 70. *17 bis, pl. Armes. 04 71 60 22 50. www.saint-flour.com.*

Occupying a spectacular site★★, St-Flour comprises two little towns; one perched on a huge rock; the other a

modern, busy place at its foot. Although all the interest is in the Upper Town, it is more convenient to park, eat and stay in the Lower Town.

At the eastern end of the Upper Town with its old lava-built houses stands the 15C **cathedral★**. From the Terrasse des Roches nearby there are extensive **views** over the rich grasslands of the Planèze de St-Flour, an inclined plateau.

Viaduc de Garabit★★

12km/7.4mi S of St-Flour.

This daring steel structure carries the Clermont-Ferrand-Millau railway across the Truyère valley with its many hydro-electric works built in the **gorges★★** gouged in the granite plateaux. Its central arch is 116m/381ft across. The viaduct was built from 1882–84 by Gustave Eiffel.

Site du Château d'Alleuze★★

26km/16mi W from Garabit via the Mallet viewpoint and the Grandval Dam.

The square keep and round towers of this most romantic of ruins loom menacingly over the lake held back by the Grandval Dam.

ADDRESSES

STAY

Chambre d'Hôte M. et Mme Prudent – *R. des Nobles. 04 71 40 75 36. 6rms.* In the heart of Salers, this stunning 17C house has a charm all its own. The simple rooms are comfortable, the pretty garden looks out towards the volcanoes, and breakfast is served either outdoors or in a handsome room typical of the region, unless you'd rather be served in bed.

Hôtel Le Gerfaut– *rte de Puy Mary – 1km/0.5mi NE via the D 680. 04 71 40 75 75. www.salers-hotel-gerfaut.com. Open Mar–Oct. 25rms.* €11.50. Above the town, a modern and functional place to sleep peacefully. The rooms have all been refurbished and some are equipped with balconies or terraces with views over the valley.

Vichy★

Allier

Pleasantly sited in the Allier valley, and well endowed with lush parks and luxurious thermal establishments, as well as high-quality entertainment, racing, a casino and good shopping, Vichy is a world-famous spa town. The virtues of the waters drew visitors here in Roman times and again from the 17C onwards.

A BIT OF HISTORY

The Roman spa town here was relatively small. In medieval times, the river crossing was commanded by a castle and later the town grew during the reign of Henri IV.

It began to flourish as a spa resort from the 17C onwards, and the renowned letter writer Madame de Sévigné came here during the latter part of the century, soon to be followed by the daughters of Louis XV. It was the visits of Napoleon III during the 1860s, however, which really placed Vichy in the top rank of spa towns.

More recently, Vichy gave its name to the Nazi collaborationist government of France led by Marshal Pétain, whose regime ruled the country from Vichy under close German supervision from 12 July 1940 until 20 August 1944.

▶ **Population:** 25 691
 Michelin Map: 326 H 6
 Info: 19 rue du Parc. ℰ04 70 98 71 94. www.ville-vichy.fr.
 Location: The town is 70km/43.mi NE of Clermont-Ferrand.

Vichy's reputation was somewhat tarnished by this episode, but its fortunes were revived by the damming of the Allier in the 1960s which created a town-centre lake for watersports.

SIGHT
Le Quartier Thermal (Spa)★

The florid spa architecture of the second half of the 19C is well represented by a number of constructions such as the Grand Casino of 1865, the Napoleon Gallery (Galerie Napoléon) of 1857, the covered galleries bordering the park (Parc des Sources), which formed part of the 1889 Paris Universal Exhibition before being re-erected here, and the Great Baths (Grand établissement thermal) of 1900.

EXCURSIONS
Riom★★

▶ *Riom is 63km/39mi SW of Vichy along the D 984 and D 2009.*

Château de Lapalisse

J. Damase/MICHELIN

193

Taste the natural spring water

S. Sauvignier/MICHELIN

The Vichy Springs

Vichy's mineral and thermal springs contain mainly bicarbonate of soda and carbonic acid. The main springs belong to the State and are operated by a contracting company founded in 1853. The waters here are used to treat conditions of the liver, gall bladder and stomach, diabetes, migraines, nutritional and digestive disorders, and also rheumatological complaints.

Waters from the Grande Grille, Hôpital and, in particular, Célestins springs are bottled and exported the world over.

Hot springs – These are the basis of the Vichy drinking cures. The **Grande Grille** is named after the grille which used to protect it from thirsty animals. The bubbling water (temperature 40°C/104°F) comes up from a depth of 1 000–1 200m/3 280–4 028ft. The **Chomel** (temperature 41°C/106°F) is named after the doctor who captured the spring in 1750 and managed the waters. A third hot spring, the **Hôpital** (temperature 33°C/91.4°F), rises in a rotunda-shaped pavilion behind the Casino.

Cold springs – Part of the regimen includes drinking the water. The **Parc** (temperature 24°C/75°F) gushes forth in the Parc des Sources. The **Lucas** (temperature 24°C/75°F) is named after the doctor and inspector who bought the spring at the beginning of the 19C on behalf of the State. The **Célestins** has a temperature of 21.5°C/71°F.

Thermal establishments – The Centre Thermal des Dômes can provide up to 2,500 people with thermal and related treatments each morning. The Callou pump room, like that of the Célestins, boasts the latest technical innovations.

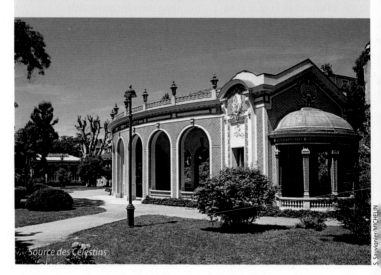

Source des Célestins

S. Sauvignier/MICHELIN

🛈 *27 place de la Fédération.*
📞 *04 73 38 59 45. www.riom.net.*
The old town of Riom, market centre of the Limagne district, still reflects the splendour of bygone days with its black stone houses and fountains. Be sure to have a leisurely wander in the Old Town.

Quartier Ancien (Old Town)

The medieval town was the capital of the Duchy of Auvergne, then in the 16C and 17C an administrative and legal centre, giving it a heritage of fine houses. Note the 16C **Maison des Consuls**★ *(5 r. de l'Hôtel de Ville)*; and the Renaissance **clock tower** and 16C **Hôtel Guimoneau**★ in Rue de l'Horloge. A ring of boulevards is built on the former ramparts enclosing the Old Town.

Rue du Commerce

The modern sculptures made of lava contrast with the traditional decoration of the houses using the same material (No 36 has 17C caryatids). 16C **Église Notre-Dame-du-Marthuret**★ houses the splendid late 14C sculpture – **Virgin with a bird**★★★, a masterpiece of harmonious proportion with a graceful Madonna and infant Jesus holding a bird in his hand.

Additional Sights

Ste-Chapelle★ *(r. Jean de Berry)* – remarkable 15C stained-glass windows.
Musée régional d'Auvergne★ *(10 bis r. Delille)* – folk art and local customs.
Musée Francisque Mandet★ *(14 r. de l'Hôtel de Ville)* – 17–18C French and Flemish painting and decorative arts.

Église de Mozac★

◗ *2km/1.2mi W. of Riom.*
This ancient abbey was founded towards the end of the 7C by St Calminus, becoming subordinated to Cluny in 1095. Until its collapse in 1460, the abbey church was one of the finest in Auvergne.
Of the building of 1095, all that remains are arches and pillars and the north aisle, together with the 47 capitals **(chapiteaux**★★) which are the oldest and perhaps the most beautiful in the whole of the province. They are products of a

workshop which was active from the end of the 11C until the middle of the 12C and which enjoyed considerable influence. Those depicting Jonah (first bay of the nave), the Apocalypse (on the ground in the choir) and the Centaur (third pillar on the left) are justly famous, but it is the capital showing the Resurrection which is truly outstanding (on the ground at the end of the nave). The Shrine of St Calminus **(châsse de Saint Calmin**★★) in champlevé enamel is an exquisite example of Limoges work with chased and gilded inlay figures.

Église de Marsat

◗ *3km/1.8mi SW of Riom.*
The church here has one of Auvergne's great works of medieval art, a 12C **Black Virgin**★★ (in the choir of the north chapel).
Few will be untouched by this depiction of Mary as a simple countrywoman, holding out the Child in a maternal gesture of great dignity.

Château de Tournoël★★

◗ *8km/5mi W of Riom.*
This is one of the province's most celebrated castles. It dominates the town of Volvic, famous for its lava quarry and, of course, its spring water (on sale worldwide), whose exceptional purity is due to the filtering effect of one of the lava flows from the Puy-de-la-Nugère. Picturesquely perched on a crag, the castle dates from the turn of the 13C and was first owned by Guy II the Count of Auvergne.
It has two keeps, one round, one square, joined together by ancillary buildings now in ruins. Mullioned windows of Renaissance date look down onto the courtyard, some of them blocked up to avoid window tax.

Gour de Tazenat★

◗ *22km/14mi NE of Riom.*
This lovely upland lake (32ha/79 acres, 60m/196.8ft deep) in its wooded setting marks the northern limit of the Auvergne volcanoes, one of whose craters it now fills.

Château de Lapalisse★★

▶ *Town and château are 25km/ 15.5mi NE of Vichy.*

🏛 *26 r. Winston Churchill, Lapalisse. 𝄐04 70 99 08 39.*

The little crossroads town (pop 3 332) has grown up at the foot of the château which has commanded the crossing of the Besbre since the 11C. Its most famous owner was Jacques II de Chabannes (1470–1525), a Marshal of France who distinguished himself in the conquest of Milan but who was killed by a blast from a harquebus received during the Battle of Pavia.

Visit

🍃 *Guided tours (1hr) Apr–Sept daily 9am–noon, 2–6pm; Oct Sat–Sun only 9am–noon, 2–6pm. Reservations required. ⬬€6. 𝄐04 70 99 37 58.*

Little remains of the medieval castle. The present building, started at the beginning of the 16C, is very much in the style of the early Renaissance, the work of Florentine craftsmen brought from Italy by Jacques.

The courtyard façade is enlivened by heraldic motifs and polychrome brick-work, by sandstone courses on the tow-ers and around the windows, by brack-eted lintels and mullioned windows, by medallions in the portal of the central tower, by foliated scrolls, pilasters and Corinthian capitals.

Inside, there is interesting Louis XIII fur-niture in the main reception room. The **Salon doré**★★ has a coffered ceiling and 15C Flemish tapestries. The chapel, built in granite, is in Flamboyant style, and there is a fine timber ceiling in the service range **(communs)**.

Moulins★

Allier

Moulins, on the River Allier, is the quiet, charming capital of the Bourbonnais region dominated by the twin spires of its Flamboyant Gothic cathedral and the Église du Sacré Coeur. Le Pal Amusement Park is well worth a visit – especially if you have children in tow. Activities on offer include horse riding, kayaking and golf.

A BIT OF HISTORY

The city was founded by the Bourbon lords at the end of the 11C. In time, the Bourbons rose to the rank of dukes. The 15C was the duchy's golden age, with many artists commissioned to work here. The independence of the Bourbonnais became an irritant to the king and François I took advantage of the supposed treason of Charles III, the Ninth Duke, to confiscate his estates. After a series of battles against the French forces, Charles was killed (1527) and the Bourbonnais attached to the French Crown.

▶ **Population:** 20 470
◔ **Michelin Map:** 326 H 3
▯ **Info:** 11 r. François Péron. 𝄐04 70 44 14 14. www. moulins-tourisme.com.
▶ **Location:** Moulins sits in the centre of the country, 54km/34mi N of Vichy and 58km/36mi S of Nevers.

SIGHT
Cathédrale Notre-Dame★

Pl. des Vosges. ⏰*Open year-round daily 9am–noon, 2–6pm.* 🍃*Guided tours available.* ⏰*Closed 1 Jan, 1 May, 14 Jul, 25 Dec.* ⬬*€2 donation suggested. 𝄐04 70 20 89 65.*

From the 17C arcaded covered market there is a good view of the cathedral, which has exemplary **stained-glass windows**★★ depicting famous figures from the Bourbons' court. Among the works of art diplayed in the cathe-dral is the **Triptych by the Master of Moulins**★★★, from about 1498 – a tri-umph of late Gothic painting. The Mas-ter has never been conclusively identi-

Forêt de Tronçais

©World Pictures/Photoshot

fied. The poses of the figures depicted suggest the Flemish School, while their faces recall the work of Florentine masters. Note also the **Jaquemart**★ (bell tower). The **Mausolée du Duc de Montmorency**★ (☞ *guided tours available; ℘04 70 48 51 18)* dating from 1585–1632, is not to be missed.

EXCURSION
Forêt de Tronçais★★★
◐ *The forest lies N of Montluçon, and is easily reached on autoroute A71.*
🏛*Pl. du Champ-de-Foire, Cérilly. ℘04 70 67 55 89. http://paysdetroncais.free.fr.*
This splendid oak forest, regarded by many as one of the finest in France, if not Europe, lies at the southeastern end of the great plains of central France, bounded by the rivers Allier and Cher.

A Bit of History
Today's forest passed into the hands of the French Crown when François I put an end to the independence of the Bourbonnais in 1527.
A steady process of deterioration set in which was reversed by the great Colbert in 1670; anxious to maintain the supply of ship timber for the expanding French navy, he instituted measures for the conservation and renewal of the woodland. However, in 1788 an iron foundry was opened, and to satisfy its demands for charcoal, two-thirds of the area was converted from high forest to a coppice regime. In 1832 a new policy of conservation was adopted, and since 1928 six blocks of high forest totalling 650ha/1 606 acres have been managed on a long rotation of 225 years.

Visit
The forest consists largely of sessile oak. The finest stands are called the **Hauts-Massifs**★★★; here there are a number of exceptional trees with their own names, some more than 300 years old. East of the Gardien clearing are the Carré, Émile-Guillaumin and Charles-Louis-Philippe oaks, and to the west of the Buffévent clearing in the Richebout block are other venerable trees called Jacques-Chevalier, de la Sentinelle and des Jumeaux.
The Tronçais region straddles the boundary between the north and south of France. To the north is the langue d'oïl, four-wheeled carts, and slate or flat-tiled roofs; to the south, the langue d'oc, two-wheeled carts, and pantiled roofs in the Roman fashion.

Additional Sights
Séries de l'Ouest★ – Western forest stands.
Futaie Colbert★ – Colbert Stand.
Étangs de St-Bonnet★
Pirota et Saloup★ – ponds.

BRITTANY

Populated by Celts since its birth, Brittany retains many affinities with the other Celtic lands fringing the Atlantic. Its identity, quite distinct from that of the rest of France, is expressed in its language (Breton, akin to Welsh), traditions and landscape. The province's long and mysterious past makes itself felt in the abundance of prehistoric remains, menhirs, dolmens and megaliths. Granite distinguishes Breton building whether in church or castle, harbour wall or humble house, and is used to great effect.

Highlights

1 Village set in aspic:
   Locronan (p213)

2 Spectacular coastal landscape:
   Pointe-du-Raz (p214)

3 Small inland sea near Vannes:
   Golfe de Morbihan (p219)

4 Medieval town of **Josselin**
   (p220)

5 Megaliths at **Carnac** (p221)

Geography – Brittany has an extraordinarily indented coastline, called "Armor" (country near the sea) by the Gauls. Its cliffs, rocky headlands and offshore islands are battered by Atlantic breakers, while its narrow drowned valleys, *abers,* and sandy bays are washed by tides of exceptional range. Inland is the "Argoat" (country of the wood), once thickly forested, now a mixture of *bocage*, heath and moor.

History – The Channel coast is punctuated by historic towns, elegant resorts, dramatic corniches and headlands. The original Celts were subjugated by the Romans in the 1C AD, but fresh waves of Celtic settlers arrived here from Cornwall following the collapse of the Roman Empire and the country remained anarchic until 799, when Charlemagne took control.

The Duchy of Brittany was soon established and independence achieved in AD 845. Although later Dukes paid homage to the French monarch, this autonomy was retained till the late 15C following the marriage of Anne of Brittany to the King. The Bretons were enthusiastic supporters of the Revolution and helped put down those who revolted against the new state.

Economy – Much of France's fishing fleet operates from Brittany. Other industries include food processing and car manufacturing. Tourism is vitally important and many summer visitors are attracted to the resorts on the Atlantic and Channel coasts.

🕮*See the Michelin Green Guide Brittany for hotel and restaurant suggestions.*

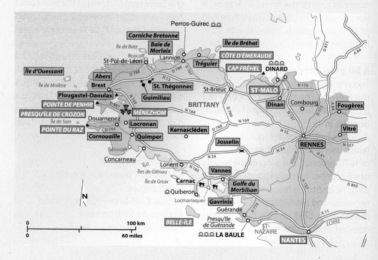

Rennes★★

Ille-et-Vilaine

The city of artistic, architectural and historical interest, founded by the Gauls, became capital of Brittany in the 16C.

A BIT OF HISTORY

Du Guesclin's Beginnings (14C)
Bertrand Du Guesclin was born in a castle southwest of Dinan. The eldest of 10 children, he entered a tournament at Rennes at age 17 and unseated several opponents. From this humble victory, he went on to defeat far greater opponents. In the service of France, he freed Périgord from English rule in 1370, and Normandy in 1378.

In the 18C there was no running water in the town and therefore no way of fighting fires. In December 1720 an accidental fire caused by a lamp falling into a carpenter's shavings destroyed much of the town.

SIGHTS

Palais du Parlement de Bretagne★★

pl. du Parlement de Bretagne.
Guided tours only (1hr30); reservations at the tourist office.
Closed 1 May. €7. 02 99 67 11 66.
www.parlement-bretagne.com
Brittany's Parliament initially had its seat in Rennes for part of the year and Nantes for the other, before finally the decision was taken in 1561 to establish a single seat in Rennes.

Le Vieux Rennes★

The old town was devastated in 1720 by a great fire that raged for eight days and engulfed almost 1 000 houses. Enough buildings were spared to make a walk through the old part of Rennes an architecturally rewarding experience.

The medieval houses crowd together in the narrow streets, identifiable by their timber construction, their projecting upper floors and their sculptured decoration. No 3 r. St-Guillaume, called the **Du Guesclin House**, has a deeply carved door flanked by figures of St

▶ **Population:** 211 778
Michelin Map: 309 L-M 6
Info: 11 r. St Yves.
02 99 67 11 11.
www.tourisme-rennes.com.
▶ **Location:** Rennes lies 105km/66mi N of Nantes, and 152km/95mi W of Le Mans.
Timing: Rennes is not a city to rush around; allow a full day or more to get the most from your visit.

Sebastian and one of his tormentors. The **Hôtel de Brie★** (8 r. du Chapitre) is of such refinement that it has been attributed to Mansart.

Les Champs Libres★

10 cours Alliés. Open Tue–Fri noon–7pm (Tue until 9pm), Sat-Sun 2–7pm.
€7. 02 23 40 66 00.
www.leschampslibres.fr.
This cultural centre brings together three institutions: the Musée de Bretagne, the Espace des Sciences and the library. The ultra-modern building is the work of architect Christian de Portzamparc.

Cathédrale St-Pierre

Carrefour de la Cathédrale. Open 9am–noon, 3–6pm. 02 99 78 48 80.
The third built on the site since the 6C, this cathedral was finished in 1844 after 57 years' work. The previous building collapsed in 1762 except for the two towers in the Classical style flanking the façade.

The **interior★** is very rich, its stucco facing covered with paintings and gilding. The cathedral contains a masterpiece: the gilded and carved wood **altarpiece★★** in the chapel before the south transept.

Musée des Beaux-Arts★

20 quai Émile Zola. Open Tue 10am–6pm, Wed–Sun 10amnoon, 2-6pm.
Closed Mon and public holidays.
€6. 02 23 62 17 45.
www.mbar.org.

The permanent collection rooms at the Museum of Fine Arts have recently been restyled, extended and enriched with new works that have never been shown. It now contains fine examples of painting, sculpture, drawing, prints and objects from the 14C to the present.

EXCURSIONS
Fougères★★
▶ Distance from Rennes 51km/32mi.

🏠 2 r. Nationale. ℘02 99 94 12 20. www.ot-fougeres.fr.

In the 19C Fougères was the most industrialised town in Brittany, having abandoned cloth-making in favour of shoe production. The area formed part of the frontier region taken from the Franks in AD 850 by **Nominoé** (🔗 see VANNES).

Château de Fougères★★
pl. Pierre Symon. 🕐Open daily except Mon: May–Sept 10am–1pm, 2–7pm (Jul–Aug daily 10am–7pm); Oct–Apr: 10am–12.30pm, 2-5.30pm. 🕐Closed Jan and 25 Dec. ⊙€7.50. ℘02 99 99 79 59. www.chateau-fougeres.com.

The first fortifications date from the 10C. In the 13C the castle's mighty towers served to protect Brittany from Capetian France. After its important role in the War of the Breton Succession (🔗 see JOSSELIN) in the 14C, the castle was partly demolished by Richelieu.

Vitré★★
▶ Distance from Rennes 40km/25mi.

🏠 pl. du Gen.-de-Gaulle, 35500 Vitré. ℘02 99 75 04 46. www.ot-vitre.fr.

This is the best-preserved "old world" town in Brittany; its fortified castle, its ramparts and its small streets have remained just as they were 400 or 500 years ago, giving the town a picturesque and evocative appeal that is long remembered. The old town is built on a spur, commanding the deep valley of the Vilaine on one side and a railway cutting on the other; the castle stands proudly on the extreme point. From the 15C to the 17C, Vitré was one of the more prosperous Breton cities; it made hemp, woollen cloth and cotton stockings that were sold not only in France, but also in England, Germany, Spain and even America and the Indies. Gathered together to form the powerful brotherhood known as "Marchands d'Outre-Mer", the Vitré tradesmen of this period commissioned the building of highly distinctive houses with half-timbering, many of which can still be seen today.

Château★★
🕐Open Apr–Sept daily 10.30am–12.30pm, 2–6.30pm; Oct–Mar daily except Tue and Sun am, 10.30am–12.15pm, 2–5.30pm. ⏴Guided tours available. 🕐Closed 1 Jan, Easter Sun, 1 Nov and 25 Dec. ⊙€4. ℘02 99 75 04 46. www.ot-vitre.fr.

The château, dating from the 11C, was rebuilt from the 13C to the 15C. The entrance is guarded by a drawbridge and entrance fort (Châtelet) flanked by two big machicolated towers.

The St-Laurent Tower houses the **Musée St-Nicolas**, which contains 15C and 16C sculpture from the houses of Vitré, the 15C tomb of Gui X (a local lord) as well as 16C Flemish and 17C Aubusson tapestries.

Combourg★
▶ Distance from Rennes 38km/24mi.

🏠 pl. Albert-Parent, 35270 Combourg. ℘02 99 73 13 93.

This picturesque old town stands at the edge of Lac Tranquille, a large lake, and is dominated by an imposing feudal castle. Those who want to take only a quick look at the castle from the outside should walk along the local road that branches off the Rennes road and runs beside the lake.

Château★
🕐Open daily except Sat. ⏴Guided tours (45min): Apr–Sept 2–5.30pm (Jul–Aug, daily 10.30am, 11.15am 2–5.30pm); Oct 2–5pm. ⊙€7. ℘02 99 73 13 93. www.combourg.net.

The exterior of the castle looks like a powerful fortress with its four massive towers, pepper-pot roofs, crenellated parapet walk and thick walls slit by narrow openings.

St-Malo★★★
Ille-et-Vilaine

The **site**★★★ of the walled town of St-Malo on the east bank of the Rance is unique in France, making the ancient port one of the country's great tourist attractions.

A BIT OF HISTORY

The town's prosperity began in the 16C. In 1534, **Jacques Cartier** had set out from here on the voyage which led to the discovery and naming of Canada; very soon a thriving commerce had begun, based on furs and fish. Local ship-owners began to build themselves fine manor houses in the surrounding countryside, as well as tall timber-built residences in the town itself. By the 1660s their boats were trading in the Pacific, and their ever-increasing wealth enabled them to build in granite. Parisian architectural fashions began to prevail over local traditions. Anticipating the coming naval rivalry between England and France, Colbert became aware of the vulnerability of his country's western coasts; in 1689, Vauban was commissioned to strengthen the defences of St-Malo.

In the 19C, the invention of floating docks ended the advantage which the great tidal range of the port had long given its ship-builders and -repairers.

SIGHTS

Old Town and Ramparts★★★

From the ramparts there are fine views of the Rance valley and towards Dinard on the far side of the estuary. Within the walls is the old town, almost entirely rebuilt in its original form after near-total destruction in 1944. Solid walls of granite, relieved by horizontal bands between each storey, steep mansard roofs and formidable chimney stacks combine to give an effect of harsh dignity and strong identity. The houses along the Rue de Dinan and those facing the walls are particularly fine.

Cathédrale St-Vincent

pl. J. de Chantlon.

▶ **Population:** 49 823
◔ **Michelin Map:** 309 J 3
▪ **Info:** espl. St-Vincent. ☏ 08 25 135 200. www.saint-malo-tourisme.com.
▶ **Location:** St Malo is on Brittany's northern coast 70km/44mi NNW of Rennes.
P **Parking:** Park near the port by the Esplanade St-Vincent.
◔ **Timing:** Walk right around the town on top of the ramparts in about 2hr. Spend another 2hr seeing the château and cathedral.
▪ **Kids:** Le Grand Aquarium.

The nave vault of 1160 is one of the oldest in Brittany, albeit rebuilt after the last war. Note the **stained-glass windows**★ by Jean Le Moal.

Le Grand Aquarium★★

ave du Général Patton. ◔*Open daily Apr–Jun and Sept 10am–7pm; mid-Jul–mid-Aug 9.30am–10pm; early Jul and late Aug 9.30am–8pm; rest of the year 10am–6pm.* ◔*Closed mornings of 25 Dec and 1 Jan, 2 weeks in Jan, 2 weeks Nov (call to check).* ⊜€14 (children €9). ☏02 99 21 19 00. www.aquarium-st-malo.com.

The aquarium offers a fascinating experience as well as presenting collections of great scientific interest, as visitors trace the history of great sailors from St-Malo. Attractions of special interest include the ring (**Anneau**), a remarkable round aquarium containing 600 000 litres in which shoals of pelagic species of fish swim endlessly; and a life-size reconstruction of a sunken wreck (**Vaisseau englouti**) with sharks.

ADDITIONAL SIGHTS

Musée d'Histoire de la Ville et d'Ethnographie du Pays Malouin★

espl. Felicité Lamennais.
◔*Apr–Sept 10am–12.30pm, 2–6pm, rest of the year Tue–Sun 10am–noon, 2–6pm.* ◔*Closed 1 Jan, 1 May, 1 and*

11 Nov and 25 Dec. ⊚€5.50. ℘02 99 40 71 57. History of the town and its famous men.

Quic-en-Groigne Tower★
(pl. Vauban). Wax museum.

⭐ Fort National★
Access by Plage de l'Éventail at low tide only (check with tourist office), 15min on foot there and back. ☞Guided tours (45min) Easter, Whitsun, Jun–Sept daily at low tide (variable times). ⊘Closed during high tide. ⊚€4. ℘02 72 46 66 26. www.fortnational.com.
Historical monument built in 1689 by the great military architect Vauban to protect the port of St-Malo.

EXCURSIONS
⛭ Côte d'Émeraude★★★
The name Emerald Coast has been given to Brittany's picturesque northern shore from Cancale **(headland – Pointe du Grouin**★★**)** to **Le Val André**★★ and includes some famous beaches: Dinard, St-Lunaire, Paramé etc. and the city of privateers, St-Malo.

The Emerald Coast scenic road runs through the major resorts (Dinard, St-Malo) and offers detours to the tips of the numerous headlands, including **Fort de Latte**★★, **Cap Fréhel**★★★ and **Cap d'Erquy**★ from which the views of the jagged coastline are in places quite spectacular.

Dinard★★★
⊙ *This smart resort is on the left bank of the Rance across from St-Malo.*
🛈*2 bd Féart.* ℘02 99 46 94 12. www.ot-dinard.com.
On the magnificent estuary of the River Rance opposite St-Malo, Dinard, once a small fishing village, is an elegant resort with sheltered sandy beaches and luxuriant Mediterranean vegetation flourishing in the mild climate.

The resort came into being when a wealthy American called Coppinger built a château here in 1850. He was followed two years later by a British family, who in turn attracted many of their fellow-countrymen. By the end of the 19C its reputation rivalled that of Brighton; sumptuous villas and luxuri-

ous hotels abounded, frequented by an international smart set.

Promenades lead from **Plage de l'Écluse**★ (or **Grande Plage**), a fine beach bordered by hotels, the casino and convention centre, to the **Plage du Prieuré**. From the **Pointe du Moulinet**★★, the view extends as far as Cap Fréhel to the west and the ramparts of St-Malo to the east. In summer, the **Promenade du Clair de Lune**★ with its pretty parterres and Mediterranean plants forms an attractive setting for evening concerts.

⛭ Fort La Latte★★
⊙*Open Apr–Sept 10.30am–6pm (Jul–Aug 10.30am–7pm); Oct–Mar 1.30–5.30pm.* ⊚€5 *(children €3).* ℘02 96 41 57 11. www.castlelalatte.com.
This stronghold, built by the Goyon-Matignons in the 14C, remodelled in the 17C and restored in the early 20C, has kept its feudal appearance. It stands on a spectacular **site**★★, separated from the mainland by two gullies, which are crossed by drawbridges.

Follow the lane to the fort; you will pass a menhir known as **Gargantua's Finger**. Cross the thick walls and go to the *Tour de l'Échaugette* and the cannon-ball foundry.

From the parapet walk, there is a **panorama**★★ of Sévignés Cove, Cap Fréhel, the bay of La Frênaye, Pointe de St-Cast, the Hébihens archipelago, and the walls of the fort.

Dinan★★
⊙ *Dinan is at the top of the Rance estuary, about 30km/18.6mi S of St-Malo.* 🛈*9 r. du Château.* ℘02 96 87 69 76. www.dinan-tourisme.com.
Dinan is a gem of a town, surrounded by ramparts and guarded by a castle.

The great hero of the town is **Bertrand du Guesclin** (c.1315–80), a redoubtable warrior. Jean le Bon (John the Good) had been taken prisoner by the English at the Battle of Poitiers in 1356. During the four years of captivity he spent in England he became aware of the extent to which feudal rights imposed limitations on royal power, and conceived the

St-Malo - view of the city from the Fort National

R. Mattès/MICHELIN

idea of a body of knights attached to the monarch. In pursuit of this aim, he took Du Guesclin into his service shortly after his release and return to France.

This middle-aged knight had until then experienced little but rebuffs and difficulties due to his modest ancestry, lack of means and exceptionally ugly appearance. John's successor, Charles V, kept him on, doubtless in view of his great popularity and reckless bravery and his implacable hatred of the English (which at one point in his youth had led him to support Charles of Blois).

In 1366, after ridding France of the "Free Companies" (marauding bands of mercenaries), he was made High Constable of France. He freed Périgord from English rule in 1370 and Normandy in 1378. In 1379 he handed his sword to the king rather than use it against his rebellious Breton compatriots. In 1380 he died beneath the walls of Châteauneuf-de-Randon in the south.

La Vieille Ville

The houses of the old town cluster together behind the long circuit of walls, built by the Dukes of Brittany in the 14C to defend their domain against the Normans, the English, and, after the accession of Louis XI, the French.

Château★

pl. du Guesclin. ◷*Open Jun–Sept daily 10am–6.30pm; Oct–Dec and Feb–May daily 1.30–5.30pm.* ◉€4. ℘*02 96 87 58 72.*

Begun by Duke John IV about the middle of the 14C. Its 15C towers project outwards in order to facilitate enfilading fire. The exceptionally fine machicolations of Duchess Anne's Keep (Donjon de la Duchesse Anne) are of interest.

Basilique St-Sauveur

pl. St-Sauveur.

The west front is much influenced by the Poitiers version of the Romanesque. In the north aisle is the Evangelists' Window, a fine example of late 15C Breton glass, famous for its yellows. In the north transept is the cenotaph containing the heart of Du Guesclin.

Vieilles maisons

Duke John was happy to let Dinan run its own affairs, and the town's prosperity is reflected in the rebuilding of many old timber houses in stone. A most picturesque townscape results from the many buildings with overhanging upper storeys, angle-posts, half-timbering, arcades and granite side-walls.

The most interesting houses are on Rue de l'Apport (the 15C Mère Pourcel House), **Place des Merciers★** (triangular gables and porches), **Rue du Jerzual★** which links the main part of the town with the port (15C and 16C shops where craftsmen have worked for six centuries) and on Place du Guesclin (17C and 18C town houses).

St-Brieuc★

Côtes-d'Armor

The town is built 3km/1.8mi from the sea on a plateau deeply cleft by two water courses: the Gouëdic and the Gouet. Bold viaducts span their valleys. The Gouet is canalised and leads to the commercial and fishing port of Légué. St-Brieuc is the administrative, commercial and industrial centre of the *département* (Côtes-d'Armor). The markets and fairs of the town are much frequented, especially the Fair of St-Michael (Foire St-Michel) on 29 September. On Saturdays, a market is held in front of the cathedral. The peaceful provincial city has retained some fine timber-framed houses.

▶ **Population:** 47 971
- **Michelin Map:** Local map 309 F3 – Côtes-d'Armor (22).
- **Info:** 7 r. St-Gouéno, 22000 St-Brieuc. ✆08 25 00 22 22. www.baiedesaint brieuc.com.
▶ **Location:** St-Brieuc is crossed by the N 12, which comes from Dinan (60km/37mi E) and goes to Brest (145km/90mi W). The D 786 follows the coast, serving the resorts of the Côte d'Émeraude.
👥 **Kids:** A walk through the Galerie des Oiseaux at the Maison de la Baie.
🕐 **Timing:** Allow a day to visit the town and beaches.
👁 **Don't Miss:** The exceptional views from pointe du Roselier.

SIGHTS

Cathédrale St-Étienne★

This great cathedral of the 13C and 14C has been reconstructed several times and restored in the 19C; its mass bears striking witness to its original role of church fortress. The front is framed by two great towers complete with loopholes and machicolations and supported by stout buttresses. The two arms of the transept jut far out and are protected by towers with pepper-pot roofs.

The nave with its seven bays was rebuilt in the 18C. The harmonious three-sided chancel has an elegant triforium with quatrefoil balustrade and trefoil arches above the great arcades.

In the south aisle, note the carved wooden altar by Corlay (c.1745) in the Chapel of the Holy Sacrament. The south arm of the transept is lit by fine 15C stained-glass windows and in the small chapel stands the tomb of St William (d.1234). The stained-glass windows represent the Glorification of Mary. Note too the 16C organ loft, the 18C pulpit and the Stations of the Cross carved in granite by Saupique (1958).

Old Houses

The area to the north of the cathedral still retains many 15–16C half-timbered and corbelled houses. Walk through place du Martray, rue Fardel (at the corner of place au Lin: the Ribeault mansion); at No 15, the house known as the "mansion of the dukes of Brittany"; Nos 17, 19, 27, 29, 31, 32 and 34 are also worth a look); rue Quinquaine (No 9) and rue de Gouët (Nos 6, 16, 22).

Tour du St-Esprit is an interesting Renaissance structure with a pepper-pot octagonal corner tower, and has been carefully restored.

Fontaine de St-Brieuc is sheltered by a lovely 15C porch, and stands against the east end of the Chapelle of Notre-Dame-de-la-Fontaine. Brieuc, the Welsh monk who came to the region in the 5C, is believed to have settled here.

Tertre Aubé★

The hill commands a fine **view**★ of the vallée du Gouët, crossed by the viaduct which carries the road to Paimpol; also of the partly hidden port of Légué, below, and, to the right, of St-Brieuc Bay and the ruined tower of Cesson.

EXCURSIONS
Cap Fréhel★★★

▶ *Between St-Brieuc and Dinard, on the Emerald Coast.* 🅸 *pl. de Chambly, 22240 Fréhel.* ☎*02 96 41 57 23. www.paysdefrehel.com.*

The **site** of this cape is one of the grandest on the Breton coast. Its red, grey and black cliffs rise vertically to a height of 70m/230ft and are fringed with reefs on which the swell breaks heavily.

Overlooking the English Channel, legend has it that in ancient times you could walk to the UK from here! Of course, scientists have since proven otherwise.

This wild, protected site covers 400ha/988.4 acres of heathland and includes an ornithology park.

Panorama

The coastal panorama is vast in clear weather: from the Pointe du Grouin, on the right, with the Cotentin in the background, to the Île de Bréhat, on the left. The famous outline of Fort la Latte is visible on the right.

🚶 Tour du Cap
30min walk.

At the extremity of the headland stands the **lighthouse**, built in 1950 and lit automatically nowadays by a xenon flash lamp; the light carries only 200m in foggy weather, but it can be seen 120km/75mi away when it is clear.

From the gallery at the top of the tower, there is an immense view of the horizon: you may see Bréhat to the west, Jersey to the north, Granville, a part of the Cotentin Peninsula and the Îles Chausey to the northeast. At a point 400m from the lighthouse a siren mounted in a shelter gives two blasts every minute in foggy weather.

After passing the furthest point where the siren stands, you can look down on the **Fauconnière rocks**, crowded with seagulls and cormorants; the contrast between the mauvish-red of the rocks and the blue or green of the sea is striking. Near the Restaurant de la Fauconnière, take a steep path on the right; halfway down it reaches a platform from which there is another fine view of the Fauconnière rocks and the sea.

Tréguier★★

▶ *72km/45mi NW of St-Brieuc.*
🅸 *1 pl. Général Leclerc.* ☎*02 96 92 30 19. www.ville-treguier.fr.*

Tréguier is a little medieval city, overlooking the estuary of the Jaudy and Guindy rivers, one of the drowned valleys characteristic of the Breton coast. The town and its surroundings were no strangers to misfortune. In 1345–47. the area was devastated by the English allies of Jean de Montfort in retribution for having supported Jeanne de Penthièvre in the War of the Breton Succession. In 1592 it was pillaged by the Catholic Leaguers for having taken the side of Henri IV, then punished again in 1789 for its oppostion to taxes and reforms introduced at the French Revolution.

Cathédrale St-Tugdual★★

Begun in 1339, this is one of the finest buildings of its kind in Brittany, Anglo-Norman in style in spite of the use of the local granite. The exterior is notable for its Romanesque Tour d'Hastings and the balustrades adorning the slate roofs, as well as for the two porches on the south side; the larger one with its statues of the Apostles is known as the Porche du Peuple, while the other with its much-eroded statuary is the Porche des Cloches.

Within, the Lanceolate version of the Gothic survives in the three-storey elevation. A frieze sculpted in white tufa runs underneath the blind triforium; in the south transept there is a graceful window (**Grande Verrière**★) with Flamboyant Gothic lancets (**fenêtre**★) adorned with a depiction of the Mystic Vine symbolising the Church in Brittany. In the ambulatory is a 13C wooden figure of Christ, and the nave has a copy of the tomb of St Ives built by Duke John V. The **cloisters** (**cloître**)★ of 1458 are among the few to survive in Brittany. Timber-roofed and with a carved frieze, it has 48 elegant arches giving onto a hydrangea-planted courtyard.

Lannion★

Côtes-d'Armor

Lannion, spread out on both banks of the River Léguer, has retained its typical old Breton character. From the bridge, there is a good view of the port and of the vast Monastère Ste-Anne. The Centre de Recherches de Lannion and the Centre National d'Études des Télécommunications, where research is undertaken in telecommunications and electronics, have been built north of Lannion at the crossroads of the road to Perros-Guirec and that of Trégastel-Plage. Lannion's annual organ festival takes place in Église St-Jean-du-Baly (16–17C).

SIGHTS
Old Houses★

The beautiful façades of the 15C and 16C houses, half-timbered, corbelled and with slate roofs, may be admired especially at *pl. du Général Leclerc* (Nos 23, 29, 31, 33), *r. des Chapeliers* (Nos 1-9), *r. Geoffroy-de-Pont-Blanc* (Nos 1 and 3) and *r. Cie-Roger-de-Barbé* (Nos 1 and 7). At the corner of the latter, on the left, a granite cross has been sealed in the wall at the spot where the *Chevalier de Pont-Blanc* distinguished himself in the heroic defence of the town during the War of Succession.

▶ **Population:** 20 610

Michelin Map: Local map 309 B2 - Côtes-d'Armor (22).

Info: 2 quai d'Aiguillon, 22300 Lannion. ✆02 96 46 41 00. www.ot-lannion.fr.

Location: The town is crossed by the D 786 which links Morlaix (38km/ 23.5mi W) and Paimpol (35km/22mi E), passing by Tréguier.

Timing: Explore old Lannion in the morning and the outskirts in the afternoon.

Parking: Ursulines car park is free all year.

Don't Miss: The medieval old town, the market on Thursday morning and Séhar point for the views.

Église de Brélévenez★

The church was built on a hill by the Templars in the 12C and remodelled in the Gothic period.

Note the curious **Romanesque apse** decorated with round pillars, carved capitals and modillions. The bell tower dates from the 15C. The Romanesque crypt, remodelled in the 18C, contains an 18C **Entombment**★, in which the subjects are depicted life-size.

La Côte de Granit Rose

The Pink Granite Coast boasts a remarkable stretch of pink-coloured rocky coastline between Trégastel and Trébeurden. While there are many places in the world that have pink or red rock, there are only two other places that have the same type of pink granite found at the northern Brittany coast: the Bavella range of mountains in southeast Corsica, and in southeast China. Due to the fragility of this spectacular environment, the Pink Granite Coast has been designated a conservation area with dedicated footpaths to protect the rock from the impact of erosion created by human activity.

It's not just the vivid pink and orange tints that are spectacular along the Côtes-d'Armor's Pink Granite Coast; wind, rain and the tide have carved the rocks here into extraordinary shapes. Local imagination has given names to many of the rocks dotted along the shore, such as Napoleon's Hat, the Gnome, the Witch, the Elephant, the Whale, the Ram, the Rabbit, the Tortoise and the pile of crêpes.

St-Pol-de-Léon ★

Finistère

St-Pol is one of the main market-gardening centres of the rich band of fertile soils running all round the Breton coast from St-Malo to St-Nazaire. Where the wind can be kept out, the otherwise mild climate allows excellent crops of vegetables to be grown, artichokes, onions, early potatoes, cauliflowers, salad vegetables... eagerly bought in the markets of Paris and on the far side of the English Channel. Mechanisation means that much of the characteristic pattern of tiny fields bounded by stone walls is doomed to disappear.

▶ **Population:** 7 332
✆ **Michelin Map:** 308 H
▯ **Info:** pl. de l'Evêché.
  ☎02 98 15 05 69.
  www.saintpoldeleon.fr.
◐ **Location:** The town is in western Brittany, 5km/3mi S of Roscoff.

SIGHTS

Chapelle du Kreisker ★

2 r. Verderel.

The chapel was rebuilt around 1375; in the 15C, when the coastal towns were prospering from their sea-borne trade, it housed the meetings of the town council. In about 1430, Duke John V of Brittany tried to introduce the Gothic style into Brittany in order to boost his prestige. But the response of the Breton architects was to adapt Flamboyant Gothic to local ways; they shunned highly designed and decorated façades which were difficult to reconcile with the dour qualities of the granites of the region, and favoured a flattened apse. They thereby eliminated the problems caused by vaults with a circular or polygonal plan, as well as enabling the interior to be lit by a single large window. In addition, the use of a coffered ceiling and a lightweight slate roof allowed them to dispense with flying buttresses. The chapel was subsequently enlarged, and, between 1436–1439, given its **belfry** (**clocher**★★), the finest in the province. Interest in it has increased owing to the loss of the tower of Notre-Dame-du-Mur at Morlaix on which it is supposed to have been modelled. In its vertical emphasis, it is reminiscent of the churches of Normandy; it has a pointed steeple and pinnacles so delicate they had to be tied into the main structure by braces to enable them to resist the force of the wind.

Ancienne Cathédrale ★

r. de Morlaix.

The old cathedral was erected on 12C foundations in the 13C and 14C. This fine building with its characteristically Breton balustraded belfry was restored by the Dukes of Brittany from 1431 onwards. Seven bays of the nave still have their original vaults; the nave itself was built in Caen stone, a clear indication of Norman influence. Norman too is the inspection gallery which runs below the triforium.

In the north side of the chancel, below the funerary niches, are a number of wooden reliquaries with skulls dug up in a nearby cemetery, while in the sanctuary a palm tree carved in wood contains a ciborium for the Host (1770).

EXCURSIONS

Roscoff ★

◐ *5km/3mi N.*

The harbour town with its fishing fleet and important export trade (vegetables) to Britain also has ferry services linking Brittany to Plymouth and Cork. It is a flourishing resort and a medical centre using sea-water treatment.

The town centre is an agreeable place to explore, and is often overlooked by visitors. Here, not far from the harbour, is the church of **Notre-Dame-de-Kroaz-Batz**★ with its remarkable lantern-turret belfry (**clocher**★) of Renaissance date. Inside, four alabaster **statues**★ grace the altarpiece of one of the altars in the south aisle.

Scene from the Passion on the Calvary, St-Thégonnec

Enclos Paroissial de St-Thégonnec★★

◯ *The village lies 12km/7.4mi SW of the town of Morlaix, in northern Brittany.*

The parish close at St-Thégonnec is among the most famous of these typically Breton monumental groupings of church, cemetery, calvary and ossuary. The magnificent 17C parish close at St-Thégonnec was to be the last of the great parish closes of Brittany. By good fortune, the village has managed to preserve it in fine condition.

Although of older origin, parish closes began to develop in this form during the second half of the 16C. They formed a useful tool for the Catholic Church, trying to promote a veneration of apostles and saints in opposition to Brittany's heritage of local cults.

Their effectiveness was increased by the presentation of their subject matter somewhat in the manner of a strip cartoon, with exaggerated features and dramatic gestures.

This parish close is approached through a Renaissance **triumphal arch★ (porte triomphale)** (1587), lavishly decorated with cannon balls, shells, pilasters and little lanterns. The **calvary★★ (calvaire)** dates from 1610. It is the work of Rol-land Doré, and the last of its type to be carved from the mica-rich igneous rock known as **kersanton**. On the lower arm of the cross are figures of angels collecting Christ's blood, while the base shows scenes of the Passion and Resurrection. Note particularly the depiction of Christ's tormentors and also the symbolic use of clothing, with Our Lord and His followers dressed according to Christian tradition, while the representatives of worldly power wear the fashions of the time of Henri IV. The **funerary chapel★ (chapelle funéraire)** of 1676 illustrates traditional decorative motifs in the province (altarpiece with spiral columns and a Holy Sepulchre in painted oak).

The 15C **church★ (église)** was rebuilt and refurnished several times in the 17C and early 18C. The **pulpit★★ (chaire)** has a polygonal base (1683) carved by master carpenters from the naval yards at Brest, as well as a fine medallion at the back and a Louis XV sounding-board.

Enclos Paroissial de Guimiliau★★

◯ *8km/5mi SW.*

This example of a parish close pre-dates the one at St-Thégonnec by some 30 years. The **calvary★★ (calvaire**, 1581) has an attractively naïve quality; its 200 figures are full of a sense of vigorous movement and are carved in a robust way which recalls the sculpture of the Romanesque period.

Also of interest is the terrifying sculpture showing the Gates of Hell, with the struggling figure of Lost Kate (Catel Gollet in Breton), the flirtatious serving-girl who failed to reveal all at Confession. The funerary chapel of 1642 has an outdoor pulpit of earlier (15C) date.

The **church★ (église)** has a Renaissance **porch★★** dating from 1606; the arching depicts scenes from the Old and the New Testaments. Panelled vaulting is a feature of the interior, which has a Baroque **baptistery★★ (baptistère)** with a canopy and spiral columns decorated with pampres and foliage.

With its sculpted panels of about 1675, the **pulpit★ (chaire)** is also in the Baroque style.

Brest★

Finistère

An ancient port built on a magificent natural roadstead that, being nowhere less than 10m/33ft deep, is almost an inland sea, Brest remains wedded to its maritime tradition.

A BIT OF HISTORY

Although used as a port by Gauls and then Romans, the importance of Brest was firmly established from the 13C onwards. A French garrison moved in and has been there ever since.

At the beginning of the 17C, Richelieu's wish was to have French naval forces which could be permanently ready for action. He founded the naval dockyard and its first warship was launched in 1634. The Rue de Siam, running in a straight line between the arsenal and Place de la Liberté, formed the main axis of the ancient town and its fame was spread worldwide by the sailors who frequented it. The town had to be completely rebuilt after World War II, in which it suffered four years of air attack and a 43-day siege.

SIGHTS

🚹🚺 Océanopolis★★★

Port de Plaisance du Moulin Blanc.
♿🕐*Hours vary for each exhibition; call ahead.* ⬟€16.20 (child €11). ✆*02 98 34 40 40.* www.oceanopolis.com.

▶ **Population:** 146 143
⏱ **Michelin Map:** 308 A 4, E 4-5
ℹ **Info:** pl. de la Liberté. ✆02 98 44 24 96. www.brest-metropole-tourisme.fr.
◗ **Location:** The town is 71km/42mi N of Quimper.
🚹🚺 **Kids:** One of the town's principal attractions is the giant Océanopolis centre.

In this ultra-modern building, shaped like a giant crab, visitors discover the marine life of Brittany's coastal waters in the saltwater aquariums (downstairs), and the many sea birds of the coast in their nesting places on the cliff face (entrance level).

Cours Dajot★

This fine promenade was laid out in 1769 on the old ramparts. It gives splendid **views**★★ of the activity of the port and of the great roadstead of 150sq km/ 58sq mi.

Musée des Beaux-Arts★

24 r. Traverse. 🕐*Open Tue–Sat 10am– noon, 2–6pm, Sun 2–6pm.* 🕐*Closed public holidays (except 14 Jul and 15 Aug).* ⬟€4. ✆02 98 00 87 96.

Océanopolis

© Camera Lucida/Alamy

The collections illustrate the advances made by the painters of the Pont-Aven School, for example *Yellow Sea (Mer jaune)* by Lacombe, as well as a curious study of the town of Ys (⌚ *see QUIMPER*), Manet's *Parrots*, and *Bouquet of Roses* by Suzanne Valadon.

EXCURSIONS
Calvaire de Plougastel-Daoulas★★
▶ *11km/6.8mi E, S of the church.*
The calvary was built from 1602 to 1604 by the Priget brothers to mark an outbreak of plague four years earlier. Its 180 figures are sculpted in the round; a certain stiffness of posture is set off by the size of the heads and the vigorous expressions.

The Abers★
The term *aber* is of Celtic origin and is found in Scottish and Welsh place names. In Brittany *abers* are picturesque, fairly shallow estuaries on the low, rocky northwest coast of Finistère. The entrance to the **aber Wrac'h** is guarded by the small seaside resort of the same name near which there are fine views of the lighthouse on Vierge Island, the tallest in France (82.5m/270ft). A **scenic road**★ runs along the rugged coastline through a number of charming resorts.

Île d'Ouessant★★
The island is open to pedestrians and cyclists only, and reached from the coast of Brittany by a 15min flight from Brest or by ferry from Brest (2hr15min), Le Conquet (30min–1hr) or Camaret (1hr15min). Almost all ferry crossings are early in the morning. ▪ *Bourg de Lampaul.* ✆*02 98 48 85 83. www.ot-ouessant.fr.*
Most of the island's male residents are professional seamen, many in the navy. The few fishermen trap lobsters. The population lives in scattered hamlets or in the little capital of Lampaul, with its tiny harbour and the mausoleum where the Proella crosses representing those lost at sea are assembled.

The island is a fragment of the Léon plateau on the mainland. Two outcrops of granite running northeast–southwest enclose a sunken area of mica-schist much eroded by the sea to form the Baie de Lampaul and the Baie du Stiff. Where there is shelter from the wind, camellias, aloes and agaves can grow, but the characteristic vegetation of the island is heather and dwarf gorse. The meagre grasses nourish a small flock of sheep.
◔*For all ferry information, contact* **Compagnie Maritime Penn Ar Bed** (✆*02 98 80 80 80. www.pennarbed. com). For flight information, contact* **Finistair** (✆*02 98 84 64 87. www.finistair.fr).*

🏃 Côte Sauvage★★★
4hr round-trip on foot starting at Lampaul.
The headlands and inlets of Ushant's rocky northwestern coastline have a rugged and dramatic beauty. The most spectacular locations include Keller Island (Île de Keller), Penn-ar-Ru-Meur and the Cadoran islet (Îlot de Cadoran). The 300 or so vessels which pass each day are guided by five great lighthouses.
The one at **Creac'h**, which houses the **Centre d'Interpretation des Phares et Balises** (♿◔*open daily Apr–Sept 10.30am–6.30pm; Nov–Dec 1.30–5pm, Jan–Mar and Oct 1.30–5.30pm, excl. holidays;* ◔*closed winter holidays, Easter and 1 Nov;* ✆*02 98 48 80 70),* a historical museum on lighthouses and beacons, is the most powerful in the world; together wth its counterpart at Land's End in Cornwall it marks the western limit of the English Channel. The light at **Stiff** gives a splendid **view**★★ over the rolling sea. The lighthouses play a vital role: over the last hundred years over 50 wrecks have been recorded.

Crozon Peninsula
▶ *Crozon Peninsula (Presqu'île de Crozon) lies between Brest to the N and Douarnenez Bay to the S.*
The peninsula is a place of craggy cliffs and golden sand beaches, windswept

Tas de Pois, Pointe de Penhir

R. Mattes/MICHELIN

moorland and tiny coves, not least at **Morgat** a little to the south of the main town Crozon.

The **beach**★ here is a gentle arc, backed by a scattering of brightly painted shops and bars, which provide everything you need for a short break or an uncomplicated, *encore le pastis*, life style. The nearby **LaGrange holiday village** is perfectly placed.

Pointe de Penhir★★★

Penhir Point is the most impressive of the four headlands of the Crozon Peninsula, which has some of the finest coastal landscapes in the whole of Brittany. The processes of coastal erosion have worn away the sandstone matrix from which the cliffs were formed, exposing the seams of quartzite. In rough weather, the violence of the waves crashing against the variously coloured rocks makes a magnificent spectacle.

Camaret-sur-Mer★

At the end of the peninsula, Camaret-sur-Mer is a dizzy little place favoured by artists, and with brightly coloured shop and restaurant fronts that would do Scotland's Tobermory proud. Just before reaching Camaret, a little diversion takes you to the **Alignements Mégalithiques de Lagatjar**★, Crozon's answer to the question that is Carnac.

Cap de la Chèvre★★

From the former German observation point there is a fine view over the Atlantic: (left to right) Pointe de Penhir, Tas de Pois, the Île de Sein, Cap Sizun, Pointe du Van and Pointe du Raz to the south of Douarnenez Bay.

A **monument**, representing the wing of an aircraft, is dedicated to the aircrew personnel of Aéronautique Navale killed or missing in active service.

Pointe des Espagnols★★

From here there is a remarkable **panorama** that includes the Brest Sound, the town and harbour of Brest, the Elorn estuary, the Pont Albert-Louppe, the Presqu'île de Plougastel, and the end of the roadstead. The point owes its name to the Spanish garrison that occupied the area for a brief period in 1594 and built a fort on the headland.

Pointe de Dinan★★

A fine **panorama** can be seen from the edge of the cliff. Skirting the cliff to the right is the enormous rocky mass of **Dinan Castle**, joined to the mainland by a natural arch.

Les Petites Grottes

These small caves at the foot of the spur between Morgat and Le Portzic beaches can be reached at low tide.

Quimper★★

Finistère

Quimper is in Brittany's far west and is the capital of Finistère. It lies in a pretty valley at the junction (*kemper* in Breton) of two rivers, the Steir and the Odet.

A BIT OF HISTORY

The town was first of all a Gaulish foundation, sited on the north bank of the Odet estuary. Towards the end of the 5C BC, Celts sailed over from Britain (hence the area's name of Cornouaille, i.e. Cornwall) and drove out the original inhabitants. This was the era of the legendary King Gradlon and of the fabulous city of Ys which is supposed to have sunk beneath the waves of Douarnenez Bay. The town has a long tradition of making faïence (fine earthenware), and is a centre of Breton folk art.

VISIT

Cathédrale St-Corentin★★

The cathedral is dedicated to Saint Corentin, one of the figures responsible for founding Brittany after the fall of the Roman Empire. Much of the cathedral is Gothic, although the magnificent twin spires were added only in the 19th century. Much of the interior decoration – furnishings, reliquaries and statues – was stripped away during the Revolution and the Reign of Terror (1793), and while the lime-washed interior that remains may not suit some tastes, it does leave the cathedral with a bright and appealing atmosphere. Unusual, perhaps, the central nave and choir are not in a straight line.

Le Vieux Quimper★

The medieval town lies between the cathedral and the Odet and its tributary, the Steyr. There are fine old houses with granite ground floors and timber-framed projecting upper storeys.

Musée des Beaux-Arts★★

40 pl. St-Corentin. ♿ ⏱*Open daily except Tue 10am–noon, 2–6pm (Jul–Aug daily 10am–7pm).* ⏱*Closed 1 Jan,*

▶ **Population:** 67 274
🚗 **Michelin Map:** 308 G 6-7
ℹ **Info:** pl. de la Résistance. 📞02 98 53 04 05. www.quimper-tourisme.com.
▶ **Location:** 72km/45mi SE of Brest, and 69km/43mi NW of Lorient.
👁 **Don't Miss:** The Old Town.

1 May, 1 and 11 Nov and 25 Dec. 💶€4.50. 📞02 98 95 45 20. *www.musee-beauxarts.quimper.fr.*
This Fine Arts Museum contains a collection of paintings representing European painting from the 14C to the present. The museum has its own unique atmosphere, largely due to the mixing of natural and artificial lighting, in which it is possible to view the works in – quite literally – a new light.

On the ground floor, two rooms are devoted to 19C Breton painting: *A Marriage in Brittany* by Leleux; *A Street in Morlaix* by Noël; *Potato Harvest* by Simon; *Widow on Sein Island* by Renouf; *Flight of King Gradlon* by Luminais; and *Fouesnant Rebels* by Girardet.

One room is devoted to **Max Jacob** (1876–1944), who was born and grew up in Quimper. His life and work are evoked through literature, memorabilia, drawings, gouaches, and in particular a series of portraits signed by his friends Picasso, Cocteau and others.

Faïenceries de Quimper HBHenriot

r. Haute. 🚶*Guided tours (French and English) Mon–Fri at 10.30am and 2.45pm.* ♿ 💶€5. 📞02 98 90 09 36. *www.hb-henriot.com.*
The 300-year-old faïence workshops were bought in 1984 by Paul Janssens, an American citizen of Dutch origin. Earthenware is still entirely decorated by hand with traditional motifs such as Breton peasants in traditional dress, birds, roosters and plants.

A tour of the workshops enables visitors to discover in turn the various manufacturing stages, from the lump of clay to the firing process.

A few concessions have been made to modern practices: the clay mixture is no longer prepared in house and the ovens are electrically heated. There is a shop on site.

Musée Départemental Breton★

1 r. de Roi Gradion; ⏱*Open Jun–Sept daily 9am–6pm; Oct–May Tue–Sat, 9am–noon, 2–5pm, Sun 2–5pm;* ⏱*Closed Easter Mon, 1 and 8 May, 25 Dec.* ⬛€4. *(no charge Sun Jan–May, Oct–Dec).* ✆*02 98 95 21 60. http:// museedepartementalbreton.fr.*

The museum, housed in the former palace of the Bishops of Cornwall, is the most remarkable monument after the Cathedral of Quimper, and presents a synthesis of the archaeology, folk and decorative arts of Finistère. It is an excellent introduction to the discovery of the département.

EXCURSIONS
La Cornouaille★★

Although the area today is limited to the coast and immediate hinterland west of its capital Quimper, Cornouaille was once the Duchy of medieval Brittany, stretching as far north as Morlaix. Brittany's "Cornwall" juts out into the Atlantic just like its counterpart across the Channel.

The spectacular coastline with its two peninsulas, **Presqu'île de Penmarch**★ and **Cap Sizun**★★, culminates in the breathtaking **Pointe du Raz**★★★.

Locronan★★

▶ *E of Douarnenez and NE of Quimper.*
🏛 *pl. de la Mairie, 29180 Locronan.*
✆*02 98 91 70 14. www.locronan.org.*
🅿*You must park outside the village.*

Locronan is firmly rooted in times past. This used to be a major centre for woven linen, of the type required for sails by the French, Spanish and English navies. As a result, the centre of the village is endowed with splendid examples of Breton architecture that mostly date to the 18C, and was largely built at the behest of wealthy sail merchants. In the 19C, competition from Vitré and Rennes, coupled with the general economic downturn of the period, brought ruin and stagnation for Locronan. Just how wealthy a place this must have been is self-evident if you study the quality of the opulent architecture, especially in the place de l'Église.

It takes a while to register, but there is something not quite right about Locronan. And then you notice that there are no spaghetti tangles of telephone cables festooned from building to building, no television aerials or satellite dishes, no road markings, no permanent road signs; in fact, nothing that visually places the setting in the 21C.

Museum

On the Châteaulin road. ⏱*Open Jul– Aug, 10am–1pm, 2–7pm, Sun and holidays 2–6pm; rest of the year Mon– Fri 10am–noon, 2–6pm.* ⬛€2.
✆*02 98 91 70 14.*

The museum houses Quimper faience, sandstone objects, local costumes,

---

The *Troménies*

The **Petite *Troménie*** consists of a procession that makes its way to the top of the hill, repeating the walk that St-Ronan, a 5C Irish saint, according to tradition, took every day, fasting and barefooted. The **Grande *Troménie*★★** takes place every sixth year on the second and third Sundays in July *(next in 2013)*. Carrying banners, the pilgrims go around the hill (12km/7.5mi), stopping at 12 stations.

At the different stations each parish exhibits its saints and reliquaries. The circuit follows the boundary of the former Benedictine priory – built on the site of the sacred forest or "Nemeton", which served as a natural shrine – founded in the 11C, which was a place of retreat. Hence the name of the *pardon Tro Minihy* or Tour of the Retreat, gallicised as *Troménie*.

exhibits relating to the *Troménies* (*see p213*) and to ancient crafts, pictures and engravings by contemporary artists of Locronan and the surrounding area.

Montagne de Locronan★

▶ *2km/1.2mi E of Locronan.* ◷*Open only during the Troménies held every year on the 2nd Sun in July, and the Grandes Troménies held every six years from the 1st to the 2nd Sun in July.* ✆*02 98 91 70 14.*

From the top (289m), crowned by a **chapel** (note the stained-glass windows by Bazaine), you will see a fine **panorama**★ of Douarnenez Bay. On the left are Douarnenez and the Pointe du Leydé; on the right Cap de la Chèvre, the Presqu'île de Crozon, Ménez-Hom and the Monts d'Arrée.

Ste-Anne-la-Palud

▶ *8km/5mi NW of Locronan. Leave Locronan by D 63 to Crozon. After Plonévez-Porzay, turn left.* ◷*Open Easter–1 Nov daily 9am–8pm; rest of the year Sun only.* ✆*02 98 92 50 17.*

The 19C **chapel** contains a much-venerated painted granite statue of St Anne dating from 1548. The *pardon* on the last Sunday in August, one of the finest and most picturesque in Brittany, attracts thousands. On the Saturday at 9pm the torchlit procession progresses along the dune above the chapel.

Pointe du Raz★★★

▶ *The point is at the farthest tip of Brittany's Cornouaille peninsula, about 51km/32mi W of Quimper.*

Raz Point is one of France's most spectacular coastal landscapes. Its jagged cliffs, battered by the waves and seamed with caves, rise to over 70m/220ft.

The **view**★★ extends over the fearsome Raz de Sein with its multitude of reefs and rocky islands (on the outermost of which is sited the lighthouse, Phare de la Vieille). The outline of the Île de Sein can be seen on the horizon. To the north lies the headland, Pointe du Van, perhaps less impressive, but having the

distinct advantage of being off the tourists' beaten track.

Concarneau★

▶ *The town is S of Quimper, in western Brittany.* 🛈*quai d'Aiguillon.* ✆*02 98 97 0144. www.tourismeconcarneau.fr.*

The growth of Concarneau is based on its importance as a fishing port. Trawlers and cargo-boats moor in the inner harbour up the estuary of the Moros, while the outer harbour is lively with pleasure craft. There are many vegetable and fish canneries and plenty of bustle as the catch is sold in the early morning at the "criée" (fish auction market).

Ville close (Walled Town)★★

On its islet in the bay, this was one of the strongholds of the ancient county of Cornouaille; as at Dinan and Guérande, its walls proclaim the determination of the citizens to maintain their independence, particularly in times of trouble (as during the War of the Breton Succession in 1341). The English nevertheless seized the place in 1342, and were thrown out only by Du Guesclin in 1373.

The granite **ramparts** (*access to the ramparts is prohibited if weather conditions are not favourable*), with their typically Breton corbelled machicolations, were started at the beginning of the 14C and completed at the end of the 15C.

They were improved by Vauban at the end of the 17C at a time when England once more posed a threat to these coasts; he lowered the height of the towers and built gun emplacements into them.

At the heart of the walled town, rue Vauban and rue St-Guénolé are a demonstration of how medieval market places arose more or less spontaneously through a simple widening of the street. A Fishing Museum, **Musée de la Pêche**★ (*3 r. Vauban;* ◷*open Feb–Mar 10am–noon, 2–6pm; Apr–Jun, Sept–Oct 10am–6pm; Jul–Aug 9.30am–8pm;* ◷*closed rest of year;* ✦€6.50, child €4; ✆*02 98 97 10 20; www.musee-peche.fr*), is nearby.

Lorient

Morbihan

The modern city of Lorient boasts proudly of being the site of five ports: the fishing port of Keroman; a military port, with dockyard and submarine base (capacity for 30 submarines); a passenger port, with ships crossing the roadstead and sailing to the Île de Groix; the Kergroise commercial port, which specialises in the importing of animal foodstuffs; and the Kernevel pleasure boat harbour, with a wet dock located in the centre of the city: it is the starting point for transatlantic competition. An annual Interceltic Festival (Festival Interceltique, *see Calendar of Events*) is held in Lorient.

▶ **Population:** 59 830
Michelin Map: Local map 308 KB - Morbihan (56).
Info: 6 quai de Rohan, 56100 Lorient. ℘02 97 84 78 00. www.lorient-tourisme.fr.
Location: 69km/43mi SW of Brest, and 56km/35mi W of Vannes.
Kids: *La Thalassa* fishing trawler and exhibition; Pont-Scorff Zoo.
Timing: Use the Batobus: very practical and pleasant "boat-buses" with six itineraries. But a few hours wandering on foot won't go amiss.
Parking: A modern town, there are plenty of car parks – the first half-hour is free in blue zones.

A BIT OF HISTORY

The India Company – After the first India Company, founded by Richelieu at Port-Louis, failed, Colbert revived the project in 1664 at Le Havre. But as the Company's ships were too easily captured in the Channel by the British, it was decided to move its headquarters to the Atlantic coast. The choice fell on "vague and vain" plots of land located on the right bank of the Scorff. Soon afterwards, what was to be known as the "Compound of the India Company" was born. Since all maritime activities were focused on India and China, the installations built on that site bore the name *l'Orient* (French for the East). In those days, the arrogant motto of the India Company – *Florebo quocumque ferar* (I shall prosper wherever I go) – was fully justified by the flourishing trade which it exercised. But a new naval war loomed ahead, so Seignelay turned the "Compound" into a royal dockyard patronised by the most famous privateers (Beauchêne, Duguay-Trouin).

In the 18C, under the stimulus of the well-known Scots financier Law, business grew rapidly; 60 years after its foundation, the town already had 18 000 inhabitants. The loss of India brought the Company to ruin, and in 1770 the State took over the port and its equipment. Napoleon turned it into a naval base.

During WWII, Lorient was occupied by the Germans on 25 June 1940. From 27 September 1940 the city was subjected to bombardments, which intensified as the war raged on, culminating in a hugely destructive offensive in August 1944. The fighting between the entrenched German garrison and the Americans and locally based Free French Forces, which encircled the Lorient "pocket", devastated the surrounding area.

When the townspeople returned on 8 May 1945, all that greeted them was a scene of utter desolation.

VISIT

Ancien Arsenal

Until 2000, the naval dockyard was located in the former India Company's area; four docks were used for the repair of warships. Abandoned by the navy, the area is being modernised. The Breton television channel Breizh has located its headquarters along quai du Péristyle.

Église Notre-Dame-de-Victoire

Better known to the locals as the church of St-Louis, it stands in place Alsace-Lorraine, itself a successful example of modern town planning.

The church is built in reinforced concrete and has very plain lines. It is square with a flattened cupola roof and a square tower flanking the façade. The beauty of the church lies in its **interior**★.

Little panes of yellow and clear glass reflect light into the building from the top of the rotunda, and the bays in the lower section consist of brightly coloured splintered glass.

Enclos du Port de Lorient

Enter through the "Porte Gabriel". Information on tours available from the tourist office: ☎*02 97 84 78 00. www.lorient-tourisme.fr.*

A tour of the dockyards recalls the heyday of the India Company: the Hôtel des Ventes, built by Gabriel in 1740, has been entirely restored in the original style. The **Tour de la Découverte** (1737), flanked by the Admirality mills (1677), once served as a watchtower. Climb the 225 steps to enjoy the superb **view**★ of the roadstead.

👥 La Thalassa

quai de Rohan. 🕐*Open Apr Mon–Fri 9.30am–12.30pm, 2–6pm, Sat–Sun 2–6pm; May–Jun Tue–Fri 9.30am–12.30pm, 2–6pm; Jul–Aug daily 10am–7pm; Sept Tue–Fri 9.30am–12.30pm, 2–6pm, Sat–Mon 2-6pm; Oct Mon–Fri 9.30am–12.30pm, 2–6pm, Sat–Sun 2-6pm.* 🕐*Closed rest of year.* ◉◉*€7 (children €5.50).* ☎*02 97 21 10 14. www.la-thalassa.fr.*

After sailing the seas of the world (nearly 38 times round the globe), this ship, launched in 1960 by Ifremer, is enjoying well-deserved retirement in Lorient. A tour of the three decks gives visitors a good idea of life on board, techniques of navigation, trawler fishing and oceanographic research. The tour continues on land with an exhibition devoted to the fishing industry in Lorient.

Port de Pêche de Keroman

Partly reclaimed from the sea, the port of Keroman is the only French harbour designed and equipped for commercial fishing; it is the leading port in France for the value and variety of fish landed. It has two basins set at right angles: the **Grand Bassin** and the **Bassin Long** (totalling 1 850m/1.1mi of docks). The Grand Bassin is sheltered by a jetty used by cargo steamers and trawlers. The basin has two other quays, one with a refrigerating and cold-storage plant for the trawlers and fish dealers; and the other, as well as the quay at the east end of the Bassin Long, where the trawlers unload their catch. In front of the quays is the 600m/655yd-long **market hall** *(criée)* where auctions are held, and, close behind it, the fish dealers' warehouses which open onto the car park, where lorries destined for the rest of France are loaded. There is also a **slipway** with six bays where trawlers can be dry-docked or repaired.

The port of Keroman sends out ships for all kinds of fishing throughout the year. The largest vessels go to sea for a fortnight, and carry their own ice-making equipment (which can make up to 400t a day) to the fishing grounds.

Base de Sous-marins Keroman★

🕐*Guided tours (1hr30min): all year, Sun, 3pm; school holidays daily at 3pm.* 🕐*Closed Jan.* ◉€*7.50.* ☎*02 97 02 23 29. www.lorient-tourisme.fr.*

The submarine base is named in honour of a WWII maritime engineer who, by appearing to collaborate with the Germans, was able to keep abreast of activities on the base and inform Allies. When he was discovered, he was executed.

The three blocks were built in record time. The first two (1941) have slots for 13 submarines. The third (1943) has a reinforced concrete roof 7.5m/24.5ft thick. At the end of WWII, the French Navy took over the base for their Atlantic submarine operations, but have since abandoned it for this purpose. The last dry-dock operation took place in December 1996, and the *Sirène*, the

Frescoes on the vault, Kernascléden church

© Florian Monheim/age fotostock

last active submarine, left the base for the Toulon port in February 1997.

The *Flore* is the only ship remaining; it has no military purpose but is kept up for display between blocks one and two. The navy has progressively turned over the dockyards to the city of Lorient, and various projects for the use of the area are under way or being considered.

EXCURSIONS

Larmor-Plage⌂

◉ *6km/3.7mi S of Lorient by the D 29.*

Looking out over the ocean, across from Port-Louis, Larmor-Plage has lovely, fine, sandy beaches much appreciated by the people of Lorient.

The parish **church**, built in the 12C, was remodelled until the 17C. The 15C porch, uncommonly situated on the north façade because of the prevailing winds, contains statues of the Apostles and above the door a 16C painted wood Christ in Fetters.

The old road from Larmor follows the coast fairly closely, passing many small seaside resorts. After Kerpape the drive affords extensive views of the coast of Finistère, beyond the cove of Le Pouldu and over to the Île de Groix.

In the foreground are the coastal inlets in which lie the little ports of Lomener, Perello Kerroch and Le Courégant and the large beach of **Fort-Bloqué** dominated by a fort (privately owned). Go through **Guidel-Plages** on the Laïta estuary. From Guidel make for the Pont de St-Maurice (6km/3.7mi there and back) over the Laïta. The **view**★ up the enclosed valley is magnificent.

Hennebont

◉ *17km/10.5mi NE of Lorient. Route passes through Lanester.*

Hennebont is a former fortified town on the steep banks of the River Blavet.

The 16C basilica, **Basilique Notre-Dame-de-Paradis**, has a big **bell tower**★ and is surmounted by a steeple 65m/216ft high. At the base of the tower is a fine Flamboyant porch ornamented with niches leading into the nave, which is lit up by a stained-glass window by Max Ingrand.

Kernascléden★★

◉ *The village is about 34km/21mi N of the coastal town of Lorient.*

The small village has a beautiful church with remarkable 15C frescoes. Built in granite between 1430 and 1455, the **church**★★ typifies the Breton version of Flamboyant Gothic. It has two **porches** on the south side (one of them with statues of the **Apostles**★).

Inside there is a fine window at the east end. The **frescoes**★★ are striking: the choir vault depicts 24 scenes from the Life of the Virgin.

Vannes★★

Morbihan

▶ **Population:** 51 759
♿ **Michelin Map:** 308 O 9
▯ **Info:** quai Tabarly. ☎08 25 13 56 10. www.tourisme-vannes.com.
◐ **Location:** Vannes is a lively, popular resort on the SE coast of Brittany. The historic centre is by the cathedral and Pl. Henri IV.
☺ **Don't Miss:** A boat trip on the Gulf.
👥 **Kids:** Adults and kids will love the Aquarium du Golf.

Vannes is a pleasant city in the shape of an amphitheatre at the highest point to which tides flow at the head of the Morbihan Gulf. The picturesque old town, enclosed in its ramparts and grouped around the Cathedral, is a pedestrian zone where elegant shops have been established in old half-timbered town houses.

A BIT OF HISTORY

In pre-Roman times, it was the capital of the **Veneti** tribe.

One of Gaul's most powerful peoples, they were intrepid sailors, crossing the seas to trade with the inhabitants of the British Isles. They nevertheless suffered a terrible defeat at sea in 56 BC at the hands of the Romans, losing 200 ships in a single day. As a result, Brittany's fate was to remain a backwater for a very long time.

In the 9C, Vannes was where Breton unity was achieved under Nominoé, who made Vannes his capital.

SIGHTS

Vieille Ville (Old Town)★★

Surrounded by ramparts (**remparts**★), the area around the cathedral, the successor to a much more ancient place of worship, still has the air of a medieval town.

Wash-houses along the ramparts

J.Malburet/MICHELIN

Among the old half-timbered houses built over a granite ground floor with pillars, arcades and lintels is a 14C market hall known as **La Cohue**★. Its upper floor served as the ducal law-court right up until 1796, the ground floor as a market until 1840.

There are fine houses bordering **Place Henri IV**★ and in the adjoining streets. Note the timber cross-braces, corbelling, granite pilasters and 16C slate-hung gables.

Cathédrale St-Pierre★

r. des Chanoines.

Of robust granite construction, it has a north aisle with a balustraded terrace and sharply pointed granite gables in Breton Flamboyant style separating the chapels. Inside, the 15C nave is covered by a heavy ribbed vault of the 18C, concealing the original timber roof.

Note in particular the stunning **stained-glass windows**★ and statuary.

Hôtel de Ville

pl. Maurice-Marchais. ☎*02 97 01 60 00. www.mairie-vannes.fr.*

This building in the Renaissance style, erected at the end of the 19C, stands in *place Maurice-Marchais*, which is adorned with the equestrian **statue** of the Constable de Richemont, one of the great figures of the 15C – for it was he who created and commanded the

French army which defeated the English at the end of the Hundred Years' War. He became Duke of Brittany, succeeding his brother in 1457, but died the following year.

Ramparts★

After crossing from the *Promenade de la Garenne* you will get a **view**★★ of the most picturesque corner of Vannes, with the stream (the Marle) that flows at the foot of the ramparts (built in the 13C on top of Gallo-Roman ruins and remodelled repeatedly until the 17C), the formal gardens and the cathedral in the background.

A small bridge, leading to Porte Poterne, overlooks some old **wash-houses**★ with very unusual roofing.

EXCURSIONS

Golfe du Morbihan★★

This little inland sea was formed when the land sank and the sea level rose as a result of the melting of the great Quaternary glaciers, drowning the valleys occupied by the Vannes and Auray rivers. The indented coastline and the play of the tides around the countless islands make this one of Brittany's most fascinating maritime landscapes.

Golfe de Morbihan en bateau★★★ (boat trips)

The best way to see the gulf is by boat. About 40 islands are privately owned and inhabited. The largest are Île d'Arz and the Île aux Moines, both communes. The Île d'Arz is about 3.5km/2mi long and has several megalithic monuments. The Île aux Moines is 7km/4.3mi long and the most populous.

It is a particularly quiet and restful resort where camellias and mimosas grow amongst the palm trees.

👤 Aquarium du Golfe★

Parc du Golfe du Morbihan. Open daily Jul–Aug 9am–7.30pm; rest of the year 2–6pm (except public holidays 10am–noon, 2–6pm); Apr–Jun and Sept 10am–noon, 2–6pm. Ticket office closes 30min before closing time. Closed 1 Jan and 25 Dec. €10.30; child €7.20. 02 97 40 67 40. www.aquarium-du-golfe.com.

More than 50 pools, in which the relevant natural environment has been reconstructed, house about 1 000 fish from all over the world (cold seas, warm seas, freshwater), which make up an incredible kaleidoscope of colour.

In one 35 000l/7 700gal tank, a coral reef has been re-created and is home to numerous species of fish which habitually frequent this environment.

A huge aquarium contains several varieties of shark and an exceptional sight: a huge 3m/9.8ft-long sawfish!

Château de Suscinio★

▶ *30km/18.5mi S of Vannes by D 780. Sarzeau*

This was once the summer residence of the Dukes of Brittany. There is a rare 13C decorated tiled floor (accessible via a spiral staircase with 94 steps). The massive buildings lining the courtyard are now partly ruined.

A gun emplacement at the foot of the northwest tower may well date from the time of the War of the Breton Succession.

Port-Navalo★

▶ *40km/25mi SW Vannes by D 780.*

The little port and seaside resort guards the entrance to the Gulf. There are fine views.

Ensemble Mégalithique de Locmariaquer★★

▶ *32km/20mi SW Vannes by N 165, D 28 and D 781.*

This group of megaliths is an important part of a programme of conservation and restoration of megalithic sites.

Three megaliths can be found on this site: the **Grand Menhir brisé** (probably broken on purpose into five pieces, after it had served as a landmark for sailors); the **Table des Marchands** (a recently restored dolmen as well as the tumulus underneath) and the **Tumulus d'Er-Grah** (excavations are under way here).

Côte Sauvage at Presqu'île de Quiberon

R. Mattes/MICHELIN

Presqu'île de Quiberon★

▶ 45km/28mi SW of Vannes by N 165 and D 768.

Quiberon used to be an island, but over the years sand has accumulated north of Penthièvre Fort to form an isthmus linking it to the mainland.

The peninsula's rocky and windswept western shore is known as the **Côte Sauvage** (Wild Coast), but to the east there are sheltered sandy beaches. The ferries for **Belle-Île★★** leave from Quiberon harbour.

Cairn de Gavrinis★★

▶ 16.5km/10mi SW of Vannes by D 101.

The tumulus, 6m/19ft high and 50m/164ft round, is made of stones piled on a hillock. It comprises a gallery with carved symbols leading to a funeral chamber.

Château de Josselin★★

▶ 45km/28mi N of Vannes by D 778.

The château is in the heart of the inland village of Josselin, W of Rennes.

Guided tours (45min) daily mid-Jul–Aug 11am–6pm; Sept 2–6pm; Oct, weekends and school hols 2–5pm; 4 Apr–13 Jul 2–6pm. €6.80. Place de la Congregation. 02 97 22 36 45. www.pays-de-josselin-tourisme.com.

This famous stronghold of the Rohan family, who have owned the castle for more than 500 years and still live here in the private apartments, has stood

guard over the crossing of the Oust for 900 years and seen many battles.

The **War of the Breton Succession**, which started in 1341, set rival heirs to the Duchy against each other, Jeanne de Penthièvre, granddaughter of Jean II of Brittany, and Jean de Montfort, Jean III's half-brother. The struggle, long and confused, overlapped with the early stages of the Hundred Years' War. Jeanne was married to Charles de Blois and her claim, supported by the Valois rulers of France, was based on established Breton custom. The ousted De Montfort allied himself to the Plantagenets who had won the great naval battle of Sluys the previous year. He was able to persuade them to set a terrible example by laying waste the area around Tréguier; this action took place during the period which also saw the triumph of English arms at Crécy and Calais.

The garrison at Josselin faced the defenders of Ploërmel Castle, 12km/7.4mi to the east; between them they ravaged the countryside without any decisive outcome. A solution to the impasse was sought by arranging a contest between 30 knights from each camp.

The **Battle of the Thirty** took place in 1351, half-way between the two towns. Ploërmel's champions consisted of four Bretons, six Germans and 20 Englishmen. Josselin emerged victorious, but even this dramatic settling of accounts did not prove decisive.

The war was finally brought to an end in 1364 by the death of Charles de Blois at the Battle of Auray. In 1365 de Montfort was acknowledged as ruler of the Duchy, albeit subject to the Capetian kings of France.

The medieval robustness of the massive walls overlooking the river contrasts with the refinement of the upper parts belonging to the reconstruction of the 15–16C. The marriage of Anne of Brittany to Charles VIII of France in 1491 had led to a lessening of tension between the Duchy and the French kingdom, and John of Laval was able to rebuild the old castle in accordance with the new ideas of Renaissance architecture. What had been a fortress now became a palace.

The transformation is particularly evident in the courtyard, where the **façade**★★ featuring an ornate roof **balustrade** has a splendid variety of motifs: pinnacles, tracery and mouldings. Inside there is an innovative staircase with straight ramps.

In the 17C the keep and five of the towers were demolished on the orders of Richelieu who announced with cruel irony "I have just thrown a fine ball among your skittles, Monsieur". A park was laid out in 1760, and in 1882 the castle was restored.

Carnac★

▶ *33km/20mi SW of Vannes by N 165, D 768 and D 119 at the base of the Quiberon Peninsula.*

🏠 *74 ave des Druides. ℘02 97 52 13 52. www.ot-carnac.fr.*

In the bleak Breton countryside just north of the little town of Carnac (pop 4 450) are some of the world's most remarkable megalithic remains.

Megaliths★★

The area containing the megaliths is divided up by roads and a number of stones have been lost, but altogether it comprises 2 792 menhirs, arranged in 10 or 11 lines – *alignements* – including the **alignements du Ménec**★★ with 1 169 menhirs, the **alignements de Kermario**★ with 1 029 and the **alignements de Kerlescan**★ with 594. There are also dolmens (burial places), cromlechs (semicircles) and tumuli (mounds). Megalithic culture flourished from about 4 670 to 2 000 BC. It was the creation of a settled population growing crops and with domestic animals (in contrast to the hunter-gatherers of Paleolithic times), who produced polished objects, pottery and basket-work and who traded in flints. The inhabitants of Carnac had commercial relations with people from Belgium and from Grand-Pressigny in the north of Poitou.

Markings on the megaliths resemble abstract art in contrast to the figurative cave-art of the Upper Paleolithic, and the orientation of the lines in a west–northeast direction adds to their enigmatic character. Various theories have been advanced about their likely religious or astronomical significance.

The tumuli and dolmens which appeared 40 centuries before the birth of Christ are collective burial places, and the mounds covering them, a thousand years older than the pyramids of Egypt, may be mankind's most ancient built monuments.

Four thousand centuries previously, the Carnac area was inhabited by prehistoric people, and, during the Lower Paleolithic, by nomads, contemporaries of the nomads of Tautavel, Terra Amata and the Ardèche Valley. In the 5C BC, the Celts moved here. In Gallo-Roman times there was the great villa of the Bosseno. Later, the area was repopulated by immigrants from Britain and monks from Ireland.

ADDITIONAL SIGHTS

Église St-Cornély★ – fine 17C Renaissance church In the centre of the village with good 17–19C decoration.
Musée de Préhistoire J.-Miln-Z.-Le-Rouzic★★ *(10 pl. de la Chapelle; ♿○open Apr–Jun and Sept Wed–Mon 10am–12.30pm, 2–6pm; Jul–Aug daily 10am–6pm; Oct–Mar Wed–Mon 10am–12.30pm, 2–5pm; ○closed 1 Jan, 5–31 Jan, 1 May, 25 Dec; ◎€5 (child €2.50); ℘02 97 52 22 04; www.museedecarnac.com).*
Tumulus St-Michel★ *(○open daily 9am–7pm; ◎no charge).*

Belle-Île★★★

Morbihan

The name alone is enticing, but the island's beauty surpasses expectations. This, the largest of the Breton islands, is a schist plateau measuring about 84sq km/32sq mi; 17 km/10.5mi long and 5–10km/3–6mi wide. Valleys cut deep into the high rocks, forming beaches and harbours. Farmland alternates with wild heath, and whitewashed houses stand in lush fields.

▶ **Population:** 4 489
🕭 **Michelin Map:** 308 L-M 10-11
🄸 **Info:** quai Bonnelle, Le Palais. ℰ02 97 31 81 93. www.belle-ile.com.
▷ **Location:** Regular car ferries linking Quibéron (Brittany) and Le Palais in 45min are operated by SMN (ℰ08 20 05 60 00. www.smn-navigation.fr). Passenger-only speed-boats operate in summer between Le Palais and Lorient (Brittany) in 60min.

A BIT OF HISTORY

Belle-Île's interest lies as much in its history as in its wonderful coastline. It is a story of constant attack and defence. In the Middle Ages the island belonged to the Counts of Cornouaille and was often raided by pirates (French as well as Dutch and English) because of its wealth in grain.

From 16C the island was constantly in danger of an English attack, and the fortifications were substantially increased. The island's proximity to the French coast gave it great strategic importance. In 1696, the English took the nearby islands of Houat and Hoëdic and at one point landed on Belle-Île itself.

Over the next decades, the English fleet was a ceaseless threat, and eventually took Belle-Île's citadel in the Seven Years' War. By the 1763 Treaty of Paris England gave back Belle-Île.

SIGHTS

Le Palais

This is the island's capital, known to locals simply as "Palais". Most of the island's amenities are to be found here. The natural harbour is dominated by the imposing citadel and fortifications, known as **Citadelle Vauban**★ (◐open Apr–Oct daily 9.30am–6pm; Jul and Aug daily 9am–7pm; Nov–Mar: daily 9.30am–noon, 2–5pm. ◌€6.10 (child €3.05); no charge 3rd weekend in Sept. ℰ02 97 31 84 17). The proximity of Belle-Île to the ports of the south coast of Brittany and the mouth of the Loire gave it great importance in the fight for the control of the high seas conducted by England and France. In 1658 the island came into the hands of chancellor Fouquet. He consolidated the defences and installed 200 new batteries.

From 1682, the great military engineer Vauban adapted the citadel following improvements in the technology of war, converting an old chapel into a powder-magazine with a projecting roof to fend off broadsides, rebuilding the old arsenal as well as laying out an officers' walk with a gallery giving fine seaviews.

Côte Sauvage★★★

The Côte Sauvage, literally "wild coast", runs from the Pointe des Poulains to the Pointe de Talud. Battered by the Atlantic waves, the schists of which the island's plateau is composed have been formed into spectacular coastal scenes.

Port-Donnant★★ has a splendid sandy beach between high cliffs but is known for its great rollers and perilous currents. The **Aiguilles de Port-Coton**★★ are pyramids hollowed out into caverns and grottoes. The different colours of the rock have been exposed by the action of the sea.

ADDITIONAL SIGHTS

Sauzon★
Pointe des Poulains★★
Port-Goulphar★

Nantes★★★
Loire-Atlantique

Nantes is Brittany's largest city, sited at the point at which the mighty Loire becomes tidal. The presence of islets (inhabited from the 17C on) in the river had long facilitated the building of bridges, making Nantes the focus of trade and movement between Lower Brittany and Poitou.

A BIT OF HISTORY

In the 9C the city was disputed between Nominoé, the first Duke of Brittany, and the Franks to the east. In 939 it was chosen as his capital by King Alain Barbe-Torte (Crookbeard). By the 14C, Nantes had become a trading port, with a fleet of 1 300 ships, but it was only in the 15C, under Duke François II, that the city reached its full importance. It was in its cathedral, on 13 April 1598, that Henri IV signed the **Edict of Nantes**, establishing equality between Catholics and Protestants, and granting privileges to the latter regarding the right to maintain fortified strongholds. Louis XIV revoked the Edict in 1685, provoking the Huguenot exodus to England, Holland and Germany and depriving France of some of its most valuable craftsmen.

In the early 18C Nantes grew rich on the "triangle" of trade importing sugar cane from the West Indies, exporting manufactured goods to Africa, and shipping slaves from Africa to the West Indies. Nantes became France's premier port until the loss of French territories abroad and the abolition of slavery. The substitution of sugar-beet for cane sugar and the increasing size of ships further led to the old port's decline. However, in the 19C and 20C the construction of larger downstream harbour facilities has contributed towards Nantes' continuing prosperity.

SIGHTS
Château des Ducs de Bretagne★★

4 pl. Marc Elder ⏱Open daily. **Castle courtyard and ramparts** Jul–Aug daily 9am–8pm (Sat 11pm); Sept–Jun

▶ **Population:** 544 932
⏱ **Michelin Map:** 316 G 4
ℹ **Info:** 3 cours Olivier de Clisson. ℘08 92 46 40 44. www.nantes-tourisme.com.
▷ **Location:** Three tramway lines and over 60 bus routes make for easy movement throughout the city.
🕐 **Timing:** You'll need at least 3hr to visit the château and the surrounding sights.
🅿 **Parking:** It is not easy to move around Nantes by car. Find parking in one of several lots surrounding the downtown area and move around the city by tramway, bus or foot.
🞷 **Don't Miss:** Find a bar or restaurant in the Ste-Croix neighbourhood for an authentic Nantes evening.
🜨 **Kids:** Planète Sauvage at Port-St-Père.

10am–7pm. **Museum** Jul–Aug daily 9.30am–7 pm; Sept–Jun 10am–6pm (no admission after 6pm). ⏱Closed Tue (till 7 Jun), Mon from 9 Jun, 1 Nov, 25 Dec, 1 Jan, 1 May. **Evening events** mid-May–mid-Sept, the courtyard, ramparts and moat gardens are open until 11pm – a chance to enjoy the Castle's illuminations. From mid-Jul–mid-Aug, open-air concerts on Tue at 8pm. ⊕Entrance is free to the Castle

Un bon vin blanc

This expression, well known for being part of a phonetics exercise for Anglo-Saxon learners of French – literally "a fine white wine" – adequately describes the local Muscadet, dry but not too sharp, perfect with seafood. The vineyards are located to the south and east of Nantes, alongside or near the Sèvre and towards Ancenis on the banks of the Loire.

Château des Ducs de Bretagne

courtyard, ramparts and moat gardens.
Museum €5. 0811 46 46 44 (when
in France), 00 33 2 51 17 49 48 (from
abroad). www.chateau-nantes.fr.

"God's teeth! No small beer, these dukes
of Brittany!" exclaimed Henri IV on seeing this massive stronghold for the first
time.

The castle was much rebuilt and
strengthened from 1466 on by Duke
François II who saw in it the guarantee
of his independence from Louis XI. His
daughter Anne of Brittany continued
the work.

The great edifice is defended by deep
ditches of considerable width, which
could be flooded when necessary, and
by six stout towers with characteristically Breton pyramidal machicolations.
The interior reflects the castle's role as
a palace of government and residence,
known for its high life of feasts and
jousting.

Many of its features are of great interest,
like the Golden Crown Tower (**Tour de la
Couronne d'or**★★), the main building
(Grand Logis) with its massive dormer
windows, the Governor's Major Palace
(Grand Gouvernement) rebuilt at the
end of the 17C, and the well (**puits**★★)
with its wrought-iron well-head incorporating ducal crown motifs.

There are two museums in the castle:
the **Musée d'Art populaire**★ featuring Breton coiffes, dress and furniture,
and the Musée des Salorges, a maritime

museum (reorganisation in progress).
Temporary exhibitions of the latter's
collections are held in the Horse-shoe
Tower (Tour du Fer-à-Cheval).

Cathédrale St-Pierre et St-Paul
pl. St-Pierre
Although the building of the cathedral
extended over a period of 450 years, it
has a great unity of style.

The use of a white calcareous tufa in the
interior★★ enhances the impression
of boldness and purity of line resulting
from the mouldings of the pillars which
soar without a break in their flight up
into the keystones of the vaults.

In the south transept of the cathedral is
the exceptionally fine tomb of François II
(**tombeau de François II**★★ – 1502).

ADDITIONAL SIGHTS
Musée des Beaux-Arts★★
(10 r. Georges Clemenceau)
Muséum d'Histoire Naturelle★★
*(le Square Loius-Bureau, pl. de la
Monnaie)*
The 19C Town★ *(pl. Royale, pl. Grasilin,
passage Pommeraye, etc.)*
Palais Dobrée★ *18 r. Voltaire*
Musée Jules-Verne★
(3 r. de l'Hermitage)
Musée archéologique★ *(18 r. Dobrée)*
Jardin des Plantes★
(pl. Charles Leroux)
Ancienne Île Feydeau *(r. Kervégan
opposite pl. du Commerce)*

EXCURSIONS
👥👤 Planète Sauvage★★
🔽 *20km/12.4mi SW, on D 758.*
www.planetesauvage.com.
This safari park at the heart of the Pays de Retz has over 1 500 animals roaming free in its 140ha/350-acre enclosure. The visit includes two circuits: one to be toured on foot, the other by car.

La Baule🏖🏖🏖
The resort stands on the N bank of the wide Loire estuary. It is reached on autoroute A11 and then by expressway from Nantes. �ℹ *8 pl. de la Victoire.* 📞 *02 40 24 34 44. www.labaule.fr.*
Perhaps the ultimate in modern seafront development on the French Atlantic, the resort of La Baule (pop 15 830) is today one of Europe's major resorts and considered to have one of its most beautiful beaches. It was only in 1879 that construction of the town began, after 400ha/1 000 acres of maritime pines had been planted to halt the steady encroachment of sand dunes.
The older houses retain much of their original charm and stand mostly hidden behind the more recent constructions along the shaded and well laid-out avenues. Water-sports, tennis, a casino and golf make this one of the most popular seaside resorts on the Atlantic Coast.

Visit
Many kilometres of beautiful and well-frequented sandy beaches are protected by the headlands, Pointes de **Penchâteau** and **Chémoulin** to the northwest and southeast respectively. The elegant promenade lined with modern buildings stretches for about 7km/4.3mi.
Numerous hotels and apartment complexes, some comfortable, others luxurious, in the proximity of delightful resorts such as **Le Croisica**, **Le Pouliguen**★ and **Pornichet**★, with their pleasure-boat harbours, make La Baule, together with its neighbour **La Baule-les-Pins**★★, the ideal spot for discovering the splendour of the **"Côte d'Amour"** and the **Guérande Peninsula**.

La Côte Sauvage
This Wild Coast is on the mainland (the other is on Belle-Île, 🐚*see BELLE-ÎLE*) and stretches from Pointe du Croisic in the west to Pointe de Penchâteau in the east. Skirted by a road and footpaths, the coastline alternates rocky parts with great sandy bays and numerous caves accessible only at low tide such as the cave of the Korrigans, the little elves of Breton legends.

Guérande★
The town lies behind beach resort La Baule. �ℹ*1 pl. du Marché au Bois.* 📞*02 40 24 96 71. www.ot-guerande.fr*
Standing on a plateau overlooking the salt marshes and secure behind its circle of ramparts, Guérande (pop 13 603) has kept its appearance as a proud medieval town.

Ramparts★
Begun in 1343, the ramparts were completed in 1476 and remain unbreached. They were flanked by six towers and pierced by four fortified gateways. In the 18C the Governor of Brittany had the moats filled in, although the north and west sections still contain water.

Collégiale St-Aubin★
pl. St.Aubin
Built between the 12C and the 16C, the church has a striking west front in granite. Embedded in a buttress on the right is an **outdoor pulpit**. Inside, the **capitals** are decorated with grotesque figures and foliage. The chancel is lit by a magnificent **stained-glass window**.

Presqu'île de Guérande★
In the Roman era, a great sea gulf stretched between the rocky island, Île de Batz, and the Guérande ridge.
Just a channel remains open opposite Le Croisic through which the sea flows at high tide.

Burgundy's unity is based more on history than on geography. Fortunately located on the trade route linking northern Europe to the Mediterranean, the territory was consolidated by its great Dukes in the 15C. It comprises a number of *pays* of varying character, though its heartland lies in the limestone plateaux stretching eastwards from the Auxerre area and terminating in escarpments, which drop down to the Saône Valley. To the east the Jura's limestone uplands run in a great arc for some 240km/150mi from Rhine to Rhône, corresponding roughly to the old province of Franche-Comté.

Highlights

1 17C Ducal Palace at **Dijon** (p228)

2 6C BC grave goods at **Trésor de Vix** (p229)

3 The 1C **Abbaye de Fontenay** (p229)

4 Flemish-Burgundian Hospital, Hôtel Dieu, at **Beaune** (p233)

5 The Benedictine **Abbaye de Cluny** (p250)

Geography – Of the Burgundian escarpments La Côte is the most renowned, with its slopes producing some of the world's finest wines. To the north is the Morvan, a granite massif of poor soils, with scattered hamlets and extensive forests. Further north and west the Nivernais stretches to the Loire and to the south the lower reaches of the Saône are bordered by the broad Bresse plain. The limestone uplands of the Jura were folded into long parallel ridges and valleys by the pressure exerted on them in the Alpine-building period (&see p91). This is a verdant landscape with extensive forests and vast upland pastures.

History – Burgundy was independent of France in the Middle Ages, but by the 15C the powerful Dukes had extended their rule to include the Jura. Later, however, the Duchy became a province of the Holy Roman Empire, annexed by France in 1674.

Economy – The name Burgundy has been synonymous with fine wines since the 14C. The region also produces cheese, cereals and poultry, although tourism is increasingly important.

In the Jura region, world-famous cheeses are produced, along with the yellow wine of Arbois.

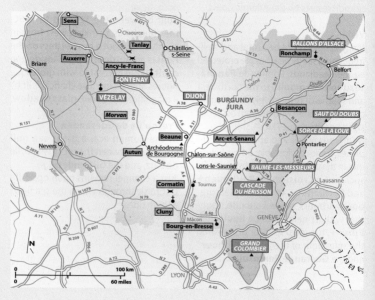

Dijon★★★
Burgundy

Close to some of the world's finest vineyards, Dijon, former capital city of the Dukes of Burgundy, straddles important north–south and east–west communication routes and has a remarkable artistic heritage.

A BIT OF HISTORY

Dijon had been the capital of Burgundy ever since the rule of Robert the Pious at the beginning of the 11C. In 1361, Philippe de Rouvres died without an heir, leaving the duchy without a ruler. In 1363, the French King Jean II le Bon (the Good) handed the duchy to his son Philippe, the first of an illustrious line of Valois Dukes who made the Burgundian court at Dijon one of the most brilliant of Europe.

Philippe became duke in 1364, at the same time as his brother Charles V le Sage (the Wise) was acceding to the throne of France. Thus from this time Burgundy and France were closely entwined. Philippe stood out as the most able of four royal brothers; cool, analytical on the one hand, well-named "le Hardi" (the Bold) on the other. His marriage in 1369 to Margaret of Flanders made him the most powerful prince of Christian Europe.

Anxious to provide a worthy burial place for himself and his successors, he founded the Champmol Charterhouse in Dijon in 1383, and set out to attract to the city the best sculptors, painters, goldsmiths and illuminators from his possessions in Flanders. His successor **Jean sans Peur** (John the Fearless) was assassinated in 1419. **Philippe le Bon** (the Good) inherited the title. From this time on, Burgundy saw its cultural importance waning in favour of the Netherlands and Flanders, where Renaissance ideas were blossoming. Nevertheless, artistic production continued throughout his 48-year reign. At the same time, Nicolas Rolin, the duke's Chancellor, was establishing the Hôtel-Dieu at Beaune.

> ▶ **Population:** 155 460
> ⚲ **Michelin Map:** 320 K 5-6
> 🄸 **Info:** 11 r. des Forges. 𝄞 0892 70 05 58. www.visitdijon.com.
> ◖ **Location:** Dijon lies 46km/29mi N of Beaune.
> 🅿 **Parking:** There are plenty of car parks around the perimeter of the city centre, and metered street parking within the city. But consider making use of the free shuttle buses called *Diviaciti* which run in the city centre from 7am–8pm Monday to Saturday.
> 🕓 **Timing:** At least one day to explore the centre without feeling rushed.

The boundaries of the Burgundian state had never been more extensive nor the life of its court more exuberant; on his wedding day in 1429, Philippe founded the Order of the Golden Fleece; never had the French king and his court, lurking in relative obscurity at Bourges, been more pitiful. But Burgundy's alliance with England had become unpopular just as Joan of Arc was awakening national sentiment. Philippe decided it was prudent to submit himself to the authority of the French king, marking the beginning of the end of the Hundred Years' War.

Charles le Téméraire (the Bold) succeeded in 1467; he was the last and perhaps the most renowned of all the Valois Dukes of Burgundy. He squandered its resources in the search for glory. Charles' death in 1477 marked the end of the great days of the Burgundian dynasty, but in the same year Mary of Burgundy, Charles' daughter, married Maximilian, Holy Roman Emperor. She was to be the mother of **Philippe le Beau** (the Fair), who in turn fathered the future Emperor Charles V. The recovery of Burgundy and the other lands making up her dowry cost France more than two and a half centuries of struggle.

LA VILLE DUCALE (THE DUCAL CITY)

Palais des ducs et des États de Bourgogne★★

pl. des Ducs-de-Bourgogne.
⊙*Open Mon–Fri 8.45am–12.15am,
Sat 9.30am–12.30pm.* ✆*No charge.*
✆*03 80 74 52 71.*

The ducal palace had been neglected since the death of Charles the Bold. In the 17C, it was restored and adapted and given a setting of dignified Classical buildings. At the time the city was keen to emphasise its parliamentary role and needed a suitable building in which the States-General of Burgundy could meet in session. The exterior of the Great Hall of the States-General (Salle des États) recalls the Marble Court (Cour de Marbre) at Versailles. By contrast, the east wing with its peristyle anticipates the architectural style of the 18C.

Musée Amora

⊙*Open year-round.* ✆*Guided tours daily (except Sun and public holidays), mid-May–mid-Sept, 3pm. Enquire at the tourist office.* ✆*03 80 44 11 41.*

This museum, created by the Amora mustard company, recounts the history of the condiment, its origins, and every aspect of its production. Dijon has become the "Mustard Capital of the World", although mustard is not farmed in France.

Musée des Beaux-Arts★★

Cour de Bar entrance, Palais des Etats de Bourgogne. ♿⊙*Open May–Oct Wed Mon 9.30am–6pm; Nov-Apr Wed–Mon 10am–5pm.* ⊙*Closed public holidays.* ✆*No charge.* ✆*03 80 74 52 09.*
http://dijoon.free.fr/mba/acc-mba.htm.
The Fine Arts Museum is housed in the former ducal palace and in the east wing of the palace of the States-General.

Salle des Gardes★★★

Palais des Etats de Bourgogne.
On the first floor, in the former Banqueting Hall. This is the ducal palace's most important interior. Its centrepiece is formed by two tombs which before the French Revolution were in the chapel of the Champmol Charterhouse. The tomb of Philip the Bold was designed by Jean de Marville; its decoration was in the hands of Claus Sluter followed by his nephew Claus de Werve who succeeded in softening somewhat the severity of Marville's conception. Flamboyant Gothic inventiveness and exuberance are expressed in the procession of hooded mourners making its way around the cloisters formed by the four sides of the monument. Nearby, the tomb (**tombeau**★★★) of John the Fearless and Margaret of Bavaria is similar in style. There are also two altarpieces, dazzling in the richness of their decoration: one, sculpted by Jacques de Baerze and painted and gilded by Broederlam, shows **Saints and Martyrs**★★★; the other, depicting the Crucifixion, has famous paintings by Broederlam on the reverse side of its panels.

A portrait of Philip the Good by Rogier van der Weyden (born in Tournai, a pupil of Van Eyck and perhaps of Campin too, then teacher to Memling) is remarkable for its psychological insight. In an adjoining room is a fine Nativity of 1425 by the Master of Flémalle.

Ancienne Chartreuse de Champmol★

Enter at 1 bd Chanoine-Kir. Follow signs for "Puits de Moïse". ⊙*Open 10am–6pm.* ✆*No charge.* ✆*03 80 42 48 01.*
All that is left of the Charterhouse is Moses' Well (**Puits de Moise**★★) and the chapel doorway (**portail de la chapelle**★), both the work of Claus Sluter, the foremost among the sculptors of the Dijon School.

Born in Holland, he learnt his skills in Brabant and worked in Dijon from 1385–1404. Moses' Well was originally the pedestal of a Calvary. The statues of Philip the Bold and Margaret of Flanders in the chapel doorway are thought to be actual portraits.

EXCURSIONS

Châtillon-sur-Seine★

▶ *83km/51.5mi N of Dijon.*
🚹 *9–11 r. de la Libération.* ✆*03 80 81 57 57. www.pays-chatillonnais.fr.*

Cloisters, Abbaye de Fontenay
© John Frumm/hemis.fr

Châtillon occupied a strategic location on the ancient north–south trade route. It was here that the Seine ceased to be navigable; as a result, the place developed all the facilities that transshipment needed, and grew prosperous on the merchandise being exchanged between Cornwall and Etruria – amber, tin, coral, ceramics.

Two major events in Chatillon's history are separated by exactly 100 years. In 1814 a Congress was held here between France and her enemies.

Napoleon rejected the terms, fighting resumed and the downfall of the Empire soon followed. In 1914 General Joffre set up his Headquarters here and issued the famous order which led to the halting of the German advance by French troops.

♟♟ Le Trésor de Vix★★

Found in the tomb of a young Celtic queen, 6C BC grave goods (the treasure of Vix) can be found on display in the **Abbaye Notre-Dame de Châtillon** (*r. de l'Abbaye; for information and opening times, contact tourist office*).

Abbaye de Fontenay★★★

▶ *The abbey is next to Montbard, in northern Burgundy.*

Tucked away in its lonely valley near the River Brenne, Fontenay is very evocative of the self-sufficient life of a Cistercian abbey of the 12C.

St Bernard (1091–1153), unhappy with the wealth and power of Cluny, found greater asceticism and spirituality at the abbey of **Cîteaux**, 23km/14mi south of Dijon. He was made responsible for establishing the abbey at **Clairvaux** on the River Aube; then, in 1118, at the age of 27, he founded **Fontenay**, his "second daughter".

Ancienne Abbaye

♿🕐*Open daily mid-Nov–mid-Apr 10am–noon, 2–5pm; mid-Apr–early Nov 10am–6pm.* 📞*03 80 92 15 00. www.abbayedefontenay.com.*

The abbey church (**église abbatiale**) was built between 1139 and 1147. It is the first example of the "monastic simplicity" characteristic of the architecture promoted by St Bernard, and is laid out in a straightforward way, with a square chancel and chapels of square plan.

🚗 DRIVING TOUR

CÔTE DE NUITS★★

▶ *Leave Dijon on D 122, known as the Route des Grands Crus.*

The Côte de Nuits road follows foothills covered with vines and passes through villages with world-famous names.

Chenôve

The Clos du Roi and Cls du Chapitre recall the former owners of these vineyards, the dukes of Burgundy and the canons of Autun. The dukes' wine cellar, **Cuverie des ducs de Bourgogne** (♿🕐*open Jul–Sept 2–7pm; rest of the* year by appointment; *03 80 51 55 00)* contains two magnificent 13C presses.

Marsannay-la-Côte

Part of the Côte de Nuits, Marsannay produces popular rosé wines, obtained from the black Pinot grapes.

Fixin

This village produces wines that some consider among the best of the Côte de Nuits appellation.

The small **Musée Noisot** (*open mid-Apr to mid-Oct Sat–Sun 2–6pm. €4.50. *03 80 52 45 62*) houses mementoes of Napoleon's campaigns.

The 10C church in nearby **Fixey** is thought to be the oldest in the area.

Brochon

Brochon, which is on the edge of the Côte de Nuits, produces excellent wines. The **château** was built in 1900 by the poet Stephen Liégeard who coined the phrase Côte d'Azur for the Provençal coast. The name has stuck long after the poet has faded into obscurity, together with his poem which was honoured by the French Academy.

Gevrey-Chambertin

This village is typical of the wine-growing community immortalised by the Burgundian writer **Gaston Roupnel** (1872–1946). It is situated at the open end of the gorge, Combe de Lavaux, and surrounded by vineyards. The older part lies grouped around the church and château whereas the Baraques district crossed by N 74 is altogether busier.

The famous Côte de Nuits, renowned for its great red wines, starts to the north. In the upper village is this square-towered fortress **château** (*open Jun–Sept; guided tours (1hr) 10am–noon, 2–6pm; €6; *03 80 34 36 77. http://chateaudegevrey.free.fr*), lacking its portcullis; it was built in the 10C by the lords of Vergy.

Chambolle-Musigny

The road from Chambolle-Musigny to Curley passes through a gorge, Combe

Ambin, to a charming beauty spot: a small chapel stands at the foot of a rocky promontory overlooking the junction of two wooded ravines.

Vougeot

Vougeot red wines are highly valued. The walled vineyard of Clos-Vougeot, owned by the abbey of Cîteaux from the 12C up to the French Revolution, is one of the most famous of La Côte.

Since 1944 the **Château du Clos de Vougeot**★ (*open daily: Apr–Sept 9am–6.30pm; Oct–Mar 9–11.30am, 2–5.30pm; closed 1 Jan, and 24–25 and 31 Dec. €4.50. *03 80 34 36 77. www.closdevougeot.fr*) has been owned by the **Confrérie des Chevaliers du Tastevin** (Brotherhood of the Knights of the Tastevin).

The château was built in the Renaissance and restored in the 19C. The rooms visited include the Grand Cellier (12C cellar) where the *disnées* (banquets) and the ceremonies of the Order are held, the 12C cellar containing four huge wine-presses, the 16C kitchen with its huge chimney, and the monks' dormitory with a spectacular 14C roof.

Vosne-Romanée

These vineyards produce only red wines of the highest quality. Among the various sections *(climats)* of this vineyard, Romanée-Conti and De Richebourg have a worldwide reputation.

Nuits-St-Georges

This attractive little town is surrounded by the vineyards to which it has given its name. The fame of the wines of Nuits goes back to Louis XIV.

When the royal doctor advised him to take some glasses of Nuits and Romanée with each meal as a tonic, the whole court wanted to taste it.

The **museum** (*open May–Oct daily except Tue 10am–noon, 2–6pm; €2.30; *03 80 62 01 37*), in the cellars of an old wine business, shows items found in the Gallo-Roman settlement excavated at Les Bolards near Nuits-St-Georges.

ADDRESSES

🏨 STAY

B & B Hôtels – *5 r. du Château.* ✆*03 892 707 506. www.hotel-bb.com.* 🛏*55rms.* ⊑*€6.* If you don't mind the rather formulaic character of chain hotels, you'll have a happy stay in this town-centre hotel.

Hostellerie le Sauvage – *64 r. Monge.* ✆*03 80 41 31 21. www.hotellesauvage.com.* 🅿*22rms.* ⊑ *€6.50.* This 15C coaching inn has a prime spot, just a ten-minute walk from the Ducal Palace and in the middle of a lively quarter with a great café and restaurant scene.

Hôtel Montigny – *8 r. Montigny.* ✆*03 80 30 96 86. www.hotelmontigny.com. Closed 18 Dec–2 Jan. WiFi. 28rms.* ⊑ *€7.50.* Efficiently run hotel near the town centre with secure parking.

Hôtel Victor Hugo – *23 r. Fleurs.* ✆*03 80 43 63 45. www.hotelvictorhugo-dijon.com. WiFi. 23rms.* ⊑ *€6.* A friendly place with bright, smartly decorated and well-kept rooms.

Hôtel Wilson – *1 r. de Longvic.* ✆*03 80 66 82 50. www.wilson-hotel.com. WiFi. 27rms.* ⊑ *€12.* This former post house has retained its traditional charm and charisma.

Hôtel Du Nord – *pl. Darcy.* ✆*03 80 50 80 50. www.hotel-nord.fr. Closed 17 Dec–2 Jan. 27rms.* ⊑ *€11.50.* Right on the bustle of Dijon's central shopping square.

🍴 EAT

Le Chabrot – *36 r. Monge.* ✆*03 80 30 69 61.* If you're after traditional tastes and a laid-back ambience, this bistro is right up your street.

La Comédie – *3 pl. du Théâtre.* ✆*03 80 67 11 62. www.la-comedie.com.* This bistro appeals to those seeking traditional flavours and atmosphere.

Le Dôme – *16 bis, r. Quentin.* ✆*03 80 30 58 92.* This modern restaurant deals in traditional and contemporary cooking, with a good showing of Burgundian specialities.

L'Émile Brochettes – *16 pl. Émile-Zola.* ✆*03 80 49 81 04.* This quirky cavern-style restaurant looking onto lovely place Émile Zola celebrates the kebab in all of its savoury and sweet forms.

La Mère Folle –*102 r. Berbisey.* ✆*03 80 50 19 76.* This small, town-centre restaurant offers regional specialities. Convivial atmosphere, good service and 1930s-style décor.

Le Bistrot des Halles – *10 r. Bannelier.* ✆*03 80 49 94 15. Closed Sun and Mon.* A typical bistro a stone's throw from the covered market.

Le Bento – *29 r. de la Chaudron-nerie.* ✆*03 80 67 11 50. Lunch set menu €16. Sun noon–6pm.* Japanese food fans should try this place – the chef invents new sushi, sashimi and maki dishes every day.

La Dame d'Aquitaine – *23 pl. Bossuet.* ✆*03 80 30 45 65. www.ladame daquitaine.fr. Closed Mon lunch and Sun.* In the town centre, a paved courtyard and a long flight of steps descend to a superb 13C vaulted dining hall.

Le DZ'Envies – *12 r. Odebert.* ✆*03 80 50 09 26. www.dzenvies.com.* This contemporary gastronomic bistro on the market square reworks French cuisine with Japanese and North African touches.

🍸 ON THE TOWN

Theatres and Opera – Full programme of plays and comedy at the Théâtre du Sablier (*R. Berbisey*), the Théâtre du Parvis-St-Jean (*Pl. Bossuet*), the Bistrot de la Scène (*R. D'Auxonne*). In May the city hosts the Rencontres Internationales du Théâtre.

L'Agora Café – *10 pl. de la Libération.* ✆*03 80 30 99 42. Open Tue–Sat 11.30am–2am.* Piano-bar in a former 16C convent chapel with a laid-back vibe.

☕ TAKING A BREAK

Comptoir des Colonies – *12 pl. François-Rude.* ✆*03 80 30 28 22. Open Mon–Sat 8am–7.30pm.* Colonial-style tea shop, with a large sunny terrace.

Maison Millière – *10 r. de la Chouette.* ✆*03 80 30 99 99. www.maison-milliere.fr. Open Tue–Sun 10am–7pm.* Pleasant tearoom in a former 15C fabric shop.

La Causerie des Mondes – *16 r. Vauban.* ✆*03 80 49 96 59. Open 11am–7pm, Sun Oct–Mar 3–7pm. Closed Mon.* Asian-themed décor and mood music make for an exotic take on the tearoom.

Mulot et Petitjean – *13 pl. Bossuet.* ✆*03 80 30 07 10. www.mulotpetitjean. fr. Open Mon 2–7pm, Tue–Sat 9am–noon, 2–7pm.* This Dijon institution, founded in 1796, specialises in gingerbread.

🛍 SHOPPING

Marché des Halles – *centre of town. Tue, Thu and Fri mornings, and Sat.*

Burgundy's Legendary Vineyards

The lie of the land

The Côte runs along the east-facing slopes of the "mountain", dominating the plains of the Saône at an altitude varying from 200–300m (220–330yd), and slashed by cross-cut combes in a similar layout to the blind valleys of the Jura vineyards. Only the east- and south-facing slopes of the combes are planted with vines – around 8 000 hectares of first-quality grapes; the north-facing slopes are often densely wooded. While the hilltops are crowned with scrubland or thickets, the vineyards carpet the limestone slopes, basking in the morning sunlight and well protected from cold winds. This exposure to sunlight is what determines the production of sugar in the grapes and the final alcohol content of the wine. The slopes also ensure that rain runs off, keeping the soil well drained and nicely dry – just how the vines like it – to produce top-class wines.

Burgundy's fine wines – the "grands crus"

For much of its length, the D 974 marks the dividing line between the "noble" grape varieties and the rest, with the grands crus generally planted mid-way up the slopes. Pinot Noir is the king of Burgundy grapes: it is used to make red wines, whereas the great white wines are made from the Chardonnay grape. After the devastation of the phylloxera blight in the 19C, the vineyards were entirely replanted with resistant vines grafted from North American stock. But it's an ill wind that blows no good. Paradoxically, the pesky parasites brought beneficial changes in their wake: small producers were able to buy back land from the big boys, and a reduction in the quantity of wine produced led to much-improved quality. The Côte d'Or divides into two main areas: the superstars are the Côte de Nuits and the Côte de Beaune. The wines of the Côte de Nuits are prized for their robustness, while those of the Côte de Beaune are admired for their delicacy.

The Côte de Nuits

The Côte de Nuits extends from Fixin to Corgoloin. Its vineyards cover around 3 740 hectares and produce 104 950 hectolitres annually – that's 14 million bottles, give or take. The vineyards are planted on limestone slopes rich in calcium from fossils. This is red wine country whose most famous crus, running from north to south, are Chambertin, Musigny, Clos-Vougeot et Romanée-Conti. Rich and beefy, these wines need eight to ten years to develop the incomparable body and character of the best Burgundy. To the south, the Hautes-Côtes de Nuits vineyards produce uncomplicated wines on the west-facing slopes of the Côte.

The Côte de Beaune

The Côte de Beaune stretches over 5 950 hectares from north of Aloxe-Corton to Santenay, producing not only top-notch white wines, but also superb reds. On the upper slopes, the vineyards grow in limestone-rich soil, which changes its character to brown marly earth mingling with pebbles and clay as it washes down towards the lower reaches. The bottom line is an annual production of some 214 335 hectolitres, equating to 28 million bottles. Its most prestigious crus are, in the red corner, Corton, Volnay, Pommard and Beaune; in the white camp are Meursault and Montrachet. The reds are muscular and fruity – rather like the whites, which deliver a fabulously rich intensity on the nose and palate.

Beaune★★

Right at the heart of the Burgundian vineyards lies Beaune, a name synonymous with good wine; a visit to this ancient city, which boasts a splendid architectural heritage and some fine museums, is not complete without a tour of the vineyards of La Côte.

A BIT OF HISTORY

Birth of a town – First a Gaulish centre and then an outpost of Rome, Beaune was the seat of the Dukes of Burgundy to the 14C. After the death of Charles the Bold, last Duke of Burgundy, in 1477, the town refused Louis XI's efforts to annex it and gave in only after a five-week siege.

Wine auction at the Hospices de Beaune – This is the main event of the year and draws a large crowd. The Hospices de Beaune (this name includes the Hôtel-Dieu, the Hospice de la Charité and the hospital) acquired a very fine vineyard between Aloxe-Corton and Meursault through Chancellor Rolin. The wines from this vineyard have won international acclaim. The proceeds of the auction sales, **Les Trois Glorieuses**, known as the "greatest charity sale in the world", go to the modernisation of the medical facilities and maintenance of the Hôtel-Dieu.

SIGHT

Hôtel-Dieu★★★

Open late Nov–Mar 9–11.30am, 2–5.30pm; Apr–late Nov 9am–6.30pm.
€6.70. 03 80 24 45 00.
www.hospices-de-beaune.com.
The Hôtel-Dieu in Beaune, a marvel of Burgundian-Flemish art, was founded as a hospital by Chancellor Nicolas Rolin in 1443. The building with its medieval décor has survived intact and was used as a general hospital until 1971.

Exterior

The main decorative elements of the external façade with its tall and steeply pitched slate roof are the dormer windows, the weather vanes, the delicate

- **Population:** 22 935
- **Michelin Map:** 320: I-7
- **Info:** 6 bd Perpreuil, 21200 Beaune. 03 80 26 21 30. www.beaune-tourisme.fr.
- **Location:** 46km/29mi S of Dijon.
- **Parking:** It can sometimes be difficult to park in the very centre of Beaune on busy days.
- **Timing:** Beaune is a glorious place to explore; allow a full day, or stay overnight.

pinnacles and lacework cresting of lead. The roof line is broken by the bell turret surmounted by a slim Gothic spire.
The delicate roof above the porch is composed of three slate gables terminating in worked pinnacles.
Each weather vane bears a different coat of arms. On the panelled door, note the ironwork grille and the door knocker, a magnificent piece of sculpted wrought-iron work.

Courtyard

The wings to the left and rear have magnificent roofs of coloured glazed tiles (recently restored) in geometric patterns. These roofs are punctuated by turrets and a double row of dormer windows, surmounted by weather vanes adorned with heraldic bearings and small spires of worked lead.

Interior
Grand'Salle or Chambre des Pauvres ★★★

This immense hall, used as the poor ward, has a magnificent timber roof in the shape of an upturned keel which is painted throughout; the ends of the tie-beams disappear into the gaping mouths of monsters' heads.

✎ WALKING TOURS

1 TOWN CENTRE

Among the many old houses, those at Nos 18, 20, 22 and 24 **rue de Lorraine** form a fine 16C ensemble. The town hall (**Hôtel de ville**) is in a 17C former Ursuline convent. The right wing houses two museums.

At No 10 **rue Rousseau-Deslandes** there is a house with its first floor decorated with trefoiled arcades.

Hôtel de la Rochepot★

⊶*Not open to the public.*

This 16C building has an admirable Gothic façade. In place Monge is a 14C belfry and a statue of **Gaspard Monge** (1746–1818), a local shopkeeper's son who became a famous mathematician. No 4 **place Carnot** is a 16C house with attractive sculptures.

Place de la Halle

The Hôtel-Dieu with its fine slate roof overlooks the square. Avenue de la République and rue d'Enfer lead to the former mansion of the dukes of Burgundy, dating from the 15C and 16C, now the museum of Burgundy wine.

No 13 **place Fleury** is the **Hôtel de Saulx**, a mansion with a quaint tower and an interior courtyard. The Maison des Vins (tastings) is on rue Rolin, beyond the Hôtel-Dieu.

Musée du Vin de Bourgogne★

r. d'Enfer. ◷*Open: Apr–Nov daily 9.30am–6pm; Dec–Mar daily except Tue 9.30am–5pm.* ◷*Closed 1 Jan, 25 Dec.* ✎€5.50. ✆*03 80 22 08 19.* *www.musees-bourgogne.org*

The museum is in the former mansion of the dukes of Burgundy, dating mainly from the 15C and 16C. The history of Burgundian vineyards and vine cultivation is explained in a comprehensive exhibit on the ground floor. The large first-floor room decorated with two huge Aubusson tapestries is the headquarters of the Ambassade des Vins de France.

Collégiale Notre-Dame★

The daughter house of Cluny, begun about 1120, was considerably influenced by the church of St-Lazare in Autun; it is a fine example of Burgundian Romanesque art despite successive additions.

Exterior – The façade is concealed by a wide 14C porch with three naves. The sculpted decoration was destroyed during the Revolution, but the 15C carved door panels have survived.

Walk clockwise round the church to get the best view of the chevet. Three different phases of construction – the pure Romanesque of the ambulatory and apsidal chapels, the 13C refurbishment of the chancel and the 14C flying buttresses – can be detected in the handsome proportions of the whole. The crossing tower, which is formed of Romanesque arcades surmounted by pointed bays, is capped by a dome and a 16C lantern.

Interior – The lofty nave of broken-barrel vaulting is flanked by narrow aisles with groined vaulting. A triforium, composed of open and blind bays, goes round the building, which is strongly reminiscent of Autun with its decoration of arcades and small fluted columns. Besides the decoration of the small columns in the transept, it is worth noting the sculptures on certain capitals in the nave representing Noah's Ark, the Stoning of St Stephen and a Tree of Jesse, and the Renaissance chapel with the fine coffered ceiling off the south aisle.

Tapestries★★ – In the choir behind the high altar are some magnificent tapestries which mark the transition from medieval to Renaissance art. Five richly coloured panels, worked in wool and silk, trace the whole life of the Virgin Mary in a series of charming scenes. They were commissioned in 1474 and offered to the church in 1500 by Canon Hugues le Coq.

At No 2 **rue E.-Fraysse**, the Maison du Colombier is a Renaissance house which can be seen from the square in front of the church of Notre-Dame.

2 THE RAMPARTS★

The relatively well-preserved ramparts form an almost continuous wall walk (2km/1mi).

They were built between the end of the 15C and the middle of the 16C, and are adorned with a few surviving towers and eight rustic bastions of various shapes – the double one, originally a castle, is known as the **Bastion St-Jean**. The moat is now occupied by gardens, tennis courts etc.

The north tower of the Bastion St-Jean has gargoyles and a niche occupied by a Virgin and Child. Pass the Blondeau Tower to get to the **Bastion Notre-Dame**, with a charming turret covering the spur. The line of the ramparts is broken by the 18C Porte St-Nicolas at the end of rue Lorraine.

Next come the Bastion des Filles, spoilt by the addition of an ugly new roof, and the now filled-in Bastion St-Martin forming a triangular terrace (**square des Lions**) overlooking a shaded garden.

The route now takes you past the Bastion des Dames, the **Rempart des Dames** and the now-abandoned Bastion de l'Hôtel-Dieu. The 15C Grosse Tour on the Rempart Madeleine is followed by the Bastion Ste-Anne with a turret overlooking the moat. The tour ends in front of the castle's **south tower**.

EXCURSIONS

Château de Savigny-lès-Beaune★

▶ *5km/3mi NW.* ◷*Open daily: Apr–Oct 9am–6.30pm; Nov–Mar 9am–noon, 2–5.30pm.* ⊛*€8.* ✆ *03 80 21 55 03.*

This village, known for its quality wines, has a 14C castle with some interesting collections on display. The smaller 17C château is now home to a wine-tasting and sales room and an exhibit of **Arbath endurance cars**. Visitors to the park will see 60 **jet fighter planes**, including Mirages (I to V), MIG 21 US (1962), Sikorsky helicopters and more.

The château was built by Jean de Frolois, Maréchal de Bourgogne, and restored by the Bouhier family in the 17C. An upper floor has been set aside for the **motorcycle collection★**, including over 500 models from around the world, which gives an overview of changes in mechanics and design over the 20C.

Montagne de Beaune

▶ *5km/3mi NW along D 970.*

Seen from the orientation table near the war monument south of the statue of Notre Dame-de-la-Libération, a lovely view extends over the brown-tiled roofs of the town to the vineyards beyond, and the Mâconnais hills to the south. Come in the afternoon when the light is at its best.

Vineyards of Savigny-lès-Beaune

© Jean-Baptiste Rabouan/hemis.fr

Autun★★

48km/30mi W from Beaune on D 973.
13 r. Général Demetz. ℘03 85 86 80
38. www.autun-tourisme.com.

Flanked by wooded hills, this dignified country town in northern Burgundy has a cathedral, museums and Roman remains that bear witness to its past.

Autun was founded by the Emperor Augustus, half a century after Caesar's conquest of Gaul. Rome itself was taken as the model for the new town; its walls (6km/4mi in length) soon sheltered fine civic buildings (a theatre, an amphitheatre) and a thriving commercial life. From their stronghold at Bibracte on Mont Beuvray 29km/18mi away to the west, the Gallic Aedui tribe watched the city's growth with fascination and ended up moving there themselves. In the Middle Ages the city consolidated itself on the upper part of its site.

Cathédrale St-Lazare★★

The great sandstone edifice was built from 1120–46 and named after the friend of Christ whom He raised from the dead and whose relics had supposedly been brought here from Marseille shortly before. Though its external appearance was altered by the addition of a tower and steeple in the 15C, it remains essentially a building of the Burgundian Romanesque style; its barrel-vaulted nave having slightly pointed arches (an early example) and a blind triforium designed to enliven an otherwise bare wall. With a gallery identical to that of the city's Roman Arroux Gate (Porte d'Arroux), this triforium is evidence of the continuing Roman influence well into the 12C.

The glory of the cathedral is its 12C Burgundian sculpture, most of it the achievement of Master Gislebertus, who came from Vézelay in 1125 and worked here for 20 years. The **tympanum (tympan)**★★★ over the central doorway dates from about 1135 and has the Last Judgement as its subject. It exhibits supreme mastery of technique and the boldness of its design outshines all other contemporary work. Look carefully, for example, at the joy of the saved, the agony of the damned and the use of scale in the treatment of the figure of Christ, the Apostles and other figures. The same mastery is evident in the **capitals (chapiteaux)**★★ in the nave and the chapterhouse, where more capitals (originally in the choir) are displayed at eye level.

Musée Rolin★

5 r. des Bancs. Open daily except Tue: Apr–Sept 9.30am–noon, 1.30–6pm; Oct–mid Dec 10am–noon, 2–5pm (Sun 2.30–5pm); 15 Feb–Mar 10am–noon, 2–5pm (Sun 2.30–5pm). Closed 14 Jul and 15 Dec–14 Feb. €5. ℘03 80 22 08 19. www.autun.com.

The 20 rooms contain many noteworthy exhibits. Two rooms (8 and 9) are devoted to masterpieces of Roman **statuary**★★, mostly by the two great sculptors of the Burgundian School, Gislebertus and Martin, a monk. Gislebertus' **Temptation of Eve**★★ expresses sensuality through the curves of the body and the plants; the carving adorned the lintel of the north door of the cathedral before 1766. Martin created part of the **tomb of St Lazarus**, which took the form of a miniature church and stood behind the altarpiece in the chancel of the cathedral until it was destroyed during the changes made by the canons in 1766. The surviving figures from the main group, which depicted the Resurrection of Lazarus, are the slim and poignant figures of St Andrew and Lazarus' sisters, Martha (who is holding her nose) and Mary. The rest of the work is represented by a few fragments supplemented by a sketch.

The first floor houses 14C and 15C sculptures from the Autun workshops and works by French and Flemish Primitive painters. The room devoted to the Rolin family contains the famous 15C painting of the **Nativity**★★ by the Master of Moulins.

15C Burgundian statuary is represented by the **Virgin**★★ of Autun in polychrome stone and a St Catherine attributed to the Spanish sculptor Juan de la Huerta who worked in the region during the reign of Philip the Good.

Gallo-Roman Town

The ruins of the **Roman Theatre** were once the largest theatre in Gaul (capacity: 12 000).

Porte St-André★ is where the roads from Langres and Besançon meet. It is the sole survivor of four original gates in the Gallo-Roman fortifications, which were reinforced with 54 semicircular towers.

Porte d'Arroux was the Roman Porta Senonica, leading towards Sens and the Via Agrippa, which ran from Lyon to Boulogne. The upper arcading dates from the time of Emperor Constantine.

Nevers★

▶ *152km/95mi W of Beaune by D 978.*
🛈 *Palais Ducal r. Sabatier. ℘03 86 68 46 00. www.nevers-tourisme.com.*

From the red sandstone bridge spanning the Loire, there is a fine view of the old town of Nevers set in terraces on its limestone hill. Its tall town houses with their roofs of slate and tile are dominated by the high square tower of the great cathedral and the graceful silhouette of the ducal palace.

Nevers was known for its pottery in the Middle Ages. Artistic pottery seems to have been brought here in the 1560s by Italian craftsmen. In the time of Louis XIII and Louis XIV the town was a centre of faïence production, with 12 manufactories producing some of the finest Blue Persian work ever made. There is a fine **collection★** of Nevers pottery in the museum **(musée municipal)**. Nevers flourished as a port until the 19C when the Loire ceased to be navigable.

Following her visionary experiences at Lourdes, Bernadette Soubirous came to Nevers in 1866 to enter the convent of **St-Gildard★** here.

Palais Ducal★

r. Sabatier.
The former residence of the Dukes of Nevers is a fine example of French Renaissance architecture.

Église St-Étienne★

This splendid Romanesque church has a magnificently tiered east end and a beautiful overall pattern of windows in the style of the great abbey church of Cluny. The height of the interior is particularly impressive for a building of its date (1063–97).

Chalon-sur-Saône★

▶ *30km/19mi S of Beaune by A 6.*
🛈 *4 pl. du Port Villiers. ℘03 85 48 37 97. www.uk.chalon-sur-saone.net*

Chalon is the urban centre for the fertile lowlands bordering the Saône River as it makes its way between the Jura and the Massif Central. Its most famous son is the father of photography, Joseph Nicéphore Niépce (1765–1833)

The river is fed by a number of canals; at Corre it is joined by the Eastern Canal (Canal de l'Est – completed 1882), at Pontailler by the canal from the Marne (1907), and at St-Jean-de-Losne by both the Rhine-Rhône Canal (1833) and the Burgundy Canal (1832).

But it is only at Chalon, where it is joined by the Central Canal (completed 1790), that it becomes one of Europe's great commercial waterways, flowing south to join the Rhône at Lyon. Long before the present age, however, the Saône had been an important commercial route; a large number of amphora bases were found at Chalon, proof that wine was imported here from Naples before the introduction of the vine to Burgundy by the Romans.

Since the 18C the banks of the river have been a favoured site for industry, which includes the heavy engineering firm Schneider du Creusot as well as electrical works and nuclear power plants.

The Origins of Photography – Joseph Nicéphore Niépce was a native of Chalon. His restlessly inventive disposition had already led him to design an internal combustion engine in 1807. He lacked talent as a draughtsman, but was fascinated by lithography. At the age of 48 he set himself the task of recording images through the spontaneous action of light. He was familiar with the optics of the camera obscura, which had been studied by the Arab physicist El Hazen (11C), by Leonardo da Vinci and by various 18C men of science, among them Jacques Charles, husband of Lamartine's Elvire. After three years' work he succeeded in making and fixing a positive image, and on 28 May 1816 he sent his brother a print made at his home in St-Loup-de-Varennes (7km/4.3mi south); this was the very first photograph.

Daguerre popularised Niepce's discovery and others developed it (e.g. Fox Talbot and Bayard). Progressive refinement and invention have led from Niepce's simple apparatus to photography as an art form, to the Hasselblad used in lunar exploration and to the snapshots in the family album.

Musée Nicéphore Niépce★★

28 quai des Messageries. ⏰*Open daily except Tue: Sept–Jun 9.30am–11.45am, 2–5.45pm; Jul–Aug 10am-6pm.* ⏰*Closed public holidays.* 👁*No charge.* 📞*03 85 48 41 98.www.museeniepce.com.*
The museum is housed in the 18C Hôtel des Messageries on the banks of the Saône. The rich collection comprises photographs and early photographic equipment, including the earliest cameras ever made, which were used by Joseph Nicéphore Niépce, as well as his first heliographs. There are also works by well-known contemporaries of Niepce in the world of photography.

ADDRESSES

🛏STAY

🍽🍽 **Chambre d'hôte La Cadolle** – *Grande-Rue, 21200 Bouze-les-Beaune. 6km/3.7mi northwest of Beaune on D970.* 📞*03 80 26 08 99. www.lacadolle.com. Closed Dec and Jan.* 🅿 🚭. *3rms.* This delightfully renovated stone house offers three rooms with original wood parquet flooring. Those on the first floor open onto their own little balconies, while the third has a more cosy character. All in all, a nice little set-up run by welcoming owners.

🍽🍽 **Hôtel Grillon** – *21 rte de Seurre.* 📞*03 80 22 44 25. www.hotel-grillon.fr. Closed 1–7 Dec and all Feb. WiFi. 17rms.* 🚭 *€10.* A spruce little bolthole tucked

away in a walled garden, with attractive personal touches in the bedrooms. There's a lounge-bar in the cellar, and a flowery alfresco terrace for summery breakfasts.

🍽🍽 **Hôtel Le Parc** – *13 r. du Golf, 21200 Levernois. 6km/3.7mi southeast of Beaune on D970.* 📞*03 80 24 63 00. www.hotelleparc.fr. Closed 31 Jan–13 Mar.* 🅿 *Wi-Fi. 17rms.* 🚭 *€8.* Charming hotel clad with Virginia creeper and bursting with flowers in summer. The two buildings are separated by a patio. The grounds at the back look out over fields.

🍽🍽🍽 **Hostellerie du Château de Bellecroix** – *20 chemin de Bellecroix, 71150 Chagny. 18km/11mi southeast of Beaune on D974 then N6.* 📞*03 85 87 13 86. www.chateau-bellecroix.com. Closed 15 Dec–13 Feb and Wed (except Jun–Sept). 19rms.* 🚭 *€16.* The two towers of this 18C château stand amid wooded parkland. Nearby lie the turrets of a former 12C Knights Templar building of the Order of Malta. Bedrooms come with antique furniture.

🍽🍽🍽🍽 **Hôtel Le Cep** – *27 r. Maufoux.* 📞*03 80 22 35 48. www.hotel-cep-beaune.com. WiFi. 64rms.* 🚭 *€19.* Ravishing 16C house in the old quarter. Cosily old-fashioned bedrooms are named after famous vintages from the Côte-d'Or. Breakfast is served in the vaulted cellar or in the courtyard with its pretty Renaissance arcades.

🍴EAT

🍽 **Aux Vignes Rouges** – *4 bd Jules-Ferry.* 📞*03 80 24 71 28. www.auxvignesrouges.com. Closed Mar and Wed.* Two dining rooms in a stone-vaulted cellar done out with a natural look are the setting for regional cuisine built on fresh local produce.

🍽🍽 **Le Bénaton** – *25 Faubourg Bretonnière.* 📞*03 80 22 00 26. www.lebenaton.com. Closed Thu lunch and Sat lunch Apr–Nov, and Wed.* Small, tranquil restaurant with a covered terrace for warm days. Delicious meals made with fresh seasonal produce are great value for money.

🍽🍽 **Caveau des Arches** – *10 bd de Perpreuil.* 📞*03 80 22 10 37. www.caveau-des-arches.com. Closed Sun and Mon.* Savour fine classic Burgundy cooking in the cosy vaulted dining rooms of this restaurant on the ramparts.

🍽🍽 **La Ciboulette** – *69 r. de Lorraine.* 📞*03 80 24 70 72. Closed Mon and Tue.* Two cheerful dining rooms furnished with green rattan and wood panelling. Appetising menu of traditional dishes given a Bourguignon spin.

La Cuverie – 5 r. Chanoine-Donin, 21420 Savigny-lès-Beaune. ℘03 80 21 50 03. Closed Tue and Wed. This 18C stone wine cellar with bourguignon furniture and a snazzy collection of cafetières is just the job for traditional dining featuring local produce.

Le Jardin des Remparts – 10 r. Hôtel-Dieu. ℘03 80 24 79 41. www.le-jardin-des-remparts.com. Closed Sun and Mon except public holidays. ⊞. Comfy dining rooms and a delightful garden terrace in this 1930s house up against the ramparts. Contemporary cooking using top-class materials.

Ma Cuisine – passage Ste-Hélène. ℘03 80 22 30 22. Closed Wed, Sat and Sun. Located along a tiny street, this small dining room sports the colours of Provence. Regional bottles on the wine list.

Via Mokis – 1 r. Eugène Spüller. ℘03 80 26 80 80. www.viamokis.com. Masterfully creative cooking served on small plates, or *mokis*, in a trendy bistro setting. Good choice of wines by the glass. Spacious, individual, modern rooms, and there's a basement spa.

Le P'tit Paradis – 25 r. Paradis. ℘03 80 24 91 00. Closed Sun and Mon. Dining room and terrace by a flower garden. Modern cuisine with regional flair and wines from boutique producers.

☞ TAKING A BREAK

Bouché – 1 pl. Monge. ℘03 80 22 10 35. Open Tue 8am–8pm, Sun 8am–1pm and 3–8pm. Inside this pretty tearoom are lovely gift boxes to fill with tantalising house specialities – chocolate "snails", candied chestnuts and fruits. At table, you're spoilt for choice with 20 or so speciality sweets.

Palais des gourmets – 14 pl. Carnot. ℘03 80 22 13 39. Open daily 7am–7.30pm (7pm Oct–Apr and closed Tue). This delightful patisserie-tearoom serves many local delicacies, including *cassissines* (blackcurrant jelly flavoured with blackcurrant liqueur).

☺ ON THE TOWN

Le Bistrot Bourguignon – 8 r. Monge. ℘03 80 22 23 24. www.restaurant-le bistrotbourguignon.com. Open Tue–Sat 11am–3pm, 6–11pm. Closed mid–Feb to mid–Mar. Relax on the terrace or sink into a comfy armchair in this old house as you sip a glass of wine to the mellow strains of classic jazz.

♀ WINE LOVERS' PARADISE

L'Athenaeum de la Vigne et du Vin – 5 r. de l'Hôtel-Dieu. ℘03 80 25 08 30. www.athenaeumfr.com. Open daily 10am–7pm. Closed 25 Dec and 1 Jan. This book-shop has a reputation as the best on oenology, Burgundy and gastronomy. Also wine-related items from corkscrews to cellarman's knives.

Cave Patriarche Père & Fils – 5–7 r. du Collège. ℘03 80 24 53 79. www.patriarche.com. Open daily 9.30–11.30am, 2–5.30pm (Nov–Mar Sat–Sun 5pm). Closed 24, 25, 31 Dec and 1 Jan. Burgundy's largest cellars are housed in a former convent dating from the 14C. Guided tours and tasting sessions.

Caves de La Reine Pédauque – Porte St-Nicolas. ℘03 80 22 23 11. www.reine-pedauque.com. Open end Nov–Mar daily 10am–noon, 2–5pm; Apr–Nov daily 9.30am–12.30pm, 2–7pm. Closed Christmas and Jan. After exploring the 18C vaulted cellars, go for a wine tasting around an imposing, round, marble table.

La Cave des Cordeliers – 6 r. de l'Hôtel-Dieu. ℘03 80 25 08 85. Open daily Oct–Apr 10.30–11.30am, 2–5.30pm; May–Sept 9.30am–noon, 2–6pm. Closed 25 Dec and 1 Jan. The Couvent des Cordeliers, built in 1242, provides a splendid backdrop to these wine cellars, which you can visit before tasting six fine wines.

Le Comptoir Viticole – 1 r. Samuel Legay. ℘03 80 22 15 73. www.comptoirviticole.com. Open daily 8am–noon (9am Mon), 2–7pm. Closed Sun and public holidays. Wine-buff heaven in a shop selling all manner of wine-making kit.

Marché aux Vins – 2 r. Nicolas Rolin. ℘03 80 25 08 20. www.marcheauxvins.com. Open Jul–Aug daily 9.30am–5.45pm, rest of the year daily 9.30–11.45am, 2–5.45pm. Closed 25 Dec and 1 Jan. Wine market in Beaune's oldest church offering 18 wines of between 3 and 15 years of age.

Vins de Bourgogne Denis-Perret – 40 r. Carnot. ℘03 80 22 35 47. www.denis perret.fr. Open May–Oct Mon–Sat 9am–7pm, Sun 9am–noon; rest of the year Mon–Sat 9am–noon, 2–7pm. Five wine-growers and a group of landowners have teamed up to offer you some of the most prestigious names from the Burgundy region.

Auxerre★★
Burgundy

A port on the River Yonne, surrounded by rustic, wooded farm country and hillsides planted with vines and orchards, the city was once an important staging post on the great Roman highway which led from Lyon to Boulogne via Autun and Lutetia (Paris).

▶ **Population:** 39 456

Michelin Map: 319 E-F-G 5

Info: quai de la République. ℰ03 86 52 06 19. www.ot-auxerre.fr.

Location: Auxerre lies 149km/93mi NW of Beaune, and 78km/49mi SW of Troyes.

VISIT
Abbaye St-Germain★

2 bis, pl. Saint-Germain. ◐*Open daily except Tue: May–Sept 10am-6.30pm; Oct–Apr 10am–noon, 2–6pm.* ◐*Closed 1 Jan, 1 May, 1 and 11 Nov, 25 Dec.* ≋€4.50. ℰ03 86 18 05 50. *www.auxerre.culture.gouv.fr.*

The city's famous Benedictine abbey is named after bishop St Germanus (378–448), born in Auxerre. A small basilica was probably erected over the saint's tomb in the 6C by Clothilde, the wife of King Clovis. It was extended in 841 to include an outer nave and a crypt.

The abbey **crypt★** houses a raised cavity which was hollowed out in the 9C to hide the tomb from raiding Norsemen. In addition there is a false tomb designed to lead them astray. In part of the crypt dating from Merovingian times (6C), there are two oak beams on Gallo-Roman columns and also a 5C monogram of Christ. From the Carolingian period (8–10C) there is a **fresco** showing the bishops of Auxerre, floor-tiling, and, most moving of all, a capital based crudely on the Ionian Order, proof of the aesthetic poverty of the time.

Cathédrale St-Étienne★★

◐*Open 7.30am–6pm.* ⚒*Tour of the treasury and crypt from Easter–1 Nov daily 9am–6pm (Sun 2–6pm); rest of the year daily except Sun 10am–5pm.* ℰ03 86 52 23 29.

The fine Gothic cathedral was built between the 13C and 16C to replace the existing Romanesque one. The building was practically finished by 1525.

West front – The Flamboyant style façade has four storeys of arcades sur-mounted by gables. The sculptures on the doorways (13–14C) were mutilated in the 16C during the Wars of Religion, and the soft limestone has weathered badly.

Interior – The nave, built in the 14C, was vaulted in the 15C. The choir and the ambulatory date from the beginning of the 13C. In 1215, the cathedral's Romanesque choir was pulled down; rising above the 11C crypt is the beautiful piece of architecture built to replace it, completed in 1234.

Romanesque crypt★ – The crypt, the only remaining part of the 11C Romanesque cathedral, has 11–13C frescoes.

Treasury★ – The many interesting exhibits include a collection of 12–13C chased enamels, manuscripts, 15–16C books of hours and miniatures.

Musée Leblanc-Duvernoy

◐*Open May–Sept Wed–Fri 10am–noon, 2–6pm; Sat and Sun 10am–6.30pm; rest of year times vary.* ◐*Closed 1 Jan, 1 and 8 May, 1 and 11 Nov, 25 Dec.* ≋€2.50. ℰ03 86 18 05 50. This museum is mainly devoted to faïence ware, with many exhibits from French or local ceramicists. It also houses 18C Beauvais tapestries depicting scenes from the life of the Emperor of China.

EXCURSIONS
Briare

▶ *The Briare canal is reached 70km/44mi SW of Auxerre.*

pl. Charles de Gaulle. ℰ02 38 31 24 51. *www.briare-le-canal.com.*

Briare is a busy town on the banks of the Loire, known for its ceramic floor mosaics and its stoneware.

Pont-Canal★

The Loire was used by river traffic from the 14–19C, but the navigation companies found it difficult to cope with the river's irregular flow on the one hand, and shallowness on the other.

To rectify this, and as part of his policy of economic unification, Henri IV began building the Briare Canal in 1604; completed in 1642, it linked the basins of the Loire and the Seine via its junction with the River Loing at Montargis. It was the first connecting canal in Europe.

The Loire Lateral Canal (1822–38) extends it south to Digoin. It crosses the Loire at Briare on an aqueduct built 1890–94 (58 years after those at Le Guétin and Digoin). The channel is the longest in the world and rests on 15 granite piers designed by Gustave Eiffel.

Sens★★

▶ 80km/50mi NW of Auxerre.
🚩 pl. Jean-Jaurès. ℘03 86 65 19 49.
www.office-de-tourisme-sens.com.

The once-important old town is girded by boulevards that replaced the ancient ramparts. In the city centre stands the first of France's great Gothic cathedrals. The tribe of the Senones, who gave the town its name, was of the most powerful in Gaul. In 390 BC they even invaded Italy and seized Rome.

Its central position in relation to Burgundy, Champagne and the Île-de-France gave Sens considerable importance for centuries; for a long time it was the Bishop of Sens who crowned French kings.

Cathédrale St-Étienne★★

148 r. de la Résistance.

In its general conception this is the very first of France's great Gothic cathedrals, its foundations laid in the years 1128–30, though most building took place between 1140 and 1168.

The influence of the Romanesque can be discerned in a number of features, like the slightly pointed "Burgundian" arches of the nave, a series of twin openings at tribune level with a false gallery, and, in the side chapels, a combination of rounded and pointed arches. But it is the Gothic which is decisive. Following the collapse of the south tower of the west front in 1268, the building was restored and altered, with the probable addition of flying buttresses. In the 13C and 14C, the clerestory windows were given extra height; then, in the 15C and 16C, the transepts were built in Flamboyant style.

Inside, the eye is drawn to the **stained glass**★★, which is 12C in the ambulatory and north side of the choir, while the Jesse Tree and St Nicholas in the south transept and the rose window of the north transept are all Renaissance works by master glaziers from Troyes. The ambulatory, the chapels opening off it, and the choir all have very fine grilles of wrought and gilded ironwork (18C).

Museum, Treasury and Palais Synodal★

🕐 Open Wed, Sat–Sun 10am–noon, 2–6pm; Mon, Thu, Fri 2–6pm.
🕐 Closed Tue, 1 Jan and 25 Dec.
💷 €4.50. ℘03 86 83 88 90.

The Musées de Sens are housed in the **Old Archbishop's Palace** (16–18C) and the Synodal Palace which stand on the south side of the cathedral.

François I and Henri II wings – These 16C galleries are devoted to the history of Sens and the Sens district. The first rooms display prehistoric and proto-historic articles: Paleolithic stone tools, Neolithic house and burials (7 500 to 2 500 BC), Bronze Age objects (2 500 to 750 BC) including the treasure of Villethierry (jeweller's stock), many Iron Age weapons and ornaments.

The basement contains pieces of **Gallo-Roman stonework**★ reused in the building of the town walls of Sens: architectural pieces, sculptures, tombstones. Excavations under the courtyard have revealed the foundations of a 4C bath-house and a collection of bone combs. Sculpture from the 18C is displayed on the first floor: reliefs from the Porte Dauphine erected in memory of the dauphin, Louis XV's son, and of the dauphin's wife, as well as parts of a rood screen removed from the cathedral in the 19C.

White Wines of Chablis

Chablis has been made in Burgundy since the 12C, when the vineyards stretched as far as the eye could see. Tending them was the population's sole occupation, and the source of an enviable prosperity. Today, the land is used more selectively, and the soil is the determining factor in the appellation on the bottle, which is a reference to the silica, limestone and clay content of the soil (as in Champagne), rather than to domaines, or specific vineyards (as in Bordeaux, for example).

The best vintages are the Grands Crus, mostly grown on the steep hillsides of the east bank: Vaudésir, Valmur, Grenouilles, Les Clos, Les Preuses, Bougros and Blanchots. Rich in aroma yet dry and delicately flavoured, distinguished by their golden hue, these generally bloom after three years in the bottle, but are rarely kept more than eight. Premier Cru wines are grown on both banks of the river; lighter in colour and less full-bodied, they are best aged three years, never more than six. More than half of the production, bearing the Appellation Chablis Contrôlée label, is very dry and pale, to be aged one to three years before reaching its best.

Often described as crisp or fresh, a good Chablis made exclusively from Chardonnay grapes is delightful with oysters, freshwater fish, ham or chicken dishes with creamy sauce. Lesser vintages, including hearty Bourgogne Aligoté or fruity Petit Chablis, are best enjoyed young with local country fare (grilled sausage, crayfish) or regional cheese (Chaource, St-Florentin) and fresh bread.

Cathedral treasury (Trésor)★★ (access via the museum) – One of France's richest treasure houses, containing a magnificent collection of materials and liturgical vestments: the shroud of St Victor, a 13C white silk mitre embroidered with gold thread, St Thomas à Becket's alb; handsome 15C high warp tapestries (Adoration of the Magi and Coronation of the Virgin); ivories (5C and 6C pyx, the 7C liturgical comb of St Lupus, an 11C Byzantine coffret and a 12C Islamic one) as well as gold plate (late 12C ciborium).

Synodal Palace – A beautiful 13C palace restored by Viollet-le-Duc. The great vaulted chamber on the ground floor was the seat of the ecclesiastical tribunal (officialité). In the 13C two bays served as a prison and there are still traces of graffiti on the walls.

Chablis

◗ 21km/13mi E of Auxerre.
℘03 86 42 80 80. www.chablis.net.
This small town, with the feel of a big village, is tucked away in the valley of the River Serein, between Auxerre and Tonnerre. Chablis is the capital of the prestigious wine-growing region of lower Burgundy. Thanks to its many old buildings, harking back to its heyday in the 16C, it still has a medieval feel. The annual wine fair and the village fairs of November and late January, held in honour of St Vincent, patron of wine-growers (see Calendar of Events), recall the town's lively commercial past.

The **Église St-Martin** (open Jul–Aug Mon–Fri 11am–1pm, 3–6pm; Fri–Sat 11am–1pm, 2.30–6pm; Sun 2.30–6pm. ℘03 86 42 80 80) dates from the late 12C. It was founded by monks from St-Martins-des-Tours, who carried their saint's relics with them as they fled the Normans.

Château d'Ancy-le-Franc★★

◗ The château stands in N Burgundy countryside, SE of Tonnerre.
🏠 18 pl. Clermont-Tonnerre. ℘03 86 75 14 63. www.chateau-ancy.com.
Open late end Mar–mid-Nov Tue–Sun. €9. Guided tours (50min) late Mar–mid-Nov Tue–Sun 10.30am, 11.30am, 2pm, 3pm, 4pm; Apr–Sept at 5pm. €9.

This dignified château marks the end of the early, Italian-influenced French Renaissance in all its brilliance. Designed by Sebastian Serlio, Italian architect invited to France in 1541 by

François I, the château was begun in 1546 and completed 50 years later.

The exterior gives an impression of great order, combining symmetry with a masterly handling of spaces and surfaces according to the rules of the Golden Section. The courtyard is particularly subtle, with deeply sunken twin pilasters topped by Corinthian capitals and separating scalloped niches.

The interior is equally fine. There are ancient bindings in the library, secret cabinets from Italy, dell'Abbate's *Battle of Pharsalus* and oval medallions by Primaticcio representing the Liberal Arts.

Vézelay★★★

▶ *Vézelay is W of Avallon.*
🛈 *r. St-Étienne. ℘03 86 33 23 69.*
www.vezelaytourisme.com.

The quiet and picturesque little village of Vézelay climbs a steep slope among the northern foothills of the Morvan countryside, overlooking the Cure valley. Its fame is due to the majestic basilica which numbers among the greatest treasures of France. The Celts were the first to settle this hilltop site. In 878 an abbey was founded here, and in 1050 it was dedicated to Mary Magdalene, whose remains were supposedly here, and the place soon became one of France's great pilgrimage destinations. It was here that St Bernard preached the Second Crusade in 1146. In 1279, however, the monks of St-Maximin in Provence claimed to have discovered the bones of Mary Magdalene in a cave; the certification of the relics as authentic led to the decline of Vézelay as a place of pilgrimage; it was pillaged by the Huguenots, razed at the time of the French Revolution and given its *coup de grâce* by lightning.

Basilique Ste-Marie-Madeleine★★★

pl. de la Basilique. ⓧ*Closed during Church services.* ⊜*No charge.*
℘*03 86 33 39 50. http://vezelay.cef.fr.*

First built between 1096 and 1104 and restored following the fire of 1120. The principal external features are the fine Romanesque body of the church (to which flying buttresses were added in the 13C), **Tour St-Antoine**, and a particularly harmonious chevet with radiating chapels. From the terrace, there is a fine **view**★ over the valley of the river Cure.

In the dimly lit narthex (1140–60) is the marvellous **tympanum**★★★ of the central doorway, dating from around 1125. Proportion is used to reinforce the meaning of the composition; for example, the figure of Christ is of superhuman size.

The Romanesque nave is unusually large and well lit. The greatest contribution to the basilica's decoration is made by the many **capitals**★★★ adorning the pillars; these were sculpted in the 12C.

Aerial view of Vézelay with Basilique Ste-Marie-Madeleine

J. Damase/MICHELIN

Besançon★★

Jura

The capital of the Franche-Comté occupies a superb **site**★★★ on a meander of the River Doubs, overlooked by a rocky outcrop on which Vauban built a fortress which has resulted in the town being an outstanding example of 17C military architecture. The birthplace of the writer Victor Hugo, Besançon is also known for its many museums and fine architecture.

▶ **Population:** 121 671
⚫ **Michelin Map:** 321 G 3
▪ **Info:** 2 pl. de la 1ére-Armée-Française. ℘03 81 80 92 55. www.besancon-tourisme.com.
◗ **Location:** 109km/68mi NE of Beaune.
◔ **Timing:** The historic centre of town lies within the circle *(la boucle)* of the Doubs river. Shops and restaurants can be found on Grande-Rue, near the bridges. The modern town is on lower ground across the river. Allow half a day or more to appreciate everything.

A BIT OF HISTORY

A 2C triumphal arch called the Black Gate (Porte Noire) survives from a Gallo-Roman settlement (Vesontio) first mentioned by Julius Caesar as the home of the Gaulish *Sequani* tribe: the modern Grande-Rue still follows the course of its main street in the heart of old Besançon. Later the town became an important archbishopric.

The city is closely connected with the Holy Roman Empire and was given the title of Imperial Free City in 1184. Through inheritance and marriages, in the 15C and 16C the town – like the rest of Franche-Comté – became part of the Austro-Spanish empire. It marked a high point in the province's commercial life, illustrated by the rise of the Granvelle family. Although born into the humblest of peasant families, the son Perrenot was given an education, rose rapidly, becoming chancellor to Charles V, and built himself the Palais Granvelle. In 1674 Louis XIV conquered the Franche-Comté, made Besançon its capital and had Vauban construct the citadel.

SIGHTS
Palais Granvelle★

This fine example of civil architecture of the 16C has a three-storey façade, divided by five horizontal bands of decoration, and a high mansard roof with crowstep gables.

Its proportions and decorative details are those of the Early Renaissance (basket-handle arches, mouldings) while other features are quite new (Tuscan columns, and the superposition of Ionic and composite orders).

Citadel and Museums★★

99 r. des Fusillés-de-la-Résistance. ◔*Open daily except Tue: Nov–Mar 10am–5pm; Apr–Oct 9am–6pm (Jul–Aug 7pm).* ◔*Closed 25 Dec, 1 and 14 Jan.* ⊛€9. ℘03 81 87 83 33. www.citadelle.com.

From 1675-1711 Vauban constructed this mighty fortress. Its great mass is best appreciated from the sentry-walk along the encircling ramparts. The building houses a zoo and the Musée d'Histoire naturelle (aquarium, insectarium, climatorium, noctarium).

Musée des Beaux-Arts et d'Archéologie★★

1 pl. de la Révolution. ◔*Open daily except Tue: 9.30am–noon, 2–6pm (Sat–Sun 9.30–6pm).* ◔*Closed 1 Jan, 1 May, 1 Nov, 25 Dec.* ⊛€5 (free on Sun and public holidays). ℘03 81 87 80 49. www.musee-arts-besancon.org.

The museum houses a diverse collection of artistic, historical and archaeological displays. Most important is the priceless 14–17C art collection of the Granvelle family. A room on the first floor provides plenty of evidence of the long tradition of clock and watch-making in the Franche-Comté. Most of the great clock-making firms are represented at Besançon. Many of the important advances in the art from 17C to the present have been made here or nearby.

ADDITIONAL SIGHT

♣♣ Musée des Maison Comtoises

▶ 15km/9.5mi E on D 464 to Nancray. Allow half a day for your visit. ○Open Jul–Aug daily 10am–7.30pm; May–Jun and Sept 10am–6.30pm; mid-Mar–Apr and Oct–early Nov 1-6pm. ○Closed mid-Nov–Mar. ▧€7.50. ℘03 81 55 29 77. www.maisons-comtoises.org.

This open-air museum has reconstructed 30 typical Franche-Comté houses to demonstrate rural architecture and the country way of life as it was in the 17C to 19C. There are organic vegetable gardens, orchards and rare breeds of animals to encourage sustainability and biodiversity. Regular demonstrations and festivals are held on-site.

EXCURSIONS

Saut du Doubs★★★

▶ On the border 10km/6mi E of Morteau. ⊟ r. Berçot, 25130 Villers-le-Lac. ℘03 81 68 00 98. www.villers-le-lac-info.org. ⊛ The waterfall is at its best viewed in autumn after heavy rain. Allow at least an hour at the falls.

Bursting out of the Chaillexon lake, the waters of the Doubs plunge down in a magnificent drop, known as "le Saut du Doubs", one of the most famous natural phenomena you can admire in the Franche-Comté.

From the raised level of the lake, the Doubs tumbles to its natural level in a noisy and turbulent cascade of spume. There is a **boat service** (○open daily Apr–Oct; during Mar and Nov call for information. ▧€12.50, children €8.90. ℘03 81 68 13 25; www.sautdudoubs.fr) from Villers-le-Lac. The boats follow the river's meanders as they gradually open up to form the Chaillexon Lake; then they take their passengers through a gorge, the most picturesque part of the trip. From the landing-stage, take the path (🚶30min round-trip on foot), which leads to the two viewpoints overlooking the Saut du Doubs.

Villers-le-Lac★

This small town in the Doubs valley, where the river spreads to form the **Lac de Chaillexon★**, is the starting point of boat excursions to the **Saut du Doubs★★★** waterfall.

Two slopes on either side of the River Doubs crumbled in and blocked a part of the valley, creating a natural dam which in turn formed the lake. There are two principal parts to it: in the first, the water is a single, open stretch between the gentle slopes of the valley; in the second, it lies between abrupt limestone cliffs which divide this part of the lake into a number of basins.

Le Saut du Doubs

G. Magnin/MICHELIN

In the town, the interesting **Musée de la Montre**★ (♿⏱open school holidays daily except Tue 10am–noon, 2–6pm; ☞€5.50;. ℘03 81 68 44 53) celebrates the history of watchmaking, a long-standing tradition of the Jura region on both sides of the Franco-Swiss border.

Arc-et-Senans★★

▷ The royal saltworks of Arc-et-Senans are located in Jura, not far from the River Loue. They are situated SW of Besançon and N of Arbois.

🏛 Institut Claude-Nicolas Ledoux. ℘03 81 54 45 45. www.salineroyale.com.

Erected 1775–80, the Classical buildings of the former royal saltworks are an extraordinary essay in utopian town planning of the early Industrial Age and are on UNESCO's World Heritage List.

In 1773, the King's Counsel decreed that the royal saltworks should be built at Arc-et-Senans, drawing on the salt waters of Salins.

Only the cross-axis and half the first ring of buildings envisaged by the visionary French architect **Claude-Nicolas Ledoux** (1736–1806), inspector general of other saltworks, were actually completed; what we see today is however enough to evoke the idea of an ideal 18C city.

His plan was ambitious; a whole town laid out in concentric circles with the Director's Residence at the centre, flanked by storehouses (Bâtiments des sels), offices and workshops, and extending out to include a church, a market, public baths and recreational facilities. Ledoux's vision makes him one of the forerunners of modern architecture and urban design and while the enterprise was never really viable, being closed down in 1895, the amazing buildings of the Saline Royale remain.

Saline Royale (Royal Saltworks)★★

The complex today consists of the gatehouse, Director's Residence, courtyard, coopers' building and salt storehouses. The **gatehouse**, which features a peristyle of eight Doric columns, now houses the reception and a bookshop. Badly damaged by fire in 1918 and a subsequent dynamite attack, the **Director's Residence** has been the object of much-needed restoration; its rooms are now used for conferences. Its basement contains a display on the saltwork operations.

The semicircular **courtyard** is today a lawn; firewood was once unloaded for storage here. In the **coopers' building** architectural models, photographs and prints depict Ledoux' ideas about an ideal society. The old **salt storehouses** have been converted into venues for concerts and other events.

Pontarlier

▷ The town lies near the Swiss border at the foot of the Jura mountains.

🏛14 bis r. de la Gare. ℘03 81 46 48 33. www.pontarlier.org.

Between the 13C and 17C this proud upland town (pop 18 360), which still commands the internationally important Besançon-Lausanne highway, was the capital of the area known as the Baroichage.

This statelet, consisting of Pontarlier and the 18 surrounding villages, enjoyed an independent regime of republican character which was only extinguished by Louis XIV's conquest of the Franche-Comté.

Cluse de Pontarlier★★

▷5km/3mi S. of Pontarlier.

The Jura has many such cluses – lateral clefts through the high ridges separating two valleys that facilitate communication between valley communities. This example, with the road and railway tightly squeezed together in the narrow defile, is strategically located on the route to Switzerland and overlooked by the Larmont and Joux forts high above (the Cluse de Joux is one of the Jura's most beautiful cluses).

Lac de St-Point★

▷ 8km/5mi S of Pontarlier.

Nearly 7km/4.3mi long, it is the largest lake in the Jura, fed by the waters of the River Doubs and attractively sited among mountain pastures and pine forests.

Source de la Loue★★★

▶ *16km/10mi W. of Pontarlier*

The River Loue rises in one of the blind valleys that penetrate deeply into the high plateau of the Jura.

In its setting of high cliffs and luxuriant vegetation, it is one of the region's finest natural sites.

Grand Taureau★★

▶ *11km/7mi E. Leave Pontarlier S along N 57 and turn left onto a minor road climbing to the ski resort of Montagne du Larmont.*

This is the highest point (1 323m/4 340ft) of the Larmont mountains, less than 1km/0.5mi from the Franco-Swiss border. The **view**★ from here stretches over Pontarlier and the Jura plateaux to the west.

Chapelle de Ronchamp★★

▶ *Ronchamp is a small former mining town bordering Alsace.*

🏛 *Rue Chapelle, Ronchamp.* 🖉*03 84 20 65 13. www.chapellederonchamp.fr.*

Built by **Le Corbusier** (1887-1965), the Chapelle Notre-Dame-du-Haut on its hilltop site is one of few great works of religious architecture produced by the early 20C Modern Movement.

The apparent simplicity of the building's curving lines and asymmetrical surfaces can be deceptive, as can the architect's subtle use of light falling from the "periscopes" in the side chapels, filtering in from the base of the convex vault or streaming through the irregular wall-openings which constitute the building's main decoration. Only slowly does one come to appreciate the fusion of feeling and technology.

ADDRESSES

🏠 STAY

⊜⊜ **Hôtel Siatel Chateaufarine Hôtel du Nord** – *8 r. Moncey.* 🖉*03 81 81 34 56. www.hotel-du-nord-besancon.com. 44rms.* 🍴*€7.* Situated in the historic quarter, this hotel dating from the 19C is a perfect base for venturing out into the old town.

⊜⊜ **Hôtel Foch** – *7 bis av. Foch.* 🖉*03 81 80 30 41. www.hotel-foch-besancon.com. 27rms.* 🍴*€7.50.* The rather severe façade of this large building on the corner reveals a well-run hotel.

⊜⊜ **Citotel Granvelle** – *13 r. Lecourbe.* 🖉*03 81 81 33 92. www.hotel-granvelle.fr.* ♿ *30rms. WiFi;* 🍴*€8;.* This stone building has an ideal location just a few steps from the historic town centre.

⊜⊜ **Hôtel Siatel** – *3 Chemin des Founottes.* 🖉*03 81 80 41 41. www.hotel siatel.com.* ♿🅿 *40rms. WiFi;* 🍴*€7.* A functional hotel close to a busy main road, but the identical rooms are well sound-proofed. The dining room offers buffets, traditional meals and grills.

⊜⊜⊜⊜ **Mercure Parc Micaud** – *3 av. Ed.-Droz.* 🖉*03 81 40 34 34. www.mercure.com.* 🅿 *91rms.* 🍴*€15.* Opposite the Doubs River, close to the old town where Victor Hugo was born in 1802. Rooms suit the demands of a business clientele; there is a decent bar and the modern-styled restaurant has a view to the gardens of the casino.

🍴 EAT

⊜ **Le Cavalier Rouge** – *3 r. Mégevand.* 🖉*03 81 83 41 02. www.cavalierrouge.com. Closed Sun.* A trendy urban atmosphere and speedy service.

⊜ **Au Petit Polonais** – *81 r. des Granges.* 🖉*03 81 81 23 67. Open lunch Tue–Sun; evenings Thu–Sat. Closed Mon.* A simple, unpretentious setting for traditional local cuisine. Warm, congenial atmosphere.

⊜ **La Femme du Boulanger** – *8 r. Morand.* 🖉*03 81 82 09 56. Closed Sun.* This friendly tea room and baker's café offers sandwiches made with Poilâne bread, salads and a dish of the day served both lunchtimes and evenings.

⊜ **Miam** – *8 r. Morand.* 🖉*03 81 82 09 56. Closed Sun.* A very chic, designer restaurant which will whisk your palate far away from the banks of the Doubs River.

⊜⊜ **La Source** – *4 r. des Sources, 25170 Champvans-les-Moulins. 8km/5mi NW of Besançon.* 🖉*03 81 59 90 57. www.lasource-besancon.com. Closed Wed eve except Jun–Aug, Sun eve and Mon.* Big bay windows bathe the main room on the mezzanine with light. Regional and traditional food is served.

Lons-le-Saunier★

Jura

The capital of the Jura is a spa town with an interesting heritage, and makes a good base for excursions to the vineyards or the Jura plateau. The local *Vin Jaune* or yellow wine is similar in taste to dry sherry.

▶ **Population:** 19 053

Michelin Map: 321 D 6

Info: pl. du 11-novembre. ℰ03 84 24 65 01. www.ville-lons-le-saunier.fr.

Location: Near the Swiss border. 85km/53mi SW of Besançon.

SIGHT
Rue du Commerce★
The town was ravaged by fire between 25 June and 4 July 1636 when it was attacked by Condé on Richelieu's orders. Seven years later, the population was amnestied by Mazarin and allowed to return. The Rue du Commerce was rebuilt in accordance with a detailed plan in the second half of the 17C; it is elegantly laid out on a slight curve and is famous for its great variety of shops with their attractive displays.

What might have been a monotonous piece of planning reflects instead a local love of independence and appreciation of good design. Note particularly the high roofs with their mansards and tall chimneys, the 146 stone arcades (some of them of Romanesque date) of many different shapes and sizes, the trapdoors leading to the cellars, sculpted heads, and balconies and window decoration in wrought iron.

No 24 is the birthplace of Rouget de l'Isle, composer of the *Marseillaise*, the French national anthem. A museum in the Hôtel-de-Ville has a collection of his songs.

A statue of the great man by Bartholdi (the designer of the Statue of Liberty in New York harbour) can be found on the Promenade de la Chevalerie. Erected in 1882, it was declared a National Monument in 1992 for the bicentennial celebrations of the *Marseillaise* song.

EXCURSIONS
Cirque de Baume★★★
▶ *19km/11.8mi E.*

This is one of the most spectacular of the blind valleys characteristic of the western rim of the Jura.

The action of water has been particularly significant here in undermining the upper beds of limestone, which have caved in, thus forming the impressive gorge we see today. The viewpoint at Roches de Baume *(near the D 471)* gives splendid prospects over this great natural amphitheatre marking the boundary between the high plateau of the western Jura and the Bresse plain.

Cascade du Hérisson★★★
▶ *E of Lons-les-Saunier, and approached from the villages of Bonlieu, Doucier or Ilay, and then reached on foot.*
6 Grande-rue, Clairvaux-les-Lacs.
℘03 84 25 27 47. www.juralacs.com.

High up at the foot of the cirque of Chaux-de-Dombief is little Lake Bonlieu, drained by the River Hérisson (hedgehog). The river crosses the narrow Frasnois plateau, then drops via a series of rapids and falls through its famous wooded gorge to the Champagnole plain below.

The path climbs over a series of limestone outcrops laid down over a period of 35 million years during Jurassic times; it is they that form the succession of splendid falls, the **Éventail★★★** (Fan Falls), the **Grand Saut★★** (Great Leap), Château Garnier, the **Saut de la Forge★** and Saut Girard.

☺ Walking Tours ☺

Follow the marked **Sentier des Cascades** footpath which starts 8km/5mi E of Doucier as far as the Ilay crossroads (3hr round-trip).

Bourg-en-Bresse★★

Jura

Bourg is the capital of the Bresse area, famous in France for its high-quality poultry, which bears its own label of authentification.
It is situated to the west of the Jura Mountains on the River Reyssouze, a tributary of the Saône.

A BIT OF HISTORY

Little is known about Bourg until it was awarded the status of a free town in 1250. Passed between Savoy and France several times, it finally became French in 1601.

"Fortune infortune fort une" – The sad motto of **Margaret of Austria** (1480–1530) can be translated (less poetically) as "Fate very hard on one woman." As a child of two, Margaret lost her mother, Mary of Burgundy. At three, she was chosen by Louis XI as the wife of the Dauphin Charles VIII because of her Burgundian inheritance; a form of wedding took place. Then, at the age of 11, she was repudiated by the Crown and the marriage was annulled. At the age of 21 she married John of Castile who died after less than a year.

At 24 she remarried, this time to Philibert le Beau. He too soon died. From then on Margaret's life was devoted to prayer and to quietly caring for the domains she had inherited. Her rule was marked by diplomacy, prudence and wisdom. As a result, in 1508 her father, the Emperor Maximilian, made her Regent of the Low Countries. Margaret, still only 26 years old, moved to Brussels, but also set about transforming the humble priory of Brou into a monastery, partly to fulfil a vow made 24 years earlier by her mother-in-law, Margaret of Bourbon, partly to symbolise her love for her husband.

SIGHT
Monastère royal de Brou★★

63 bd de Brou. ⏱*Open daily: Apr–Jun 9am–12.30pm, 2–6pm; Jul–Sept 9am–6pm; Oct–Mar 9am–12.30pm, 2–5pm.*

▶ **Population:** 40 972
◔ **Michelin Map:**
328 C-D-E 34
ℹ **Info:** 6 ave Alsace Lorraine. ℘04 74 22 49 40. www.bourg-en-bresse.fr.
▶ **Location:** 37km/23mi E of Macon and 82km/51mi NE of Lyon.

⏱*Closed 1 Jan, 1 May, 1 and 11 Nov, 25 Dec.* ☞€7. ℘04 74 22 83 83. *www.brou.monuments-nationaux.fr.*
The church – now deconsecrated – was built from 1513 to 1532 in exuberant Flaboyant Gothic style. The work was undertaken by a Flemish master builder and a team of artists and craftsmen, mostly from Flanders, where Margaret was now living. The interior decoration was already much influenced by the Renaissance. In the elegant nave, built of pale stone from the Jura, a finely sculptured balustrade was substituted for the more usual triforium.

The stone **rood screen★★** has three basket-handle arches and is profusely decorated with leaves, cable-moulding and scrolls. The 74 **choir stalls★★** were built by local carpenters. An array of statuettes represents biblical figures. In the **Margaret of Austria chapel★★★** an altarpiece is a masterwork of amazing craftsmanship. There are also superb **stained-glass windows★★**.

The three **tombs★★★** give the church its truly regal character. On the right is that of Margaret of Bourbon, in a Gothic niche with Flamboyant decoration. Philibert the Fair's elaborate tomb is completely Renaissance in character. Margaret of Austria's tomb forms part of the parclose screen; she is first shown lying in state on a black marble slab, then, underneath, in her shroud. Its richly carved canopy incorporates her motto.

The **museum★** *(same opening hours as the church)* is housed in the monastic buildings which are ranged around two-storey **cloisters★**, unique in France. On the ground floor of the small cloisters the sacristy and the chapterhouse, now one room, are used for temporary exhibitions. The great cloisters lead to the second chapterhouse, now the museum reception. A staircase leads up to the dormer where the old monks' cells now house collections of paintings and decorative art. The cells on the south side are devoted to 16–18C art, including a fine portrait of Margaret of Austria★ painted by B Van Orley c.1518.

EXCURSIONS
Cluny★★
◉ *A climb to the top of the Tour des Fromage gives the best view of the town and its historic structures.*
🏛 *6 r. Merciere.* 📞 *03 85 59 05 34.* *www.cluny-tourisme.com.* 🅿 *Plenty of parking available at pl. de l'Abbaye and pl. du Marche.*

The conditions for the future renown and prosperity of the great **Abbaye de Cluny**★★ existed at the very moment of its foundation.

The abbey, founded in 910, deep in forest and far removed from the centres of power in either France or Germany, was subject to no authority other than that of the pope himself. It answered – like its daughter houses and other dependencies – to no one but its elected abbot. It thus became a powerful instrument for the papacy.

Cluny's development was rapid, its prestige immense and its influence preeminent. In under a century, the abbey had amassed considerable power as well as much property and already had 1 184 daughter- and dependent houses. One hundred and fifty years later their numbers had risen to 3 000, scattered all over Europe.

For two and a half centuries this capital of monasticism found leaders of exceptional calibre, some of whom ruled for up to 60 years. The decline of the order began in the 13C, but its prosperity lasted until the 18C.

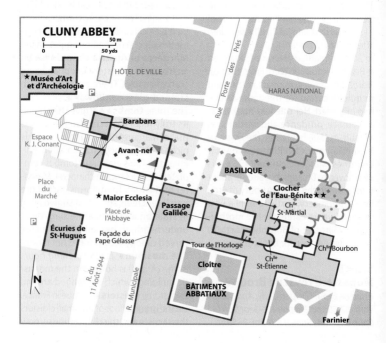

CLUNY ABBEY

View of the Rhône and Lac de Bourget from the Grande Colombier, the Bugey

© Camille Moirenc/hemis.fr

Abbaye Bénédictine de Cluny

Palais Jean de Bourbon. ⊙*Open daily: May–Aug 9.30am–6.30pm; Sept–Apr 9.30am–noon, 1.30–5pm.* ⊙*Closed 1 Jan, 1 May, 1 and 11 Nov, 25 Dec.* ⊙€7. ℘*03 85 59 15 93.*
http://cluny.monuments-nationaux.fr.
The abbey church, started 1088, was completed in 1130. It was destroyed during the Revolution. All that remains are the lower parts of two towers; the bell tower known as "the Holy Water" **(Eau bénite★★)**, an octagon, and another known as the Clock Tower (Tour de l'Horloge); of the great transept, the south arm with its two chapels and an octagonal vault (32m/105ft high); of the minor transept, the chapel (Chapelle de Bourbon) with sculpted heads of the Prophets. Reduced in height, the flour store *(Farinier)* has a fine 13C timber roof, and eight capitals from the abbey. The abbey buildings were rebuilt in the 18C.

Château de Cormatin★★

⊙ *13km /8mi N of Cluny.*
⊙*Guided tours (45min) daily: Apr–mid-Jun 10am–noon, 2–5.30pm; mid-Jun–mid-Sept 10am-noon, 2–6.30pm; mid-Sept–mid-Nov 10am–noon, 2–5.30pm.* ⊙€9 (children €4.50). ℘*03 85 50 16 55.*
www.chateaudecormatin.com.
The château, probably built by Jacques II Androuet du Cerceau, is a good example of the Henri IV style (late 16–early 17C): the monumental gates framed by antique orders, the basement built of stone and the windows decorated with mouldings. The mannerist style which evolved in the literary salons under Louis XIII (1610–43) reached its peak with the gilding and the lapis-lazuli decoration of the St Cecilia Room **(Cabinet Ste-Cécile★★★)**.

Grand Colombier★★★

⊡ *r. de la Mairie, Culoz.* ℘*04 79 87 00 30. http://culoz.interarb.com/colom.*
At 1 571m/5 154ft, the Grand Colombier forms the highest point in the Bugey area. The viewpoint at the summit is one of the finest in the whole of the Jura.
⊙*It's possible to drive almost to the top. Leave the car in the car park and continue to the summit on foot. It's a tough climb.*

From Virieu-le-Petit to Culoz

⊙ *29km/18mi.*
The road rises steeply, passing first through splendid pine forests. At the summit, with its cross and triangulation point, there is the widest of panoramas, taking in the Jura, the Dombes plateau, the valley of the Rhône, the Massif Central and the Alps.
In the distance the Grand Fenestrez, crowned by an observatory **(Observatoire★★)**, rears up from the Culoz plain, which can be reached by car via a boldly designed hairpin road.

CHÂTEAUX OF THE LOIRE

Rising far to the southeast in the Massif Central, France's longest river, the Loire, was once a busy waterway. Many of the towns along its banks bear traces of this former activity: from Orléans, once the Loire's foremost port, Blois, Tours, Langeais and Saumur. As with other great rivers, navigation was never easy and, once the railways came, the Loire was left to its caprices. Nowadays the region is famous for its magnificent Renaissance châteaux, which adorn the banks of the Loire's tributaries, the Indre and the Cher.

Highlights

1 Exceptional tapestry of Angers' **Tenture de l'Apocalypse** (p253)
2 Château partly built on a bridge: **Chenonceau** (p266)
3 French Gothic style: **d'Azay le Rideau** (p267)
4 Formal gardens (Jardins) at **Villandry** (p268)
5 First of France's Classical palaces: **Chambord** (p272)

Geography – This "garden of France", as the Loire Valley has been called, has also been called "a home-spun cloak with golden fringes", a reference to the contrast between the fertile valleys of the Loire and its tributaries and the low plâteaux that separate them. From Orléans onwards the Loire exercises its greatest attraction, with gentle landscapes and soft light.

History – Following the withdrawal of the Romans the Franks occupied the region. Viking incursions affected Tours and Angers during the 9C, but until the 12C most of the area was held by powerful barons. After 1202 King Philippe-Auguste was able to take charge following the seizure of the territory from King John of England. In the late medieval period the region was involved in the Hundred Years' War with much of the Loire falling into English hands again. During the 16C, however, the great château-building period began as part of the new ways of thinking about art and architecture ushered in by the Renaissance and exemplified by the magnificent edifices at Chenonceau, Azay, Blois and Chambord, their elegance and architectural exhuberance contrasting with the sterner fortresses of an earlier age, like the great castle at Angers. Other buildings have white tufa walls and slate roofs; around Amboise and Tours are troglodytic dwellings.

Economy – The Loire Valley is a major agricultural region, cultivating vines, cereals, rapeseed, sugar beet and sunflowers. Manufacturing is important, with the production of car parts, ball bearings and tyres made possible partly by the establishment of three nuclear power plants and partly by excellent communications. Tourism, also vitally important, is based on the châteaux and the great cathedrals of Orléans and Tours.

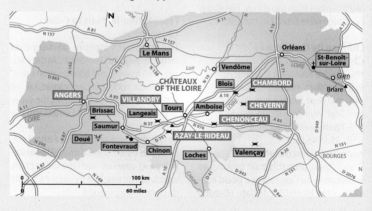

Angers★★★

Maine-et-Loire

This dynamic and cultured city on the River Maine was once the capital of a mighty Plantagenet kingdom encompassing all of England and half of France.

A BIT OF HISTORY

On 9 June 1129, Geoffrey Plantagenet married William the Conqueror's grand-daughter Mathilda, whose inheritance of both Normandy and England made her the most desirable of brides. Twenty-three years later another significant marriage took place, between Henry II, Geoffrey's son, and Eleanor of Aquitaine, the divorced wife of Louis VII.

Two months later Henry became king of England, thereby extending the frontiers of the Angevin state to Scotland in the north and the Basque country in the south. By contrast, the Capetian kingdom to the east cut a sorry figure; its capital, Paris, seemed little more than an overgrown village in comparison with Angers.

In 1203, with the 81-year-old Eleanor living in retirement at Fontevraud, King Philippe Auguste succeeded in incorporating Anjou into the French kingdom, together with Normandy, Maine, Touraine and Poitou, all territories of John Lackland. In 1471, King **René** let Anjou pass into the hands of Louis XI.

SIGHTS

Château★★★

2 prom. du Bout-du-Monde ⏰*Open daily: May–early Sept 9.30am–6.30pm; early Sept–Apr 10am–5.30pm. Last admission 45min before closing.* ⏰*Closed 1 Jan, 1 May, 1 and 11 Nov, 25 Dec.* 👣*Guided tours available (2hr).* 🎫*€8.* 📞*02 41 86 48 77. http://angers. monuments-nationaux.fr.*

Built by Louis IX from 1228 to 1238 on the surviving Roman foundations, this splendid fortress was intended to counter any threat from the nearby Dukes of Brittany. With 17 towers in alternating courses of dark schist and white freestone, they must have constituted a

▸ **Population:** 152 969
🚲 **Michelin Map:** 317 E-F-G 4
🅸 **Info:** 7 pl. du Président-Kennedy. 📞02 41 23 50 00. www.angers-tourisme.com.
▷ **Location:** mid-way between Nantes (88km/55mi SW) and Le Mans (94km/59mi NE).
🅿 **Parking:** Parking is available by the château on Esplanade du Port-Ligny.
🏅 **Don't Miss:** The 14C Tenture de l'Apocalypse and other tapestries.
🕐 **Timing:** After visiting the château (2hr), allow at least half a day to walk through the Old Town. A fun way to discover the city is a tour on the Petit Train, which drives around to all the main sights. There are also Taxi Tours, and guided Discovery Tours on foot.

formidable deterrent. The moats were dug in 1485 by Louis XI. During the Wars of Religion (1562–98), the towers were reduced in height and terraces added to give the defenders a clear field of fire. A purpose-built gallery at the heart of the château displays the **Tenture de l'Apocalypse**★★★, a tapestry, originally 168m/550ft long and 5m/16ft high, the oldest and most important to have been preserved. Jean Lurçat (1892–1966), who discovered it in 1938 and whose artistic career was inspired by it, called it "one of the greatest works of Western art". The 76 extant scenes are based on the Apocalypse of St John, and are impressive in their masterly scale, composition and design. Commissioned by the Duke of Anjou Louis I, this superb tapestry was executed in 1375–80 by master weaver **Nicolas Bataille**.

In the Governor's Lodging, a fine collection of Flemish tapestries includes the 16C *Lady at the Organ* and *Penthesilea*, and the richly coloured late 15C three-part *Tenture de la Passion et Tapisseries*

Château d'Angers

© Liane Matrisch/Dreamstime.com

mille-fleurs★★, with graceful angels carrying the instruments of the Passion.

Cathédrale St-Maurice★★

The cathedral stands in a charming district of old houses.

The characteristically elegant Angevin vault is notable in the 12C vaulting of the nave, with its transverse arches with double roll mouldings by Normand le Doué. By the end of the century the vaulting has become lighter; the number of ribs increases, springing from slender columns, as in the choir and transepts. At the beginning of the 13C it reaches its peak of development: lateral support is dispensed with; the structure dissolves into a graceful web of liernes, as in the hospital ward of the former **hôpital St-Jean**★ (St John's Hospital), resting on a small number of slim columns, as in the early 13C ceiling of the choir of the Église St-Serge.

Musée Jean-Lurçat et de la Tapisserie contemporaine★★

4 bd Arago. ⓖ⊙Open Jun–Sept daily 10am–6.30pm; Oct–May Tue–Sun 10am–noon, 2–6pm. ⊙Closed 1 Jan, 1 May, 14 Jul, 1 and 11 Nov, 25 Dec; ⊜€4. ℰ02 41 05 38 00. http://musees.angers.fr.

The former St John's Hospital, founded in 1174 and in use for 680 years, now houses the **Musée Jean-Lurçat**. In the hospital ward with its Angevin vaulting is Lurçat's series of tapestries known as **Le Chant du Monde**★★ (The Song of the World), ten huge compositions symbolising the contradictions of the modern world. Lurçat's achievement marked the revival of the art of tapestry.

Logis Barrault (Musée des Beaux-Arts)

This beautiful late 15C residence housing a **Fine Arts Museum** was built by Olivier Barrault, the King's Secretary, Treasurer to the Brittany States and Mayor of Angers. In the 17C it was taken over by the seminary, whose pupils included **Talleyrand** (ⓖsee VALENÇAY), the future Bishop of Autun.

Monastery buildings★

pl. Michel-Debré. ⊙Open Mon–Fri 9am–5.30pm. ⊜No charge. ℰ02 41 81 49 49.

The abbey buildings, extensively restored in the 17C and 18C, presently house local government offices. On the left side of the courtyard is a glazed-in **Romanesque arcade**★★, part of the cloisters, with sculptures of remarkably refined craftsmanship. The door with sculpted arch mouldings led to the chapterhouse; the arcades support a gallery from which those monks who had no voice in the chapter could listen to the proceedings.

EXCURSIONS
Château de Brissac★★

▶ *Brissac lies 18km/11.2mi from Angers.*
▪ *8 pl. de la République, Brissac-Quincé.*
Guided tours (45min) Apr–Jun and Sept–Oct daily except Tue 10am–12.15pm, 2–6pm; Jul–Aug daily 10am–6pm; Nov–Mar call for hours. €9.
02 41 91 21 50. www.brissac.net.

The château, set in a fine park shaded by magnificent **cedar trees**★, is unusual both for its height and for the juxtaposition of two buildings, one of which was intended to replace the other rather than stand next to it. Be sure to see the tapestries inside the château.

As the original building had been damaged during the Wars of Religion, Duke Charles de Cossé commissioned a new residence designed by Jacques Corbineau, the architect responsible for the citadel at Port-Louis in Lorient.

Work ceased on his death in 1621 and the château was left as we see it today. There is an unfinished main façade flanked by medieval towers. The central pavilion and the left wing are abundantly ornamented with rusticated pilasters and statues in niches. The right wing, which would have replaced the Gothic tower, was never built.

The 17C French painted **ceilings** are often embellished with sculptures; the walls are hung with superb **tapestries**. The Louis XIII staircase leads to the imposing guard room (Salle des Gardes), to the bedchamber where Louis XIII and his mother, Marie de' Medici, had a short-lived reconciliation after the Battle of Ponts-de Cé (1620), and to the Hunt Room (Chambre des Chasses), hung with magnificent 16C Flemish tapestries. North of Brissac, on the road to Angers, stands a fine windmill with a chamber hollowed out at ground level.

Château de Serrant★★★

▶ *The château is located off the N23 20km/10mi west of Angers, just before Saint-Georges-sur-Loire.*
Take the 1hr guided tour of the château before taking the excursion to the abbey at St-George.

Although built over a period of three centuries, 16C to 18C, this sumptuous moated mansion has great unity of style and perfection of detail. Its massive domed towers and the contrast between the dark schist and the white tufa give it considerable character.

The Château

Guided tours (1hr) mid-Mar–May and mid-Sept–mid-Nov Wed–Sat 1.30–5.15pm, Sun and public holidays 9.45am

Library, Château de Serrant

The Birthplace of the French Motor-Car Industry

In the second half of the 19C **Amédée Bollée** (1844–1917), a local bell-founder, began to take an interest in the incipient motor-car industry. His first car (*L'Obéissante*) was completed in 1873. Later he built the *Mancelle*, the first car to have the engine placed in front under a bonnet and to have a transmission shaft. The Austrian emperor, Franz-Josef, went for a ride in the *Mancelle*.

Bollée's son Amédée (1867–1926) devoted himself mainly to racing cars; they were fitted with **Michelin** tyres and reached 100kph/62mph. After WWI he began to produce an early form of piston rings, which became the main line of manufacture in his factory.

On 27 June 1906, the first prize on the Sarthe circuit was won by Szisz driving a Renault fitted with Michelin detachable rims.

In 1908 his brother, Léon Bollée, invited **Wilbur Wright** to attempt one of his first flights in an aeroplane at Les Hunaudières. When asked how the aircraft had performed, Wright replied, "Like a bird". In 1936 Louis Renault set up his first decentralised factory south of Le Mans in the Arnage plain.

–noon, 1.30–5.15pm; Jun–mid-Sept daily 9.15am–5.15pm (English tour at 1pm). ◉€9.50. ✆02 41 39 13 01. www.chateau-serrant.net.

The **Château de Serrant** was begun in 1546 by Charles de Brie supposedly after drawings by Philibert Delorme, the architect responsible for the construction of Fontainebleau.

The castle was bought by Hercule de Rohan, Duke of Montbazon, in 1596, and sold in 1636 to Guillaume Bautru whose granddaughter married the Marquis of Vaubrun, Lieutenant-General of the king's army. On the death of her husband, the Marchioness continued construction work until 1705. She commissioned Jules Hardouin-Mansart to build the beautiful chapel in memory of her husband, and Coysevox to design the mausoleum. During the 18C, the property was acquired by Antoine Walsh, a member of the Irish nobility who followed James II into exile in France and became a shipowner in Nantes.

Interior

In addition to the superb Renaissance staircase surmounted by coffered vaulting, the whole interior is very attractive. The **apartments**★★★ are magnificently furnished and this exceptional collection of furniture was added to the list of Historic Monuments. Sumptuous Flemish and Brussels tapestries hang in the reception rooms which contain rare pieces of furniture such as the unique ebony cabinet by Pierre Gole (17C) adorning the Grand Salon. Note also 17C, 18C and early 19C furniture by prestigious cabinet-makers (Saunier, JE de Saint-Georges) and Empire-style furniture by Jacob, upholstered with Beauvais tapestry, commissioned for Napoleon and Josephine's visit.

There are fine paintings representing the French and Italian schools, a bust of the Empress Marie-Louise by Canova (Empire-style bedroom on the first floor), and two terracotta nymphs by Coysevox in the sumptuous **Grand Salon**★★.

The **library**★★★ houses 12 000 volumes. Some of the books are marked with the Trémoille seal showing four T's symbolising the main estates owned by the family: Trémoille, Thouars, Talmont and Tarente. Opening onto the main courtyard, the chapel built by Jules Hardouin-Mansart contains the magnificent white-marble funeral monument of the Marquis de Vaubrun killed at the battle of Altenheim (1673).

St-Georges-sur-Loire

▶ *2km/1mi by N 23.*

St-Georges, on the north bank of the Loire, is situated not far from the famous vineyards, the **Coulée de Serrant** and the **Roche aux Moines**, where some of

Anjou's finest white wines are produced. The **abbey** (open Jul–Aug Tue–Sun 11am–12.30pm, 2.30–6.30pm; rest of the year by request, enquire at town hall; 02 41 72 14 80) was founded in 1158 by the Augustinian Order. The building dates from 1684 and contains a grand staircase with a wrought-iron banister and the chapterhouse with original wainscoting.

Le Mans★★

The city centre is the old quarter on the left bank of the Sarthe.

 Hôtel des Ursulines, 19 bis, r. de l'Étoile. 02 43 28 17 22. www.ville-lemans.fr.
 There is usually plenty of parking space in Place des Jacobins.

Le Mans, a large, modern provincial capital, hosts several fairs and events every year, most famously the 24hr Grand Prix, the "24 Heures de Mans".

An old town, enclosed by ramparts in the 4C, Le Mans was part of the Plantagenet estates. It has long been the site of trade fairs and festivals, which today include a Spring Fair (late Mar–early Apr), a great Four-Day Fair (mid-Sept) and an Onion Fair (first Fri in Sept). As a result, Le Mans has a long gastronomic tradition; local specialities include potted pork (*rillettes*), plump pullets (*poulardes*), capons (*chapons*) accompanied by cider, as well as the delicious reinette apple.

Vieux Mans★★

The historic centre of Le Mans stands on the site of a Celtic settlement, overlooking the lowlands on either side of the Sarthe. This part of the city is still enclosed within its 4C Gallo-Roman ramparts, some of the few extant in western France.

Cathédrale St-Julien★★

This magnificent building makes a fine spectacle from Place des Jacobins. Its Gothic **chevet**★★★, supported on intricate Y-shaped two-tier buttresses, is a spectacular demonstration of the boldness and ambition of its architect. The transition from nave to choir is one of the clearest demonstrations

anywhere – even for the architecturally uninitiated – of the great technical and stylistic changes which took place over a period of some 160 years. The arches of the south porch are pleasingly decorated, and the **doorway**★★ has splendid statue-columns. The Gothic choir was completed in 1254. The whole is lit on three levels by 13C **stained-glass windows**★★; in the chapels opening out onto the outer ambulatory, in the inner ambulatory and in the clerestory. Note how in the south transept (1385–92) the junction has been effected between the Gothic choir and the older, Romanesque, transept.

Churches

Several of Le Mans' churches are worth a visit, including: **Église de la Couture**★ (22 r. Berthelot); **Église Ste-Jeanne d'Arc**★ (pl. George-Washington) and **Notre-Dame de L'Épau**★ (r. de l'Esterel).

Museums

Le Mans has its fair share of museums: discover old Le Mans with historical maps and pictures at **Musée de la Reine Bérengère**★ (7–3 r. de la Reine-Bérengère au Mans; 02 43 47 38 51); visit the half-timbered 16C house **Maison du Pilier Rouge** (Grand Rue); admire the paintings at **Musée de Tessé**★ (2 av. de Paderborn-au-Mans; 02 43 47 38 51).

Motor-Racing Circuits

 To the S of Le Mans between N 138 and D 139.

Le Mans 24-hour Race

In 1923 Gustave Singher and Georges Durand launched the first Le Mans endurance test which was to become a sporting event of universal interest and an ideal testing ground for car manufacturers.

The difficulties of the circuit and the duration of the race are a severe test of the quality of the machine and of the endurance of the drivers.

The track has been greatly improved since the tragic accident in 1955 when 83 spectators died and 100 were injured. Whether seen from the stands or from the fields or pine woods that surround the track, the race is an unforgettable experience: the roaring of the engines, the whining of the vehicles hurtling up the Hunaudières section at more than 350kph/200mph, the smell of petrol mingled with the resin of the pine trees, the glare of the headlights at night, the emotion and excitement of the motor car enthusiasts. ⊙Every year there is also a Le Mans 24-hour motorcycle race and a Le Mans 24-hour truck race. A Grand Prix de France motorcycle race is held here regularly.

Circuit des 24 Heures

The 24-hour circuit (13.6km/8.5mi long) begins at the Tertre Rouge bend *(virage)* on N 138. The racetrack, which is about 10m/33ft wide, is marked in kilometres. The double bend on the private road and the Mulsanne and Arnage hairpin bends are the most exciting hazards on the 24-hour course. In 1972 the course was laid out to give a better view.

○ *From the main entrance to the track on D 139 a tunnel leads to the Bugatti circuit and the museum.*

Circuit Permanent Bugatti

♿⊙○*Guided, individual and group tours – see website .* ℰ02 43 40 24 30. www.lemans.org.
Apart from being used by its school for racing drivers, the track is also a permanent testing ground for teams of racing-car drivers and motorcyclists who use it for private trials.

Musée des 24 Heures du Mans – Circuit de la Sarthe★★

9 pl. Luigi Chinetti
♿⊙*Open: Jun–Aug 10am–6pm; Sept– May 11am–5pm.* ⊙*Closed 24, 25 31 Dec, 1 Jan.* ⊛€8 (10-18 years: €6).℘02 43 72 72 24. www.lemusee24h.com.
Rebuilt in 1991, the Motor Museum displays 110 vehicles in an extremely modern and instructive setting.
The section on racing cars, in particular those that won the Le Mans 24-hour race, presents a superb collection of outstanding automobiles, including a 1924 Bentley, a 1949 Ferrari, a 1974

Matra, a 1983 Rondeau, a 1988 Jaguar, a 1991 Mazda and a 1992 Peugeot.

ADDRESSES

⌂ STAY

⊝ **Chambre d'hôte La Ferme Chauvet** – *72430 Chantennay-Villedieu. 3km/2mi E of village.* ℘02 43 95 77 57. *5rms.* 🍽.
All modern comforts at a reasonable price; working farm.

⊝ **Chambre d'hôte Le Fresne** – *72300 Solesmes.* ℘02 43 95 92 55. www.lefresne.com. *3rms.* 🍽. Discover the delights of a working farm; rooms are in an annex.

⊝ **Chambre d'hôte Mme Bordeau** – *Le Monet . 72190 Coulaines . 5km/3mi N of Le Mans.* ℘02 43 89 45 56. *2rms.* 🍽.
A chance to stay in the countryside, but not too far from town. This typical regional house has been restored but has retained its original character.

⊝ **Chambre d'hôte Le Petit Pont** – *3 r. du Petit-Pont . 72230 Moncé-en- Belin. 11km/6.8mi S of Le Mans on D 147 towards Arnage, then D 307.* ℘02 43 42 03 32. *5rms. Evening meal* ⊝⊝. The rooms are simply decorated and well equipped. The property is situated on a working farm.

⊝ **Chambre d'hôte La Truffière** – *72430 Asnières-sue-Vègre. 2km/1mi NE of Asnières-sue-Vègre.* ℘02 43 95 12 16. *3rms.* 🍽. On a working farm; regional cuisine.

⊝⊝ **Chambre d'hôte Grand Talon** – *3 rte des Chapelles. 49800 Andard, 11km/ 6.8mi E of Angers on N 147 (towards Saumur) then D 113.* ℘02 41 80 42 85. *3rms.*
This elegant 18C house just outside Angers, decked out with leafy vines of Virginia creeper, is a haven of peace. You can picnic in the park, or relax in the lovely square courtyard. The rooms are pretty and the owners extend a very warm welcome.

⊝⊝ **Hôtel Cavier** – *La Croix-Cadeau– 49240 Avrillé, 8km/5mi NW of Angers on N 162.* ℘02 41 42 30 45. *43rms.* ⊒ €10.
The sails of this 18C windmill still turn! Inside its old stone walls is the dining room, near the original machinery. Modern bedrooms in a recent wing. Terrace next to the outdoor pool.

⊖⊜ **Hôtel Mail** – *8 r. des Ursules, Angers.* ⌕*02 41 25 05 25. www.hotel-du-mail.com. 26rms.* ⎚ *€9.* The thick walls of this former Ursuline convent in a peaceful street prevent the noise from the nearby town centre from penetrating. The fairly spacious rooms have a personal touch and are under the sloping roof on the top floor.

⊖⊜ **Le Progrès** – *26 r. Denis-Papin, Angers.* ⌕*02 41 88 10 14. www.hotelleprogres.com. Closed 7–15 Aug, 24 Dec–3 Jan. 41rms.* ⎚ *€7.50.* Conveniently located near the train station, this is a friendly place with modern, well-lit and practical rooms. Before setting out to tour the château, enjoy your coffee in the breakfast room, with its décor inspired by the bright colours of Provence.

⛴ EAT

⊖ **La Ferme** – *2 pl. Freppel, Angers.* ⌕*02 41 87 09 90. Closed Sun eve and Wed. Reservations required.* A well-known restaurant near the cathedral, where you can enjoy traditional local cooking in a simple setting. The terrace is one of the nicest in town.

⊖⊜ **Le Fontainebleau** – *12 pl. St-Pierre . Angers.* ⌕*02 43 14 25 74. Closed Tue.* A rustic atmosphere with walls dating from 1720, this restaurant in Old Mans offers modern cuisine according to the season. Faultless table settings and friendly welcome.

⊖⊜ **Le Grenier à sel** – *26 pl. de l'Eperon.* ⌕*02 43 23 26 30. Closed Sun-Mon.* Right in the town centre, this former salt store now houses a restaurant serving modern cuisine. Menu changes daily.

⊖⊜ **Mercure Batignolles** – *r. Pointe.* ⌕*02 43 72 27 20. Closed Mon lunch.* Establishment housing modern, practical and well-kept rooms; those to the rear are quieter. Garden with crazy golf. Dining room decorated with photographs recalling the legendary Le Mans 24-hr race. Traditional repertory.

⊖⊜ **Provence Caffé** – *9 pl. du Ralliement, Angers.* ⌕*02 41 87 44 15. Closed Sun and Mon. Reservations required.* This popular restaurant next to the Hôtel St-Julien is often full both at lunchtime and in the evenings. The patron is from the south of France and the menu reflects this, with its Mediterranean flavours. The dining room has a Provençal atmosphere too. Carefully prepared cuisine at moderate prices.

⊖⊜ **Le Relais** – *9 r. de la Gare, Angers.* ⌕*02 41 88 42 51. Closed Sun and Mon.* The woodwork and the murals in this charming tavern recall the vineyard and the harvest. The traditional cooking is satisfying and simple, at affordable prices.

🛒 SHOPPING

Maison du Vin de l'Anjou – *5 bis, pl. Kennedy, Angers.* ⌕*02 41 88 81 13. www.vinsdeloire.fr.* In the centre of town, near the château, this wine shop offers a good selection of Anjou and Saumur wines, which you can taste.

La Petite Marquise – *22 r. des Lices, Angers.* ⌕*02 41 87 43 01.* Does *Quernons d'Ardoise* mean anything to you? If you don't know about this delicious local speciality of nougatine and chocolate made to look like roof slates, then head to this little shop where they were first created.

🏃 OUTDOOR LEISURE ACTIVITIES

Les Croisières au Mans – *101 quai de l'Amiral-Lalande, Le Mans –* ⌕*02 43 80 56 62.* Make your reservation through the tourist office for a boat trip or cruise (with a meal) on the Sarthe. A different way of discovering Le Mans and its surroundings.

Maison de l'Environnement – *Parc de loisirs du Lac de Maine, ave du Lac de Maine, Angers –* ⌕*02 41 22 32 30.* This nature information centre organises various activities including environment-awareness courses.

Public Gardens and Parks – Anger's Jardin des Plantes, Jardin du Mail, Jardin Médiéval, French-style gardens in the moat and Parcs de l'étang St-Nicolas on the outskirts of town. *Open daily.*

Boat Trips – Possibilities include a combined tourist-train ride and mini boat trip on the River Maine and a candlelit dinner/cruise. *Batellerie promenade l'Union, cale de la Savatte. 49100 Angers.* ⌕*02 41 42 12 12.*

Saumur★★
Maine-et-Loire

Lying on the banks of the Loire, beneath its imposing fortress, Saumur is famous for its Cavalry School, its wines (especially sparkling wines), its medal makers and its mushrooms (production of which is 42 percent of the national figure).

A BIT OF HISTORY

Charles the Bald built a fortified monastery in the 9C to house the relics of St Florent, but it was not long before it was destroyed by the Vikings. In the 11C Saumur was the subject of numerous conflicts between the Count of Blois and the Count of Anjou. In 1203, the town was captured by Philippe Auguste.

In the late 16C and early 17C the town enjoyed its true heyday. It was one of the great centres of Protestantism. Henri III gave it as a stronghold to the king of Navarre, the future Henri IV, who appointed as governor **Duplessis-Mornay**, a great soldier, scholar and fervent Reformer, who was known by the Roman Catholics as the Huguenot Pope. In 1611 a general assembly of the Protestant churches was held there to consolidate their organisation following the death of Henri IV and the departure of Sully. Louis XIII grew alarmed at the Protestant danger and ordered the town walls to be demolished in 1623. The Revocation of the Edict of Nantes in 1685 dealt Saumur a fatal blow; many of the inhabitants emigrated and the Protestant church was demolished.

École d'application de l'arme blindée et de la cavalerie (EAABC) – It is interesting to note the mementoes of officers who served in the cavalry of the African Army between 1830 and 1962: Bugeaud, Gallifet, Charles de Foucault, who was an officer before he became a recluse, Lyautey, Henry de Bournazel and Leclerc de Hauteclocque.

▶ **Population:** 29 632

◉ **Michelin Map:** 317: I-5

▤ **Info:** pl. de la Bilange, BP 241, 49418 Saumur. ✆02 41 40 20 60. www.ot-saumur.fr.

◗ **Location:** Saumur lies 65km/40mi SE of Angers, 32km/20mi NE of Chinon.

◉ **Don't Miss:** Every year a tattoo using horses and motor transport is given by the **Cadre Noir** on the vast place du Chardonnet (◉*see Calendar of Events in PLANNING YOUR TRIP*). Repeat performances are given in the Riding School of the National Equitation Centre in Terrefort.

◔ **Timing:** You can easily fill a day in Saumur.

VISIT
Old Town★

The narrow twisting streets between the castle and the bridge still follow their original course; in some areas the old houses have been preserved whereas in others new constructions have been built in the medieval style or are resolutely modern but full of surprises (*south of St Peter's Church*).

Along the main shopping street, rue St-Jean, and in the square, **place St-Pierre**, half-timbered houses and 18C mansions with wrought-iron balconies stand side by side.

Église St-Pierre

The church is Plantagenet Gothic except for the west front which collapsed in the 17C and was rebuilt. The Romanesque door in the south transept leads into the interior which is hung with two series of 16C **tapestries**★.

Hôtel de Ville★

Only the left-hand section of the town hall is old (16C). Originally the Loire flowed past the foundations and the building was a bridgehead and part

of the town walls, hence its military appearance.
The façade facing the courtyard is in the Gothic Renaissance transitional style with some fine sculpture.

Église Notre-Dame-de-Nantilly★

This is a fine Romanesque church. Louis XI added the right aisle. A pillar on the left in the same aisle bears an epitaph composed by King René d'Anjou.
The 12C painted wooden statue of Our Lady of Nantilly was placed in the apse on the right of the chancel. The organ case dates from 1690. There are fine **tapestries**★★ dating from the 15C and 16C except for eight in the nave which were made at Aubusson in the 17C.

SIGHTS

Château★★

Interior closed for maintenance. Exterior: open Jul–Aug Tue–Sun 10am–6pm; Apr–Jun and Sept 10am–1pm, 2–5.30pm. €3. 02 41 40 24 40. www.saumur.fr.

The château is compact and solid, and despite being a fortress is decorated in the style of a country house with machicolations and balustrades at the windows overlooking the courtyard.
A succession of fortresses has been erected on the promontory. The present building, which succeeded Louis IX's castle, was rebuilt at the end of the 14C. The interior was altered in the 15C by René d'Anjou and external fortifications were added in the late 16C by Duplessis-Mornay.
Under Louis XIV and Louis XV it was the residence of the governor of Saumur; it subsequently became a prison and then barracks, and it now houses two museums.

Musée de la Cavalerie

Open Mon–Thu 9am–noon, 2–5pm, Sat, Sun 2–6pm. 02 41 83 69 23.

In 1763 the Carabiniers Regiment, a crack corps recruited from the best horsemen in the army, was sent to Saumur. The present central building was constructed between 1767 and 1770 as their barracks. This museum's rich display of souvenirs, created in 1936 from Barbet de Vaux collections, traces the heroic deeds of the French Cavalry and the Armoured Corps since the 18C.

Musée des Blindés

Via boulevard Louis-Renault; follow the signposts. Open daily: Jan–Apr, and Oct–Dec Mon–Fri 10am–5pm, Sat–Sun and public holidays 11am–6pm; May–Jun and Sept, 10am–6pm; Jul–Aug 9.30am–6.30pm. €7. Guided visits (no charge) in Apr–early May 10.30am, 2pm, 4pm; Jul–Aug Mon–Fri 10am, 3pm. Closed 1 Jan, 25 Dec. 02 41 83 69 95. www.museedesblindes.fr.

This museum and information centre on tanks houses over 100 vehicles (tanks,

Pont Cessart over the Loire, with Château de Saumur on the left

© Jean-Philippe Delisle/Fotolia.com

armoured vehicles, artillery equipment), many of which are still in working order, coming from a dozen or more countries. The most prestigious or rare exhibits are the **St-Chamond** and the **Schneider** (the first French tanks), the Renault FT 17 (French tank used in the very last stages of the WWI), the Somua S 35, the B1bis (issued to the 2nd Armoured Division under General de Gaulle in 1940) and German tanks dating from the French Campaign until the fall of Berlin (Panzers III and IV, Panther, Tiger), the Comet A 34 (the British tank used in the Normandy landing), the Churchill A 22, the Sherman M 4 and AMX 13 and 30.

EXCURSIONS
Fontevraud l'Abbaye★★
◗ *The abbey occupies the heart of the village of the same name, which is 15km/9.3mi SE of Saumur, close to the Loire and Vienne rivers.*

🏛 *Place Saint-Michel.* 📞*02 41 51 79 45. www.abbayedefontevraud.com.*

Fontevraud Abbey, close to the hearts of the Plantagenets, stands on the borders of Anjou, Tourraine and Poitou. Despite the ravages of history, it remains the largest group of monastic buildings in France, having retained some interesting features typical of Anjou architecture, in particular the lofty vaulting of the abbey church and the impressive

Abbey church of Fontevraud

A. Cassaigne/MICHELIN

kitchen. There is a good view of the Abbey from the Loudun road on the south side of the village.

The Order of Fontevraud was founded in 1099 following the failure in France of Pope Gregory's reform, which had been designed to enhance both the competence and the respectability of the clergy. The success of the new Order was immediate and it quickly took on an aristocratic character accommodating both sexes. It was presided over by an abbess at a time when the growing cult of the Virgin Mary was influencing the status of womanhood, and the abbesses, who were members of noble families, procured rich gifts and powerful protection for the abbey. The Plantagenets chose the abbey as their last resting place and Eleanor of Aquitaine, her husba,nd Henry II and her son Richard the Lionheart were buried here. Later, the hearts of John Lackland (King John) and his son Henry III, who built Westminster Abbey, were transferred to the crypt.

Église Abbatiale★★
The Abbey Church has a vast nave with delicately carved capitals and is roofed by a series of domes, characteristic of churches found in the southwest of France. Built several decades earlier than the nave, the transept and chancel are reminiscent of the Benedictine plan: an ambulatory and radiating chapels where the luminosity and repetition of vertical lines signify the aspiration to reach up to heaven.

In the transept crossing are a number of **Plantagenet tombs**★, good examples of Gothic funerary sculpture. The figures of Henry Plantagenet, Richard the Lionheart and Eleanor of Aquitaine are in painted tufa, while the figure of Isabel of Angoulême, John Lackland's wife, is of polychrome wood.

The **kitchen**★★ is a highly individual structure (27m/89ft high), dating from around 1160 and restored in 1902. It is a rare example of a Romanesque kitchen, with a tiled roof characteristic of the Poitiers area.

Chinon★★

▶ *Chinon is 32km/20mi SE of Saumur.*
🏠 *Place d'Hofheim.* ℘*02 47 93 17 85.*
www.chinon-valdeloire.com.
Chinon occupies a sunny site on the
Vienne, surrounded by the fertile Veron
countryside, and known for the mildness
of its climate.

Le Vieux Chinon★★

The old town has kept its medieval
and Renaissance appearance. The old
gabled houses with corner turrets and
the 16C and 17C mansions, most of them
in white tufa, make up a most evocative
townscape. Many fine old buildings
stand in its main street Rue Voltaire,
including the Gothic dwelling where
Richard the Lionheart is supposed to
have died in 1199.

At the crossroads (**Grand Carroi**★★)
the oldest houses of all press closely
together. On her arrival from Vaucouleurs
on Sunday 6 March 1429, **Joan of Arc** is
thought to have used the coping of the
well-head here to dismount from her
horse. The following day she picked out
the Dauphin (the heir apparent) hiding
among his courtiers, and declared, "You
are the heir of France and true son of the
king, Lieutenant of the King of Heaven
who is King of France".

Château★★

🕐*Open daily: Jan–Mar 9.30am–5pm;*
Apr–Sept 9am–7pm; Oct–Dec 9.30am–
5pm. ✆€*7.* ℘*02 47 93 13 45.*
www.forteressechinon.fr.
The spur overlooking the town was
the site of a Gallic oppidum, then of a
fortress, long before Henry II of England
(born at Le Mans in 1133) built the present
castle to protect Anjou from Capetian
designs. The castle was taken by Philippe
Auguste in 1205 from John Lackland; it
subsequently became a royal residence,
was strengthened by Charles VII, but then
abandoned by the court at the end of the
15C and gradually dismantled.

The remains of the castle include, to the
east, St George's Fort (Fort St-Georges),
watching over the most vulnerable

approach, the Middle Castle (Château
du Milieu) which has a 14C clock tower,
the royal apartments and gardens, and
finally the Coudray Fort (Fort de Coudray)
at the far end of the spur.

Château de Langeais★★

▶ *The town and château are on the*
right bank of the Loire between Tours
and Saumur, approached by taking the
left bank road and crossing the river
into the town.
🕐*Open daily: Feb–Mar 9.30am–*
5.30pm; Apr–Jun, and Sept–mid-Nov
9.30am–6.30pm; Jul–Aug 9am–7pm;
mid Nov–Jan 10am–5pm (25 Dec
2–5pm). ✆€*8.50.* ℘*02 47 96 72 60.*
℘*02 47 96 58 22. www.chateau-de-*
langeais.com.
The castle is built on a promontory,
beneath the high walls of which are
nestled the town's white houses.

The great Angevin ruler Foulques Nerra
built a sturdy keep to command the
Loire Valley. Completed in 994, now in
ruins in the park of the château, it is considered to be the oldest such building in
the whole of France.

The château itself was built to protect
France from Brittany. In 1491, the marriage of Charles VIII of France and Anne
of Brittany ended the threat. Seen from
outside, the château still looks like a
medieval fortress, with drawbridge,
towers, battlemented sentry-walk and
almost windowless walls. But the façade
facing the courtyard has the features of
a Renaissance country house, including
pointed dormers, turrets, sculptures and
mullioned windows.

Inside, the **apartments**★★★ have kept
their medieval layout, one room commanding the next through narrow doors
and laid out along diagonal lines. The
last owner, Jacques Siegfried (a mill- and
ship-owner and banker from Le Havre),
refurnished the interior very expertly,
and Langeais gives a good impression
of aristocratic life in the early Renaissance period. The rooms contain fine
tapestries. In the Charles VIII Room is a
17C clock with a single hand.

Tours★★

Indre-et-Loire

With a civilised air, under dazzling Loire Valley skies, built in bright white tufa and roofed in black slate, the ancient city of Tours makes a perfect base for excursions into the château country.

A BIT OF HISTORY

The place originated in Gallic times, becoming an important centre of trade and administration under the Romans in the 1C AD.

Throughout the Middle Ages it was an important religious centre and was the capital of Tours (Touraine) county; indeed, Tours became the capital of France during the reign of Louis XI.

SIGHTS

Château★

25 ave André Malraux.

Not comparable in grandeur to the more typical Loire châteaux, this is a heterogeneous collection of buildings from the 4–19C.

The lower parts of the wall on the west side go back to Roman times and here too is the 11C residence of the Counts of Anjou; the Guise Tower (Tour de Guise) with its machicolations and pepper-pot roof is of the 13–15C, while the dormer-windowed Governor's Lodging (Logis du Gouverneur) is 15C and other additions were made as recently as the 17–19C.

Cathédrale St-Gatien★★

Following a fire, the cathedral was rebuilt from 1235 onwards. The work lasted all of 250 years.

As a result it demonstrates the complete evolution of the Gothic style, from a chevet in the early phase, to a Flamboyant west front, and even a lantern crowning the twin towers that is characteristic of the Early Renaissance.

The stained glass ranges in date from the 13C (high windows in the chancel) via the 14C (transept rose windows) to the 15C (rose window of the west front).

▶ **Population:** 138 783
🚲 **Michelin Map:** 317 N 4
ℹ️ **Info:** 78 r. Bernard-Palissy. ℘02 47 70 37 37. www.ligeris.com.
▶ **Location:** 80km/50mi NE of Saumur, Tours spans the Loire and fills the isthmus between the Loire and its tributary the Cher.
🕐 **Timing:** Allow half a day to visit the Old Town along the left bank of the Loire.

La Psalette★

🕐*Open Apr daily 10am–12.30pm, 2–5.30pm (Sun am by appointment); May–Aug daily 9.30am–12.30pm, 2–6pm (Sun am by appointment); Sept–Mar daily except Mon, Tue and Sun am, 10am–12.30pm, 2–5.30pm.* 🕐*Closed 1 Jan, 1 May and 25 Dec.* ☞€3. ℘02 47 47 05 19.http://la-psalette. monuments-nationaux.fr.*

This is the name given to the cathedral cloisters where canons and choir-master used to meet. The tiny Archive Room (Salle des Archives) of 1520 and the vaulted Library (Librairie) are reached by means of a spiral staircase, Gothic in structure but Renaissance in the way in which it is detailed.

Place Plumereau★

This busy and picturesque square is located at the old "meeting of the ways" (carroi); it is bordered by fine 15C residences built of stone and timber. On the corner with the Rue du Change and the Rue de la Monnaie is a carved corner post with a somewhat mutilated depiction of the Circumcision.

Musée des Beaux-Arts★★

18 pl. François Sicard. 🕐*Open daily except Tue 9am–6pm.* 🕐*Closed 1 Jan, 1 May, 14 Jul, 1 and 11 Nov, 25 Dec.* ☞€4. ℘02 47 05 68 73.

In the former Bishops' Palace (17–18C), its rooms are beautifully decorated with Louis XVI panelling and silk hangings made locally. It houses works of art from the châteaux at Richelieu and Chanteloup (now the site of the Parc de la Pagode, *see AMBOISE*) as well as from the great abbeys of Touraine. The collection of paintings consists mostly of French works of the 19–20C, but there are also two outstanding Mantegnas, a Resurrection and Christ in the Garden of Olives (late 15C).

Musée du Compagnonnage★★

8 r. Nationale and a walkway. ⏱*Open daily 9am–12.30pm, 2–6pm (Jan–Jun and mid Sept–Dec daily except Tue).* ⏱*Closed public holidays.* €5. 📞02 47 21 62 20.

The city long prided itself on its craftsmen, and even at the end of the 19C there were still three guilds jealously guarding their traditions. The museum contains many fine examples of the work of master craftsmen, such as roofers and slaters, blacksmiths and locksmiths, saddlers and carpenters.

ADDITIONAL SIGHTS

Rue Briçonnet★

This charming street is bordered by houses showing a rich variety of local styles, from the Romanesque façade to the 18C mansion.

Place Grégoire-de-Tours★

This square gives a fine view of the east end of the cathedral and the Gothic flying buttresses; to the left is the medieval gable of the **Archbishop's Palace** *(now the Musée des Beaux-Arts).*

Hôtel Gouin★ *(26 r. du Commerce)*

This mansion, a fine example of living accommodation during the Renaissance, is one of the most interesting of its kind in Tours.

Musée de la Société archéologique de Touraine★ *(26 r. du Commerce)*

L'Historial de Touraine★

(in the castle) *(25 quai d'Orléans)*

Jardin de Beaune-Semblançay★

The **Hôtel de Beaune-Semblançay** belonged to the unfortunate Minister of Finance who was hanged during the reign of François I.

Musée des Équipages militaires et du Train★ *(r. du Plat d'Etain, Quartier Beaumont)* ⏱*Open Mon–Fri*

Sept–Jul 2–5.30pm. No charge. 📞02 47 77 33 07.

In 1807 Napoleon created the service corps to remedy the problem of insufficient transport means: up to then, the army administration had resorted to using the services of civilian companies, whose efficiency left something to be desired. The museum has been set up in the **Pavillon de Condé** (the only vestiges of the abbey of Ste-Marie in Beaumont). Ten carefully laid out rooms retrace the history of the service corps.

EXCURSIONS

Amboise★★

▶ *The busy town centre rises from the S bank of the Loire.*

🛈 *quai du Gén.-de-Gaulle.* 📞02 47 57 09 28. www.amboise-valdeloire.com. 🚹 *On the edge of town kids will love the Parc des Mini-Châteaux (La Menaudière;* 📞0 2 47 23 44 57; *www.mini-chateaux.com) and the Parc de la Pagode de Chanteloup (Route de Blere.* 📞02 47 57 20 97. www.pagode-chanteloup.com).

Amboise is a bridge-town, built at the foot of an escarpment already fortified in Gallo-Roman times, on which stand the proud remains of its great château which appears at its most picturesque when viewed from the north side of the river.

Château★★

⏱*Open daily Jan and mid-Nov–Dec 9am–12.30pm, 2–4.45pm; Feb 9am–12.30pm, 1.30–5pm; Mar and Nov–mid-Nov 9am–5.30pm, Apr–Jun 9am–6.30pm; Jul–Aug 9am–7pm; Sept–Oct 9am–6pm.* ⏱*Closed 1 Jan, 25 Dec.* €10. 📞08 20 20 50 50. www.chateau-amboise.com.

The 15C saw the Golden Age of Amboise. Charles VIII was born here in 1470; from his 22nd year onwards he carried on the work begun by his father, Louis XI. By the time he left on his Italian campaign, work was well in hand on a number of projects: the round towers, the great Gothic roof of the wing overlooking the Loire, and the Flamboyant St-Hubert Chapel, which served as an oratory for

Anne of Brittany and has particularly fine Flemish door panels. In 1496 Charles returned from Italy, bringing with him not only works of art but a whole retinue of artists, architects, sculptors, cabinet-makers and gardeners.

With these Italians came a taste for anti-quity and a decorative sense unknown at the time in France (doorways resem-bling triumphal arches, inlaid ceilings, superimposed arches, etc.). Charles' liking for luxury enhanced the prestige of the monarchy; his promotion of the artistic ideas of the Renaissance was continued by Louis XII and even more by François I, under whom château life became a whirl of princely gaiety with festivals, entertainments and hunting parties. However, this first French châ-teau of the Renaissance was destined to disappear; partly demolished by the troops of Louis XIII, it was further dis-mantled on the orders of Napoleon's Senate. Now it is known only from an engraving by Du Cerceau.

Tour – From the **terrace**, there is a fine view of the Loire Valley and the slate-blue roofs of the town. Inside, the **Royal Apartments** are the only part of the château that escaped demolition from 1806–10.

Laid out in informal English style, the pleasant **gardens** are worth seeing.

Clos-Lucé★

▶ *Very near the château.* ◷*Open daily: Jan 10am–6pm; Feb–Jun 9am–7pm; Jul–Aug 9am–8pm; Set–Oct 9am–7pm; Nov–Dec 9am–6pm.* ◷*Closed 1 Jan, 25 Dec.* ◉€13 (winter €9). ✆02 47 57 00 73. www.vinci-closluce.com.

To this manor house of red brick with stone dressings François I invited **Leon-ardo da Vinci** in 1516. The great Floren-tine was then aged 64. At Amboise he neither painted nor taught, devoting himself instead to organising royal fes-tivities, designing a château at Romo-rantin, planning the drainage of the Sologne and amusing himself designing mechanical inventions, some of which have now been constructed and are in a display of "fabuleuses machines".

Château de Chenonceau★★★

▶ *14km/8.7mi S of Amboise, the château straddles the River Cher.* ◷*Open daily: Jan–mid-Feb and Nov–Dec 9.30am–5pm; mid-Feb–Mar 9.30am–6pm (7pm from mid-Mar); Apr–May 9am–7pm; Jun and Sept 9am–7.30pm; Jul–Aug 9am–8pm; Oct 9am–6.30pm (6pm from 23rd).* ◉€10.50. ✆02 47 23 90 07. www.chenonceau.com.

Chenonceau is a jewel of Renaissance architecture, built 1513–21 on the site of a fortified mill on the River Cher by Thomas Bohier, François I's treasurer. It is a rectangular building with corner-towers; it stands on two piers of the former mill resting on the bed of the Cher. The library and the chapel are pro-jecting structures to the left. Catherine de Medici's two-storey gallery is built on the elegant 60m/197ft multi-arched bridge spanning the river and provides one of the region's iconic views.

Over the years the place has been in the charge of six women, of whom three marked it strongly with their per-sonality. Catherine Briçonnet was the wife of Thomas Bohier. In his absence she supervised much of the building work. It is to her that we owe the cen-tral hall giving onto all the other rooms; its axial vault, broken by keystones, is a masterpiece. Another innovation is the introduction into the Loire Valley of an Italian staircase, that is, one that sub-stitutes ramps for Gothic spirals, and is consequently much better adapted for receptions. However, here the returns are still curved and provided with steps. In 1556 Diane de Poitiers commissioned Philibert Delorme, who had previously worked for her at Anet, to design the flower garden (to the east) as well as the bridge across the Cher.

Three years later, on the death of Henri II, Catherine de' Medici humiliated the former favourite by forcing her to exchange Chenonceau for Chaumont. Later, she added the two extra storeys to the bridge, laid out the gardens to the west and gave the windows their elaborate pediments.

Aerial view of Château de Chenonceau

F. Soreau/MICHELIN

There is much to see within the château: a fine fireplace by **Jean Goujon** (in the Salle Diane de Poitiers), the Library of 1521, the ceiling of the Green Cabinet (Cabinet Vert), the portrait of Diane by Primaticcio, the tapestries and mantelpiece of the Salon Louis XIV, a fine Renaissance creation with its wealth of scrolls, baskets of fruit, cornucopias and fantastic beasts.

Loches★★

Loches lies on the River Indre, 49km/30.4mi SE of Tours.

pl. de la Marne. 02 47 91 82 82. www.loches-tourainecotesud.com

Modern Loches lies mostly on the left bank of the Indre, at the foot of the fortified bluff that dominates the valley and that set natural limits to the growth of the medieval town.

Cité médiévale★★

The medieval town is contained within a continuous wall some 1 000m/1 100 yd long in which there are only two gates. To the south, the great square **keep**★★ (open 22 Mar–Sept daily 9am–7pm; Oct–21 Mar daily 9.30am–5pm; closed 1 Jan and 25 Dec. €7. 02 47 59 07 86) was built by the Counts of Anjou in the 11C on even earlier foundations.

In the 13C, it was strengthened by wide ditches hewn into the solid rock, by buttress towers and the Martelet Tower with its impressive dungeons,

then given additional accommodation including service buildings.

In the centre of the old town is a church, **Église St-Ours**★, with its Angevin porch built around a Romanesque portal, and pyramid vaults in its nave.

To the north is the **Château**★★ (same as for the **keep**★★. €7. 02 47 59 01 32), begun at the end of the 14C as an extension of the 13C watchtower known as **Tour Agnès Sorel**. Part of the royal apartments are medieval (Vieux logis), part Renaissance (Nouveau logis). It was in the great hall of the Vieux Logis on 3 and 5 June 1429 that Joan of Arc persuaded the Dauphin to undertake his coronation journey to Reims.

There is a tiny Flamboyant oratory, dedicated to Anne of Brittany and decorated with the ermine of Brittany and the girdle of St Francis, and, in the Charles VIII Room, a recumbent figure (**gisant d'Agnès Sorel**★) of Charles VII's "Lady of Beauty".

Château d'Azay-le-Rideau★★★

Azay lies about 25km/15.5mi from Tours in the direction of Chinon.

Open daily: Oct–Mar 10am–12.30pm, 2–5.30pm; Apr–Jun and Sep 9.30am–6pm; Jul–Aug 9.30am–7pm. Closed 1 Jan, 1 May, 25 Dec. €8. 02 47 45 42 04. http://azay-le-rideau.monuments-nationaux.fr.

Sitting in a verdant setting where the waters of the Indre act as reflecting

Château d'Azay-le-Rideau

©Jose I. Soto/Dreamstime.com

pools, this castle was built for financier Gilles Berthelot from 1518–29.

The château d'Azay-le-Rideau was built in French Gothic style. Its defences (machicolated cornice, pepperpot towers and turrets) are purely decorative. By contrast, the interior shows Italianate influences.

The decoration includes Florentine shells in the gable of the great dormer window, pilasters, moulded entablatures, and, above all, the grand staircase with straight flights and rectangular landings. The interior is also notable for the French-style ceiling in the dining room and the chimney piece in the François I Room.

Jardins et Château de Villandry★★★

⊙ Coming from Langeais, take D 16, which has scenic views. Coming from Tours, take D 288, which crosses the Loire at Savonnières.

⊙ Open: the gardens are open every day, all year, from 9am, closing hours vary; the chateau is open at 9am from mid Feb–mid-Nov, and 9.30am from mid–end Dec, closing times vary.

⊙ Closed early Jan–mid-Feb and mid-Nov–mid-Dec. ⌕ Self-guided tour with a leaflet. ⊛€9.50 (château and gardens). ℘02 47 50 02 09.

www.chateauvillandry.com.
ℹ Le Potager, Villandry. ℘02 47 50 12 66.

In 1536, Jean Le Breton, who had been France's ambassador in Italy, rebuilt the château here on the foundations of an earlier one. The new building had a number of features which made it unusual in Touraine: ditches and canals, an esplanade and a terrace, rectangular pavilions in place of round towers, and, above all, its gardens.

Château★★

The interior is distinguished by Louis XV panelling in the Great Salon and Dining Room, by the fine ramped staircase in wrought iron, and by a surprising 13C Mudejar ceiling from Spain, brought here by Joachim de Carvallo (1869–1936).

Jardins★★★

In 1906, Dr Carvallo, founder of the French Historic Houses Association (Demeure Historique), bought the Villandry estate and began to restore the gardens.

The plan of the gardens shows both the influence of the agricultural writer **Olivier de Serres** and the synthesis of the monastery garden with the Italian garden proposed by Jacques II Androuet du Cerceau.

Covering a total area of 7ha/17.3 acres, the gardens have many fascinating features. There are three terraces, one above the other, separated by shady avenues of limes and vines; the highest is the water garden with its mirror-like stretch of water, then comes an ornamental garden with box clipped into patterns symbolising the varieties of love: tragic (sword and dagger blades), fickle (butterflies and fans), tender (masks and hearts) and passionate (broken hearts). Finally there is a kitchen garden with 85 000 plants contained in clipped-box beds. The use of the humblest of vegetables (cabbage, celery), chosen for their culinary value, symbolism, therapeutic value or colour, is here raised to an art form of great delicacy and seasonal interest.

ADDRESSES

🛏 STAY

⊜⊜ **Chambre d'hôte Le Moulin Hodoux** – *37230 Luynes, 14km/8.7mi W of Tours on N 152 and minor road.* ✆*02 47 55 76 27. 5rms.* In a peaceful country setting not far from Tours, near the castle at Luynes, this 18–19C watermill provides comfortable, well-equipped rooms. In the lovely garden there are tables, chairs and a barbecue, as well as a swimming pool.

⊜⊜ **Hôtel Le Cygne** – *6 r. du Cygne.* ✆*02 47 66 66 41. Closed Christmas. 16rms.* ⊑ *€8.* One of Tours' oldest hotels (18C). Rooms have been renovated, but their character has been preserved. In winter, a fine 16C fireplace warms the little lounge. There is a pleasant family atmosphere.

⊜⊜ **Hôtel du Relais St-Éloi** – *8 r. Giraudeau.* ✆*02 47 38 18 19. 56rms.* ⊑ *€9.* Recent building with small, practical rooms. Some, with a mezzanine, are particularly suitable for families. No-frills décor and regular maintenance. Modern dining room, but traditional culinary repertoire.

⊜⊜⊜⊜ **Central Hôtel** – *21 r. Berthelot.* ✆*02 47 05 46 44. 37 rooms.* ⊑ *€13.* A quiet, comfortable hotel in the old part of Tours, near the busy pedestrian-only districts. The staff are reserved but pleasant. There is a small, peaceful garden behind the hotel and you can eat breakfast on the terrace.

🍴 EAT

⊜ **Bistrot de la Tranchée** – *103 ave Tranchée.* ✆*02 47 41 09 08. Closed Sun and Mon.* Dark wood panelling, bottles of wine, comfortable wall sofas and old-fashioned pizza ovens make up the décor of this pleasant bistro. Enjoy a good selection of small dishes typical to this type of restaurant. Definitely worth a visit.

⊜⊜ **Cap Sud** – *88 r. Colbert.* ✆*02 47 05 24 81. Closed weekends and Mon.* This little restaurant has a Mediterranean atmosphere, both in its warm décor and up-to-date cuisine. Short, well-selected wine list.

⊜⊜ **Léonard de Vinci** – *19 r. de la Monnaie.* ✆*02 47 61 07 88. Closed Sun eve and Mon. Reservations required in eve.* A taste of Tuscany in the heart of the Touraine. This Italian restaurant's claim to fame is that it doesn't serve pizzas! A chance to discover different Italian dishes, with a décor that highlights models of Leonardo da Vinci's inventions.

⊜⊜⊜⊜ **La Roche Le Roy** – *55 rte de St-Avertin.* ✆*02 47 27 22 00. www.rocheleroy.com. Closed Sun and Mon.* The restaurant in this Touraine manor house will be much appreciated by gourmets. Sample the cooking, which varies with the seasons, in the intimate dining room or the pretty enclosed courtyard in summer.

🍴 CAFÉS

Le Vieux Mûrier – *11 pl. Plumereau –* ✆*02 47 61 04 77.* This is one of the oldest cafés in place Plumereau and it has that extra hint of character that is so often missing from modern establishments.

🛒 SHOPPING

Markets – **Second-hand goods:** 1st and 3rd Fri of the month, *r. de Bordeaux;* 4th Sun in the month, *bd Bérange;* Wed and Sat mornings, *pl. de la Victoire.*

Flowers – Wed and Sat, all day, *bd Béranger.*

Au Vieux Four – *7 pl. des Petites-Boucheries.* ✆*02 47 66 62 33. www.auvieuxfour-mahou.com. Closed Sun and Mon.* This boulangerie and museum reveals the secrets of traditional bread-making.

La Chocolatière – *6 r. de la Scellerie.* ✆*02 47 05 66 75. www.la-chocolatiere.com. Closed Mon.* "Le pavé de Tours" is one of the great specialities of this exceptional maker of pâtisseries, confectionery and top-of-the-range chocolates.

Blois★★

Loir-et-Cher

Blois looks northwards to the Beauce and south to the Sologne, and is situated at that point on the Loire at which the limestone landscapes around Orléans give way almost imperceptibly to the chalk country of Touraine downstream.

Originally defended by a medieval castle, the town was transformed from 1503 onwards when the kings moved there from Amboise, bringing in their train all the trades devoted to satisfying the royal taste for luxury.

SIGHTS

Château★★★

⊙*Open daily: Jan–Mar and Nov–Dec 9am–12.30pm, 1.30–5.30pm; Apr–Jun, and Sept 9am–6.30pm; Jul–Aug 9am–7pm; Oct 9am–6pm.* ⊙*Closed 1 Jan and 25 Dec.* ⊛*8€–9.50.* ℘*02 54 90 33 32. www.chateaudeblois.fr.*
⊙*For Illustration, see p79.*

The whole development of secular French architecture from feudalism to the Classicism of Louis XIII's reign can be traced at Blois.

The medieval remains include the round towers, spiral stairways and steep-pitched roofs of the Foix Tower and the Chamber of the States-General of 1205; with its panelled ceiling, this is where the States-General held its Assemblies in 1576 and 1588.

The transition from the Gothic to the Renaissance is evident in the Charles of Orléans Gallery and particularly in the Louis XII Wing of 1498–1501. Louis had been born at Blois in 1462 and, together with Anne of Brittany, carried out a number of improvements including the construction of a new wing.

This was right up to date with its triumphal arch doorways, Italianate arabesque decoration applied to the three Gothic pillars on the courtyard side, and the use of galleries to link rooms rather than having them run directly into one another.

▶ **Population:** 49 032
⊙ **Michelin Map:**
318 C-D-E-F 5-6-7
▤ **Info:** 23 pl. du Château.
℘02 54 90 41 41.
www. bloispaysde
chambord.com.
◑ **Location:** Blois is roughly mid-way between Tours (66km/41mi SW) and Orléans (61km/38mi NE).
⊛ **Don't Miss:** Be sure to stroll in the old quarter, which rises behind the town centre.
▲▲ **Kids:** The Maison de la Mogie will entertain young ones. Or ask at the tourist office about taking a boat trip on the Loire.

Built only 15 years later, possibly by Claude de France, the François I wing exemplifies the preoccupation with ornamentation that swept in with the first phase of the French Renaissance. The work remained incomplete but the new taste for sumptuous decoration is very apparent, not only in the Façade des Loges (built in front of the old rampart) with its still-irregular fenestration, but also in Pierre Trinquart's François I staircase; though somewhat over-restored in the view of some archaeologists, this is a richly decorated masterpiece with openings between its buttresses forming a series of balconies.

The much-modified interior includes, on the first floor, Catherine de Medici's study with its secret cupboards, and on the second floor, Henri III's apartments, scene of the murder of Henri de Guise. The King's brother employed François Mansart, who, however, failed to deploy the full range of his talents, his work here being stiff rather than dignified. Building stopped when the birth of Louis XIV put paid to his uncle's hopes of succeeding to the throne.

♁♁ Maison de la Magie Robert-Houdin★

1 pl. du Chateau. ♿🕐*Open daily Apr–mid-Sept 10am–12.30pm, 2–6.30pm (Sept Mon–Fri 2–6.30pm, Sat–Sun 10am–2.30pm, 2–6.30pm).* ☞€8 *(children 6-17 years:* €6.50*).* ✆02 54 55 26 26. www. maisondelamagie.fr.

Set up in a 19C *hôtel particulier* facing the château, the Maison de la Magie enlightens visitors on the history of magic and serves as a national centre for the art of illusionism *(open to professional conjurers and researchers only)*. The museum is dedicated to the great Robert-Houdin. A six-headed dragon, operated by a highly sophisticated computer system, welcomes visitors to this attractive mansion made with tufa and painted bricks. The tour starts with a guided visit through the history of conjuring, illustrating the chronological developments in this fascinating world.

Visitors then become part of the exhibition, walking through a giant kaleidoscope and stepping into a picture gallery before they reach the foyer devoted to magicians of international renown such as Georges Méliès, who was to pave the way for special effects in the film industry. On the first floor, set against an elegant and theatrical backdrop, the **Cabinet fantastique Robert-Houdin** displays exhibits relating to the world of magic. Posters, engravings, manuscripts and miscellaneous accessories evoke Houdin's performances, which would attract large crowds of Parisian socialites to the Palais-Royal Theatre.

The **Théâtre des Magiciens**★ (400 seats set up under the château esplanade) has been especially designed for high-class conjuring acts and offers a 20min show of dazzling expertise, performed by some of the world's leading illusionists.

EXCURSIONS
Boat trips
Sailing along the Loire in a traditional boat will offer you the opportunity of observing at leisure the local fauna and flora. For information, apply to the tourist office.

Orchaise
▶ *9km/5.6mi W on D 766.*
Situated near the church, the **Priory Botanical Gardens** (🕐*open Apr–Oct Sat–Thu 3–7pm.* ☞6€. ✆*02 54 70 03 92; http://prieure.orchaise.free.fr*) boast a superb collection of rhododendrons, azaleas, camellias and peonies, as well as numerous evergreen plants.

Mulsans
▶ *14km/8.7mi NE along D 50.*
Mulsans is a small farming village on the edge of the Beauce, heralded by the village's traditional walled-in farmyards which are characteristic of this region.

The **church** has Flamboyant windows and a fine Romanesque bell-tower decorated with blind arcades and twin round-arched window openings.

There is a Renaissance gallery supported by carved wooden columns extending the full width of the nave and incorporating the porch; this is a regional feature known as a *caquetoire* where people would pause to talk after Mass.

Suèvres★
▶ *11km/7mi NE along N 152.*
The ancient Gallo-Roman city of Sodobrium hides its picturesque façades below the noisy main road on the north bank of the Loire. The **church of St-Christophe** beside the road is entered through a huge porch *(caquetoire)* where the parishioners could pause to engage in conversation. The stonework is decorated with various fishbone and chevron patterns characteristic of the Merovingian period.

The houses at No 9 and No 14 bis in rue Pierre-Pouteau date from the 15C. Turn right into a picturesque cul-de-sac, rue des Moulins, running beside the stream which is spanned by several footbridges. The washing place is at the corner of rue St-Simon; on either side of the street are traces of an old fortified gate.

Further on through the trees *(left)* emerges the two-storey Romanesque tower of the **Église St-Lubin** with its attractive south door (15C).

Château de Chambord

© Frédéric Chapron/Fotolia.com

Château de Chambord★★★

▶*The château is S of the Loire, between Beaugency and Blois, at the end of a long avenue through woodland.*

🕑*Open daily: Jan–Mar and Oct–Dec 10am–5pm; Apr–Sept 9am–6pm.*

🕑*Closed 1 Jan, 1 May, 25 Dec.* ⊗€9.50.
☎*02 54 50 40 00. www.chambord.org.*
🅘*pl. Saint Louis, Chambord.*
☎*02 54 33 39 16.*

The first of France's great Classical palaces, Chambord stands in a vast park enclosed by a wall. Beyond stretches the forest of Sologne, teeming with the game that the rulers of France have long loved to hunt.

At the age of 21, François I had just returned in triumph from his victory over the Swiss at Marignano which had given him possession of the Duchy of Milan. Dissatisfied with the old royal residence at Blois in spite of the improvements he had made, he had a vision of a dream castle to be built four leagues away on the forest edge. Leonardo da Vinci may have helped with the plans for this fabulous edifice; its feudal keep and corner towers belied its purpose as a palace of pleasure and status symbol for a Renaissance prince. The château was begun in 1519; later Philibert Delorme, Jean Bullant and the great Mansart all worked on it.

Hardly had Chambord started to rise from its foundations when the king suffered defeat and captivity at Pavia in 1525. On his return to France he judged it more suitable for a monarch to live close to his capital, at either Fontainebleau or St-Germain-en-Laye.

From the entrance there is a fine view of the keep linked to the corner towers by two arcades surmounted by galleries.

A gallery was added to the façade towards the end of the reign of François I at the same time as the two spiral staircases in the north corners of the courtyard.

The château's famous double staircase, undoubtedly conceived by Leonardo da Vinci, is justly famous for its interlocking spirals opening onto internal loggias and for its vaults adorned with salamanders, François' crest. The extraordinary roof terrace was where the king and his entourage spent much of their time watching tournaments and festivals or the start and return of the hunt; its nooks and crannies lent themselves to the confidences, intrigues and assignations of courtly life, played out against this fantastic background of pepperpot turrets, chimney stacks, dormers peeping from the roofs, false windows embellished with shells, all decorated with inset slatework and dominated by the splendid lantern.

The state rooms contain rich furnishings: wood panelling, tapestries, furniture, portraits and hunting collections.

Château de Cheverny★★★

▶ *17km/10.5mi S of Blois, the château can be seen from afar.*

⏱ *Open daily: Jan–Mar and Nov–Dec 9.45am–5pm; Apr–Jun and Sept 9.15am –6.15pm; Jul–Aug 9.15am–6.45pm; Oct 9.45am–5.30pm.* 🎫 *(château and park) €8 (children, €5)* ☎ *02 54 79 96 29. www.chateau-cheverny.com.*

🏨 *2 r. des Chenes des Dames, Cour-Cheverny.* ☎ *02 54 79 95 63.*

👪*There's a permanent exhibition on the cartoon character Tintin.*

Cheverny was built between 1604 and 1634 with that simplicity and distinction characteristic of the Classical architecture of the reigns of Henri IV and Louis XIII.

The elevation is strictly symmetrical, extending to either side of the well containing the staircase, and terminated by massive corner pavilions with square domes. The prominent slate roofs are in Louis XIII style, pierced with mansards and bull's-eye windows.

The first-floor windows are crowned with scrolls; between them are medallions of Roman emperors (Julius Caesar in the central pediment).

The elegant doorway is adorned with two concentric collars. The state rooms, served by a majestic Louis XIII ramped staircase with massive balustrades and rich sculptural decoration, contain a fine collection of furniture from the 17–19C.

Vendôme★★

▶ *The River Loir flows parallel to the Loire, to its N.*

The town's setting is complicated and unusual, the islands fitting together like a jigsaw puzzle. Rue Poterie runs north–south across the town centre. 🏨 *Hotel du Saillant, Parc Ronsard.* ☎ *02 54 77 05 07. www.chateaux-valdeloire.com/ Vendome.html.*

At the foot of a steep bluff, which is crowned by a castle, the Loir divides into several channels. Vendôme stands on a group of islands crowded with bell towers, gables and steep slate roofs.

Ancienne Abbaye de la Trinité★

Founded in 1040 by Geoffroy Martel, Count of Anjou, the Benedictine abbey expanded considerably and became one of the most powerful in France. Pilgrims flocked here to venerate the supposed Holy Tear Christ shed at Lazarus' tomb and which Martel brought back from a Crusade. The Flamboyant Gothic **abbey church**★★ has a remarkable west front, which contrasts with the plain Romanesque tower. The transept, all that is left of the 11C building, leads to the chancel and ambulatory with its five radiating chapels. In the 14C chancel are fine late 15C **stalls**★ decorated with naïve scenes. The axial chapel contains a window dating from 1140 depicting the Virgin and Child (Majesté Notre-Dame).

Château de Cheverny

© Marius Godoi/Dreamstime.com

Château de Valençay★★

▶ *The château is on D 956, between Tours and Vierzon.*

🕐 *Open daily: mid Mar–Apr 10.30am–6pm; May and Sept 10am–6pm; Jun 9.30am–6.30pm; Jul–Aug 9.30am–7pm; Oct–mid-Nov 10.30am–5.30pm.*

🕐 *Closed rest of year.* ⬤⬤ €11. ℘02 54 00 15 69. www.chateau-valencay.fr.

⌂ *Many events are held here, notably the re-enactments of 19C life in period costume in the afternoons, and evening Son et Lumière shows.*

Vast and superbly proportioned, richly furnished, and standing in an exquisite park, this is a place dedicated to the good life.

The original medieval castle was rebuilt in the 16C and the defensive features were retained as decoration. In 1803, the estate was acquired by **Charles-Maurice de Talleyrand-Périgord** (1754–1838), paid for mostly by Napoleon, at the time still First Consul.

For almost a quarter of a century, the château served as a glittering background to international diplomacy conducted by its owner, who held high offices of state from the time of Louis XVI to the Restoration.

Inside are opulent furnishings of the Régence and Empire periods, including 18C Savonnerie carpets and the round table from the Congress of Vienna.

ADDRESSES

🏠 STAY

⬤⬤ **Hôtel Anne de Bretagne** – *31 ave J.-Laigret.* ℘02 54 78 05 38 . *Closed 9 Jan–6 Feb . 28rms.* ⬜€7. This small family hotel is near the castle and the terraced Jardin du Roi. The rooms are decorated in attractive colours and well soundproofed; those on the third floor are under the sloping roof.

⬤⬤⬤ **Chambre d'hôte La Villa Médicis** – *1 r. St-Denis, Macé, 41000 St-Denis-sur-Loire. 4km/2.5mi NE of Blois on N 152 towards Orléans.* ℘02 54 74 46 38. *Reservations required in winter. 6rms.* Marie de Medici came to take the waters at the springs in the park in which this 19C villa was built, as a hotel for spa patrons at the time.

🍴/ EAT

⬤⬤ **Au Bouchon Lyonnais** – *25 r. des Violettes.* ℘02 54 74 12 87. *Closed Sun, except public holidays. Reservations recommended.* Located just at the bottom of the hill crowned by the château, this restaurant is a favourite with residents of Blois, who enjoy the rustic décor with exposed beams and stone walls. The menu features regional fare.

⬤⬤ **Au Rendez-vous des Pêcheurs** – *27 r. Foix.* ℘02 54 74 67 48. *Closed Mon lunchtime and Sun. Reservations recommended.* A provincial-style bistro in the old part of Blois. Stained-glass windows filter the light in the quiet dining room. Fish features prominently among the fresh market produce on the menu.

⬤⬤⬤ **Le Bistrot du Cuisinier** – *20 quai Villebois-Mareuil .* ℘02 54 78 06 70. You'll find a real bistro atmosphere here, simple and relaxed, and from the front dining room there is a splendid view of Blois and the Loire.

🛍 SHOPPING

Rue du Commerce and the adjacent streets in the pleasant pedestrian-only town centre *(r. du Rebrousse-Pénil, r. St-Martin)* offer all kinds of shops.

SON ET LUMIÈRE

👤👤 *Shows are put on nightly at the château from Easter–Sept from 10pm. The Wed show is in English. €7 (child €3).* ℘02 54 90 33 32. www.blois.fr.

Alain Decaux of the Académie Française wrote the texts that retrace the history of Blois – "a thousand years' history spanning ten centuries of splendour" – and they are read by famous French actors including Michael Lonsdale, Fabrice Luchini, Robert Hossein, Pierre Arditi and Henri Virlojeux. Enormous projectors, combining photographs with special lighting effects, and the very latest in sound transmission systems make for a lively, entertaining and visually stimulating show, despite there being no live actors participating in the show.

Orléans★

Loiret

Orléans grew up on the great bend in the Loire between the rich cornfields of the Beauce to the north and the heaths and forests of the Sologne to the south. For a time the city was the capital of France. Place du Martroi, with its statue of Joan of Arc, is the centre of the historic town.

▶ **Population:** 116 515
🕑 **Michelin Map:** 318 I 4
ℹ **Info:** 2 pl. de l'Etape. ℘02 38 24 05 05. www.tourisme-orleans.com.
◐ **Location:** The city lies 131km/82mi SW of Paris and 62km/39mi NE of Blois, at the closest point of the Loire to the capital.

A BIT OF HISTORY

The **Siege of 1428–29** was one of the great episodes in the history of France, marking the country's rebirth after a period of despair. It began on 12 October 1428, as the Earl of Salisbury attempted to take the bridge over the Loire and thus link up with the other English forces in central and southern France.

Lasting almost seven months, the siege was the scene of one of the first-ever (albeit inconclusive) artillery duels. On 29 April 1429, **Joan of Arc** arrived from Chinon; she skirted Orléans to the south and entered the city by the Burgundy Gate (Porte de Bourgogne), several days ahead of the army advancing along the north bank of the river. By 7 May, victory seemed assured, and on 8 May the English capitulated.

In Orléans, Joan enjoyed the hospitality of Jacques Boucher, whose fine half-timbered dwelling with its **museum** is known as **Maison de Jeanne d'Arc★** *(3 pl. de Gaulle; ℘02 38 52 99 89; www.jeannedarc.com.fr/maison/maison.htm).*

SIGHTS

Cathédrale Ste-Croix★

r. Adolphe Crespin

Construction of the cathedral lasted from the 13C to the 16C. The nave was torn down by the Huguenots in 1568, but rebuilt in composite Gothic style by **Henri IV**, mindful of the city's loyalty to him.

The woodwork (**boiseries★★**) of the choir stalls (1706) includes splendidly carved medallions and panels adorning the high backs.

Musée des Beaux-Arts★★

1 r. Ferdinand Rabier, Pl. Ste-Croix.
🕑*Open Tue–Sun 10am–6pm.*
🕑*Closed public holidays.* €3; no charge 1st Sun in the month. ℘02 38 79 21 55. www.orleans.fr.

This museum houses some of the richest collections in France, especially of French painting from the 16–20C, including Courbet, Boudin and Gauguin.

Musée historique et archéologique★

🕑*Open: Oct–Apr Wed 1.30–5.45pm, Sun 2–6pm; May–Jun and Sept Tue–Sat 1.30–5.45pm, Sun 2–6pm; Jul–Aug Tue–Sat 9.30am–12.15pm, 1.30–5.45pm, Sun 2–6pm.* 🕑*Closed 1 Jan, 1 and 8 May, 14 Jul, 1 and 11 Nov, 25 Dec.* €3, no charge 1st Sun in the month. ℘02 38 79 21 55. www.musees.regioncentre.fr.

The Museum of History and Archaeology is housed in an elegant little mansion, **Hôtel Cabu** (1550), next to another Renaissance façade.

On the ground floor is the astonishing **Gallo-Roman treasure★** from Neuvy-en-Sullias which consists of a series of expressive statues, a horse and a wild boar in bronze as well as a number of statuettes of great artistic value.

The first floor is devoted to the Middle Ages and the Classical period, as well as typical local ceramic ware. The second floor is occupied by local folklore, pewter ware, gold and silverware, and clocks. Another room presents the history of the port of Orléans, describing the various industries associated with river traffic in the 18–19C.

Maison de Jeanne d'Arc★

3 pl. de Gaulle. ○Open Tue–Sun: May–Oct 10am–12.30pm, 1.30–6.30pm. Nov–Apr 1.30–6pm. ○Closed public holidays. ◉€2; no charge 2nd Sun in the month. ℘02 38 52 99 89. www.jeannedarc.com.fr.

The tall timber-framed façade contrasts with the modernity of the square, place du Général-de-Gaulle, which was heavily bombed in 1940. The building is a reconstruction of the house of Jacques Boucher, Treasurer to the Duke of Orléans, where Joan stayed in 1429. An audiovisual show on the first floor recounts the raising of the siege of Orléans by Joan of Arc on 8 May 1429.

The centre's resources include a book library, a film library, and microfilm and photographic archives.

The old **museum** houses displays of a scientific and cultural nature. The four upper floors of the museum are devoted to the marine world, aquatic ecosystems (aquarium), reptiles and amphibians, higher vertebrates, mineralogy, geology, palaeontology and botany (greenhouses of temperate and tropical plants on the top floor).

EXCURSIONS
Artenay

⊙20km/12.4mi N on N 20.

The entrance to this large town in the Beauce region is marked by a windmill-tower with a revolving roof (19C).

A Beauce farmhouse is the setting for the ♁♁ **Musée du Théâtre forain** (♿○open Wed-Mon: Jun-Sep 10am-noon, 2-6pm. Oct-May 2-5pm. ○closed 2nd and 4th weekends in the month, 1 Jan, 1 May, 14 Jul, 15 Aug, 1 and 11 Nov, 25 Dec. ◉3€. ℘02 38 80 09 73. www.museetheatre-forain.fr), a museum devoted to the life of travelling theatre, which toured French towns and villages from the 19C to the 1970s.

Parc floral de la Source★★

⊙In Olivet take D 14 E to the Source Floral Park.

○Open end Mar–early Oct 10am–7pm; Oct–early Nov 10am–6pm; Nov–Mar 2–5pm. ○Closed 1 Jan, 25 Dec. ◉€6, (children, 6–16 years, €4). ℘02 38 49 30 00. www.parc-floral-la-source.fr.

This park was laid out in the wooded grounds of a 17C château to host the 1967 Floralies Internationales horticultural exhibition. As the seasons change, so does the display: in spring, the flower beds are in bloom with tulips, daffodils, then **irises**★, rhododendrons and azaleas; mid-June to mid-July is when the rose bushes are at their best; in September the late-flowering rose bushes come into bloom with the dahlias. The **butterfly house** is a great attraction.

The **Loiret spring**★ can be seen bubbling up from the ground. The spring is the resurgence of the part of the river which disappears underground near St-

Parc Floral de la Source

Benoît-sur-Loire. Throughout the year, flocks of cranes and emus and herds of deer roam the park, while flamingoes stalk by the banks of the Loiret.

Abbaye de St-Benoît-sur-Loire★★

▶ *The abbey is at the village of St-Benoît, beside the Loire between Gien and Orléans. A pretty way to approach it is along the riverside road, D 60.*

🏠 *44 r. Orléanais.* ✆*02 38 35 79 00.*

Enthralling by its majestic size, exquisite harmony and utter simplicity, Fleury Abbey at St-Benoît-sur-Loire is justly one of the most famous Romanesque buildings in France.

The original abbey was founded here on a river terrace well above flood level. In around AD 675, it was presented with the remains of St Benedict and of his sister, St Scholastica, brought from Monte Cassino in Italy.

Hitherto known as Fleury Abbey, the monastery rededicated itself to the founder of Western monasticism (St Benedict is St-Benoît in French).

Basilique★★

⏰*Open 9am–10.30am, 1–2.15pm, 4–6pm.* ⏰*Closed during religious services.* ✆*02 38 35 72 43. www. abbaye-fleury.com.*

Built between 1067 and 1108, the Romanesque basilica has a fine **crypt**★ with a double ambulatory and a massive central pillar containing the relics of St Benedict. The **choir**★★ is remarkable for its paving (a Roman mosaic brought here from Italy) and for the elegant arcading.Outside, the **belfry porch**★★ is one of the finest examples of Romanesque art in France.

Germigny-des-Prés★

▶ *5.5km/3.4mi NW.*

The much-restored church is the **oratory** that Abbot Theodulf built for himself. It is a typical example of Carolingian architecture of the 9C, with an unusual plan, alabaster window-panes filtering the light, and a remarkable **mosaic**★★.

Châteaudun★★

▶ *130km/80mi southwest of Paris, between Chartres (45km/28mi) to the N and Vendôme (40km/25mi) to the SW.*

On the south bank of the Loir at the point where the Perche region joins the Beauce, Châteaudun and its castle stand on a bluff, indented by narrow valleys called *cavées.*

Château★★

⏰*Open daily: Sept–Apr 10am–12.30pm, 2–5.30pm; May–Jun 10am–1pm, 2–6pm; Jul–Aug 10am–1pm, 2–6.15pm.* 🎟️*€6.50.* ⏰*Closed 1 Jan, 1 May, 25 Dec.* ✆*02 37 94 02 90.*

Châteaudun is the first of the Loire châteaux to come into sight on the road from Paris. It stands on a bluff rising steeply above the Loir. Crude and fortress-like from the outside, the buildings resemble a stately mansion when seen from the courtyard. The keep, which is 31m/102ft high without the roof, dates from the 12C; it is one of the earliest circular keeps, and one of the most impressive and best preserved.

The **basement rooms** extend into the Dunois wing. Two of these rooms, beautifully decorated with intersecting ribbed vaulting, housed the kitchens, each with a double fireplace running the whole width of the room.

The **south oratory** collection of 15 **statues**★★ is an excellent example of the work produced in Loire Valley workshops in the late 15C.

The **Aile de Dunois** was begun towards 1460 and is built in the true Gothic tradition, although the interior furnishings suggest a desire for comfort following the Hundred Years' War. The huge living rooms have massive overhead beams and are hung with tapestries, including, on the first floor, a superb series from Brussels depicting the Life of Moses.

The **Aile de Longueville** was built between 1510 and 1520 by François II de Longueville and then by his brother the Cardinal on foundations which date from the preceding century, but it was never completed.

CORSICA

Kallisté, the name given to Corsica by the ancient Greeks, means "most beautiful", and even today the French refer to it as L'Île de Beauté. This mountainous island lies some 170km/105.6mi off the coast of mainland France. With its intense light, its superbly varied and dramatic coast and its wild and rugged interior, it is a place of distinct natural identity, enhanced by the succession of peoples who have been attracted here to settle or to rule; these have included megalith builders and mysterious Torreans, Greeks and Romans, Pisans and Genoese, French and British, though the somewhat absurd interlude of the Anglo-Corsican Viceroyalty of 1794–96 seems to have left little trace.

Highlights

1 Sheer rock walls rising above pines in **Aiguilles de Bavella** (p280)

2 Jagged granite rocks on the coast at Porto and the **Calanches de Piana** (p281)

3 The upper town **(Ville Haute)** of **Bonifacio** perched on high cliffs (p282)

4 Finger of mountains pointing into the sea: **Cap Corse** (p284)

5 Pisan-style striped church: **San Michele de Murato** (p285)

Geography – The gulfs of Corsica's west coast are of extraordinary beauty, the jagged headlands and precipitous cliffs rising from the Golfe de Porto being especially memorable. The Cap Corse promontory prolongs the island's backbone of schistic rocks 40km/25mi northwards into the sea.

The coastal plains of Bastia and Aléria to the east constitute the only substantial areas of flat land. The interior is penetrated by a network of narrow and winding roads as well as by a remarkable 1m/3ft-gauge railway. Here are villages of tall granite houses overlooking deep gorges, as well as forests of oak, Corsican pine and sweet chestnut. Above the tree line rise the high bare summits, all the more imposing because of their proximity to the sea.

History – Remarkably Corsica has been part of France only since the late 19C, and before that it had a succession of occupiers including Greeks, Romans, Byzantines, Saracens (who gave the island its symbol, the Moor's Head) and finally the Genoese. During the War of Independence in the 19C the nationalist movement, led by the Cosican hero Pasquale Paoli, had some success, but despite the support of the British during the rather absurd Anglo-Corsican Viceroyalty of 1794–96, the island was absorbed into France in 1796. Corsica's most famous son is, of course, Napoleon Bonaparte, and he is celebrated in every town.

Economy – Corsica is an unspoilt Mediterranean island, and this, allied with beautiful mountains, a magnificent coastline and an agreeable climate, attracts the many tourists who are the mainstay of the economy. The island does also produce honey, chestnuts, cheese, wine and sausages, which are mostly exported to mainland France. The nationalist movement remains active, and in 2003 a referendum which would have given Corsica more independence was narrowly defeated.

Ajaccio★★
Corse-du-Sud

Ajaccio occupies a natural amphitheatre looking out over its splendid bay. The town was founded in 1492 by the Office of St George which governed Corsica on behalf of the Republic of Genoa. Native Corsicans were forbidden residence there until 1553, when, in the course of the first French intervention in the island, it was taken by the legendary military adventurer Sampierro Corso (1498–1567), born in the village of Bastelica, 25km/15.5mi to the northeast.

▶ **Population:** 65 883
🜨 **Michelin Map:** 345 A-B 7-8
ℹ **Info:** 3 bd du Roi-Jérôme, 20181 Ajaccio (Aiacciu). ℘04 95 51 53 03. www.ajaccio-tourisme.com.
◖ **Location:** Ajaccio is on the W coast of Corsica, 82.4km/51mi SW of Corte along the N 193. Place Foch is the heart of town. The tourist office has information on guided tours.

A BIT OF HISTORY

It was here, at 1am on 13 September 1943, that the first Free French forces to land on the territory of France disembarked from the submarine *Casabianca*, under Commander L'Herminier.

Ajaccio's historic importance is due above all to its being the birthplace of **Napoleon Bonaparte**. The town continues to revere the memory of its "glorious child prodigy". Born on 15 August 1769, the son of Charles-Marie Bonaparte and Letizia Romolino, he entered the military school at Brienne (*Aube*) at the age of 10. At 27 he married Josephine Tascher de la Pagerie, widow of General Beauharnais, before directing the Italian campaign (Battle of Arcole) and, two years later, the expedition to Egypt. In 1804, taking the title of Napoleon I, he crowned himself Emperor of the French.

On 26 August the following year he launched the *Grande Armée* (Grand Army) against Austria from the encampment at Boulogne whence he had threatened England with invasion. By 1807, at the age of 38, he dominated Europe.

It was then, however, that coalitions originally formed to resist the French Revolution were turned against the Empire. England was deeply involved in them all, in the colonies and on the high seas as well as in Europe. Though bloated and prematurely aged, Napo-leon rose to the challenge, never more formidable than from 1809 on, the years of struggle against the Fifth and Sixth Coalitions. But France and her Emperor were out of touch with a changed Europe. There was now a strong desire for national independence among the peoples of Europe. The Napoleonic Age was brought to a close on 18 June 1815 by the Battle of Waterloo. On 15 July Bonaparte sailed to exile on St Helena, where he died on 5 May 1821.

SIGHTS
Old Town

It is the heart of Ajaccio's old town that holds the most interest. Here, a network of ancient streets spreads north and south from place Foch, which itself opens out to the seafront close by the port and marina. Place de Gaulle is essentially the town centre, and from here the main highway, cours Napoléon, extends parallel to the sea in a north-easterly direction.

Salon Napoleonien

Hôtel de Ville, Place Foch. ♿🕐*Open mid Jun–mid-Sept Mon–Fri 9–11.45am, 2–5.45pm; mid-Sept–mid-Jun Mon–Fri 9-11.45am, 2-4.45pm.* ⬤€2.50. ℘04 95 51 52 62. www.napoleon.org.

Situated in the Hôtel de Ville, this early 19C Restoration-style room displays paintings and sculptures relating to the Imperial era in addition to coins and medals also from the period.

Village of Zonza and the Aiguilles de Bavella

H. Le Gac/MICHELIN

Maison Bonaparte

r. St-Charles ○*Open daily: Apr–Sept 9am –noon, 2–6pm; Oct–Mar 10am–noon, 2–5pm.* ∞€6. ℘04 95 21 43 89. www. musees-nationaux-napoleoniens.org

A typical house of the Genoese quarter, the Bonaparte family moved here from Italy in 1743. Napoleon is supposed to have been born on a couch in the ante-chamber on the first floor.

The family enjoyed a reasonable stand-ard of living. In May 1793, the Bona-partes, loyal to Republican ideas, were forced by the followers of Pascal Paoli to abandon the house, which was sacked and the adjoining family properties laid waste. On her return to Ajaccio in 1798, Napoleon's mother put the house back in order with the help of her half-brother, Abbot Fesch (a future cardinal). The work was financed in part by a grant from the Directory, in part by sums sent to his brother Joseph by Napoleon (now in Egypt), enabling him to acquire the upper storeys and the adjoining house. On his return from Egypt on 29 September 1799, Bonaparte stopped off at Ajac-cio to see the family home. He is sup-posed to have slept in the alcove on the second floor. After six days he slipped away via a trap-door, never to see his birthplace again. A diverse collection of memorabilia is displayed.

Palais Fesch: musée des Beaux-Arts

50–52 r. Cardinal Fesch. ○*Open: Oct– Apr Mon, Wed, Sat 10am–5pm, Thu–Fri noon–5pm (Sun, 3rd weekend of month, noon–5pm); May–Sept Mon, Wed, Sat 10.30am–6pm, Thu, Sun noon–6pm, Fri noon–6pm.* ∞€8. ℘04 95 26 26 26. www.musee-fesch.com.

The building was constructed for Car-dinal Fesch, uncle of Napoleon I, in order to establish an Institute of Arts and Sciences. Born in Ajaccio in 1763, the cardinal died in Rome in 1839, and bequeathed to his home town more than 1 000 works of art. The museum is the most important in France after the Louvre as regards Italian painting.

Place Maréchal-Foch

This fine square, the focus of Ajaccio's outdoor social life, is shaded by palm trees; its upper part is dominated by a marble statue by Laboureur of Napoleon as First Consul.

EXCURSIONS
Aiguilles de Bavella★★★

◐ *The Aiguilles rise above the Col de Bavella, the mountain pass on D268, which runs from Sartène in SW Corsica to Solenzara on the southeast coast. The nearest community is Zonza.*

▪ *There is no tourist office nearby, but the Mairie (town hall, ℘04 95 78 66 87) in Zonza can assist with information. For more on this region of Corsica, see www.alta-rocca.com.*

The Bavella Pass is the starting point for many walks and trails for all levels of ability, and is on the long-distance path GR20 (◖*see right*). It is one of the most dramatic locations in Corsica. From the Bavella Pass, Col de Bavella, there is an awesome view of the jagged Bavella or Asinao Peaks in a spectacular, stark setting; the changing light plays on the sheer rock walls rising above the pine trees at the base.

Forêt de Bavella★★

The dense forest growing at an altitude of 500m–1 300m (1 640ft/4 265ft) has been damaged repeatedly by fire and

Walking in Corsica

The scope for walking in Corsica is great, but it covers a vast range of terrain including rough, stony mountainsides, exposed airy ridges, rock slabs, earth-based paths through woodland and pastureland, sandy beaches and numerous river crossings, the latter generally achieved by fording. Most paths have clear waymarking, although numbering of them is rare. Waymarking uses the conventional system of painted stripes on rocks common to anyone who has walked elsewhere in France.

The GR20, the so-called high-level route, is a tough and unremitting trail that heads high into the mountains and stays there for days. The landscape through which it passes is awesome, passing from Calenzana in the north to Conca in the south, a distance of around 190km/118mi.

Two excellent guides are *Walking in Corsica*, by Gillian Price, and *GR20 – Corsica* by Paddy Dillon, both available from www.cicerone.co.uk.

has been extensively replanted with maritime and laricio pines, cedars and fir trees. A hunting preserve shelters herds of wild sheep which can be glimpsed perched high up on the sheer rocks. Just before the pass are low buildings formerly used as sheep-pens, and an inn, **Auberge du Col**, which is the starting-point for walks around the pass to the Trou de la Bombe and La Pianona.

Col de Bavella

The mountain ridge crowning the island is indented by the Bavella Pass marked by a cross and the statue of **Notre-Dame-des-Neiges**.

The setting and the panorama over the summits are spectacular.

To the west the Bavella Peaks rise above the forest of twisted pine trees, while to the east the rock wall of Calanca Murata and the jagged ridge of red rock of Punta Tafonata di Paliri stand out against the backdrop of the Tyrrhenian Sea.

Golfe de Porto★

The Gulf is the large bay on the shores of which the town of Porto stands, in western Corsica.
ℹ *Qtr. de la Marine,* ☎ *04 95 26 10 55. www.porto-tourisme.com.*
The Bay of Porto is one of the most splendid destinations on the Corsican coast, owing to its sheer size, range of colours and varied natural sights. Imposing cliffs of red granite contrast with the

deep-blue waters. The area is part of a nature park, Parc naturel régional de Corse, listed as a World Heritage Site.

Calanches de Piana★★★

Boat trips (1hr30min) leaving from Porto. 🕐*Easter–Oct: departure 2pm, 4pm, 6pm. www.otpiana.com.*
The deep creeks *(calanches)* dominating the Bay of Porto are remarkable; the chaotic landscape is shaped by erosion of the granite, jagged rocks and spherical cavities known as "taffoni", and integral feature of the picturesque landscape of Corsica.

A road (D 81), which runs through the calanche for 2km/1.2mi, affords splendid viewpoints over the rock piles and the sea. Starting from the terrace of the **Chalet des Roches bleues**, several walks lasting about one hour allow visitors to admire at close range the distinctive form of some of the rocks: the Turtle, the Bishop, a human head and a castle.

Réserve Naturelle de Scandola★★★

The Presqu'île de Scandola rises between the Punta Rossa to the south and the Punta Nera to the north.
The majestic massif is of volcanic origin and features numerous taffoni.

Bonifacio★★★
Corse-du-Sud

Projecting into the sea on Corsica's southern tip, the old town occupies the top of a high wedge of rock with exceptional views, while the harbour and new town at the foot of the cliff is the busy centre of commerce and actiivity.

> ▶ **Population:** 2 925
> ◔ **Michelin Map:** 345 D-E 11
> ▤ **Info:** 2 r. Fred Scamaroni.
>   ℘04 95 73 11 88.
>   www.bonifacio.fr.
> ◑ **Location:** At the southern tip of the island: 122km/ 76mi S of Ajaccio.

A BIT OF HISTORY

Greek and Roman remains have been found at Bonifacio but the town's history really begins when Bonifacio, Marquis of Tuscany, gave it his name in AD 828. Its strategic position controlling the Western Mediterranean was appreciated by the Genoese, who took it in 1187.

The town was besieged many times, most notably in 1420 by King Alfonso V of Aragon. Legend has it that his soldiers cut the famous stairway of 187 steps into the cliff-face in the course of a single night.

VISIT
Site★★★

Bonifacio is magnificently sited on a long, narrow promontory protecting its "fjord" in the far south of Corsica and it is reached from the rest of the island across a vast, arid plain.

The town is divided in two, the **"Marine"**★, the port quarter offering a safe anchorage for warships, fishing boats and pleasure craft, and the **Upper Town**★★ overlooking the sea from 60m/200ft-high cliffs.

Its old houses, many of them with four or five storeys, are joined together by what appear to be flying buttresses but are in fact rainwater channels feeding the town's cisterns. The great loggia of the Church of Ste-Marie-Majeure is built over a huge cistern with a capacity of 650cu m (c.140 000 gal); under Genoese rule this is where the affairs of the town were deliberated upon by four elders, who were elected for three months at a time. Twice a week the *podesta*, the mayor, who lived opposite, would mete out justice from here.

Parc Marin International des Bouches de Bonifacio★★

The Nature Reserve of Bonifacio was founded at the initiative of the Ministry of Environment and Territorial Collectivity of Corsica, to preserve and enhance the natural heritage of this strait.

This reserve is home to marine and coastal environments and exceptional landscapes: the Lavezzi islands, Cerbicales, Bruzzi Moines, and the cliffs of Bonifacio.

Coastline

With 70km/44mi of coastline, Bonifacio has numerous sandy beaches, coves, islands, archipelagos, fishing ports and marinas. Worthy of a visit are the Bay of **Rondinara**★★★, regarded by many as the **most beautiful beach in France** (and the third most beautiful beach in Europe (www.onbeach.fr)), Fazzio, Sant'Amanza, and the wild beaches of Tonnara and Petit Sperone.

EXCURSIONS
Grotte du Sdragonato★

▶ *45min by boat.*

The dragon's cave is dimly lit by a shaft in the shape of Corsica in reverse. 12km/7.4mi away across the sometimes choppy waters of the Bonifacio Straits (Bouches de Bonifacio) is Sardinia. The trip gives good views of the high limestone cliffs of the promontory and of the King of Aragon's steps.

Filitosa★★

▶ *The site, overlooking the Taravo valley, is located in the commune of Sollacaro, 17km/10.5mi N of Propriano, in southern Corsica.*

View of Bonifacio from the sea

S. Sauvignier/MICHELIN

🚹 *Place St Marcel. ℰ 95 37 18 07.*
www.frotsi-corse.com.
This fascinating site was discovered in
1946; the beginnings of Corsican history
are all visible here, from the Neolithic
to the Megalithic and the Torreen, and
finally to the Roman.

Station Préhistorique★★

🕐 *Apr–mid-Oct: 9am–7pm. Preferably*
in the middle of the day: good light to
study the sculptures and engravings.
Sound recordings in 4 languages.
👓 *€5. ℰ 04 95 74 00 91.*
By the path leading to the prehistoric
site stands the superb menhir known
as **Filitosa V**, bearing, in front, a long
sword and an oblique dagger, and,
behind, anatomical or clothing details.
A stone wall built by the Megalithic
people encloses the site. Within it, four
striking groups of monuments testify
to the domination exercised by the Tor-
reens: the **East Monument** which they
filled in; the remains of **huts** (*cabanes*)
which they re-used, the circular **Central Monument**, and the fragments
of menhir-statues. The latter had been
made by the Megalithic people; the Tor-
reens cut them up and re-used them,
face downwards, in the construction
of the Central Monument, doubtless to
signal their supremacy.
Some of them, however, have been
placed upright again, and Filitosa IX
and XIII frame the way into the Central
Monument.

The **West Monument** is Torreen, and is
built on Megalithic foundations.
The five menhir-statues near an age-old
olive tree on the far slope of the valley
mark the end of the Megalithic period
in this area.

Sartène★

▶ *The town is 51km/31.7mi NW of*
Bonifacio. 🚹 *Place de la Libération.*
ℰ *04 95 77 74 01. www.sartene.fr.*
The writer Prosper Mérimée thought
Sartène, 305m/1 000ft above the Bay
of Valinco, the "most Corsican of Cor-
sican towns".

Place de la Libération

The shady square is the focus of local life.
It is overlooked by the **Église Ste-Marie**,
built in granite. To the left of the main
entrance are the chains and the heavy
cross of oak borne by Catenacciu, the
anonymous red-robed penitential figure
at the centre of the nocturnal procession on Good Friday. This **procession du
Catenacciu**★★ is probably the island's
most ancient ceremony.

Vieille ville (Old Town)★★

Go through the arch of the town hall
(Hôtel de ville) and take the street opposite (Rue des Frères-Bartoli). The narrow
stone-flagged alleyways, some stepped
or vaulted, are lined by tall granite-
built houses with a fortress-like air. The
Quartier de Santa Ann★★★ has this
kind of characteristic townscape.

Bastia★★

Haute-Corse

The overriding impression of Bastia, the island's most successful commercial town, is one of aged distress and charm. Thankfully, the town's industry lies to the south, among the lowlands. Bastia has two ports which co-exist amicably and between them portray the old and the new aspects of this time-worn place.

▸ **Population:** 44 091.
- **Michelin Map:** 345 F 3.
- **Info:** place St-Nicolas ✆04 95 54 20 40. www.bastia-tourisme.com.
- **Location:** Bastia lies on the northeaastern coast of the island, 57.5km/92mi NE of Ajaccio.
- **Timing:** Half a day would ordinarily suffice to explore Bastia, but its old port and centre are charismatic and you may find yourself wanting to linger.

SIGHTS
Old Town (Terra Vecchia)
The old quarter, the Terra Vecchia, consists of a tightly packed mishmash of streets, Flamboyant Baroque churches and lofty tenements, displaying crumbling ochre walls against a scented backdrop of maquis-covered hills.

Bastia dates from Roman times, when a camp was established at Biguglia to the south, close by a freshwater lagoon. Little remains of this former colony, but the site is worth a day-trip for the well-preserved pair of Pisan churches at Marana, rising from the southern fringes of Poretta airport. Bastia began to thrive under the Genoese, when wine was exported to the Italian mainland from Porto Cardo, as the old port was originally called. Despite the fact that in 1811 Napoléon made Ajaccio the capital of the island, initiating a competitiveness between the two towns that is evident to this day, Bastia soon developed the stronger trading position with mainland France. The Nouveau Port, created in 1862 to the north of the town to cope with the increasing traffic with France and Italy, became the mainstay of the local economy, exporting chiefly agricultural products from Cap Corse, Balagne and the eastern plain.

Citadel and ramparts
Place du Donjon.
Constructed in the 15–17C by the Genoese, the citadel of Bastia is almost a town in its own right, known as Terra Nova, which you enter through the Louis XVI gate, which gives onto the place du Donjon. Entrenched behind the citadel walls, the villagers lived peacably for nearly three centuries, and styled the centre on the grid plan of Roman cities. Today, the houses seem to be stacked above one another, presenting a colourful picture to the port. The narrow streets have great allure, beckoning like an impatient child, leading into a maze of alleyways that confuse and amuse in equal measure.

EXCURSIONS
Cap Corse★★★
▸ *Cap Corse can be reached from either the east or the west coast. The city of Bastia stands at the base of the "finger" on the east coast.*
Port de Plaisance, Macinaggio.
✆*04 95 35 40 34. www.ot-rogliano-macinaggio.com.*
Make time to visit the superb covered market, near the Old Port, daily except Monday. Take a picturesque drive along the coast to discover villages clinging to defensive sites, tiny sandy beaches, and marinas nestling in an inlet.

Cap Corse is the finger of mountain range that prolongs the island's ridge of rock 40km/24.8mi into the sea.

A Seafaring People – In contrast to the rest of the Corsican population, local inhabitants responded to the call of the sea and took up trade and travel to distant lands. In the 19C they set up the first trading-posts in North Africa.

A large number emigrated to South America; many became prosperous and built great houses in colonial or Renaissance style in their native village. These styles have influenced the architecture of the region.

This northernmost part of Corsica is in fact its sunniest and is ideal for walking and cycling. The east side of the Cap has small villages like Erbalunga nestling in coves, while on the west side the villages of Nonza and Canari are on higher ground.

Corte★

Corte sits high in the rocky interior of the island. 🅸 *Citadelle de Corté.* 🕿 *04 95 46 26 70. www.corte-tourisme.com.*
Corte owes its fame to its **site**★ among gorges and ravines, as well as to two great men, Gaffori and Paoli, who were instrumental in making it one of the strongholds of Corsican patriotism.
Jean-Pierre Gaffori (1704–53) was born here. He was a member of the Triumvirate elected as "Protectors of the Nation", who took up arms against Genoa.

In 1746, supported by his indomitable wife Faustine, he succeeded in wresting the town from the Genoese. In 1750 they returned, taking the citadel but failing to overcome the resolute defence of the old town; Gaffori's house still bears the marks made by the Genoese guns.

In June 1751, Gaffori was made "General of the Nation" and granted executive power. But two years later he was killed in an ambush, betrayed by his brother. After this an appeal was made for **Pascal Paoli** (1725–1807), then in exile in Italy, to return to his native land. He was proclaimed "General of the Nation" in his turn. By 1764, the island was united under his leadership, with only the Genoese coastal forts holding out against him.

For 14 years he made Corte his capital, drew up a constitution, founded a university, minted money, reformed the system of justice, encouraged industry and stimulated agricultural production. Having failed to put down the Corsicans' long struggle for independence (1729–69), the Republic of Genoa requested the intervention of France. A mission of conciliation arrived, headed by the future French Governor, Marbeuf. Paoli unwisely prevaricated and was bypassed by events; on 15 May 1768, by the Treaty of Versailles, Genoa provisionally gave up its rights over the island to France. Paoli proclaimed a mass uprising, but was defeated at **Ponte Nuovo** on 8 May 1769.

Paoli went into exile, spent mostly in England, where he was lionised by the court of George III. Amnestied at the outbreak of the French Revolution, he met with a triumphal reception in Paris before returning to Corsica.

Later, after his denunciation as a counter-revolutionary, he sought aid from the English. Nelson's victories over the French at St-Florent, Bastia and Calvi did not, however, fulfil Paoli's hopes of independence under the English Crown, but led to the short-lived Anglo-Corsican kingdom and renewed exile in London for Paoli. He died there in 1807.

Ville Haute★

Dominated by the **citadel**★ perched high up on its rock, old Corte, with its cobbled, stepped streets and tall houses, still has the air of the island's capital it once was.

In the Place Paoli stands the statue of the great man, in bronze. Further up is the Place Gaffori, where, behind the monument to the General of the Nation, is his house. A ramp opposite the National Palace (Palais National) leads to a **viewpoint**★ on a peak standing out from the main promontory on which the citadel is built. It offers a fine view of the town in its setting bordered by the river valley, Gorges du Tavignano.

Église San Michele de Murato★★
Michelin map 345-E-4
The church and village of Murato are 54.6km/34mi NE of Corte. On its hilltop site just north of the village of Murato in the Bevinco valley, this 13C Romanesque church is Pisan in style, of uneven stripes of beautiful green serpentine and white limestone blocks.

DORDOGNE BERRY LIMOUSIN

The Dordogne, with its hills, its mature and varied agricultural landscapes, its deciduous woodlands and its mellow stone buildings, is not unlike parts of southern England, albeit with a more genial climate and a general atmosphere of good living. Little touched by industrialisation or mass tourism, the regions of Berry and Limousin seem to represent the quintessence of rural France. Berry centres on Bourges which, with its great cathedral, was once the seat of the French court. The Limousin is the name of the old province around Limoges forming the northwestern extremity of the Massif Central.

Highlights

1   Palace of wealthy financier, Jacques Coeur, at **Bourges** (p289)
2   Tranquil riverside village and Abbey: **Brantôme** (p297)
3   World famous prehistoric cave painting at **Grotte de Lascaux** (p301)
4   Pilgrimage site clinging to a cliff **Rocamadour** (p303)
3   Medieval bridge with towers at Cahors: **Pont Valentré** (p306)

Geography – The Dordogne incorporates the Périgord region which forms a plateau dissected by the Dordogne; along the banks grow maize, tobacco, sunflowers and cereals. In Quercy the thick layers of Jurassic limestone form *causses*, covered by scrubby oaks and carob trees, which are dissected by dry valleys and spectacular canyons.

The vast limestone plateau, which forms Berry's heartland, is devoted to arable farming, making a contrast with the *bocage* of the Boischaut and the Brenne marshlands. Much of the Limousin is quiet countryside drained by rivers flowing westwards to the Dordogne and the Saintonge. In contrast is the Montagne, its name derived more from the rigour of the climate than the altitude since nowhere does it rise above 1 000m/3 280ft.

History – The Dordogne area has been settled since the very earliest times as evidenced by its renowned cave paintings at Lascaux and Font-de-Gaume. As well as stunning examples of medieval settlement, such as Rocamadour, there are numerous reminders of Anglo-French struggle, from the planned towns, or *bastides*, like Monpazier, Domme, Villefranche-du-Périgord and Beaumont, to rugged strongholds such as Beynac and Castelnaud. The Limousin and the Berry, like the Dordogne, were

The Dronne at Brantôme

C. Labonne/MICHELIN

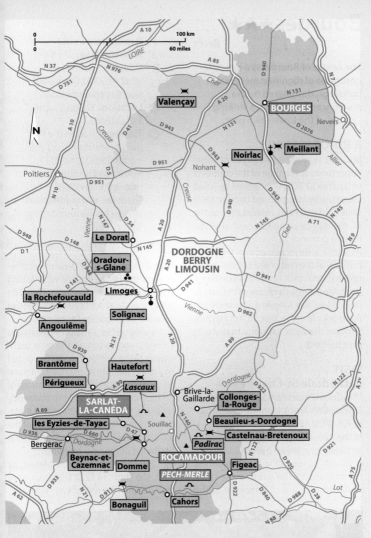

both part of Aquitania in Roman times and were later ruled by the Franks. Also contested during the Hundred Years' War, they were eventually annexed to France during the reign of Henry IV.

Economy – The climate of the Dordogne enables the successful cultivation of crops and production of foie-gras, while the Lot Valley, west of Cahors, is renowned for its "black" red wine. Tourism is very important and the area is much loved by northern Europeans. Berry and Limousin are largely rural; agriculture is the mainstay of both, but tourism is important and the porcelain industry at Limoges is as prominent today as ever.

This section also covers towns in Quercy. Although less well known to tourists than its neighbour the Périgord, tourism is of increasing importance here, with more than 1 million visitors per year visiting Rocamadour and 400,000 exploring the cave systems. Today, Quercy comprises all of the Lot and part of Tarn et Garonne départements, stretching from the Massif Central in the east to the plains of Aquitaine in the west and from the Limousin in the north to the Midi-Pyrénées in the south.

Bourges★★★

Berry

The centre of Bourges is a majestic ensemble of dignified medieval buildings, dominated by the magnificent cathedral, a striking symbol of the town's rich past.

A BIT OF HISTORY

Bourges was already a place of some importance at the time of the conquest of Gaul; in 52 BC it was sacked by Julius Caesar, who is supposed to have massacred 40 000 of its inhabitants. In the 4C the city became the capital of the Roman province of Avaricum.

Its significance increased over the years, but only at the end of the 14C did it take on a national role, under Jean de Berry. He made Bourges a centre of the arts to rival Dijon and Avignon, commissioning works like the Très Riches Heures, perhaps the most exquisite miniatures ever painted.

VISIT

Cathédrale St-Étienne★★★

Guided tours Apr–Sept 8.15am 7.15pm; Oct–Mar 8.15am–5.45pm. €8. 02 48 65 49 44.

In the 12C, Bourges was the seat of an archbishopric linked by tradition to the royal territories to the north, whereas the regions to the south west came under the sphere of influence of the

- **Population:** 71 022
- **Michelin Map:** 323 K 4-6
- **Info:** 21 r. Victor Hugo. 02 48 23 02 60. www.bourges-tourisme.com.
- **Location:** 122km/76.5mi S of Orléans.
- **Timing:** A ride on the P'tit train touristique gives you a good look at the city's history and architecture (Apr–mid-Nov daily). There are also guided tours offered by the tourist office (*see p289*).

Angevin kingdom. The great new cathedrals of the Île-de-France were taking shape, and the Archbishop, Henri de Sully, Primate of Aquitaine, dreamed of a similar great edifice for his city.

In drawing up his plans, the anonymous architect exploited all the new techniques of the Gothic in order to control and direct the thrusts exerted by and on his great structure. Other innovations of his included leaving out the transepts, retaining six sexpartite bays and incorporating the Romanesque portals of the old cathedral into the north and south doorways of the new building.

By 1200 the crypt was completed, by 1215, the choir. In 1220 the great nave with its splendid row of two-tiered fly-

Stained-glass windows depicting Joseph's dream, Cathédrale St-Étienne

S. Sauvignier/MICHELIN

ing buttresses was ready. Overenthusiastic restoration at the start of the 19C included the remodelling of the external gables and the unfortunate addition of round windows, balustrades and pinnacles.

The huge west front has five doorways, anticipating the nave and four aisles adorned with the radiating motifs of the High Gothic (mid-13–14C) style; they were begun in 1230. Ten years later the two right-hand portals were in place. By 1250, the central portal (Last Judgement) had been finished. But 60 years later, subsidence made it necessary to prop up the South Tower by means of a massive pillar-buttress and to strengthen the west front. This was to no avail; on 31 December 1506, the north tower fell into ruins. Guillaume Pellevoysin, the new architect, worked for 30 years on its replacement and on the construction of the two left-hand portals; he included many architectural and decorative features of the Early Renaissance.

The east end has the Gothic windows of the lower church inserted between the base of the chapels and the buttresses. Three-sided chapels radiate out from the outer ambulatory, while the inner ambulatory is spanned by the first tier of the double flying buttresses; the upper spans pierce the structure to hold the vault of the choir in place. The Lanceolate Gothic style here reaches a high point in its development.

Inside, the nave and four **aisles**, completed in 1270, make a striking impression by virtue of their great height and the light filtering through the stained glass. The outer aisles, lined by chapels, are already 9m/29.5ft from floor to vault; the inner aisles, with a blind triforium, reach 21m/68.9ft, while the nave rises to a full 37.1m/121.7ft. With no gallery, and limited by the great size of its arches, it is covered by a sexpartite vault; the alternating sequence of major and minor piers is cunningly disguised by the shafts wrapped around the columns. Beneath the choir a **crypt**★★ of the same layout takes up a 6m/19.6ft change in level of the ground. A fine example of a 13C crypt, it has an outer

ambulatory with triangular vaulting and arcades mounted on twisted diagonal arches to allow the keystones to be set properly. ◗◖Guided tours (45min); daily except Sun am: Apr and Sept 9.45–11.45am, 2–5.30pm; May–Jun 9.30–11.30am, 2–6pm; Jul–Aug 9.30am–12.30pm, 2–6pm; Oct–Mar 9.30–11.30am, 2–4.45pm. ☼Closed 1 Jan, 1 May, 1 and 11 Nov, 25 Dec. ∞€7 (combined ticket with Palais Jacques-Cœur, €9.50). ℘02 48 65 49 44.

The stained glass (**vitraux**★★★) – some of the finest in the whole of France – demonstrates the whole evolution of the art of glass-making between the 12C and 17C. The 13C windows in the choir recall the techniques of the master glass-makers of Chartres. The great nave is illuminated by light streaming in through all its windows.

Palais Jacques Cœur★★

10 bis, r. Jacques Coeur. ☼Open daily: May–Jun 9.30am–noon, 2–6.15pm; Jul–Aug 9.30am–12.30pm, 2–6.30pm; Sept and Apr 10am–12.15pm, 2–6pm; Oct–Mar 9.30am–noon, 2–5.15pm. ☼Closed 1 Jan, 1 May, 1 and 11 Nov, 25 Dec. ∞€7 (combined ticket with cathedral tour, €9.50). ℘02 48 24 79 42. www.palais-jacques-coeur.monuments-nationaux.fr.

The son of a Bourges fur-trader, **Jacques Cœur** (1395–1456) started out as a goldsmith, first at the court of Jean de Berry, then with Charles VII. He soon became aware of the economic recovery just beginning and of the opportunities opening up in the Mediterranean.

Before long he had many commercial interests and he supplied the royal court with luxury goods and became the king's Minister of Finance. At the peak of his career at the age of 50 he decided to build himself a worthy residence.

His palace, begun in 1445, was completed in the short space of 10 years. It shows how the will to build had revived after the stagnation due to war and also demonstrates the success of the Flamboyant Gothic style. It is a sumptuous building, incorporating certain pioneering comforts like a bathhouse and an arcaded courtyard.

Other innovations that it contributed to the evolution of late medieval domestic architecture included the provision of a large number of rooms with independent access, sculptures indicating the purpose of the rooms served by the various staircases, and, in the chapel, two oratories reserved for the proprietor and his wife.

ADDITIONAL SIGHTS

Musée du Berry★ (4 r. des Arènes)
This quiet, unpretentious museum, housed in the Hôtel Cujas, contains **archaeological collections**★ (dating from prehistory to the end of the Gallo-Roman period), sculpture, furniture and pottery.

Musée des Meilleurs Ouvriers de France (pl. Etienne Dolet) Housed in the former archbishop's residence, this unusual museum contains exceptionally fine objects made by gifted craftsmen.

Musée Maurice-Estève★ (r. Edouard Branly) Since 1987, this museum, located in the Hôtel des Échevins, has been home to a unique collection of 130 works in oil and on paper.

Musée des arts décoratifs★ (Hôtel Lallemant) This magnificent Renaissance mansion has retained the name of Jean Lallemant, the rich cloth merchant who had it built. It now houses the **Musée des Arts Décoratifs**.

Jardin des Prés-Fichaux★ (bd de la République) A beautiful garden has been laid out on marshland between

the river and the close of St-Ambroise Abbey where the Protestants used to gather in the 16C to sing.

EXCURSIONS
Château de Meillant★★

⏵ *The castle is located 39km/24.2mi S of Bourges.* 🕐 *Open daily: 9.30am–noon, 2–6pm (Jul–Aug 9.30am–6pm).* 🕐*Closed mid Nov–Feb.* ◉€.50. ✆02 48 63 32 05. www.chateau-de-meillant.com.

This château is a fine example of how stylistic change was allied to the growing desire for domestic comfort towards the end of the 15C, to transform what had been a typical medieval castle into an agreeable country residence.

The medieval south front lapped by the waters of a moat is the only remnant of the old fortress built in the early 14C by Étienne de Sancerre; the towers retain their narrow loopholes although the wall-walk has been demolished.

The ornate east façade, which is in a different style recalling that of the châteaux of the Loire, includes two projecting stair turrets in the late Gothic style featuring a pierced balustrade at the base of the roof, dormer windows adorned with carvings, chimneys with elaborate Gothic balustrades, and in particular the splendidly decorated tower (Tour du Lion) by Giocondo, one of Michelangelo's assistants.

The interior, notably the formal dining room (Grande Salle à Manger) and the Bishop of Amboise's chamber, is furnished with period pieces, fireplaces, tapestries and carpets.

Abbaye de Noirlac★★

⏵ *The abbey is just outside the town of St Amand-Montrond.*
🕐*Open daily: Feb-Mar 2-5pm; Apr-Sep 10am-6.30pm; Oct- 23 Dec 2-5pm.* 🕐*Closed 24 Dec–31 Jan.* ◉€7. ✆02 48 62 01 01. www.abbayedenoirlac.fr.
Between the River Cher and the Meillant Forest, this 12–14C abbey is one of the best-preserved medieval monasteries in France. It occupies an exceptional setting for the Gregorian chants, concerts and cultural events that take place here.

The perfect simplicity of the **abbey church** dates from 1150–60. It follows the plan of the great abbey at Clairvaux. The modern glass is the work of Jean-Pierre Raynaud, aided by craftsmen from Chartres and Bourges. The Gothic cloisters were added in the 13C.

Sancerre★

⊘ *46km/28.7mi NE of Bourges via D955.* ℹ *Nouvelle Place.* ℘*02 48 54 08 21* *www.ville-sancerre.fr.*

High above the banks of the River Loire, Sancerre roosts above St-Satur and St-Thibault. From this **vantage point**★, a wide panorama embraces the river and the Nivernais to the east, and Berry to the west. This little city, reigning over a land of trim vineyards and frisky goats, is renowned for its delicious white wine, flinty in flavour, and its little round cheeses, especially those from Chavignol. The steep streets of the town are enticing for their tempting food shops, restaurants and wine merchants.

A strategic location – Sancerre, already well known in Roman times has long stood watch over the Loire. It may have been the 9C residence of Robert le Fort, an early member of the Capetian dynasty. Later, the city played an important role in the Hundred Years' War, as the gateway to Berry, placed between the Burgundians and the English. Charles VII, the so-called king of Bourges, assembled 20 000 warriors there, personally commanding them for a time.

Sancerre became a stronghold of Protestantism, withstanding the assault of royal forces. The Treaty of St-Germain (1570) and the St Bartholomew's Day Massacre (1572) had no effect on those who held to their reformed views of religion, and refused to give in.

So, on 3 January 1573, the Maréchal de La Châtre, accompanied by 7 000 men, laid siege to Sancerre. After an intense artillery preparation, an assault took place on three fronts, but the local resistance was strong.

Capitulation came after seven long months of struggle. The population's surrender was accepted with honour, and they were allowed the freedom of their religion.

Sancerre wine – "Wine," wrote Balzac in 1844 in *La Muse du Département*, "is the main industry and the most important trading item of this land, which produces many generous vintages of rich bouquet, so similar to those of Burgundy that an untrained Parisian palate cannot taste the difference. Sancerre wines are therefore popular in Parisian cabarets where they flow steadily, which is a good thing, as they cannot be kept more than seven or eight years."

Vineyards are planted on every hill where the sun shines. The Sancerre label is only applied to white Sauvignon wines, and to red and rosé wines made from the Pinot grape.

Old Town

Visitors will enjoy strolling in the old neighbourhoods, where many of the interesting houses and vestiges are marked with informative signs. There are many architectural details to attract the eye.

Esplanade de la Porte César★★

From this terrace, there is a great **view**★★ over the vineyards, St-Satur and the viaduct, St-Thibault and the Val de Loire, and even farther afield to the Puisaye region of woods and lakes, between the Loire and the Loing, north-east of Sancerre.

Tours des Fiefs

This 14C cylindrical keep is the only vestige of the château of the counts of Sancerre, a Huguenot citadel bitterly defended during the 1573 siege.

From the top, there is a wide **scenic view**★ of the Loire Valley and the hills of Sancerre.

ADDRESSES

⌂ STAY

⊜⊜ **Chambre d'hôte Château de Bel Air** – *Lieu-dit le Grand-Chemin, Arcay. 16km/10mi S of Bourges on the D 73.* ℘*02 48 25 36 72. 6rms.* Surrounded by spacious grounds, this 19C château is both calm and comfortable.

Hôtel Christina – *5 r. Halle.* ☎*02 48 70 56 50.* *71rms.* This hotel is the perfect base for discovering the city centre.

Hôtel les Tilleuls – *7 pl. Pyrotechnie.* ☎*02 48 20 49 04. Closed 26 Dec–3 Jan.* *39rms.* Situated in a quiet part of town. Children's play area in the garden. Solarium.

Best Western Hôtel d'Angleterre – *1 pl. des Quatre-Piliers.* ☎*02 48 24 68 51.* *30rms.* The city's former court of justice is located close to the Palais Jacques-Cœur.

ⵞ/ EAT

Le Bourbonnoux – *44 r. Bourbonnoux.* ☎*02 48 24 14 76. Closed Sun eve Nov–Jun, Sat lunch, Fri.* The restaurant is in a street lined with craft shops, just a few steps away from St-Étienne Cathedral.

Le Bistro Gourmand – *5 pl. de la Barre.* ☎*02 48 70 63 37. Reservations recommended.* A delightful bistro specialising in regional and Lyonnais cuisine.

La Courcillière – *r. de Babylone.* ☎*02 48 24 41 91. Closed Wed, Tue eve.* Located in the Les Marais district just a stone's throw from the city centre. Down-to-earth and reasonably priced cuisine.

D'Antan Sancerrois – *50 r. Bourbounnoux.* ☎*02 48 65 96 26. Closed Sun, Mon.* This pretty bistro used to be home to a 15C alderman who kept company with the Duchesse de Berry.

⵷ BARS / ⵞ CAFÉS

Pub des Jacobins – *Enclos des Jacobins.* ☎*02 48 24 61 78. Closed Sun.* This piano-bar is wholeheartedly devoted to jazz. Top-quality concerts are held here once a month.

Pub Jacques Cœur – *1 r. d'Auron.* ☎*02 48 70 72 88.* This 16C half-timbered residence, now a pub, was built on the site where Jacques Cœur, a wealthy and influential 15C merchant and councillor to King Charles VII, was born.

ⵗⵛ ENTERTAINMENT

Maison de la Culture de Bourges – *pl. André-Malraux.* ☎*02 48 67 74 70. www.mcbourges.com.* This lively and popular venue hosts plays, dance performances and classical music and jazz concerts.

Les Nuits Lumières de Bourges – ☎*02 48 23 02 60. Every eve in Jul-Aug and during the Printemps de Bourges festival.* A walk through the historic city centre at night to view illuminated buildings.

ⵜⵝ LEISURE ACTIVITIES

Base de Voile du Val-d'Auron – *23 chemin Grand Mazières.* ☎*02 48 20 07 65. Closed Oct–Apr and Mon.* This watersports centre at the Val d'Auron Lake offers swimming, canoeing, fishing, rowing, and more.

ⵉ SHOPPING

The main shopping area is in the pedestrianised zone that includes rue Coursarlor and rue Mirebeau (near the Palais Jacques-Cœur), and rue Bourbonnoux and rue Moyenne (near the cathedral).

Markets – Every Sat morning, the listed **Halle au Blé** comes to life with 200 stallholders selling all types of food. A permanent daily market is also held at the **Halle St-Bonnet**, selling fresh seasonal produce, local cheeses and other regional specialities.

La Maison des Forestines – *3 pl. Cujas.* ☎*02 48 24 00 24.* This chocolate/confectionery business founded in 1825 occupies an attractive Haussmann-style building.

Épicerie du Berry – *41 r. Moyenne (Îlot Victor-Hugo).* ☎*02 48 70 02 38.* This small boutique at the foot of the cathedral sells only regional products.

Limoges★

Limousin

A dynamic regional capital with a long history, and a great tradition of high-quality enamel, ceramics and porcelain, Limoges is a lively university town with a notable heritage, and a place synonymous with affluence and prosperity.

A BIT OF HISTORY

Limoges originated as a ford over the River Vienne at a meeting point of Roman highways, but remained a small provincial centre, specialising in ceramics, until the early 19C, when the manufacture of porcelain moved here from St-Yrieix where there were kaolin deposits but no workforce.

It became a prestigious industry, the town's name synonymous with the highest quality porcelain. The town was the birthplace of the Impressionist painter Auguste Renoir (1841–1919).

SIGHTS

Musée Municipal de l'Évêché – Musée de l'Émail★

pl. de la Cathédrale. ◔*Open daily except Tue 10am–noon, 2–5pm (Jun, 6pm; Jul–Aug, every day, 6pm).* ◔*Closed public holidays.* ☞*No charge.* ✆*05 55 45 98 10.*

The museum is housed in the former Bishops' Palace and features a stunning collection of some 300 *champlevé or cloisonné* enamels *(ground floor)* by Limoges masters. The palace gardens, **Jardins de l'Évêché★**, include a themed and a "wild" garden.

▸ **Population:** 142 425
◔ **Michelin Map:** 325 E 5-6
▪ **Info:** 12 bd Fleurus. ✆05 55 34 46 87. www.limoges-tourisme.com.
◑ **Location:** On the north bank of the River Vienne, Limoges is 125km/78.5mi SE of Poitiers, and 171km/107mi W of Clermont-Ferrand.
◔ **Don't Miss:** The Adrien-Dubouchée porcelain museum.
◔ **Timing:** A basic circuit of its principal sights will not consume more than half a day, but with attendant visits to its parks and ancient buildings, you need at least a whole day.

Musée Adrien-Dubouché★★

8 bis, pl. Winston Churchill. ◔*Open daily except Tue: 10am–12.25pm, 2–5.40pm.* ◔*Closed 1 Jan, Dec 25.* ☞€*4.50.* ✆*05 55 33 08 50.* www.musee-adriendubouche.fr.

This remarkable collection of international importance features items illustrating the evolution of pottery from ancient times to today, with many examples of the finest Limoges ware.

Ville and Cité

Early in its history, Limoges developed two rival centres, known as Cité and Ville (or Château). Overlooking the Vienne, **La Cité** is the historic core of Limoges.

Limoges Enamel

In the 12C Limoges became an important centre of production, partly due to the variety of minerals found in the area. The technique consists of crushing leadglass, coloured with metal oxides, applying it to a metal surface, then heating it to a temperature of up to 800°C/1 472°F, resulting in a crystalline effect. In the 12C Limoges specialised in *champlevé* enamels, in which the enamel is poured into grooves let into a copper surface, then polished level with the metal. In the 14C painted enamels made their appearance. In the reign of François I, Léonard Limosin was made Director, and enamels of great brilliance and colour were produced.

It spreads out around the **Cathédrale St-Étienne**★, which has a fine portal (**portail St-Jean**★) and which has kept its **rood screen**★ of 1533, now located at the west end of the nave. In the chancel are a number of **tombs**★.

The **Château** quarter, or Ville, serves as the modern centre of Limoges, with busy shopping streets. **St-Michel-des-Lions**★ is an old hall-church that has retained its original rectangular plan.

EXCURSIONS
Le Dorat★★

▶ *Le Dorat is in a rural location 58km/ 36mi N of Limoges.* 🛈*17 pl. de la Collégiale.* ℘*05 55 60 76 81.*

Le Dorat lies in the gently rolling countryside of the old province of Marche, whose patchwork of pastureland feeds the yellowish-fawn Limousin cattle bought and sold in the great market at **St-Yrieix-la-Perche**. The little town has a collegiate church of impressive size and harmonious proportions.

Collégiale St-Pierre★★

🕐*Open year-round daily.* 👣 *Guided tours Mon–Sat except public holidays 10am–noon, 2.30–6pm.* ℘*05 55 60 72 20.* 🎫*No charge.*

The great edifice was rebuilt in Romanesque style over a period of 50 years beginning in 1112. It is firmly rooted in its region by virtue of its siting, the coarse granite from which it is built, and by a number of characteristic Limousin features. These include the massive square west tower flanked by bell turrets, the portal with its scalloped archivolts, the openwork lantern (inspired by the one built 50 years earlier at St-Junien, but vastly more original), and the mouldings used in the arches and arcades through out the building.

Oradour-sur-Glane★★

▶ *The site is located 24km/15mi NW of Limoges.*

Access to the ruins of the martyred village is via the Centre de la Memoire. The centre offers a permanent exhibit dedicated to the rise of Nazism and the massacre of the villagers.

🕐*Open daily: Feb and Nov–mid-Dec 9am–5pm; Mar–mid-May and mid-Sept–Oct 9am–6pm; mid-May–mid-Sept 9am–7pm.* 🎫*€8.* ℘*05 55 43 04 30 www.oradour.org.*

🔍*Don't miss the Centre de la Mémoire, at the entrance to the ruined village.*

Scene of a horrific massacre, Oradour was chosen by the Germans for its very innocence and insignificance in order to terrorise ordinary French people.

This small country town where the 642 inhabitants were massacred in a revenge attack by retreating Germans on 10 June 1944 is preserved unchanged as a fascinating and deeply moving memorial. The stark walls of the burnt-out village have been kept as a sombre reminder. Harassed by the Resistance, the troops made a characteristically brutal example of this entirely innocent place, massacring its inhabitants (men, women and children), and laying waste the village itself. The victims are buried in the village cemetery; a memorial commemorates the terrible deed. Only six escaped.

Solignac★★

▶ *Solignac is 10km/6.2mi S of Limoges.* 🛈*pl. Georges Dubreuil.* ℘*05 55 00 42 31.*

The 12C abbey church, robust and harmonious, has multiple domes. As well as being among the last of their kind to be built in Aquitaine, these are some of the finest examples to be seen in the region. There is an extraordinarily deformed dome over the choir and one of ovoid shape covering the north transept.

Eglise Abbatiale★★

Founded in 632 by St Eligius and rebuilt around 1175, the abbey church shows Limoges influence in its use of granite, but its domes are based on the ones at Souillac in Quercy.

From the steps of the porch, there is a view of the interior, beautifully proportioned. Among the last of their kind, the pointed arches and pendentives are some of the finest examples in the region.

ADDRESSES

🏨 STAY

🛏 **Hôtel de la Paix** – *25 pl. Jourdan.*
℘05 55 34 36 00. 31rms. This Napoleon III
-style hotel in the heart of the city features
an entertaining phonographic collection.
Bright and airy bedrooms, some with
wicker furnishings.

🛏🛏🛏 **Hôtel Jeanne-d'Arc** – *17 ave du
Gén.-de-Gaulle. ℘05 55 77 67 77.
www.hoteljeannedarc-limoges.fr.
Closed 21 Dec–8 Jan. 50rms. ☕€8.*
This pleasant, well-located hotel is close
to the city's famous train station. The
well-mantained bedrooms and pleasant
breakfast room have managed to retain
their old French charm.

🍴 EAT

🍽🍽 **Le Bœuf à la Mode** –
*60 r. François-Chenieux. ℘05 55 77 73 95.
www.leboeuf-alamode.com. Closed Sat
lunch, Sun and public holidays.* If you love
meat, then this is definitely the place for
you! Excellent cuisine served in a friendly
and traditional ambience.

🍽🍽 **Chez Alphonse** – *5 pl. de la Motte.
℘05 55 34 34 14. Closed Mon eve, Sun and
public holidays.* Tucked away behind the
halles, this bistro is a popular local haunt.
Tables are decorated with chequered
tablecloths and a menu is written up on
the blackboard.

🍽🍽 **L'Escapade du Gourmet** – *5 r. des
71ème-Mobiles. ℘05 55 32 40 26. Closed Sat
lunch, Sun and Mon.* A Belle-Époque décor
of wood, frescoes, moulded ceilings and
coloured glass is the backdrop to this
popular traditional restaurant located
between the château and the Cité
Episcopale. Classical French cuisine.
Good value for money.

🍽🍽 **Le Pont St-Étienne** – *8 pl. de
Compostelle. ℘05 55 30 52 54. Reservations
required at weekends.* Attractive bay
windows with views of the old stone
bridge and the river. The à la carte menu
features a number of imaginatively named
dishes. Summer terrace.

🍽🍽 **Les Petits Ventres** – *20 r. de la
Boucherie. ℘05 55 34 22 90. Closed Sun and
Mon.* Classic, high-quality French cuisine
is to the fore in these two typical 15C
houses, run by two enthusiastic owners.
Traditional dishes based on liver, tongue,
pig's trotters, tripe, etc.

🍷 BARS / 🍸CAFÉS

Brasserie Artisanale St Martial –
8 pl. Denis-Dussoubs. ℘05 55 79 37 98. This
brewery (in the true sense of the term)
perpetuates an old local tradition. Beer has
been brewed in the region since the 18C;
in the 19C there were no fewer than 50
brewers in the Limoges area.

**Café des Anciennes Majorettes de la
Baule** – *27 r. Haute-Vienne. ℘05 55 34
34 16. Closed Mon, and mid-Jul–mid-Aug.*
This renowned local bar is the venue for
regular concerts and plays.

L'Irlandais – *2 r. Haute-Cité. ℘05 55 32 46
47.* This lively Irish pub is jointly run by a
fisherman from Brittany who has travelled
the world and established a bakery and a
pub in Ireland, and by a concert violinist
who has played in royal circles. Over
recent years they've hosted jazz, Celtic
music and other concerts here.

🛒 SHOPPING

Most of the city's shops are located
in the area around the castle.
The main boutiques selling porcelain
are along boulevard Louis-Blanc and
along the streets heading west from
the city centre.

Le Pavillon de la Porcelaine –
*Av. du Prés.-John-Kennedy – ℘05 55 30 21 86.
www.haviland-limoges.com.* Factory
outlet of Haviland, makers of prestigious
porcelain sets. A wide choice of tableware
on sale.

Buissières – *27 r. Jean-Jaurès. ℘05 55 34
10 44.* At this chic confectioner's, the Art
Deco décor is almost worth a visit on its
own. Chocolates, pastries and desserts,
including the house speciality black
chocolate with chestnut cream.

Périgueux★★

Dordogne

Périgueux is an ancient town built in the fertile valley of the River Isle. Its long history can be traced in its urban architecture and two distinctive districts, each of which is marked by the domes of its sanctuary: the Cité district, overlooked by St Stephen's tiled roof, and the Puy St-Front district, with the Byzantine silhouette of the present cathedral bristling with pinnacles. There is a good overall view of the town from the bridge beyond Cours Fénelon to the southeast. Périgueux's gastronomic specialities, with truffle and foie gras occupying prize position, have become famous around the world and attract many visitors.

A BIT OF HISTORY

Five distinct historical periods have contributed to the formation of this ancient town.

First was the Gaulish settlement which prospered in Roman times under the name of Vesunna; its site, the "Cité", is marked by the amphitheatre gardens and St Stephen's Church (St-Étienne).

In the Middle Ages, the quarter known as "Puy St-Front" became established on a rise to the north; the cathedral was built here and the area became the heart of Périgueux, eventually, in 1251, absorbing the older Cité.

In the 18C, the provincial governors, the Intendants, were responsible for a planned northward extension of the city, which linked the two districts by means of broad streets lined with public buildings. At the end of the 19C, the station area was developed, and more recently vast modern suburbs have grown up on the outskirts.

SIGHTS

St-Étienne-de-la-Cité★

Two of the domes of the original sanctuary have survived. The earlier is thought to have been built in 1117.

▶ **Population:** 30 458
Ⓒ **Michelin Map:** 329 F 4
🔲 **Info:** 26 pl. Francheville, Tour Mataguerre. ℘05 53 53 10 63. www.tourisme-perigueux.fr.
◉ **Location:** Périgueux is 93km/60mi SW of Limoges.
🅿 **Parking:** Underground car parks at pl. Montaigne, pl. Francheville and espl. du Théâtre.

The second dome, half a century later, is altogether lighter.

Cathédrale St-Front★

Of the original early Romanesque church there remain only two small octagonal domes at the eastern end of the nave. The church was an important stopping-place for pilgrims on their way to Santiago de Compostela since it was here that the remains of St Front, the apostle of Périgord, could be seen. His tomb dates from 1077.

The cathedral was virtually rebuilt from 1852 onwards by Abadie, the architect who designed the Sacré-Cœur in Paris.

St-Front District★★★

The old artisans' and merchants' district has been given a face-lift. A conservation programme for safeguarding this historic area was set up, and the area has been undergoing major restoration. Its Renaissance façades, medieval houses, courtyards, staircases and shops are gradually being brought back to life; the pedestrian streets have rediscovered their role as commercial thoroughfares. Place du Coderc and place de l'Hôtel-de-Ville are colourful and animated every morning with their fruit and vegetable market, whereas place de la Clautre is where the larger Wednesday and Saturday markets are held.

During the winter, the prestigious truffle and foie gras markets held in place St-Louis attract hordes of connoisseurs.

Domes and turrets of Cathédrale St-Front and view towards St-Front District

© Christophe Boisvieux/age fotostock

Vesunna – Musée Gallo-Romain de Périgueux

🕐 *Open daily Jul–Aug, 10am–7pm; Apr–Jun and Sept, Tue–Fri 9.30am–5.30pm, Sat–Sun and public holidays, 10am–12.30pm, 2.30–6pm; Oct–Mar, Tue–Fri 9.30am–12.30pm, 1.30–5pm, Sat–Sun, 10am–12.30pm, 2.30–6pm.* 🕐 *Closed 2 wks in Jan.* ✆€6. 🖉05 53 53 00 92. www.vesunna.fr.

Designed by Jean Nouvel, this museum houses the remains of an opulent Gallo-Roman residence covering 4 000sq m/ 4 784sq yd. Built in the centre of a garden, it is like a large glassed-in inner courtyard reflecting the surroundings and blending perfectly with them. On one side, a mezzanine on two storeys overlooks the ancient *domus*. This section of the museum is devoted to the ancient town of Vesunna: a scale model of the town in the 2C shows how extensive it was in Roman times – the residence can easily be located near the sanctuary and the forum.

Wooden footbridges enable visitors to wander through the house. Digs have revealed the presence of a 1C building, considerably extended in the 2C. Elaborate murals can be seen on the base of the walls of the primitive house. The frieze surrounding the central pond, on the other hand, was painted when the house was extended. Along the way, the daily life of the inhabitants is illustrated: hypocaust heating system, decoration, water distribution (oak water pump) and various handicrafts.

EXCURSIONS
Brantôme★★

▶ *27km/17mi N of Périgueux on D 939.*
🛈 *Abbaye de Brantôme.* 🖉05 53 05 80 52. www.ville-brantome.fr.

Brantôme lies in the midst of lush countryside, in the charming Vallée de la Dronne, north of the town of Périgueux. Its old abbey and picturesque setting make it one of the most delightful little places in Périgord.

This riverside village has old dwellings with slate roofs built like manor houses, a crooked bridge seen across the tranquil surface of the water, and great trees growing on the lawns of its lovely gardens. The 18C abbey has a fine west front and a Romanesque **bell tower**★★.

Château de Hautefort★★

▶ *The castle is 41km/25.4mi E of Périgueux.* 👍🕐 *Open Sat–Sun and public holidays: Mar and Oct–mid-Nov 2–6pm; Apr–May 10am–12.30pm, 2–6.30pm; Jun–Aug 9.30am–7pm; Sept 10am–6pm.* 🕐 *Closed mid-Nov–Feb.* ✆€8.50. 🖉05 53 50 51 23. www.chateau-hautefort.com.

The elegant château rises up proudly on its hilltop site, overlooking its extensive and well-kept grounds. In the 16C, an

Château de Hautefort

ancient fortress was strengthened, and, a century later, reconstructed in Renaissance and Classical style. It has been further restored since a fire in 1968. The interior has fine Flemish tapestries saved from the flames, a 17C Felletin landscape, good pieces of furniture and unusual paved floors. The tower has magnificent **chestnut timberwork★★**.

ADDRESSES

STAY

⊜⊜ **Comfort Hôtel Régina** – *14 r. Denis-Papin (opposite the railway station). ℘05 53 08 40 44. 41rms.* It is easy to spot this hotel, thanks to its yellow façade. The rooms are small, functional and colourful.

⊜⊜ **Hôtel-Restaurant L'Écluse** – *at Antonne-et-Trigonant, 10km/6.2mi NE of Périgueux. ℘05 53 06 00 04. 43 rooms.* The River Isle flows gently past the hotel's small waterfront. Rooms on the main façade have balconies which overlook the river.

⅋/EAT

⊜ **Au Bien Bon** – *15 r. des Places. ℘05 53 09 69 91. Closed Sat lunch, Sun, Mon and public holidays.* The menu here is firmly influenced by seasonal local products.

⊜ **Au Temps de Vivre** – *10 r. St-Silain. ℘05 53 09 87 18. Closed eves (except summer 7–9.30pm), Sun and Mon. Reservations recommended.* Tucked away in a pleasant street in the old town, this restaurant serves daily specials, plus savoury and sweet pies.

⊜⊜ **Le Clos Saint-Front** – *5 r. de la Vertu. ℘05 53 46 78 58.* This old house, with its exposed beams, fireplace and Louis XVI furniture, is now home to an elegant restaurant which is resolutely devoted to Périgourdine cuisine with an inventive twist.

⊜⊜⊜ **Hercule Poireau** – *2 r. de la Nation. ℘05 53 08 90 76. Closed Sat–Sun.* In a vaulted 16C cellar, this place is popular with locals, who come here for the varied menu, which includes several healthy options.

🛒 SHOPPING

Le Relais des Caves – *44 r. du Prés.-Wilson. ℘05 53 09 75 00.* The friendly proprietor sells a wide selection of wines from across France, including a few very special vintages.

Stéphane Malard – *8 r. de la Sagesse. ℘05 53 08 75 10.* Behind the window arcades of his shop, Stéphane sells the region's finest delicacies, including confits, foies gras, duck magret and wines.

Markets – *pl. de Clautre: Wed and Sat morning; pl. de la Clautre* (food), *pl. Bugeaud and pl. Franche-Ville* (clothing)*; pl. du Coderc* (food); duck and goose products from Dec–Feb.

Sarlat-la-Canéda★★★

Dordogne

This attractive old Dordogne market town has narrow medieval streets lined with restored Gothic and Renaissance houses.

A BIT OF HISTORY

Sarlat is the capital of the Périgord Noir (Black Périgord) country, a fortunate and abundant region between the Dordogne and Vézère rivers.

The town grew up around the Benedictine abbey founded in the middle of the 9C. The wealth of the surrounding countryside poured into the town, enabling it to support a prosperous population of merchants, clerics and lawyers. Sarlat reached its peak during the 13C and 14C. The town long played host to fairs and markets, which still take place every Saturday, when the stalls are loaded with seasonal produce, poultry, cereals, horses, nuts, geese, foie gras, truffles and other goods.

OLD SARLAT★★★

Sarlat's old district was cut into two in the 19C by the Traverse (rue de la République).

The town houses are quite unique: built with quality ashlar-work in a fine golden-hued limestone, with interior courtyards; the roofing, made of heavy limestone slabs (*lauzes*), necessitated a steeply pitched framework so that the enormous weight (500kg per sq m – about 102lb per sq ft) could be supported on thick walls.

Over the years new floors were added: a medieval ground floor, a High Gothic or Renaissance upper floor and Classical roof cresting and lantern turrets.

This architectural unit escaped modern developments and was chosen as one of the new experimental national restoration projects, the goal of which was to preserve the old quarters of France's towns and cities. The project, begun in 1964, has allowed the charm of this small medieval town to be re-created.

▶ **Population:** 9 871
Michelin Map: 329 I 6
Info: r. Tourny. ☎05 53 31 45 45. www.sarlat.com.
Location: 64km/40m SE of Périgueux.
Parking: There are plenty of car parks; spaces also in the old town, except Sat.
Timing: It might be tempting to whizz around this lovely town in an hour or so. But allow at least half a day or more.
Don't Miss: Saturday market, which fills the town centre with a glorious array of local produce.

Cathédrale St-Sacerdos

St Sacerdos' Church was built here in the 12C. In 1504 Bishop Armand de Gontaut-Biron had the church razed, in order to build a cathedral. However, the bishop left Sarlat in 1519 and the construction work was not completed for more than a century.

Typical house in old Sarlat

J. Damase/MICHELIN

EXCURSIONS

Beynac-et-Cazenac★★

▶ *The castle and village are on the N bank of the Dordogne, 12km/7.4mi S of Sarlat.* ⏱*Open daily Jun–Sept 10am–6.30pm; Oct–Feb 10am–dusk; Dec–Feb noon–dusk.* ◉€7.50. ℘05 53 29 50 40. ⊛*As well as the château, the beautiful Renaissance village at the foot of the cliff is also worth visiting.*

One of the great castles of Périgord, **Château de Beynac** is famous for its history, its architecture and for its panoramic setting on top of a rugged rock face.

Defended on the north side by double walls, the castle looms over the river from a precipitous height of 150m/492ft. Crouching benath its cliff is a tiny village, once the home of poet Paul Eluard.

A square keep existed here as early as 1115; it was strengthened at the time of the great rivalry between the Capetians and the Plantagenets.

Domme★★

▶ *The village is S of the River Dordogne, 12km/7.4mi from Sarlat.* 🚩 *pl. de la Halle.* ℘05 53 31 71 00. www.ot-domme.com.

One of the many medieval fortified towns *(bastides)* founded in southwest France by both French and English, Domme was laid out by Philippe le Hardi (the Bold) in 1281. The normal rectangular plan of such settlements was here distorted in order to fit it to the rocky crag overlooking the Dordogne 145m/475.7ft below.

A Royal Bastide – Domme was founded by Philip the Bold in 1283 in order to keep watch on the Dordogne Valley and check the desire for expansion of the English established in Gascony. The king granted the town important privileges including that of minting coins and Domme played an important role during the Hundred Years' War. In the 17C, its wine-growing and river-trading activities were thriving and its markets were renowned throughout the region.

Panorama★★★

There are splendid views over the alluvial valley of the Dordogne from the Barre belvedere or, better still, from the cliff-top walk (Promenade des Falaises) just below the public gardens. All around is an opulent landscape of castles, well-wooded slopes dotted with stone-built villages, lush meadows, walnut trees and corn.

American writer Henry Miller described the area as perhaps the nearest thing to Paradise on Earth.

Les Eyzies-de-Tayac★★

▶ *The village is in the heart of the Dordogne region, 20km/12.4mi from Sarlat.* ⊛*The best of the many fascinating sites are Grotte de Font-de-Gaume, Grotte du Grand Roc and the Musée National de la Préhistoire. The sites are not all in the village – they are mostly spread along the Vézère Valley. It is rewarding to spend a full day in the area.*

The village occupies a grandiose setting of steep cliffs crowned with evergreen oak and juniper, at the confluence of two rivers.

In the base of the cliffs are caves that were prehistoric habitations, where the art and crafts of our distant ancestors can still be seen.

Grotte du Grand-Roc★★

Laugeri-basse, 24620 Les Eyzies de Tayac. ↝*Guided tours (30min) Apr–Oct 10am–6pm (Jul–Aug 9.30am–7pm).* ◉€7.50. ℘05 53 06 92 70.

The cave is set in a magnificent cliff overlooking the Vézère, and is renowned for its stalagmites and stalactites which display considerable variety.

Musée National de Préhistoire★

⏱*Open Oct–May daily except Tue 9.30am–12.30pm, 2–5.30pm; Jun and Sep daily except Tue 9.30am–6pm; Jul–Aug daily 9.30am–6.30pm.* ⏱*Closed 1 Jan and 25 Dec.* ◉€5. ℘05 53 06 45 65. www.musee-prehistoire-eyzies.fr.

Comprehensive displays of prehistoric artefacts in an old 13C fortress with good views.

Grotte de Font-de-Gaume ★

Just outside village on road to St-Cyprien; footpath to cave entrance. ◷*Open daily except Wed: Mar and Oct 9.30am–noon, 2–5.30pm; Apr–Sept 9am–noon, 2–6pm; Nov–Feb 10am–noon, 2–5pm.* ◷*Closed 1 Jan, 1 and 11 Nov, 25 Dec.* ◈*€5.50.* ℘*05 53 06 86 00.* ⊕*Advance booking essential; only 200 visitors allowed per day.*

Since its discovery in 1901, dozens of polychrome paintings have been found in the tunnel-like Grotte de Font-de-Gaume.

Abri de Laugerie-Haute

▶ *On D 47 where it turns away from the Vézère.* ⚭⚑*Guided tours by appointment; call for other opening times.* ◷*Closed public holidays.* ⓘ *Information at the Grotte de Font-de-Gaume.* ℘*05 53 06 86 00.*

Representing 7 000 years of civilisation, this rock shelter was used during the Upper Palaeolithic period as a workshop for flints.

Grotte de Lascaux

▶ *The cave is situated 2km/1.2mi S of the village of Montignac, and 26km/16mi S of Sarlat.* ◷*The actual Lascaux cave is closed to the public. However, a replica, known as Lascaux II, is open for visits at Montignac, just 200m away.* ℘*05 53 05 65 65.* www.lascaux.culture.fr.

The world-famous cave paintings of Lascaux were discovered by accident on 12 September 1940 by a young man looking for his dog, which had disappeared down a hole.

The Paintings – Most of the paintings in the cave appear to date from the end of the Aurignacian period, others from the Magdalenian. They cover the walls and roofs of the cave with a bestiary of bulls, cows, horses, deer and bison, depicted with such skill as to justify Abbot Breuil's epithet "the Sistine Chapel of prehistoric times".

Unfortunately, the damage caused by visitors was such that the caves were closed to the public and a full-size replica was constructed.

Bergerac★

▶ *49km/30.5mi S of Périgueux.* ⓘ *7 r. Neuve-d'Argenson, 24100 Bergerac.* ℘*05 53 57 03 11.* www.ville-bergerac.com.

Spread out on both banks of the Dordogne where the river tends to be calmer and the valley widens to form an alluvial plain, this distinctly southern town is surrounded by prestigious vineyards and fields of tobacco, cereals and maize. A project to restore the old quarter has seen the embellishment of a number of Bergerac's 15C and 16C houses.

Intellectual/commercial crossroads – The town's expansion began as early as the 12C. Benefiting from the town's situation as a port and bridging point, the local merchants profited from successful trade between the Auvergne and the Limousin and Bordeaux on the coast. This flourishing city and capital of the Périgord became one of the bastions of Protestantism as its printing presses published pamphlets which were widely distributed. In August 1577 the Peace of Bergerac was signed between the king of Navarre and the representatives of King Henri III; this was a preliminary to the Edict of Nantes (1598). Despite this, in 1620, Louis XIII's army took over the town and destroyed the ramparts. After the Revocation of the Edict of Nantes (1685), the Jesuits and Recollects tried to win back their Protestant disciples. A certain number of Bergerac citizens, faithful to their Calvinist beliefs, emigrated to Holland, a country where they had maintained commercial contacts. Bergerac was the capital of Périgord until the Revolution, when the regional capital was transferred to Périgueux, which also became Préfecture of the Dordogne *département*.

In the 19C, wine-growing and shipping prospered until the onslaught of phylloxera and arrival of the railway.

Bergerac today – Essentially an agricultural centre, Bergerac is the capital of tobacco in France and, as a result, the Experimental Institute of Tobacco and the Tobacco Planters Centre of Advanced and Refresher Training are located here. In addition, the 12 000ha/29 650 acres of vineyards surrounding the town produce wine with an *appellation d'origine contrôlée* (which means it is of an officially recognised vintage) including: Bergerac, Côtes de Bergerac, Monbazillac, Montravel and Pécharmant. The Regional Wine Council, which establishes the *appellation* of the wines, is located in the Recollects' Cloisters. The main industrial enterprise of the town is the powder factory producing nitro-cellulose for use in such industries as film-making, paint, varnish and plastics.

Famous citizens – Oddly enough, the Cyrano of Edmond Rostand's play was inspired by the 17C philosopher **Cyrano de Bergerac** whose name had nothing to do with the Périgord town. Not discouraged in the slightest, the townspeople took it upon themselves to adopt this wayward son and erect a statue in his honour in place de la Myrpe.

SIGHTS
Musée d'anthropologie du Tabac★★
pl. du Feu. ⚙️🕐*Open Tue–Fri 10am–noon, 2–6pm; Sat 10am–noon, 2–5pm; Sun 2.30–6.30pm (mid-Nov–mid-Mar Mon–Fri only).* 🕐*Closed public holidays.* ⊛€4 *(combined ticket with the Musée du Vin and the Musée Costi, €5).* ☎05 53 63 04 13.

This remarkable and beautifully presented collection, which includes satirical engravings, traces the history and evolution of tobacco through the centuries. On the **second floor** works of art depicting tobacco and smokers are displayed. *Two Smokers* from the 17C Northern French School, *Three Smokers* by Meissonier, and the charming *Interior of a smoke den* by Teniers the Younger, are among the works exhibited.

A section is devoted to the cultivation of tobacco (planting, harvesting, drying etc), with special reference to the Bergerac region.

Another room is set aside to display the techniques used to manufacture smoking accessories both in the past and throughout the world.

Musée Régional du Vin et de la Batellerie★
5 rue des Conférences. ⚙️🕐*Open Tue–Sun 10am–noon, 2–5.30pm, Sat 10am–noon, Sun 2.30–6.30pm (mid-Nov–mid-Apr, Mon–Fri only).* 🕐*Closed public holidays.* ⊛€3. ☎05 53 63 04 13.

This museum is located at the end of place de la Myrpe. On the first floor, the importance of barrel-making to the Bergerac economy is explained. The section on wine shows the evolution of the Bergerac vineyards over the centuries and the type of houses the wine-growers lived in. On the second floor there are models of the various kinds of river boats, *gabares*, flat-bottomed boats sometimes with sails.

Musée Donation Costi
pl. de la Petite Mission. ☎05 53 63 04 13. This third Bergerac museum was created thanks to the gift of the sculptor Constantin Papachristopoulos, whose work it displays.

Maison des Vins – Cloître des Récollets
🕐*Open all year (exc. Jan) mid–Jun to Aug, every day 10am–7pm; Sept–mid Jun, daily except Mon, 10.30am–1pm and 2–6pm.* ⊛*No charge.* ☎05 53 63 57 55.

The brick and stone cloister building was built on 12C foundations. The interior courtyard has a 16C Renaissance gallery beside an 18C gallery where exhibitions devoted to wine are staged.

There is a fine view of the Monbazillac vineyards from the sumptuously decorated great hall on the first floor.

The wine-testing laboratory includes the wine-tasting room *(open to visitors)*, where all the Bergerac wines are tasted annually to determine whether they are worthy of the *appellation d'origine contrôlée* – the AOC mark on the label.

The AOC system is a method of ensuring the quality of wine, and here one can learn how it works. The vineyards on the banks of the Dordogne cover 12 000 hectares/29 653 acres, producing wine for the 13 local appellations including Bergerac and Montravel.

Rocamadour★★★
Quercy

Clinging dramatically to the sheer cliffs of the gorge cut by the little River Alzou, the tiny medieval town of Rocamadour is one of the most visited places in the Dordogne. All around stretches the **Causse de Gramat**★, a vast limestone plateau, known as good sheep country and for its pâté de foie gras.

A BIT OF HISTORY

Long ago, Rocamadour was chosen by a hermit, Saint Amadour, as his place of retreat.

From the 12C onwards, and above all during the 13C, Rocamadour was one of the most popular places of pilgrimage in the whole of Christendom. Just as they do today, souvenir stalls tempted the throngs of tourists, among them Henry III of England, who is said to have experienced a miraculous cure here.

VISIT

A stairway with 216 steps leads to the Place St-Amadour (**or Parvis des églises**) around which are grouped seven sanctuaries, including the Chapel of Notre-Dame or Miraculous Chapel. The stream of pilgrims eventually dried up, unsurprisingly, in view of the

▶ **Population:** 698

♿ **Michelin Map:** 337 F 3

ℹ **Info:** The tourist office is at L'Hospitalet. ✆ 05 65 33 22 00. www.rocamadour.com.

▷ **Location:** 53km/33mi S of Brive-la-Gaillarde. You can enter Rocamadour only on foot, so park on the plateau and walk into town (or pay and take the elevator), or take the little train (fee). To reach Place St-Amadour (and the seven sanctuaries), take the stairway at Via Sancta or the elevator.

☺ **Don't Miss:** The view of Rocamadour from the Hospitalet belvedere *(2km/1.2mi NE)*, or from the Couzou road. The castle, rising 125m/410ft above the valley floor.

destruction which was caused by the great rock-fall of 1476 and completed by the Huguenots a century later.

In the 19C, the place was restored by the Bishops of Cahors in an attempt to revive the pilgrimages.

Rocamadour

© Lucio Pompeo/iStockphoto.com

EXCURSIONS
Gouffre de Padirac★★

▶ *The Gouffre lies about 2km/1.2mi from the village of Padirac, in the Lot département.*

Padirac Chasm (Gouffre de Padirac) provides access to wonderful galleries hollowed out of the limestone mass of the Gramat plateau (Causse de Gramat) by a subterranean river. A tour of this mysterious river and the vast caves adorned with limestone concretions leaves visitors with a striking impression of this fascinating phenomenon.

The chasm served as a refuge for the people living on the *causse* during the Hundred Years' War and the Wars of Religion, but it would appear that it was towards the end of the 19C, following a violent flooding of the river, that a practicable line of communication opened between the bottom of the well and the underground galleries.

The spelaeologist, **Edouard A Martel**, was the first to discover the passage, in 1892. He then undertook nine expeditions and finally reached the Hall of the Great Dome.

Padirac was opened to tourists for the first time in 1898. Since then, numerous spelaeological expeditions have uncovered 22km/13.6mi of underground galleries. The 1947 expedition proved by fluorescein colouring of the water that the Padirac River reappears above gound 11km/6.8mi away where the Lombard rises, and at St George's spring in the Montvalent Amphitheatre near the Dordogne.

During the expeditions of 1984 and 1985, a prehistoric site was discovered, with bones of mammoths, bison, bears and other animals, all found to date from between 150 000 and 200 000 years ago. Among the bones were chipped flints dating from between 30 000 and 50 000 years ago.

Thanks to the efforts of **Guy de Lavaur** (1903–86), the total known length of the subterranean network at Padirac rose from 2km/1.2mi to 15km/9.3mi.

Visit

Exhibited in the entrance hall are copies of some of the bones found in the prehistoric site.

The chasm is like a gigantic well of striking width and depth to the rubble cone formed by the collapse of the original roof. With its walls covered in vegetation and the overflow from stalagmites, it is one of the most atmospheric of France's underground domains.

The Grand Pilier, Grande Pendeloque of the Lac de la Pluie and the **Salle du Grand Dôme** are among the most striking of all natural monuments of the underground world.

The underground river flows beneath the surface of the plateau, to reappear on the surface near the natural amphitheatre at Montvalent on the Dordogne.

Souillac★

▶ *Along the N 20, 29km/18mi E of Sarlat-la-Canéda and 39km/24mi S of Brive-la-Gaillarde.*

🛈 *bd Louis Jean Malvy.* ☎ *05 65 37 81 56.* *www.tourisme-souillac.com.*

At the confluence of the Corrèze and the Dordogne, in the centre of a fertile region, Souillac is a small town bustling with trade and tourists.

After the Benedictines settled in the plain of Souillès (*souilh* meaning bog or marshland where wild boar wallow), they transformed the marsh into a rich estate. **Souillac Abbey** was plundered and sacked several times by the English during the Hundred Years' War and the Wars of Religion, but rose from its ruins each time thanks to the tenacity of its abbots. During the Revolution, its buildings were used for storing tobacco.

Abbey church
pl. de l'Abbaye

Dedicated to Mary, Mother of Christ, this became a parish church to replace the church of St Martin, destroyed during the Wars of Religion. Built in the 12C, the church is related to the Romanesque cathedrals of Angoulême, Périgueux and Cahors with their Byzantine inspiration, but it is more advanced in the lightness of its columns and the height of its arcades than the others. From place de l'Abbaye one can admire the attractive east end with its five pentagonal, apsidal chapels and an unusual tower on the other side of the building.

The disfigured bell tower, which is all that remains of the church of St Martin, is now the town hall belfry.

Musée National de l'Automate★

Open Apr–May and Oct daily except Mon 10am–noon, 3–6pm; Jun and Sept 10am–noon and 3–6pm; Jul–Aug 10am–7pm; Nov–Mar daily except Mon and Tue 2.30–5.30pm. €5.50 (children 5–12, €3).
05 65 37 07 07.

The museum contains some 3 000 objects, including 1 000 automata donated by the **Roullet-Decamps** family, who for four generations were leaders in the field. In 1865 Jean Roullet created his first mechanical toy: a small gardener pushing a wheelbarrow. Note especially the **Jazz band** (1920), a group of electric automata with black musicians performing a concert.

Beaulieu-sur-Dordogne★★

Beaulieu is in the Limousin region, some distance upriver from the popular Dordogne resorts.
pl. Marbot. 05 55 91 09 94.
http://otbeaulieu.free.fr.
Rising from the River Dordogne, picturesque Beaulieu has a fine church and former abbey.

Église St-Pierre★★

This is the church of a former Benedictine abbey. Its **doorway**★★, dating from 1125, has as its theme the opening stages of the Last Judgement, with the dead being summoned from their graves. The Treasury in the north transept houses a remarkable 12C Romanesque **figure of the Virgin**★ in a 13C shrine.

Collonges-la-Rouge★★

20km/12.4mi SE of Brive, in the Limousin region. Cars are not allowed in the village in summer. Use the car park by the old station.

Collonges-la-Rouge boasts mansions, old houses and a Romanesque church built of red sandstone; the surrounding countryside is dotted with nut orchards and vineyards. In the 13C the village was granted franchises and other privileges by the county of Turenne. In the 16C it became a holiday centre for county dignitaries who built charming mansions and residences flanked by towers and turrets.

The exclusive use of the traditional building stone and the balanced proportions of the various structures give a harmonious character to the town. Some are of special interest: the **Maison de la Sirène** with an elegant carved porch; the imposing mansion **Hôtel des Ramades de Friac**; the **Château de Benge**; and the elegant **Castel de Vassinhac**★.

Château de Bonaguil★★

54km/33.5mi W of Cahors.
Open Dec–Feb school holidays only 2–5pm; Mar–May and Oct daily 10am–12.30pm, 2–5.30pm; Jun and Sept daily 10am–12.30pm, 2–6pm; Jul–Aug daily 10am–7pm; Nov Sun and school holidays 10.30am–12.30pm, 2–5pm. Closed 25 Dec and 1 Jan. €7. 05 53 71 90 33.
www.bonaguil.org.
This majestic fortress on the border of Périgord Noir (Black Périgord, so-called because of its extensive woods) and Quercy, makes a stunning sight. It exemplifies the state of military architecture of the late 15C and the 16C.

The castle was enlarged in 1445 around the existing 13C keep, and further extended between 1482 and 1520. It is unusual in that underneath its old-fashioned appearance of a traditional stronghold it is actually remarkably well adapted to the new firearms then coming into use, and thus has loopholes for both cannon and muskets.

Furthermore, it was conceived not as an offensive establishment but as a place of refuge, able to withstand any attack, with its firearms used in a purely defensive role. In 1480–1520 this was something new, and it anticipated the concept of the fort.

Cahors★★

Quercy

Impressively sited on a promontory almost completely surrounded by a bend in the River Lot, Cahors enjoyed fame and fortune in the Middle Ages and is a pleasant country town today. Cahors is well known for its "black" wine.

SIGHTS

Pont Valentré★★

The city's merchants were responsible for building this superb six-arched stone bridge; its construction lasted from 1308 to 1378. Its fortifications are a reminder of the importance attached to the defence of Cahors by Philippe le Bel (the Fair), whose relationship with the city was based on an act of pariage (equality between a feudal lord and a town).

Cathédrale St-Étienne★

pl. Chapou.
The cathedral is one of the first of the domed churches of Aquitaine. The 13C **north door★★** shows Christ beginning to rise, while the angels are stilling the fears of the disciples.

✿ WALKING TOUR
Chapelle St-Gausbert

⏰*Open Sat 3–5pm or by prior arrangement. Contact the Tourist Office.* ☎*05 65 53 20 65.*
16C paintings in the style of the Italian Renaissance decorate the ceiling of this former chapterhouse, while 15C paintings representing the Last Judgement adorn the walls. The chapel also contains the Cathedral Treasury. Enter the inner court of the former arch-deaconry of St John through the door in the northeast corner of the cloisters.

▶ *On leaving the cathedral, follow rue Nationale past the covered market.*

Rue Nationale

This was the main thoroughfare of the active Badernes Quarter. At No 116, the panels of a lovely **17C door** are decorated with fruit and foliage. Across the way, the narrow **rue St-Priest** has kept its medieval appearance. It leads to place St-Priest which boasts a beautiful outside wooden staircase in Louis XIII style (No 18).

▶ *Turn right.*

Rue du Docteur-Bergounioux

At No 40 a 16C town house has an interesting Renaissance façade opened by windows influenced by the Italian Renaissance style.

▶ *Retrace your steps and continue straight on.*

Rue Lastié

Note the Rayonnant windows at No 35. At No 117, a 16C house has kept its small shop on the ground floor above which are twin bays. At the far end of the street, the pretty brick houses have been recently restored.

▶ *Turn left.*

Rue St-Urcisse

The late-12C church of St-Urcisse is entered through a 14C doorway. Inside, the two chancel pillars are decorated with elegant historiated capitals.

▶ **Population:** 21 157
⏱ **Michelin Map:** 337 E 5
ℹ **Info:** pl. Mittérrand. ☎05 65 53 20 65. www.tourisme-cahors.com.
▶ **Location:** 112km/70mi N of Toulouse via the D 820 or A 20.
🅿 **Parking:** Several car parks around the town centre.
🕐 **Timing:** Allow at least half a day to explore the town, and another day to visit the nearby villages and vistas of the Lot Valley. For a different perspective on the town, take a boat trip on the Lot.
👁 **Don't Miss:** Pont Valentré.

Note the 13C half-timbered house (No 68) with its *soleilho* (open attic), in which laundry was hung out to dry.

▷ *Turn right.*

Maison de Roaldès
The mansion is also known as Henri IV's Mansion because it is said that the king of Navarre stayed there during the siege of Cahors in 1580. The house dates from the end of the 15C and was restored in 1912. In the 17C it became the property of the Roaldès, a well-known Quercy family.

▷ *Turn back then right onto rue de la Chantrerie.*

La Daurade
This varied set of old residences around the Olivier-de-Magny square includes the Dolive House (17C), the Heretié House (14–16C) and the so-called Hangman's House (Maison du Bourreau), with windows decorated with small columns (13C).

▷ *Turn right then walk down the street on the right.*

Pont Cabessut
From the bridge there is a good **view**★ of the upper part of the city, the Soubirous district. The towers bristling in the distance are: Tower of the Hanged Men or St John's Tower, the bell tower of St-Bartholomew, John XXII's Tower, Royal Castle Tower and the Pélegry College Tower.

Tour du Collège Pélegry
The College was founded in 1368 and at first took in 13 poor university students; until the 18C, it was one of the town's most important establishments. The fine hexagonal tower above the main building was constructed in the 15C.

▷ *Follow the narrow lane to the left; it runs onto rue du Château du Roi. Turn right then right again past the prison.*

Tour du Château du Roi
Near Pélegry College stands what is today the prison and was once the governor's residence. Of the two towers and two main buildings erected in the 14C, the remaining massive tower is known as Château du Roi.

▷ *Return to the prison, follow the street opposite and turn right.*

Ilôt Fouillac
This area has undergone an extensive programme of redevelopment. By getting rid of the most run-down buildings, a square has been cleared. Its sides are decorated with **murals**, and it is brightened by a particularly interesting **musical fountain**.

▷*Turn right towards rue des Soubirous.*

Tour Jean-XXII
This tower is all that remains of the palace of Pierre Duène, brother of John XXII. It is 34m/112ft high and was originally covered in tiles. Twin windows pierce the walls on five storeys.

Église St-Barthélémy
This church was built in the highest part of the old town, and was known until the 13C as St-Etienne de Soubiroux, *Sancti Stephani de superioribus* (St Stephen of the Upper Quarter), in contrast to the cathedral built in the lower part of the town. The church was rebuilt to its present design in several stages. The belfry, the base of which dates from the 14C, has no spire, and it is built almost entirely of brick.
The nave, with its ogive vaulting, was designed in the Languedoc style. In the chapel nearest the entrance, on the left, a marble slab and bust call to mind that John XXII was baptised in this church. The cloisonné enamels on the cover of the modern baptismal font depict the main events in the life of this famous Cahors citizen.

▷ *Walk to boulevard Gambetta and head north.*

Barbican and Tour St-Jean★

The ramparts, constructed in the 14C, cut the isthmus formed by the meander of the River Lot completely off from the surrounding countryside.

Remains of these fortifications can still be seen and include a massive tower at the west end, which sheltered the powder magazine, and the old gateway of St-Michel, which now serves as entrance to the cemetery.

It is on the east side, however, where the N 20 road enters the town, that the two most impressive fortified buildings remain: the barbican and St John's Tower. The barbican is an elegant guard house which defended the Barre Gateway; St John's Tower ,or the Tower of the Hanged Men *(Tour des Pendus)*, was built on a rock overlooking the River Lot.

EXCURSIONS
Figeac★★

◯ *70km/43.5mi W of Cahors via D 653.*
🛈 *Hôtel de la Monnaie, pl. Vival, 46102 Figeac. ℘05 65 34 06 25. www.tourism-figeac.com.* 🅿 *Parking in centre.*

Sprawled along the north bank of the Célé, Figeac developed at the point where the Auvergne meets Upper Quercy. A commercial town, it had a prestigious past, as is shown in the architecture of its tall sandstone town houses.

Le Vieux Figeac★

The old quarter, surrounded by boulevards tracing the line of the former moats, has kept its medieval town plan with its narrow and tortuous alleys.

The buildings, of elegant beige sandstone, exemplify the architecture of the 13C, 14C and 15C. Generally the ground floor was opened by large pointed arches and the first floor had a gallery of arcaded bays. Underneath the flat tiled roof was the soleilho, an open attic, which was used to dry laundry, store wood, grow plants, etc. Its openings were separated by columns or pillars in wood or stone, sometimes even brick, which held up the roof. Other noticeable period architectural features to be discovered during your tour of the old quarter are: corbelled towers, doorways, spiral staircases and some of the top storeys, which are half-timbered and of brick.

Musée Champollion★

pl. Champollion. ◷*Open Apr–Sept daily except Mon 10.30am–12.30pm, 2–6pm (Jul–Aug daily 10.30am–6pm); Oct–Mar daily escept Mon 2–5.30pm.* ◷*Closed 1 Jan, 1 May, 25 Dec.* ⬤€4. ℘*05 65 50 31 08. www.ville-figeac.fr.*

Museum devoted to Jean-François Champollion. Permanent exhibits include hieroglyphs and letters written by Champollion to his brother. Learn how and why people started writing.

Prehistoric painting in Grotte du Pech-Merle

E. Larribere/MICHELIN

Grotte du Pech-Merle★★★

▶ *The cave is located 7km/4.3mi N of St. Cirq-Lapopie and 32km/19.8mi E of Cahors.*

🌤*Guided tours (1hr) Apr–Nov 9.30am –noon, 1.30–5pm. Tour limited to 700 visitors per day (reservations recommended 3 days in advance in Jul and Aug).* ⊕€8 (children, €4.50). ☎05 65 31 27 05. www.pechmerle.com.

Sited high above the River Célé just before it flows into the Lot, the Pech-Merle cave is one of the most fascinating in terms of prehistory and spelaeology.

On the lower level of the cave are **paintings** of a fish, two horses covered in coloured dots, and "negative hands" (made by stencilling around hands placed flat against the rock). Something like a three-dimensional effect is produced by the way in which the Late Perigordian artists integrated their work with the irregularities of the rock surface. There are also representations of bisons and mammoths, as well as petrified human footprints from the Early Magdalenian. The upper level has strange, disc-like concretions, "cave pearls", and eccentrics with protuberances defying the laws of gravity.

ADDRESSES

🏠 STAY

⊖**Chambre d'hôte le Clos des Dryades** – *46090 Vers. 19km/11.8mi NE of Cahors on the D 653, towards St-Cirq-Lapopie and the D 49 road to Cours.* ☎05 65 31 44 50. *5rms, 3 gîtes.* Nestled deep in the woods, this house with its tiled roof is the perfect place to get away from it all. The rooms are comfortable and the large swimming pool is a great place to cool off on a hot summer's day. Two self-catering cottages are also available.

⊖**Hôtel Les Chalets** – *46090 Vers, 14km/9mi E of Cahors on the D 653.* ☎05 65 31 40 83. *23rms.* This small modern hotel situated in an attractive leafy setting is particularly welcoming. The bedrooms, with balconies or small gardens, overlook the river.

⊖⊖**Hôtel A l'Escargot** – *5 bd Gambetta.* ☎05 65 35 07 66. *Closed Feb school hols, Dec and Sun out of season. 9rms.* Near the Tour Jean-XXII, this hotel occupies the old palace built by the pontiff's family. Functional bedrooms with colourful furnishings, plus a renovated breakfast room.

🍴 EAT

⊖⊖**Auberge du Vieux Douelle** – *46140 Douelle, 8km/5mi W of Cahors on the D 8.* ☎05 65 20 02 03. The dining room in the vaulted cellar of this popular inn, known locally as "Chez Malique", is decked out with bright red tablecloths.

⊖⊖**Le Dousil** – *124 r. Nationale.* ☎05 65 53 19 67. *Closed Sun and Mon.* This wine bar near the town's covered market offers an extensive list of over 100 vintages. The décor includes a traditional zinc counter and stone walls.

⊖⊖**La Garenne** – *In Saint-Henri, 7km/ 4.5mi N towards Brive.* ☎05 65 35 40 67. *Closed Mon eve and Tue eve (except Jul–Aug) and Wed.* This typically Quercy-style building once served as a stable. But the main attraction here is the delicious regional cuisine.

⊖⊖**Le Rendez-Vous** – *49 r. Clément-Marot.* ☎05 65 22 65 10. *Closed 28 Mar– 14 May, Sun and Mon. Reservations recommended.* Located close to the cathedral, Le Rendez-Vous has developed a reputation for modern cuisine.

🛒 SHOPPING

Market – A traditional market is held on Wednesday and Saturday mornings at **Place Chapou**, with farmers' stalls selling a range of local produce.

Les Délices du Valentré – *21 bd Léon-Gambetta.* ☎05 65 35 09 86. Try the *Coque de Cahors*, a *brioche* with candied citron and flavoured with orange water, and *Cabecou*, a chocolate sweet.

FRENCH ALPS

Stretching from the Mediterranean to Lac Léman (Lake Geneva), the French Alps display all the varieties of mountain scenery, from the tranquility of bare rock and eternal snow to the animation of densely settled valleys. Here, human habitat show close adaptation to natural conditions. Centuries of endurance and ingenuity have overcome formidable obstacles and brought all possible resources into play, not only settling valley floors, but pushing grazing and cultivation to its highest limits and developing widely varied local traditions of living and building.

Highlights

1 Sea of ice above Chamonix: **Mer de Glace** (p319)
2 High road through the Alps: **Route des Grandes Alpes** (p321)
3 Spectacular view of Grenoble from **Fort de la Bastille** (p329)
4 Natural fortress: **Massif du Vercors** (p331)
5 Europe's most spectacular gorge: **Grand Canyon du Verdon** (p333)

Geography – The north of the French Alps is marked by the great sweep of Lac Léman. To the south rise the Alps of Savoy, first the Chablais and Faucigny country and beyond that the famous peaks and glaciers around Mont Blanc. Westward lie other graceful stretches of water, Lake Annecy and Le Bourget Lake. An important communication route is formed by the Sub-Alpine Furrow, a broad and prosperous valley in which Grenoble sits, and the western rampart of the Alps is formed by a succession of massifs including the Vercors. Briançon is close to the Italian border and further south still the scene is often one of striking severity, bare rock rising from vegetation of Mediterranean character. Geologists divide the French Alps into four main areas: the **Préalpes**, or Alpine foothills, consisting almost entirely of limestone rocks formed during the Secondary Era, except in the Chablais area; the **Alpine trench**, a depression cut through marl, lying at the foot of the central massifs; the **central massifs**, consisting of very old and extremely hard crystalline rocks.

The tectonic upheavals of the Tertiary Era folded the ancient landmass, creating "needles" and high peaks, which are the highest of the whole Alpine range. From north to south, these massifs are: the Mont Blanc, Belledonne, Grandes Rousses, Écrins and Mercantour; the **intra-Alpine zone**, forming the axis of the Alps. It consists of sedimentary rocks transformed and folded by the violent upheavals which took place in the area. It includes the Vanoise, the Briançonnais

Cycling in the Gorges de la Bourne, parc naturel régional du Vercors

© Franck Guiziou/hemis.fr

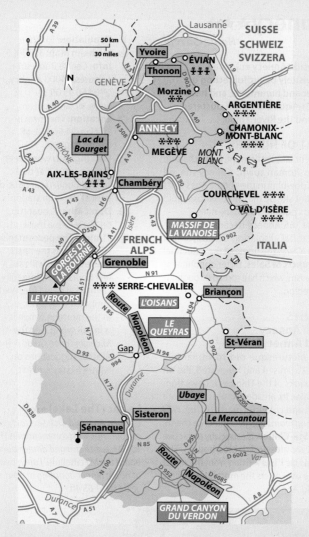

and the Queyras as well as the upper valleys of the Tarentaise, the Maurienne and the Ubaye.

History – The Alps have been inhabited since the Stone Age, but it was the Romans who first made an impact on the region as they sought to control the trade routes through the mountains. After the Romans the area was subject to Barbarian invasions before eventually becoming the County of Savoy which, during the 15C, was integrated with Piedmont and became the Duchy of Savoy.

Economy – Traditionally the Alps were an area of cattle rearing, and observed the traditional summer practices of transhumance, when man and beast would head into the high mountain pastures, returning just before the onset of winter. Now year-round tourism is of major importance, with many activities available in summer as well as the traditional winter sports such as skiing and snow-boarding.

The French Alps contain a number of National and Regional Parks where flora and fauna abound amid a landscape of considerable beauty.

Annecy★★★
Haute-Savoie

Lakeside Annecy enjoys an exquisitely beautiful setting of water and mountains, and has a picturesque old centre clustered around the River Thiou.

A BIT OF HISTORY
Ancient lake settlement, then a hillside Gallo-Roman town, Annecy moved back downhill in the Middle Ages to its present site by the Thiou, whose rapid waters powered its many mills.

In the 16C Annecy became the regional capital, displacing Geneva, and in the 17C was the home of the influential **St Francis of Sales**, bitter opponent of Calvinism, which had spread throughout the region.

SIGHTS
Vieil Annecy (Old Annecy)★★
The picturesque old town, largely pedestrianised and renovated, lies on the banks of the Thiou as it flows from the lake. Its arcaded houses, Italianate wells and colourful markets *(Tue, Wed and Sun mornings)* give immense charm. **Rue Ste-Claire**★ is especially attractive with arcades and gabled houses. The **Palais de l'Isle**★ rising from the midst of the river offers the most famous view of Old Annecy.

▶ **Population:** 51 970

⌾ **Michelin Map:** 328 J-K 5

▤ **Info:** Centre Bonlieu,1 r. J.-Jaurès, 74000 Annecy. ℘04 50 45 00 33. www.lac-annecy.com.

◖ **Location:** The town is 39.4km/24.5mi NE of Lac du Bourget.

🅿 **Parking:** You won't need the car; leave it at the central Bonlieu car park, or park at the train station.

⬟ **Don't Miss:** A boat trip on the lake is a must.

◷ **Timing:** The pedestrianised Old Annecy is the heart of the city, and will take a few hours to explore fully. On market days (Tue, Wed, Sun), visit Old Annecy in the morning, when it is in full swing. See the *Michelin Green Guide French Alps* for suggestions on where to stay and eat.

Le Lac (The Lake)★★★
◷*Open Apr–mid-Oct: several types of boat trips with commentaries (1hr).* ⬤€13. *Lunch trip and dinner-dance on board the MS Libellule. Lunch boarding at noon; dinner boarding at 8pm.* ℘04 50 51 08 40.

Lac Annecy at Talloires

© Pierre Jacques/hemis.fr

www.annecy-croisieres.com.

A road runs around the edge of this lovely lake, giving wonderful views. Fine vista from the **Avenue d'Albigny**, in Annecy. There are several pleasant small resorts on the lakeside, notably **Talloires**★★★, overlooking the narrows dividing the Grand Lac to the north from the Petit Lac to the south.

ADDITIONAL SIGHTS
Musée-Château d'Annecy★

○*Open Jun–Sept daily 10.30am–6pm; Oct–May, daily except Tue 10am–noon, 2-5pm.* ○*Closed public holidays.* €*5.50.* 04 50 33 87 34.

This handsomely restored former residence of the lords of Geneva, from a junior branch of the House of Savoie, dates from the 12C to the 16C. The castle was damaged by fire several times, abandoned in the 17C, then used as a garrison before being restored with the help of public funds.

To the right of the entrance stands the massive 12C Tour de la Reine, with 4m/13ft-thick walls; this is the oldest part of the castle. From the centre of the courtyard, you face the austere living quarters of the Logis Vieux (14–15C), with its stair turret and deep well; to the left is the early Renaissance façade of the Logis Nemours (16C) and to the right the late-16C **Logis Neuf**, which housed the garrison of the castle.

At the end of the courtyard are the 15C Logis and **Tour Perrière**, which house the **Observatoire régional des lacs alpins**, illustrating the various aspects of mountain lakes including the effects of pollution on the fauna and displaying archaeological finds.

The Logis Vieux and the Logis Nemours house an interesting **museum of regional art** on three floors linked by a spiral staircase. Note the remarkable fireplaces facing each other in the vast kitchen, the splendid guardroom with its rows of columns, and the great hall. There are collections of art, carved glass and popular art including pottery, earthenware, glassware and furniture.

Conservatoire d'Art et d'Histoire de la Haute-Savoie

○*Open Jun–Sept daily 10am–6pm; rest of year,Mon–Fri 10am–noon, 2–5pm.* ○*Closed public holidays.* *No charge.* 04 50 51 02 33.

This art and history museum, situated just south of the castle, is housed in a fine 17C building, extended in the 19C. The collections include numerous paintings and engravings depicting landscapes of Haute-Savoie, as well as 18C and 19C paintings.

In the chapel, the Cité de l'image en mouvement (CITIA) has an **exhibit of animated films**; for more than 20 years Annecy has hosted an annual festival of animation. ○*Open Jun–Sept daily 10.30am–6pm; rest of year daily except Tue 10am–noon, 2–5pm.*

Jardins de l'Europe★

At the time of the annexation of Savoie to France, these gardens were laid out as an arboretum with species from Europe, America and Asia. You can admire several huge **sequoias** and a ginkgo biloba, also called "maidenhair tree". From the banks of the Thiou, the embarkation point for the lake cruisers, you can look up to the massive castle buildings.

Musée Paccard★

214 rte du Piron, Sevrier (5km/3mi S). ○*Open Mon–Sat 10am–12.30pm, 2.30–6.30pm (Sun and public holidays 2.30–6.30pm) (Oct–May closes noon and 5.30pm).* €*5 (children 6–18 years* €*3.50).* 04 50 52 47 11.

This museum was created by the **Paccard bell-foundry**, which has made bells for almost two centuries. It explains the manufacturing process and traces the history of this ancient craft through a collection of bells dating from the 14C to the 19C.

You can also learn about the history of two very large bells that were made in Annecy : the *Savoyarde* in Montmartre's Sacré-Cœur in Paris (1891) and the *Jeanne d'Arc* in Rouen Cathedral.

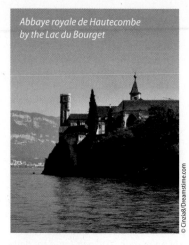

Abbaye royale de Hautecombe by the Lac du Bourget

© Cinzia8/Dreamstime.com

EXCURSIONS
Lac du Bourget★★

▶ *The lake is 39km/24.5mi SW of Annecy. The ideal base for a tour of the lake is Aix-les-Bains, a famous resort with lively streets, opulent hotels near the spa baths, and an attractive lakeshore.*

🛈 *pl. Maurice Mollard, Aix-les-Bains. ℘04 79 88 68 00.www.bourgetdulac.com.*

Enclosed within an impressive mountain setting, this is France's largest, deepest and most celebrated natural lake, lying in a glaciated valley between the Jura and the Alps. On its eastern shore is the elegant spa town of Aix-les-Bains. The lake is best seen from La Chambotte a little further north.

The lake and its banks form a rich and unusual habitat for wildlife. In its waters live around 50 species of fish, including pollans, migratory members of the salmon family, and crayfish. Its varied birdlife includes 300 or so cormorants which winter on the west bank at La Grande Cale.

The poet Lamartine (1790–1867) wrote movingly about the beauty of the lake, and of Mme Lulie Charles Julie whom he met here in October 1816. The popular spa Aix-les-Bains is one of the best-equipped resorts in the Alps, and has been known for its health-giving waters for over 2 000 years. Queen Victoria visited here three times.

Abbaye royale de Hautecombe★★

On the west bank of the lake. ⏱*Open Wed–Mon 10am-–1.15am, 2–5pm. ℘04 79 54 58 80.*

Jutting into the lake, the abbey (founded 1125) houses the tombs of 42 princely members of the House of Savoy. The abbey's little harbour has an unusual 12C building **(grange batelière)** with covered moorings, allowing goods to be unloaded and stored under the same roof.

Chambéry★★

▶ *10km/6.2mi S of Lac du Bourget.*
🛈 *24 bd de la Colonne. ℘04 79 33 42 47. www.chambery-tourisme.com.*
✍*Don't miss the many fascinating trompe-l'œil decorations around the town.*

The well-restored old centre recaptures something of Chambéry's past splendour as the capital of Savoy.

Château de Chambéry

This fortress was occupied by the counts of Savoy in 1285, who expanded it during the 14C to serve as their residence and seat of administration.

The **Sainte-Chapelle**★, adjoined to the château, displays Flamboyant Gothic architecture (👁*guided tours (1hr) daily; ☞€4; ℘04 79 70 15 94*).

Musée Savoisien★

sq. Lannoy de Bissy. ⏱*Open Wed–Mon 10am–noon, 2–6pm.* ⏱*Closed public holidays.* ☞*€3.50 (no charge 1st Sun of the month). ℘04 79 33 44 48.*

The museum houses interesting exhibits of prehistory, religious art and regional ethnography.

Fontaine des Éléphants (Elephants' Fountain)
r. de Boigne.

This famous – and originally disliked – landmark was erected in 1838. The shape of the Savoyan cross is achieved by the truncation in a column of the forelimbs of four elephants.

Aix-les-Bains ♨♨♨

Aix-les-Bains lies at the foot of Mont Revard, on the eastern shore of Lac du Bourget. Follow A 41 and A 43, 10km/6.25mi from Chambéry.

pl. Maurice-Mollard, 73100 Aix-les-Bains. ℘04 79 88 68 00. www.aixles bains.com.

The town-hall car park is located at the heart of the town, near spas, gardens and pedestrian malls.

After touring the town, stop by the Faure museum for the bronze sculptures by Rodin.

This well-known spa, which specialises in the treatment of rheumatism and respiratory ailments, is also one of the best-appointed tourist centres in the Alps, with lively streets, splendid palace hotels near the baths and attractive lake shores.

Taking the waters: a fashionable pastime – Aix's health-giving waters have been famous for almost 2 000 years. The Romans excelled in the art of hydropathy and the baths were at once a social club, a casino and a fitness club. The name of the town comes from *Aquae Gratianae*, "the waters of Emperor Gratianus".

During the Middle Ages, the baths were severely neglected. Taking the waters became fashionable again in the 16C, but the first real establishment dating from the 18C was only equipped with showers.

The treatment offered became more sophisticated in the 19C with the introduction of the steam bath and shower-massage, a technique brought back from Egypt by Napoleon's doctors.

The splendour of Aix-les-Bains at the turn of the century – The expansion of the spa town, which began in 1860, reached its peak during the Belle Époque. Luxury hotels were built in order to attract the aristocracy and the crowned heads of Europe: the "Victoria", for instance, welcomed Queen Victoria on three occasions, whereas the Splendide and the Excelsior counted among their guests a maharajah from India, the Emperor of Brazil and Empress Elizabeth ("Sissi") of Austria-Hungary. Most of the buildings in the spa town were designed by an architect from Lyon, Jules Pin the Elder (1850–1934), whose masterpiece was undoubtedly the Château de la Roche du Roi. After WWII, most of these magnificent hotels closed down for economic reasons.

THE SPA TOWN

The life of the spa town is concentrated round the baths, the municipal park with its vast open-air theatre, the Palais de Savoie and the new casino, as well as along the lake with its beach and marinas. Rue de Genève, rue du Casino and adjacent streets form the shopping centre of the town.

THE ROMAN TOWN★
Arc de Campanus

Erected by a member of the "Pompeia" family, this arch stood 9m/30ft high in the centre of the Roman town. The remains of the **Roman baths** can only give a rough idea of their former splendour (24 different kinds of marble were used to decorate them).

Temple de Diane

This remarkable rectangular Roman monument has its stones set in place without mortar. Note the classic Italianate façade on the former **Grand Hôtel** (1853) on the corner.

Musée Faure★

&. *Open daily 10am–noon, 1.30–6pm. Closed Tue, public holidays and 22 Dec–3 Jan. €4. ℘04 79 61 06 57.*
In 1942, Dr Faure bequeathed to the town a rare collection of paintings and sculptures including a large number of works by the Impressionists and their predecessors.

Thermes nationaux and caves

Open May–Oct. Guided tours (1hr) daily at 3pm, except Sun and Mon. Closed public holidays. €4. ℘04 79 35 38 50.
Inaugurated in 1783, renovated and enlarged during the 19C, the baths were completed by the Nouveaux Thermes in 1934, and modernised in 1972; these are open to visitors.

Évian-les-Bains ⚓⚓⚓

Haute-Savoie

Poetically known as the "pearl of Lake Geneva", Évian is remarkably well situated between the lake and the foothills of the Préalpes du Chablais. The resort town, renowned for its old palaces and thermal spas, climbs up from the flat lake area like an amphitheatre, with steep little roads parting in every direction. You can enjoy splendid architecture, walks or simply lazy evenings by the lake, and the town makes a fine base to explore the Chablais.

▶ **Population:** 8 366

⏱ **Michelin Map:** 328 M2

ℹ **Info:** pl. de la Porte d'Allinges, 74500 Évian-les-Bains. ☎04 50 75 04 26. www.ville-evian.fr.

▶ **Location:** Évian-les-Bains is about 45min from exit 15 of A 40, or 10km/6.25mi from Thonon-les-Bains.

✦ **Don't Miss:** A boat ride on Lake Geneva is a delightful experience. The amazing panorama from the Pic de Mémise.

👪 **Kids:** The Pré-Curieux is both fun and educational.

🕐 **Timing:** You can spend quite a few hours strolling along the waterfront.

THE LAKESIDE★

The most enjoyable walk in Évian. Firstly, because of the rare trees that border the lake, along with lawns and pretty flowerbeds. Next, because it is here that you will find the important buildings of the **palais Lumière**, the **villa Lumière**, today's town hall, and the **casino**.

All along the promenade up to the pleasure port Les Mouettes, the water in **musical fountains** plays in time to the music. Behind you, appearing through the chestnut groves of Neuvecelles, are the grand hotels, stacked up on the lower slopes of the Gavot.

Église Notre-Dame-de-l'Assomption

Typical of early Gothic art in Savoie (end of 13C), the church has been rebuilt and restored frequently. A few columns survive from the original construction.

Villa Lumière (hôtel de ville)

Once owned by Antoine Lumière, father of the cinema pioneer, this grand 1896 villa now houses the town hall; the ground-floor rooms and the **grand staircase**★ are especially elegant, while the next-door **theatre** is a splendid relic of 19C excess.

Also on the lakeside, on the same site as the château de Blonay, willed to the town in 1877, are the **casino,** built in 1911 by the same architect as for the **buvette Cachat**, and the **palais Lumière**, a thermal spa until 1984 when it was converted to a cultural centre.

Buvette Cachat (Information Centre about Évian water)

🕐*Open mid Jun–mid-Sept daily 10.30am–12.30pm, 3–7pm; mid-May–mid-Jun and end Sept Mon–Sat 2.30–6.30pm.* 👛 *Free.* ♿ ☎*04 50 26 93 23.*
The centre is housed in the former pump room (1905) of the **Cachat spring**, an Art Nouveau building surmounted by a cupola. The spring is named after its owner, who improved the installations in 1824.

Parc Thermal

The new baths are situated in the **Parc thermal**. The pump room, designed by Maurice Novarina, was erected in 1956, and the Espace Thermal in 1983. This is partly built below ground in order to preserve the appearance of the park.

Jardin Anglais

Beyond the harbour where yachts find a mooring and where the lake's pleasure boats come alongside, the Jardin anglais offers a view of the Swiss shore.

Yvoire by Lac Léman

© Gérard Labriet/Photononstop

Le Pré Curieux Water Gardens★

♿👤🚻🅿🚤*May–Sept Wed–Sun (Jul–Aug, daily) at 10am, 13.45pm and 3.30pm.* 💶*1€0 (children €8).* 📞*04 50 70 15 44.* *www.precurieux.com.*

This pretty garden demonstrates the rich variety of marshland ecosystems. You reach the elegant, colonial-style villa on a solar-powered boat.

EXCURSIONS

The nearby town of **Amphion-les-Bains** (4km/2.5mi to the west) was the first spa resort of the Chablais region, which became fashionable as early as the 17C, when the Dukes of Savoie regularly took the waters.

The medicinal properties of Évian water were discovered in 1789, when a gentleman from Auvergne realised it was dissolving his kidney stones. The water, filtered by sand of glacial origin, is cold (11.6°C/52.8°F) and low in minerals.

As well as for drinking it is prized for its beneficial effects on kidney disorders and rheumatism.

You can visit the very modern **bottling factory** (*Guided tour (1hr30) by appointment at the Évian information centre.* 📞*04 50 84 86 54*), which produces an average of 5 million litres of water per day, the highest output of any producer.

Yvoire★★

▶*26km/16mi W along the shore from Évian-les-Bains.* 🏚*Place de la Mairie.* 📞*04 50 72 80 21.*

This picturesque village, bedecked with flowers, has retained its medieval character. It enjoys a magnificent site on the shores of Lake Geneva (Lac Léman), at the tip of a headland separating the Petit Lac and the Grand Lac.

Village Médiéval (Old Town)★

🚷*Pedestrian access only.*

Rebuilt in the 14C on the site of a former fortress, Yvoire has kept part of its original ramparts, including two gates protected by towers and its castle (🔒 *closed to the public*) with a massive square keep framed by turrets. The bustling streets lined with old houses and craft shops lead to delightful squares decked with flowers which afford fine views of the lake.

Jardin des Cinq-Sens★

Le Labyrinthe. ♿🕐*Open Sat–Sun and public holidays all year, 10am–7pm, and Mon–Fri Apr–May and Sept 11am–6pm; Jul–Aug 10am–7pm; Oct 11am–5pm.* 💶*€10.* 📞*04 50 72 88 80.* *www.jardin5sens.net.*

The former kitchen garden of the castle has been turned into a reconstruction of a medieval enclosed garden, situated in the centre of Yvoire's Old Town.

Chamonix-Mont-Blanc★★★

Haute-Savoie

Chamonix lies at the foot of the famous 3 000m/9 842ft Chamonix Needles (Aiguilles de Chamonix) at a point where the glacial valley of the Arve widens out. All around are the high mountains of the Mont Blanc Massif. This is the most renowned of the massifs of the French Alps because of its dramatic relief, crystalline rocks and glacial morphology. The top of the great White Mountain is just visible from the town.

▶ **Population:** 9 359
⚲ **Michelin Map:** 328 M-O 5
🛈 **Info:** 85 pl. du Triangle de l'Amitié. 𝄞04 50 53 00 24. www.chamonix.com.
▶ **Location:** Chamonix is 101km/63mi E of Annecy.
🕐 **Timing:** You can wander aimlessly for hours, although there are really only two main streets.
👁 **Don't miss:** A ride up the Aiguille du Midi and to Montenvers, but be sure to check the weather in advance. See the *Michelin Green Guide French Alps* for suggestions on where to stay and eat.

RESORT

Already the mountaineering capital thanks to its Compagnie des Guides, Chamonix has also become one of the best-equipped ski resorts in the Alps. The development of the town as a skiing destination began when the first Winter Olympic Games were held here in 1924. Today, the Chamonix Valley offers a mixture of architectural styles and incessant traffic throughout the high season. Hardly beautiful in itself, its main attraction lies in its magnificent landscapes, lively atmosphere and numerous opportunities to practise sports and enjoy cultural events.

Rue du Dr-Paccard, extended by rue Joseph-Vallot, is the town's main artery. The short rue de l'Église, perpendicular to it, leads to the church at the heart of the old town and to the **Maison de la Montagne**, which houses the offices of the Compagnie des Guides.

In the opposite direction, avenue Michel-Croz leads past the **statue** of Docteur Michel Gabriel Paccard to the station and the newer districts of Chamonix lying on the left bank of the Arve. A **bronze sculpture** by Salmson, depicting the naturalist Horace Bénédict de Saussure (1740–99) and the mountain guide Jacques Balmat (1762–1834) admiring Mont Blanc, decorates the widened Pont de Cour.

Musée Alpin

89 avenue Michel-Croz. ♿🕐*Open daily 2-7pm (school holidays 10am-noon, 2-7pm).* 🕐*Closed mid- to end May.* 🎫*€6 (ticket gives free access to Espace Tairraz).* 𝄞04 50 53 25 93.

This museum illustrates the history of the Chamonix Valley, daily life in the 19C, the conquest of Alpine summits, scientific experiments and early skiing in the valley.

Espace Tairraz

Rocade du Dr. Payot 🕐*Open Jan-Jun 2–7pm (school holidays 10am–noon, 2–7pm).* 🎫*6€ (entrance to Musée Alpin gives free admission to Espace Tairraz).* 𝄞04 50 55 53 93.

The space is shared between the 👥 **Musée des Cristaux**, with remarkable examples of crystal from Mont Blanc and around the world, and temporary exhibits about the regional heritage.

SIGHT

The tongue of the Glacier des Bossons hangs 500m/1 650ft above the valley on the approach to Chamonix. The Geneva naturalist **Horace Benedict de Saussure** based himself here in the course of his scientific studies in Savoy. In 1760, he offered a reward for the first ascent of

Mer de Glace and the Montenvers Railway

© Pierre Jacques/hemis.fr

Mont Blanc. On 8 August 1786, Dr Michel Paccard and Jacques Balmat reached the summit, thereby inaugurating the age of mountaineering, as well as the development of the town as an Alpine resort.

EXCURSIONS

Aiguille du Midi ★★★

Cable car: *Runs daily subject to weather conditions: see website for more specific details: http://www. compagniedumontblanc.fr/pages/ excursion_schedules.html.*
Trip in two stages: Chamonix–Plan de l'Aiguille and Plan de l'Aiguille–Aiguille du Midi. ⊗€42.50 round-trip.
The **panorama**★★★, especially from the central peak (3 842m/12 605ft), is staggering, taking in Mont Blanc, Mont Maudit, the Grandes Jorasses, and the dome of the Goûter whose buttresses are buried in 30m/100ft of ice.
The **Vallée Blanche**, also known as the Giant's Glacier (Glacier du Géant), can be reached by taking the cable-car *(téléférique)* to Pointe Helbronner. From here can be seen the glacial cirques with their flanks worn down by the incessant attacks of the ice.

Mer de Glace ★★★

Montenvers train: *Runs daily subject to weather conditions.* ⊗€25 *includes train, cable car and visit to the ice grotto.*
The view from the upper station of the railway built in 1908 takes in the whole of this "sea of ice". The glacier is

7km/4.3mi long, in places 200m/656ft thick, and moves 90m/295.2ft a year.
The rocky material it carries with it scores and scratches the mountain walls on either side as well as giving the glacier its characteristic rather grimy appearance (as the ice evaporates grit is left on the surface). At the foot of the glacier this material is deposited, forming a terminal moraine.
Beyond, the eye is led from one peak to another; this **panorama**★★★ is one of the most beautiful in the region.

Argentière ✳✳✳

▶ *8km/5mi northeast of Chamonix.*
Contact 24 Route du Village, 74400 Argentière. ℘04 50 54 02 14.
www.chamonix.com.
At 1 252m/4 108ft, Argentière is the highest resort in the Chamonix Valley; with its annexes of Montroc-le-Planet and Le Tour, it forms an excellent holiday and mountaineering centre offering a wide choice of expeditions to the Massif du Mont Blanc and Massif des Aiguilles Rouges. The slopes of the upper Arve Valley provide pleasant walks through a fringe of larch woods.
A legend in the French Alps, **Armand Charlet** (1900–75), a native of Argentière, was held to be the king of mountain guides until the early 1960s. He set a record, which has never been equalled, by climbing the Aiguille Verte more than 100 times.

Aiguille des Grands-Montets★★ 🚠

Access by the Lognan and Grands-Montets cable cars. 📞*04 50 54 00 71. www.compagniedumontblanc.com. About 2hr30min return.*

The **panorama**★★★ is breathtaking. The view extends to the Argentière Glacier over which tower the Aiguille du Chardonnet and Aiguille d'Argentière to the north, Mont Dolent to the east, Aiguille Verte and Les Drus to the south, with the Aiguille du Midi, Mont Blanc and Dôme du Goûter further away.

Col de Balme★★ 🚠

Access all year round by the **Col de Balme** *gondola.* 📞*04 50 54 00 58. www.compagniedumontblanc.com. Allow 10min to walk from the lift to the pass.*

The **view**★★ extends northeast to the Swiss Alps and southwest to the Chamonix Valley surrounded by the Aiguille Verte, Mont Blanc and the Aiguilles Rouges massif.

CHAMONIX VIEWPOINTS BY CABLE CAR
Aiguille du Midi★★★ 🚠

Minimum 2hr return.

The Aiguille du Midi cable car, suspended part of the time 500m/1 640ft above ground, and the gondola form the most thrilling attraction in the French Alps.

Plan de l'Aiguille★★ 🚠

This midway stop, situated at the foot of the jagged Aiguilles de Chamonix, is the starting point for walks. Good view of the upper parts of the Mont Blanc massif.

Le Brévent★★★ 🚠

Minimum 1hr30 min return by gondola (to Planpraz, 20 min) then by cable car (Planpraz–Brévent 20 min).

Planpraz★★ relay station offers a splendid view of the Aiguilles de Chamonix and an excellent lunch. From Le Brévent, the **panorama** extends over the French side of the Mont Blanc massif.

La Flégère★ 🚠

Cable car Les Praz–La Flegère (15min) plus l'Index chair lift (20min).

From Les Praz, there is an impressive **view** of the Aiguille Verte and the Grandes Jorasses summits closing off the Mer de Glace depression.

Les Houches

▶ *Les Houches is 6km/3.75mi south of Chamonix on D 213.*

🗓 *BP 9, 74310, Les Houches.*
📞*0450 55 50 62. www.leshouches.com.*

The view of the massif from this resort at the foot of Mont Blanc is spectacular. Les Houches has extended across the widest and sunniest part of the Chamonix Valley, while still keeping its village character. Even if the setting is not on a par with Chamonix, Les Houches is a pleasant family resort; well equipped and ideal for skiers who prefer not to take on the steeper, high-altitude slopes.

Ski area 🎿🚡

The resort offers skiers a wide range of difficulties in the Lachat, Bellevue and Prarion areas, and 110 snow cannon are on standby to make good any lack of snow. The famous "green run" (black in fact!) requires a high level of skill. There are, in addition, some 30km/18.6mi of cross-country skiing trails.

Bellevue★★

1hr there and back including a 15min cable-car ride.

🚶 It is possible to continue up to the Nid d'Aigle (*Glacier de Bionnassay*) and go back down via St-Gervais on board the Tramway du Mont Blanc.

The Nid d'Aigle★★ (Glacier de Bionnassay)

Allow 3hr there and back by the Tramway du Mont Blanc (🕐see above). This journey provides a good introduction to high-altitude mountain landscapes by opening up the wild setting of the Bionnassay Glacier stretched out at the foot of the Aiguilles de Bionnassay (*spectacular avalanches*) and of the Aiguille du Goûter. **View** of the massifs surrounding the Bassin de Sallanches.

Route des Grandes Alpes★★★

Among the many routes inviting visitors to explore the French Alps, this high-altitude road is the most famous. Rarely far from the frontier, the Great Alpine Road links Lake Geneva with the Riviera, crossing mountain passes as it leaps from valley to valley. The route is open from end to end during the summer months only.

- ⌖ **Michelin Map:** 332, 334, 340 and 341
- ▣ **Info:** Association Grande Traversée des Alpes, 14 r. de la République, Grenoble. ℘04 76 42 08 31. www.grande-traversee-alpes.com.
- ◖ **Location:** From Thonon-le-Bains to Menton, across 25 mountain passes.

🚗 DRIVING TOUR

◖ *734km/458mi.*

Thonon-les-Bains★★

From the Place du Château the view extends over the great sweep of **Lake Geneva (Lac Léman**★★★**)**. On the Swiss shore to the north rise the terraces of the great Lavaux vineyard, and beyond are the mountains of the Vaudois Alps (to the east) and the Jura. Saint Francis of Sales once preached in St Hippoly-tus' Church (Église St-Hippolyte); its vault **(voûte**★**)** has retained its original stucco and 18 painted medallions, together with the stucco decoration of

Port of Rives and Château de Rives

© Nicolas Thibaut/Photononstop

its false pillars (visible from the adjoining basilica), all done by the Italian crafts-men who restored the interior in Rococo style in the 18C.

The road rises in a series of steps through the damp beech woodland of the gorges cut by the River Dranse de Morzine. This marks the transition between the gen-tly rolling hill country fringing the great lake and the **Chablais**★★ massif, a com-plex of high ridges and peaks, with rich pastures grazed by Abondance cattle. The most spectacular part of the route is known as the **Gorges du Pont du Diable**★★, marked by a number of rock-falls, one of which has formed the bridge attributed to the Evil One.

Morzine★★

◖ *33km/20.5mi SE of Thonon*

The valleys around the resort are dot-ted with hamlets; the chalets have patterned balconies. All around grow sombre forests of spruce.

After the pass at Les Gets, the small industrial town of Tanninges marks the beginning of the **Faucigny**★★ country. Drained by the Giffre, this is a landscape of pastures and sprucewoods, fashioned by the action of glacial moraines on cal-careous rocks deposited here far from their point of origin.

Cluses

◖ *29km/18mi SW of Morzine.*

The town commands the most impor-tant lateral valley *(cluse)* in the French Alps. The River Arve has cut down directly through the folded rocks of the **Aravis** range to make its gorge. Clocks and watches and precision metal products are made here.

The upland Sallanches basin is bounded to the north by the dramatic peaks of a number of ranges, but dominating all is the great mass of Mont Blanc itself, the "Giant of the Alps".

La Clusaz★★

⊙ 44km/27.3mi SW of Cluses.

The most important ski resort in the **Massif des Aravis** owes its name to the deep gorge, or cluse, downstream of it, through which the Nom torrent gushes. The village, situated in the middle of pine forests and mountain pasture, is tightly huddled around the big church characterised by its onion-dome tower. The jagged outlines of the Aravis mountains can be seen in the distance.

In the summer, La Clusaz offers excellent walking, and in winter plenty of thrills for ski enthusiasts.

Two-Day Programme

By driving hard it is indeed possible to get from Thonon to Menton in two days, but to do so would be to deprive yourself of a number of sights that in themselves would make the trip worthwhile. They include Chamonix with the Aiguille du Midi and the Vallée Blanche, La Grave and the splendid viewpoint at Le Chazelet, St-Véran.

Five-Day Programme

Thonon–Beaufort
144km/89.4mi –allow 5hr30min including sightseeing.
Beaufort–Val d'Isère
71km/44mi – allow 3hr including sightseeing.
Val d'Isère–Briançon
180km/111.8mi – allow 7hr30min including sightseeing.
Briançon–Barcelonnette
133km/82.6mi – allow 6hr30min including sightseeing.
Barcelonnette–Menton
206km/128mi – allow 6hr including sightseeing.

At the top of the climb out of the valley, Val d'Arly, the Notre-Dame de Bellecombe road gives good views, first of the whole Aravis massif, then of the wooded gorges cut by the Arly.

Col des Saisies

⊙ 18km/11mi SE of La Clusaz.

At this point the route leaves the Sub-Alpine Furrow *(Sillon alpin)*; from here as far as St-Martin-d'Entraunes to the south of the Cayolle Pass *(Col de Cayolle)*, its course lies entirely within the High Alps *(Grandes Alpes)*.

The broad depression of the **Saisies Pass**, 1 633m/5 357ft high, is one of the most characteristic Alpine grazing grounds to be seen along the route; it is browsed by sturdy little reddish-brown cattle as well as by the dark-brown Tarines breed and the white-spotted Abondances. The landscape is studded with innumerable chalets.

Beaufort

⊙ 18km/11mi SE of Col des Saisies.

This little crossroads town (its church has fine woodcarvings and interesting sculptures) has given its name to the **Beaufortain★★** country, an area of folded limestone beds on a base of ancient crystalline rocks. Virtually continuous forest cover forms a background to sweeping alpine past-ures. Above the 1 450m/4 757ft contour, the pastoral economy is marked by the seasonal movement of the herds up and down the slopes. The village of **Boudin★** *(7km/4.3mi S)* is particularly picturesque.

Cormet de Roselend★

⊙ 20km/12.4mi SE of Beaufort.

This long valley, 1 900m/6 200ft high, links the Roselend and Chapieux valleys. It is a vast, treeless, lonely place, dotted with rocks and a few shepherds' huts.

A rushing mountain stream descends the steep valley, **Vallée des Chapieux★**, in a series of abrupt steps towards **Bourg-St-Maurice**. This strategically sited town commands the routes coming down from the Beaufortain country and the Little St Bernard (Petit-St-Bernard) and Iseran passes. Around it is the **Tarentaise**★★ country of the upper Isère Valley where transhumance is still practised. By the time the route reaches Ste-Foy in the upper Tarentaise, the landscape has become more mountainous in character. The Tignes Valley (Val de Tignes) is characterised by gorges and glacial bars; the avalanche protection works are impressive, as is the **Tignes Dam**★★, a major engineering feat of the 1950s.

Val d'Isère★★★

◗ *50km/31mi SE of Cormet de Roselend*
In its high valley, 1 000m/3 281ft above Bourg-St-Maurice, this is the most important town in the upper Tarentaise. With an excellent sunshine record, the resort is surrounded by splendid mountain landscapes; to the south and west are the glaciers and peaks (several rising to more than 3 500m/11 483ft) of the Vanoise National Park, much favoured by walkers.

As the road climbs amid the crystalline massifs, it gives views of the imposing peaks of the Gran Paradiso in Italy to the left and of the Vanoise massif (Grande Motte peak) to the right.

Col d'Iseran★

◗ *16km/10mi SE of Val d'Isère.*
2 770m/9 088ft. The road across this high pass is the only link between the Tarentaise and the **Maurienne** country to the south which centres on the long

valley of the River Arc. Industry is more important here than agriculture. The location of settlements has been determined by the sharp breaks in slope marked by glacial bars.

Modane

◗ *55.5km/34.5mi SW of Col d'Iseran.*
This is a border town at the French end of rail and road tunnels into Italy. At Valloire, the route once more enters the ancient Hercynian mountains and begins to climb towards the Galibier Pass.

Col du Galibier★★★

◗ *52km/32.3mi SW of Modane.*
2 642m/8 668ft. From the viewing table there is a superb panorama which takes in the Maurienne country (to the north), and the Pelvoux region (to the south), which is separated from the Briançonnais country by the high ridge of the Massif des Écrins. The pass marks the dividing line between the northern and southern part of the French Alps.
At the pass, **Col du Lautaret**★★, with its fine views of the Meije mountains, turn right in the direction of La Grave in the Romanche Valley, then turn left at the entrance to the second tunnel.

Oratoire du Chazelet★★★

◗ *23km/14.3mi W of Col du Galibier.*
From the viewing table, the view extends over the high peaks of the Écrins

Val-d'Isère

National Park from the Col des Ruillans on the right to the broken ridges of the Meije (including le Doigt de Dieu). The upper course of the glacier, fed by frequent snowfall, is of a staggering whiteness.

La Grave★

⊙ *5km/3mi E of Oratoire du Chazelet.*

The village has a particularly fine **site**★★ in the Romanche Valley at the foot of the Meije. A two-stage cable-car ride takes the visitor to the col on the western flank of Mont du Râteau, from where there are unforgettable views over the Meije and the Écrins glaciers.

Back at the Col du Lauteret, the route now enters the southern part of the French Alps. At Monêtier in the Guisanne Valley, it re-enters the sedimentary zone of the High Alps; oak, beech and ash reappear, the valleys open out and the whole landscape takes on a lighter air.

Briançon★★

⊙ *38km/23.6mi SE of La Grave.*
⊙ *See BRIANÇON*

Col d'Izoard★★

⊙ *14km/8.7mi SE of Briançon.*
2 361m/7 746ft.

The pass is in a desolate setting fringed by dramatic peaks. From the viewing tables magnificent views extend over the Briançonnais to the north and the Queyras country to the south.

The road descends in a series of hairpin bends through a strange landscape of screes and jagged rocks known as the **Casse Déserte**★★.

At this high altitude, the processes of erosion are greatly accelerated by the extremes of temperature to which the rocks are exposed.

The high **Queyras**★★ country is centred on the valley of the River Guil.

Closed off downstream from the outside world by a series of narrow gorges, and cut off from main communication routes, it has fine examples of Alpine houses. Above Château-Queyras, the valley sides are sharply differentiated; the gentler south-facing slopes are covered with well-watered meadows, while the north-facing slopes grow only larches and Arolla pines.

Saint-Véran★★

⊙ *34km/21mi SE of Col d'Izoard.*

Lying between the 1 990m/6 528ft contour and the 2 040m/6 693ft contour, this is the highest village in France and the third highest in Europe. Its chalets, timber-built on a basement of schist, are a unique example of adaptation to the rigours of a high-altitude mountain life which combines arable cultivation and grazing, forestry, and the exercise of craft skills during the long winters. The south-facing dwellings are sited in groups, most with hay-barns and balconies on which cereals are ripened.

Saint-Véran

The village has a strange sculpture showing Christ's Agony. The little town of **Guillestre**, with its church characterised by a beautiful **porch**★, is situated at the end of the **Combe du Queyras**★★, a canyon carved out by the clear waters of the Guil.

Embrun★

▷ *51km/31.6mi SE of Saint-Véran.*

High up on its terrace overlooking the River Durance as it emerges from the mountains, the little town was once the seat of an archbishop. From the Place de l'Archevêché there are fine views over the valley slopes with their well-cultivated terraced fields. The torrents entering the main valley have spread their debris over its floor in alluvial fans. The upper slopes are gouged by deep ravines, while dominating the scene are sombre high mountain crests.

The former **Notre-Dame Cathedral**, the finest church in the whole of the Dauphiné Alps, dates from the 12C. It has fine black-and-white marble stonework, and the **north porch**★ is supported on pretty pink columns.

Col de Vars

▷ *38.5km/24mi E via N 94/D 902.*

2 111m/6 893ft. This pass forms the gateway to the Ubaye Valley. The valley floor, littered with boulders and studded with ponds, is grazed by sheep.

Beyond the pass, the south-facing slopes with their scattered hamlets are given over to stock-farming. In its upper reaches, the River Ubaye has cut deeply into the dark schists. Near La Condamine, the 19C Fort Tournoux seems part of the high rock on which it is built. After Jausiers, the route enters the Barcelonnette basin; the valley pastures are interspersed with woodland and the scene becomes more cheerful.

Barcelonnette★

▷ *31km/19mi SW of Col de Vars.*

The little capital of the Ubaye district was laid out as a bastide on a regular plan in 1231 by Raimond Béranger, Count of Barcelona. It belonged to the House of Savoy until passing to France

under the provisions of the Treaty of Utrecht in 1713. On the edge of town are the houses of the "Barcelonnettes" or "Mexicans", locals who made their fortunes in the textile trade in Mexico before returning home. A museum, **Musée de la Vallée**, traces the history of the migrations.

The road climbs around the flank of Mont Pelat, the highest (3 035m/10 164ft) peak in the Provence Alps.

Col de la Cayolle★★

▷ *30km/18.6mi SE of Barcelonnette.*

2 327m/7 635ft. This pass links the Ubaye country and the Upper Verdon to the upper reaches of the Var. From the top there are views over the deep valley of the Var towards the Grasse Pre-Alps in the far distance.

THE UPPER VALLEY OF THE RIVER VAR★★

The source of the Var is on the left as the road drops away from the pass to follow the river through the sombre mountains.

At **St-Martin-d'Entraunes** the route passes from the High Alps into the sedimentary zone, the Pre-Alps of **Provence**. Downstream from **Villeneuve d'Entraunes** water coursing through drainage channels draws attention to the changes that take place in the landscape of the countryside around **Guillaumes**.

Gorges de Daluis★★

▷ *3.5km/2mi S of Guillaumes.*

These deep gorges have been cut by the river into thick beds of red porphyry and Urgonian limestone, giving striking colour effects. The road from **Guillaumes** to **Beuil** leads to the **Gorges du Cians** in the upper stretch of the River Var.

The road climbs steadily to the **Col de Valberg** offering views of the different sides of the valley: woody to the north, compared to the southern one covered with vineyards and fruit trees. The descent towards **Roubion** from the **Col de Couilloie** (1 678m/5 503ft) reveals the valleys of **La Vionèse** and **La Tinée**.

After the impressive **site**★★ of **Roubion** (the village is perched 1 300m/4 264ft up on a ridge), the road travels through a red schistose landscape, enlivened by several waterfalls.

Roure★

 12.4km/7.7mi E of Roubion.

This village is characterised by its architectural unity: houses with red schist walls and limestone tile roofs *(lauze)*. The route then follows the River Vionèse until it flows into the River Tinée at **St-Sauveur-sur-Tinée**. Outside the village, on the left, a small road leads to the striking **site**★ of **Ramplas**, a village built on a ridge.

La Bolline

 22km/13.7mi SE of Roure via D 2205/D 2265.

This pleasant summer resort is situated in the middle of a chestnut grove.

La Colmiane

 8km/5mi E of La Bolline.

The chalets and hotels of this winter sports resort are set amidst a wonderful larch forest. From the **Col de St-Martin**, there is a possibility of taking a chairlift up to the **Pic de Colmiane**★★ (beautiful **panorama**★★ from the top).

St-Martin-Vésubie★

 8.4km/5.2mi E of La Colmiane.

A Baroque church and channelled stream flowing down the Rue du Docteur-Cagnoli characterise this famous mountaineering centre from which visitors can go rambling in the **Vallon du Boréon**★★ or the **Vallon de la Madone de Fenestre**★.

La Bollène-Vésubie

 16km/10mi SE of St-Martin-Vésubie.

The concentric streets of this peaceful village, in the middle of a beautiful chestnut grove, converge on the church, which crowns the hill. The forest, **Fôret de Turini**★★, which spreads across the valleys of the Vésubie and the Bévéra, demarcates the southern border of the Parc national du Mercantour.

Le Massif de l'Authion★★

 32.5km/20.2mi SE of La Bollène-Vésubie.

North of the **Col de Turini**, this massif constitutes a wonderful natural fortress which seems to stand guard over the roads between the Vésubie and Roya valleys. This strategic value has caused it to be, throughout the centuries, the stage for several conflicts. In April 1945, it was the last sector of France to be liberated. A stele commemorates the fierceness of the combat.

After crossing the forest of Turini, the river Bévéra winds its way towards the **Gorges du Piaon**★★ where the corniche road overlooks the river. Before reaching the gorges, the road goes through **Moulinet**, a charming village set in a verdant valley before passing the **Chapelle de Notre-Dame-La-Menour** with its Renaissance façade on the left.

Sospel★

 28.6km/17.7mi SE of Le Massif de l'Authion.

This Alpine resort was a bishopric during the Great Schism and a stop on the Salt Road linking Turin with the coast. Old houses line both banks of the Bévéra which is traversed by an ancient fortified bridge.

On the Nice road, 1km/0.6mi from the centre of the village stands the **Fort St-Roch**, one of the last elements of the "Alpine Maginot line" built in the 1930s. The road follows the old railway line which used to link Sospel to Menton, along the course of the Merlanson, a tributary of the Bévéra. On the opposite side of the valley, the road to Nice via the **Col de Braus** winds its way, amidst olive groves, towards the capital of the French Riviera.

Menton★★

 21km/13mi SE of Sospel.

 See MENTON

Courchevel★★★
Savoie

Courchevel is undoubtedly one of the major and most prestigious winter sports resorts in the world. Founded in 1946 by the Conseil général de la Savoie (regional council), it played a leading role in the development of the **Trois Vallées**※※※ complex.

Émile Allais, who was the downhill world champion in 1937, was the first to introduce to French resorts the idea of grooming ski runs. Après-ski activities are just as exciting: art exhibitions, classical and jazz concerts, an impressive number of luxury shops, sports centres, fitness clubs and famous nightclubs. However, Courchevel also owes its reputation to the quality of its hotels and gastronomic restaurants, unrivalled in mountain areas. Even in summer, when Courchevel changes radically and becomes a peaceful resort, this diversity sets it apart.

THE RESORTS

The Trois Vallées 🚡🎿, comprising Courchevel, Méribel, Les Menuires, Val Thorens and several smaller resorts, is the largest linked ski resort in the world, having 200 lifts on a single pass and 600km/375mi of ski runs.

At Courchevel, snow cover is guaranteed from early December to May, owing to the north-facing aspect of the slopes and an impressive array of more than 500 snow cannons.

There are excellent runs for beginners along the lower sections of the Courchevel 1850 ski lifts (Verdon, Jardin Alpin). Advanced skiers prefer the great Saulire corridor and the Courchevel 1350 area. Cross-country skiers can explore the network of 130km/81.25mi of trails linked across the Trois Vallées area.

The Courchevel area includes four resorts on the slopes of the Vallée de St-Bon, among pastures and wooded areas, in a vast open landscape framed by impressive mountains.

▶ **Population:** 2 000
⏱ **Michelin Map:** 333 M5
ℹ **Info:** Le Coeur de Courchevel. BP 37, 73122 Courchevel. 📞04 79 08 00 29. www.courchevel.com.
◗ **Location:** The drive is 50km/31.25mi from Albertville to Courchevel, partly on D 91 with its spectacular panoramic views.
🚠 **Don't Miss:** The cable-car trip up the Saulire is a high point of any visit; a guided tour in the mountains: 📞04 79 01 03 66.
🕐 **Timing:** The "Forfait de loisir" gives access to many activities. See the *Michelin Green Guide French Alps* for suggestions on where to stay and eat.

Le Praz 1300
Ski jumps used during the 1992 Olympic Games are close to the old village. A picturesque 7km/4.3mi-long forest road leads to the resort of **La Tania**.

Courchevel 1550
Family resort situated on a promontory near woodlands.

Moriond-Courchevel 1650
Sunny resort where urban architecture contrasts with traditional chalets.

Courchevel 1850
Courchevel 1850 is the main resort of the complex as well as the liveliest and most popular. There is an impressive **panorama**★ of Mont Jovet, the Sommet de Bellecôte and the Grand Bec peaks.

EXCURSIONS
La Saulire★★★
Access from Courchevel 1850 by the Verdon gondola and the Saulire cable car. The well-equipped summit links the Courchevel and Méribel valleys and is

the starting point of a dozen famous runs. Non-skiers can take a gondola to Méribel or Mottaret and a cable car to Courchevel.

From the top platform, the view embraces the Aiguille du Fruit in the foreground, the Vanoise Massif and glaciers further away, the Péclet-Polset Massif to the south, the Sommet de Bellecôte and Mont Pourri to the north with Mont Blanc on the horizon.

Sommet de la Saulire

Alt 2 738m/8 983ft. 1hr return on foot.
This excursion is recommended in summer to tourists at ease in mountain conditions. The summit can be reached from the cable-car station, along a wide path and a steep lane on the right.

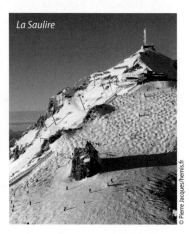

La Saulire

© Pierre Jacques/hemis.fr

Massif de la Vanoise★★★

Numerous Neolithic monuments, cairns and stone roads high on the mountains show that this magnificent landscape has been a centre of human activity for many tens of thousands of years.

This famous massif lies between the valleys of the Arc and the Isère. It was proclaimed a national park in 1963.

La Vanoise Massif, which is dotted with charming villages and lovely forests, remains nonetheless a high mountain area with over 100 summits in excess of 3 000m/9 842.5ft.

The massif is noted for its diverse fauna (marmots, ibexes, chamois) and flora (around 2 000 species).

VISITS

Val-d'Isère★★★ – a prestigious winter sports resort with impressive views.
Rocher de Bellevarde★★★ –
Access by cable railway. Views of the Tarentaise and Mont Blanc.
Refuge de Prariond★★ – *2hr round-trip on foot.* A pleasant walk with varied landscapes (gorges, rock faces).
Réserve naturelle de la Grande Sassière★★ – A backdrop of lakes and glaciers frames Tignes Dam. The park boasts a wealth of animal and plant species which may be easily observed. From the Saut car park, walks to **Lac de la Sassière★★** *(1hr on foot)* and the **Glacier de Rhême-Golette★★** *(2hr30min)*, at an altitude of 3 000m/ 9 842ft.
Tignes★★★ – *Alt. 2 100m/6 889ft.* Resort around a lake in a **site★★** dominated by the breath-taking view of the Grande Motte Glacier (3 656m/11 994ft). Seasoned ramblers may want to tackle **Col du Palet★★**, **Pointe du Chardonnet★★★** *(very steep slope)* or the **Col de la Croix des Frêtes★★**, the **Lac du Grattaleu★**, **Col de Tourne★**.
Peisey-Nancroix★ – This village, nestling in the lush **Vallée de Ponturin★**, opens onto the park and is linked to the skiing area of Les Arcs.
Lac de la Plagne★★ – *4hr round-trip on foot.* A route in a delightful, flowery setting, at the foot of the Bellecôte summit, 3 417m/11 269ft) and Mont Pourri (3 779m/12 398ft).
Pralognan★ – *Alt. 1 410m/4 626ft.* One of the main stopping places for ramblers in La Vanoise Massif.
Col de la Vanoise★★ – *4hr round-trip. Alt. 2 517m/8 260ft.* Views of the Grande Casse (3 855m/12 647ft).
Col d'Aussois★★★ – *Alt. 2 916m/9 567ft. Ascent 5hr.* Sweeping panorama. These two passes may also be reached from Termignon and Aussois en Maurienne.
Réserve naturelle de Tuéda★ – Beautiful pine forest by Tuéda Lake.
Cime de Caron★★★ – *round-trip by cable car and cable railway. Alt. 3 198m/10 550ft.* Panorama of the Écrins, Tarentaise and Mont Blanc.

Grenoble★★

Isère

Capital of the French Alps, Grenoble is a flourishing modern city of broad boulevards at the confluence of the Drac and Isère rivers.

A BIT OF HISTORY

The vast quantities of material brought down by the restless River Drac ("that most brutal, most violent of Alpine tributaries": R Blanchard) formed an alluvial fan on which by the late 3C a fortified Roman town was sited.

Development of the town was held back by the precarious nature of its communication links; though Grenoble was well sited on the roads leading from the Rhône Valley to Turin and Cannes, frequent floods and challenging gradients made travelling an uncertain business. In the reign of Henri IV the city was captured by Lesdiguières, commander of the armies of Piedmont and Savoy, who re-fortified it. Later fortifications doubled the area of the city to the south.

SIGHTS
Fort de la Bastille
Access by cable car. Allow 1hr.
The fort was built in the 16C to protect the approaches to the city, and strengthened in the 19C. It has the best **view**★★★ over the town in its magnificent setting.

▶ **Population:** 159 307
Michelin Map: 336 H 6 -7
Info: 14 r. de la République. ℘04 76 42 41 41. www.grenoble-tourisme.com
Location: Grenoble lies 104km/65mi SE of Lyon.
Don't Miss: A walk along the heights of the Bastille is a highlight of any trip.
Timing: The Notre-Dame district comes to life in the evening.
Kids: The beach at La Bifurk.

Vieille Ville (Old Town)★
The Roman town lay close to the present-day Place Granette (celebrated by Stendhal) and on either side of the Grande-Rue, itself a Roman road.
By the 13C the town had spread northeastwards as far as the Isère, where today a number of courtyards and porches dating from the 16C can be found (No 8 Rue Brocherie, Nos 8 and 10 Rue Chenoise).

Musée de Grenoble★★★
Open Wed–Mon 10am–6.30pm. Closed public holidays. €5, no charge 1st Sun of the month. ℘04 76 63 44 44. www.museedegrenoble.fr.

View of Grenoble with Fort de la Bastille and the cable car

© Ludovic Maisant/hemis.fr

On the bank of the Isère in the heart of the old town, this Fine Arts museum has a remarkably plain and sober appearance. Huge windows look out on massive sculptures which enhance the parvis and the Parc Michallon, outside the north building.

This is one of France's most important provincial museums, with painting from the 16C to the 20C, including an exceptionally rich collection of modern art. The collections include fine modern works like Matisse's *Interior with Aubergines* and Picasso's *Woman Reading* as well as Old Masters like de Champaigne's *John the Baptist*, Rubens' *Pope Gregory surrounded by Saints* or de La Tour's *St Jerome*. Most art movements after 1945 are represented: Abstraction lyrique, New Realism, "Supports-surfaces", Pop Art and Minimalism.

ADDITIONAL SIGHTS
Musée archéologique, église St-Laurent★★
(⊶*Closed for restoration*).
₰04 76 44 78 68.
Rare in Europe, this archaeological museum is housed in a disused church ranked among the top historic monuments of France. The Merovingian **crypt** is unique and splendid testimony to the art and architecture of the Middle Ages.

Musée de la Résistance et de la Déportation★
14 r. Hébert. ◷*Open daily except Tue am, 9am-6pm (Jul-Aug 10am-7pm, Tue 1.30-7pm).* ◈*No charge.* ₰*04 76 42 38 53. www.resistance-en-isere.fr.*
The Museum of the Resistance and Deportation is intended as a museum of history. The Grenoble Resistance movement and the story of deportation are covered, from aspects of the local history to the men who were involved and the events that took place.

Note the three doors on the first floor that are the remains of the Gestapo dungeons, covered with Resistance graffiti. A large relief map illustrates the activites of the Resistance forces and the events that hallmarked this troublesome time.

Musée dauphinois★
30 r. Maurice Gignoux. ♿ ◷*Open daily except Tue: Oct–May 10am–6pm; Jun–Sept 10am–7pm.* ◷*Closed 1 Jan, 1 May, 25 Dec.* ◈*No charge.* ₰*04 57 58 89 01. www.musee-dauphinois.fr.*
This interesting regional museum is located in a 17C **convent of the Visitation of Ste-Marie-d'En-Haut** clinging to the side of a hill in a superb setting. The main galleries are devoted to the Dauphinois heritage, and display a fine collection of domestic furniture and traditional tools, symbolic of rural life in the Alps.

The history of skiing is also illustrated in a comprehensive account of the impact of this winter sport on daily life in the mountains. The wealth and quality of the themed exhibitions make this museum of particular importance in the history of the region.

A visit to the museum also enables you to discover a part of the original convent, the **chapel★★**, a real gem of Baroque art completed in 1662 for the beatification of St Francis de Sales.

EXCURSIONS
L'Oisans★★★
▶ *The region is largely within the Parc National des Écrins, between the rivers Romanche and Drac.*
L'Oisans is the second-highest massif in France, after Mont Blanc. Its population is grouped in villages sited on high terraces reached by spectacular narrow roads.

Les Écrins
These bare mountains between the valleys of the Romanche, Drac and Durance look down on more than 100sq km/38.6sq mi of glaciers.

The Route des Grandes Alpes (◉ *see ROUTE DES GRANDES ALPES*) gives fine views of the north and east faces of the massif (from the Col du Galibier, the Oratoire du Chazelet, and from La Grave), cut by isolated valleys with their typical way of life and served by long cul-de-sac roads; the best known is the valley of the Vénéon leading to La Bérarde.

Bassin du Bourg d'Oisans★

Until the 13C the fertile basin was a glacial lake, now filled in by material brought down by the Romanche and its tributary, the Vénéon. This is the economic centre of the region.

Vallée du Vénéon★★★

○ 31km/19mi from Bourg-d'Oisans to La Bérarde.

The road up to La Bérarde is a lesson in glacial geomorphology made more dramatic by the scale of the great U-shaped valley and the ruggedness of its high granite walls, moraines, waterfalls in hanging valleys, and compact little villages, before reaching La Bérarde, now a climbing centre.

Massif du Vercors★★★

○ The area is to the W and SW of Grenoble. 🏠 La-Chapelle-en-Vercors. ℘04 75 48 22 54. www.vercors.fr; www.vercors.com.

Rising above Grenoble like a fortress, the massive limestone plateau of the Vercors forms the largest regional park in the northern Alps.

The Vercors is the most extensive of the Pre-Alpine massifs. Protected by sheer cliffs, it is a natural citadel, inside which grow fine forests of beech and conifers interspersed with lush pasturelands. In places, the immensely thick limestone has been cut into by the rivers to form deep and spectacular gorges.

In 1944, the Resistance in these mountains numbered several thousand.

In June of that year, the Wehrmacht stepped up its assault on the Resistance, and brought in parachute troops on 21 July. With many of their number lost, the surviving members of the Resistance were given the order to disperse on 23 July. 700 of the inhabitants and defenders of the Vercors had died; several of its villages lay in ruins.

North of the rebuilt village of **Vassieux-en-Vercors** is a National Cemetery with the graves of some of those who died during that terrible summer, and at the Col de Lachan stands a monument to the fallen (Mémorial du Vercors).

The **Vercors Regional Natural Park**★★★ (℘04 76 94 38 26. www.parc-du-vercors.fr) is France's largest natural reserve; there are no roads, no villages, only shepherds and forestry workers, along with 65 species of mammals, 135 species of birds and 17 species of reptiles. The flora is extremly diverse with 1 800 species, of which 80 are protected. There are 60 species of orchids alone.

Gorges de la Bourne★★★

○ 18.7km/11.6mi N of Vassieux-en-Vercors.

The unusually regular walls of the gorge open out downstream. Its entrance is marked by the old cloth town of Pont-en-Royans with its houses clinging picturesquely to the rock face.

Combe Laval★★★

○ 24.6km/15.3mi SW of Gorges de la Bourne.

One of the finest sights in the Vercors. The road clings dizzily to a vast limestone wall rising 600m/1 968.5ft above the upper valley of the Cholet.

Grands Goulets★★★

○ 17.7km/11mi SE of Combe Laval.

An epic piece of construction dating from 1851, the narrow road was hewn directly from the rock. From its upper section it is possible to see the river beginning the process of eroding an as yet intact geological formation. The village of Les Barraques-en-Vercors was destroyed by enemy action in 1944.

Col de Rousset★★

○ 22.6km/14mi S of Grands Goulets. Go to the southern entrance to the disused tunnel.

The pass marks the climatic as well as the morphological boundary between the northern and southern Alps.

There are spectacular views, not only of the road twisting its way downwards, but also of the great limestone walls protecting the Vercors, of the Die Valley 960m/3 149.6ft below, and of a succession of bare ridges extending into the far distance.

Briançon★★
Hautes-Alpes

The highest town in Europe (1 321m/4 334ft), Briançon is best viewed from the terraces of the UNESCO site, La Fort de Salettes, where stands the 9m/29.5ft-high **statue of France**★ sculpted by **Antoine Bourdelle.**

A BIT OF HISTORY

Since ancient times, two great routes into Italy have met here, one coming from the Romanche Valley via the Col de Lautaret, the other following the Durance up from Embrun. The strategic value of the site was appreciated by the Gauls. It seems likely that the survivors of the Germanic tribes routed by the Roman general Marius outside Aix-en-Provence found their way here, and Briançon may have provided a refuge too for some of the persecuted members of the Vaudois, a 15C sect. The town played an important commercial and military role, the latter enhanced by the presence of great rock bars lending themselves naturally to fortification.

SIGHT
Ville Haute (Upper Town) ★★

In January 1692, the War of the League of Augsburg had been raging for six years; mercenaries in the pay of Vittorio-Amadeo II, Duke of Savoy, invaded the

▶ **Population:** 12 103
Ⓖ **Michelin Map:** 334 H 3
▤ **Info:** 1 pl. du Temple.
   ℰ 04 92 21 08 50.
   www.ot-briancon.fr.
◗ **Location:** Briançon lies 118km/73.3mi SE of Grenoble. After arriving at the town, follow signs to "Briançon Vauban" to find the Old Town.

Dauphiné and torched Briançon – only two houses out of 258 escaped the fire. Vauban was working in Burgundy, but was immediately dispatched by Louis XIV to Briançon with a brief to rebuild the town and make it impregnable.
A week sufficed for the great engineer to draw up his plans, but age and ill health made it impossible for him to supervise their execution.
With its gate (Porte Pignerol) and its fortified church, Briançon-Vauban, in contrast to the lower town Briançon-Ste-Catherine, still has the look of a frontier town of Louis XIV's reign, while its narrow, steeply sloping streets, especially the **Grande Gargouille**★ (also known as the Grande Rue), express the drama of its precipitous site. East of town, the **Pont d'Asfeld**★ (bridge) was built in 1734 and is also part of the town's collection of UNESCO sites.

View of Briançon with Collégiale Notre-Dame

Grand Canyon du
Verdon★★★
Alpes-de-Haute-Provence

The modest-looking River Verdon has cut Europe's most spectacular canyon through a remote, wild landscape.

GEOGRAPHY

The canyon extends 26km/16mi from the meeting point of the Verdon with the Jabron in the east to where it flows into Ste-Croix Lake in the west at the Galetas bridge.

The opposite rims of the canyon are between 200–1 500m (656–4 921ft) apart. Its depth varies from 250–600m (820–1 968ft), while the width of its floor ranges from 8–90m (26–295ft). The height of the canyon's walls impresses on one the sheer scale of the Jurassic sedimentation, in terms of both time and the quantity of material deposited.

VISIT

La Corniche Sublime★★★
South bank scenic route.

The steep and twisting (20km/12.4mi) road was engineered so as to open up the most spectacular views. They include: the **Balcons de la Mescla**★★★ overlooking the swirling waters where the Verdon is joined by the Artuby; the bridge, Pont de l'Artubya, linking sheer walls of rock; the Fayet tunnels above the Étroit des Cavaliers (Knights' Narrows), and the **Falaise des Cavaliers**★ (Knights' Cliff) 300m/982.2ft high.

La route des Crêtes★★★
North bank scenic route.

The road (23km/14.3mi long) links a series of viewpoints overlooking the most spectacular section of the canyon. Further eastwards, the viewpoint known as the **Point Sublime**★★★ dominates the downstream section of the canyon and the impressive narrows, the **Couloir de Samson**★★★.

Castellane★
See ROUTE NAPOLÉON.

- **Michelin Map:** 334 E-F 10
- **Info:** Maison des Gorges du Verdon, La Palusur-Verdon. ℰ04 92 77 32 02. www. lapaludsurverdon.com.
- **Location:** The gorge is best reached from Castellane on the east side or Moustiers-Ste-Marie on the west. On the north side, the canyon can be followed on D 952 and D 23, while the spectacular D 71 (the Corniche Sublime) runs along the south side.
- **Timing:** The road on either side is slow and tiring, so allow a full day.

Moustiers-Ste-Marie★★

The small town is the centre for the Valensole plateau. It has an extraordinary **site**★★ at the foot of a cleft in the limestone cliff, across which a knight returning from the Crusades stretched the chain which can still be seen today. The church has a **tower**★ with arcading in Lombard style.

Faïence was introduced here in 1679; the most sought-after pieces were fired at high temperatures (*see LIMOGES*) and are decorated with charming hunting scenes in blue.

WALKING IN THE GRAND CANYON★★★

1 SENTIER MARTEL★★★

Between the Chalet de la Maline and the Point Sublime, GR 4, known as the Sentier Martel, offers those who do not mind a tiring day's hike an unforgettably close contact with the Grand Canyon.

Chalet de la Maline to the Point Sublime
5hr walk, along a difficult itinerary – headtorch essential. GR 4 is marked in white and red.

From the steps going down to the river, there are fine views of the Pas de l'Estellié.

View of the Grand Canyon du Verdon from the Corniche Sublime

▷ *Ignore the path branching off to the right towards the Estellié Footbridge; it leads to the Restaurant des Cavaliers and the Corniche Sublime.*

At the Pré d'Issane (*after 1hr 30min walking*), the path runs close to the river and follows it through the Étroit des Cavaliers with sheer cliffs towering 300m/984ft above. The gorge widens and the path reaches the Talus de Guègues, a scree framed by steep slopes. Continue upstream past the vast Baumes-aux-Bœufs Cave and take the second path to the right leading to the **Mescla★★★** (*30min return*), where the flow of the Verdon mixes with that of the Artuby. There is a splendid view upstream of the Défilé des Baumes-Frères.

▷ *Retrace your steps to the intersection and turn right.*

The path winds its way up to the Brèche Imbert (*steps*): superb view of the Baumes-Frères and the Barre de l'Escalès. The canyon, overlooked by very high cliffs, becomes wider and the walk (*1hr30min*) is a bit monotonous, until the cliffs narrow. The **Chaos de Trescaïre**, on the right, is an extraordinary jumble of fallen rocks. The hilltop village of Rougon can be seen in the distance. Next come two tunnels; inside the second, metal steps lead to the **Baume-aux-Pigeons★**, a vast cave, 30m/98ft high, situated at the foot of a high cliff. From the bottom of the stairs, you can see, on the opposite bank, the huge blocks which fell when the roof caved in. This cave and the collapsed roof indicate that in the past the Verdon flowed partly underground. From the last opening, there is a view of the **Couloir Samson★★**, a very narrow corridor with smooth vertical sides. Beyond the tunnel, the path goes over the footbridge across the Baou and climbs to the parking area. The walk ends at the **Belvédère du Point Sublime★★★**.

▷ *Walk to the inn where you can call a taxi. You can join D 952 from the Auberge du Point Sublime by taking short cuts.*

If you wish to go to La Palud-sur-Verdon without going past the Point Sublime, take the path on the left just before the footbridge over the Baou; it goes up along the south bank of the stream and joins D 952 4km/2.5mi from La Palud-sur-Verdon.

② SENTIER DE DÉCOUVERTE DES LÉZARDS

👥 From Point Sublime★★★

🚶 This well-marked nature trail starts from the Plateau des Lauves. A small explanatory booklet is available at the

Auberge du Point Sublime or at the tourist office in La Palud-sur-Verdon. Another itinerary leads to the Pont de Tusset along GR 49.

3 BELVÉDÈRE DE RANCOUMAS★★

East bank starting from Point Sublime★★★
3hr 30min return. It is possible to start from the Point Sublime car park and to walk south, following GR 49 markings, or to drive towards the Couloir Samson (D 23B) and park the car on the last bend before the straight stretch ending in the car park.

🚶 2km/1.2mi before reaching the car park, take GR 49 on the left, marked in white and red; it leads through an oak forest down to the **Pont de Tusset**★, a bridge dating from the early 17C.

The path starts rising through a forest of pines, maples and beeches, then joins a wide track.

Leave the marked path and follow the track on the right; it crosses a stream before reaching the ruins of Encastel. Go up to the edge of the cliff.

The natural Belvédère de Rancoumas offers a striking **panorama**★★ of the whole Falaise de l'Escalès with the Sentier Martel running below. The **Mourre de Chanier**, the highest summit of the Verdon region, soars in the distance to the northwest.

◯ *Return along the same route.*

EXCURSION
Sisteron★★
◯ *Sisteron is located on the Route Napoléon between Gap and Digne.*
🏢 *Hôtel de Ville.* ☎ *04 92 61 36 50. www.sisteron.com.*

The lofty citadel of Sisteron, sternly guarding a narrow ravine and looking down on the clustered lanes of the 14C town, still makes an impressive spectacle despite the battering it took from Allied bombing raids during 1944.

Sisteron lies on the Route Napoleon and the River Durance and is the main mountain gateway to Provence.

The town is situated between the Laragne Valley to the north and the valley of the middle Durance to the south. As well as marking the historic boundary between Dauphiné and Provence, this is also the northern limit of the cultivation of the olive.

Citadel★
🕐 *Open daily: Apr and Oct 9am–6pm; May 6.30pm; Jun and Sept 7pm; Jul–Aug 7.30pm.* 🎫 *€6.* ☎ *04 92 61 27 57. www.citadelledesisteron.fr.*

There is nothing left of the 11C castle. The keep and the watch-path are late 12C and the mighty walls set around the rock are the work of **Jean Errard**, Henri IV's chief military engineer. New defences, designed by **Vauban**, Louis XIV's military engineer, in 1692, were added to the powerful 16C fortifications. Part of the citadel, including the chapel, was damaged by bombing in 1944 but later tastefully restored.

A marked tour leads up a succession of steps and terraces, offering views of the town and the Durance Valley, and on to the watch-path. Walk on below the keep, where Jan Kazimierz, Prince of Poland, was imprisoned in 1639, to reach the terrace and enjoy the bird's-eye **view**★ of the lower part of town, the reservoir and the mountains dominating the horizon to the north.

Walk to the north side of the citadel, to the **"Guérite du Diable"** offering an impressive **view**★ of the Rocher de la Baume. The steps leading downwards were once part of an underground staircase, built to link the citadel to the Porte de Dauphiné, destroyed in 1944.

👥 Musée Terre et Temps★
6 pl. Gén-de-Gaulle. 🕐 *Open Tue–Sat: Mar–Sept, 9am–noon, 2–6pm; late Sept –Nov 9–10m, 3–6pm.* 🎫 *No charge.* ☎ *04 92 61 61 30.*

In the Visitandine chapel, this museum, set up by the Réserve Géologique de Haute-Provence, explores the development of the idea of time, from geological time to modern timepieces. A Foucault's pendulum shows the rotation of the Earth.

FRENCH RIVIERA

The Riviera's abundant sunshine, exotic vegetation and dramatic combination of sea and mountains have made it a fashionable place of pleasure since its "discovery" in the 19C. The coast is densely built up, the resorts linked by triple corniche roads. Further north are the Maritime Alps, dissected by the upper valleys of the Var, Tinée, Vésubie and Roya. To the west of Nice the coast flattens out, forming wide bays with fine beaches, before again rising beyond Cannes to higher ground.

Highlights

1 The fascinating old quarter of Nice: **Le Vieux Nice** (p337)
2 Exciting drives and fine views: **Corniches de la Riviera** (p340)
3 The capital of the city of Monaco: **Le Rocher** (p343)
4 Ancient village in natural amphitheatre: **Saorge** (p348)
5 Stunning red porphyry outcrop: **Massif de L'Estérel** (p353)

Geography – The bustle of the coast is in contrast to the quieter charm of the interior, with its olive groves, spectacular gorges and hill villages. There is no defined boundary for the Riviera, but it is widely accepted as extending from the border with Italy, west to St-Tropez. Between Nice and Menton, the Pre-Alps plunge into the sea while the limestone plâteaux of the Provence tableland are separated from the sea by two massifs, Estérel and Maures. Its coastline has great promontories extending into the sea defining wide bays like that of the Gulf of St-Tropez. The Toulon coast is characterised by vertical cliffs, and a number of attractive beaches; to the north rise the limestone heights of the Provençal Ranges.

History – Although preceded by the Ligurians and Greeks, the Romans had established themselves in the region by the 1C AD and evidence of their presence can be seen today at Fréjus and Cimiez (Nice). In the Middle Ages Provence changed hands several times and did not become part of France until the late 15C. Nice remained part of Savoy and was not restored to France until 1860.

Economy – The Riviera, also known as the Côte d'Azur, is dominated by tourism, which began in the 19C.

This most important industry is why Nice, the largest city in the region, has France's second-busiest airport. After tourism, the best-known industry on the Riviera is perfume, but there is a burgeoning industry, just a short distance inland, that produces olives and olive oil; that, too, is a major contributor to the local economy.

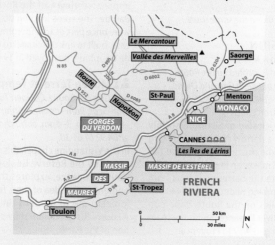

Nice★★★

Alpes-Maritimes

Enclosed by an amphitheatre of hills, extending around a beautiful blue bay, the capital of the Riviera has artistic treasures, countless attractions, distinctive cuisine, a wonderful climate and a magnificent setting that has long attracted visitors year round.

A BIT OF HISTORY

Some 400 000 years ago, bands of elephant hunters made their encampments on the fossil beach at Terra Amata, 26m/85.3ft above the present level of the sea. In the 6C BC, Celto-Ligurians settled on the castle hill; a little later it was the turn of merchants and sailors from Marseille, who established themselves around the harbour. These were followed by the Romans, who favoured the Cimiez district. In 1388, aided and abetted by the **Grimaldi** family, Count Amadeus VII of Savoy (1360–91) incorporated Provence into his domain and made a triumphal entry into Nice.

As a result of the alliance of 1859 between France and Sardinia, Napoleon III undertook to help drive out the Austrians from the Lombardy and Veneto regions; in return, France was to receive from the House of Savoy the lands to the west of the Alps and around Nice, which had once been hers. A plebiscite produced an overwhelming vote in favour of a return to France (25 743 for, 260 against) and the ceremony of annexation took place on 14 June 1860.

SIGHTS

Le Vieux Nice★

The core of the city, huddling at the foot of the castle hill, has a lively, utterly Mediterranean character.

Château

The landscaped slopes of the castle hill, with their umbrella pines shading pleasant walks, reach a height of 92m/301.8ft. The summit provided a place of refuge for the denizens of Cimiez at the time of the fall of the Roman Empire. In

▶ **Population:** 348 556

Michelin Map: 341 E 5

Info: 5 Promenade des Anglais. ✆08 92 70 74 07. www.nicetourisme.com.

Location: Nice is 27km/17mi W along the coast from the border with Italy.

Parking: Parking is difficult. On arrival, park in one of the many large underground car parks.

Don't Miss: A stroll along the Promenade des Anglais; the panorama from the château hill.

Timing: At least a full day: spend the morning on the oceanfront and in Vieux Nice; reserve the afternoon for Cimiez, and, if you have time, choose an art museum according to your taste – Matisse, Chagall, the Musée des Beaux-Arts, or the Musée d'Art Moderne et d'Art Contemporain.

the 12C, the Counts of Provence built a castle here which was subsequently strengthened by the Angevin princes and the Dukes of Savoy but was demolished by Louis XIV in 1706.

From the top there is a fine **view**★★ over the city, the Pre-Alps and the bay (Baie des Anges).

Place Garibaldi

The square is named after the great fighter for Italian unity who was born in Nice. The ochre walls and arcading of the buildings along its sides recall

---

A Bit of Advice

A 1-, 2- or 3-day sightseeing **Nice Riviera Pass** grants free entry to many sights, guided tours, and shopping and dining advantages in the greater Nice area. €24, €26 and €54.

© haak78/Bigstockphoto.com

Nice Carnival

The **Nice Carnival**★★★ is one of the biggest celebrations in the region, with two weeks of parades, confetti battles, fireworks and masked balls *(veglioni)*. The **floral parades**, or *batailles de fleurs,* offer a picturesque spectacle and attract huge and excited crowds, drawn by the colourful fruit and flowers.

The tradition dates back a long way in Nice, with references as long ago as 1294, on the occasion of the visit of the Count of Provence, Charles II. Nice Carnival has always been a welcome diversion from social tensions and conflicts, which were constantly breaking out as a result of Nice's geographical location and disputed ownership. Until the end of the 18C, the carnival took place after the Lenten fast in the form of local festivities in the old part of the city.

After a break of several years, caused by the wars of the Revolution and the Empire, the first parade of carnival floats took place in 1830 in honour of the royal visit of King Charles Félix to Nice and the return to Sardinian sovereignty. The modern form of carnival dates back to 1873, with the establishment of the various stages of the festivities and the setting of a different official theme every year.

Carnival-going families from Nice belong to long lines of tradition verging on outright dynasties. Each "stable" of carnival floats has its own characteristics. On average, about one tonne of papier-mâché is used in the making of each float. Famous painters from this area have also played their part in enriching the carnival decorations. The festivities begin with the triumphal entry of "Sa Majesté Carnaval" about mid-February, normally three weeks before Shrove Tuesday, or Mardi Gras, and extend well into March. An effigy of the King of the Carnival is later ceremonially burned to mark the end of the carnival season. During the intervening period celebrations are in full swing, with parades of carnival floats accompanied by people in costumes sporting huge comical heads made of papier-mâché.

More, and up-to-date, information about the Carnival is available at *www.nicecarnaval.com*.

the urbane elegance characteristic of Piedmontese town planning in the 18C.

Cathédrale Ste-Reparate

This is a fine example of the Baroque style as it developed in Nice. The west front, a pleasant mixture of greens and yellows, is decorated with niches and medallions, topped by an imposing entablature and supported by but-tress-pillars with composite capitals. The **interior**★ is enlivened by an elaborate cornice, and in the choir is a frieze out-lined in white and gold and decorated with little figures of angels.

Place Masséna

The linear park laid out on what was once the bed of the River Paillon is inter-rupted by this square, begun in 1815. Its buildings, with their façades rendered in reddish ochre and their arcades, recall the planned urban spaces of Turin.

Site archéologique gallo-romain★

&. ⓞOpen Wed–Mon 10am–6pm. ⓞClosed 1 Jan, Easter Sunday, 1 May, 25 Dec. ⊜No charge. ☛Guided tours (1–2hr) ⊜€5. ℘04 93 81 59 57. www.musee-archeologique-nice.org. The Cimiez district originated in the Roman settlement whose growth soon eclipsed that of the older town laid out around the harbour. The archaeological site consists of medium-size amphithea-tres and the area around the baths.

Monastère de Cimiez★

The monastery church possesses a Pietà of 1475; though an early work of Louis Bréa, and executed in Gothic style, it is one of his finest achievements, notably in its portrayal of the grieving Mary. To the left of the choir is a later work by the same artist, a Crucifixion (1512) which heralds the Renaissance.

Musée Matisse★★

&. ⓞOpen Wed–Mon 10am–6pm. ⓞClosed 25 Dec, 1 Jan, Easter Sunday, 1 May. ⊜No charge. ☛Guided tours €3. ℘04 93 81 08 08. www.musee-matisse-nice.org.

The museum is housed in the Villa des Arènes; it traces the artist's evolution, from a still-life (Nature morte aux livres, 1890) to the Fauteuil de Rocaille (1947) and the Nu bleu (1952).

Musée Marc-Chagall★★

&. ⓞOpen daily except Tue: 10am–6pm (Nov–Apr 5pm). ⓞClosed 1 Jan, 1 May, 25 Dec. ⊜€7.50 (free 1st Sun in the month). ℘04 93 53 87 31. www.musee-chagall.fr. The museum was designed to display the 17 great paintings making up the artist's Biblical Message (painted bet-ween 1954 and 1967).

ADDITIONAL SIGHTS

Promenade des Anglais ★★ – This wide promenade, facing due south and flanking the sea along its entire length, provides wonderful views of the Baie des Anges. Until 1820 access to the shore was difficult, but the English colony, numerous since the 18C, undertook the construction of a coastal path which now carries its name.

Musée des Beaux-Arts ★★ – ⓞOpen daily except Mon 10am–6pm. ⓞClosed 1 Jan, Easter Sun, 1 May, 25 Dec. ⊜No charge. ℘04 92 15 28 28. www.musee-beaux-arts-nice.org.Since 1928 the Fine Arts Museum has been housed in an 1878 residence built in the Renaissance style of 17C Genoese palaces for the Russian princess Kotschoubey. The museum displays a rich collection of art acquired through donations around a nucleus of works sent to Nice by Napoleon III in 1860.

Musée d'Art Moderne et d'Art Contemporain★★ – ⓞOpen daily except Mon 10am–6pm. ⓞClosed 1 Jan, Easter Sunday, 1 May, 25 Dec. ⊜No charge. ℘04 93 62 61 62. www.mamac-nice.org. Designed by Yves Bayard and Henri Vidal, the Museum of Modern and Contemporary Art is made up of four square towers with roof-top terraces linked by glass passageways. The collections present French and American avant-garde art movements from the 1960s to the present.

Musée d'Art et d'Histoire – Musée Masséna★ – ⊙*Open daily except Tue 10am–6pm.* ⊜*No charge.* ✆*04 93 91 19 10.* This museum and gardens was built in 1898, modelled on Italian residences of the First Empire, made after plans by Georg Tersling and the Niçois A Messian for Victor Masséna, great-grandson of the Marshal. In 1919 his son André gave it to the town. In 2007 the new exhibit rooms opened, featuring the **chronological history of Nice** from the 19C to the 1930s presented on two floors. A library on the top floor houses over 30 000 photos and 3 000 maps.

EXCURSIONS
Corniches de la Riviera★★★
◖*Circular tour of 41km/25.4mi.*

The Lower Corniche road skirts the foot of Mont Boron, giving fine views over Villefranche-sur-Mer and its bay.

The highly indented coastline is the result of the recent folding and subsequent drowning of the limestone Pre-Alps.

Both **Cap Ferrat**★★ and the nearby headland, Pointe St-Hospice, offer splendid views of the Riviera with its corniche roads; the village of Èze-Bord-de-Mer, the fashionable resort of Beaulieu, Cap d'Ail can all be identified, and rising out of the sea in the distance is Cap Martin. Clinging like an eagle's nest to its inaccessible rock spike, **Èze**★★ seems the very archetype of a hill village. It was

inhabited by the Ligurians and by the Phoenicians, then fortified against raiders from the sea.

In 1706 both the village and its castle were demolished on the orders of Louis XIV, but it was rebuilt after 1760.

Vallée des Merveilles★★
The whole of the site known as the Vallée des Merveilles consists of seven distinct regions around Mont Bégo: the Vallée des Merveilles itself, which is the largest; the Vallée de Fontanalbe, which is narrower; the Valmasque, Valaurette, Lac Sainte-Marie, Col du Sabion and Lac Vei del Bouc.

At the foot of **Mont Bégo** lies a region of glacial lakes, valleys and rocky cirques formed during the Quaternary Era, cut off by the scarce roads and harsh mountain climate. In this dramatic landscape is the Vallée des Merveilles, famous for the thousands of prehistoric rock engravings found there.

The Engravings – The name Bégo is derived from an Indo-European root which means the sacred mountain *(Be)* inhabited by the bull-god *(Go)*.

The region of Mont Bégo is an **open-air museum** comprising over 40 000 engravings. Cut into the rock face worn smooth by glacial erosion 15 000 years ago, the linear engravings date from the Gallo-Roman period through the Middle Ages to the present. The most interesting ones to the archaeologists date back to the early Bronze Age.

Cap Ferrat

©MguvanDreamstime.com

Magic Mountain

The engravings reveal the preoccupations of the Ligurian people who lived in the lower valleys and made pilgrimages to Mont Bégo, which they believed had divine powers. The engravings have five themes: horns, arms or tools, anthropomorphs, geometric figures and other unidentified images.

The mountain cult was linked to that of the bull; drawings of horns and bovine creatures feature in half the engravings. Ploughs and harnessed animals suggest that agriculture was practised, and crisscross patterns may represent parcels of land. There are many representations of weapons matching those excavated on nearby archaeological sites. The rare human figures have been given names: Christ, the Wizard, the Chieftain, the Dancer. Others, of a more enigmatic nature, are open to interpretation, such the Tree of Life at Fontanalbe (guided tours only).

The Mercantour National Park
04 93 16 78 88.
www.parc-mercantour.eu.
Created in 1979, and once part of the hunting grounds of the kings of Italy, Mercantour is now twinned with the Parco Naturale delle Alpi Marittime across the border in Italy. These two parks work together to protect their natural and cultural heritage.

WALKS
VALLÉE DES MERVEILLES
▶ *10km/6mi north of St-Dalmas-de-Tende by D 91. Leave the car at Lac des Mesches.* ⚑ *8hr.*
Take the signposted footpath to the Refuge des Merveilles and then to Lac Long, the starting point for a guided tour of the Arpette area. It is possible to spend the night at the refuge (reservation necessary). Return by the same route.

Fontanalbe
▶ *12km/7.4mi north of St-Dalmas-de-Tende by D 91. Park in Casterino.* ⚑ *5hr. Easier walking than the first walk; more suitable for families.*
Start south of Casterino by the information panel *(sign: Fontanalbe),* taking the wooded path west and continuing to the refuge. Bear left of the refuge building and continue to Lac Vert, the starting point for self-guided tours of the Sentier du Découverte. For a guided tour of the engravings continue along the side of the lake to the guides' hut at **Lacs Jumeaux.**

By staying overnight at the Fontanalbe refuge it is possible to climb the foothills of Mont Bégo as far as the Baisse de Fontanalbe (alt. 2 568m/8 423ft) – fine views of the three lakes in the Valmasque valley. It is possible to continue towards the Valmasque Refuge or to return to Casterino by the outward route.

ADDRESSES

🛏 STAY

🛏 **Clair Hotel** – *23 bd Carnot, Impasse Terra Amata.* *04 93 89 69 89. 10rms.* ⚏ *€8.* This converted schoolhouse near the archaeological museum has rooms all on one floor (in the old classrooms) and a Mediterranean garden terrace where breakfast is served in the summer.

🛏 **Star Hôtel** – *14 r. Biscarra.* *04 93 85 19 03. www.hotel-star.com. Closed 15 Nov–24 Dec. 20rms.* ⚏ *€7.* Small hotel away from the bustling town centre offering simple accommodations, some with a balcony. Close to the Nice-Étoile shopping centre.

🛏🛏🛏 **La Pérouse** – *11 quai Rauba-Capéu.* *04 93 62 34 63. www.hotel-la-perouse.com. 58rms.* ⚏ *€21.* A prime seaside location overlooking the Baie des Anges from the foot of the Château hill, this cosy Provençal-style hotel features a heated swimming pool and grill restaurant set within a garden against the rocky hill.

🍴 EAT

🍴 **La Tapenade** – *6 r. Ste-Réparate.* *04 93 80 65 63. Closed Mon.* Curious décor re-creating a typical street from the south of France, with its shutters, terracotta flower pots and strings of garlic.

Lou Balico – *20/22 ave St-Jean-Baptiste.* *04 93 85 93 71. www.loubalico.com. Closed lunch in Jul–Aug.* Three generations of the same family have been serving classic Niçois dishes in this cosy dining room.

L'Escalinada – *22 r. Pairolière.* *04 93 62 11 71. www.escalinada.fr. Closed 15 Nov–15 Dec.* Nestling in the old quarter, this charming restaurant offers attractively presented regional cuisine.

Le Pain Quotidien – *3 r. St-François-de-Paul (Cours Saleya). 04 93 62 94 32. Closed Tue.* This country-style restaurant specialising in brunch has long wooden tables where guests sit side by side, an original formula conducive to a friendly, convivial atmosphere. .

La Table d'Alziari – *4 r. François-Zanin. 04 93 80 34 03. Closed Sun–Mon.* Unpretentious family restaurant set up in a small alley of the old district. Typical dishes from Nice and the Provence area.

Grand Café de Turin – *5 pl. Garibaldi. 04 93 62 29 52. www.cafede turin.com. Closed Tue.* This brasserie, which is over 200 years old, has become an institution in Nice.

NIGHTLIFE

Casino Ruhl – *1 prom. des Anglais.* *04 97 03 12 22. www.lucienbarriere.com.* The casino boasts 300 slot machines and has facilities for French and English roulette, blackjack, stud poker, etc. American bar.

Le Relais – *Hôtel Negresco, 37 prom. des Anglais. 04 93 16 64 00.* The sumptuous decoration of this bar belonging to the legendary Negresco Hotel has remained the same since 1913. Piano bar every evening.

La Trappa – *2 r. Jules Gilly. 04 93 80 33 69.* A lively tapas bar with deep, comfortable settees and red walls awaits you at La Trappa, open since 1886. Sip a Cuban cocktail while you listen to Latin-American music (DJ weekends). Friendly atmosphere and local wine list.

Le Livingstone at Grand Hotel Aston – *12 ave Félix Faure. 04 92 17 53 00.* A chic rooftop bar providing panoramic vistas over the city.

SHOPPING

Markets – There are street markets all over town, including: **Fish market** – *pl. St-François; Tue–Sun 6am–1pm;*

Flower market – *Cours Saleya; Tue–Sun 6am–5.30pm;* **Marché aux Puces** (Flea market) – *pl. Robilante Tue–Sun 10am–6pm;* **Marché de la Brocante** (Antiques) – *Cours Saleya Mon 7.30am–6pm.*

Alziari – *14 r. St-François-de-Paule.* *04 93 85 76 92. www.alziari.com.fr.* One of the best addresses in town for olive oil and regional specialities.

La Maison de l'Olive – *18 r. Pairolière.* *04 93 80 01 61.* Marseille soaps made from pure olive oil, lotions and scents for the body and home, and regional products.

À l'Olivier – *7 r. St-François-de-Paule.* *04 93 13 44 97.* Every brand of French olive oil with the AOC label is sold in this boutique, originally opened in 1822, in Nice since 2004.

Confiserie Auer – *7 r. St-François-de-Paule.* *04 93 85 77 98. www.maison-auer.com.* A gorgeous vintage boutique selling candied fruit and crystallised flowers from the Nice region, as well as chocolates, and calissons from Aix.

Confiserie Florian – *14 quai Papacino.* *04 93 55 43 50. www.confiserieflorian.com. Guided tours of the factory 9am–noon, 2–6.30pm.* Candied fruit, lemon, orange and grapefruit preserve, chocolates and sweets, crystallised petals and delicious jams made with rose, violet and jasmine blossom.

Maison Poilpot – Aux Parfums de Grasse – *10 r. St-Gaétan. 04 93 85 60 77.* This traditional perfumery produces more than 80 different fragrances, including popular Mediterranean scents such as mimosa, rose, violet and lemon.

L'Art Gourmand – *21 r. du Marché.* *04 93 62 51 79.* This Old Nice boutique has nougats, calisson, candied fruit, cookies, pastries, ice cream and northern France specialities.

EVENTS

Nice Carnival – *see p338.*

Fête de la Mer et de la St-Pierre – Celebrating the sea and St-Peter on the port and Quai des Etats-Unis the last weekend in June.

Nice Jazz Festival – The Roman amphitheatre is the venue for the jazz festival in the last two weeks of July. *08 92 68 36 22. www.nicejazzfestival.fr.*

Principauté de
Monaco★★★

The Principality of Monaco, world-famous haunt of the super-rich, is a sovereign state. Inhabited since prehistoric times and later a Greek settlement (5C BC) and a Roman port, its history really began when the Grimaldi family bought it from the Republic of Genoa in 1308. Prince Rainier III ruled the principality from 1949–2005 with the assistance of a National Council. His only son Prince Albert then took power, but because he has no children, it seems certain that the line of succession will pass to Rainier's daughter, Princess Caroline. Four districts make up the town: Monaco-Ville, the historic seat of the Principality; Monte-Carlo, the district surrounding the casino; La Condamine, around Port Hercule and Fontvielle, the new industrial area built on land reclaimed from the sea.

SIGHTS
Le Rocher (The Rock)★★
This is the historic core of the principality, and its prestigious capital, the miniature city of Monaco. It is built on a rocky peninsula 60m/196.8ft above the sea.

▶ **Population:** 33 015
⚭ **Michelin Map:** 341 F 5
Info: 2a bd des Moulins. ☎00 377 92 16 61 66. www.visitmonaco.com.
Location: The territory includes the Old Town or Monaco Ville on the Rock (Rocher de Monaco); the new town of Monte-Carlo and the port area at La Condamine linking the two.
🅿 **Parking:** Park in the underground garage (parking des Pêcheurs creusé) of Le Rocher, and take the lift up to the Old Town on the Rock.
Don't Miss: The Musée Océanographique or the Palais Princier.
🕐 **Timing:** Allow 3hr in Old Monaco before visiting Monte-Carlo, where you can try your luck in the casino. November is very busy, especially around the 19th, Monaco's National Day.
Kids: Musée Océanographique; Collection des Voitures Anciennes; Musée National des Automates et Poupées d'Autrefois à Monaco.

Le Rocher

© Alex Treflow/Bigstockphoto.com

👥 Musée Océanographique★★

ave St-Martin. 🦽🕐Open daily Jan–Mar, and Oct–Dec 10am–6pm; Apr–Sept 9.30am–7pm (Jul–Aug 7.30pm). 🕐Closed day of F1 Grand Prix. ☞€14 (children, €7). 📞00 377 93 15 36 13. www.oceano.mc.

The museum was founded by Prince Albert I, a leading light in the early days of oceanography. The imposing rooms house the skeletons of large marine mammals, such as whales and sea-cows, as well as stuffed specimens.

A splendid **aquarium**★★ teems with rare tropical and Mediterranean species of marine life. A live coral reef from the Red Sea is a unique exhibit. The museum is also a research centre, with exhibits of marine laboratories, the technology of underwater exploration and applied oceanography.

Cathédrale

ave St-Martin. 🕐Open daily winter 8am –6pm; summer until 7pm. 📞00 377 93 30 87 70. www.cathedrale.mc.

The neo-Romanesque building, constructed with white stone from La Turbie between 1875 and 1903, contains a number of early paintings of the **Nice School**★★, including a St Nicholas altarpiece by Louis Bréa: 18 sections in glowing colours surrounded by Renaissance carving of leaves and dolphins.

Palais Princier (Prince's Palace)★

State Apartments 🕐Open daily: Apr 10.30am–6pm; May–Sept 9.30am–6.30pm; Oct 10am–5.30pm. ☞€9.
Museum of Napoleonic Souvenirs 🕐open Tue–Sun mid-Dec–May 10.30am–12.30pm, 2–5pm; Jun–Sept daily 9.30am–6.30pm; Oct–11 Nov daily 10am–5pm. 🕐Closed 12 Nov–16 Dec, 25 Dec, 1 Jan. ☞€4. 📞00 377 93 25 1831. www.palais.mc .

The oldest parts of the Palace are 13C although the buildings on the south side are in 15–16C Italian Renaissance style. The formidable perimeter is built into the vertical rock and a monumental doorway with the Grimaldi Arms completes the the ensemble.

The palace overlooks a square called the **Place du Palais**★, ornamented with cannon presented by Louis XIV. With its medieval battlements and walls strengthened by Vauban, the palace makes a most picturesque composition. The imposing gateway leads into the Court of Honour with its arcades; inside the Palace is the Throne Room and state apartments decorated with fine furniture and hung with signed portraits by Old Masters.

Monte-Carlo★★★

Europe's gambling capital was launched by François Blanc, director of the casino in Bad Homburg in Germany.

The place's success has led to building at a very high density indeed, but Monte-Carlo retains its attractiveness with its luxurious casino, its sumptuous villas, its de luxe shops and its pretty gardens. From the fine **terrace**★★ of the Casino, the view extends from Monaco to the Bordighera headland in Italy.

Jardin Exotique★★

bd du Jardin-Exotique. 🕐Open mid May–mid-Sept 9am–7pm; mid-Sept–mid-May 9am–6pm. 🕐Closed 19 Nov, 25 Dec. ☞€7. 📞00 377 93 15 29 80.

This exceptional collection (900 varieties) of cacti, some more than a century old, clings dramatically to the cliffs above Monaco, cascading down a steep rock face with huge candelabra-like euphorbia, giant aloes, "mother-in-law cushions" and Barbary figs. Down 279 steps is the **Grotte de l'Observatoire**★, adorned with stalactites and stalagmites. Tools and prehistoric animal bones excavated at the site are on display in the **Musée d'Anthropologie Préhistorique**★ *(access through the Jardin Exotique).*

The Rainier III Gallery contains regional collections including animals which once roamed the Riviera before the climate changed, such as reindeer, mammoths, cave bears and even hippos.

ADDITIONAL SIGHTS
Musée Napoléonien et des Archives du Palais★ – *pl. du Palais.* 🕐Open

daily: Dec–Apr 10.30am–5pm; Apr–Oct 10am–6pm. **○***Closed 1 Jan, 25 Dec.* ⊚€*4.* ☏*00 377 93 25 18 31. www.palais.mc.* One wing of the Palace is devoted to a museum on Napoleon, including genealogical charts showing how the Bonapartes are related to the Grimaldi princes. There are many of the Emperor's personal souvenirs and documents. The upper floor is devoted to the history of Monaco, with the charter granted by Louis XII recognising the Principality's independence on display.

Nouveau Musée National de Monaco★ – *bd du Jardin Exotique.* **○***Open daily 10am–6pm.* ⊚€*6.* ☏*00 377 98 98 48 60. .www.nmnm.mc.* The New National Museum, housed in the charming Villa Paloma built by Charles Garnier and fronted by a rose garden dotted with sculptures (formerly home to the collection of dolls and automata), has, since 2009, hosted temporary exhibitions on the history and culture of the Principality.

Collection des Voitures Anciennes★ – *Fontvieille.* ♿ **○***Open daily 10am–6pm.* **○***Closed 25 Dec.* ⊚€*6 (children, €3).* ☏*00 377 92 05 28 56. www.palais.mc.* About 100 old vehicles and carriages from the royal collection are on display. On the first level are the barouches used by Prince Charles III. Next is the De Dion Bouton (1903), the first car owned by Prince Albert I, a Rolls-Royce Silver Cloud given by Monégasque tradesmen to Prince Rainier on his wedding day in 1956, and a 1952 Austin London taxi converted for Princess Grace. The 1929 Bugatti (winner of the 1st Grand Prix)and a 1989 Ferrari F1 (600hp) have pride of place in the hall dedicated to Formula 1.

Musée des Timbres et des Monnaies – *Fontvieille.* ♿**○***Open daily Oct–Jun 10am–5pm; Jul–Sept 10am–6pm.* ⊚€*3.* ☏*00 377 93 15 41 50* Housed in a very modern setting, this museum contains stamps made in the Principality together with the Princes' collections and rare stamps.

ADDRESSES

🛏STAY

🛏 **Hôtel de France** – *6 r. de la Turbie.* ☏*00 377 93 30 2464. www.monte-carlo. mc/france. 27rms.* ⊊ €*10.* Charming, soundproofed rooms decorated in Provençal hues, and a modern breakfast lounge enhanced with metal and wood furniture.

🛏 **Columbus Hôtel** – *23 ave des Papalins.* ☏*00 377 92 05 922 22. www.columbushotels.com. 181rms.* ⊊ €*25.* Clean, contemporary lines and a soothing palette are combined with cosy fabrics and warm wood furnishings. A lounge bar and Italian-style brasserie with terrace seating attract fashionable locals. Access to a private pool; the heliport is just a block away.

🛏 **Metropôle** – *4 ave de la Madone.* ☏*00 377 93 15 15 15. www.metropole.com. 141rms.* ⊊ €*37.* This 1886 hotel got a complete face-lift by the hot Parisian designer Jacques Garcia, with luxurious fabrics and timeless style. The outdoor pool and solarium have views overlooking the rooftops of the Place du Casino. The restaurant is managed by leading French chef Joël Robuchon.

🍴EAT

🍴 **Polpetta** – *2 r. Paradis.* ☏*00 377 93 50 67 84. Closed Sat lunch & Tue.* A small Italian restaurant offering three different settings in which to enjoy a tasty tagliatelle alla carbonara or vitello al funghi: the verandah giving onto the street, the rustic-style dining hall or the cosy, intimate room at the back.

🍴 **La Maison du Caviar** – *1 ave St-Charles.* ☏*00 377 93 30 80 06. Closed Sat lunch and Sun.* This prestigious house has been serving choice caviar to Monaco residents for the past 50 years. In an unusual setting made up of bottle racks and wooden panelling, you can also purchase salmon, foie gras or bœuf strogonoff. Definitely worth a visit.

🍴 **Vistamar** – *Hôtel Hermitage, Square Beaumarchais.* ☏*00 377 98 06 98 98. www.hotelhermitagemontecarlo.com. Closed for lunch Jul–Aug.* An elegant restaurant specialising in fresh seafood, with one of the best panoramic views of the Principality from its top-floor terrace.

🍽🍽🍽🍽 **Zebra Square** – *Grimaldi Forum, 10 ave Princesse-Grâce.* 📞*00 377 99 99 25 50. Closed 3 weeks in Feb.* This stylish restaurant has the same sleek décor as its Parisian namesake, featuring modern fusion cuisine and panoramic views over the sea from the terrace. At night the bar is packed with a young and trendy crowd.

NIGHTLIFE

Casino de Monte-Carlo – *pl. du Casino.* 📞*00 377 98 06 21 21. www.montecarlo casinos.com. Open daily from 2pm.*🎟*€10.* This is Europe's leading casino, with over a million euros in annual profits, attributed to gambling and not to slot machines as is the case in other casinos. The gambling salons and lavish dining hall Le Train Bleu, decorated in the style of the Orient Express, are truly impressive. The terrace overlooking the sea is a haven of tranquillity, whether or not you have broken the bank!

Bar le Vistamar – *Hôtel Hermitage, Square Beaumarchais.* 📞*00 377 98 06 98 98. www.hotelhermitagemontecarlo.com.* This famous bar has been patronised by many celebrities over the years. Its superb terrace affords beautiful views of Monaco harbour. The specialities of the house are American cocktails, particularly with champagne!

Sass Café – *11 ave Princesse-Grace.* 📞*00 377 93 25 52 00. www.sasscafe.com.* Exclusive bar-restaurant with a cosy atmosphere where members of the local jet set drop in for a fancy vodka or champagne cocktail before meeting up at Jimmy'z.

Le Jimmy'z – *26 ave Princesse-Grâce.* 📞*00 377 92 16 20 00. Reservations recommended.* Formal evening wear is expected in this legendary small but select club where the wealthy love to congregate, whether they come from banking, advertising, fashion, film or the entertainment world. A unique, magic experience.

Stars'N'Bars – *6 quai Antoine 1er.* 📞*00 377 97 97 95 95. www.starsnbars.com.* This is the great American bar-of-the-moment, more relaxed than the Principality's other establishments, and catering to a younger clientele eager to drink beer, eat a hamburger or two, play billiards, surf on the internet and dance the night away. The decoration features the paraphernalia of stars. Rock concerts are organised on a regular basis. Terrace with a view of Monaco harbour.

Grimaldi Forum – *10 ave Princesse-Grâce.* 📞*00 377 99 99 20 00. www.grimaldiforum. com.* This 1 800-seat auditorium plays host to headlining events throughout the year, including performances by the Monte Carlo Ballet and the Monte Carlo Philharmonic Orchestra.

ENTERTAINMENT

Le Cabaret – *pl. du Casino.* 📞*00 377 92 16 36 36. www.montecarloresort.com. Shows mid-Sept–mid-Jun Wed–Sat from 10.30pm; bar/restaurant open from 8.30pm.* This cabaret, run by the Monte-Carlo Casino, presents nightly flamenco, jazz or pop concerts.

BOAT TRIPS

👥 **Aquavision** – *quai des Etats-Unis, Port Hercule.* 📞*00 377 92 16 15 15. Departures several times daily throughout the season.* 🎟*€12 (child €8).* Views of the sea depths, and marine fauna and flora, with commentary in four languages.

SHOPPING

All the famous fashion brands have boutiques in Monte-Carlo. Find shops specialising in traditional goods in the narrow streets of the Rock (*Le Rocher*) opposite the palace. Boutique du Rocher in Avenue de la Madone is the official shop for local crafts.

EVENTS

Highlights of a packed calendar are:

Monte-Carlo Rally – *Held every year since 1911 (late Jan).*
Feast of Ste-Dévote – *Feast day of Monaco's Patron Saint (27 Jan).*
Sciaratù Carnival – *Monégasque festival (week of Mardi Gras).*
Spring Arts Festival – *Art, music, theatre and dance festival (Apr).*
Formula 1 Monaco Grand Prix – *Race in the Principality's winding streets (late May): 78 laps of a 3.34km/2.08mi circuit.*
National Day – *Picturesque procession and cultural displays (19 Nov).*

Menton★★

Alpes-Maritimes

Between mountain and Mediterranean, Menton stretches out agreeably on its sunny site★★ on the lower slopes of a picturesque natural amphitheatre of mountains. The town is known for its citrus groves and its dazzling annual Lemon Festival (during Carnival).

A BIT OF HISTORY

On the cliffs around are the remains of fortifications and human settlement going back to Neolithic times. The town was bought by the Grimaldi family of Monaco in the 14C, then incorporated into the French kingdom when the county of Nice was annexed.

SIGHTS
Hôtel de Ville

The town hall is a pretty building in Italianate style, with pilasters and Corinthian capitals and a cream-coloured cornice contrasting with the rosy rendering of the walls. The **Salle des mariages**★ was decorated by Cocteau in 1958 and can be visited duiring normal office hours for a small fee.

Vieille Ville★★

The old town nestles underneath the hill just above r. Longue and r. St-Michel and is fragrant with orange trees,

- ▶ **Population:** 29 327
- **Michelin Map:** 341 F 5
- **Info:** 8 ave Boyer. ✆04 92 41 76 76. www.menton.fr.
- ▶ **Location:** Menton is the last town on the Riviera before the Italian border, 29km/18mi E of Nice. It is divided into a modern beach resort and an old town.
- **Don't Miss:** Gardens in the Garavan district and nearby countryside.

whose alignment marks the course of the Roman Via Giulia Augusta. Parvis St-Michel★★ is a charming square in the Italian style, laid out on two levels by the Grimaldis, whose monogram can be seen in the pebble mosaic forming the paving. It is bordered by a number of houses in the local style, by a pink-walled chapel (Chapelle de la Conception), and by the **Basilique St-Michel** ★ (⊙*open Mon–Fri 10am–noon 3–5.15pm; Sat–Sun 3–5.15pm)*, a fine Baroque building dating from the middle of the 17C, extensively restored after the earthquake of 1887.

THE SEAFRONT AND BEACHES★★

▷ *Start from the Casino Municipal.*

Menton with Basilique St-Michel Archange

© Taylor Richard/Sime/Photononstop

Promenade du Soleil★★

The wide **Promenade du Soleil★★** facing the sea follows the shore beneath the old town.

The **harbour**, used by local fishermen and tourists alike, is flanked by the **Jetée Impératrice-Eugénie** and **Quai Napoléon-III** and its lighthouse. The far end of the port, home to Volti's sculpture of St Michael, commands pleasant **views**★ of old Menton. In the distance you can admire the Italian coastline.

The gravel beach of **Plage des Sablettes** is dominated by Promenade de la Mer and **Quai Bonaparte**. From the top, there is a nice view of the old quarter. A huge flight of steps leads up to the church of St-Michel.

The luxurious residential suburb of **Garavan**, running between Promenade de la Mer and Boulevard de Garavan, has many examples of the eclectic architecture of the Belle Époque (like the Fondation Barriquand-Alphand, d'Abel Gléna on Boulevard de Garavan). The marina can accommodate boats up to 40m/132ft. The pretty 17C Baroque **Chapelle St-Jacques** houses a municipal gallery of contemporary art.

ADDITIONAL SIGHTS
Musée des Beaux-Arts
(Palais Carnolès)★ – ⓒOpen Wed–Mon 10am–noon, 2–6pm. ⬚No charge. ℘04 93 35 49 71. This former summer residence of the princes of Monaco was built in the 17C in the spirit of the Grand Trianon of Versailles.

After heavy remodelling in the 19C it was restored by the Danish architect Georg Tersling and decorated with frescoes on antique themes. The original stuccowork and gilding have survived in the Grand Salon de Musique and the Salon Bleu.

The first floor is dedicated to the collection of **early religious art** by French, Italian and Flemish masters, including Bréa, da Vinci, Luini and Orsi. There are also modern works by Suzanne Valadon, Kisling and Camoin. A collection of **contemporary and modern work** is housed on the ground floor.

Musée Jean-Cocteau – ⓒOpen Wed–Sun 10am–noon, 2–6pm. ⬚€3. ℘04 93 35 49 71. This 17C bastion, built by Honoré II of Monaco, was restored and converted into a museum by Cocteau, the "Prince of the Poets", in 1957. The artist designed pebble mosaics in traditional Menton style on several themes and wrought-iron display cases. In the entrance hangs an Aubusson tapestry, *Judith and Holophernes*, which Matisse described as the "only truly contemporary tapestry".

EXCURSIONS
Roquebrune-Cap Martin★★
▶2km/1.2mi SW.

Roquebrune is a most picturesque hilltop village (**village perché★★**), where the tourist can stroll through the small streets towards the **keep**★ From the top, wonderful **panorama**★★ of the sea, Cap Martin, the Principality of Monaco and the Mont Agel.

Saorge★★

▶ *The village is high in the back country of the Riviera, close to the Italian border.* 🛈 *ave Docteur Joseph Davéo. ℘04 93 04 51 23. www.saorge.fr.*

The **gorges**★★ of the Upper Roya form a spectacular **setting**★★ for the village clinging to the steep, south-facing slopes which rise abruptly from the river far below.

Saorge was originally a Ligurian settlement and then later a Roman colony. In the Middle Ages the town was said to be impregnable, but it has yielded twice since: in 1794 to the French and again in April 1945.

Saorge is dominated by the belfries of its churches and monasteries, overlooking terraces and balconies, old houses with open-fronted drying lofts and roofs tiled with heavy stone slabs. A maze of stepped and tunnelled streets completes this highly picturesque townscape.

Route Napoléon★★

This scenic highway follows the route taken by Napoleon on his return from Elba in 1815. it leads from the Riviera northwest through the Pre-Alps and is marked along its length by the flying eagle symbol inspired by Napoleon's remark: "The eagle will fly from steeple to steeple until he reaches the towers of Notre-Dame".

A BIT OF HISTORY

The Emperor escaped from Elba on 26 February 1815, landing on the beach at Golfe-Juan on 1 March.

2 March: After a brief overnight stop at Cannes, Napoleon and his band halted outside Grasse and took to the mule tracks. The night was spent at Seranon.

3 March: Midday halt at Castellane and overnight in Barrème.

4 March: The party rejoined the highway at Digne, and passed the night at the Château de Malijai.

5 March: The Emperor lunched at Sisteron, then continued. Overnight at Gap.

6 March: At Les Barraques, Napoleon declined the offer of the local peasants to join his force. Overnight at Corps.

7 March: Near Laffrey, the way was barred by troops. Ordered to fire, they hesitated, then broke ranks to shouts of "Vive l'Empereur!" Escorted by the men of the 7th Regiment, Napoleon made a triumphal entry into Grenoble at 7pm.

🚗 DRIVING TOUR

GOLFE-JUAN TO GRENOBLE

336km/208.7mi – allow a whole day.

Leading across the southern Pre-Alps to the long valley known as the Sub-Alpine Furrow, the route can be followed throughout the year.

- **Michelin Map:** 341 B 5-D 6
- **Info:** ℰ04 76 68 15 16. www.route-napoleon.com.
- **Location:** The route starts at Golfe-Juan and ends at Grenoble, via Grasse, Digne and Gap, a distance of 336km/209mi. The highway following the route is mainly the D 6085.
- **Timing:** Napoleon covered the journey in just six days; today's motorists could do it in one very tiring day, when realistically, three or four would allow for better appreciation of the route.

Leave Golfe-Juan to the NE on Avenue de la Liberté (D 6007) for 5km/3mi until you reach Antibes.

Antibes★★

The first settlement here was a trading post founded by Greek merchants from Marseille in the 4C BC. Reconstructed in the 16C, the **Château Grimaldi** dates from the 12C, when it was built on the site of a Roman encampment to protect the coast from the incursions of Barbary pirates. Inside, the **Musée Picasso**★ *(Picasso Museum, 4 r. des Cordiers. ℰ04 92 90 54 20)* has a superb selection of the master's works, including ceramics, drawings, prints and tapestries *(The Lobster, Two Nudes and a Mirror)*, as well as paintings *(Still Life with Watermelon)*. The town was purchased from the Grimaldi family by Henri IV because of its strategic position in relation to the Kingdom of Savoy. It was fortified first by François I, then by Vauban. To the west of the **Cap d'Antibes**★★ stretches the fine sandy beach of Golfe-Juan.

Go E until you hit D 635; follow it N onto La Provençale (A 8/E 80); continue on to Pénétrante Grasse Cannes(D 6185). Once you reach D 9, continue NW to Grasse. 28.5km/17.7mi.

View of Grasse

Grasse★★

Prettily located on the slopes of the Grasse Pre-Alps, the Old Town (**Vieille Ville**★) has picturesque streets lined with tall Provençal houses. Grasse's most famous son is **Jean-Honoré Fragonard** (1732–1806), a painter known for witty depictions of the frivolities of 18C court life. The Salle Fragonarda in the Villa-Musée Fragonard has two of the artist's self-portraits as well as his *Landscape with Washerwomen* and *Three Graces*.

For the past three centuries, Grasse has been the world's most important centre of the perfume industry, with perfume manufacturers open to the public and two museums, the **Musée international de la Parfumerie** (2 bd du Jeu de Ballon; www.museesdegrasse.com) and the **Musée d'Art et d'Histoire de Provence** (2 r. Mirabeau).

To the north of the **Pas de la Faye** with its **view**★★ over mountains and Mediterranean, the road enters Haute Provence through the Seranon valley.

▷ *Leave Grasse NW onto ave Gaston de Fontmichel (D 6085); road becomes D 4085. Continue through La Garde and Chaudanne until you reach Castellane. 64km/39.7mi.*

Castellane★

The sheep-grazed valley in which the town is situated is overlooked by the "Roc", a limestone cliff. The Castellane Pre-Alps extend over a wide area; they consist of a series of bare ridges through which the River Asse has cut a deep valley. To the north rise the Digne Pre-Alps, a harsh landscape with a meagre mantle of garrigue vegetation, deeply scored by the beds of torrents.

A complex geological history has produced a series of folded ridges through which the rivers have cut deep gorges, as well as long crests of pale rock to the east and broad fertile valleys to the north.

▷ *Head NW on bd Saint-Michel; continue towards D 4085. Bear left on to N 85 (direction Grenoble). Continue N through Châteauredon until you hit Digne-les-Bains. 52km/32mi.*

Digne-les-Bains★

Digne spreads out along its valley **site**★ at the foot of the rise on which its old town is situated. There are dramatic **views**★ of the whole area from the hill-top village of **Courbons**★.

In the Place General-de-Gaulle is a memorial to **Pierre Gassendi** (1592–1655), born at nearby Champtercier. This natural philosopher devoted much of his scientific work to studying the properties of sound.

At **Malijai**, the route enters the **Durance basin**, an alluvial plain lying between the Valensole plateau to the east and the Vaucluse to the west. The Durance is the great river of the southern Alps, tracing its meanders through the gravel terraces on which a prosperous agricultural pattern has developed, favoured by the mildness of the climate.

▶ *Leave Digne-les-Bains to the SW along N 1085 for 6km/3.7mi or so; at roundabout take 2nd exit onto N 85 (direction Grenoble). Follow N 85 as it winds NW and becomes D 4. At Briasc, move onto L'Autoroute du Val de Durance (A 51/E 712) heading N following Durance River. Sisteron is about 6km/3.7mi from Briasc.*

Sisteron★★ – ♿ See SISTERON.

▶ *Head out of Sisteron NW on A 51/ E 712. The road merges into N 85. Bear NE until you reach Gap. 50.5km/31.4mi.*

Gap★

Gap is pleasantly sited in the valley carved out by the glacier which was the ancestor of the Durance.

The town's prosperity was built on the rich soils of its agricultural hinterland, one of the most fertile areas of the southern Alps. Founded by the Gauls, Gap became a staging-post along the Roman road from Turin to Valence, then a fortified cathedral town.

The **Col Bayard** links the southern and northern Alps. To the north is the beginning of the Sub-Alpine Furrow which the road enters by way of the Drac Valley. This is an ancient highway, once travelled by merchants on their way to the fairs at St-Bonnet.

▶ *Leave Gap N by N 85; follow N 85 as it bears NE until you reach Corps.*

Corps

A small bustling town in the Sub-Alpine Furrow. The road passes through areas of well-cultivated farmland interrupted by glacial bars, one of which has been used in the siting of the **Barrage de Sautet★★**, with its deep lake hemmed in by high canyon-like walls; far below its surface is the hidden confluence of the Drac with the Souloise. Around La Mure, the Trièves country is overlooked by the

broad summit of Mont Aiguille, also known as the "unclimbable mountain", although it was actually conquered as long ago as 1492.

▶ *Leave Corps NW by r. des Fosses (D 1085) and continue for 24.5km/15mi. Turn left at D 1085/r. de Breuil and keep following D 1085 for about 14km/9.3mi N, passing Lac de Pierre-Châtel, Lac de Petichet and Lac de Laffrey until you reach Laffrey.*

Laffrey★

Just south of the village lies the spot known as "Prairie de la Rencontrea", where the vain attempt was made to bar Napoleon's progress northwards. The road now descends towards Vizillea and Grenoble.

ADDRESSES

♥/EAT

🍽🍽 **Nounou** – *On the beach at Golfe-Juan.* ℘*04 93 63 71 73. www.nounou.fr. Closed Nov–Mar.* Regional cuisine and seafood specialities.

CERAMICS

Tour of traditional pottery workshops – *Closed Sat–Sun.* 🚳*No charge. Information at the tourist office* ℘*04 93 63 82 58.*

Pottery classes – *Espace Grandjean, bd des Deux-Vallons. Closed winter, Sat–Sun in summer.* ℘*04 93 63 07 61.* Pottery classes for kids and adults at the fine arts school (10, 20 or 30 hours).

♥ EVENTS

Fête de la Poterie – This pottery festival takes place on the second Sunday in August.

Biennial International Festival of Ceramic Art – ℘*04 93 64 34 67, http://biennale.vallauris.free.fr.* Even-numbered years Jul–mid Oct.

Cannes★★★
Alpes-Maritimes

A charming old quarter, chic town centre and glamorous beachside promenade make Cannes one of the most enjoyable places on the Riviera. Spread out between the Suquet Heights and La Croisette Point on the shore of La Napoule Bay, Cannes also owes its popularity to an exceptionally beautiful setting. Star of the Côte d'Azur, Cannes became known as early as 1834 for its mild climate, making it the preferred winter salon of the world's aristocracy. Framed to the west by the red rocks of the Esterel and across the bay by the forested Îles de Lérins, this beautiful setting forms the backdrop to the palm-lined beaches of La Croisette and the world-famous Cannes Film Festival.

A BIT OF HISTORY

In 1834, the former Lord Chancellor of England, Lord Henry Brougham, was on his way to Italy when he was prevented from entering the County of Nice, then part of Italy, due to a cholera epidemic. Forced to wait, he made an overnight stop at a fishing village called Cannes. Enchanted by the place, he built a villa here and returned to it every winter, establishing a trend among the English aristocracy and stimulating Cannes' first period of growth, ultimately leading to its establishment as a holiday resort.

SIGHTS

Boulevard de la Croisette ★★

Locals and visitors congregate along this wide, attractive seafront road, with delightful gardens along its centre. To one side extends the splendid sandy beach and broad promenade, while the landward side of the boulevard is lined with the dignified and impeccably maintained façades of four luxury "palace" hotels and exclusive boutiques. At the eastern end of La Croisette is a marina, busy with yachts and pleasure craft, and at its western end another, overlooked by the Festival and Confer-

▶ **Population:** 73 903

◔ **Michelin Map:** 341 B-D 5 and D P-Q 5

▯ **Info:** Palais des Festivals, 1 bd de la Croisette. ✆04 92 99 84 22; Gare SNCF. ✆04 93 99 19 77; pl. du Marché 1 r. Pierre Sémard. ✆04 92 99 84 22. www.cannes.fr.

▷ **Location:** Cannes is situated 34.4km/21.3mi along the coast SW of Nice.

⊛ **Don't Miss:** The superb covered market.

◕ **Timing:** As a town Cannes is extensive; the heart of town is in a narrow strip close to the sea, while the centre of the action is the Palais des Festivals et des Congrès.

TOURS AND TRANSPORTATION

TAM – ✆0800 06 01 06. These buses operate between **Cannes** and **Nice**, including a direct service to the airport. **Train Station** – *SNCF Gare de Cannes.* ✆0891 70 30 00. www.ter-sncf. com/paca. This train station is served by local and national trains including **TGV** and regional **TER** trains (service between **Mandelieu-La-Napoule** and **Vintimille**). The Carte Isabelle day rail pass offers excellent value along the **Côte d'Azur** between Fréjus and Vintimille *(1 Jun–30 Sept; €12, family passes also available).* **Trans Côte d'Azur** – *Quai Laubeuf.* ✆04 92 98 71 30. www.trans-cote-azur.com. Regular service to the **Île Ste-Marguerite** (15min), plus seasonal tours to l'**Île de Porquerolles, Monaco, Saint-Tropez, San Remo, la Corniche d'Or,** etc.

ence Centre (Palais des Festivals et des Congrès) where the **Cannes International Film Festival** is held every May – the town's most spectacular and prestigious event.

Le Suquet

Le Suquet, the old town area of Cannes, climbs a steep hill beside the Old Port. The lower streets of this area are today the centre for nightlife and restaurants. From a terrace in front of the Tour du Mont Chevalier, there is a fine **view**★ over beach and bay, the Lérins Islands and the Esterel Heights.

The 11C Cannes castle today houses the remarkable **Musée de la Castre** ★★ (Le Suquet; ℘04 93 38 55 26; ⊶guided tours (1hr) available), an eclectic 19C private collection of exceptional ethnographic artefacts taken from cultures around the world.

EXCURSIONS
Les Îles de Lérins★★

The peaceful **islands** (boat service from Cannes) are clad in a rich vegetation of pines, cypresses and eucalyptus and have a fascinating historic and archaeological heritage. The fine view back to the coast of the mainland stretches from Cap Roux to Cap d'Antibes.

Île Ste-Marguerite★★

There are fine **forest walks** as well as through the botanical collection and along the avenue, Allée des eucalyptus géants. **Fort Royal** was built for coastal defence by Richelieu.

The fort served as a prison for Protestants, and also for the mysterious Man in the Iron Mask (1687–98), whose identity has never been established with certainty. From the terrace there is an extensive **view**★ of the coast.

Massif de l'Esterel★★★

▶ 40km/24.8mi W by N 98.

The Esterel stretches along the coastline of the Var between Cannes and Fréjus, and encompasses several small villages and resorts such as St-Raphaël.

🛈 The tourist offices of St-Raphaël-Agay, Fréjus, Mandelieu and Le Muy work with the National Office of Forestry to organise tours of the forests in the Massif de l'Esterel. ℘04 94 19 52 52. www.saint-raphael.com. 🅿 Except in high season around the major towns, free parking is relatively easy to find near walking trailheads.

⚠ It is advisable to remove all valuables from your car when walking.

⚠ Don't miss the panoramic view from the Pointe de l'Esquillon, the scenic port in Agay, and for the robust hikers, the views from the Pic de l'Ours. You could easily drive through the Esterel along N 98 coastal road from Cannes to Fréjus in less than an hour, with a pause for a short walk at Dramont or the Point d'Esquillon. For the longer walks plan for at least a half day, and be prepared with enough drinking water, food and appropriate footwear.

The Esterel between St-Raphaël and La Napoule is an area of breathtaking natural beauty. One of the loveliest parts of

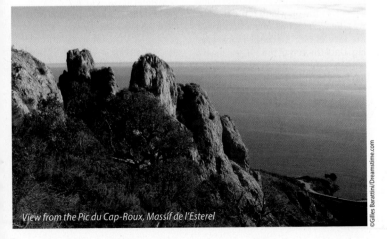

View from the Pic du Cap-Roux, Massif de l'Esterel

©Gilles Barattini/Dreamstime.com

Provence, it was opened to large-scale tourism by the Touring Club's creation in 1903 of the scenic road known as the Corniche d'Or (Golden Scenic Route). The fiery red of the rocks forms a strong contrast with the deep blue of the sea, while the bustling life along the coast contrasts with the seclusion of the inland roads.

The Massif – The massif's jagged relief of volcanic rock (red porphyry) worn by erosion dips vertically into the deep blue sea between La Napoule and St-Raphaël. The rugged coastline is fringed with rocks, islets and reefs.

From **Mont Vinaigre**★★★, its highest peak (alt 618m/2 027ft), a vast panorama unfolds over the surrounding area. The pine and cork-oak forests clothing the wild and lonely massif have been ravaged by fire in recent years.

Via Aurelia – The Esterel was bordered to the north by the Via Aurelia (Aurelian Way), one of the most important routes of the Roman Empire, connecting Rome and Arles via Genoa, Cimiez, Antibes, Fréjus and Aix. Paved, cambered, and more than 2.5m/8ft wide, the road made use of many bridges and other civil engineering works to create the shortest route possible. At the end of each Roman mile (1 478m/1 617yd) distances would be indicated by a tall milestone – one is on display in St-Raphaël (Musée Archéologique).

Esterel Gap – The road skirting the north side of the Esterel, which for many years was the only land route to Italy, was rife with highwaymen; "to survive the Esterel Gap" became a local saying. Until the end of the 19C the massif remained the refuge of convicts escaping from Toulon.

RESORTS

Stretching more than 30km/18.6mi between St-Raphaël and La Napoule, the striking landscape of the Corniche de l'Esterel is punctuated by several pleasant seaside resorts.

The small resort of **Boulouris**, where villas are dotted among pines in beautiful gardens, has several little beaches and a harbour.

Agay borders a deep port, the best in the Esterel, used in earlier times by the Ligurians, the Greeks and the Romans. The scenic bay of the **Rastel d'Agay** is lined by a large, sunny beach.

The resort of **Anthéor** is dominated by the three peaks of the Cap Roux range. Just before the Pointe de l'Observatoire is a **view** inland of the red rocks of St-Barthélemy and Cap Roux.

Le Trayas is divided into two parts: one terraced on wooded slopes, the other by the seashore. The creeks and inlets which mark the coast include many small beaches, the largest of which lies at the end of Figueirette Bay.

Miramar is an elegant resort with a private harbour in Figueirette Bay.

La Galere is built on wooded terraces on the slopes of the Esterel where it forms the western limit of La Napoule Bay. Below the road, the seaside development of **Port-la-Galère** (private port), an astonishing design by the architect Jacques Couelle, seems to merge into its rocky environment.

Théoule-sur-Mer is sheltered by the Théoule promontory. It has three small beaches. The crenellated building on the shore, now a château, used to be a soap factory in the 18C.

ADDRESSES

🛏 STAY

🍽 **Hôtel Alnea** – *20 r. Jean de Riouffe.* ✆*04 93 68 77 77. www.hotel-alnea.com. Closed 3 weeks in Dec. 14rms. 🍽 €7.50.* A family-run establishment with simple well-kept and colourful rooms. Located just a couple of minutes from La Croisette in the heart of Cannes.

🍽🍽 **Hôtel Appia** – *6 r. Marceau.* ✆*04 93 06 59 59. www.appia-hotel.com. Closed 21 Nov–28 Dec, 5–14 Jan. 32rms. 🍽 €7.* Practicality takes precedence over comfort in this downtown hotel where the well-kept, smallish rooms are both air-conditioned and soundproofed. Pristine bathrooms.

🍽🍽🍽 **Villa l'Églantier** – *14 r. Campestra.* ✆*04 93 68 22 43. 3rms.* Impressive white villa dating from 1920, surrounded by palm trees and other exotic species, dominating the city of Cannes. The large, peaceful rooms are all extended by a terrace or a balcony.

ᵗ/ EAT

🍴 **Le Côte d'Azur** – *3 r. Jean-Daumas. 📞04 93 38 60 02. Closed evenings and Sun.* Modest restaurant with a friendly ambience and cosy setting with period furnishings. The traditional cooking attracts a great many locals.

🍴🍽 **Aux Bons Enfants** – *80 r. Meynadier. Closed 1 Dec–2 Jan.* Simplicity, generosity and congeniality are the hallmarks of this informal establishment where there's no telephone and customers are required to pay in cash. A true locals' hangout since 1935, with tasty Mediterranean dishes.

🍴🍽 **Le Comptoir des Vins** – *13 bd de la République. 📞04 93 68 13 26. Closed a fortnight in Feb and a fortnight in Sept; all Sun.* This handsomely stocked wine boutique leads to a colourful dining area where light snacks can be served, washed down with a glass of wine.

🍴🍽🍷 **Le Caveau 30** – *45 r. Félix-Faure. 📞04 93 39 06 33. www.lecaveau30.com.* Large restaurant comprising two dining rooms done up in the style of a 1930 brasserie. The terrace overlooks a shaded square popular among *boules* players. Fish and seafood are the specialities of the house.

🍴🍽🍷 **Fred l'écailler** – *7 pl. de l'Étang. 📞04 93 43 15 85. http://fredlecailler.com.* A large neon sign marks the entrance to this rustic-style restaurant whose walls are draped with fishing nets. The tiny square affords a glimpse of village life with its bustling activity and daily games of *pétanque*. Fine selection of freshly caught fish and seafood.

🍴🍽🍷 **Au Poisson Grillé** – *8 quai St-Pierre, Vieux Port. 📞04 93 39 44 68. www.poisson-grille.com.* Appropriately located in the old port, this fish restaurant was opened back in 1949. It serves grilled fish alongside many other Mediterranean dishes, in a warm setting of varnished wood evoking the interior of a luxury cabin. Attentive service at affordable prices.

🍸 NIGHTLIFE

The best way to get to know this glamorous city is to frequent its luxury hotel bars: order a cocktail on the terrace of the Carlton Hotel, on the beach of the Majestic or in the piano bar of the Martinez.

L'Amiral – *73 la Croisette. 📞04 92 98 73 00. www.hotel-martinez.com.* Attached to the Martinez Hotel, this bar is by far the most popular meeting place along the coast. It owes its reputation to the head barman and to Jimmy, the American piano player. Live music every evening from 8pm.

🛒 SHOPPING

Market – *Marché de Forville; Tue–Sun 7am–1pm.* Fine stalls displaying fresh regional produce. **Allées de la Liberté** – Flower market every morning. Popular flea market on Saturdays. **Shopping streets** – *r. Meynadie.* Tempting window displays of food and craftwork in lively pedestrian area. Rue d'Antibes: luxury clothes and luggage. **Cannolive** – *16 r. Vénizelos. 📞04 93 39 08 19.* This shop boasts an incredible choice of Provençal products: household linen, *tapenades*, crockery, *santons*, soap, and even Lérina liqueur from the nearby islands.

🏃 LEISURE ACTIVITIES

Watersports Plongée Club de Cannes *(46 r. Clémenceau; 📞04 9338 6757).*

Beaches – Not all the beaches on La Croisette charge a fee (details of prices are listed at the top of the steps), or belong to a hotel (located opposite). There are also three free beaches, one of which is located behind the Palais du Festival. The other public beaches lie west of the old port, on Boulevard Jean-Hibert and Boulevard du Midi, at Port Canto and on Boulevard Gazagnaire beyond La Pointe.

Ponton Majestic Ski Nautique – *10 bd de la Croisette. 📞04 92 98 77 47. http://majesticskiclub.online.fr.* Water-skiing and parasailing.

🎭 EVENTS

Cannes International Film Festival – 11 days in May; free open-air cinema on the beach. *📞01 53 59 61 00. www.festival-cannes.com.*

Nuits Misicales du Suquet – Mid- to late Jul; classical concerts on the esplanade in front of the Église du Suquet. *📞04 92 99 33 83. www.nuitsdusuquet-cannes.com.*

St-Tropez★★

Var

After half a century of fame, the little town of St-Trop' (as the locals call it) is still in fashion, thanks to an exquisitely picturesque harbour, a stunning location, and a constant stream of artists, journalists and photographers.

VISIT

Celebrities can sometimes be spotted in St-Tropez and the atmosphere is created by an impressive array of luxury charter yachts moored in the picturesque harbour, which teems with life.

The old fishing village, which was discovered by writer **Guy de Maupassant** and his friend painter **Paul Signac**, and went on to attract Matisse and major post-Impressionist artists as well as the writer **Colette**, remains a fashionable resort frequented by writers and artists and more recently by celebrities from the entertainment world.

Two *Bravades*, or "acts of defiance", take place each year in May. The first is a religious procession in honour of St-Tropez, while the second commemorates an event of local history which took place in 1637.

Musée de l'Annonciade★★

pl. Georges Grammont. ○*Open Jun–Sept Wed–Mon 10am–noon; Oct and Dec–May 10am–noon, 2–6pm.* ○*Closed 1 Jan, 1 May, Ascension Day, 25 Dec;* ◈€6. ℘04 94 17 84 10.

The museum, in an old house delightfully positioned on a bend in the quayside, has an impressive permanent collection, including post-Impressionist pictures of St-Tropez and also some remarkable temporary exhibitions.

EXCURSIONS
St-Tropez Peninsula★★

St-Tropez is located on the north coast of the peninsula. Its east coast is fringed with popular sandy beaches, notably the famous **Plage de Pampelonne**. The south coast has some scenic rocky headlands. The interior is hilly and rustic,

▶ **Population:** 5 364
◉ **Michelin Map:** 340 O 6
▤ **Info:** quai Jean-Jaurès.
℘0892 68 48 28.
www.ot-saint-tropez.com.
▷ **Location:** St-Tropez, 86km/54mi from Cannes, can be reached on the congested road that encircles the peninsula. The easiest approach is by the short passenger ferry from Port Grimaud across the bay.
Ⓟ **Parking:** Use the large car parks on the edge of town.

with small vineyards, pine copses and two charming old villages commanding wide views, **Ramatuelle** and smaller **Gassin**. A **footpath** extends around the coast of the whole peninsula.

Massif des Maures★★★

The long, low parallel ranges of the massif unfold from Fréjus to Hyères. Its fine forests of pine, cork oak and chestnut trees have often been devastated by fire. Chapels, monasteries and small villages are dotted in the hinterland, while the coast is fringed by coves, bays and small beach resorts.

Abbaye du Thoronet★★

▷ *The abbey can be reached from autoroute A 8, junction 13.* ♿ ○*Open daily: Apr–Sept 10am–6.30pm, Sun 10am–noon, 2–6.30pm; Oct–Mar Mon–Sat 10am–1pm, 2–5pm, Sun 10am–noon, 2–5pm.* ○*Closed 1 Jan, 1 May, 1 and 11 Nov, 25 Dec.* ◈€7. ℘04 94 60 43 90/98.http://thoronet.monuments-nationaux.fr.

Of the "Three Cistercian Sisters of Provence" (the others are Silvacane and Sénanque), Le Thoronet is the earliest; it was founded in 1136, when St Bernard was still alive. It is one of the most characteristic of Cistercian abbeys, as well as one of the most austere.

The plain architecture of the abbey is unrelieved by decoration, save in the chapterhouse, where just two roughly sculpted capitals relieve the prevailing rigour. The abbey **church**★ has a simple beauty. Built from 1160 onwards, it has remarkable stonework which was cut and assembled without the use of mortar (notably in the oven-vaulted apse). The **cloisters**★ of about 1175 have kept their four barrel-vaulted walks; the change of level is more obvious here than in the church and is still causing problems of subsidence.

ADDRESSES

🛌 STAY

😑🍽 **Bello Visto** – *pl. deï Barri, Gassin, 8km/5mi SW of St-Tropez.* 𝄢*04 94 56 17 30. Closed Jan and Nov. 9 rms.* ⌶ *€8.* There's truth in the name of this small family-run out-of-town hotel and restaurant at the top of Gassin village. Most rooms, like the terrace, profit from a "beautiful vista" over the Massif des Maures and the gulf of St-Tropez. Dining room with Provençal cuisine.

😑🍽🍽 **Hôtel Lou Cagnard** – *ave Paul-Roussel.* 𝄢*04 94 97 04 24. www.hotel-lou-cagnard.com. Closed 1 Nov–26 Dec. 19 rooms.* ⌶ *€11.* Enjoy breakfast in the shade of a mulberry tree in the tiny garden of this pretty Provençal house, just off Place des Lices. At night you'll be lulled to sleep by the chirping of cicadas. Modest prices, for St-Tropez.

😑🍽🍽🍽 **Hôtel de La Ponche** – *3 r. des Remparts.* 𝄢*04 94 97 02 53. www.laponche.com. Closed 2 Nov–3 Apr. 18rms.* ⌶ *€20.* The rooms of this cosy hotel occupy four village houses formerly belonging to fishermen; the blue one was a favourite of actress Romy Schneider's. The rooftop terraces nestle between the citadel and the bell tower, and the warm, bright hues, combined with considerate service, make the Hôtel Ponche an absolute must.

🍽 EAT

😑🍽 **Leï Salins** – *rte des Salins.* 𝄢*04 94 97 04 40.* Open-air beach restaurant offering a tasty bill of fare consisting of salads and grilled, freshly caught fish. Charming seaside location coupled with attractive surroundings.

😑🍽🍽 **Leï Mouscardins** – *1 r. Portalet.* 𝄢*04 94 97 29 00. Closed Wed off-season.* Tucked away behind the harbour, near Tour du Portalet, this restaurant pays homage to Mediterranean tradition. It has a faithful following of food lovers, lured by its creative and lovingly prepared cuisine, presented to you in two dining rooms opening out onto St-Tropez Bay.

😑🍽🍽 **Régis Restaurant** – *19 r. de la Citadelle.* 𝄢*04 94 97 15 53.* Pasta in all shapes and sizes, cooked in various ways, as well as sushi and wok stir-fries, attract a regular clientele to this restaurant located on a steep, narrow street in St-Tropez.

😑🍽🍽 **La Table du Marché** – *38 r. Georges-Clemenceau.* 𝄢*04 94 97 85 20. www.christophe-leroy.com/tablemarche sttropez.* Gourmets will love this temple of gastronomy located near Place des Lices, open all day. In addition to the restaurant offering traditional French cuisine, La Table du Marché is also known for its home made pastries that can be purchased on the premises.

🍸 NIGHTLIFE

Bar du Château de la Messardière – *rte de Tahiti.* 𝄢*04 94 56 76 00.* This bar belongs to one of the Riviera's most prestigious hotels. Cosy ambience in the piano bar of this former 18C private residence.

Le Bar du Sube – *15 quai Suffren sur le Port.* 𝄢*04 94 97 30 04.* Right on the quayside, one of the most beautiful bars in town.

Sénéquier – *quai Jean-Jaurès.* 𝄢*04 94 97 20 20.* The pavement terrace and crimson chairs of this tea room are famous throughout the world – or so say the locals! Renowned personalities such as Jean Marais, Errol Flynn and Colette would come here for the many delights on offer.

🛍 SHOPPING

Markets – *Tue and Sat, pl. des Lices.*

Shopping streets – *r. Clemenceau, r. Gambetta and r. Allard* offer an impressive selection of local arts and crafts: pottery, glassware, etc.

Les Sandales Tropéziennes – *16 r. Georges Clemenceau.* 𝄢*04 94 97 19 55.* The Rondini house has been crafting St-Tropez sandals since 1927. The distinctive, namesake model in natural leather is the most popular, but the snakeskin version sells well, too!

Le Petit Village – *at La Foux roundabout, follow signs to Grimaud/Cogolin.* 𝄢*04 94 56 32 04.* This showroom brings together wines from eight prestigious vineyards on the St-Tropez peninsula, just off the busy La Foux intersection.

Toulon★★

Var

Backed by high hills whose summits are crowned by forts, Toulon is France's second most important naval base, set in one of the Mediterranean's most beautiful harbours. The Old Town of Toulon is located on the Old Port, or Vieille Darse, bounded to the east by Cours Lafayette, to the west by Rue Anatole-France and to the north by Rue Landrin. The greater Toulon area includes the towns surrounding the harbours (Grande Rade and Petite Rade) as well as the Bay of Lazaret formed by the peninsula of the Presqu'île de St-Mandrier. The Old Town is accessible to pedestrians only.

- ▶ **Population:** 169 010
- ⓖ **Michelin Map:** 340 K 7
- ▪ **Info:** 334 ave de la République. ℘04 94 18 53 00. www.toulon tourisme.com.
- ◖ **Location:** The city is 64km/39.7mi E of Marseille.
- ℗ **Parking:** The largest parking areas are located on the Place d'Armes, Place de la Liberté/Palais Liberté, and at the Centre Mayol.
- ⊛ **Don't Miss:** A boat trip around the immense natural harbour *(rade)* is especially enjoyable (1hr; €9. ℘04 94 93 07 56). Also don't miss the winding streets of the Old Town and Old Port around the Arsenal and Quai Cronstadt.

SIGHTS
La Rade★★

Construction of Toulon's Old Port (Darse Vieille) began under Henri IV. Richelieu appreciated the strategic advantages of the roadstead and ordered the building of the first naval installations. In the reign of Louis XIV, the base was extended and the New Port (Darse Neuve) laid out by Vauban. In the 19C, the Mourillon extension and the Castigneau basin were built, completing the naval base which had become the home port of the French Mediterranean Fleet.

Port★

To the west of the Quai Cronstedt (landing-stage for boat trips) is the **Navy Museum** (Musée de la Marine). Once the entrance to the old Arsenal, its doorway is a Louis XV masterpiece; it is flanked by sculptures of Mars and Bellona and has marble columns with Doric capitals framing tableaux of maritime motifs. The balcony of the former **Town Hall** is supported by two splendidly muscular **Atlantes**★, the work of Pierre Puget.

Mont Faron★★★

This distinctive yet small massif rising behind the town is the easternmost of the limestone ranges which were raised up in Provence on the fringe of the great earth movements associated with the formation of the Alps.

A telepherique travels over pine-clad slopes to the summit, an exciting experience, with thrilling views of Toulon, the inner and outer anchorages, the St-Mandrier and Cap Sicié peninsulas and Bandol. (bd Amiral Vence. ⊛€7. ℘04 94 92 68 25).

Musée-mémorial du Débarquement en Provence★

♿ⓞ*Open daily except Mon: 10am–1pm, 2–5.30pm (May–Sept 6.30pm).* ⊛€4. ℘04 94 88 08 09.

From the tower, Tour Beaumont, there are fine views inland as well as a magnificent seaward **panorama**★★★ over the Hyères Islands, the Toulon roadstead and the whole of the coast between Sanary and Bandol.

The diorama explains the course of the landings which took place on the night of 14–15 August 1944, and of the subsequent liberation of the coast between Antheor and Marseille.

EXCURSIONS
Hyères★

The palm trees and mild climate of this southernmost Riviera resort are a good indication of what has attracted winter visitors to Hyères (aka Hyères-les-Palmiers) for more than a century. Its magnificent villas and Belle Époque palace hotels reveal the faded glory of the town once populated by wealthy aristocrats. Excavations on the coast reveal that Greeks from Marseille set up a trading station called **Olbia**, which was succeeded by a Roman town **Pomponiana**, and then a convent called **St-Pierre-d'Almanarre** during the Middle Ages, when the inhabitants moved further up the hill.

The town became a well-known resort in the 19C. In the 20C, tourism led to the development of the beaches, although Hyères is a lively town throughout the year.

Beaches

The long sandy beach of **L'Almanarre** is near the ancient site of the Greek town of Olbia and used by many surfing schools. The Route du Sel (accessible only in summer) leads along the peninsula, passing a vast salt marsh and then the Étang des Pesquiers, home to many aquatic birds.

Boats leave from the **port** for the Îles d'Hyères. The old port of Hyères, **Ayguade-le-Ceinturon**, is where St Louis disembarked on his return from the Seventh Crusade. It is now a pleasant resort area with two sand beaches.

Jardins Olbius-Riquier

○Open daily 7.30am–5pm (summer until 8pm). ⊘No charge.

The extensive gardens grow a rich variety of tropical plants, palms and cacti. In the **greenhouse** more fragile species can be seen together with a few rare animals.

Villa de Noailles

○Open daily except Mon–Tue and public holidays 1–6pm (Fri 3–8pm). ⊘No charge. ✆04 94 01 84 40. www.villanoailles-hyeres.com.

In 1923 the Noailles, a rich couple of art patrons, commissioned ths winter villa from the Belgian architect Mallet-Stevens. With its covered swimming pool and 60 or so rooms, it was one of the first modern homes on the Riviera, and became a favourite rendez-vous for avant-garde artists of the 1920s (Picasso, Giacometti, Man Ray, Dalí). The city restored the villa in 1986, and temporary exhibitions are held on the first floor.

Îles d'Hyères★★★

⊘No matter which island you visit, be sure to take plenty of drinking water.

These popular Côte d'Azur islands off the Hyères harbour are just a short sea crossing from the coast, and offer many beautiful scenic walking trails, sandy beaches and rocky inland hills. These islands are also known as the **Îles d'Or** due to the fact that in certain lights their mica shale rocks cast golden reflections.

Île de Porquerolles★★★

Porquerolles was called Protè (First) by the Greek settlers who came to live along its shores. The best way to discover the island is by bicycle (hired in the village). The north coast has sandy beaches bordered by pine trees, heather and scented myrtle; the south coast is steep and rugged with one or two inlets that are easily accessible.

Île-de Port-Cros★★★

Port-Cros Island is hillier, more rugged, and higher above the sea than its neighbours, and its lush vegetation is unrivalled on the coast. A few fishermen's cottages, a bunch of shops and a small church adorn the area around the bay, which is commanded by Fort du Moulin (aka the "Château"). Port-Cros, together with Île de Bagaud and neighbouring islets is designated a **Parc National**.

Île du Levant

The island consists of a rocky spine rimmed by vertical cliffs. Ninety percent of the island is occupied by the Marine Nationale (⊘access is forbidden). Much of the rest is used for private nudist beaches.

Languedoc-Roussillon follows the arc of the coastal plain from the mighty Rhône to the massive barrier of the Pyrénées. Adjoining the Languedoc-Roussillon on its western edge, the Midi-Pyrénées stretches from the mountains of the south to the Massif Central in the north. It is a hugely diverse area, ranging from seaside resorts to mountain villages and rural hamlets, not to mention some large towns and cities in both regions.

Highlights

1 The magnificent meander of the **Cirque de Navacelles** (p364)
2 Fortified Templar settlement on the Causses: **La Couvertoirade** (p365)
3 Restored Medieval walled city of **Carcassonne** (p387)
4 The last stronghold of the Cathars: **Château de Montségur** (p390)
5 Abbey on an eagle's eyrie: **St-Martin-du-Canigou** (p397)

Geography – Along the southern edge of the Massif Central stretch the Grands Causses, whose corniche roads offer unforgettable views. The Cévennes to the east consist of granite summits and deep, narrow valleys that merge with the scrubby *garrigues*. The plains of Lower Languedoc and Roussillon are bordered by a chain of brackish lakes, separated from the Mediterranean by sandy bars. The south of the region is dominated by the Pyrénées mountain range. To the west the Garonne flows through the heartland of the Midi-Pyrénées, and, to the north, the Lot meanders through the wine region of Cahors.

History – The Languedoc-Roussillon plain was used by Hannibal after he crossed the Pyrénées en route to Rome (214 BC). By the 2C AD, the Romans were in control but eventually the region was ruled by the Counts of Toulouse. Following the Cathar heresy, French kings took control; the region has been part of France since then.

Languedoc nevertheless saw the rise of a number of traditions particular to the area, as well as a Romance language – Langue d'Oc – used by wandering poets (troubadours), who composed plaintive songs typically of unrequited love and travelled around southern France, entertaining the court nobility during the 11C to 13C. Today the term Occitan is used and comprises several major dialects; street signs in Occitan can be seen today in many of the regions' towns. Its similarity to Catalan, the national language of neighbouring Andorra and an official language of Spain, facilitated a certain degree of cultural exchange that is still

View of La Cité, Carcassonne

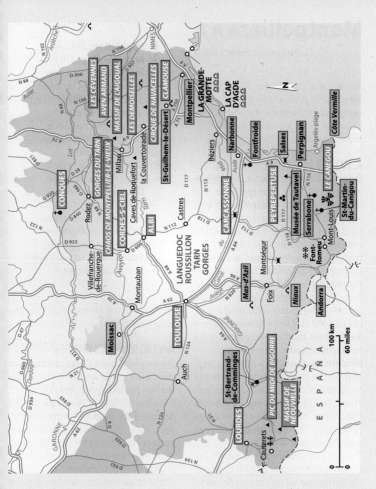

evident today in the *sardana* dances accompanied by *cobla* orchestras at festivals such as those at Céret.

Today – The economic diversity of Languedoc-Roussillon and the Midi-Pyrénées is as vast and varied as its geography, ranging from artisanal crafting of fine leather goods or the casting of church bells at the Hérault foundry at Hérépian, to the high-tech wonders of the aeriopace industry around Toulouse, as well as bio and nano technologies. In this part of France, you're never far from vineyards, the mainstay of the local economy. Much of the Midi-Pyrénées is given over to agriculture and tourism. Languedoc-Rousillon is the fourth most visited tourist area in France. With some 15 million visitors a year,

one-third from outside France, tourism is a huge economic player, with summer beach-going on Languedoc's "sunshine coast," cultural tourism, sybaritic spas like d'Amélie-les Bains at Vallespir and ski resorts like Cerdagne et le Capcir. The region's booming demographics pose a challenge to the protection and management of the environment, ecosystem and natural resources, and have stimulated a concerned consciousness and the growth of sustainable wind and solar energy development and technology. Air Languedoc-Roussillon is the first regional association in France created to control the quality of the air, and the Cerbère-Banyuls natural marine reserve is another environmental protection initiative.

Montpellier★★

Languedoc-Roussillon

As capital of Languedoc-Roussillon, Montpellier is an administrative centre and university city with beautiful historical districts and superb gardens.

A BIT OF HISTORY

Origins – Montpellier had its beginnings with two villages: Montpellieret and Montpellier. In 1204 Montpellier became a Spanish enclave and remained so until 1349 when John III of Majorca sold it to the king of France for 120 000 *écus*. After that, the town developed quickly by trading with the Levant. In the 16C, the Reformation arrived in Montpellier, and Protestants and Catholics in turn became masters of the town. In 1622 royal armies of Louis XIII laid siege to Montpellier's fortifications and Richelieu built a citadel to keep watch over the rebel city.

Modern Montpellier – After the Revolution the town became the simple *préfecture* of the Hérault *département*. When the French returned from North Africa after 1962, the city regained its dynamism. The high-speed (TGV) rail makes Paris only 4hr away.

The city's dynamism is reflected in the **Corum** conference and concert centre, the **Antigone** district that is linked to old Montpellier by the Triangle and Polygone shopping centres, and the new **Odysseum** leisure district.

PROMENADE DU PEYROU★★

The upper terrace of the promenade affords a sweeping **view**★ of the Garrigues, Cévennes, Mediterranean and Mont Canigou.

The key feature of the Promenade du Peyrou is the ensemble of the *château d'eau* and St-Clément aqueduct. On Saturday, Promenade des Arceaux becomes a flea market.

The late-17C **Arc de Triomphe** depicts the victories of Louis XIV and major events from his reign: the Canal du Midi, revocation of the Edict of Nantes, the capture of Namur in 1692 and the United

▶ **Population:** 256 344

Ⓖ **Michelin Map:** 339 I-7

🄸 **Info:** 30 allée De-Lattre-de-Tassigny (espl. Comédie), 34000 Montpellier. ℘04 67 60 60 60. www.ot-montpellier.fr.

Ⓞ **Location:** 170km/106mi west of Marseille.

Ⓐ **Don't Miss:** Place de la Comédie; a walk in the Old Town; the view from the promenade du Peyrou; the Neoclassical architecture of Quartier Antigone; Musée Fabre.

Ⓞ **Timing:** At least a full day to explore the centre.

Provinces of the Netherlands kneeling before Louis XIV.

ANTIGONE DISTRICT★

Starting from place de la Comédie (east side), walk to the Antigone district via the Polygone shopping centre.

Catalan architect **Ricardo Bofill** designed the bold new Antigone district. This vast Neoclassical housing project combines prefab technology with harmonious design. Behind a profusion of entablatures, pediments, pilasters and columns are low-income housing, public facilities and local shops, arranged around squares and patios.

Place du Nombre-d'Or continues with the cypress-lined **place du Millénaire**, place de Thessalie then place du Péloponnèse. The vista stretches from the "Échelles de la Ville" past the crescent-shaped buildings of **esplanade de l'Europe**, to the **Hôtel de Région**, converted into a dock for Port Juvénal.

Cathédrale St-Pierre

Ⓞ*Open daily except Sun afternoon.*

Towering like a fortress, the cathedral seems more massive with the adjacent façade of the Faculty of Medicine. It is the only church in Montpellier not completely destroyed during the Wars of Religion. Although built in the Gothic style, the cathedral is reminiscent of the single-nave Romanesque churches along the coast.

Faculté de Médecine

The Montpellier Faculty of Medicine occupies a former Benedictine monastery founded in the 14C by order of Pope Urban V. The Faculty houses two museums (* *see Museums below*).

Jardin des Plantes

**Open Jun–Sept daily except Mon noon–8pm; Oct–May daily except Mon noon–6pm. *04 67 63 43 22.*
The oldest botanical gardens in France, created in 1593 for the Montpellier Faculty of Botany for the study of medicinal plants, contain various Mediterranean species such as the nettle tree, holm-oak and mock privet (phillyrea). A large ginkgo biloba planted in 1795 is a graft from the first ginkgo plant introduced to France by Antoine Gouan.

MUSEUMS

Musée Fabre★★

*39 bd Bonne-Nouvelle. *Open daily except Mon 10am–6pm (Wed 1–9pm; Sat 11am–6pm). *Closed 1 Jan, 1 May, 25 Dec. ⊕€6. *04 67 14 83 00. http://museefabre.montpellier-agglo.com.*
The museum was founded in 1825 with the generosity of the Montpellier painter **François-Xavier Fabre** (1766–1837) and displays Greek and European ceramic ware, and paintings from the Spanish, Italian, Dutch and Flemish schools. Early-19C French painting features works by the *luminophiles* (light-lovers), Languedoc painters who captured the region's superb light on canvas.

Musée Languedocien★

*7 r. Jacques-Cœur. *Open mid-Jun–mid-Sept daily except Sun 3–6pm. Rest of year except Sun and public holidays 2.30–5.30pm. ⊕€6. *04 67 52 93 03. www.musee-languedocien.com.*
The medieval room houses Romanesque sculpture and capitals from the St-Guilhem-le-Désert cloisters. Other museum highlights are a 13C Vias lead font, 17C Flemish tapestries, beautiful Languedoc

cabinets, Sèvres porcelain, archaeological artefacts and folk art.

Musée Atger★

*2 r. de l'École-de-Médecine, first floor, access (signposted) via the Houdan staircase. *Open Mon, Wed, Fri 1.30–5.45pm. *Closed Aug. ⊕No charge. *04 67 41 76 40.*
This museum contains drawings bequeathed by Xavier Atger (1758–1833) and works by artists of the 17C and 18C French School, the 16C, 17C and 18C Italian School, and the 17C and 18C Flemish School.

EXCURSIONS

Sète

▷*36km/22.5mi SW of Montpellier.*
The main strolling and shopping streets are found on the east side of the "island"; beaches to the west.
▯*60 Grand'Rue Mario-Roustan, 34200 Sète. *04 67 74 71 71. www.ot-sete.fr.*
Guided tours of the town organised by the Sète tourist office cover the themes of "Façades and canals", "Old Sète" and "The fish market auction". ▯**Parking:** *You'll find lots near the canal fringing Sète on the east.*
Don't miss the trip up Mont St-Clair for memorable views of the surrounding area. Stroll about the town before heading up to Mont St-Clair. If your time allows, head for the beach or take a cruise on the lagoon or in the harbour area.

Sète was built on the slopes and at the foot of Mont St-Clair, a limestone outcrop 175m/541ft high, on the edge of the Thau lagoon. Once an island, it is linked to the mainland by two narrow sand spits. The new town, east and northeast of Mont St-Clair, runs right up to the sea itself and is divided up by several canals. Sète is the scene of the famous *joutes nautiques*, jousting tournaments, particularly well attended on the day of St-Louis in August.

Vieux port★

The old harbour, with its picturesque fishing boats and yachts, is the most interesting part of Sète port.

Quai de la Marine is lined with fish and seafood restaurants, with terraces overlooking the Sète canal. It is the departure point for various **boat trips** around the coastline and harbour.

A little farther down, fishermen and bystanders are summoned by the **"criée électronique"** (electronic auction) when the boats come in at around 3.30pm. It is worth taking a stroll round the other basins and the canals as well. Sailing is practised at high level near the St-Louis pier. **Promenade de la Corniche** – This busy road, leading to the Plage de la Corniche, situated 2km/1mi from the centre of town, cuts around the foot of Mont St-Clair with its slopes covered by villas. **Plage de la Corniche** – This 12km/7.5mi-long sandy beach stretches across a conservation area.

Massif de l'Aigoual★★★
◗ Rising high at the heart of the Cévennes National Park, the Aigoual summit, 37km/23mi S of Florac, is reached on the steep D 118.
Maison de l'Aigoual, L'Espérou. ℘04 67 82 64 67. www.causses-aigoual-cevennes.org.
◗ Choose a fine day for your visit – otherwise mist may reduce the view.

The immense forces involved in the formation of the Alps in the Tertiary Era acted on the ancient granitic foundation of this landscape, uplifting it to form a massif which reaches its highest point at **Mont Aigoual★★★**.

Subsequent erosion, all the more vigorous because of high precipitation and the low elevation of the surrounding country, has created a landscape of long straight ridges cut by deep ravines. These well-watered highlands make a striking contrast to the arid landscapes of the neighbouring *causses* where any rainfall is immediately absorbed by the porous limestone.

From 1875 onwards a massive programme of reafforestation was undertaken by the state; the forest today covers some 140sq km/54sq mi.

Tree growth is particularly vigorous on the more exposed western slopes. In the last 20 years conifers have been added to the beeches planted in the 19C. There are sweet chestnuts too, the traditional tree of the Cévennes, growing at high altitudes of 600–900m/1 968–9 842ft.

A **panorama★★★** extends over the Causses and the Cévennes from the viewing table at the top of the meteorological station

The clearest days are in winter, when it is sometimes possible to see both Mont Blanc (*◗ see MONT BLANC*) and the Maladeta Massif in the Pyrénées.

Grotte des Demoiselles★★★
◗ The caves are in the upper Hérault Valley near the town of Ganges.
Guided tours (1hr) Nov–Feb daily 2pm, 3pm, 4pm (Sun 10am, 11am, 2pm, 3pm, 4pm); Mar and Oct daily 2.30pm, 3.30pm, 4.30pm (Sun and public holidays 10am, 11am, noon, 1.30pm, 2.30pm, 3.30pm, 4.30pm); Apr–Jun and Sept daily 10am, 11am, noon, 1.30pm, 2.30pm, 3.30pm, 4.30pm, 5.30pm; Jul–Aug daily continuous from 10am–6pm. €9.50 (children, 12–17, €7). ℘04 67 73 70 02. www.demoiselles.com.

The cave, discovered in 1770, contains an enthralling underground landscape. Deposition of calcium carbonate within the cave has produced extraordinary forms, from stalactites and stalagmites and translucent draperies, to the great columns and huge organ-case of this underground cathedral.

◗ Take a sweater; the temperature in the caves is a constant 14°C/57°F.

Cirque de Navacelles★★★
◗ The site is reached by turning off the road between Lodève and Ganges, in the Hérault département.

This spectacular 300m/984ft-deep basin, separating the Causses – high plateaux – de Larzac and Blandas marks the former course of the River Vis before it cut through the base of the meander. On the outer sweep of the meander great screes have been formed; the upper parts of the cliffs are made up of exceptionally thick beds, thinning out at the lower levels where traces remain of old buildings and terraces on the marl and clay deposits. On the valley floor a pretty single-arched bridge leads to the village of Navacelles, which once had a priory. The little settlement clings to a rocky outcrop in order to conserve as much as possible of the belt of cultivable land in the former bed of the river. In contrast to the harsh conditions prevailing on the arid causses, the valley floor has a mild microclimate, which allows figs to be grown.

St-Guilhem-le-Désert★★

▶ *The village is in the Hérault gorge, and can be approached via Gignac and Aniane if coming from the E or S, via St-Félix and Montpeyroux if coming from the N or W.*

🏛 ℘04 67 57 70 17. www.saint-guilhem-le-desert.com. 🅿 *All cars must be left in the village's car park (charge).*

The eponymous Guilhem was born in the mid-8C and renowned for his talent in handling weapons as well as his intelligence and piety. He was brought up with the sons of the Carolingian king, Pepin the Short, and his friendship with one in particular, Charles, the future Charlemagne, was to last until his death. In its remote and dramatic **site**★ where the Val de l'Infernet runs into the valley of the Hérault, this 9C **village**★ grew up around an abbey founded by William of Aquitaine. This timeless place centres on a huge and ancient plane tree in the village centre, from which narrow streets radiate and disappear into inviting corners.

L'Abbaye et le Musée du Cloître★

🕐*Open May–Sept daily except Sun am 10.30am–noon, 1–6pm.*

This is a Romanesque structure of striking simplicity, famed for its possession of a fragment of the True Cross *(in the south transept)*. It has a doorway with dog-tooth moulding, and an apse with massive buttresses and an elegant little arcade. Inside, the width of apse and transept is the result of a rebuilding undertaken in the 11C. Of the 11–12C cloisters, nothing remains apart from the ground floor of the north walk and part of the west walk.

Grotte de Clamouse★★★

▶ *3km/1.8mi S.*

🎫*Guided tours (1hr15min) daily Jul–Aug 10.30am–6.20pm; Jun and Sept 10.30am–5.20pm; Feb–May and Oct–Nov 10.30am–4.20pm.* ⊛€9 *(children, 12–18, €7.70.* ℘04 67 57 71 05. www.clamouse.com.

The caves, a UNESCO World Heritage Site, run beneath the Larzac plateau and were carved by an extensive network of underground streams. There are remarkable stalactites and stalagmites, but best of all are the splendid crystallisations in varied shapes.

😊 *Take a sweater; the temperature inside is 17°C/62.6°F.*

La Couvertoirade★

▶ *The village stands to one side of the highway, which crosses Larzac.*

🕐*Open daily Mar and Oct–mid-Nov 10am–noon, 2–5pm; Apr–Jun and Sept 10am–noon, 2–6pm; Jul–Aug 10am–7pm.* ⊛€3. 🎫*guided tours (40min)* ⊛€5. 🅿*Park at the village car park, the payment for which gives admission to the walled village.* 🏛 ℘05 65 58 55 59. www.lacouvertoirade.com.

High up on the lonely Larzac limestone plateau *(causse)*, this old fortified settlement once belonged to the Knights Templar. It has many robustly built houses, typical of the region, with cisterns, outside stairways leading to the main floor, and a vaulted sheep-pen at ground level. Most date from the 17C. The towers and the sentry-walk of the **ramparts** are particularly interesting. Go through the north gateway and, taking great care, climb the steps at the foot of the Renaissance house, following the watch-path round to the left to the round tower for a view over the town and its main street, rue Droite.

Also see the **fortified church** constructed in the 14C, which is an integal part of the town's defences and has two disc-shaped stelae showing different representations of the cross, and a graveyard with unusual disc-shaped gravestones.

Gorges du Tarn ★★★

Tarn Gorges

The deep gorges cut by the Tarn through the harsh limestone plateaux *(causses)* to the south of the Massif Central make up one of France's most spectacular natural landscapes. The source of the Tarn lies high (1 575m/5 167ft) in the granitic uplands of Mount Lozère; tumbling torrent-like down the slopes of the Cévennes, the river then enters the most spectacular section of its course at **Florac**.

THE AREA

The Tarn River – 381km/237mi long – flows through gorges and canyons, joined by side valleys such as the Jonte and the Dourbie, in Millau.

Escape from the valley bottom is by means of roads that twist and turn up the precipitous slopes to join the roughly planed surface of the Causse Méjean; its porous limestone is deeply fissured and hollowed out to form the caves for which the region is famous.

Most visitors come here when the summer sun is beating down, but the scene is best appreciated in spring and autumn, when the vegetation and local wild life are flourishing. The spectacle

Stalagmites, Grotte de l'Aven Armand

A. Cassaigne/MICHELIN

- ⚅ **Michelin Map:** 330 H-J 8-9 and 338 L-N 5
- ▤ **Info:** Le Bourg, Le Rozier. ℰ05 65 62 60 89. www.officedetourisme-gorgesdutarn.com.
- ▷ **Location:** The River Tarn rises on Mont Lozère and runs through the Cévennes before reaching the Causses country, where it has carved its plunging gorge between the limestone plateaux. The road runs at the top of the cliffs. There are small villages, notably Ste-Énimie, along the gorge, but no communities of any great size.
- ⊘ **Don't Miss:** Pause at the Point Sublime to get the full picture of the Tarn gorge.
- ⊕ **Timing:** The road along the gorge is narrow, difficult, and in season can be congested. Allow several hours to cover the full distance.

of winter should not be missed, when every feature has its frosty outline.

The hostile landscape here has been humanised by centuries of determined human effort. Thus there are villages on the flatter patches of cultivable land which occur on the valley bottom and sides (Ste-Énimie, La Malène, Les Vignes) and the castles of lords and robber-barons on the more easily defended sites overlooking the river. On the plateau above are isolated farms based on the better soils of the little depressions known as dolinas; the drystone walls once made by piling up the boulders collected laboriously from the fields are now supplemented by electric fences, and the thoughtless forest clearance of the 19C is being made good by the planting of Austrian pines.

No trace of the underground realm of chasms (**Aven Armand**★★★) and

Kayaking at Les Détroits

© Pierre Jacques/hemis.fr

caverns is visible at the surface; those who venture into this unsuspected world are rewarded by the extraordinary spectacle presented by the dissolution of the limestone, and by the strange forms of stalactites and stalagmites.

EXCURSIONS

Les Détroits (The Straits)★★
◖ *36km/22.3mi NE of Gorges du Tarn.*
This is the narrowest part of the valley, hemmed in by plunging cliffs of coloured limestone and slightly to the east of La Malène.

Cirque des Baumes★★★
◖ *2.4km/1.5mi NW of Les Détroits.*
Below Les Détroits, the gorge widens, forming a magnificent natural amphitheatre.

Le Point Sublime★★★
◖ *Just W of Cirque des Baumes.*
This splendid viewpoint above the Cirque des Baumes overlooks both the Tarn Canyon and the Tarn Causse.

Grotte de l'Aven Armand★★★
◖ *43km/27mi NE of Millau, Aven Armrand is in the plateau country S of the Gorges du Tarn.*
⟶ *Guided tours only: late Mar–early Nov 10am–noon, 1.30–5pm (10 Jul–Aug 9.30am–6pm).* ✆€9.50. ℘04 66 45 61 31 or ℘04 66 45 60 33. www.aven-armand.com.

☺*The temperature inside is 10°C/50°F.*
One of the wonders of the underground world, this immense cavern is reached down a 200m/656ft tunnel in the bleak Causse Méjean.
Deep within the arid limestone of the Causse Méjean, subterranean waters have created a vast cavern, 60m wide and 120m long (197 x 394ft), its floor littered with rock fallen from its roof. Four hundred stalagmites, some up to 30m/97.5ft high and christened the "Virgin Forest", make an extraordinary spectacle.

Millau★
◖ *116km/72.5mi N of Montpellier.*
At the northern edge of the Larzac plateau. All main roads lead directly to the centre of town. 🄸*1 pl. du Beffroi.*
℘*05 65 60 02 42. www.ot-millau.fr.*
☺*Take a trip out of town to the Aire de Vision to see the beautiful 2.5km/1.5mi Millau Viaduct, part of the A 75 autoroute.*
Millau huddles between two high limestone plateaux, the Causse du Larzac and the Causse Noir, at the meeting-point of the Tarn and the Dourbie.
The site of a ford in ancient times, it acquired a bridge in the Middle Ages and became a trading centre of some importance. Today it is a lively provincial town, with a southern air, close to a remarkable modern viaduct soaring over the Tarn Valley.

During the 1C AD, Millau, then known as Condatomagus, was a Roman centre for earthenware production with over 500 potters.

Terra sigillata ware – bright red-glazed pottery decorated with floral, geometric or historiated patterns of Hellenistic influence – was produced. As early as the 2C AD, the milk of the Larzac ewes was made into a gourmet blue cheese in the nearby caves at Roquefort. Their wool and skins were also turned to advantage, including the manufacture of fine gloves at Millau. Today Millau's gloves are still exported around the world and the industry has expanded into the designer market, producing gloves and shoes for well-known high-street labels as well as diverse leather goods and furnishings. In a sheltered valley with a mild climate, Millau's streets are attractive, with plane trees, fountains and a bustling air.

The **Musée de Millau**★ *(pl. du Mar-Foch;* ○*open Jul–Aug 10am–6pm; rest of year 10am–noon, 2–6pm daily except Sun and public holidays;* ○*€5 (no charge 1st Saturday of the month);* ✆*05 65 59 01 08)* is housed in the 18C Hôtel de Pégayrolles. Its **palaeontology** section includes fossils from secondary marine sediments and the 4m/13ft-long 180-million-year-old skeleton of a plesiosaurus marine reptile from Tournemire. There is a remarkable collection of Gallo-Roman **earthenware**★, found at Graufesenque, including moulds and potters' chisels and accounts books. The **Maison de la Peau et du Gant**★ includes exhibits on glove-making and a magnificent collection of evening gloves.

Chaos de Montpellier-le-Vieux★★★
○ *18km/11.2mi NE.*

This extraordinary "ruined city" in fact made entirely of natural rocks, has a bewildering variety of rock formations (the Sphinx, the Elephant, the Gates of Mycaenae).

Caves de Roquefort★
○ *25km/15.5mi SW.* ○*Open Jan–Mar 10am–noon, 1.30–4.30pm; Apr–10 Jul 9.30am–noon, 1–5pm; 11 Jul–early* Sept 9.30am–6.30pm; early Sept–Oct 9.30am–noon, 1.30–5pm; Nov–Dec 10am–noon, 1.30–4.30pm. ○*€5.* ✆*05 65 58 54 38. www.roquefort-societe.com.*

The name of the market town of Roquefort, located between Millau and St-Affrique, is synonymous with one of the most famous of French cheeses: the delicious blue-veined Roquefort. In accordance with AOC Roquefort regulations, all production of the cheese must take place underground, in natural caves in which the temperature and humidity are constant. Roquefort cheese is produced exclusively from full-fat, untreated ewe's milk.

Millau Viaduct/Millau Bridge★★★
This amazing cable-stayed construction, completed in 2004 and designed by the British architect Norman Foster, spans the 2km/1.2mi-wide Tarn Gorge near Millau. The world's tallest road bridge, it forms part of the A 71-A 75 autoroute from Paris to Béziers.

ADDRESSES

⌂ STAY

○ **Hotel de la Capelle** – *7 pl. de la Capelle.* ✆*05 65 60 14 72. www.hotel-millau-capelle. com. 45 rooms.* ○ *€9.* This hotel has two distinct advantages: reasonable prices and an air of tranquillity.

⛍ SHOPPING

Cave des Vignerons des gorges du Tarn – *ave Causses 12520 Aguessac. 5km/3mi from Millau.* ✆*05 65 59 84 11.* This co-op produces wines with the Vin délémité de qualité supérieure (VDQS) label côtes de Millau (red and rose).

⚐ SPORTS AND RECREATION

Walking – The main waymarked footpaths are the GR 62 ("Causse Noir-Lévezou-Rouergue") and several PR, "Causse Noir" (13 itineraries around Millau for rambling and mountain biking), "Millau et les causses majeurs", "St-Affrique-Vallée du Tarn-Pays de Roquefort" (footpaths around St-Affrique, Camarès and Roquefort).

Conques★★★

Midi-Pyrénées

This tiny medieval town has a splendid **hillside site**★★ best seen from the rock, Rocher du Bancarel (3km/1.8mi south).

SIGHTS
Église St-Foy★★
Completely rebuilt between 1045 and 1060, this is one of the oldest Romanesque pilgrimage churches on the route to Santiago de Compostela.

Its abbey had a chapel and hospice at Roncesvalles to serve the pilgrims as they made their way across the Pyrénées. Within, the spacious nave is flooded with light from the south tribune windows. The dimensions of the transept are exceptional and the ambulatory with its annular barrel vault is also remarkable.

The **tympanum**★★★ above the west door with its wealth of sculpture forms a striking contrast to the overall plainness of the west front. Traces of the original colouring can still be made out. It shows how sculpture had evolved away from the static solemnity characteristic of Burgundy and Languedoc, towards the greater freshness and spontaneity evident in the capitals of the churches of the Auvergne. It may be that the weighing of souls taking place below the figure of Christ is an expression of the idea – entirely new at the beginning of the 12C – of the personal nature of the Last Judgement.

Trésor★★★
The treasury is among the most important in Europe. Its most precious object is the reliquary statue of St Faith (Ste-Foy). The saint's relics had been brought to Conques at the end of the 9C, when they were venerated by prisoners and by the blind. The statue was put together and added to over a long period; some of its features probably go back as far as the last years of the Roman Empire and consist of reused elements of Roman date (face-mask, intaglio work

in precious stones, jewels); the gold and engraved crystal are of the Merovingian and Carolingian periods (7–9C).

At the close of the 10C the revered statue was renovated here at Conques and adorned with enamels, cabochons and other precious stones. Four more of the treasures are of exceptional significance: the initial "A" given to the abbey, it is said, by Charlemagne (a fragment of the Holy Cross decorated in the 11C with intaglio work and with chased and gilded silver); two portable altars, one, St Faith's, in alabaster and chased silver, the other, Abbot Begon's, from the beginning of the 12C, in porphyry and silver inlaid with niello; and the reliquary of Pope Pascal with filigree work and diadems, also from the early 12C.

EXCURSION
Cordes-sur-Ciel★★★
▶ *The village is 69m/43mi SW of Conques and 25km/15.5mi NW of Albi.* ℘05 63 56 00 52. *www.cordes-sur-ciel.org.*
Nestling at the top of the peak, Puech de Mordagne, Cordes occupies a most attractive **site**★★ overlooking the Cérou Valley.

The superb row of **Gothic houses**★★ dating from the 13C and 14C testify to the wealthy past of this quaint little town. Notice the **Maison du Grand Fauconnier**★ and the **Maison du Grand Veneur**★. For more than 50 years, artists and craftsmen have contributed to preserving and restoring local tradition.

▶ **Population:** 288
⌖ **Michelin Map:** 338 G-3.
ℹ **Info:** Office de tourisme de Conques – r. du Chanoine-Benazech, 12320 Conques. ℘05 65 72 85 00. www.conques.fr.
▷ **Location:** 39km/24mi N of Rodez.
Ⓟ **Parking:** Outside the village.
⊘ **Don't Miss:** Spectacular view from the site du Bancarel.

Albi★★★

Midi-Pyrénées

From the bridges spanning the Tarn to the extraordinary cathedral, **Albi** "the red" is made of brick, which owes its rosy hue to the clays dug from the river's bed.

A BIT OF HISTORY

At the start of the 13C, the city was one of the centres of the dualist Cathar doctrine, dubbed the "Albigensian heresy" by a fearful Church.

The subsequent "Albigensian Crusade" of 1209 was directed on the spiritual side by St Dominic and commanded militarily by the fearsome Simon de Montfort; on the ground, armies moved in from north and east to commit the terrible atrocities of Béziers, Carcassonne, Minerve and Lavaur. The Capetian kings took advantage of the troubles from 1208–1229, to gain a foothold in Languedoc, but Catharism itself was finally stamped out only by the Inquisition and the ghastly funeral pyre at Montségur (*see CHÂTEAU DE MONTSÉGUR*).

SIGHTS
Cathédrale Ste-Cécile★★★

5 bd Sybille. Open daily Jun–Sep 9am–6.30pm; Oct–May 9am–noon, 2–6.30pm. €3. 05 63 43 23 43.
Construction of the cathedral, extending over two centuries, began in 1282 at a time when work on the neighbouring Berbie Palace, the bishops' residence, and on that of the Dominicans at Toulouse, was already well advanced. For the bishops, the status of the Church was inextricably linked to its temporal power and they therefore gave their cathedral the appearance of a for-

> ### 😊 Albi Pass 😊
>
> This visitors' card gives numerous discounts at sites and monuments, shops and attractions. Valid for a year, it costs €6.50 from the tourist office.

▶ **Population:** 51 275
🕐 **Michelin Map:** 338 D 6, E 7
🛈 **Info:** Palais de la Berbie, pl. Ste-Cécile, Albi. 05 63 49 48 80. www.albi-tourisme.fr.
▶ **Location:** Albi is 77km/ 47.8mi NE of Toulouse.
🕐 **Timing:** The town was built around the cathedral, and, to better understand the massive proportions of the cathedral, view it from a distance, preferably the bridge across the Tarn (the Pont du 22-Août), or from one of the streets of Old Albi. But the town is such a delight to explore that you need at least a whole day to do it justice.
😊 **Don't miss:** Enjoy a boat trip on the river to appreciate the beauty of the city at its best.

tress. In the 19C the formidable edifice acquired the three upper storeys of its keep-like bell tower, its machicolations and its inspection gallery.

Inside, the perfect simplicity of the single broad nave with its Southern French Gothic side chapels passes almost unnoticed, such is the exuberance of the Flamboyant decorative scheme. The **rood screen★★★**, one of the few to have survived, is also one of the most sumptuous. In the 15C and 16C all the greater churches possessed such a screen; it separated the clergy, in the choir, from the lay worshippers in the nave; during services readings would be given from its gallery. This example dates from 1485, as does the screen closing off the **choir**; its arches and gables, columns and arcading all show the extraordinary skill and attention to detail of the craftsmen who worked the white limestone. The naturalistic poses and facial expressions typical of Gothic art are here brought to a fine pitch. Old Testament figures are on the outside, those from the New Testament on the side of the choir, where there are two rows of 66 stalls. The vaults were painted from 1509 to 1512 by Bolognese artists; they repay study with binoculars.

The hallucinatory **Last Judgement** is a masterpiece of late 15C mural painting; it was unfortunately disfigured by the installation in the 17C of the great organ. But it is nevertheless possible to admire the upper part depicting the Heavenly Kingdom: on the left the Apostles, haloed in gold, and the saints as well as the elect bearing the book of their life held open; on the right the damned, punished by their sin itself.

Palais de la Berbie★

The former Bishops' Palace houses the **Musée Toulouse-Lautrec★★**(○*open daily: Jan 10am–noon, 2–5pm; Feb–Mar and Nov–Dec 10am–noon, 2–5.30pm; Apr–May 10am–noon, 2–6pm; Jun 9am– noon, 2–6pm; Jul–Sept 9am–6pm; Oct 10am–noon, 2–6pm;* ○*closed Tue Oct– Mar, 1 Jan, 1 May, 1 Nov, 25 Dec;* ≈*€5.50;* ℘*05 63 49 58 97),* devoted to the life and art of Henri de Toulouse-Lautrec (1864– 1901). The Collection was bequeathed to Albi by the artist's mother, Comtesse Alphonse de Toulouse-Lautrec, and other family members. Born in Albi at the Hôtel du Bosc, Toulouse-Lautrec was crippled in early life by two accidents. He is revealed here as one of the great painters of everyday life; his vision of the depravity and decadence of late 19C Paris is communicated with

restraint and compassion (*Jane Avril, Mademoiselle Lucie Bellanger, Au bal de l'Élysée-Montmartre*).

EXCURSIONS
Rodez★

⊙ *The town is on a meeting of highways between Languedoc and Auvergne.*

🅸 *pl. Foch.* ℘*05 65 75 76 77. www.ot-rodez.fr.*

Once the capital of the Rouergue, Rodez is situated on the borders of two very different regions, the dry Causses plateaux and the well-watered Ségale hills. The ancient town stands on a rocky spur high above the meanders of the River Aveyron. Its layout reflects the medieval rivalry of secular and ecclesiastical power: the cathedral and castle districts were both fortified.

Cathédrale Notre-Dame★★

The 13C red sandstone edifice has a fortress-like west front, once a bastion in the city wall.

It has Flamboyant Gothic portals and a magnificent **bell tower** ★★★. The interior was completed in the 16C but still in the style of the 13C. Note the 15C former **rood screen**★ and the superb 17C carved wooden **organ case** ★. The choir **stalls**★ are by André Sulpice (15C).

Musée Fenaille★★

○ &*Open mid Jun–mid-Sept, Tue, Thu, Fri 10am–1pm, 1.30–6pm, Wed, Sat noon– 6pm, Sun 2–6pm; mid–Aug, daily 10am*

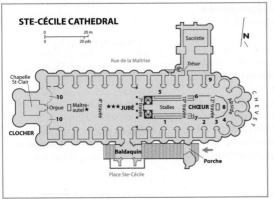

STE-CÉCILE CATHEDRAL

0   20 m
0   20 yds

Rue de la Maîtrise

Chapelle St-Clair

Orgue   Maître-autel ★   ★★★ JUBÉ   Stalles   CHŒUR

CLOCHER

Baldaquin   Porche

Place Ste-Cécile

Sacristie

Trésor

Chevet   Abside

N

1 Judith
2 Prophet Zephaniah
3 Prophet Isaiah
4 Prophet Jeremiah
5 Esther
6 Charlemagne
7 Constantine
8 Statue of Virgin and Child
9 Chapelle Sainte-Croix
10 Painting of the Holy Family
11 Chapelle du Rosaire
12 Last Judgement

–1pm, 1.30–6pm. ⏱Closed Mon, and 1 Jan, 1 May, 1 Nov, 25 Dec. ⌨€3. ✆05 65 73 84 30. www.musee-fenaille.com. The museum is housed partly in the oldest mansion in Rodez and partly in an adjacent modern building which blends harmoniously with its neighbour. Inside are the most extensive collections concerning the Rouergue region, each section displaying a time scale for easy reference. In order to follow the exhibition's chronological order, start on the third floor in the modern building devoted to prehistory. Note in particular the menhirs from south of Aveyron.

Bozouls★

▶ 20km/12mi NE of Rodez.
🅿 pl. de l'Hôtel-de-Ville, 12340 Bozouls. ✆05 65 48 50 52. www.bozouls.com. Bozouls is distinguished from afar by its modern church (1964), south of D 20. Its sanctuary in the shape of a ship's prow houses a statue of the Virgin Mary by local sculptor Denys Puech.

Trou de Bozouls★ – The terrace next to the war memorial affords the best view of this 800m/2 600ft canyon, hollowed out of the Causse de Comtal by the River Dourdou. From the town hall, walk round the south side of the "Trou" for the **Ancienne Église Ste-Fauste**. The church's 12C nave, with its raised, semicircular barrel vaulting, was originally roofed with heavy limestone slabs (lauzes). Under this enormous weight, the pillars sagged and the roof was replaced by a timber-frame one in the 17C.

Villefranche-de-Rouergue★

On the western edge of the Massif Central, the town is at a meeting point of three highways. The town centre is Place Notre-Dame, beside the church.
🅿 Promenade de Guiraudet. ✆05 65 45 13 18. www.villefranche.com. The ancient bastide of Villefranche, with its rooftops clustered around the foot of the massive tower of its church, lies at the bottom of a green valley surrounded by hills, at the confluence of the Aveyron and the Alzou.

Bastide★

The old town on the north bank of the River Aveyron has kept many of the typical features of a planned urban foundation of the 13C. Its cobbled streets, connected by narrow alleyways, are laid out on a grid pattern, and there is a central square **(Place Notre-Dame★)** with covered walks, dominated by a large metal figure of Christ.

The tall, severe houses are characteristic of the Rouergue area; a number of them have high open balconies with provision for drying grain. The President Raynal House (Maison du Président Raynal) with its 15C façade is particularly striking, and the Maison Dardennes has a fine galleried courtyard. The fortified church **(Église Notre-Dame★)** has splendid ironwork around the font.

Chartreuse St-Sauveur★

▶ Take D 922 towards Najac.
15C Gothic charterhouse, with "Great" and "Small" cloisters.

ADDRESSES

🛏 STAY

⊜⊜**Chambre d'hôte à la Ferme "Naussens"** – 81150 Castanet. ✆05 63 55 22 56. Closed Nov–mid Apr. 5rms. A warm and convivial welcome awaits at this farm in the midst of vines. Simple, traditional, family-style cooking.

⊜⊜**Hôtel du Midi** – 1 r. Béteille, Rodez. ✆05 65 68 02 07. www.hotelmidi.com. Closed 20 Dec–6 Jan. 🅿 34rms. ⌨€7.50. Restaurant⊜⊜. Facing the cathedral, this hotel has simple, well-kept and well-lit rooms.

⊜⊜**La Régence George V** – 27–29 ave du Maréchal-Joffre, Albi. ✆05 63 54 24 16. www.laregence-georgev.fr. 20rms. ⌨€7. It is worth searching out this cosy establishment with its typical local style in the station district. Rooms are a generous size and some have a fireplace.

⊜⊜⊜**Cantepau** – 9 r. Cantepau, Albi. ✆05 63 60 75 80. www.hotelcantepau.fr. 33rms. ⌨€9. Wicker furniture, subdued hues and fans give this hotel a colonial feel following its recent revamp.

🍴🍴🍴 **Hôtel Mercure** – *41 bis, r. Porta, Albi.* ☎*05 63 47 66 66. www.mercure.com. 56rms.* � *€12.* This modern hotel has an original setting, in an old 18C red-brick mill on the banks of the Tarn.

ℜ/EAT

🍴 **Auberge de l'Ady** – *1 ave du Pont-de-Malakoff (near the church) in Valady (20 km/ 12mi N of Rodez).* ☎*05 65 72 70 24. Closed Sun evening, Tue evening and Mon; Jan.* Auberge at the heart of a pretty village, serving local and regional cuisine.

🍴 **Salon de Thé de la Berbie** – *17 pl. Ste-Cécile, Albi.* ☎*05 63 54 13 86.* This attractive tea room, opposite the cathedral, serves a wide range of tea, coffee, pastries, ice-cream sundaes and pancakes.

🍴 **Le Table du Sommelier** – *20 r. Porta, Albi.* ☎*05 63 46 20 10. www.latabledu sommelier.com. Closed Sun–Mon.* The proprietor sets the scene here perfectly, with cases of wine piled high in the entrance and rustic dining room with mezzanine floor. This wine-focused bistro serves refined cuisine using the freshest ingredients.

🍴🍴 **Le Poisson d'Avril** – *17 r. d'Engueysse, Albi.* ☎*05 63 38 30 13. Closed Sun.* This restaurant in a typical old Albi house 200m/220yd from the cathedral has an unusual interior décor designed like the inside of a barrel, with wooden beams. Prices are moderate and food is not heavy.

🍴🍴 **Le Robinson** – *142 r. Édouard-Branly, Albi.* ☎*05 63 46 15 69. Closed Mon–Tue.* This isle of green on the banks of the Tarn is accessible from the Pont Neuf. Dating from the 1920s, the old-fashioned dance hall has an exuberant charm.

🍴🍴🍴 **Jardin des Quatre Saisons** – *19 bd de Strasbourg, Albi.* ☎*05 63 60 77 76. www.lejardindesquatresaisons.fr. Closed Sun for dinner and Mon.* A friendly welcome from the owners awaits, along with a good selection of wines and traditional cuisine.

TOURS

Guided Tour of the Old Town (45min) organised by the tourist office, Jul–Aug Mon–Sat. Book at the tourist office.

Walks – Three walks allow the visitor to discover Albi : the *circuit Pourpre* (purple) goes through the heart of old Albi and takes in the main historic sites, characters and monuments; the *circuit Or* (gold) focuses on the growth of Albi over two thousand years;

the *circuit Azur* (azure) leads along the banks of the Tarn, taking in the Pont Vieux and the Pont Neuf.

🛒 SHOPPING

In the streets of Albi's Old Town (especially *rues Mariès, Ste-Cécile* and *Verdrusse*) is a variety of antique shops and boutiques. Also, visitors cannot miss the many shops selling local food and drink specialities, including foie gras, confits, anis biscuits and other pâtisserie.

L'Artisan Pastellier – *5 r. Puech-Bérenguier, Albi.* ☎*05 63 38 59 18. www.artisanpastellier.com.* Pastels were for centuries an important industry in the region. Near the Maison du vieil Alby, this shop is a poem in blue. Made from pastel leaves, this irresistible colour is used to shade local crafts and fabrics. Calligraphers and artists will also be in their element here among inks, paints and pastels of natural pigments.

Marché biologique (Organic market) – *pl. F.-Pelloutier, Albi.* A big range of local organic produce.

Markets– *pl. Ste-Cécile*. A big market is held on Saturday on place Ste-Cécile: fruit, vegetables, foie gras (in season), mushrooms, garlic from Lautrec, charcuterie from Lacaune and Gaillac wines.

Patisserie Galy – *7 r. Saunal, Albi.* ☎*05 63 54 13 37. Closed Sat–Mon, public holidays.* One of the popular pastry cooks of the old quarter, with many local specialities.

🏃 LEISURE ACTIVITIES

Boat Trip on the Tarn (Berges du Tarn) ☎*05 63 43 59 63. www.albi-croisieres. com. Open Jun–Sept daily 11am–11.45am. €6.* The boat is a flat-bottomed barge, a *gabarre*, used for transporting goods until the 19C. Leaving Albi's old harbour at the foot of the ramparts, the barge travels along the Tarn past the old Albi mills.

🎭 EVENTS

Carnaval – *Feb.*
Coupe de France des Circuits – *Mar.* Motor Festival.
Marathon d'Albi – *Apr.*
Free Organ Concerts in the Cathedral – *Wed and Sun afternoons in Jul and Aug.*
Festival de Tarot – *Aug.*
Le Grand Prix automobile d'Albi – *Sept.*

Toulouse★★★

Haute-Garonne

A vibrant regional capital, attractive with its red-brick architecture, Toulouse is a lively university town with a thriving high-tech industrial sector and, at the same time, plenty of attractions for the visitor to enjoy.

A BIT OF HISTORY

Toulouse has long been the focus of very diverse influences. The city was the capital of the Visigothic kingdom, and enjoyed considerable prosperity between the 9C and 13C under the Raymond dynasty, whose court was considered to be one of the most cultured in Europe.

Their extensive territories were known as the "Langue d'Oc". In the 13C, the whole domain of the Raymonds – most of present-day Languedoc and parts of the Midi-Pyrénées and Provence – embraced Catharism. This stance gave the Capetian kings an opportunity, with the authority of the pope, to launch the Albigensian Crusade against Catharism. The Crusade put an end to the power of the Raymonds, broke up their territories, and enabled the Capetian kings to push their frontier southwards into Languedoc.

In 1323, Europe's oldest literary society was founded here to further the cause of the language of southern France (Langue d'Oc). Later, in the 16C, the city flourished again because of a boom in what at the time was the most widely

- ▶ **Population:** 446 340
- **Michelin Map:** 343 G 3
- **Info:** Donjon du Capitole. 0892 180 180. www.uk.toulouse-tourisme.com.
- ▶ **Location:** Toulouse lies between Bordeaux (243km/152mi to the W) and Narbonne (150km/94mi to the E).
- **Parking:** Cars can be parked free of charge in the "Transit car parks"; you then take the bus or metro into the city.
- **Don't Miss:** From the St-Michel bridge, there's a great view of the city, especially towards the end of the day when the sun picks up the warm red tones of the brickwork.
- **Timing:** If you plan on visiting most of the museums, consider buying a Toulouse en Liberté City Pass (€10, child €5). Take a guided tour of Toulouse first, to get a better idea of where you want to spend your time in France's fourth-largest urban centre; three days will fly by.

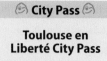

City Pass

Toulouse en Liberté City Pass

This city pass entitles the bearer to discounts on dining, accommodation, entertainment, museum entry, car rental, excursions and shopping. Enquire at the tourist office. Valid for 1 year: €10 adult, €25 family (2 adults, 2 children), €5 child.

cultivated of all dye plants, woad, which yielded a blue-black colour.

As early as 1917, strategic industries like aircraft manufacturing were being set up in southwestern France, as far away as possible from the country's vulnerable eastern border. In the inter-war period, Toulouse became the starting point of France's first scheduled air service. The city has remained the focus of France's aeronautics industry.

SIGHTS

Basilique St-Sernin★★★

pl. Saint-Sernin. Open daily 10am–noon, 2–6pm. **Crypt** opens Mon–Sat 10am–11.30am, 2.30–5pm; Sun 2.30–

Place du Capitole
© José Manual Herrado/Office de Tourisme de Toulousea

5pm. ℘05 61 21 70 18. www.basilique-st-sernin-toulouse.fr.

The great church was built to honour the memory of the Gaulish martyr St Sernin (or Saturninus). A first phase of construction lasting from around 1080–1118 was in a mixture of brick and stone, a second phase in brick alone.

St-Sernin was one of a number of major Romanesque pilgrimage churches on the route to Compostela. St-Sernin's octagonal bell tower is particularly characteristic of the area, with five levels of twin arches built in brick, the upper two of which are provided with little pediments.

Église des Jacobins★★

69 r. Pargaminières. ⛄ ◷Open daily 9am–7pm. ℘05 61 22 21 92. www.jacobins.mairie-toulouse.fr.

This was the first church of the Preaching Friars, an order founded in 1215 by St Dominic, and intended to help in the fight against Catharism. To the poverty demanded by St Francis of his followers, Dominic added a knowledge of theology and a training in eloquence, which enabled his disciples to attempt to overcome their opponents in argument.

The church is the key building in the evolution from 1230 onwards of Southern French Gothic as influenced by the mendicant orders. The size of the edifice, combined with the impossibility of providing it with external support (because of ownership and circulation problems), ruled out the construction of a single nave. The architect resorted to the expedient of a marvellous ribbed vault and the **"palm-tree"** of the chancel with its splendid array of 22 radiating arches. All this in 1292, 170 years before the great pointed vaults of the Late Gothic.

The tower dates from 1298 and became the model for the towers of the major churches of Southern France.

Capitole★

This is Toulouse's City Hall, its name being derived from the "capitouls" or consuls who administered the city when it was ruled by the Raymonds. With its Ionic pilasters and alternating use of brick and stone, it is a fine example of the urban architecture of the 18C.

Cathédrale St-Étienne★

pl. Saint–Etienne. ◷Open Mon–Sat 8am–7pm, Sun 9am–7pm. ⬦No charge. ℘05 61 52 03 82.

There is a fascinating contrast here between the nave completed in 1212, a vast hall in the Mediterranean tradition designed to accommodate large numbers of people, and the chancel, begun 60 years later on the pattern of the Gothic churches of Northern France. The architect of this later addition was Jean Deschamps, who took it upon himself to propagate this style throughout Languedoc once it had become part of the Capetian realm. The nave and chancel are not aligned on the same axis and hardly seem to form part of a whole. The original plan had envisaged a more or less total reconstruction, but in the event the old nave was retained, and the link between it and the chancel cleverly improvised by some architectural virtuosity in what should have been the north transept.

Musée des Augustins★★

&. ⊙ Open daily 10am–6pm (Wed 9pm). ⊙Closed 1 Jan, 1 May, 25 Dec. ⊜€3 (free 1st Sun in the month). ℘05 61 22 21 82. www.augustins.org.
The museum is housed in the former convent, with a famous **Pietà** and superb collection of **Romanesque sculpture**★★★ (mostly 12C), much of it in grey Pyrénéan marble.

ADDITIONAL SIGHTS
Hôtel d'Assezat★★

This, the finest private mansion in Toulouse, was built in 1555–57 according to the plans of Nicolas Bachelier, the greatest Renaissance architect of Toulouse, for the Capitoul d'Assézat, who had made a fortune from trading in dyer's woad. Today, it houses the donation of private art collector Georges Bemberg, the **Fondation Bemberg** (&. ⊙open daily except Mon 10am–12.30pm, 1.30–6pm (Thu 9pm); ⊙closed 1 Jan and 25 Dec; ⊜€5; ℘05 61 12 06 89; www.fondation-bemberg.fr).
This impressive collection comprises painting, sculpture and objets d'art from the Renaissance to the 20C.

Muséum d'Histoire Naturelle★★

⊙Open daily except Mon 10am–6pm. ⊙Closed 1 Jan, 1 May, 25 Dec. €6. ℘05 67 73 84 84. www.museum.toulouse.fr.
The natural history museum has extensive collections, most notably of ornithological, prehistoric and ethnographical exhibits.
Take this opportunity to discover the **Jardin des Plantes**, the **Jardin Royal**

and the **Grand Rond**, well-laid-out gardens that make a very pleasant place for a stroll.

Musée St-Raymond★★

&. ⊙Open Jun–Aug 10am–7pm; Sept–May 10am–6pm. ⊜€3 (no charge 1st Sun in month). ℘05 61 22 31 44.
This museum, housed in one of the buildings of the old Collège St-Raymond (13C), rebuilt in 1523 and restored by Viollet-le-Duc, displays its collections of archaeology and antique art.

Musée Paul-Dupuy★

⊙Open daily except Tue 10am–6pm (Oct–May 5pm). ⊜3€ (no charge 1st Sunday in month). ℘05 61 14 65 50. www.mairie-toulouse.fr.
This museum is devoted to the applied arts from the Middle Ages to the present: metal and wood work, clock-making, weights and measures, coins, musical instruments, enamel work, gold plate, costumes and weapons.

Cité de l'espace★

⊥ Parc de la Plaine, along the eastern side of the ring road. ⊙Open early Jul–Aug 9.30am–7pm; rest of year 9.30am–5pm (weekends and school holidays 9.30am–6pm). ⊜€24.50–27 (children 5–15 years, €19–20.50). ℘0 820 377 223. www.cite-espace.com.
Visible from quite a distance, thanks to the rocket standing there and to a surprising contemporary sculpture which serves as the Exposition Pavilion (the work of Henri-Georges Adam – 1904–67), the Cité de l'espace is a place for discovering, experimenting and learning about the universe.

EXCURSIONS
Canal du Midi

▷ The Canal runs from Sète on the Languedoc coast to Toulouse, then joins the Canal Lateral to the Garonne and then on to Bordeaux.
It is hard to believe that this calm, beautiful, even elegant waterway, now so popular for leisurely boating holidays, was a daunting engineering achievement enabling the transport of

industrial goods directly between the Mediterranean and the Atlantic.

The notion of a canal between the Atlantic and the Mediterranean enabling shipping to avoid the long route via Gibraltar had preoccupied not only the Romans but also François I, Henri IV and Richelieu. The natural obstacles, however, seemed insurmountable.

Then in 1662, Pierre-Paul Riquet (1604–80) succeeded in interesting Colbert in overcoming them. The canal was to prove his ruin; all the work was carried out at his own expense and he died six months before the opening. The completed Canal du Midi is 240km/149mi long and has 103 locks; It proved a huge commercial success – too late for the great man.

Becoming obsolete in the late 19C, the canal provides a perfect illustration of pre-industrial techniques. It passed into state ownership in 1897 and today is used mainly by leisure craft. In 1996 it was named as a World Heritage Site by UNESCO.

Auch★

◗ *Auch lies 76.4km/47.4mi W of Toulouse.*
🖪 *1 r. Dessoles. ℘05 62 05 22 89. www.auch-tourisme.com.*
🏛*The Escalier Monumental is a majestic flight of 232 steps linking the river to the town centre.*

Auch is an attractive, pleasantly busy local capital in the heart of Gascony. Auch began in ancient times as a fortified Basque settlement beside the River Gers. For 2 000 years it served as a staging post on the old Toulouse–Bordeaux highway; its position avoided the treacherously shifting course of the River Garonne to the north. It owes some fame to the story of *The Three Musketeers* – the real d'Artagnan, Charles de Batz, was from this district.

Cathédrale Ste-Marie★★

pl. de la République. ◷*Open daily.*
◷*Closed during Mass. ℘05 62 05 72 71. http://auch.paroisse.net.*
The cathedral's ambulatory contains a masterly series of Renaissance **stained-glass windows★★**, completed in 1517, and remarkable for their sophisticated use of colour (subtle nuances and gradations and half-tones, all in strong contrast to the pure colours, rigidly separated, of the Gothic), and for the way in which the central figure of each window is surrounded by vignettes elucidating its symbolism and prefiguration (a characteristic humanist device of the time). Adam and Eve, Jonah, and the Nativity are exceptionally fine.

The **choir stalls★★★** are an inspired work completed in 1554, illuminated by 1 500 different figures in an extraordinary wealth of detail. The backs are carved with representations of biblical and other personages; more faces crowd the dividers, elbow-rests, the panels and niches of the backs and the misericords.

Montauban★

◗ *The town is 55.3km/34.3mi N of Toulouse (autoroute A 62).*
🖪 *4 r. du Collège. ℘05 63 63 60 60. www.montauban-tourisme.com.*
On the boundary between the hillsides of Bas Quercy and the rich alluvial plains of the Garonne and the Tarn, the old bastide of Montauban, built with a geometric street layout, is an important crossroads and a good point of departure for excursions into the Aveyron gorges. The almost exclusive use of pink brick lends the buildings here a distinctive character, which is also found in most of the towns and villages in Bas Quercy and the Toulouse area.

Place Nationale★

The square, formerly the Place Royale, dates from the foundation of the town in the 12C. After fire destroyed the wooden roofs or *couverts* above the galleries in 1614 and again in 1649, the arcades were rebuilt in brick in the 17C. The square features a double set of arcades with pointed or round-arched vaulting. The inner gallery was a covered passageway while the outer gallery was occupied by market stalls.

The ornate elements and warm tones of the brick soften the overall effect, which would otherwise be rather austere.

Musée Ingres★

19 r. de l'Hôtel-de-Ville. ○*Open daily except Mon from Palm Sunday–late Oct 10am-noon, 2-6pm; Jul–Aug daily 10am-noon, 1.30-6pm; late Oct–Palm Sunday daily except sun am and Mon.* ○*Closed public holidays.* €4 *(no charge 1st Sun in month).* €05 63 22 12 91. www.amis-museeingres.com.

Devoted to Jean-Auguste-Dominique Ingres' works, the museum is housed in a former bishop's palace. The first floor features some of the artist's best examples of his paintings: *Ruggiero freeing Angelica, Ossian's Dream, Jesus among the Doctors*, along with a selection of his 4 000 **drawings**.

Moissac★★

○ *70km/44mi NW of Toulouse, via A 62.* ☐ *6 pl. Durand de Bredon.* €05 63 04 01 85. www.moissac.fr.

Moissac is situated on a low rise overlooking the fertile flood plain near the meeting point of the Tarn with the Garonne. The place is famous for the white Chasselas dessert grape, which grows here in abundance.

Église St-Pierre★

The former Benedictine abbey church, founded in the 7C, was consecrated in 1063 and the **cloisters**★★ completed 35 years later. It subsequently served as a model for similar work all over Europe. The church's **south doorway**★★★ is a triumph of Romanesque sculpture.

St-Bertrand-de-Comminges★★

○ *St-Bertrand lies 112km/70mi SW of Toulouse, S of A 64, junction 17.* ☐ *22 pl. Valentin-Abeille, Montréjeau.* €05 61 95 80 22. http://otimontrejeau. ifrance.com.* ☐ *In July and August park either under the trees in Grand Place and take the steps, or park near Porte Majou, from which a "little train" (€1) makes the climb easy!*

This is one of the most picturesque and charming villages in the Pyrénéan foothills, perched on an isolated hilltop, encircled by ancient ramparts and dominated by an imposing cathedral.

St-Bertrand-de-Comminges

A substantial town was founded here in 72 BC by Pompey. In AD 585 the Burgundians descended on the place and laid it waste. For centuries the site lay abandoned, until in 1073 St Bernard saw its potential for the building of a cathedral and monastery.

Here the rules of the religious reforms of Pope Gregory VII were applied, making the little city the spiritual centre of Comminges, endowing the awkwardly shaped county (sandwiched as it was between the territories belonging to the House of Foix-Béarn and dotted with enclaves) with a religious significance far outweighing its political importance.

Cathédrale Ste-Marie-de-St-Bertrand de Comminges★

€05 61 89 04 91. www.cathedrale-saint-bertrand.org.

The Romanesque portal of the cathedral is made up of several independently sculpted panels showing the Adoration of the Magi and a figure of St Bertrand without a halo, recalling the work of the School of Toulouse at St Sernin.

The **cloisters**★★ are built over the 12–15C ramparts; the south side is open, giving fine views over the Upper Garonne countryside, and there is a famous pillar in primitive style with statues of the four Evangelists.

There are splendid choir stallsaa of 1535 in Renaissance style.

ADDRESSES

🛌 STAY

Hôtel le Capitole – *10 r. Rivals, Toulouse.* ✆*05 61 23 21 28. www.capitole-hotel.com. 33rms.* 🍽 *€8–10.* Situated very near to the Place du Capitole, this old mansion has a brick façade that has recently been redone. Some of the spacious bedrooms are sparkling new, and half are air-conditioned. A bonus: breakfasts are served 'til noon.

Hôtel Castellane – *17 r. Castellane, Toulouse.* ✆*05 61 62 18 82. www.castellane hotel.com. 53rms.* 🍽 *€8.50.* This small hotel close to the Capitole is slightly set back from the main thoroughfare. The simple, practical rooms are housed in three different buildings.

Hôtel de France – *5 r. d'Austerlitz, Toulouse.* ✆*05 61 21 88 24. www.hotel-france-toulouse.com. 64rms.* 🍽 *€8.* In business since 1910, this attractive hotel is situated a few steps from Place Wilson. The rooms are of various sizes; though not luxurious, they are shipshape and affordable. Some of the largest come with a balcony.

Hôtel Ours Blanc – *25 pl. Victor-Hugo, Toulouse.* ✆*05 61 23 14 55. www.hotel-oursblanc.com. 38rms.* 🍽 *€7.* Situated opposite the marché Victor-Hugo, this hotel has simple yet comfortable rooms (recently renovated) which are air-conditioned and soundproofed; bright breakfast room with some attractive pictures embellishing its walls.

Hôtel Mermoz – *50 r. Matabiau, Toulouse.* ✆*05 61 63 04 04. www.hotel-mermoz.com. 52rms.* 🍽 *€14.* The inner flower garden of this hotel near the city centre provides a haven of calm. Many decorative touches, notably portraits of pilots, bring aviation's early years to mind.

Citiz Hôtel – *18 Allées Jean Jaurès, Toulouse.* ✆*05 61 11 18 18. www.citizhotel.com. 56rms.* 🍽 *€10.* Only 2 minutes from Place Wilson, this renovated hotel is a marvel of contemporary design, and, considering its central location, very peaceful. Complimentary parking in adjacent underground car park; excellent buffet breakfasts.

🍽 EAT

La Cave des Blanchers – *29 r. des Blanchers, Toulouse.* ✆ *05 61 22 47 47. Closed Tue.* An attractive spot, situated among other restaurants on a street which is very popular in the evenings.

Regional cuisine blending characteristic sweet and sour flavours.

La Faim des Haricots – *3 r. du Puit Vert, Toulouse.* ✆ *05 61 22 49 25. Closed Sun.* A mere stone's throw from the Capitole, this vegetarian restaurant gives diners a choice of varied, plentiful fixed-price menus at painless prices.

Jean Chiche – *3 r. St-Pantaléon, Toulouse.* ✆ *05 61 21 80 80.* This pleasant pâtisserie and tearoom is close to the Capitole. The menu o ffers a choice of around a dozen light meals, plus cakes and ice creams.

Bon Vivre – *15 bis, pl. Wilson, Toulouse.* ✆ *05 61 23 07 17. www.lebonvivre.com.* With its terrace giving onto Place Wilson and an attractive interior decorated with photos of Gers (where the proprietor was born), this is an appealing spot with a solid traditional menu.

Le Chapon Fin – *3 Pl. des Récollets, Rodez.* ✆*05 63 04 04 22. www.lechaponfin-moissac.com. Closed Mon between Nov and Easter.* This establishment on the market square pampers its customers. The dining room in contemporary pastels serves classic cuisine.

Le Châteaubriand – *42 r. Pargaminières, Toulouse.* ✆*05 61 21 50 58. Closed Sun.* The atmosphere in this little restaurant in old Toulouse is particularly pleasant. Cosy interior with a parquet floor, red-brick walls, a huge mirror and house plants.

Chez Simone – *r. du Musée, St-Bertrand-de-Cominges.* ✆*05 61 94 91 05. Closed Toussaint and Christmas school holidays, and evenings off-season.* A couple of streets from the cathedral, Simone offers simple family fare.

Grand Café de l'Opéra – *1 pl. du Capitole, Toulouse.* ✆ *05 61 21 37 03. www.brasserieopera.com. Closed Sun.* The brasserie of the Grand Hôtel de l'Opéra is the essential place to see and be seen.

Le Mangevins – *46 r. Pharaon, Toulouse.* ✆*05 61 52 79 16. Closed Sun.* In this local tavern where salted foie gras and beef are sold by weight, the bawdy, fun atmosphere is enhanced by ribald songs. There is no menu, but a set meal for hearty appetites.

La Régalade – *16 r. Gambetta, Toulouse. 05 61 23 20 11. Closed Sat–Sun.* Located between the Capitole and the Garonne, this small restaurant's pink brick façade leads to a pleasant interior of exposed beams, modern art, wood furniture and bistro chairs.

⊜⊜🍽 **Brasserie "Beaux Arts"** –
*1 quai Daurade, Toulouse. 𝄢 05 61 21 12 12.
www.brasserielesbeauxarts.com.* The
atmosphere of a 1930s brasserie with
bistro-style chairs, wall seats, retro
lighting, wood panelling and mirrors.

⊜⊜🍽 **Le Colombier** – *14 r. Bayard,
Toulouse. 𝄢05 61 62 40 05. www.restaurant-
lecolombier.com. Closed public hols and Sun.*
Opened in 1874, this is an essential
stopping point for culinary pilgrims in
search of authentic cassoulet.

⊜⊜🍽 **La Madeleine de Proust** –
*11 r. Riquet, Toulouse. 𝄢05 61 63 80 88.
www.madeleinedeproust.com. Closed Sun.*
Childhood memories inspire the original,
carefully designed décor of this restaurant
featuring waxed tables, antique toys, an old
school desk and a time-worn cupboard.

⊜⊜🍽🍽 **L'Envers du Décor** – *22 r. des
Blanchers, Toulouse. 𝄢05 61 23 85 33.
www.enversdudecor.info. Closed Sun; Mon–
Tue for lunch.* Cuisine of the southwest
with some exotic touches is served in this
restaurant in a busy street not far from the
Garonne.

⊜⊜🍽🍽 **En Marge** – *8 r. Marge, Toulouse.
𝄢05 61 53 07 24. www.restaurantenmarge.
com.* Excellent French cuisine located
in the old district. Chef Frank Renimel
produces a new menu every fortnight.

⊜⊜🍽 **7 Place St-Sernin** – *7 pl.
St-Sernin, Toulouse. 𝄢 05 62 30 05 30.
www.7placesaintsernin.com. Closed Sat
lunch, Sun.* This pretty 19C house typical
of Toulouse stands opposite the basilica.
Bright red and yellow Catalan colours,
contemporary furniture and a display of
paintings from a local art gallery garnish
the dining room. Contemporary cuisine.

🎭 NIGHTLIFE

The bimonthly magazine *Toulouse
Culture* lists all upcoming events.

Place du Capitole – The famous central
square of the city is a pedestrian-only
meeting place surrounded by alluring
brasserie terraces.

Le Bibent – *5 pl. du Capitole, Toulouse.
𝄢05 61 23 89 03.* Classified as an historic
monument due to its Belle Époque décor,
this roomy café has a superb terrace giving
onto Place du Capitole.

Au Père Louis – *45 r. des Tourneurs,
Toulouse. 𝄢05 61 21 33 45. Closed Sun &
public holidays.* First opened in 1889 and
now a registered historical building, this
wine bar is a local institution.

🛒 SHOPPING

Toulouse markets – **Saturday mornings:**
organic farmers' market in Place du
Capitole. **Sunday morning:** farmers'
market around Église St-Aubin; L'Inquet,
a renowned flea market around the
Basilique St-Sernin. **Wednesday and
Friday** (Nov–Mar): geese, ducks and
foie gras are sold in Place du Salin.
Shopping streets – The main shopping
streets are Rue d'Alsace-Lorraine, Rue
Croix-Baragnon, Rue St-Antoine-du-T.,
Rue Boulbonne, Rue des Arts and the
pedestrian sections of Rue St-Rome,
Rue des Filatiers, Rue Baronie and Rue
de la Pomme.

🚶 LEISURE ACTIVITIES

Bateau Mouche Le Capitole – *quai
de la Daurade, Toulouse. 𝄢05 61 25 72 57.
www.toulouse-croisieres.com.* Embark upon
this pleasure steamer for a cruise on the
Garonne.

Péniche Baladine – *quai de la Daurade,
Toulouse. 𝄢05 61 80 22 26. www.bateaux-
toulousains.com.* Canal du Midi cruises
depart at 10.50am and 4pm; Garonne
cruises at 2.30pm, 5.30pm and 7pm.

Parc Toulousain – On an island in the
River Garonne, Parc Toulousain has 4 pools
(3 outdoors); the Stadium; the Parc des
Expositions and the Palais des Congrès.

🎪 EVENTS

Fête de la Violette – *mid-Feb.
𝄢05 61 11 02 22.* Growing, selling,
exhibiting… the ideal opportunity to
learn all about the flower that is the
city's emblem.

Le Marathon des mots – *mid-Jun.
𝄢05 61 99 64 01. www.lemarathondes
mots.com.* Literary festival.

Piano aux Jacobins – *Sept.
𝄢05 61 22 40 05. www.pianojacobins.com.*

Le Printemps de Septembre –
*Sept–Oct 𝄢05 61 14 23 51.
www.printempsdeseptembre.com.*
Festival of photography and visual arts.

Festival Occitania – *Sep-Oct.
𝄢05 61 11 24 87. http://festivaloccitania.com.*
Regional culture celebrated through
various media (cinema, poetry, song).

Le Marché de Noël – *Dec. 𝄢05 61 87 55 06.
www.midexpo.fr.* Toulouse Christmas
market.

Lourdes★★★

Midi-Pyrénées

This little market town, sited at the meeting point of mountain and plain, became a pilgrimage place of world renown in the 19C.

GEOGRAPHY
The town's setting
The summit of the **Béout** mountain is littered with great erratic blocks that give some idea of the power of the Quaternary glaciers.

The **view**★ is an object lesson in physical geography; it extends northwards from the exits of the Lavedan valleys over the morainic terraces through which the Pau torrent winds its sinuous course, to the glacial rock-bar on which the castle is sited, and finally to the great terminal moraine which forces the stream to make an abrupt turn to the west.

A BIT OF HISTORY
On 11 February 1858, **Bernadette Soubirous** (1844–79), while preparing for her First Communion, is said to have had the first of the 18 visions that led to Lourdes becoming a centre of the cult of Mary, with the grotto and its surroundings attracting pilgrims, and with a special place reserved for the lame and the sick, who come in the hope of a miraculous cure.

In 1866, the building of the first sanctuary was begun, and in 1871 the upper basilica was constructed.

- ▶ **Population:** 15 797
- ⚙ **Michelin Map:** 324 L 4
- 🗊 **Info:** pl. Peyramale. ℘05 62 42 77 40. www.lourdes-infotourisme.com.
- ◐ **Location:** The town is in the central Pyrénées area, 20km/12.4mi S of the town of Tarbes.
- ◔ **Timing:** About an hour will suffice to explore the town centre.

VISIT
Château Fort★
◷*Open Apr–Sept 9am–noon, 1.30–6.30pm (Jul–Aug 9am–6.30pm); Oct–Mar 9am–noon, 2–6pm.* ◷*Closed 1 Jan, 1 and 11 Nov, 25 Dec.* ✑€5 *(children, 6–11 €3).* ℘05 62 42 37 37. www.lourdes-visite.fr.

The fortress guarding the gateway to the Central Pyrénées, a fine example of medieval military architecture, was the state prison in the 17C and 18C. The Pointe du Cavalier (Rider's Bluff) panorama covers the valley of the Pau torrent and Pyrenean chain.

The **Pyrenean Folk Museum**★ exhibits local costumes, musical instruments, fine ceramics, a Béarnaise kitchen, *surjougs* (harness bells on wooden frames) and displays on palaeontology and prehistory.

THE PRACTICAL PILGRIM
Tourist train – A small train runs from late Mar–early Nov; departures from place Mgr-Laurence *every 20min 9am–noon and 1.30–6.30pm; 8–11pm.*♿ Accessible to persons of impaired mobility. €5.50 (children €2.70).

Pilgrimage – Before 5am, only the path to the Calvary is open (Les Lacets entrance). At 9am, pilgrims group on the Esplanade du Rosaire to celebrate the *Queen of Heaven (Easter to 31 Oct)*. Then the grotto opens. Thousands of votive candles flicker along the path and in front of the entrance and pilgrims seeking miracle cures immerse themselves in blue marble pools. At 4.30pm, the Holy Eucharist is borne from the Chapelle de l'Adoration to the Esplanade du Rosaire and the blessing of the sick begins.

Grotto area

The site of the visions is the **Grotto of the Miracles**, where the most moving manifestations of faith take place.

In the summer months the great local, national and international pilgrimages are held here. The degree of spirituality is evident in the scale of the ceremonial and the devotion of the participants.

In neo-Byzantine style, the **Basilica of the Rosary** has two curving approach ramps that have fixed the image of the great building in the popular mind.

The **crypt** is a realm of devotion, contemplation and silence. The **Upper Basilica** is dedicated to the Immaculate Conception and has a vast nave of five bays.

EXCURSIONS

Grottes de Bétharram★★

Saint-Pé-de-Bigorre. 14km/8.7mi W. Open 25 Mar–Oct daily 9am–noon, 1.30–5.30pm; 11 Feb–late Mar Mon–Fri 2.30–4pm. €13. 05 62 41 80 04. www.grottes-de-betharram.com.

This is one of the most popular natural attractions in the Pyrénées area. The caves comprise five separate galleries, one above the other.

Notable features include the vast roofs of porous rock of the upper level, a striking column which is still growing and is a typical example of the evolution of stalagmites and stalactites; a collapsed pot-hole 80m/262ft deep; and a narrow fissure through which the river flows.

Pic de Pibeste★★★

2hr20min climb from Ouzous on D 202.

This peak – alt. 1 349m/4 426ft – provides one of the best viewpoints in the central Pyrénées.

Tarbes

19km/12mi NE of Lourdes by N 21.

Tarbes has been the capital of Bigorre since the 9C. Tarbes is also an important trading centre and the traditional home of fairs and markets, as well as the second-largest university centre in the Midi-Pyrénées region after Toulouse.

Pic du Jer★

59 av. Francis-Lagardère; the mountain summit is SE of Lourdes.

A **funicular railway** offers a **panorama** of the central Pyrénées (*open Jul–Aug 9am–8pm, Mar–Jun and Sept–Nov 9.30am–6pm; €9.50 return (children 12–18, €8); 05 62 94 00 41*) rising to 948m/3 110ft.

Le Béout★

Alt. 791m/2 595ft. S of Lourdes.
Take the footpath from the Cité-Secours-St-Pierre rescue centre.

The **view** of Lourdes, Pic du Jer, Pic de Montaigu, the Argelès Valley, and Bat-Surguère and Castelloubon valleys is splendid. Continue along the ridge to the far end to admire the Pic du Midi de Bigorre, Lac de Lourdes, Pic Long in the Néouvielle massif, the Marboré Cylinder and Monte Perdido.

Parc National des Pyrénées★★★

The park extends for more than 100km/60mi along the French border region from Vallée d'Aspe in the west to Vallée d'Aure in the east.
Seven Maisons du Parc and several other seasonal outposts offer maps, brochures and tourist information (see Useful Addresses).

The Pyrénées National Park was created in 1967 with the aim of preserving the beauty of the natural environment. The Parc National des Pyrénées and its peripheral area attract thousands of tourists every year. In winter, the mountains are a kingdom where skiers reign – children and adults, beginners and experts alike. In summer, both experienced and occasional walkers take to the mountain trails. Although the park can be toured by car, it can be a convoluted process, and so the countryside is better appreciated on foot.

Geology – The park itself is surrounded by a peripheral area of 206 000ha/795sq mi, including 86 municipalities in the Hautes-Pyrénées and Pyrénées-Atlantiques *départements*.

The development programme in this area has concentrated on revitalising the pastoral economy of the mountain villages and improving tourist facilities. The park provides shelter for 4 000 izards, a local species of chamois, particularly in the valleys of Ossau and Cauterets, where they can be easily spotted, as well as more than 200 colonies of marmots. It is now very rare to catch sight of one of the few remaining brown bears, but it is not unusual to see royal eagles or huge bearded vultures in flight in a region still frequented by wood grouse, ptarmigan and Pyrenean muskrats.

Pic du Midi de Bigorre★★★

▶ *The Pic is a landmark in the Gascon Pyrénées, rising SE of Lourdes.*
🕐*Departures every 15min 1–12 Oct, 25 Oct–6 Nov, end Nov–Jan Wed–Mon, Feb–20 Apr, May Wed–Mon 10am–3.30pm, last descent 5.30pm; Jun–Sept 9am–4.30pm, last descent 7pm.* ✆€30.
🛈℘0825 00 2877. www.picdumidi.com.
☺*Subject to change due to weather.*
Don't miss the observatory for its **panorama**★★★ *views of the Pyrénées.*
A vertiginous mountain road winds over the Tourmalet Pass (Col du Tourmalet). From the top (2 114m/6 935ft) a toll road leads to Les Laquets; from here a cable car or a rough path (2hr round-trip) gives access to the summit of the Pic du Midi de Bigorre, now reduced in level to the 2 865m/9 400ft contour in order to accommodate the television transmitter.

Observatoire et Institut de Physique du Globe du Pic du Midi

The factors favouring the siting here of an observatory include the great height, the purity of the atmosphere and the all-round viewing possibilities. The observatory, founded by General Nansouty, was originally intended for botanical and meteorological studies, but the astronomical function was soon added. It was here in 1706 that the first observations were made of the solar corona during a total eclipse of the sun. At the beginning of the 20C, the great observatory dome and reflecting telescopes were added.

Today, it is used for lunar mapping and research into the solar corona, cosmic radiation and nocturnal luminescence. At the **summit**, which can only be reached by cable car (Level 4), a glassed-in gallery and several terraces offer the most impressive panorama in the Pyrénées.

Lac de Gaube

Walks in the Pyrénées

Vallées des Cauterets

Lac de Gaube★★ – *1hr 30min round-trip by GR 10 rambling path, upstream from Pont d'Espagne. The* **Gaube chairlift** *(⊙open Jul–Aug 9.15am–5.45pm; May–Jun and Sept 9.45am-5.30pm; ⊙closed Oct–mid-Dec; ⊚€6.50 round-trip (€7 for Puntas gondola and Gaube chairlift); ℘05 62 92 52 19) from Plateau de Clots can be taken most of the way, followed by a 20min walk to a bar-café by the lake.* At the top of the chairlift, nature information panels describe forest flora and fauna and the izard, a local species of chamois. The austere yet beautiful site provides a view of the Vignemale massif and glaciers. A footpath along the river's west bank looks onto Pique Longue du Vignemale, 3 298m/10 820ft, one of the highest peaks in the Pyrenees.

Vallée du Marcadau★★ – ⊙ *6.5km/4mi. 6hr round-trip on foot from the Pont d'Espagne parking area.* Once a favourite route for crossing into Spain, this path has grass-covered shoulders and meandering mountain streams, alternating with glacial thresholds and twisted mountain pines. The Wallon refuge stands at an altitude of 1 866m/6 122ft, and beyond it is a cirque of pastureland scattered with lakes. Marcadau means market place, which this once was.

Vallée de Lutour★ – ⊙ *6km/3.6mi. Take the Pont d'Espagne road as far as a series of hairpin bends. Just before the Le Bois thermal establishment, turn sharply left onto the narrow, steep forest road to La Fruitière.* The track offers glimpses of the upper Lutour falls, then emerges into peaceful pastureland.

Vallée de Gavarnie

Cirque de Gavarnie★★★ – *3hr on foot there and back.* At the end of the village, take the unsurfaced path then follow the true left bank of the *gave* (mountain stream). Cross an old stone bridge and walk up through the woods, with the river now to your right. The last part of the walk climbs through mixed vegetation to the first rocky folds marking the approach of the Cirque itself. Then the Cirque de Gavarnie comes into view. Gazing at its majesty of sheer walls and tiered snow platforms, Victor Hugo exclaimed: "It is both a mountain and a rampart; it is the most mysterious of structures by the most mysterious of architects; it is Nature's Colosseum – it is Gavarnie!"

The mounted Driving Tours end at the Hôtel du Cirque but it is possible to continue, on foot *(1hr30min there and back)*, to the Grande Cascade. This impressive waterfall is fed by meltwater from the frozen lake on Monte Perdido on the Spanish side of the frontier. The cascade drops 422m/1 385ft into the void.

Cirque de Gavarnie

© Doug Pearson/age fotostock

Brèche de Roland (Roland's Gap) – *4–5hr on foot there and back – for experienced mountain walkers only: beware of the névés Sept–early Jul. Follow the marked path starting E of Port de Boucharo.* The path follows the Haute Route des Pyrénées and fords a waterfall at the foot of the Taillon glacier. From the pass admire the Grande Cascade of the Cirque de Gavarnie. Beyond the Sarradets refuge, the climb to the gap is long and more difficult due to snow and *névés*. The breach named after the gallant 8C knight Rolland offers a **view** of Monte Perdido and the barren Spanish side.

Massif de Néouvielle★★★

The Massif de Néouvielle is the ideal area for family walks as well as for more demanding treks in the mountains. There are numerous marked itineraries, and appropriate topoguides are on sale in local shops or in the **Maison du Parc** in Saint-Lary-Soulan (*℘05 62 39 40 91)*; information is available from the **Bureau des Guides** in Saint-Lary-Soulan (*℘05 62 40 02 58 or 05 62 39 41 97)*.

Col (or hourquette) d'Aubert★★ – *3hr on foot to the pass. From the Lac d'Aubert parking area, follow the marked path that skirts the lake by the NE. Alt. 2 498m/8 196ft.* This pass links the depression cradling the Aubert and Aumar lakes with the desolate Escoubous coomb on the slopes towards Barèges. There is a remarkable **view**★★ of the tiered lakes at the foot of Pic de Néouvielle.

Hiking in the Massif de Néouvielle

H. Le Gac/MICHELIN

ADDRESSES

STAY

Cazaux – *2 chemin Rochers, Lourdes.* ℘*05 62 94 22 65. http://hotelcazauxlourdes. site.voila.fr. Closed 9 Oct–8 Apr. 20rms.* ⬜€6 This small hotel just outside the town centre offers scrupulously kept, fresh-looking rooms, a friendly welcome and reasonable prices among other things. It is near the market.

Chambre d'hôte M. and Mme Vives – *28 rte de Bartrès, Loubajac, 6km/ 3.7mi NW of Lourdes on D 940 towards Pau.* ℘*05 62 94 44 17. www.anousta.com. Closed mid-Nov–mid-Feb. 5rms.* If you like the countryside, peace and quiet and a farm atmosphere, this is the place for you. Sheep, chickens and ducks are raised and consumed here against a stunning backdrop of the Pyrénées. Four rooms with beams and sloping ceilings; two others with a terrace. Fine garden and children's play area.

Chambre d'hôte Les Rocailles – *Omex, 4.5km/3mi SW of Lourdes on D 13 then D 213.* ℘*05 62 94 46 19. Closed Nov–Easter. 3rms.* You'll adore this sweet little place! The owner used to be a costume designer at the Paris Opera and has decorated this small stone house with taste and refinement. Warm woods blend harmoniously with shimmering fabrics.

Chambre d'hôte Le Grand Cèdre – *6 r. du Barry, St-Pé-de-Bigorre.* ℘*05 62 41 82 04. www.legrandcedre.fr. 4rms.* This lovely 17C manor is sure to charm you. Each room is in a different style: Art Deco, Louis XV, Henri II, Louis-Philippe. Dining room, music room and superb park with a glasshouse and a vegetable garden.

Hôtel Les Cimes – *1 pl. d'Ourout 65400 Argelès-Gazost.* ℘*05 62 97 00 10. www.hotel-lescimes.com. 24rms.* This family-run hotel is located at the southern end of the town, and is an ideal spot from which to explore the Gave de Gavarnie, the routes up to the Pont d'Espagne, and the Col du Tourmalet.

Hôtel Solitude – *3 passage St-Louis Ave, Lourdes.* ℘*05 62 42 71 71. Closed 6 Nov–31 Mar. 356rms.* This large, imposing modern hotel on the banks of the Pau, a Pyrénéan stream, has a small rooftop swimming pool. The dining room is a rotunda and has a terrace overlooking the river. The rooms with their little red armchairs are comfortable. We recommend those on the side of the river.

Mercure Hôtel Impérial – *3 av. du Paradis, Lourdes.* ℘*05 62 94 06 30. www.mercure.com. Closed 16 Dec–31 Jan. 93 rooms.* ⬜€12. This 1935 hotel, which has been completely renovated in its original Art Deco style, is near the cave. The rooms are pleasant and furnished in soothing mahogany tones. Large classic-style dining room and drawing room opening onto a small garden.

EAT

Pizza Da Marco – *47 r. de la Grotte, Lourdes.* ℘*05 62 94 03 59.* This is a pleasant place, decorated with photos and engravings. The pizzaïolo is set up in the front room, but it is nicer to sit in the other room. Crispy pizza and efficient service.

Le Magret – *10 r. 4 Frères-Soulas, Lourdes.* ℘*05 62 94 20 55. www.lemagret. com. Closed Mon.* This little restaurant occupies a rustic-style dining room with exposed beams and straw-bottomed chairs. Pilgrims and locals alike can enjoy traditional southwest cuisine without pretension.

Brasserie de l'hôtel de la Grotte – *66 r. de la Grotte, Lourdes.* ℘*05 62 94 58 87. www.hotel-grotte.com. Closed 25 Oct–9 Apr. Reservations required.* Agreeable contemporary surroundings comprising ochre-coloured dining room, veranda and terrace, and a menu to suit all budgets, plus a more formal adjacent restaurant.

LEISURE ACTIVITIES

Sarl La Truite des Pyrénées – *65400 Lau -Balagnas.* ℘*05 62 97 02 05. Apr–Sept 9am– noon, 3pm–7pm; Oct–Mar daily except Sun 9am–noon, 3pm–6pm; closed 1 & 11 Nov.* Everything you need to know about trout fishing (equipment and instruction available), and a shop and exhibition.

Lac de Lourdes – *Leave town W along D 940 and turn left onto the path leading to the edge of the lake via l'Embarcadère restaurant.* Lying at an altitude of 421m/ 1 381ft, the 11m/36ft-deep glacial lake offers water-sports facilities (non-supervised bathing), fishing and golf (Lourdes 18-hole golf course to the south). From the shores of the lake there are fine views of the Pyrénéan foothills. A footpath runs round the lake.

Voie Verte des Gaves – This is a 17km/ 10.6mi-long cycle track between Lourdes and Soulom to the west. *Information from Association française de développement des Véloroutes et Voies Vertes – Délégation Grand Sud-Ouest – 5 av F.-Collignon, 31200 Toulouse.* ℘*05 34 30 05 59 – www.af3v.org.*

Carcassonne★★★

Aude

A visit to fortified Carcassonne, a UNESCO World Heritage Site, is a return to the Middle Ages. On Bastille Day (14 July) a dramatic fireworks display makes the stunning citadel seem to go up in flames. The romantic old town contrasts sharply with the commercial Ville Basse (lower town), a *bastide* town, where Carcassonne shows off its role as the centre of the Aude *département*'s wine-growing industry.

A BIT OF HISTORY

The site of the Cité was first fortified by the Gauls; their entrenched camp served Roman, Visigoth and Frank in turn. In the 9C, Carcassonne became the capital of a county, then of a viscounty subject to the County of Toulouse. In common with the rest of the South of France it enjoyed a long period of prosperity which was brought to an end by the Crusade against the "Albigensians" – Cathars. On 1 August 1209 the army of crusaders under Simon de Montfort arrived at the walls of Carcassonne and besieged the city. Within a fortnight, the attackers had seized the Viscount, Raymond-Roger Trencavel, and the town capitulated.

WALKING TOUR

LA CITÉ★★★

The "Cité" of Carcassonne on the Aude's east bank is the largest fortress in Europe. It consists of a fortified nucleus, the Château Comtal, and a double curtain wall: the outer ramparts, with 14 towers, separated from the inner ramparts (24 towers) by the outer bailey, or lists *(lices)*. A resident population of 139, and school and post office, save Carcassonne from becoming a ghost town. *Leave the car in one of the car parks outside the walls in front of the gateway to the east, Porte Narbonnaise. 2hr tour of the ramparts aboard a* **tourist train** *(& ☉ open May–Sept tours (25min, leaving from the Porte Narbonnaise) with explanation of the defence system*

- **Population:** 49 142
- **Michelin Map:** 344 E-F 3
- **Info:** 28 r. de Verdun. ℰ04 68 10 24 30. www.carcassonne-tourisme.com.
- **Location:** The city lies 93km/58mi SE of Toulouse and 59km/37mi W of Narbonne.
- **Parking:** Visitors are not allowed to drive in the Cité: use the large car parks outside the walls in front of the Porte Narbonnaise.
- **Don't Miss:** The view of the Cité from a distance, especially from *autoroute* A 1, is spectacular.
- **Timing:** Half a day to visit the fortified Cité, and the same for the modern town.

☺ Guided Tours ☺

There are several guided tour options in the Cité. Contact the tourist office for details.

10am–noon, 2–6pm; €7 (children €3) ℰ04 68 24 45 70) or a **horse-drawn carriage** *(☉ open Apr–Nov: discovery of the ramparts in a caleche (20min), with historical commentary; €7 (children €4); rte de la Cavayère, Montlegun, Carcassonne; ℰ04 68 71 54 57; www.carcassonne-caleches.com.*

Porte Narbonnaise

On either side of the gateway to the original fortified town are two massive Narbonne towers, and, between them, a 13C statue of the Virgin Mary. Inside, the 13C rooms restored by Viollet-le-Duc house **temporary exhibitions** of modern art.

Rue Cros-Mayrevieille

This street leads directly to the castle, although you might prefer to get there by wandering along the narrow winding

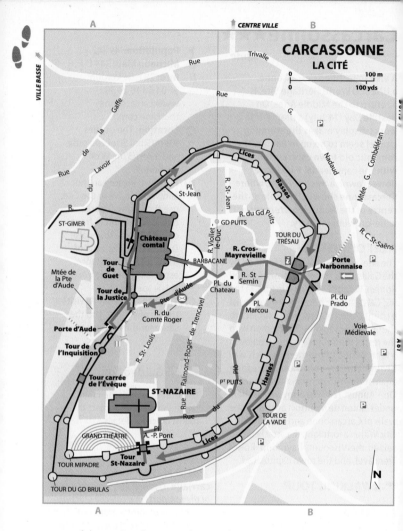

streets of the medieval town, with its many crafts and souvenir shops.

Château Comtal

🕐⏰🎫 Apr–Sept 9.30am–6.30pm; Oct–Mar 9.30am–5pm. 🕐Closed 1 Jan, 1 May, 1 and 11 Nov, 25 Dec. 🎫€9 (no charge 1st Sunday of the month from Nov–Mar). 📞04 68 11 70 72. www.monum.fr.

The castle was originally the palace of the viscounts, built in the 12C by Bernard Aton Trencavel. It became a citadel after Carcassonne was made part of the royal estate in 1226. Since the reign of St Louis IX, it has been defended by a large semicircular barbican and formidable moat.

▶ Leave the castle and follow rue de la Porte d'Aude on the left.

Porte d'Aude

A fortified path, the Montée d'Aude, weaves from the church of St-Gimer up to this heavily defended gateway. The west and north sections of the outer bailey are called the "lices basses". The **Tour de l'Inquisition** was the seat of the Inquisitor's court, and its central pillar with chains and cell bear witness to the tortures inflicted upon heretics.

The Bishop's **Tour carrée de l'Évêque** was much more comfortably appointed.

▶ *Return towards the Porte d'Aude and continue along the Lices Basses.*

The itinerary takes you past the **Tour de la Justice**. The Trencavels, protectors of the Cathars, sought refuge here with the count of Toulouse during the Albigensian Crusade. This circular tower has windows whose tilting wooden shutters enabled those inside to see (and drop things on) attackers.

▶ *Walk beneath the drawbridge by the Porte Narbonnaise and continue SE.*

The "lices hautes"

The wide gap between the inner and outer ramparts, edged with moats, was used for weapons practice and jousting. Beyond Porte Narbonnaise, note the three-storey Tour de la Vade on the outer curtain wall to the left.

This fortified tower kept watch over all of the eastern ramparts. Carry on to the Tour du Grand Brulas, on the corner opposite the Tour Mipadre.

Tour St-Nazaire

This tower's postern was only accessible by ladders. A well and an oven are still in evidence on the first floor. At the top of the tower is a viewing table.

▶ *Enter the Cité through the Porte St-Nazaire.*

Basilique St-Nazaire★

All that remains of the original church is the Romanesque nave. The basilica's **stained-glass windows**★★ (13–14C) are considered the most impressive in the south of France.

Remarkable **statues**★★ adorn the pillars around the chancel walls, and one of the most eye-catching bishops' tombs is that of Pierre de Roquefort (14C).

▶ *Return to the Porte Narbonnaise via rue du Plô.*

EXCURSIONS

Castres★

▶ *Castres is 70km/43.5mi E of Toulouse.*
🏠 *2 pl. de la République.* ✆*05 63 62 63 62. www.tourisme-castres.fr.*

This industrial town on the **Agout** River has fine 16–17C mansions, a Goya museum, and is a good base for exploring the Lacaune and Montagne Noire hill country. The Castres area is the French wool carding centre; its wool industry is second only to Roubaix-Tourncoing.

Musée Goya★

Hôtel de Ville. ◷*Open Sept–Jun Tue–Sun 9am–noon, 2–5pm; Jul–Aug daily 10am–6pm.* ◷*Closed 1 Jan, May, 1 Nov, 25 Dec.* ◉*€2.50 (no charge 1st Sun of the month (Oct–May)).* ✆*05 63 71 59 30.*
Set up on the second floor of the former episcopal palace (now the Town Hall), this museum specialises in Spanish painting and possesses several outstanding works by Goya: *Self-Portrait, The Disasters of War, Francisco del Mazo* and *The Junta of the Philippines led* by Ferdinand VII.

Foix★

▶ *Foix is 90km/56mi SW of Carcassonne.* 🏠 *29 r. Delcassé.* ✆*05 61 65 12 12. www.tourisme-foix-varilhes.fr.*
In the Middle Ages this hill town was important as the capital of the colourful Counts of Foix. Ruggedly set against a skyline of jagged peaks and three castle towers, it overlooks the Plantaurel hills. Its old narrow streets radiate from Rue de Labistour and Rue des Marchands, starkly contrasting with the 19C administrative area fanning out from the Allées de la Villote and the Champ de Mars.
Once part of the Duchy of Aquitaine, the Foix region became a county in the 11C. At the conclusion of the Albigensian Crusade, the Counts, who had favoured the heresy, were obliged to submit to the king of France under the terms of the Treaty of Paris (1229).
Until the late 19C the Ariège River was panned for gold, and many local iron foundries were supplied by the mine at La Rancié until 1931.

Château de Montségur on the peak

Panorama★

From the **Château** (⊙*open Jan 10.30am –noon, 2–5.30pm; Feb–Apr and Oct–Dec 10.30am–noon, 2–5.30pm; May, Mon–Fri 10.30am–noon, 2–5.30pm, Sat–Sun and public holidays 10am–noon, 2–6pm; Jun–Sept daily 10am–6pm (Jul–Aug 6.30pm); ⊙closed public holidays; ⊛€4.60; ℘05 34 09 83 83)* rock high above the river there are extensive views over the surrounding region.

Parc Pyrénéen de l'Art Préhistorique (Tarascon-sur-Ariège) ★★

▶ *At Lacombe, on the road to Banat via the N 20.*

The park, devoted to cave paintings – there are some 12 decorated caves in the Ariège area – comprises a distinctive modern building housing a display area, the Grand Atelier, and an open space with exhibits featuring water and rock. An audio-tour of the Grand Atelier gives a comprehensive account of the discoveries of cave paintings.

Grotte du Mas-d'Azil★★

▶ *In the Ariège hills, 31km/19mi NW of Foix.*

◗◖*Guided tours (45min) year-round; call or see website for opening hours. ⊛€6.50, includes museum visit. ℘05 61 69 97 71. www.grotte-masdazil.com.*

This cave is one of the outstanding natural phenomena of southwestern France, as well as a very important prehistoric site. In 1887 Édouard Piette discovered evidence of human habitation during the Azilian period (9 500 BC). Research continued under Abbé Breuil, Mandement, Boule and Cartailhac.

Château de Montségur★

▶ *The small village of Montségur is 56.6km/35mi N of Ax-les-Thermes, in the foothills of the eastern Pyrénées. ℘05 61 03 03 03. www.montsegur.org.*

It was on this fearsome peak that the last episode of the Albigensian Crusade took place, when its Cathar defenders were massacred and Languedoc eclipsed by the power of the French kingdom.

Catharism – the name is derived from a Greek word meaning "pure" – was based on the principle of the total separation of Good and Evil, of the spiritual from the material. Its adherents comprised ordinary believers and the *"Perfecti"*, the latter living lives of exemplary purity in the light of God. Their austerity contrasted sharply with the venality and laxity of the Catholic clergy.

In the early 13C the local **Cathars** built a castle here to replace an old, sincedemolished fortress. Forty years later, following the ravages of the Albigensian Crusade against the Cathars, the stronghold was occupied by 400 adherents to the faith, from whose ranks was drawn the fierce band which marched on Avignonet to put to the sword the members of the Inquisition meeting there. This sealed the fate of Montségur; in the absence of Louis IX, who was dealing with disturbances in Saintonge, Blanche of Castille ordered the Crusaders to put the castle to siege. On 2 March 1244, the resistance of the defenders was overcome, but 200 of the faithful refused to retract their beliefs, even after being granted a fortnight in which to reconsider. On 16 March, they were brought down from the mountain to be burnt on a huge pyre.

Château

🕐*Open daily Feb and Dec 11am–4.30pm; Mar 10.30am–5.30pm; Apr 10am–6.30pm; May–Jun 10am–6.30pm; Jul–Aug 9am–7.30pm; Sept 9.30am–6.30pm; Oct 10am–6pm; Nov 10.30am–5pm.* 🕐*Closed Jan and 25 Dec.* ⊛€4.50.

This imposing castle was rebuilt in a pentagonal structure due to the shape of the limestone rock on which it sits.

Musée Historique et Archéologique

🕐*Same opening times as the château.*
As well as medieval period furniture and objects found in the vicinity of the castle, this museum also has two skeletons and a cast of the cross of Morency.

ADDRESSES

🏠 STAY

⊜ **Camping Le Martinet Rouge** – *11390 Brousses-et-Villaret* ℘*04 68 26 51 98 Reservations advised for Jul–Aug. 35 places.* In a fabulous setting in the Montagne Noire. Swimming pool.

⊜⊜ **Hôtel Espace Cité** – *132 r. Trivalle* – ℘*04 68 25 24 24. 48rms.* Modern hotel at the foot of the citadel, with bright and functional rooms.

⊜⊜ **Hôtel Montmorency** – *2 r. Camille -St-Saens.* ℘*04 68 11 96 70. www.hoteldu chateau.net.* 🅿 *Reservation advised in summer. 20rms.* ⊡€*12.* Close to La Cité. Very smart rooms, well furnished, but simple.

⊜⊜ **Chambre d'hôte L'Olivette** – *r. Pierre-Duhem, 11160 Cabrespine.* ℘*04*

68 26 19 25. 3rms. Charming simplicity; located not far from the gouffre de Cabrespine.

⊜⊜ **Auberge du Château** – *Château de Cavanac, 11570 Cavanac* ℘*04 68 79 61 04. www.chateau-de-cavanac.fr. Closed Jan–Feb and 2 wks in Nov. 24rms.* ⊡€*12. Restaurant* ⊜⊜. Beautiful rooms with view over vineyard; fine restaurant serving own wines.

⊜⊜🍽 **Chambre d'hôte La Maison sur la Colline** – *Lieu-dit Ste-Croix.* ℘*04 68 47 57 94. Closed 1 Dec–15 Feb. Reservation recommended in summer. 5rms.* This restored farm has a spectacular hillside view of the Cité from its garden.

⊜🍽 **Hôtel la Bergerie** – *Allée Pech-Marie, 11600 Aragon.* ℘*04 68 26 10 65. www.labergeriearagon.com.* 🅿 *8rms.* ⊡€*10. Restaurant* ⊜🍽. In a lovely village; rooms have views over vineyard.

⊜⊜🍽 **Hôtel le Donjon and les Remparts** – *2 r. du Comte-Roger.* ℘*04 68 11 23 00. www.bestwestern.com.* 🅿 *62rms.* This hotel combining old stonework and renovated décor occupies part of a 15C orphanage.

🍽 EAT

⊜ **Le Bar à Vins** – *6 r. du Plo.* ℘*04 68 47 38 38.* In the heart of the medieval Cité, this wine bar's shady garden has a view of the St-Nazaire basilica.

⊜⊜ **La Tête de l'Art** – *37 bis, r. Trivalle* ℘*04 68 47 36 36. Closed Sun in winter. Reservations recommended at weekends.* This restaurant, specialising in pork dishes, also exhibits works of modern painting and sculpture.

⊜⊜ **Auberge de Dame Carcas** – *3 pl. du Château* ℘*04 68 71 23 23. Closed Jan, noon and Wed.* This popular establishment in the medieval Cité has a generous menu.

⊜⊜ **La Marquière** – *13 r. St-Jean.* ℘*04 68 71 52 00. Closed Wed and Thu.* Roughcast building near northern ramparts. Serves traditional cuisine.

⊜⊜🍽 **Comte Roger** – *14 r. St-Louis.* ℘*04 68 11 93 40. www.comteroger.com. Closed Sun and Mon.* Your stroll through La Cité may well lead you to this sheltered spot.

Narbonne★★

Aude

Narbonne, which in its time has been the ancient capital of Gallia Narbonensis, the residence of the Visigoth monarchy and an archiepiscopal seat, is now a lively Mediterranean city playing an important role as a wine-producing centre and a road and rail junction.

A BIT OF HISTORY

The history of this ancient Mediterranean city is a long one, reaching back many centuries BC. After the defeat of Hannibal, the Roman Empire chose Narbonne to be the commercial centre of the Celtic province, with an artificial port created by diverting an arm of the River Aude. Finally it was made the capital of Gallia Narbonensis (today's Languedoc and Provence regions) and flourished right up to the end of the Empire and the arrival of the Visigoths, who made it the capital of their kingdom.

Trading activity continued (Muslim raiders found the city still worth looting in 793), and medieval shipping made use of the extensive shallow lagoons lining the coast behind the rampart of sand bars. However, in the 14C, the city's large and long-established Jewish community was expelled; the famous port silted up, and the town's prosperity came to an abrupt end. The construction of the

▶ **Population:** 52 252
◔ **Michelin Map:** 344 I-J 3
▯ **Info:** 31 r. Jean Jaurès.
  ℘04 68 65 15 60.
  www.mairie-narbonne.fr.
▷ **Location:** 61km/38mi E of Carcassonne and 96km/60mi SW of Montpelier.
▯ **Parking:** The central area is a pedestrian zone. The two nearest car parks are on quai Victor-Hugo and beneath cours Mirabeau.
✿ **Don't Miss:** The Palais des Archevêques.
◔ **Timing:** Explore early in the morning in summer before it's too hot.

Canal du Midi in the 17C, the coming of the railway in the 19C, and the development of tourism on the Languedoc coast in the 20C halted the process of decline.

SIGHTS

Cathédrale St-Just-et-St-Pasteur★★

◔*Open daily Oct–Jun 9am–noon, 2–6pm; Jul–Sept 10am–7pm.*
℘*04 68 32 09 52.*
The present building was begun in 1272, but halted later in order to preserve the ramparts which would have been

Cathédrale St-Just-et-St-Pasteur

breached to build the nave. The choir remains, its vaulting reaching the dizzy height of 41m/135ft.

The lofty cloisters (1349–1417) are built in crumbling limestone on the site of a Carolingian church. The cathedral **treasury** has a wonderful late-15C **Flemish Tapestry**★★ in silk and gold thread, a 10C ivory missal plaque and a rare marriage casket in rock crystal with intaglio decoration.

Palais des Archevêques

🕐 *Open daily Oct–Mar Tue–Sun 10am–noon, 2–5pm; Apr–Sept 10am–12.15pm, 2–6pm.* ⊘€5.50. 🖉04 68 90 30 30.

Many building styles are represented here, including the 12C **Old Palace** (Palais Vieux), the 13C **Madeleine Tower** (donjon de la Madeleine) and **Gilles Aycelin Tower (donjon Gilles Aycelin**★), the 14C **St Martial Tower** (tour St-Martial) and Palais Neuf (🕐*Open daily Oct–Jun 9am–noon, 2–6pm; Jul–Sept 10am–7pm. 🖉04 68 32 09 52)*, and the 17C Archbishops' Residence (Résidence des Archevêques) with its Louis XIII staircase to the City Hall (Hôtel de Ville), which has a 19C façade.

ADDITIONAL SIGHTS
Archaeological Museum★★

Palais Neuf. 🕐*Open Apr–Sept 9.30am–12.15pm, 2–6pm; Oct–Mar daily except Mon 10am–noon, 2–5pm.* ⊘€5.50. *(Museum Pass €8).* 🖉04 68 90 30 54.

Narbonne undoubtedly possesses one of the finest collections of **Roman paintings**★★ in France.

Museum of Art and History★

🕐 *As for the Archaeological Museum.*

This museum occupies the old episcopal apartments where Louis XIII stayed during the siege of Perpignan in 1642.

Lapidary Museum★

🕐 *As for the Archaeological Museum.*

This is in the deconsecrated 13C church of Notre-Dame-de-la-Mourguié. The magnificent exterior has projecting buttresses and a crenellated chevet.

Basilique St-Paul

This basilica was built on the site of a 4–5C necropolis near the tomb of the city's first archbishop. The **chancel**★, begun in 1224, is notable for the height of its supporting structure and vaults.

EXCURSION
Abbaye de Fontfroide★★

🕞 *15km/9.3mi SW.*

This former Cistercian abbey nestles in a quiet, restful corner of the countryside. The fine flame-coloured shades of yellow ochre and pink in the Corbières sandstone which was used to build the abbey enhance the serenity of the sight, particularly at sunset.

Réserve Africaine de Sigean★

🕞 *18km/11m S of Narbonne and 54km/34m N of Perpignan by the N 9. After Sigean follow signs.*

This **safari park** owes much of its unique character to the wild landscape of coastal Languedoc, with its *garrigues* dotted with lagoons, and to the fact that for each species large areas have been set aside, which resemble their native environment as closely as possible.

Visit by Car

Please observe the safety instructions displayed at the entrance. 🕐*Open Apr–early Sept 9am–6.30pm; rest of year opens at 9am, with varying closing hours – see website for details.* ⊘€27 *(children, 4–14, €21).* 🖉04 68 48 20 20. www.reserveafricainesigean.fr.

The route for visitors in cars goes through four areas, reserved for free-ranging animals: **African bush** (ostriches, giraffes, impalas), **Tibetan bear park**, **lion park** and **African savannah** (white rhinoceros, zebras, ostriches etc).

Visit on Foot

🚶 Walking round the safari park, visitors will come across the fauna of various continents – Tibetan bears, dromedaries, antelopes, zebras, cheetahs, alligators – and, near the lagoon of L'Oeil de Ca, birdlife such as flamingoes, cranes, ducks, white storks, sacred ibis, macaws, swans and pelicans.

Perpignan★★

Languedoc-Roussillon

▶ **Population:** 118 845
◉ **Michelin Map:** 344 I 6
▣ **Info:** Palais des Congrès, pl. Armand Lanoux. ☏04 68 66 30 30. www.perpignantourisme.com.
◉ **Location:** 64km/40mi S of Narbonne, Perpignan, the most southerly city in mainland France, lies on the banks of the River Têt and its tributary the Basse.
🅿 **Parking:** There are plenty of car parks in the town.
◷ **Timing:** Ideally you should spend a whole day in Perpignan in order to get the unique flavour of culture, cuisine and tradition that links this part of France with Spain.

Perpignan, once the capital city of the counts of Roussillon and the kings of Majorca, is an outlying post of Catalan civilisation north of the Pyrénées, and a lively commercial city, with shaded walks lined with pavement cafés. The economy is largely based on tourism, wine and olive oil, and the production of cork, wool and leather.

A BIT OF HISTORY

In the 13C the city prospered from growing trade with the eastern Mediterranean. In 1276, it became capital of Roussillon, part of the Catalan kingdom of Majorca. When the kingdom broke up, Roussillon became part of the principality of Catalonia. From 1463, the French Crown tried in various ways to take possession of Roussillon, but met fierce resistance from the local inhabitants. The province was briefly given to the monarchs of Spain, who fortified it heavily. Local people rebelled against Spanish rule too, and in 1640 Richelieu offered Roussillon a degree of autonomy if it would become part of France, which it agreed to do, leading to the Siege of Perpignan as the Spanish tried to retain the city. The French victory was ratified by the Treaty of the Pyrénées.

SIGHTS
Palais des Rois de Majorque★

4 r. des Archers. ◷Open daily Jun–Sept 10am–6pm; Oct–May 9am–5pm. ◷Closed 1 Jan, 1 May, 1 Nov, 25 Dec. ☞€4. ☏04 68 34 96 29.
The origin of this characteristically Catalan palace lay in the desire of James I of Aragon to make his younger son ruler of the "Kingdom of Majorca" with its mainland seat in Perpignan. Flints and pebbles are used to make decorative patterns in the brickwork. See the great hall known as the Salle de Majorque, the lower Queen's Chapel (Chapelle de la Reine) with traces of medieval frescoes, and the royal apartments.

Rue de la Loge★

The civic buildings make a fine architectural group along Rue de la Loge. The **Loge de Mer**★ once housed the tribunal regulating Perpignan's sea trade. Its walls are of the finest stonework, with tall Gothic arches at ground level. The **Hôtel de Ville**★ has been rebuilt a number of times. The upper floor is made of bands of pebbles held in place by brick coursing.
The Renaissance courtyard has arcades and 18C wrought-iron grilles. The **Députation**★, once the seat of the Catalan "Corts", has a high arched doorway and window-openings with delicate marble columns.

Le Castillet★

pl. de Verdun. ◷Open Wed–Mon Oct–Apr 11am–5.30pm; May–Sept 10am–6.30pm. ◷Closed public holidays. ☞€4. ☏04 68 35 42 05.
This pink brick citadel dates from the reign of Peter IV of Aragon, while the adjacent Notre-Dame Gate was built during the occupation of the city by Louis XI. The **Casa Pairal** is now a Cata-

lan folk museum, the **Joseph Deloncle Musée catalan des Arts et Traditions populaires**.

Cathédrale St-Jean★

pl. Léon Gambetta. ⏰*Open daily 9am–noon, 3–7pm.* 📞*04 68 51 33 72.*

Work on the cathedral was begun by Sancho of Aragon in 1324 but the building was completed only in 1509. The bell tower is topped by an 18C wrought-iron cage housing a great 15C bell.

Inside, the altarpieces of the high altar and the north chapels are fine work of the 15C and 16C.

EXCURSIONS

Musée de Tautavel (Centre européen de préhistoire)★★

▶ *27km/16.7mi NW of Perpignan, 9.4km/5.8mi NE of Estagel.*

⏰*Open 10am–12.30pm, 2–6pm (Jul–Aug 10am–7pm).* ⬷€8. 📞*04 68 29 07 76. www.tautavel.com.*

After the discovery in the 1970s of fragments of human skull at Tautavel, this little village gave its name to **"Tautavel man"**, hunters living about 450 000 years ago. Highlights of the excellent museum are a reconstruction of the skeleton and a copy of the cave where the bones were found.

La Côte Vermeille★★

Between Argelès Beach and the Spanish border, small towns and ports huddle in bays along the mountainous coast. The picturesque port **Collioure★★**, below its royal castle, attracted artists of the Fauve School in the early 20C. **Banyuls** is famous for its sweet wine. In the hills above, the Madeloc Tower enjoys a wide **panorama★★** of the Côte.

Fort de Salses★★

▶ *20km/12.4mi N of Perpignan.*

Rising strangely above the surrounding vine-covered plain north of Perpignan, this huge and intriguing brick fortress, originally 15C, was adapted by Vauban in the 17C to meet the demands of modern artillery.

Les Corbières★★

ℹ 📞*04 68 45 69 40. www.corbières-sauvages.com·* ⊘ *Don't miss the chateaux de Peyrepertuse, Quéribus and Puilaurens.*

Corbières is best known for its ruined castles and its wine, and for a massif landscape showered with luminous Mediterranean light. The spiny, sweet-smelling *garrigue* covers much of the countryside.

Vines have overgrown the area east of the Orbieu and around Limoux, the region producing sparkling white *blanquette*. The **Corbières** has been awarded the *Appellation d'Origine Contrôlée* for its fruity, full-bodied wines (mainly red, some white and rosé) with bouquets evocative of local flora.

The region's widely differing soil types produce a variety of grapes – Carignan, Cinsaut and Grenache – making any *dégustation* tour a real voyage of discovery. The red wines of neighbouring **Fitou**, also an *Appellation d'Origine Contrôlée*, are dark and robust with a hint of spiciness.

Many local villages have their own wine cooperatives and encourage customers to taste their wares, but private producers often require reservations.

Mont-Louis★

High in the Pyrénées, east of Font-Romeu and Andorra. ℹ *3 r. Lieutenant Pruneta.* 📞*04 68 04 21 97. http://mont-louis.net.*

Mont-Louis occupies a strategic site at the meeting point of three valleys. To the north is the valley of the Aude; its broad upper course is known as the **Capcir**. To the southwest is the Sègre, a tributary of the Ebro, which here flows through the **Cerdagne**, an upland basin; its elevated position diminishes the apparent height of the surrounding peaks, and its high sunshine level led to the construction here in 1949 of the first "solar furnace" **(four solaire)** using parabolic mirrors. Finally, to the west, is the valley of the Têt, which flows out of the Lac des Bouillouses to form the **Conflent**, the major routeway linking the Cerdagne with Perpignan.

The site's importance was confirmed following the **Treaty of the Pyrénées** in 1659, which made the Pyrénées the legal as well as the natural boundary of France. Louis XIV set about giving his newly acquired lands some more solid protection than that afforded by a signature; the great Vauban carried out his survey of Roussillon and the Cerdagne in 1679, and, from 1681 onwards, directed the construction of Mont-Louis.

Four Solaire (Solar Furnace)

Guided tours Nov–Jan 10am–4pm; Feb–mid-Jun 10am–5pm; end Jun 10am –6pm; Jul-Aug 10am–6pm; early–mid-Sept 10am–8pm; mid Sept–Oct 10am– 5pm. €6. 04 68 04 14 89. www.four-solaire.fr.

Since 1949 the solar furnace has used the sun's reflected light to generate heat and power. Its 546 mirrors focus on one point, where the temperature reaches 3 500°C/6 332°F.

Principat d'Andorra★★

There are few towns or roads. A single highway crosses the territory through the capital, Andorra La Vella. 26 ave de l'Opéra 75001 Paris. 01 42 61 50 55. www.tourisme-andorre.net.

No mere tax-free shopping haven, this tiny Catalan-speaking nation in the high Pyrénées is also a wild, scenic land of lofty plateaux and precipitous valleys. Andorra was through the centuries a possession of Catalan counts and bishops, and from 1278 was shared between the Count of Foix and the Bishop of Urgell ("co-principality"). In 1993 it was given the freedom to abandon its former feudal status and become an independent state. Despite a remote location, It is prospering with hydroelectric power and all-year-round tourism.

Andorra la Vella is a bustling commercial town. Away from the main road, the town's heart preserves quiet old streets; to the east it merges with Escales.

Port d'Envallra★★ is the highest pass in the Pyrénées (2 409m/7 903ft). It marks the watershed between the Mediterranean and the Atlantic. There is a superb **panorama**.

Château de Peyrepertuse★★★

The site is 47km/29mi NW of Perpignan. On D 14, S of Duilhac, look out for the 3.5km/2mi narrow access road that leads to the site.

Open daily Feb–Mar and Nov–Dec 10am–5pm; Apr–Jun and Sept 9am– 7pm; Jul–Aug 9am–8pm; Oct 10am– 6pm. Closed for 3 weeks in Jan. €6. 06 71 58 63 36. www.chateau-peyrepertuse.com.

The dramatic barrier of the Corbières was defended by a number of strongholds of which the ruins of the Château de Peyrepertuse, separated into two distinct castles on their rocky promontory, are the most imposing.

The Lower Castle (Château Bas) to the east came under Aragonese rule in 1162. In 1240, it surrendered to the Seneschal of Carcassonne acting in the name of the king. Under the terms of the Treaty of Corbeil in 1258, it became part of the fortified French border facing Spanish Roussillon.

The northern curtain wall running to a dramatic point, together with the ruins of the main building, the keep and chapel, give an idea of the changes that took place over the centuries. On the far side of the open area separating the two castles, a monumental stairway has been hewn into the rock.

The royal castle raised on this western height is known as St George's Castle. It was built in the course of a single campaign, probably by Philip the Bold. There are remains of a cistern and a chapel. From its western extremity the view extends over the fortifications capping the neighbouring crests.

In 1659, the incorporation of Roussillon into France by the Treaty of the Pyrénées stripped Peyrepertuse of its strategic importance.

Abbaye de St-Martin-du-Canigou★★

The abbey lies 2.5km/1.5mi S of Vernet-les-Bains. Saint Martin du Canigous, Casteil. 04 68 05 50 03. http://stmartinducanigou.org.

Park the car in Casteil, then follow a steep road uphill (1hr round-trip).

The abbey of St Martin on Mont Canigou, an eagle's eyrie at 1 055m/3 461ft above sea level, is one of the great sights of the eastern Pyrénées.

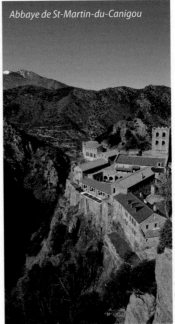

Abbaye de St-Martin-du-Canigou

© Yvann K/Fotolia.com

Site★★★

To appreciate St-Martin's unusual site, after reaching the abbey (30–50min on foot round-trip from Casteil – uphill walk), take a stairway to the left which climbs through the woods.
Turn left past the water outlet. There is an impressive view of the abbey, which lies in the shadow of the Canigou until the late morning. It stands in an imposing site above the Casteil and Vernet valleys.

Abbey

Guided tours only, in French: Jun–Sept Mon–Sat 10am–noon, 2–5pm, Sun and religious holidays 10am–12.30pm, 2–4pm; Oct–May Tue–Sat 10am–11am, 2–4pm, Sun and religious holidays 10am–12.30pm, 2–4pm. €5.
This Romanesque abbey, built on a rocky pinnacle at an altitude of 1 094m/3 589ft from around 1001–09, grew up around a monastic community founded here in the 11C.
After falling into disuse at the Revolution, it was restored from 1902–32 and extended from 1952–72. At the beginning of the 20C, all that remained of the **cloisters** were three galleries with crude semicircular arches. As part of the restoration, a south gallery has been rebuilt overlooking the ravine, using the marble capitals from an upper storey which was no longer extant.
The **lower church** (10C), dedicated to Notre-Dame-sous-Terre in accordance with an early Christian tradition, forms the crypt of the **upper church** (11C). The latter, consisting of three successive aisles with parallel barrel vaults, conveys an impression of great age with its rugged, simply carved capitals. On the north side of the chancel stands a bell tower crowned by a crenellated platform.
Near the church, two tombs have been hollowed out of the rock: the tomb of the founder, Count Gulfred de Cerdagne,

which he dug out with his own hands, and that of one of his wives.
The abbey is now home to nuns and priests, who lead the tours, which are supposed to be in silence.

Prieuré de Serrabone★★

The steep winding road up to Serrabonne is a turning (near Ille-sur-Têt) off the mountain highway from Perpignan to Font-Romèu.
Boule d'Amont. Open daily 10am–6pm. Closed 1 Jan, 1 May, 1 Nov, 25 Dec. €3. 04 68 84 09 30. In a wild and stony setting among austere mountains, this former priory contains superb Romanesque sculpture, its severity relieved by delicate pink marble.
The chapel gallery (**tribune★★**) of about 1080, originally intended to serve as the choir, was moved to the centre of the nave at the beginning of the 19C. It is an unusual feature to have survived and has wonderful decoration in low relief as well as exceptionally richly carved capitals. A delightful south-facing **gallery★** (Promenoir des Chanoines) overlooks the ravine far below.

NORMANDY

Taking its name from the Norsemen or Normans, this old dukedom extends from the edge of the Paris Basin towards the Breton peninsula. To many it is reminiscent of southern England with its shared heritage of glorious Norman architecture and lush, pastoral countryside. There is great diversity in the buildings here; Norman masons fashioned the fine Caen limestone into great churches while humbler structures were built from cob, chalk, pebbles in mortar, brick, timber, shingles and thatch.

Highlights

1 Gothic architecture at **Rouen**'s Cathédrale Notre-Dame (p399)

2 Castle above the Seine: **Château Gaillard** (p402)

3 The old town and picturesque port: **Vieux Honfleur** (p406)

4 11C masterpiece of tapestry: **The Bayeux Tapestry** (p414)

5 The Romanesque Benedictine abbey of **Mont-St-Michel** (p418)

Lower Normandy (Basse-Normandie) is built of the old rocks from the Primary Era. In the north, the Cotentin Peninsula projects into the English Channel dividing the Bay of the Seine from the Gulf of St-Malo. To the southeast lies the *bocage* (pasture) – its hedgebanks offered excellent cover to the Germans in 1944. On either side of the Seine Valley extends Upper Normandy (Haute-Normandie), centred on the historic city of Rouen. To the south is the Pays d'Auge, quintessential *bocage* country, famous for its ciders, cheeses and calvados, while to the north stretches the vast chalk plain of the Pays de Caux, bordered by the Channel coast with its white cliffs and hanging valleys.

History – Originally occupied by Celts, by the 1C BC the Romans were establishing towns here. The collapse of the Roman Empire led to occupation by the Franks, but raiding Vikings took over c. 911. Normandy remained independent until 1204 before becoming a French dukedom subject to English control for long periods, until 1469 when it became a province of France. The 15–17C saw the discovery of new territories by Norman sailors, such as Quebec. More recently, on 6 June 1944, Normandy beaches were the scene of what became known as the "D-Day Landings".

Today – The major economies are dairy farming, agriculture and, in Upper Normandy, industry; products include calvados and cider. Tourism is also a major contributor to the economy.

Rouen★★★

Seine-Maritime

Rouen, capital of Upper Normandy, has undergone a remarkable campaign of restoration that has given new life to the old city's network of narrow, winding streets lined with magnificent half-timbered houses. With its skyline of towers, spires and fine buildings, it offers a wealth of artistic delights and is a city of first-rate museums – the Musée de Beaux-Arts alone is worth the trip. Rouen sits in a lovely valley surrounded by high hills, from which there are extensive views over the city and the Seine. Established at the lowest point on the Seine which could be successfully bridged, Rouen developed into a hugely successful port and industrial centre.

▶ **Population:** 111 805
◔ **Michelin Map:** 304 G 5
▯ **Info:** 25 pl. de la Cathédrale. ℘02 32 08 32 40. www.rouen tourisme.com.
◑ **Location:** The city stands on both banks of a curve in the River Seine, 133km/83mi NW of Paris.
◔ **Timing:** Allow 1–2 hours for a walk through Old Rouen with its beautiful 15–18C half-timbered houses. The quays on the north bank and the surrounding streets are the city centre.
◌ **Don't miss:** The Musée des Beaux-Arts is, in such a busy city, a relaxing place to be – the collection is excellent, too.

A BIT OF HISTORY

Rouen has been important since Roman times owing to its position as the lowest bridging point on the Seine; the alignment of its two main streets (Rue du Gros-Horloge and Rue des Carmes) still reflects the layout of the early city.

Although Rouen is the birthplace of a number of scientists, it is men of letters and artists who have contributed most to Rouen's fame. Gustave Flaubert (1821–80) was the son of Rouen's chief surgeon and lived in and around the city. His major works include *Madame Bovary* (1857), in which the village of Ry (20km/12.4mi east) is described under the name of Yonville.

SIGHTS

Cathédrale Notre-Dame★★★

◔*Open Apr–Oct Mon 2–6pm, Tue–Sat 9am–7pm, Sun 8am–6pm; Nov–Mar Mon 2–6pm, Tue–Sat 9am–noon, 2–6pm, Sun 8am–6pm.*
◔*Closed 1 Jan, 1 May, 11 Nov. www.cathedrale-rouen.net.*

This is one of the finest achievements of the French Gothic; it was rebuilt after a fire in 1200. Thanks to the generosity of John Lackland, Duke of Normandy, as well as the king of England, recon-

struction was swift; the transepts were extended and the choir enlarged.

The spaciousness of the interior is striking. The choir, with 14 soaring pillars and delicate triforium, is a masterpiece of harmonious proportion.

The great edifice seems to have been under repair for most of its existence for varied reasons: the Hundred Years' War, another fire in 1514, the Religious Wars, the hurricane of 1683, the Revolution, the burning-down of the spire in 1822, and the aerial bombardment of the night of 19 April 1944. This most recent disaster threatened the whole structure; restoration work is still under way.

Vieux Rouen★★★

All around the cathedral and the Rue du Gros Horloge approaching it is Vieux Rouen.

The old town's narrow streets, many of them pedestrianised, are lined with more than 800 timber-framed houses, large and small, elegant or picturesquely askew, all characteristic examples of medieval building techniques. Until 1520, the upper floors jutted out

Houses in Vieux Rouen

for reasons of economy and greater floor-space. Bustling **Rue du Gros-Horloge**★★, lined with old houses and given over to pedestrians, is one of the city centre's main attractions. The Gros-Horloge clock on its arch has only one hand; next to it is the belfry, from the top of which there is a fine view over the city and its surroundings.

Rue St-Romain★★ is one of the most fascinating streets, with many timber-framed houses dating from the 15C to the 18C. No 74 is a Gothic building with 15C windows.

Place du Vieux-Marché★

This modern complex on the edge of the Old Town occupies the site where Joan of Arc, aged 19, was burned at the stake following her trial as a heretic; 25 years later she was rehabilitated. In the centre of the square is the great Cross of Rehabilitation, marking the place where Joan of Arc was burned. There is also a covered market and a church incorporating **stained-glass windows**★★ of 16C date.

Église St-Maclou★★

When compared with the cathedral, the church provides striking evidence of the evolution of the Gothic style. It was begun in 1437 and is a fine example of the Flamboyant style at its purest. Nevertheless its decoration is of the Renaissance (doors, stairs, gallery and organ-case). At the north corner of the west front is a fountain with two

manikins performing the same act as their counterpart at Brussels, albeit with somewhat less finesse.

Aître St-Maclou★★

This is a rare example of a medieval plague cemetery. It is enclosed by half-timbered buildings decorated with macabre carvings showing the Dance of Death, skulls and crossbones, grave-diggers' tools etc.

Église St-Ouen★★

Built in the 14C, this former abbey church marks the peak of achievement of the High Gothic style. Its architect was complete master of the forces acting on his building, leading them at will via ogee arches on to flying buttresses weighted by pinnacles, thence to foundations beyond the walls.

The structural problem solved, he was then able to concentrate on designing the shell of the building. With no structural role, walls could become windows, flooding the interior with light and thereby encouraging an increasingly literate congregation to follow the service with the missals now coming into use. A few years on, and the Gothic had fulfilled its architectural potential; its final phase, the Flamboyant, delights in ornamental excess rather than innovation.

Musée des Beaux-Arts★★★

&.◐*Open Wed–Mon 10am–6pm.* ◐*Closed public holidays.* ◌€5. ☎*02 35 71 28 40. www.rouen-musees.com.*

The museum has a magnificent collection of 15–20C painting, especially in the earlier period, as well as fine sculpture, and other pieces including furniture and gold-work. See Gérard David's *Virgin and Saints*, an oil painting on wood, one of the masterpieces of Flemish Primitive art, as well as several choice pieces from the French School: *Diana Bathing* by François Clouet, The *Concert of Angels* by Philippe de Champaigne, and *Venus Arming Aeneas* by Nicolas Poussin. Other outstanding works from European countries are *The Adoration of the Shepherds* by Rubens, *St Barnabé Healing the Sick* by Veronese, and especially *Democritus* by Velasquez.

Musée de la Céramique★★

◷*Open Wed–Mon 10am–1pm, 2–6pm.* ◉€3 *(no charge 1st Sun of the month).* ✆02 35 07 31 74. www.rouen-musees.com.
The 17C Hotel d'Hocqueville houses this museum, which presents the history of Rouen pottery with outstanding faïence collections. The work of Masséot Abaquesne, the first faïence-maker in Rouen in the mid-16C, is represented. Rouen pottery enjoyed great popularity in the 18C. The liking for chinoiserie and lambrequin ornament, and a desire to replace metal plates and dishes with ceramics, helped assure Rouen's success with ewers, fountains, spice pots.

ADDITIONAL SIGHTS
Palais de Justice★★

This splendid 15C and early 16C Renaissance building was built to house the Exchequer of Normandy (law courts). Renovated in the 19C, it was badly damaged in August 1944.
The **main court** – excavations have revealed a 12C Jewish place of worship – is flanked by two wings, the **façade**★★ (1508–26) of which is exquisite.
The decoration of the façade, is typical of the Renaissance: the base is quite plain but the ornamentation increases on each floor so that the roof line is a forest of chiselled stone with pinnacles, turrets, gables and flying buttresses. The left-wing stone staircase leads to

the **Salle des Procureurs** (Prosecutors' Room). This large room has a splendid modern panelled ceiling.

Musée Le Secq des Tournelles★★

◷*Open Wed–Mon 10am–1pm, 2–6pm.* ◷*Closed public holidays.* ◉€3. ✆02 35 88 42 92. www.rouen-musees.com.
The Wrought Ironwork Museum is housed in old Église St-Laurent, a fine Flamboyant building, and is exceptionally rich. The nave and transept contain large items, such as balconies, signs, railings, etc., and, in the display cabinets, locks, door knockers and keys. Note their evolution from Gallo-Roman times. The north aisle includes displays of locks, belts and buckles from the 15C to 19C. The south aisle exhibits a large variety of domestic utensils and tools.
The first floor is devoted to accessories such as jewels, clasps, combs and smoking requisites.

Jardin des Plantes★

▷*2.5km/1.5mi. Leave Rouen by avenue de Bretagne.* ♿◷*Open daily 8.30am-8pm in summer; 8am–dark in winter. Greenhouses 9–11am, 1.30–4.30pm.* ◉*No charge.* ✆02 32 18 21 30.
This beautiful 10ha/25-acre park, originally designed in the 17C, contains around 3 000 plant species inside the conservatories and **tropical hothouses** and a further 5 000 out in the open air. A star attraction is the **Victoria Regia**, a giant water lily from the Amazon, whose large, flat leaves can reach a diameter of 1m/3.3ft in summer. Its flowers bloom, change colour and die the same day.

EXCURSIONS
Abbaye du Bec★★

▷*The abbey sits beside the Risle, S of the Seine, about 40km/25mi from Rouen.* ▮✆02 32 43 72 60. www.abbayedubec.com.
This once-prestigious abbey produced two great archbishops of Canterbury. In 1042 **Lanfranc** (1005–89) appeared at the abbey. This great yet humble man had been a distinguished teacher. Three

years later, he started teaching again, making Le Bec one of the intellectual centres of the West.

After the Conquest, Lanfranc, who had become Duke William's Counsellor, was made Archbishop of Canterbury and Primate of all England. His successor at Le Bec was **St Anselm** (1033–1109), philosopher and theologian. His *Proslogion*, written here in 1078, is considered a great source of Western thought. In 1093 he became Archbishop of Canterbury. During the Revolution, the building was vandalised and the monks expelled.

Since 1948, when Bec-Hellouin became a functioning abbey again, considerable reconstruction has taken place, particularly of the St-Nicolas Tower of 1467 and the Abbot's Lodging of 1735. But the great Abbey Church, whose 42m/140ft choir was one of the wonders of the Christian world, has gone, though its spiritual power is undiminished.

Les Andelys★★

▶ *Les Andelys lies 39km/24mi SE of Rouen. The château rises beside picturesque waterside Petit Andelys. Grand Andelys extends away from the river.*

🏠*r. Philippe Auguste.* 📞*02 32 54 41 93. http://office-tourisme.ville-andelys.fr.*

The white castle rising beside Les Andelys commanded the Seine Valley on the border of Normandy. Its strategic position was valued by Richard theLionheart, Duke of Normandy as well as King of England. In 1196, he decided to break his agreement with the king of France, and construct a mighty fortress of his own. Within the year, so legend has it, the work was complete.

Château Gaillard★★

▶ *Accessible by car from Grand Andelys or on foot (30min climb) from Petit Andelys.* 🕐*Open Apr–early Nov, daily except Tue 10am–1pm, 2–6pm.* 🕐*Closed 1 May.* ⊛€3.50. 🎧*Guided tours 4.30pm daily, and 11.30am on Sun.* ⊛€5.50.

Despite its 17 towers, thick walls, three rings of defences and a moat, King Philippe Auguste succeeded in taking the castle in 1274 after a siege of only eight months. This victory enabled him to incorporate Normandy, Maine, Anjou and Touraine into the French kingdom. In 1419 Henry V of England took it back. La Hire, companion to Joan of Arc, won it again for France ten years later, only to lose it to Henry once more.

Abbaye de Jumièges★★★

▶ *Jumièges is on a big loop of the River Seine just W of Rouen.*

The great abbey in its splendid setting on the Lower Seine forms one of the most evocative groups of ruins in France. The abbey was founded in the 7C and within 50 years housed 700 monks and 1 500 lay-brothers. Its great wealth was based on the generosity of the Merovingian rulers and on tithes drawn from a vast area. Destroyed by the Vikings, the abbey was raised again in the early 11C, but suffered in the Wars of Religion. The monks were scattered at the outbreak of the Revolution.

In 1793 it was auctioned and a purchaser started dismantling it to re-use the stone, blowing up the chancel and lantern-tower in the process. In 1852 a new owner saved it from complete destruction, but by then the great edifice was already a ruin.

Évreux★★

▶ *The town is 56km/35mi S of Rouen.* 🏠*1 ter Place de Gaulle.* 📞*02 32 24 04 43. www.ot-pays-evreux.fr.*

The history of Évreux could read like a series of unmitigated disasters, from the burnings and sackings perpetrated by Vandals, Vikings and Plantagenets, to the devastation wreaked from the air by Luftwaffe (in 1940) and Allied air forces (in 1944). But after each disaster, the townspeople have re-created prosperity from ruin.

Evidence of this spirit can be seen in the promenade laid out on the old Roman rampart on the banks of the river Iton, and in the treatment of the Clock Tower (Tour de l'Horloge) which was built by Henry V in 1417, two years after his victory over the French at Agincourt.

Cathédrale Notre-Dame★

19 r. Charles Corbeau. ○*Open 8.30am–7pm.* ℘*02 32 24 04 43.*

The cathedral, begun in the 12C, is essentially a harmonious Gothic building of the 13C. Much restoration had to take place after John the Good's siege in 1356 and during the reign of Louis XI (1461–83). In the 16C the aisles of the nave were rebuilt in Flamboyant style, and after WW II much of the upper part of the cathedral was replaced. It has many beautiful 13–14C stained-glass windows★.

Dreux★

○ *Dreux is 85km/52.8mi W of Paris via N 12, and 48km/29.8mi E of l'Aigle.*
🛈℘*02 37 46 01 73. www.ot-dreux.fr.*

Dreux is set on the boundary between Normandy and Île-de-France; it is a lively regional market town earning its living from diverse industrial activities. The town is the final resting place of members of the Orléans family, one of France's royal lines; they can be viewed in the crypt of the Royal Chapel of St-Louis where their tombs comprise an impressive collection of 19C sculpture. Nearby, the Eure Valley contains lovely surprises, notably the château of Anet. Dreux rose to importance when the Normans settled west of the River Avre and Dreux Castle had to defend the French frontier against a very belligerent neighbour. The castle, which stood on the hill now occupied by St Louis' Chapel, was besieged many times. It was dismantled on the orders of Henri IV, who razed the town in 1593.

Église St-Pierre

○*Open daily 9am–noon, 2–7pm.*

Built in the early 13C and partly damaged during the Hundred Years' War, St Peter's Church was heavily remodelled from the 15C to the 17C. The façade dates from the 16C. Of the two towers designed to flank it, only the left one was actually completed. The gate, chancel and left arm of the transept are 13C. The right arm of the transept dates from the 16C to the 17C.

The church interior is notable for its fine 15C and 16C **stained-glass windows**, to be found especially in the side chapels.

Chapelle royale St-Louis

Guided tours (1hr) Jul–Aug Wed–Mon 9.30am–12.30pm, 1.30–6.30pm; Apr–Jun and Sept 9.30am–noon, 2–6pm. ○€*7.* ℘*02 37 46 07 06.*

Before the Revolution this site was occupied by the Collegiate Church of St Stephen (St-Étienne). In 1783 it received the remains of members of the Toulouse-Penthièvre families.

In 1816 the dowager Duchess of Orléans, widow of Philippe Égalité, erected a chapel in the Neoclassical style. It was enlarged by her son Louis-Philippe (1773–1850) when he became king, and the exterior was embellished with bell turrets and Gothic pinnacles. The building as a whole is a monument to the 19C for both the quality of its architecture and the work of talented artists.

The side windows make it possible to admire the stained-glass representations of the patron saints of France and the royal family: *(left)* St Philip, St Amelia, St Ferdinand (the heads are portraits). The stained glass in the apse illustrates the life of St Louis. On the lower level, five extremely rare **glass panes painted with enamels**★★ catch the visitor's attention. They were made in the Sèvres workshops, as was the other glasswork.

Musée d'Art et d'Histoire Marcel-Dessal

○*Open Mon, Wed–Fri 2–6pm (Sun Apr–Sep 2–6pm; Oct–Mar 1st Sun of month).* ○*Closed public holidays* ○€*2.50.* ℘*02 37 50 18 61. www.musees.regioncentre.fr.*

Set up in a neo-Romanesque chapel, the museum displays furnishings taken from the Collégiale St-Étienne, a 12C church which stood on the site of the Royal Chapel. Shown alongside local archaeological exhibits, dating from prehistoric, Gallo-Roman and Merovingian times, are exhibits evoking the history of the Dreux region.

ADDRESSES

🛏 STAY

Hôtel des Carmes – *33 pl. des Carmes.* ☎*02 35 71 92 31. www.hoteldescarmes.com. 12 rooms.* ⊆*€8.50.* Situated in the town centre, not far from the cathedral, this hotel is an appealing halt. The delightfully decorated reception area hints of Bohemia, and the clutter-free bedrooms are charming and well fitted out.

Hôtel Versan – *3 r. Jean-Lecanuet.* ☎*02 35 07 77 07. www.rouen-hotel-versan.com. 34 rooms.* ⊆ *€9.* A practical address on a busy boulevard not far from the town hall. The rooms are all similar, functional and well equipped.

Hôtel Dandy – *93 r. Cauchoise.* ☎*02 35 07 32 00. www.hotel-dandy-rouen. federal-hotel.com. Closed 26 Dec–2 Jan. 18 rooms.* ⊆ *€11.* Situated in a pedestrian street downtown, close to place du Vieux-Marché, this little hotel decorated with care has a certain charm. The rooms, rather too cluttered for some tastes, are quite cosy. Breakfast served in a pretty little room.

🍴 EAT

Les Maraîchers – *37 pl. du Vieux-Marché.* ☎*02 35 71 57 73. www.les-maraichers.fr.* A restaurant with Parisian bistro airs in a half-timbered house. Wall seats, a bar, tables set close to one another, old advertising plaques, hat and jug collections – nothing's missing! Improvised cuisine. Norman-style second dining room on the ground floor.

Pascaline – *5 r. de la Poterne.* ☎*02 35 71 18 30. www.pascaline.fr. Reservations recommended.* Located next to the courthouse, this restaurant with a bistro façade is very nice. Brasserie décor with handsome wood counters, long seats and yellow walls.

Le Beffroy – *15 r. Beffroy.* ☎*02 35 71 55 27. Closed Sun eve and Tue. Reservations required.* This 16C Norman half-timbered house offers the choice between three pretty dining rooms, all equally inviting. A fine address for savouring plentiful fare prepared with quality ingredients.

La Couronne – *31 pl. du Vieux-Marché.* ☎*02 35 71 40 90. www.lacouronne.com.fr.* The décor of this 14C house on the market place is simply superb: beams, carved woodwork, hearths and frescoes.

🎵 NIGHTLIFE

Le Bateau Ivre – *17 r. des Sapins.* ☎*02 35 70 09 05. http://bateauivre.rouen.free.fr. Closed Sun–Tue and Aug.* Ever on the lookout for new talents, this bar has been livening up Rouen nightlife for the past 20 years. Concerts Fridays and Saturdays, ballads and poetry Thursdays, café-theatre or French songs Tuesday evenings.

Bar de la Crosse – *53 r. de l'Hôpital.* ☎*02 35 70 16 68. Closed Sun, Mon, fortnight in Aug and public holidays.* When spending time in Rouen, pay a visit to this small, unpretentious bar. It owes its fine reputation to its singular atmosphere; between concerts and exhibits, laughter abounds, and it isn't unusual to see tourists and regulars chatting here like old friends.

La Taverne St-Amand – *11 r. St-Amand.* ☎*02 35 88 51 34. Closed 3 weeks in Aug & Sun.* Transformed into a bar 30 years ago, this 17C house attracts painters, writers and actors.

🎭 SHOWTIME

Théâtre de l'Écharde – *16 r. Flahaut.* ☎*02 35 89 42 13.* Theatre with 100 seats where the troupe's creations and shows for young theatregoers are performed.

Théâtre des Deux Rives – *48 r. Louis Ricard.* ☎*02 35 70 22 82. www.cdr2rives.com. Ticket office open Tue–Sat 2–7pm. Closed Jul–Aug.* Classical and modern theatre.

🛒 SHOPPING

Markets – pl. Saint-Marc (*Tue, Fri and Sat all day*); Place des Emmurés (*Tue and Sat all day*); Place du Vieux-Marché (*daily except Mon, mornings*).

Faïencerie Augy-Carpentier – *26 r. St-Romain.* ☎*02 35 88 77 47.* The last handmade and hand-decorated earthenware workshop in Rouen. They offer copies of many traditional motifs on white and pink backgrounds, from blue monochrome to multicoloured, and from lambrequin to cornucopia.

Maison Hardy – *22 pl. du Vieux-Marché.* ☎*02 35 71 81 55.* In this alluring delicatessen, the Hardys offer Rouen specialities such as terrine de canard, duck being a highly prized fowl in this city (also known for its mutton). Mr Hardy's andouilles de Vire and his Caen tripe cooked in calvados and cider, specialities from Normandy, have clinched his reputation.

Le Havre★

Seine-Maritime

Destroyed in WWII and rebuilt in a very striking modern style, this city is one of Europe's most important ports.

A BIT OF HISTORY

By 1517, the harbour at Harfleur *to the east* had silted up. To remedy this François I ordered the building of a new port, which was to be called "Havre-de-Grâce" (Harbour of Grace). The marshy site selected by Admiral Bonnivet seemed unpromising, but his choice was a happy one since the tide remained at the flood two hours longer here than elsewhere. The port area subsequently spread some 20km/12.4mi upstream with a parallel industrial development of chemical, engineering and motor industries, shipyards and refineries.

The town and its region have an important Impressionist history and feature in several Impressionist works, notably Claude Monet's *Terrace at Ste-Adresse* (in the Metropolitan Museum in New York), a key work. The old town and resort of **Ste-Adresse**★★ is still a pleasant place; from the clifftop at La Hève there are fine views out over the estuary and the English Channel.

Le Havre today comprises a large port and industrial area, the residential district of Ste-Adresse and the old port of Harfleur. The newer part of town centres around the Espace Niemeyer, which provides a modern architectural face-lift to Place Gambetta.

SIGHTS

Quartier Moderne (Modern Town)★

During the bombing that preceded Le Havre's liberation on 13 September 1944, the old centre was obliterated and more than 4 000 people were killed; the besieged Germans completed the destruction by dynamiting the port. The architect Auguste Perret (1874–1954), already famous for his innovative work with reinforced concrete, was given the

▶ **Population:** 181 332
⚹ **Michelin Map:** 304 A 5
⬛ **Info:** 186 bd Clemenceau.
  ✆02 32 74 04 04.
  www.lehavretourisme.com.
◐ **Location:** Le Havre is 42.6km/26.4mi SW of Fécamp and 88km/55mi W of Rouen.
🅿 **Parking:** Between the Bassin du Commerce and the Espace Niemeyer (pl. du Gén.-de-Gaulle).
◷ **Timing:** Spend 2hr walking around the modern town starting from the place du Général-de-Gaulle.
⊛ **Don't miss:** The Musée des Beaux-Arts André-Malraux is worth seeking out.

task of rebuilding the devastated town from scratch. His initial concept involved a vast deck covering all the new city's services (energy, pipelines, gas, traffic). This bold scheme was rejected, so Perret laid out the town largely using the old street pattern, but in an uncompromisingly modern idiom which remains striking.

Among the highlights of Perret's remarkable work are **Place de l'Hôtel de Ville**★, one of the largest squares in Europe; **Avenue Foch**★, with a vista down to the sea, and **Église St-Joseph**★, whose interior walls are a lattice of stained glass.

Musée des Beaux-Arts André-Malraux★

♿◷*Open Wed–Fri and Mon 11am–6pm, Sat–Sun 11am–7pm.* ◷*Closed 1 Jan, 1 May, 14 Jul, 11 Nov, 25 Dec.* ◉€5 *(no charge 1st Sat of month).* ✆*02 35 19 62 62. www.ville-lehavre.fr.* The glass and metal building looks out to the sea through a monumental concrete sculpture known locally as Le Signal. The roof, designed to provide the best possible light to the galleries inside, consists of six sheets of glass covered by an aluminium sun blind.

The museum presents a fine **collection**★ of works by **Raoul Dufy** (1877–1953), who was born in Le Havre, and **Eugène Boudin** (1824–98), a native of Honfleur.

EXCURSIONS
Honfleur★★

*Honfleur is reached via the **Pont de Normandie**★★, a soaring cable-stayed bridge crossing the Seine with a record-setting main span of 856m/2 808ft between 214m/705ft-high towers. The town is on the seafront at the mouth of the Seine.* ⓘ *quai Lepaulmier.* ℘*02 31 89 23 30. www.ot-honfleur.fr.*

Honfleur lies at the foot of the **Côte de Grâce**★★ hill, overlooking the wide waters of the Seine estuary. With its old harbour, its church, its characterful old houses and lanes combining in a singular harmony, it is truly the most picturesque of ports.

Many maritime ventures began on the quayside at Honfleur. Paulmier de Gouneville sailed from here to Brazil in 1503, and in 1506 Jean Denis explored the mouth of the St Lawrence River.

In 1608 Samuel de Champlain set out to found Quebec City, and in 1681 La Salle started the voyage which was to make him the first European to descend the Mississippi all the way to the sea, thereby opening up those vast territories to which he gave the name Louisiana in honour of his king, Louis XIV.

Great artists have appreciated the soft light and breadth of sky over the Seine estuary as seen from Honfleur.

The town appealed to English watercolourist Richard Parkes Bonington, locally born Eugène Boudin and later to Claude Monet and the other Impressionists. Erik Satie composed some of his music in Honfleur, and several distinguished writers have lived and worked here.

Le Vieux Honfleur (Old Honfleur)★★
The streets and quaysides of the ancient port are full of character. The **old harbour**★★ shelters a fishing fleet as well as yachts and pleasure craft.

A richly varied townscape is formed by the fine stone residences along the Quai St-Etienne, the narrow, slate-faced houses on the Quai Ste-Catherine, the church (Église St-Etienne), and the Governor's House (Lieutenance), all seen against the foreground of masts and rigging.

Nearby is the **Église Ste-Catherine**★ with its detached **bell tower**★ *(r. des Logettes;* ⓞ *open mid-Mar–mid-Nov Wed–Mon 10am–noon, 2–6pm;* ⓞ*closed May, 14 Jul;* ⓢ€2.50; ℘*02 31 89 11 83).* The church was rebuilt after the Hundred Years' War by the ships' carpenters. All around are houses built in like fashion: a fine group of timber buildings, unusual in Western Europe.

Rue Haute, a former pathway outside the fortifications, has kept many fine houses of brick, stone and timber once lived in by shipbuilders.

Musée Eugène Boudin

ⓞ*Open mid-Mar–Sept Wed–Mon 10am–noon, 2–6pm; rest of the year Mon, Wed–Fri 2.30–5pm, Sat–Sun 10am –noon, 2.30–5pm.* ⓞ*Closed 1 Jan– 10 Feb, 1 May, 14 Jul, 25 Dec.* ⓢ€3. ℘*02 31 89 54 00. www.ville-honfleur.fr.* This museum houses temporary exhibitions of Impressionist works from Normandy. There is also a room devoted to the works of the French Impressionist painter, Eugène Boudin (1824–98).

Lisieux★★

▶ *The town is a short distance inland from Honfleur.*
ⓘ*11 r. d'Alençon.* ℘*02 31 48 18 10. www.lisieux-tourisme.com.*

Lisieux, on the east bank of the Touques, is the market centre of the prosperous Auge region. It is also a well-known pilgrimage centre. The town is famous in France for Ste Thérèse de Lisieux (1873–97), canonised in 1925.

Manor Houses of the Pays d'Auge

With its closely packed hedgerows, thatched cottages and old manors, the Pays d'Auge is a countryside of great charm. The farmhouses and manors of this tranquil landscape are set within an enclosure planted with apple trees and defined by a hedge.

All the buildings are timber-framed, from the house itself to the cider-press, apple-store, stables and dairy grouped around it.

Among the finest are the moated site at Coupesarte *(16km/10mi SW)* and Château Crèvecœur★ *(18km/11mi W)* with its museum devoted to the story of petroleum research (Musée de la recherche pétrolière).

Étretat★★

🅱 *pl. Maurice Guillard.* ℘*02 35 27 05 21.* *www.etretat.net.*
Sited where a dry valley in the chalk country of the Caux region meets the sea, Étretat was a humble fishing village well into the 19C. It was then favoured by writers such as Maupassant and painters like Courbet and Eugène Isabey.

Falaise d'Aval★★★

🅟 *1hr round-trip on foot from the end of the promenade.*

▶ *Take the steps and then the path to the clifftop known as Porte d'Aval.*

There are fine views of the magnificent Manneport Arch, the solitary 70m/229.6ft Needle (Aiguille), the long shingle beach and the Amont Cliff on the far side of the bay. The play of colours changes constantly with the time of day and conditions of sky and sea.

Falaise d'Amont★★

🅟 *1hr round-trip on foot from the end of the promenade.*
At the end of the promenade, the memorial was put up to mark the spot from which two aviators, Nungesser and Coli, were last glimpsed as they set out in their "White Bird" (*Oiseau Blanc*) on their attempt to make a non-stop westward crossing of the Atlantic (8 May 1927).

Fécamp★★

▶ *The town is on the N Normandy coast, 43km/27mi from Le Havre.*
🅱 *quai Sadi Carnot.* ℘*02 35 28 51 01.* *www.fecamptourisme.com.*
Today the fishing industry dominates Fécamp, but as early as the 11C the town had seen considerable monastic activity. Guy de Maupassant (1850–93) used the town as the setting for many of his short stories.

Abbatiale de la Sainte-Trinité★★

The ancient abbey church marks an important stage in the evolution of Gothic architecture in Normandy.
Built mostly between 1168 and 1219, it was influenced by the developments in the Île-de-France (use of tribunes as in the churches derived from St-Denis outside Paris, the combination of flying buttresses and triforium pioneered at Chartres, which made the tribunes

Falaise d'Aval

G. Targat/MICHELIN

redundant and which here is seen in the south wall of the chancel).

Norman regionalism reasserts itself however in a number of ways: in the slender lantern-tower high above the crossing, and in the inspection gallery at the base of the triforium windows.

ADDITIONAL SIGHTS
Palais Bénédictine★★

The building, designed by Camille Albert in the late 19C, is a mixture of neo-Gothic and neo-Renaissance styles. The **museum** displays a large collection of objets d'art: silver and gold work, ivories, Nottingham alabasters (late-15C), wrought-iron work, statues and many manuscripts.

The Gothic Room is covered by a fine pitched roof made of oak and chestnut, shaped as the upturned hull of a ship; it houses the library: 15C Books of Hours with fine **illuminations**, numerous **ivories**, a collection of **oil lamps** dating from the early days of Christianity and a Dormition of the Virgin, a painted low-relief wooden carving of the German School.

Musée des Terre-Neuvas et de la Pêche★

&♿ⓄOpen Jul–Aug daily 10am–6.30pm; Sept–Jun Wed–Mon 10am–noon, 2–5.30pm. ⓄClosed 1 Jan, 1 May, 25 Dec. ♿€3. ℘02 35 28 31 99.

The Newfoundland and Fishing Museum evokes memories of the Fécamp fishing industry. The lower gallery explores the great adventure of the cod fishermen on the Newfoundland banks in the days of the sailing ship and the dory, a flat-bottomed craft rising at bow and stern.

One room is devoted to shipbuilding, featuring a model of the *Belle Poule*, the naval training ship built in Fécamp in 1931. Exhibits trace the development of fishing methods and types of craft.

Dieppe★★

🏠Pont Jehan Ango. ℘02 32 14 40 60. www.dieppe.fr.

The nearest seaside resort to Paris, Dieppe is sometimes referred to as Plage

de Paris. Its famous sea-front lawns were laid out in 1863 by Empress Eugénie and Napoleon III.

Dieppe's history as a major port goes back to the 11C, the English wool trade, and the import of spices from the Orient. As early as the 14C, Dieppe sailors were landing on the coast of the Gulf of Guinea and Jean Cousin was exploring the South Atlantic. In 1402 Jean de Béthencourt founded the first European colony on the Canary Islands. Jean Ango (1480–1551), whose privateers once captured a fleet of 300 Portuguese vessels, equipped many a voyage of discovery to remote shores.

🏛♿ ESTRAN Cité de la Mer★

ⓄOpen daily 10am–noon, 2–6pm. ♿€6 (children, €3.50). ℘02 35 06 93 20. http://estrancitedelamer.free.fr.

This museum is dedicated to the maritime history of Dieppe as a port.

Château-Musée de Dieppe (Dieppe Castle Museum)

ⓄOpen Oct–May Wed–Mon 10am–noon, 2–5pm; Jun–Sept until 6pm. ⓄClosed 1 Jan, 1 May, 1 Nov, 25 Dec. ♿€4. ℘02 35 06 61 99. www.musees-haute-normandie.fr.

Housed in a 15C fortress, this museum's collection includes fine art, archaeology, ethnology, history, music and ceramics. About a thousand ivory items created by Dieppe craftsmen are also on display.

Côte d'Albâtre (Alabaster Coast)★
From Dieppe to Étretat

▶ 104km/64.6mi

Sheer white cliffs cut into by dry valleys (valleuses) drop to sandy beaches.

Little resorts – **Pourville-sur-Mer, Ste-Marguerite-sur-Mer** and **Veules-les-Roses** – are sited at the seaward end of a series of lush valleys.

In **Varangeville-sur-Mer**, the graveyard of the 11–15C church overlooks the sea and shelters the tomb of the Cubist painter, **Georges Braque**. The stained glass of Chapelle St-Dominique (on the outskirts) by the artist are of interest.

Caen★★★

Calvados

Tough and enduring, the city of Caen rebuilt itself after being almost destroyed by bombing during WWII. Today the city proudly preserves an impressive historical legacy, while being committed to peace and the future.

A BIT OF HISTORY
Caen Stone
The light limestone quarried locally was used not only here but in great buildings of the Normans in England (Canterbury Cathedral, the White Tower at the Tower of London and Westminster Abbey).

The City of the Normans
After the invasions of the Norsemen in the 9C and 10C, and the establishment of the duchy of Normandy, Benedictines built the first major religious buildings in Normandy. Caen's architectural heritage reveals the affection felt for the city by William, Duke of Normandy, and his wife Mathilda, who chose this as their residence. They married in 1053, against papal opposition, which arose because they were cousins.

This led to their excommunication until they made amends by William founding the Abbey for Men and Mathilda the Abbey for Women.

SIGHTS
L'Abbaye-aux-Hommes★★
Guided tours (1hr30min) daily 9.30am, 11am, 2.30pm and 4pm. €3. *02 31 30 42 81.*
The church of the Abbey for Men was founded by William the Conqueror; it was begun in 1066 and took 12 years to build. The west front with its soaring towers (the octagonal spires were added in the 13C) dates from this time. The nave is vast; it is a fine example of Romanesque construction with great square bays divided in two by minor piers and with high galleries over the aisles. The great lantern-tower over

▶ **Population:** 112 790
Michelin Map: 303 E-J 3-4
Info: pl. St-Pierre. *02 31 27 14 14.* www.tourisme.caen.fr.
▶ **Location:** 15km/9mi inland from the coast and ferry terminal at Ouistreham, and 94km/59mi from Le Havre.
Don't Miss: The Mémorial de la Paix and the Abbaye-aux-Hommes.
Timing: Allow 2hr for the château and the nearby museums, 2hr for the abbeys, and 2hr for the Peace Memorial.

the crossing is probably the work of Lanfranc and William themselves; in its simple perfection it is a masterpiece of Romanesque art.

The choir, which was extended and altered in the 13C, is a very early example of Norman Gothic which set the standard for buildings all over the duchy.

Château Ducal★
Guided tours Jul–Aug Fri. No charge. 02 31 27 14 14.
This great fortress, perched on a bluff overlooking the city, was built by William in 1060, and subsequently strengthened and extended.

From its ramparts there are extensive views over Caen. The château houses **Caen's Musée des Beaux-Arts★★**.

Abbaye-aux-Dames ★★
Open daily 2–5.30pm. Guided tours (1hr) daily 2.30pm and 4pm. No charge. 02 31 06 98 98.
The Norman building, with its nave of nine bays, round-headed arches, and blind arcades in the triforium, was founded by Mathilda in 1062 as the church of the Abbey for Women.

As at St Stephen's, the upper storey was altered when the timber roof was replaced by sexpartite vaulting.

Le Mémorial★★

&⊙*Open mid-Feb–mid-Nov daily 9am –7pm; mid-Nov–24 Dec daily except Mon 9.30am–6pm; 26–31 Dec daily 9.30am–6pm.* ⊙*Closed 1st 2 weeks of Jan and 25 Dec.* ∞€*18.50.* ℘*02 31 06 06 45. www.memorial-caen.fr.*

The memorial erected by the city, which in 1944 was at the centre of the Battle of Normandy, takes the form of a Museum for Peace; it is primarily a place of commemoration and of permanent meditation on the links between human rights and the maintenance of peace.

The façade of the sober building of Caen stone, facing Esplanade Dwight-Eisenhower, is marked by a fissure which evokes the destruction of the city and the breakthrough of the Allies in the Liberation of France and Europe from the Nazi yoke. It stands on the site of the bunker of W Richter, the German general, who on 6 June faced the British-Canadian forces.

The main events of WWII, the causes and the issues at stake, are presented in the light of the latest historical analysis. The collection includes a particularly imaginative display, centred on a spiral ramp on such themes as the inter-war years and the advance of Fascism; the use of extensive archive material, including a gripping panoramic projection of D-Day seen simultaneously from the Allied and the German standpoints; as well as moving testimonies by witnesses of and participants in the drama. Lived experience is given priority so that the impact of WWII can be appreciated on a human level.

The **Mur de la Liberté** (Wall of Freedom) pays tribute to the hundreds of thousands of American soldiers who fought for freedom in Europe.

Musée de Normandie★★

Château. ⊙*Open daily 9.30am–6pm.* ⊙*Closed Tue (Nov–May) and public holidays.* ℘*02 31 30 47 60. www.musee-de-normandie.caen.fr.*

This great museum displays the history of the Normandy region, its culture and people.

Église St-Pierre★

A mix of Gothic and Renaissance architecture make this church quite fascinating. The main church was built in the 13C–14C and the Renaissance **east end**★★ was added in the early 16C.

Hotel d'Escoville★

This is a fine example of a typical 16C Caen townhouse, which has undergone various bouts of restoration over the years. The tourist office is now housed here.

Musée des Beaux-Arts★★

Located within the château. &⊙*Open Wed–Mon 9.30am–6pm.* ⊙*Closed public holidays.* ∞€*3–7.* ℘*02 31 30 47 70. www.mba.caen.fr.*

Situated within the precinct of William the Conqueror's castle, the Fine Arts Museum offers its collections from a chronological, thematic and geographical point of view. Large religious paintings and imposing historical and allegorical scenes hang in vast halls, bathed in light, whereas works of religious fervour and smaller paintings are essentially displayed in the small cabinets.

EXCURSIONS
Deauville ⌂⌂⌂

▶ *Located 94km/59mi from Rouen and 43km/27mi from Le Havre, Deauville lies on the Côte Fleurie.* ⊟ *Place de la Mairie.* ℘*02 31 14 40 00. www.deauville.org.fr.*

Deauville, a popular resort since the mid-19C, is known for the luxury and refinement of its various establishments and the elegance of its entertainments. Events of the summer season include racing (including the Grand Prix), the polo world championship, regattas, tennis and golf tournaments, galas, and the international yearling fair. Every year, in early September, the city hosts the prestigious **American Film Festival**.

The Resort

The season in Deauville opens in July and ends with the Deauville Grand Prix on the fourth Sunday in August and the Golden Cup of the international polo championship. Horse racing takes place

Deauville

© Veni/iStockphoto.com

alternately at La Touques and Clairefontaine and the international yearling sales are held in Deauville in August.

The coming and going on the **Planches** is the most distinctive feature of beach life in Deauville. Lined with elegant buildings such as the Pompeian Baths and the Soleil Bar, where stars and celebrities like to be seen, the Planches draws fashionable strollers.

Between the casino and the Planches, the Centre International de Deauville is a remarkable ensemble of suspended gardens, fountains and transparent façades which welcomes all kinds of professional, cultural and festive events. A walk along the seafront boulevard Eugène-Cornuché will prove that Deauville is not called the "beach of flowers" *(plage fleurie)* for nothing.

Deauville Port

The port is enclosed on the west side by a breakwater extending from the beach to the mouth of the Touques and on the east by a jetty marking the port entrance to the channel. The deep access channel means that the port is accessible 80 percent of the time. It consists of three docks, entered through a double lock, which provide deep water moorings and ample capacity: 800 berths along 4 000m/4 376yd of quays. At the centre are the slate-roofed marinas, the Deauville harbour master's office, an annexe of the Marina Deauville Club (quai des Marchands, near the lock) and space for shops and hotel services.

La Suisse Normande★★

The Suisse Normande takes in the Orne Valley as well as the Noireau, the Vère, the Rouvre and the Baize. 🚹 *Place du Tripot, Clécy.* 🕿 *02 31 69 79 95. www.ot-suisse-normande.com.*

This extraordinary name denotes an area straddling the **Orne** and **Calvados** regions. It has neither mountains nor lakes in the Swiss sense and does not even include Normandy's highest points, but nevertheless draws tourists to its attractive landscape. The River Orne, as it cuts its way through the ancient rocks of the Armorican Massif, produces a kind of hollow relief through which flows a pleasantly winding river course bordered by steep banks surmounted by rock escarpments.

Located in the midst of Calvados *bocage* country south of Caen and extending into the Orne *département*, the Suisse Normande lies between the towns of Condé-sur-Noireau, Thury-Harcourt and **Putanges**; some extend the range eastwards to Falaise and the rugged Ante Valley. Deeply eroded valleys and escarpments appear in stark contrast with the flat plain around Caen.

The curious name Suisse Normande was coined by tourism promoters in the 19C, as the train, followed by an improved road, brought city-dwellers into the area. Switzerland, then as now, evoked images of inspiring scenery, clean air, vigorous sports and healthy living. The branding was not too far-fetched, as the rivers and canyons still attract canoeists, walkers and anglers.

Tourists notwithstanding, the Suisse Normande is resolutely rural, with pastures for horses and cattle, fields of rapeseed, winding roads between ancient hedgerows, swathes of forest and picturesque little villages.

Thury-Harcourt

The town, rebuilt, stands on the banks of the Orne and is now a tourist centre for the Suisse Normande to the south. Thury adopted the name Harcourt from the Harcourt family, who came from the town of Harcourt in the county of Évreux; in 1700 Thury became the Harcourt ancestral seat.

Near the ruins of the Harcourt family château, burnt by the Germans in 1944, the **park**★ has walkways bordered with trees, shrubs and flower beds.

Clécy★

This township, the tourist centre of the Suisse Normande, is close to some of the most picturesque beauty spots in the Orne Valley.

♿♨ Musée du Chemin de fer miniature

♿🌫Guided tours (45min), call for times. ⊙7€ (children, 5€) ℘02 31 69 07 13. www.chemin-fer-miniature-clecy.com.

Model locomotives and wagons as well as a play area, fast food and visit to nearby lime kilns.

ADDRESSES

🛏 STAY

☞ **Hôtel St-Étienne** – 2 r. de l'Académie. ℘02 31 86 35 82. www.hotel-saint-etienne.com. 11rms. ⊆ €7. This house, going back to the Revolution, is located in a quiet district close to the Abbaye-aux-Hommes. Note the fine wooden staircase with its beautiful

woodwork and the smart bedrooms, some of them with fireplaces.

☞🛏 **Hôtel Bernières** – 50 r. de Bernières. ℘02 31 86 01 26. www.hotelbernieres.com. 17rms. ⊆€6. Don't miss the discreet entrance of this hotel, with its convivial welcome, charming breakfast room and drawing room and delightful bedrooms.

☞🛏 **Le Bristol** – 31 r. du 11-Novembre. ℘02 31 84 59 76. www.hotelbristolcaen.com. 24rms. ⊆ €9. Those who prefer to be at a distance from the bustle of the centre will appreciate this hotel just a minute from the Orne and the racetrack.

🍴 EAT

☞ **Le Bouchon du Vaugueux** – 12 r. du Graindorge. ℘02 31 44 26 26. Closed Sun–Mon. This tavern (bouchon) is situated near the château and old Caen. Crowded tables add to the friendly ambience.

☞🛏 **L'Insolite** – 16 r. du Vaugueux. ℘02 31 43 83 87. www.restaurant-linsolite. com. Closed Sun–Mon except Jul–Aug, public holidays. Reservations recommded. Take time to discover this half-timbered 16C house with its unusual décor combining rustic frescoes, mirrors and dried flowers. Fish and seafood dishes on the menu.

☞🛏 **P'tit B** – 15 r. Vaugueux. ℘02 31 93 50 76. Charming 17C house with a rustic interior artfully modernised, including a superb fireplace. Relaxed atmosphere, a view of the kitchen, and seasonal dishes.

🛍 SHOPPING

Charcuterie Poupinet – 8 r. St-Jean. ℘02 31 86 07 25. For authentic tripes à la mode de Caen, visit Poupinet, where you can buy this speciality in jars.

Stiffler – 72 r. St-Jean. ℘02 31 86 08 94. www.stifflertraiteur.com. Closed Mon, Tue. At the deli counter, find delicious, prepared dishes and salads for a quick lunch.

Markets – Marché St-Pierre (Sun) r. de Bayeux (Tue), bd Leroy (Wed, Sat), bd de la Guérinière (Thu), Marché St-Sauveur (Fri), Christmas Market (Dec).

🤸 LEISURE ACTIVITIES

♿♨ **Festyland** – bd Péripherique 50 N, exit for Carpiquet, 14650 Carpiquet. ℘02 31 75 04 04. www.festyland.com. Closed Oct–Mar. €16 (children, €14). This family leisure park has some 30 attractions. Three daily shows (including a circus show) for young children.

The D-Day Landings

Dawn of D-Day – The formidable armada, which consisted of 4 266 barges and landing craft together with hundreds of warships and naval escorts, set sail from the south coast of England on the night of 5 June 1944; it was preceded by flotillas of minesweepers to clear a passage through the mine fields in the English Channel. As the crossing proceeded, airborne troops were flown out and landed in two detachments at either end of the invasion front. The British 6th Division quickly took possession of the Bénouville-Ranville bridge, since named Pegasus Bridge after the airborne insignia, and harried the enemy positions between the River Orne and the River Dives to prevent reinforcements arriving. West of the River Vire the American 101st and 82nd Divisions mounted an attack on key positions such as Ste-Mère-Église or opened up the exits from Utah Beach.

American troops landing on the Normandy shores on 6 June 1944

© UPPA/Photoshot

British Sector – Although preliminary bombing and shelling had not destroyed Hitler's Atlantic Wall, the British forces succeeded in disorganising German defences. Land forces were able to reach their objectives, divided into three beachheads: **Sword Beach** – The Franco-British commandos landed at Colleville-Plage, Lion-sur-Mer and St-Aubin. They captured Riva-Bella and the strongpoints at Lion and Langrune and then linked up with the airborne troops at Pegasus Bridge. The main strength of the British 3rd Division then landed. This area, exposed to the Germans' long-range guns in Le Havre, became the crucial point in the battle. **Juno Beach** – The Canadian 3rd Division landed at Bernières and Courseulles, reaching Creully by 5pm. They were the first troops to enter Caen on 9 July 1944. **Gold Beach** – The British 50th Division landed at Ver-sur-Mer and Asnelles; by the afternoon they were sufficiently established so the artificial Mulberry harbour could be brought into position. The 47th Commandos advanced and captured Port-en-Bessin during the night of 7 June. On 9 June the British sector joined up with the Americans from Omaha Beach. On 12 June, after the capture of Carentan had enabled the troops from Omaha and Utah beaches to join forces, a single beachhead was established.

American Sector – A mighty Allied armada of over 4 000 specially made craft, together with hundreds of warships and naval escorts, sailed from the south coast of England on the night of 5 June 1944. The following morning they arrived: it was D-Day. The liberation of France, and of Europe, had begun. **Omaha Beach** – Here the US 1st Division made its first contact with French soil and here the bloodiest engagement of D-Day was fought. **Utah Beach** – This beach, northeast of Carentan, entered history following the landing of American forces on 6 June 1944. Despite murderous fire from the Germans, the American 4th Division managed on 12 June to link up with the forces who had landed at Omaha Beach.

The Normandy invasion, and its significance in European and world history, is marked all along this coastline by cemeteries, monuments and museums.

Bayeux★★

Calvados

The Bayeux Tapestry still presents its unique record of the events of 1066 and the Battle of Hastings. Its home, the former capital of the Bessin, was the first French town to be liberated (7 June 1944) in WWII. The town escaped damage during the war, leaving a cathedral and old houses – many tastefully restored – as well as a pedestrian precinct, for explorers in the 21C.

A BIT OF HISTORY

First a Roman town, then an early episcopal city until the 9C when it became a Norse-speaking Viking city, Bayeux was the "cradle of the Dukes of Normandy" and home of William, who invaded and conquered England.

Almost 900 years later the invasion came the other way when on 6 June 1944 the Allies landed on the Normandy beaches. On 7 June Bayeux became the first French town to be liberated and here on D-Day + 7, General de Gaulle made his first speech on French soil.

SIGHTS

≜≜ The Bayeux Tapestry (Tapisserie de la Reine Mathilde)★★★

&⚲ *Open daily mid-Mar–mid-Nov 9am–6.30pm (May–Aug, 7pm); mid-Nov–mid-Mar 9.30am–12.30pm, 2–6pm.* ⚲*Closed 1 Jan, 2nd week in Jan, 25 Dec.* ⚌€8 *(children, €4).* ℘*02 31 51 25 50. www.tapisserie-bayeux.fr.*

Beautifully displayed in specially designed premises, it is most likely that this extraordinary masterpiece of embroidery was made by talented nuns – in fact noble Saxon women who had chosen the convent – in England, soon after the Conquest in 1066.

Using a style similar to today's strip cartoon, its 72 scenes, or pictures, recount the epic of the Norman invasion with striking truthfulness; in addition, it is an irreplaceable source of information on the ships, weapons, clothes and way of life of the mid-11C.

▶ **Population:** 13 949
⚲ **Michelin Map:** 303 H 4
▯ **Info:** Pont St-Jean.
℘02 31 51 28 28.
www.bayeux-tourism.com.
▷ **Location:** 30km/18.6mi from Caen, the town is just inland from the Omaha and Arromanches Landing Beaches.
≜≜ **Kids:** Special child-friendly audioguides are available to help youngsters enjoy the Bayeux Tapestry.

Cathédrale Notre-Dame★★

≪∾*Guided tours of Cathedral 10.30am, 11.45am, 2.30pm, 3.45pm, 5pm.* ⚌€4. ℘*02 31 51 28 28.*

Numerous changes contributed to this impressive edifice. The Romanesque vaulted crypt and lower nave date from the 11C. The 12C added intricate stonework including profusely decorated walls and cornerstones as well as rib-vaulting in the aisles.

In the 13C (the High Gothic period) further elegant additions were made, including the superb chancel with radiating chapels, transepts with three-pointed arches, and a gallery with a fretwork design.

Hôtel du Doyen

A huge 17C porch leads into the 18C mansion, which houses the collection of the **Baron-Gèrard Museum**, which is closed for repairs.

Musée Baron-Gérard

⚭*Closed for renovation until 2012.*

Bayeux was once an important manufacturing centre for porcelain. Founded in 1812 by J Langlois, the workshop's famous glazing (red, gold and blue) made the reputation of the town. Production ended in 1951. The museum displays several of these decorated porcelain pieces

The upstairs rooms contain furniture and painting, mainly 15C and 16C Italian and Flemish Primitive works, and 17–19C

Detail of the Bayeux Tapestry – Harold's Oath to Duke William of Normandy

© Image Asset Management/age fotostock

French works including those of Philippe de Champaigne, David, Baron François Gérard, Boudin and Caillebotte.

Musée-Mémorial de la Bataille de Normandie★

♿⏱*Open Mar–Apr 10am–12.30pm, 2–6pm; May–Sept 9.30am–6.30pm; Oct–Dec 10am–12.30pm, 2–6pm.* ⏱*Closed 2 weeks in Jan.* €6.50 *(children, €4).* ☎02 31 51 46 90.

Situated on the line that separated the British and American sectors in 1944, the Memorial Museum recalls the dramatic events of summer 1944.

Two large galleries, named Overlord and Eisenhower, explain the chronology of the Battle of Normandy and give a detailed account of the equipment and uniforms of the various nations involved in the conflict.

The closing of the Falaise Pocket is illustrated by a diorama re-creating the village of Chambois where, on 19 August, part of the 90th US Infantry Division joined forces with the 1st Polish Armoured Division.

A great variety of heavy equipment is exhibited. Note in particular the Churchill MK VII tank (GB); the anti-tank armoured vehicle called Destroyer M 10 (US); the anti-tank Jagdpanzer (Germany); a quadruple 20mm German Flak gun as well as a Caterpillar D 7 Bulldozer.

The Norman Conquest

Edward the Confessor (c.1003–66) died without a clearly designated heir to the English throne. Harold Godwinson (c.1022–66) claimed that Edward had left England in Harold's "protection" on his deathbed. William the Bastard, Duke of Normandy (Edward's distant cousin, c.1028–87), claimed that Harold had sworn on sacred relics at Bayeux to support his own claim to the throne and had therefore perjured himself of this oath. Having secured the support of Pope Alexander II and his barons by the promise of English lands and titles, and with the resources of the cities of Caen and Rouen at his disposal, William organised a punitive expedition in just seven months.

The Norman fleet was assembled at **Dives**; its 600 ships carried 8 000 soldiers and cavalry who were landed on the coast at Pevensey Bay on 28 September 1066. On 14 October, William won the **Battle of Hastings**, the Saxon army routed and the claimant Harold dead. Duke William had become what history has renamed him, William the Conqueror.

William was crowned King of England at a ceremony in Westminster Abbey on 25 December. The situation was ambiguous: William was both King of England and Duke of Normandy; the latter title made him a vassal to the King of France. Difficulties soon arose, becoming more serious in 1152 due to the divorce of Louis VII and Eleanor of Aquitaine, only to be resolved at the end of the Hundred Years' War.

ADDRESSES

🛏 STAY

😑😑 **La Ferme des Châtaigniers** – *Vienne-en-Bessin, 7.5km/4.6mi E of Bayeux via D 126.* ☏*02 31 92 54 70. 3rms.* Set apart from the farmhouse, this converted farm building contains simple, yet pleasant, comfortable rooms. Guests have the use of a fitted kitchen. Peace and quiet is guaranteed in this house set in the fields.

😑😑 **La Ferme de Fumichon** – *Vaux-sur-Aure, 3km/1.8mi N of Bayeux via D 104.* ☏*02 31 21 78 51. www.fermedefumichon.com. 4rms.* Once part of Longues-sur-Mer Abbey, this fortified 17C farm, with its square courtyard and characteristic porch, is today a dairy and cider-making farm. The attic rooms are plain but pleasant.

😑😑 **Hôtel Reine Mathilde** – *23 r. Larcher.* ☏*02 31 92 08 13. www.hotel-reine mathilde.com. Closed 15 Nov–15 Feb. 16rms. ⬜€7.* If you wish to stay in the old town, this small family hotel is conveniently situated a stone's throw from the cathedral and the famous tapestry. Exposed beams and light-wood furniture. Plain rooms, some of them with sloping ceilings.

😑😑😑 **Chambre d'hôte Le Moulin de Hard** – *Area called "Le Moulin de Hard", 14400 Subles, 6km/3.7mi SW of Bayeux.* ☏*02 31 21 37 17. 3 rooms. ⬜⬜.* Large rooms in a restored 18C watermill near a small river with a beautiful garden.

😑😑😑 **Chambre d'hôte Manoir de Crépon** – *Anne-Marie Poisson, Crépon, 14km/8.7mi NE of Bayeux via D 12.* ☏*02 31 22 21 27. www.manoirdecrepon.com. Closed 10 Jan–10 Feb. 4rms.* This 17C and 18C house is typical of the area, with its oxblood-coloured roughcast. You will like the stone floors and fireplaces, the vast, tastefully furnished bedrooms and the authentic atmosphere of the former kitchen converted into a breakfast room.

😑😑😑 **Hotel Le Bayeux** – *9 r. Tardif.* ☏*02 31 92 70 08. www.lebayeux.com. 30rms. WiFi. ⬜€9.50.* Functional and well-kept facilities in a modern style, hidden in a quiet side street.

🍴 EAT

😑😑 **Hostellerie St-Martin** – *6 pl. Edmond Paillaud, Creully.* ☏*02 31 80 10 11. Closed 1–14 Jan.* Today it's a restaurant, but in the past the large vaulted rooms dating from the 16C housed the village market. Exposed stone, a fireplace, sculptures and a view of the wine cellar make up the curious décor. Classic cuisine. A few bedrooms.

😑😑 **Le Petit Bistrot** – *2 r. du Bienvenu.* ☏*02 31 51 85 40. Closed Sun, Wed, Mon (low season).* An inventive cuisine prepared by a keen chef is the main attraction of this small establishment facing the cathedral. Original dishes inspired by Mediterranean cuisine are served in a Provençal-style décor with an ochre colour scheme, watercolours and drawings.

😑😑😑 **Le Pommier** – *38–40 r. des Cuisiniers.* ☏*02 31 21 52 10. www.restaurant lepommier.com. Closed 14 Dec–18 Jan, Sun (Nov–Mar).* No place could be more centrally located, near the cathedral, its inviting apple-green façade announcing its rich Norman cuisine: smoked ham, *tripes à la mode de Caen*, cream sauces and, of course, apples. There are also vegetarian dishes. The vaulted dining-room with stone walls adds charming authenticity.

😑😑😑 **La Rapière** – *53 r. St-Jean.* ☏*02 31 21 05 45. Closed mid-Dec–mid-Jan, Wed & Thu.* A 15C house situated in old Bayeux. A lovely, rustic interior and tasty food using local produce.

🛒 SHOPPING

Markets – *r. St-Jean. Open Wed 7.30am – 2.30pm; and pl. St-Patrice Sat 6.30am–2.30pm.* Bayeux's two markets are quite different, each with its own charm.

St-Jean pedestrian street **Wednesday** market features some 25 stalls including greengrocers, butchers, fishmongers, cheesemakers and honey-sellers.

On the Pl. St-Patrice, every **Saturday**, some 120 merchants offer their wares, about half of them foodstuffs.

Naphtaline – *14, 16 parvis de la Cathédrale.* ☏*02 31 21 50 03. www.naphtaline-bayeux.com. Closed Jan–Feb & Sun.* Three boutiques housed in a fine 18C building offer antique and modern lace, Bayeux porcelain and reproductions of traditional tapestries woven on Jacquard looms.

🍸 NIGHTLIFE

Café Inn – *67 r. St-Martin.* ☏*02 31 21 11 37.* Coffee beans are roasted on the spot and 75 sorts of tea are served in a bustling ambience. Light meals of salads, omelettes and quiches are offered as prelude to the delicious *Tarte Tatin*, an upside-down apple pie.

Coutances★★

Manche

On its hilltop overlooking the woodlands and pastures *(bocage)* of the Cotentin Peninsula, Coutances, the religious and judicial centre of the peninsula, is dominated by its remarkable cathedral.

SIGHT
Cathédrale Notre-Dame de Coutances★★★

○*Open all year: Summer Mon–Fri 9.30am–6.30pm, Sat 10am–12.30pm, 2–6pm, Sun 10am–1pm; rest of year: Mon–Fri 9.30am–12.30pm, 2–6pm, Sat 10am–12.30pm, 2–5pm, closed Sun.*
http://cathedralecoutances.free.fr.

The present building (1220–75) made use of some of the remains of Geoffroy de Montbray's Norman cathedral, as well as drawing on the experience gained in the then recently completed abbey at Fécamp.

The west front is framed by two towers, whose soaring lines are emphasised by the tall, narrow corner turrets. The great octagonal lantern rises imposingly over the crossing; it, too, is flanked by turrets, and has strikingly delicate ribbing and slender openings. Within, the nave has clustered piers and highly moulded arches, a triforium with double openings and tall windows behind the typically Norman balustraded inspection gallery. The transept is in a more advanced style. Built in 1274, it is a masterpiece of ingenious construction. The columns of a second gallery support the ribs of the vault, and light floods in through 16 windows.

Jardin des Plantes★

&○*Open Jul–mid-Sept 9am–11.30pm; Apr–Jun and last half Sept 9am–8pm; rest of the year 9am–5pm.* ○*No charge.*
℘*02 33 19 08 10.*

The garden's entrance is flanked by an old cider press on one side and the **Quesnel-Morinière Museum** on the other. The terraced promenade traverses the sloping gardens with its many flower beds and pine trees. The obelisk in the

▶ **Population:** 10 760
& **Michelin Map:** 303 D 5
Info: pl. Georges Leclerc. ℘02 33 19 08 10. www.tourisme-coutances.fr.
▷ **Location:** 76km/47.2mi S of Cherbourg at a crossroads: D 972 links it to St-Lô (29km/18mi east), D 900 heads towards Cherbourg (77km/48mi N) and D 971 leads to Granville (29km/18km S).
Don't Miss: The Gothic cathedral, and the display of old Nativity crèches at the manor of Saussey.
○ **Timing:** Take 2hr to stroll around the town, and take time out to relax in the Jardin des Plantes.

centre commemorates a former mayor, Jean-Jaques Quesnel-Morinière.

EXCURSIONS
Abbaye d'Hambye★★

▷ *12km/7.4mi N of the town of Ville-dieu, in western Normandy.*
43 place de la République, Villedieu.
℘*02 33 61 05 69.*

The 12C abbey of Hambye is charmingly sited in the green valley of the Sienne. Its ruins evoke the serenity of Benedictine life. The abbey is nearly as complete as Mont-St-Michel. The best-preserved buildings include the chapterhouse, the sacristy and the parlour.

Église Abbatiale★★

○*Open Apr–Oct Wed–Mon 10am–noon, 2–6pm.* ○€4.50.
℘*02 33 61 76 92.*

The abbey buildings are dominated by the church, with slender columns and sharply pointed arches around the choir (1180–1200).

The high bell tower whose upper stage is pierced by round-headed arches was once crowned by a lantern. The monastic buildings frame former cloisters. The chapterhouse is a masterpiece of

Norman Gothic, divided into two by six central pillars, the final one gathers together the arches of the apse in a masterly way.

Lessay★

Lessay, a small town in the middle of the Cotentin Peninsula, lies on the edge of moorland country whose harsh beauty was sung by Barbey d'Aurevilly (1808–89), who helped establish a distinct Norman literature.

Église abbatiale★★

Founded in 1056, this is not only one of the most perfect examples of Romanesque architecture in Normandy, but also a tribute to the extraordinary skill and devotion of the chief architect of the Historic Monuments Institute, Yves Froidevaux, who rebuilt the church after it was blown up by the Wehrmacht in 1944.

From the east there is a fine view of the rounded apse backed by a flat gable and dominated by the massive tower.

Inside, there are the typically Norman features of great nave arches, triforium and inspection gallery running underneath the clerestory windows.

But Lessay also marks the architectural transition from groined vaults (as used in the 11C aisles) to quadripartite vaults, used somewhat crudely in the choir (end of the 11C), then with greater confidence in the nave (beginning of the 12C).

This revolutionary development led directly to the great achievements of Gothic architecture, with its high-flung vaults and walls of glass.

Mont-St-Michel★★★

Mont-St-Michel is a granite island about 900m/984yd round and 80m/262ft high. As the bay is already partially silted up, the mount is usually to be seen surrounded by huge sand banks which shift with the tides and often reshape the mouths of the neighbouring rivers. It is linked to the mainland by a causeway built in 1877. 🛈 *℘02 33 60 14 30. www.ot-montsaintmichel.com.*

Mont-St-Michel has been called "the Wonder of the Western World"; its extraordinary site, its rich and influential history and its glorious architecture combine to make it the most splendid of all the abbeys of France.

At the beginning of the 8C St Michael appeared to Aubert, the bishop of Avranches. Aubert founded an oratory on an island then known as Mont Tombe. This oratory was soon replaced by an abbey, which adopted the Benedictine Rule in the 10C, thereby assuring its importance. Two centuries later the Romanesque abbey reached its peak of development.

In the 13C, following a fire, a great rebuilding in Gothic style took place, known as *la Merveille* – the Marvel. Even though the English beseiged it during

Mont-St-Michel

the Hundred Years' War, the Mount did not fall into the invaders' hands.

L'Abbaye (Abbey)★★★

🕐 Open daily May–Aug 9am–7pm; Sept–Apr 9.30am–6pm. 🕐 Closed 1 Jan, 1 May, 25 Dec. ☞€9. 📞02 33 89 80 00. The architecture of the Abbey was determined by the constraints imposed by the rock on which it stands. Crowned as it is by the Abbey church and the buildings of the Merveille (c.1225), the result bears little resemblance to the conventionally planned Benedictine monastery.

Église★★

There is a striking contrast between the stern character of the Romanesque nave and the well-lit Flamboyant choir. The axis of the sanctuary is aligned on the rising sun on 8 May, the spring Feast of St Michael under the Eastern calendar.

La Merveille★★★

This is the group of buildings on the north side of the mount. The **salle des Hôtes**★ is a masterpiece of High Gothic. Suspended between sea and sky, the **cloisters**★★★, with their slim columns in pink granite arranged in a quincunx pattern, make a magic garden conducive to serenity and inner joy.

The **Refectory**★ is filled with light from its recessed windows. It hangs 45m/148ft high, a bold achievement on the part of its architect who was unable to use buttresses on the sheer rock-face. The vast Salle des Chevaliers★ is divided into four parts.

Jardins de l'Abbaye★

From the gardens there is a view of the north face of the mount, the "most beautiful wall in all the world", according to Victor Hugo.

ADDRESSES

🏠 STAY

☞ **Amaryllis Bed and Breakfast** – Le Bas-Pays, Beauvoir. 📞02 33 58 46 79. 5rms. ☞€6. This recently built stone house was designed as a B&B. The impeccably clean rooms feature well-equipped bathrooms and a furnished terrace.

☞ **La Tour Brette** – 8 r. Couesnon, Pontorson. 📞02 33 60 10 69. www.fraysse.phpnet.org. Closed 14–22 Mar, 1–20 Dec, Wed except Jul–Aug. 10rms. ☞€7. This small, centrally located hotel is named after the tower that used to protect Normandy from the Duchy of Brittany's assaults. The rooms are not very large but they've been recently renovated. Restaurant in a simple setting with a long, traditional menu.

☞☞ **Hôtel de Bretagne** – r. Couesnon, Pontorson. 📞02 33 60 10 55. Closed 20 Jan–5 Feb. 12rms. ☞€7. Regional-style house. Admire the lovely 18C wood panels and the grey-marble fireplace in the first room. Cosy, typically British bar and spacious, pleasantly furnished rooms.

☞☞ **Chambre d'hôte Bergerie** – La Poultière, Roz-sur-Couesnon. 📞02 99 80 29 68. www.la-bergerie-mont-saint-michel.com. 5rms. Located in the former sheepfold, the rooms are comfortable and benefit from the peaceful atmosphere of the small hamlet. The kitchen set aside for guests is very much appreciated. A self-catering cottage is also available.

☞☞ **Chambre d'hôte Mme Gillet** – 3 Le Val-St-Revert, Roz-sur-Couesnon. 📞02 99 80 27 85. 3rms. This family house overlooks the bay and offers a beautiful view of Mont-St-Michel and the surrounding countryside.

☞☞☞ **Les Vieilles Digues** – rte du Mont-St-Michel, Beauvoir. 📞02 33 58 55 30. http://bnb-normandy.com. Closed Dec, Jan. 7rms. This pretty stone house boasts spacious rooms thoughtfully furnished with handsome pieces.

🍴 EAT

☞☞ **Pré Salé** – Restaurant belonging to the Hôtel Mercure – 2km/1.2mi S of Mont-St-Michel via D 976. 📞02 33 60 14 18. www.hotelmercure-montsaintmichel.com. Located along the River Couesnon at the start of the dike, the Hôtel Mercure welcomes you into its bright dining room.

☞☞ **La Sirène** – located inside the walls. 📞02 33 60 08 60. This crêperie was an inn for many years. The frosted-glass windows, their panes separated by metal mullions, confirm the genuine flavour of the place.

Alençon★

Orne

A royal lace manufactory under Louis XIV, Alençon has a rich architectural heritage, a Fine Arts Museum with a collection of lacework and paintings from the 15–19C, and pleasant waterways and gardens surrounding the pedestrian town centre.

Alençon was liberated on 12 August 1944 due to the decisive role of the French 2nd Armoured Division in the Battle of the Falaise-Mortain Pocket.

▶ **Population:** 28 814
⏱ **Michelin Map:** 310 J-4
Info: Maison d'Ozé, pl. de la Madeleine. ✆02 33 80 66 33. www.paysdalencon tourisme.com.
▶ **Location:** From Alençon, roads lead to Paris (195km/122mi E via N 12), and to Brittany, Belgium and Spain. The A 28 leads to Le Mans (58km/36mi to the S) and to Rouen (160km/100mi to the N).
🚫 **Don't Miss:** The little villages of the Alpes Mancelles, especially St-Léonard-des-Bois and St-Céneri-le-Gérei.
⏱ **Timing:** Take a half-day in the town, then enjoy the lovely countryside in the forest of Perseigne or in the Alpes Mancelles.
👨‍👧 **Kids:** At St-Léonard-des-Bois, the domaine of Gasseau offers nature walks under the trees.

SIGHTS

Musée des Beaux-Arts et de la Dentelle★

&⏱*Open daily except Mon: Jan–Jun 10am–noon, 2–6pm; Jul–Aug 10am–6pm; Sept–Dec 10am–noon, 2–6pm.* ⏱*Closed 1 Jan, 1 May, 25 Dec.* ⊛€4. ✆*02 33 32 40 07.*

The Museum of Fine Arts and Lace houses paintings from the 15C to the 19C as well as collections of lace.

The presentation of the **lace collection**★ offers a broad review of the principal lacemaking centres in Italy and France. Its display of Alençon lace, which uses a needlepoint technique unique in France, includes the elegant creations of the Alençon lacemakers from the 17C to the present day.

There is also a collection of Cambodian objects brought back by **Adhémar Leclère** (1853–1917), a native of Alençon and 19C governor of Cambodia.

Église Notre-Dame★

The beautiful 14–15C Flamboyant Gothic Church of Our Lady was begun during the Hundred Years' War. The tower, transept and chancel were rebuilt in the 18C. The elegant three-sided **porch**★, built by Jean Lemoine from 1490 to 1506, is an example of the purest Flamboyant style. All the decoration is concentrated on the upper parts of the church.

Inside, the sweeping lines of the nave rise to the lierne and tierceron **vaulting** which is highly decorated. The lines of the triforium merge with those of the clerestory to form a unified whole.

Note the admirable **stained glass**★ by the master-glaziers of Alençon and the Maine region. The glass in the clerestory windows dates from 1530.

In place de la Madeleine, to the left of the church, is the attractive 15C **Maison d'Ozé**, now the Tourist Information Centre, where the future King Henri IV is said to have stayed in 1576.

ADDITIONAL SIGHTS

Ancien Château

From place Foch, you can see the 14C and 15C towers of the old castle, built by Jean II le Beau, first Duke of Alençon and ally of Joan of Arc. The central tower, known as the crowned tower, has an unexpected outline: the main tower with machicolations is itself crowned by a slimmer, round tower. The other two towers, which defend the main gate, can be seen from rue du Château.

Halle au Blé
🕐 *Open daily 9am–noon, 2–6pm.*
This circular grain market was covered towards the end of the 19C with a glass dome which the ladies of the town nicknamed the hoopskirt of Alençon. It is today a cultural centre.

Église St-Léonard
The rebuilding of the present church was begun in 1489 by René, second Duke of Alençon, and was completed in 1505 by his widow, Marguerite de Lorraine. Nearby *(No 10 rue Porte-de-la-Barre)* is a 15C house *(Maison à l'Étal)* with a slate-hung façade.

Chapelle Ste-Thérèse
🕐 *Open 9am–noon, 2–6pm (5pm, Nov–Mar).* 🕐 *Closed Mon, Jan.* ✏ *No charge.* 📞 *02 33 26 09 87. www.famillemartin-therese-alencon.com.*
Opposite the Préfecture (a fine 17C building and former military head-quarters) a double staircase leads to the chapel, which adjoins the house *(50 rue St-Blaise)* where St Theresa of Lisieux was born on 2 January 1873.

EXCURSIONS
Laval★
▷ *Laval is 32km/20mi S of Mayenne by D 162. Le Mans is 86km/53.4mi to the E on N 157.* 🏠*1 allée du Vieux-St-Louis.* 📞*02 43 49 46 46. www.laval-tourisme.com.*
The River Mayenne defines Laval, flow-ing gently through the centre of town, as it has since the city was founded in the year 1000. The town has a picturesque château and old half-timbered houses, and has produced many distinguished citizens.

👣 WALKING TOUR

OLD TOWN★
Place de la Trémoille
The square is named after the last of the local lords, guillotined during the Revolution. On the east side stands the

Renaissance façade of the 16C **Nouveau Château** built for the Count of Laval; it was enlarged in the 19C and now houses the law courts.

Rue des Orfèvres
The narrow street which runs south into Grande-Rue is lined with beautiful 16C overhanging houses and 18C mansions. At the T-junction stands the Renaissance house (1550) of the Master of the Royal Hunt *(Grand Veneur).*

Grande-Rue
This was the main street of the medieval city; it descends to the River Mayenne between rows of old houses, some half-timbered with projecting upper storeys, others in stone with Renaissance deco-ration.

▷ *Turn right onto rue de Chapelle.*

The street climbs between medieval and Renaissance houses to a charm-ing statue of St René in a niche *(right)* at the top.

▷ *Go straight ahead onto rue des Serruriers.*

South of the Beucheresse Gate are two slightly askew half-timbered houses.

Porte Beucheresse
In former days this 14C gate, then called Porte des Bûcherons, opened directly into the forest; its two round towers, topped with machicolations, were once part of the town walls. Henri Rousseau was born in the south tower, where his father worked as a tinsmith.

Cathédrale
The building has been altered many times, but the nave and the transept crossing are covered with Angevin vaulting, characterised by curved rib vaulting in which the keystones are at different heights.
The walls are hung with Aubusson tap-estries (early 17C) depicting the story of Judith and Holofernes in six panels. On the left pillar near the chancel is a

very beautiful triptych painted by the Antwerp Mannerist School in the 16C; it presents the Martyrdom of St John the Apostle when closed and three scenes from the life of John the Baptist when open. In the north transept there is an imposing revolving door, which was carved in the 18C.

On leaving the cathedral, walk round the east end to admire the northeast door (facing the law courts), which is decorated with 17C **terracotta statues**.

Rue de la Trinité

One of the old houses dates from the 16C and is adorned with statues of the Virgin and the Saints.

▷ *Turn left onto rue du Pin Doré, which ends in place de la Trémoille.*

Quays★

◷*The bateau-lavoir St-Julien, quai Paul -Boudet: Jul–Aug Tue–Sun 2–6pm.* ◉*No charge.*

The quays on the east bank provide the best overall **views**★ of Laval across the River Mayenne. From the **Pont Vieux**, a 13C humpback bridge, there is a more detailed view of the old town.

The **bateaux-lavoirs**, the last public wash houses in Laval, are moored along quai Paul Boudet. One of these, the **St-Julien**, has been restored.

Jardin de la Perrine★

The terraces of these public gardens command attractive views. As well as a rose garden there are many trees, ponds, waterfalls, lawns and flower beds.

The Château★

◷*Open Tue–Sun Jun–Sept 10am–6pm; rest of the year 2–5pm.* ◉€2. ☎*02 43 53 39 89. www.laval-tourisme.com.*

To the right of the railings in front of the law courts stands a noble 17C porch, next to an early 16C half-tim-bered house. Through the porch is the courtyard of the old castle enclosed by ramparts (from the top of the walls there is a picturesque **view**★ of the old town). In its present state the bulk of

the castle dates from the 13C and 15C; the windows and dormers in white tufa, carved with scrolls in the Italian style, were added in the 16C. The crypt and the keep are the oldest parts (12–13C).

Donjon

Originally separated from the court-yard by a moat, the keep was later incorporated between the two wings of the castle. Within the keep, the most interesting feature is the extraordinary **timber roof**★★, which was built c.1100 to an ingenious circular design.

Great beams, radiating from the cen-tre like the spokes of a wheel, project beyond the walls (which are over 2m/6.6ft thick) to support the wooden defensive gallery that projects out to permit defence of the gate and the base of the walls.

Bagnoles-de-l'Orne♨♨

▷ *Bagnoles is 2km/1mi N of the N 176, which links Alençon (47km/29mi SW) to Mont-St-Michel (90km/56mi W). The town comprises two distinct parts: to the W Bagnoles-Château, and E, Bagnoles-Lac.* ⓘ ☎*02 33 37 85 66. www.bagnolesdelorne.com.* ▣*Near the château, the museum, the casino and the place du Marché.*

In addition to its healing waters, Bag-noles-de-l'Orne has a lovely **lakeside setting**★ that invites calm. The lake is formed by the Vée, a tributary of the Mayenne, before it enters a deep gorge cut through the massif of the Andaines Forest. The site can be seen best by walking from Tessé-la-Madeleine to the Roc au Chien.

The spot known as Capuchin's Leap received its name when a Capuchin monk, cured of his ills by a magical spring, fulfilled a vow by making a gigantic leap (4m/13ft) between the rock spikes high above the water.

Parc de l'établissement thermal★

The park surrounding the spa building is planted with pines, oaks and chestnut trees. The Allée du Dante on the east bank of the Vée, which is often crowded with bathers, leads from the lake to the spa building. Other alleys in the park wind towards Capuchin's Leap and to the site known as the Abri Janolin. Shops line the lake-front rue des Casions.

Le Roc au Chien★

Tours by tourist train (30min): 3.15pm and 4.30pm: Jun–Sept daily; Mar–Oct Sat–Sun and public holidays. €6. 02 33 30 72 70. www.bagnolesdelorne.com. 45min round-trip on foot.

Start from the church and walk up the avenue du Château; the main gateway opens on to the avenue and the public park of Tessé. The château, built in the 19C in the neo-medieval style, now houses the town hall.

Take the avenue on the right which overlooks the Bagnoles Gorge and leads to the rocky promontory, the Roc au Chien, where there is a lovely **view**★ of Bagnoles beside the lake (left) and the spa building and its park (right).

Musée départemental des Sapeurs-Pompiers de l'Orne

Open daily Apr–Oct 2–6pm. €4. 02 33 38 10 34.

A deconsecrated church houses the Fire Brigade Museum with its collection of horse-drawn hand pumps, the oldest pre-dating 1790, badges, medals, helmets, uniforms, equipment, breathing apparatus and radios.

Château de Carrouges★★

Carrouges is 26km/16mi E of Bagnoles-de-l'Orne and 30km/18.5mi NE of Alençon. Open daily Apr–mid-Jun, Sept 10am–noon, 2–6pm; mid-Jun –Aug 9.30am–noon, 2–6.30pm; Oct–Mar 10am–noon, 2–5pm. Closed 1 Jan, 1 May, 1 and 11 Nov, 25 Dec. €7. 02 33 27 20 32.

For almost five centuries this immense château and park belonged to a famous Norman family, Le Veneur de Tillières; in 1936 it was bought by the nation.

From the **park** with its fine trees and elegant flower beds there are good views of the château.

The Conservatoire botanique des pommiers de Bretagne et de Normandie, at the entrance to the property, includes 152 varieties of apple trees.

The 16C **gatehouse**★ is an elegant brick building with decorative geometric patterns. It was almost certainly built by Jean Le Veneur, Bishop of Lisieux and Abbot of Bec, who helped fund Jacques Cartier's 1534 expedition to Canada.

The château itself is austere but imposing. Surrounded by a moat, the buildings are arranged around an inner courtyard. The stables and domestic quarters occupy the ground floor; the apartments and state rooms are on the first floor.

Inside, the **kitchen** presents an imposing array of copper pans. The **Louis XI Bedroom** was named after the king's visit on 11 August 1473.

The panelling is adorned with delicate panels of foliage highlighted in a different colour.

In the principal **antechamber** the chimney breast is decorated with a hunting scene. The remarkable fireplace in the **dining room** is flanked by two polished granite piers with Corinthian capitals. The sideboards are Louis XIV; note the Restoration chairs.

The **portrait gallery** with its Louis XIII chairs assembles past lords and owners. The **drawing room** occupies part of one of the corner towers. The straw-coloured panelling dates from the late 17C or early 18C.

The visit ends with the monumental great **staircase**★ and its brickwork vaulting and round headed arches as they wind up and round the square stairwell.

The Village

The village of Carrouges stands within the boundary of the **Parc naturel régional Normandie-Maine**.

The **Maison du Parc** (02 33 81 75 75; www.parc-naturel-normandie-maine.fr.) occupies the restored buildings of a 15C chapter of canons, an outbuilding of the château.

NORTHERN FRANCE AND PARIS

Paris is located at the centre of Île-de-France, the wealthiest of the regions of France, and from which the French state has grown due to its location defined by the rivers Seine, Aisne, Oise and Marne. Where its limestone plateaux have been cut into by the rivers, lush valleys have been formed, contrasting with the vast arable tracts of the Beauce, Vexin and Brie. A girdle of greenery surrounds the capital, made up of great forests such as those of **Fontainebleau** and **Rambouillet,** into which merge the landscapes of leisure and pleasure. Further north, landscapes are open and high-yielding arable land is broken by a number of valleys, such as that of the Somme.

Highlights

1 Rodin's bronze figures: **Monument des Bourgeois de Calais** (p432)

2 Grand'Place and Place des Héros at Arras: **Les Places** (p444)

3 French Classicism at its best: **Château de Versailles** (p483)

4 Railway carriage at Compiègne: **Clairière de l'Armistice** (p491)

5 Europe's only Disney resort: **Disneyland Paris** (p498)

Geography – Northeast is Flanders, consisting largely of low-lying reclaimed land, and having much in common with the adjoining Low Countries. Inland is the *pays noir*, stretching from Béthune to Valenciennes and running into the conurbation of Lille-Tourcoing-Roubaix. In the *pays noir*, the coal industry has now disappeared and, in its place, textile, processed food and car part industries provide much employment.

The presence of a number of islands in the Seine made a convenient crossing point for the prehistoric North–South trade route. Under the Gauls, urban development was confined to the Île de la Cité, though Roman Lutetia spread into today's Latin Quarter.

History – The Capetian kings made Paris their capital, giving it the dominant role in the country's political and cultural life – exercised ever since.

At the centre of the Revolution and the establishment of Empire which followed, Paris soon became an imperial city. Managing to avoid a great deal of damage in WW I; during WW II it was occupied by the Germans.

Away from the capital, the Île-de-France, together with Amiens, was the cradle of Gothic architecture, while to the north, Flanders has long been a battleground and was completely devastated during both world wars.

Today – the whole region is part of a highly successful modern economy, which, while heavily industrialised,

Galerie des Glaces, Château de Versailles

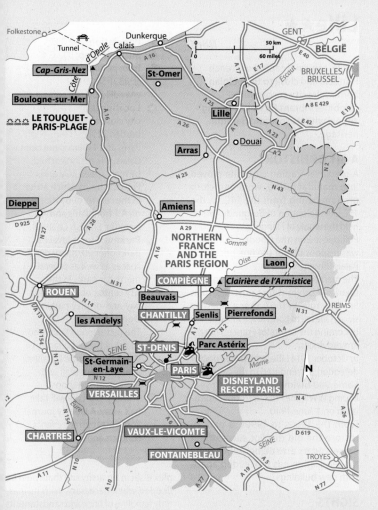

retains much woodland – especially around the capital – and there are huge tracts of agricultural land to the north, particularly in Picardy. Tourists flock to see the many attractions of Paris and the Île-de-France, bolstering its already successful tourist economy. With over 11 million inhabitants crowded into its 8 départements and hundreds of cities, Île-de-France, the most populated region of France by far, has a population in excess of some entire European countries like neighbouring Belgium, and Austria.

Culturally speaking, Picardy, comprising three separate départements, Somme, Aisne and Oise, has much more in common with Nord-Pas-de-Calais than with its southern neighbour, Île-de-France. But its geography closely links it with the Parisian Basin, its agricultural flatlands and forests. The culture of Nord-Pas-de-Calais, comprising two départements, Nord and Pas-de-Calais, has unique features of its own, such as the widespread use of Flemish.

Its rich privateer past has given birth to some of the wildest festive Carnival celebrations, not to mention a tradition of hospitality that is proverbially unequalled in France

Overall, this is a complex and vibrant region making up an interesting array of similarities and differences.

Lille★★

Nord

Lively, convivial capital of French Flanders and close to the Belgian border, the city successfully combines vibrant forward-looking appeal with its splendid Baroque heritage.

A BIT OF HISTORY

A medieval trading city, Lille moved into manufacturing, wool and cloth predominating from the 14C. In the 15C Lille belonged to Burgundy, which held the whole of Flanders; in 1454 Duke Philippe le Bon (the Good) of Burgundy was responsible for the fine brick-built Palais Rihour.

The marriage of Marie de Bourgogne to Charles V brought first Austrian, then Spanish, rule. In 1667, after a nine-day siege, Lille fell to Louis XIV, subsequently becoming the capital of France's northern provinces.

In October 1914 Lille, which was poorly defended, surrendered to the Germans. Some 900 buildings were destroyed. During WWII, the French troops capitulated on 1 June 1940.

From the 1960s to 1990s, a plan to restore the old district successfully preserved its artistic heritage, while modernisation has proceeded apace with new buildings.

SIGHTS

La Citadelle★

The Citadel is a military base.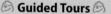
Guided tours only. May–Aug Sun 3pm. Contact tourist office for details and reservation.

Within four months of Louis XIV's troops entering the town, Vauban began to reconstruct the citadel. The great com-

---

▶ **Population:** 232 082

⚙ **Michelin Map:** 302 G 4

▤ **Info:** pl. Rihour.
℘0891 56 20 04.
www.lilletourism.com.

▶ **Location:** Lille is a large city close to the Belgian border, 220km/138mi N of Paris, and 110km/69mi from Calais. It is easily reached by high-speed TGV and Eurostar trains which arrive in the centre, or by road on A 1 from Paris and A 25 from the English Channel.

🅿 **Parking:** Street-level car parks offer 20,000 parking spaces as well as several metro car parks in the city centre, plus on-street pay-and-display parking.

☺ **Don't Miss:**
The picturesque lanes and shops of the old quarter Le Vieux Lille; Centre Euralille, a huge indoor mall with more than 130 shops.

🕐 **Timing:** Old Lille will take half a day. A weekly journal, *Sortir*, lists current events, concerts and art exhibitions.

---

plex is set in a marshy site that could be flooded when necessary. With its masterly handling of brick and sandstone, its economical design, its logical plan and its response to the geometry of artillery, it was a great masterpiece, the "Queen of citadels".

Le Vieux Lille★★

Beautiful façades of 17–18C buildings line the bustling old streets where there are numerous good little shops and brasseries. The distinctive Lille style combines brick and carved stonework.

Vieille Bourse★★

The Old Exchange designed and built in 1652–3 by the architect Julien Destrée is an example of the persistence of the Louis XIII style adapted to Flemish tastes

---

> ### ☺ Guided Tours ☺
>
> English-language walking tours of Old Lille (2hr) are on Sat at 10.15am for €9. Book at the Lille tourist office, by phone, or you can reserve online. ℘03 59 57 94 00.

(doors with broken pediments, caryatids supporting the entablatures, columns, pilasters and window-surrounds in sandstone, fruit and floral decoration and a little bell tower). The whole building proclaims the importance of textile manufacturing in the life of the city as well as paying tribute to great men and their contributions to progress with the statues lining the arcades.

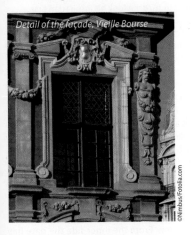
Detail of the façade, Vieille Bourse

©Nimbus/Fotolia.com

Musée des Beaux-Arts★★★

&. ⏱Open daily except Tue: Mon 2–6pm, Wed–Sun 10am–6pm. ⏱Closed public holidays. ⊜€5.50 (free 1st Sun in the month). ✆03 20 06 78 00.
www.palaisdesbeauxarts.fr.
The collection includes many masterpieces of French painting, among them the *Mystical Fountain* by Jean Bellegambe (early 16C) with its symbolic treatment of renewal and redemption, a serenely Classical *Nativity* by Philippe de Champaigne (1643), a beautifully modelled *Portrait of Madame Pélerin* by Maurice Quentin de la Tour, and another portrait, *Jean-Baptiste Forest* (1704), by Nicolas de Largillière.

Euralille

Covering an area of almost 70ha/173 acres beyond Lille city centre is a whole new urban district designed by Dutch town planner Rem Koolhaas. Since May 1993, Lille's railway station, which was renamed **Lille-Flandres**, has catered to most of the high-speed trains from Paris.

Linked by a viaduct with four arches, the new station, **Lille-Europe**, easily recognisable by its huge glass frontage, was built as part of the Paris–London and London–Brussels routes using the Channel Tunnel and for the high-speed train services between Lille and Lyon, Bordeaux, Nice, Montpellier etc.
Two towers span the new stations, the **Tour Lille-Europe WTC** designed by architect Claude Vasconi and the L-shaped **Tour du Crédit Lyonnais**★ designed by Christian de Portzamparc. The **Centre Euralille** was designed by the acclaimed French architect Jean Nouvel. Its spacious walkways and two floors contain more than 130 shops, a hypermarket, restaurants and a cultural centre called the Espace Croisé. It also has a theatre, private apartments, and a business school.

Hospice Comtesse★

⏱Open daily except Tue: Mon 2–6pm, Wed–Sun 10am–6pm. ✆03 28 36 84 00.
The hospital was built in 1237 by Jeanne de Constantinople, Countess of Flanders, to ask for divine intervention on behalf of her husband Ferrand de Portugal, taken prisoner at Bouvines. It was destroyed by fire in 1468 but was rebuilt and enlarged in the 17C and 18C. It became a hospice during the Revolution, then an orphanage. It changed again in 1939 and is today a museum of history and ethnography which also holds concerts and exhibitions.
Hospital ward – A long, sober building, rebuilt after 1470 on the old 13C foundations, flanks the main courtyard. Inside,

☺ City Pass ☺

This inclusive ticket (1 or 2 days: €20 and €30 respectively) gives you access to **metropolitan Lille's public transport** network (Transpole) plus 25 interesting sights and tourist attractions in Lille, Roubaix, Tourcoing, Villeneuve-d'Ascq and Wattrelos. Information and sales available at the tourist office.

Vauban, a Military Genius

Sébastien Le Prestre (1633–1707) was born at St-Léger *(25km/15.5mi SE of Avallon in the Morvan)*. Better known as the Marquis de **Vauban**, he was one of the truly great figures of the age of Louis XIV, a soldier who personally conducted 53 sieges, an engineer who created the French army's corps of engineers and who studied the science of gunnery, and not least an architect and town planner who redesigned ports, dug canals, spanned the Eure at Maintenon with a fine aqueduct, and built from scratch 33 new fortresses as well as improving no fewer than 300 others (many have of course disappeared).

Appointed Commissioner of Fortifications in 1678, he took his inspiration first of all from his predecessors, bringing their work to a new peak of perfection; in the case of Belfort he added a second external line of defences as well as strengthening the existing bastions by means of demilunes and a deep moat, while at Neuf-Brisach his innovations included supplementing the internal walls with bastions and placing demilunes in front of the redoubts. But above all he was able to assimilate new inventions and changes in tactics, and to adapt his designs to the particular characteristics of the site.

His main concern was to defend France's new, expanded frontiers. His work thus took him to Flanders, the Ardennes and Alsace, to the Franche-Comté, to the Pyrénées, the Alps and to many places along the country's coastline. Some of his fortresses proved their worth to the retreating French and British forces in 1940.

the immense proportions of the interior and its panelled timber **vault**★★ in the shape of an upturned boat are striking. The ward contains two beautiful tapestries, woven in Lille in 1704. One represents Baudouin of Flanders with his wife and two daughters; the other portrays Jeanne, the hospital's founder, flanked by her first and second husbands. The vault is decorated with the heraldic arms of the hospital's benefactors.

The former dormitory on the first floor has carved ceiling beams. It contains 17C Flemish and Dutch paintings and a superb 16C wooden Crucifixion from Picardy. Two rooms flanking the dormitory are filled with exhibits relating to regional history.

ADDITIONAL SIGHTS
Porte de Paris★

This gate, built from 1685 to 1692 by Simon Vollant in honour of Louis XIV, is the only example of a town gate which also served as a triumphal arch; it was formerly part of the ramparts. On the outward side, it appears as an arch decorated with the arms of Lille (a lily) and of France (three lilies). Victory stands at

the top, honoured by Fames, about to crown Louis XIV represented in a medallion. From the inner side the gate has the appearance of a lodge.

Rue de la Monnaie★

The Mint once stood in this street where the restored houses now attract antique dealers and interior decorators. On the left there is a row of 18C houses (note the apothecary's shop sign of a mortar and distilling equipment at No 3).

The houses at Nos 5 and 9 are decorated with dolphins, wheat-sheaves, palms etc.

At No 10 a statue of Notre-Dame-de-la-Treille adorns the front and at Nos 12 and 14 the crow-stepped gable has been rebuilt. Neighbouring houses date from the first third of the 17C and flank the rusticated door (1649) of the Hospice Comtesse.

Place Louise-de-Bettignies

The square bears the name of a WWI heroine. The **Demeure de Gilles de la Boé**★, at No 29 on a corner, was built in about 1636 and is a superb example of Flemish Baroque.

The abundant ornamentation includes cornices and prominent pediments. In the past this building stood on the edge of the Basse-Deûle port, in the days when there was a great deal of river traffic.

Musée d'Art Moderne★★

Open Sun at 10.30am. Consult website for individual exhibitions. 03 20 19 68 68. http://mam.cudl-lille.fr.

Lying by a lawn above Lac du Héron, the huge building (1983) by architect Rolland Simounet suggests a set of brick and glass cubes. The sculpture park displays contemporary works by **Alexander Calder** and **Picasso**. The foyer leads to the permanent and temporary exhibitions, and to the reception and other services: library, cafeteria, classrooms used for courses in the plastic arts.

The collection – Roger Dutilleul's collection, which contains over 230 works mainly from the first half of the 20C, recognised the talent of artists who were not then understood: one of the first paintings he bought was Braque's *Houses and Tree* which had just been refused entry at the Salon d'Automne.

The collection contains many Fauvist, Cubist, primitive and abstract works. The Fauvists include Rouault, Derain and Van Dongen. Cubism is represented in paintings by **Braque** and **Picasso**.

Several works by **Fernand Léger** follow his development from a 1914 landscape to his sketch for a mural (1938). One room is devoted to **Modigliani** paintings, drawings and the unique, white marble *Head of a Woman* (1913).

Works of abstract art featured are by Kandinsky, Klee and **De Staël**. De Staël knew Roger Dutilleul through the painter **Lanskoy**, who was the collector's protégé, and many examples of the latter's work are also on show. Other artists from the Paris School include **Charchoune**, **Buffet, Chapoval** and **Utrillo**.

EXCURSION
Douai★

The town is in French Flanders, close to the Belgian border. 70 pl. d'Armes. 03 27 88 26 79. www.ville-douai.fr.

The town preserves the 18C layout and grand buildings that gave it the aristocratic look that Balzac evoked.

In the 11C and 12C, Douai provided winter quarters for merchants and merchandise using the great trading routes of Northern Europe. The painter **Jean Bellegambe** (1470–1534) was born here. Around 1605, a number of Benedictine monks from England and Wales came to Douai and established the monastery of St Gregory the Great. It was here that the "Douai Bible", an English version of the Old Testament, was published in 1609. The monastery buildings were destroyed at the time of the Revolution and the community recrossed the Channel, eventually settling at Stratton-on-the-Fosse in Somerset, where they founded Downside Abbey.

One of the best **belfries★** of its kind is atop Douai's town hall (83 r. Mairie; guided tours (1hr) Mon–Sat 2pm, 3pm, 4pm, 5pm; Sun and public holidays 10am, 11am, 3pm, 4pm, 5pm (Jul–Aug daily 10am, 11am, 2pm, 3pm, 4pm, 5pm, 6pm); €3.50). Both Victor Hugo and Corot were much taken by the Gothic tower of 1390 with its elaborate crown. The Flemish Renaissance courtyard front was rebuilt in 1860.

Les fêtes des Gayants

On the Sunday after 5 July, five giant figures of the Gayant family, dressed in medieval costume, are paraded though Douai accompanied by folk groups: Gayant, the father (7.5m/24ft tall, weighing 370kg/818lbs), his wife Marie Cagenon (6.5m/21ft tall) and their children Jacquot, Fillion and Binbin. The giants appear in town on the next two days. Gayant, the oldest giant in northern France (1530), is also the most popular. The inhabitants of Douai refer to themselves in jest as "Gayant's children". www.nordmag.fr/nord_pas_de_calais/douai/gayant.htm.

ADDRESSES

🏠 STAY

Chez B&B – *78 r. Caumartin.* ✆*03 61 50 16 42. www.chezbandb.com/03.htm. Closed 15 Jul–15 Aug. 3rms.* The comfortable rooms are nicely furnished; two with sloping ceilings. Cosy sitting room.

Hôtel Flandre Angleterre – *13 pl. de la Gare.* ✆*03 20 06 04 12. www.hotel-flandreangleterre-lille.com. 44rms. ⌑ €8.* Situated opposite the train station and near the pedestrian streets, this family-run hotel presents modern rooms that are comfortable and cosy.

Hôtel Brueghel – *3–5 parvis St-Maurice.* ✆*03 20 06 06 69. www.hotel-brueghel.com. 65rms. ⌑ €9.* This Flemish-style house is conveniently located in the pedestrian part of town quite near the train station.

L'Hermitage Gantois – *224 r. Paris.* ✆*03 20 85 30 30. www.hotel hermitagegantois.com. 72rms. ⌑ €19. L'Estaminet Restaurant⌑.* Comfort, history and design in one. Delightful personalised rooms in a 14C hospice and listed building.

🍴 EAT

Le Domaine de Lintillac – *43 r. de Gand.* ✆*03 20 06 53 51. Closed Sun, Mon.* The red façade of the building will lead you directly to this rustic restaurant in old Lille. The plentiful cuisine of the Périgord region is honoured here.

Aux Moules – *34 r. de Béthune.* ✆*03 20 57 12 46. www.auxmoules.com.* A multitude of mussels (*moules*) and a few other Flemish specialities await customers in this 1930s style brasserie located in a lively pedestrian street.

Estaminet du Rijsel – *25 r. de Gand.* ✆*03 20 15 01 59. Closed Sun–Mon.* This *estaminet* is located in a street crowded with restaurants. The appealing Flemish décor features photos, posters and advertisements.

Le Passe-Porc – *155 r. de Solférino.* ✆*03 20 42 83 93. Reservations required.* The tiled floor, wall seats and enamelled plaques on the walls act as the backdrop for a remarkable collection of pigs.

La Tête de l'Art – *10 r. de l'Arc.* ✆*03 20 54 68 89. www.latetedelart-lille. com. Closed Sun & evenings except Fri–Sat. Reservations required.* A charming, lively restaurant is hidden behind a pink façade.

La Cave aux Fioles – *39 r. de Gand.* ✆*03 20 55 18 43. www.lacaveauxfioles.com. Closed Sat lunch, Sun & Public Holidays – Reservations required.* The interior is unexpectedly warm and pleasant: brick, wood, beams and paintings by area artists.

L'Huîtrière – *3 r. des Chats Bossus.* ✆*03 20 55 43 41. www.huitriere.fr. Closed Public Holidays.* A former fish-mongers, now housing three resplendent dining rooms.

🎷 NIGHTLIFE

L'Échiquier (*Bar of the Alliance Hotel*), *17 quai de Wault.* ✆*03 20 30 62 62.* This bar, installed in a former Minim convent, is attached to the Alliance Hotel.

Les 3 Brasseurs – *22 pl. de la Gare.* ✆*03 20 06 46 25. www.les3brasseurs.com.* Sample one or all of the four kinds of beer on draught drawn directly from the tuns behind the counter.

🎭 ENTERTAINMENT

Le Grand Bleu – *36 ave Max-Dormoy.* ✆*03 20 09 88 44. www.legrandbleu.com. Closed Aug. €12 (children, 6–14, €10).* This performance hall caters to a young audience. Dance, circus, theatre, story-telling, hip-hop and other nice surprises.

Orchestre National de Lille – *pl. Mendès-France.* ✆*03 20 12 82 40. www.onlille.com. Closed Aug.* Since 1976, The Orchestre National de Lille has given an average of 120 concerts per season. Performances are held in the Lille area, the Nord-Pas-de-Calais region and abroad (30 countries altogether).

Théâtre de Marionnettes du Jardin Vauban – *1 ave Léon-Jouhaux, Chalet des Chèvres in the Jardin Vauban, Armentières.* ✆*03 20 42 09 95. www.lepetitjacques.fr. Closed Oct–Mar, Sat, Mon. €4.50.* An outdoors puppet show of the Guignol tradition starring characters of local repute, such as Jacques de Lille and Jean-Jean La Plume.

🛒 SHOPPING

Marché de Wazemmes – *59000 Armentières.* Tue, Thu and especially Sun mornings, the Wazemmes market takes over the Place de la Nouvelle-Aventure.

Rue de Gand – Paved, animated and highly colourful, La Rue de Gand is well worth a visit. Butcher's shops, taverns, bars and especially restaurants serving various types of cuisine line the pavements.

Calais

Pas-de-Calais

Calais is the leading passenger port in France and the second in the world with traffic totalling 20 million passengers a year. The town gave its name to the Pas-de-Calais, the strait known on the north side of the Channel as the Straits of Dover. The history of the town has been considerably influenced by its proximity to the English coast, only 38km/23.5mi away. The white cliffs of Dover are often clearly visible from the promenade and the vast sandy beach west of the entrance to Calais harbour. Calais is the ideal starting point for excursions along the Opal Coast to Le Touquet.

A BIT OF HISTORY
The Channel Tunnel

The "Chunnel" is the realisation of more than two centuries of dreams and unfinished projects.

From utopia to reality

Over the past 250 years there have been 27 proposals, the oldest of which was made in 1750 by M Desmarets, who wanted to rejoin Britain to the mainland by a bridge, a tunnel or a causeway. From 1834 onwards, Aimé Thomé de Gamond, who is known as the "Father of the Tunnel", put forward several different propositions, all of them technically viable.

In 1880, 1 840m/over 1mi of galleries were dug out on the site called the "Puits des Anciens"; 2 000m/1.25mi were tunnelled out on the English side before the work was stopped. A fresh approach was tried in 1922. The technical progress of the 1960s gave the project a boost but a 400m/433yd gallery was abandoned once again.

During a Franco-British summit conference in September 1981, the idea of building a fixed link was again mooted by British Prime Minister Margaret Thatcher and French President François Mitterrand. In October 1985, after an international competition, four projects were shortlisted and it was the Eurotun-

▸ **Population:** 75 711
◔ **Michelin Map:** 301 E 2
▤ **Info:** 12 bd Clemenceau. ℘03 21 96 62 40. www.calais-cotedopale.com.
◑ **Location:** Calais is on the channel coast 34km/21mi NE of Boulogne-sur-Mer and 54km/34mi SW of the border with Belgium.
ⓟ **Parking:** There is plenty of metered street parking in Calais-Sud. Place d'Armes in Calais-Nord is a useful parking area.
⊛ **Don't Miss:** Rodin's remarkable *Burghers of Calais*, near the town hall.
◕ **Timing:** As well as the sights, allow plenty of time to browse Calais' excellent shops.

nel project which was finally selected, on 20 January 1986. A Franco-British treaty was signed on 12 February 1986 in Canterbury Cathedral with a view to the construction of the tunnel. The first link between France and England was established on 1 December 1990. The official opening of the tunnel and of the Shuttle service took place on 6 May 1994.

Most of the tunnel lies at a depth of 40m/130ft below the seabed, in a layer of blue chalk. The **trans-Channel link** consists, in fact, of two railway tunnels 7.60m/25ft in diameter connected every 375m/406yd to a central service gallery 4.80m/16ft in diameter built for the purposes of ventilation, security, and system maintenance. Each tunnel contains a single track along which run trains in one direction only, taking passengers and freight. The tunnels have a total length of 50km/31mi, of which 40km/24mi are beneath the Channel.

The Burghers of Calais

After his success at Crécy **Edward III** of England needed to create a power-base in France. He began the siege of

Calais on 3 September 1346, but eight months later had still not been able to breach the valiant defence led by the town governor, Jean de Vienne; in fact, it was famine that forced the inhabitants to capitulate in the end.

Six burghers, led by **Eustache de Saint-Pierre**, prepared to sacrifice themselves in order that the other citizens of Calais would be spared the sword. In thin robes, "barefoot, bareheaded, halters about their necks and the keys to the town in their hands", they presented themselves before the king to be delivered to the executioner. They were saved by the intercession of Edward's wife, Queen Philippa of Hainault.

Calais was in the hands of the English for over two centuries and liberated only in 1558, by the Duke of Guise.

This was a mortal blow to **Mary Tudor**, Queen of England, who said: "If my heart were laid open, the word 'Calais' would be engraved on it."

Calais Lace

Together with Caudry-en-Cambrésis, Calais is the main centre of machine-made lace, employing about 2 000 workers using over 350 looms. Englishmen from Nottingham introduced the industry at the beginning of the 19C; quality was improved around 1830 when the first Jacquard looms were introduced. Three-quarters of the lace made in Calais is exported. Traditional lace made with the Leavers machine is entitled to a quality label created in 1991, representing a peacock.

SIGHTS

Monument des Bourgeois de Calais★★

This famous work by **Rodin**, *The Burghers of Calais,* is located between the Hôtel de Ville and Parc St-Pierre. It dates from 1895 and exemplifies the sculptor's brilliance. Each of the six life-size figures should be admired separately: their veins and muscles exaggerated, their forms tense and haughty.

Hôtel de ville

The beautiful and graceful town hall is built of brick and stone in the 15C Flemish style yet dates only from the turn of the last century. The **belfry** (75m/246ft) can be seen for many kilometres in all directions. Inside, a **stained-glass window** recalling the departure of the English diffuses the sunlight over the grand staircase.

Place d'Armes

Before the devastation of the war, this was the heart of medieval Calais. Only the 13C **watchtower** has survived. The belfry and the town hall beside it are popular subjects for artists.

To the left is the Bassin Ouest; to the right is the Bassin du Paradis and the rear harbour used as a marina.

Burghers of Calais by Rodin, Hôtel de ville

Y. Thierry/ MICHELIN

The Lighthouse (Le phare)

Guided visits (30min) Tue–Sun 10am–noon, 2–5.30pm. €4.50 (children, €2). *03 21 34 33 34. www.pharedecalais.com.*

The lighthouse (53m/174ft tall; 271 steps) was built in 1848 to replace the watch-tower beacon.

From the top there is a surprisingly wide and splendid panoramic **view**★★ over Calais, the harbour, the basins, the town's stadium, place d'Armes and the unexpectedly large Church of Our Lady.

Musée des Beaux-Arts et de la Dentelle★

Open daily except Mon 10am–noon, 2–6pm, Sat 10am–noon, 2–6pm, Sun 2–6pm; Nov–Mar 10am–noon, 2–5pm, Sat 10am–noon, 2–5pm, Sun 2–5pm Closed public holidays. €4 *03 21 46 48 40. www.calais.fr.*

The fine arts and lace museum gives an insight into changes in sculpture over the 19C and 20C and styles of painting between the 17C and 20C.

19C and 20C sculpture features works by Rodin and the studies he made for *The Burghers of Calais.* Also works by Rodin's predecessors, including Car-rière-Belleuse, Carpeaux, Barye, and his students, Bourdelle and Maillol.

Paintings from the 17C to the 20C by the Flemish and North European schools. There are also works by modern and contemporary artists such as Jean Dubuffet, Félix Del Marle, Picasso, Fautrier, Lipchitz and Arp.

The **lace section**, in a former tulle-making factory, deals with machine-made and hand-made lace (the museum owns more than 400 000 samples of machine-made lace).

EXCURSIONS
Dunkerque

Dunkerque is 50km/31mi E of Calais; 78.8km/49mi NW of Boulogne-sur-Mer. Beffroi, r. de l'Amiral-Ronarc'h. *03 28 66 79 21. www.ot-dunkerque.fr.*

Although it was almost entirely destroyed in WW II, the rebuilt town has an attractive centre with a pleasant atmosphere, appealing bars and good shops and museums. Dunkerque (Church of the Dunes in Flemish) was originally a fishing village, whose transformation into the principal port of Flanders began as early as the 14C. It was taken by Turenne after his victory in the Battle of the Dunes in 1658, and given to England in recognition of her help in the struggle against Spain. The town was repurchased by France in 1662. It was now that Dunkerque became the abode of smugglers and of pirates pressed into the service of the king. In the course of Louis XIV's reign, a total of 3 000 foreign ships were captured or destroyed and the trade of the Netherlands completely wrecked. The most intrepid of these privateers was **Jean Bart** (1651–1702). Despite his vocation, the town is proud of him: his statue of 1848 by David d'Angers stands in the square named after him.

Demolition of the fortifications in 1713 (one of the conditions of the Treaty of Utrecht) brought about a decline in Dunkerque's fortunes, notwithstanding improvements in the port facilities. The German breakthrough at Sedan in mid-May 1940 and subsequent dash to the coast near Abbeville had led to the Allied forces in the north being trapped with their backs to the sea. Despite a magnificent rearguard action by French troops endeavouring to protect them, defeat and retreat were inevitable. The subsequent evacuation codenamed "Operation Dynamo" was turned into the "Miracle of Dunkerque", the name given to the successful evacuation from 26 May–4 June of more than 338,000 troops from the beaches of Dunkerque and its resorts of Malo, Zuydcoote and Bray-Dunes, an operation carried out in the face of intense bombardment on land and from the air. A fleet of over 900 small vessels, dubbed the "Little Ships of Dunkerque", helped to transport the troops safely back to the UK.

Le Port★★

Dunkerque is the third-largest port in France and the major French port of the North Sea with a total of over 57.7 million tonnes of traffic in 2008. The port handled 7 134 ships during the same year. A vast industrial zone has emerged, based on shipbuilding, steelworks, refineries and petrochemicals.

It is the first port in France for ore, coal copper and container fruit imports, and the second port in France for traffic with the UK. A vehicle ferry service operates between Dover and Dunkerque (Gravelines), providing an alternative to the traditional Dover–Calais route.

Belfry

⏲ *Mon–Sat except public holidays, 9.30–11.15am, 2–5pm.* 🎟 *€3 (children, 7–12, €2).* 📞 *03 28 66 79 21. www.dunkerque-tourisme.fr.*

Built in the 13C and heightened in 1440, this served as the bell tower to **Église St-Éloi** which burnt down in 1558.

This high tower contains a peal of 48 bells which play "Jean Bart's tune" on the hours and other popular tunes on the quarter-hours. The tourist office is housed on the ground floor. A war memorial has been erected under the arch opposite Église St-Éloi.

♿ 🔊 Musée Portuaire★

♿ ⏲ *Open Jul–Aug 10am–6pm. Rest of year Wed–Mon 10am–12.45pm, 1.30–6pm.* 🎟 *€10 (children, 7–12, €8).* 📞 *03 28 63 33 39. www.museeportuaire.fr.*

Laid out in a former tobacco warehouse dating from the 19C, this attractive museum gives an insight into the history and operating of the port of Dunkerque, Northern France's huge maritime gateway, through dioramas, model ships, maps, paintings, engravings and the tools once used by dockers.

In the 17C, Dunkerque became the main privateering harbour, with Jean Bart to defend it. *The Battle of Texel* (a copy of a painting by Isabey kept in the Musée de la Marine in Paris), engravings, and models of privateers' boats illustrate Bart's exploits.

Musée des Beaux-Arts★ (Fine Arts Museum)

⏲ *Open Wed–Mon 10am–noon, 2–6pm.* 🎟 *€4.50 (no charge 1st Sunday of the month).* 📞 *03 28 59 21 65.*

This museum (rebuilt in 1973) houses beautiful collections of 16–20C paintings and documents tracing Dunkerque's history. One room is dedicated to the privateer Jean Bart. Note the strange 17C money box in the shape of a chained captive from the Église St-Eloi. The money placed in it was used to buy back slaves.

Lieu d'Art et Action Contemporaine (LAAC)★

⏲ *Open Tue–Sun 10am–noon, 2–5.30pm (Apr–Oct 6.30pm).* 🎟 *€4.50.* 📞 *03 28 29 56 00.*

The museum is devoted to contemporary earthenware and glassware from 1950–80, including CoBrA, César, Soulages, Warhol and Télémaque.

Working with the theme **"Dialogues in ceramics"**, the museum aims to increase public awareness of this art form.

The Museum of Contemporary Art stands in the middle of a **sculpture park**★ designed by Gilbert Samel.

The paths climb outcrops and run down slopes, leading past great stone pieces by the sculptor Dodeigne, metal structures by Féraud and compositions by Viseux, Arman and Zvenijorovsky, all against the backdrop of the North Sea.

St-Omer★★

▶ *This northern town is 49km/30mi SE of Calais.* 🛈 *4 r. du Liond'Or.* 📞 *03 21 98 08 51. www.tourisme-saintomer.com.*

A market centre of some importance, St-Omer has kept many fine town houses dating from the Classical period.

The town lies at the junction of Inland Flanders, with its watery landscapes of poplars, elms and willows, and Coastal Flanders, won from the sea in medieval times and now dominated by industry and arable farming.

A border town, St-Omer was in turn part of the Holy Roman Empire, Flanders, Burgundy and then Spain, finally passing into French hands in 1677. The town's industry, predominantly metal-working, chemicals and glass-making, is concentrated in the Arques district. 38km/23.6mi to the south lies the site of the Battle of **Agincourt** (Azincourt), where, on 25 October 1415, France suffered its worst defeat of the Hundred Years' War at the hands of Henry V of England.

Cathédrale Notre-Dame★★
🕐*Open daily Nov–Mar 8am–5pm; Apr–Oct 8am–6pm. www.cathedrale-saint-omer.org.*
Completed at the end of the Hundred Years' War, the building shows signs of the influence of the English Perpendicular style. There are numerous high-quality **works of art**★★, including 18C woodwork, and 13C floor tiles.

Hôtel Sandelin and museum★
♿ 🕐*Open Wed–Sun 10am–noon, 2–6pm. ⊚€4.50. ✆03 21 38 00 94. www.musenor.com.*
The house was built in 1777 for the Viscountess of Fruges. It is set between a courtyard and a garden, with a huge portal and an elegant Louis XV gate.
Ground Floor – The drawing rooms overlooking the gardens form a charming suite of rooms with finely carved wainscoting, 18C fireplaces and Louis XV furnishings.
The woodcarving room (religious sculptures and medieval tapestries) and the Salle Henri Dupuis, containing ebony cabinets made in Antwerp, lead to the **Salle du Trésor** where exhibits include the famous gilt and enamelled **base of the St Bertin Cross**★ (12C), a masterpiece of Mosan art. The upper floors house a collection of local ceramics, and **Delftware**.

Jardin public★
A vast park is located on part of the old 17C ramparts, with gardens and views of the bastion, rooftops and the cathedral tower.

Côte d'Opale★
The road linking Calais and Boulogne takes the visitor along the most spectacular part of this coastline with its high chalk cliffs, heathlands and vast sandy beaches backed by dunes.

Blériot-Plage
▷ *3km/1.8mi W of Calais.*
The little resort has a fine beach stretching as far as Cap Blanc-Nez. On a cliff-top knoll is the obelisk commemorating the **Dover Patrol**, mounted continuously between 1914 and 1918 to protect the vital supply routes across the English Channel.
At Les Baraques just to the west of the resort is a monument marking **Louis Blériot's** flight across the Channel in 1909.

Cap Blanc-Nez★★
▷ *11km/6.8mi W of Calais, along D 940.*
From the top of the white cliffs the **view**★ extends from Calais to Cap Gris-Nez and right across the Channel to the English coast.

Wissant
▷ *19km/12mi W of Calais, along D 940.*
With its superb beach of fine hard sand, one of France's main centres for land yachting, Wissant enjoys its privileged position in the middle of the National Conservation Area which includes both Cap Gris-Nez and Cap Blanc-Nez.

Cap Gris-Nez★★
▷ *31km/19.2mi SW of Calais.*
This lofty limestone headland makes a contrast with the chalk cliffs to the south. It gives a **view**★ of the white cliffs of the English coast.

Wimereux
▷ *27km/16.7mi SW of Calais.*
This sizeable family resort is pleasantly situated between Cap d'Alprech to the south and the cliffs running up to Cap Gris-Nez in the north.
From the raised seafront promenade there are fine views over the Channel and along the coast from the monument (**Colonne de la Grande Armée**) to Boulogne.

Boulogne-sur-Mer★ –
♿*See BOULOGNE-SUR-MER.*

Boulogne-sur-Mer★★

Pas-de-Calais

Considered the most attractive and interesting of the "short crossing" Channel ports, Boulogne has a historic walled upper town built on the site of the Roman fortress with 13C ramparts, interesting shops and a traditional market in the lower town, and a busy quayside where fishermen's wives sell their husbands' fresh catch at traditional tiled stalls.

A BIT OF HISTORY

Boulogne's location along the chalk cliffs facing the English coast made it a cross-Channel port at an early date. It was from here that Emperor Claudius set sail to conquer Britain; he even established regular boat services to Dover and built a 12-storey landmark tower 200 Roman feet high (1 Roman ft = 2.96cm), which stood until the 16C. Fishing has long been the town's principal activity, the ship-owners' guild being regulated as early as 1203.

▲▲ SIGHTS

Nausicaä★★★

🌡🕐*Open daily 9.30am–6.30pm (Jul–Aug 9.30am–7.30pm).* 🕐*Closed first 3 weeks in Jan, 25 Dec, 1 Jan (until 2pm).* ⬠€18 (child €11.50). 🕿03 21 30 98 98. www.nausicaa.fr.

Designated as the national sea life centre, Nausicaä is an extraordinary complex, at once educational and entertaining. There are many serious elements which have an overall theme of conservation, but there are also amusements such as highly trained sea lions. Within the centre, there is a cinema, a shop, some restaurants and bar.

Ville haute★★

The upper town, Boulogne's historic district built on the site of the Roman fortress, is still surrounded by its 13C ramparts, which have a walkway on top.

▶ **Population:** 44 519

⬥ **Michelin Map:** 301 C 3

🅸 **Info:** Parvis de Nausicaä. 🕿03 21 10 88 10. www.tourisme-boulognesurmer.com.

▶ **Location:** 34km/21mi SW of Calais.

🅿 **Parking:** There are car parks by the seafront – it's much easier than trying to park in town.

⊘ **Don't Miss:** The quiet streets of Ville Haute within its ring of sturdy ramparts.

▲▲ **Kids:** Nausicaä is a family destination and kids will love it.

Basilique Notre-Dame

🕐*Open Apr–Aug daily 9am–noon, 2–6pm; Sept–Mar daily except Mon 10am–noon, 2–5pm.* 🕿03 21 99 75 98.

The basilica was built from 1827 to 1866 on the site of the old cathedral (destroyed after the Revolution) and has preserved the Romanesque crypt.

The superb, soaring **dome**★ with its circle of large statues rises behind the chancel; in the central chapel stands the wooden statuette of Our Lady of Boulogne (Notre-Dame de Boulogne), crowned with precious stones.

Crypt – ⊶*Closed for renovation until 2012–13.*

Under the basilica, a labyrinth of underground passages links 14 chambers.

Château-musée★

🕐*Open Mon–Sat 10am–12.30pm, 2–5.30pm, Sun 10am–12.30pm, 2.30–6pm.* ⬠€4.50 (free first Sun of month). 🕿03 21 10 02 20.

Formerly the residence of the counts of Boulogne, this polygonal building was the first in western Europe to abandon the traditional keep. Flanked by round towers, it protected the most vulnerable part of the ramparts facing the plateau. The archaeology of the Mediterranean is represented by an Egyptian section (sarcophagi and numerous funerary objects, the gift of Mariette the Egyptologist) and also by a beautiful group of **Greek vases**★★ dating from 5–6C BC, among them a black-figure jug portraying the suicide of Ajax.

Among the ethnographic collections, the **Eskimo and Aleutian masks**★★ brought back from a voyage to North America by the anthropologist Pinart, and the objects from the South Sea Islands including a Maori battle canoe from New Zealand, are particularly interesting.

EXCURSIONS

Colonne de la Grande Armée★★

◗ *3km/2mi north by N 1 and turn left on a small road.* ◔*The monument has been temporarily closed; check website for details.* ◔*Closed 1 Jan, 1 May, 1 and 11 Nov, 25 Dec.* ⌾€3. ✆*03 21 80 43 69. http://wimille.monuments-nationaux.fr.*
Designed by the architect **Eloi Labarre** (1764–1833) to commemorate the Boulogne Camp, the column was started in 1804 but only finished under Louis-Philippe.

On its base, a bronze low-relief sculpture portrays Field Marshal Soult offering the plans of the column to the Emperor.

A staircase *(263 steps)* leads to the square platform from where the **panorama**★★ extends over the lush countryside of the Boulogne region and, on a clear day, across the Channel as far as the white cliffs of Dover.

Le Touquet★★★

◗ *The town is on the Channel coast S of Boulogne.* 🄸 *Palais de l'Europe, pl. de l'Hermitage.* ✆*03 21 06 72 00. www.letouquet.com.*
With its casinos, grand villas, immense beach, designer stores, gourmet restaurants and luxury hotels, the "Pearl of the Opal Coast" enjoys an international reputation.

Occupied by the Germans during WWI, Le Touquet like many French towns suffered badly, especially towards the end of the war when most of the resort's hotels were destroyed.

It also had the distinction of being the most mined town in France, with over 100 000 devices to deal with at the end of the hostilities.

Seaside

Along the seafront, the **promenade** is edged by gardens and car parks. The south end leads to a yachting club and a thalassotherapy centre. The fine sand beach stretches as far as the mouth of the River Authie. The **coast road** follows the line of the dunes and leads to the marina and the water-sports club, well sheltered by Pointe du Touquet.

Sand dunes in Le Touquet-Paris-Plage

©David Hughes/Dreamstime.com

Amiens★★

Somme

The largest Gothic cathedral in France, one of the finest in the world, is the majestic centrepiece of the historic capital of Picardy.

A BIT OF HISTORY

Amiens' great legend is that of the Roman soldier who, passing near Amiens, sliced his cloak in two and gave half to a wretched beggar. Later becoming Bishop of Tours, the former soldier was eventually canonised as St Martin, patron saint of France. In 1477, on the death of Charles le Téméraire (the Bold), this ancient capital of Picardy became subject to the French Crown.

In the 17C its textile industry prospered (Amiens velvet). The city suffered in both world wars, in 1918 during the Ludendorff Offensive, in 1940 during the Battle of France. Later attractively restored and now a university town, it is again a major centre for the arts and the economy.

SIGHTS
Cathédrale Notre-Dame★★★

◷ *Open daily Apr–Sept 8.30am– 6.30pm; Oct–Mar 8.30am–5.30pm.*
Guided tours available: €5.50.
☎03 22 71 60 50.

A UNESCO World Heritage Site, this harmonious building was begun in 1220 and completed just 68 years later. The architect, Robert de Luzarches, had all the stonework cut to its finished dimensions before it left the quarry, then simply assembled it on site.

The cathedral is in Gothic Lanceolate style, with three-storey elevations including a blind triforium in nave and transept. The wonderfully elegant nave is the highest in France (42.5m/139.4ft).

😊 **City Pass** 😊

This pass offers coupons for guided tours, half-price entry to various entertainment events, recreational activities, restaurants and much more. €8 from the tourist office.

▶ **Population:** 137 375
🚗 **Michelin Map:** 301 G 8
ℹ **Info:** 40 pl. Notre-Dame.
☎03 22 71 60 50.
www.amiens-tourisme.com.
▶ **Location:** 125km/78mi S and E of Boulogne-sur-Mer. Walk across the River Somme to explore the narrow streets of Quartier St-Leu, which contain craft and antique shops, cafés and restaurants.
🅿 **Parking:** Leave the car in place St Michel, next to the cathedral, or in Saint-Leu underground car park.
😊 **Don't miss:**
The Hortillonnages; the Son et Lumière at the cathedral; the Saint-Leu district.

At an early date problems arose through water from the Somme penetrating the foundations; movement occurred along the length of the building, evidence of which can be seen in cracks in the nave near the transept. The weight of the vaults aggravated the effect; to remedy it, in the 16C a brace of Toledo steel was inserted into the triforium, heated red-hot, and allowed to cool.

For four centuries it has served its purpose admirably. The building was further strengthened by increasing the number of buttresses at the east end and by adding side chapels in the form of double aisles to the nave in order to spread the downward forces as widely as possible.

The famous slender steeple rising above the crossing was built by the master carpenter Cardon in two years (1528–29). Much of the cathedral's decoration is of very high quality indeed: the sculpture of the west front (including the noble figure of Christ known as the "Beau Dieu"), and the rose windows of the main façade, including the 16C Sea Window (rose de la Mer), of the north transept; the 14C Window of the Winds (rose des Vents); and of the south tran-

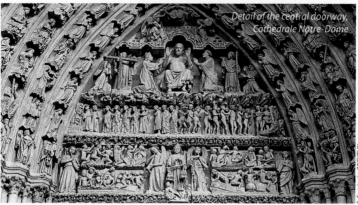
*Detail of the central doorway,
Cathédrale Notre-Dame*

S. Sauvignier/MICHELIN

sept, the 15C Window of Heaven (rose du Ciel). Inside, the wrought-iron choir screen dates from the 18C and the oak choir stalls from the beginning of the 16C. The third chapel of the north aisle houses a remarkable Romanesque Crucifixion probably influenced by oriental art. Christ's feet are nailed to the Cross separately; clad in a long robe, He wears His royal crown in glory.

The figure was carved before the arrival in Paris of the relics of the Passion (including the Crown of Thorns) purchased by St Louis.

▲▲ Chés Cabotans Puppet Theatre

ⓒ *Puppet shows mid-Oct–Mar 2–6pm; Apr–Aug 10am–noon, 2–6pm.* ⊜€8–10 (children, €4–5). ℘03 22 22 30 90. www.ches-cabotans-damiens.com.

Visiting this theatre you will get to learn a bit about famous local characters such as Lafleur and his wife Sandrine (ⓒ see Puppets panel below). While you may not understand everything that's said why not watch one of the shows given in this miniature theatre where the characters express themselves in a mixture of Picardy dialect and French?

▲▲ Hortillonnages★

⊜€5.50 (children, €4.55.
🚤 Boat trip (45min) daily Apr–Oct 1.30pm onwards. ℘03 22 92 12 18. www.somme-nature.com.

The small allotments known as **aires**, which stretch over an area of 300ha/7 491 acres amid a network of canals (or **rieux**) fed by the many arms of the Somme, have been worked since the Middle Ages by market gardeners or *hortillons*.

Puppets

Amiens' puppet shows date back to about 1785. Known in Picardy dialect as **cabotans**, the puppets are carved out of wood and are about 50cm/19.7in tall. The main character **Lafleur** is the King of St-Leu (the medieval quarter) and undoubtedly embodies all the spirit and character of the Picardy people. Since at least the 19C, this truculent, irreverent, bold character with his fiery temper has expressed plain common sense and acclaimed the proud nobility of the province in the language of his ancestors. Even from a distance, he is recognisable by his impressive stature, characteristic gait, and 18C valet's livery of fine red Amiens velvet. He is often accompanied by his wife **Sandrine** and his best friend Tchot Blaise. His motto is "Drink, walk and do nothing".

In the 19C, each of the 20 quarters in the city had its own puppet theatre. With the arrival of the cinema and sporting events at the turn of the 20C, however, the theatres gradually closed down.

At present, fruit trees and flowers are tending to replace vegetables and the gardeners' sheds are becoming week-end holiday homes. Kids will enjoy the Île-aux-Fagots, where there is an **aquarium** and an **insectarium**.

ADDITIONAL SIGHT
Musée de Picardie★★

&⏱Open daily except Mon: Tue, Fri–Sat 10am–noon, 2–6pm, Wed 10am–6pm, Thu 10am–noon, 2–9pm, Sun 2–7pm. ⏱ Closed 1 Jan, 1 and 8 May, 14 Jul, 1 and 11 Nov, 25 Dec. €5 (no charge 1st Sun in the month). ℘03 22 97 14 00.

The museum's significant collections of archaeology, medieval art and fine arts are housed in a Napoleon III building constructed between 1855 and 1867 for the Picardy Society of Antiquaries. Upon entering the central hall, visitors will not miss the rotunda and its colourful mural (1992) created by American artist Sol LeWitt (1928–2007).

EXCURSION
Parc du Marquenterre★★

▶ The Park is accessible from Abbeville via the D 940, direction Crotoy. ⏱Open daily: Apr–end Sept 10am–7.30pm; Feb–Mar, Oct–mid Nov 10am–6pm; mid Nov–Jan 10am–5pm. ⏱Closed 1 and 10–23 Jan, 25 Dec. €10. ℘03 22 25 68 99. www.parcdumarquenterre.com.
It is advisable to visit on a rising tide when the birds leave the stretches of the Baie de Somme, or during the spring and autumn migration periods. There are three different paths around the park that will take you from 45min for the shortest one to 2hrs for a more in-depth tour. The red discovery trail is tailored just for kids!

Comité Départemental du Tourisme de La Somme, 21 r. Ernest-Cauvin, 80000 Amiens. ℘03 22 71 22 71. www.somme-tourisme.com.

The Marquenterre area is an alluvial plain reclaimed from the sea, which lies between the Authie and Somme estuaries. Its name derives from *mer qui entre en terre* (sea which enters the land).

The stretches of land are made up of briny marshes, salt-pastures and sand dunes secured to the land by vegetation. Today this reserve is home to 344 species of birds, 265 species of plants, and 27 species of mammals living both on land and in the water, including a large colony of seals; the most inquisitive of them are sometimes spotted at high tide near the quayside at St Valéry-en-Somme and Le Crotoy.

Reclaimed from the sea – The process of reclaiming the land was started in the 12C by monks from **St-Riquier** and **Valloires** who erected the first dikes and attempted to canalise the rivers. Many drainage canals were built.

Perched on a hill, **Rue**, the future capital of the Marquenterre area, ceased to be an island in the 18C. During the 19C, dikes and beaches were strengthened, which allowed the development of vegetable and cereal growing.

In 1923, the industrialist **Henri Jeanson** bought an area of marshland along the coast, which his successors drained and diked using Dutch methods, so that it was eventually possible to grow bulbs. At the same time, trees were planted.

The Henson horse breed

This small, robust horse is a cross between a French saddle horse and a Norwegian Fjord pony. Its coat varies from light yellow to brown, and its mane is a mixture of black and gold. This breed was developed in 1978 in a small village of the Baie de Somme area, thanks to the determination of **Doctor Berquin**. Hensons show remarkable endurance; they can remain out in the fields all year round and cover great distances without getting tired. Their docile and affectionate behaviour makes them ideal companions for children and long-distance riders. They also fare very well in team competitions and horse shows generally.

MAKING THE MOST OF THE PARK
WHEN TO GO

Each season is interesting and enables visitors to watch different species.

Spring is the nesting season for many species such as storks, small waders (avocets, oystercatchers, plovers), greylag geese, shelduck. The herons' nesting place is particularly spectacular since five species of large waders, including spoonbills, nest at the top of pine trees.

Summer is the migrating season for black storks; it is also the time when small waders gather at high tide and when large gatherings of spoonbills, cormorants and egrets can be seen.

Autumn sees the mass arrival of many species of ducks coming to spend the winter in the park (up to 6 000 birds, some of them arriving from Russia and Finland, can be observed).

The park is the most important wader ringing centre in France, and studies on migration are carried out in cooperation with the Natonal Natural History Museum in Paris.

WHAT TO TAKE WITH YOU

Solid walking shoes, a wind- water-proof coat, and a pair of binoculars *(also available for rent at the park)*.

🐎 RIDING TOURS

👥 Espaces Equestres Henson – *34 chemin des Garennes, 80120 St-Quentin-en-Tourmont.* ✆*03 22 25 03 06. www.henson.fr.* The Henson horse-riding centre organises guided riding tours for all levels of ability, including beginners and children.

But the plans failed, and this gave rise to the idea of a bird sanctuary.

The birth of the bird sanctuary – The Marquenterre lands have always been an important habitat for migratory and non-migratory birds. Alas, it was also a paradise for hunters who brought many species close to extinction.

As a result, in 1968 the Hunting Commission created a reserve on the maritime land, to ensure the protection of the birds along 5km/3mi of coastline.

The owners of the Marquenterre estate next to the reserve decided to set up a bird sanctuary within it to allow the public to watch bird life in a natural habitat. Thirteen years later, the site became the property of the Office of Coastal Preservation. In 1994, it was granted the status of "protected nature reserve."

Discovering the Bird Sanctuary

The Bird Sanctuary covers 250ha/ 618 acres on the edge of the reserve and houses numerous species of birds, including the red-beaked shelduck, geese, terns, avocets, gulls, herons, sandpipers and spoonbills. Three marked **trails** and trained guides will help you discover the riches of the park at your own pace:

🐦 Red discovery trail – *1.5km/0.9mi.* This introductory tour of the park will offer you a close-up view of the birds that live here permanently: ducks, seagulls, geese and herons. Their calls attract wild birds of the same species. A few familiar mammals can be seen on the way – Henson horses, weasels and hares – as well as amphibians such as toads and insects such as dragonflies.

🐦 Blue observation trail – *4km/2.5mi.* This walk follows a path through the dunes to various observation hides.

🐦 Green extended observation trail – *5km/3.1mi.* An additional path shows the reserve from a completely different angle, allowing an in-depth discovery of its fauna and flora.

ADDRESSES

🏨 STAY

🛏️ Hôtel Alsace-Lorraine – *18 r. de la Morlière.* ✆*03 22 91 35 71. 14rms.* ⌓ *€7.* This comfortable, likeable little hotel hides behind an imposing carriage entrance a five-minute walk from the town centre and train station. Bedrooms, brightened with colourful fabrics, give onto the charming inner courtyard.

Hôtel Carlton – *42 r. de Noyon. ✆03 22 97 72 22. www.lecarlton.fr. 24rms. €8.50–10.* Behind the attractive 19C façade discover a modern, plush interior. Every room features waxed furniture and murals. Their simple restaurant, Le Bistrot, serves grilled meats.

Chambre d'hôte Le Petit Château – *2 r. Grimaux, Dury. 6km/3.6mi S of Amiens via N 1 dir. Beauvais. ✆03 22 95 29 52. www.le-petit-chateau.fr. 4rms.* In the countryside, 10min from central Amiens, a massive 19C residence whose comfortable guest rooms are housed in an outbuilding. The owner is happy to show his collection of old automobiles.

ⵙ/ EAT

Le Petit Poucet – *52 r. des Trois-Cailloux. ✆03 22 91 42 32. Closed Mon.* This attractive establishment is very popular with the people of Amiens who come for a slice of quiche, a *ficelle picarde* (baked crepes, stuffed and rolled), or a mixed salad for lunch, a delectable chocolate for tea, or a box of divine pastries to enjoy at home.

Le Bouchon – *10 r. Alexandre Fatton. ✆03 22 92 14 32. www.lebouchon.fr. Closed Sun eve.* A Parisian-style bistro near the railway station specialising in typically Lyonnais dishes and traditional cuisine of the region; a relaxed, "no fuss" atmosphere.

Les Marissons – *Pont de la Dodane, Quartier St.-Leu. ✆03 22 92 96 66. www.les-marissons.fr. Closed Wed and Sat for lunch, and Sun.* The place to be in the Saint-Leu quarter is this old marine workshop transformed into a restaurant. The flowery mini-garden becomes a terrace in summer, while in winter diners sit under the sloping wooden frame which has a pleasant décor of handsome beams and round tables.

GUIDED TOURS

Contact the tourist office for guided tours of the town in French, several times daily.
Barge Tours – Explore the **canals of St-Leu** in traditional style. Depart from chemin du port Cappy. *✆03 22 76 12 12.*

ⓝ NIGHTLIFE

After dark, the **Quai Belu** canalside area in the St Leu quarter is the place for pubs, discos and nightlife.
Texas Café – *13 r. des Francs-Mûriers, Quartier St.-Leu. ✆03 22 72 19 79.* This enormous Confederate-themed "saloon"

of brick and wood is always crowded and popular. Before midnight, drink (beer and cocktails), dance and sing (karaoke). After midnight, it's a disco and dance venue.

ⓔ ENTERTAINMENT

"The cathedral in living colour" – *✆03 22 22 58 90. www.amiens.fr/decouvrir/cathedrale.* The artist Skertzò uses lighting to highlight the colourful entrance on the cathedral's west side. The presentation is held mid-Jun–Sept at dusk, and during December at 7pm. Commentary in French and then English.

Comédie de Picardie – *62 r. des Jacobins. ✆03 22 22 20 20. www.comdepic.com.* This venerable old manor, entirely restored, houses a very pretty 400-seat theatre. The region's creative and dramatic hub, it produces 15 different shows for a total of 250 performances per season.

Maison de la Culture d'Amiens – *pl. Léon-Gontier. ✆03 22 97 79 79. www.maisondelaculture-amiens.com.* Two halls (1 070 and 300 seats), a movie theatre devoted to art and experimental films, and two exhibition rooms. This complex offers an unusually interesting and eclectic selection of events.

Théâtre de Marionnettes – *Chés Cabotans d'Amiens, 31 r. Édouard-David, quartier St-Leu. ✆03 22 22 30 90. www.ches-cabotans-damiens.com.* This fascinating family-orientated show, established in 1933, takes place in a veritable miniature theatre with a beautifully designed set. The puppets all have their own history and language (French or Picard).

ⓢ SHOPPING

Atelier de Jean-Pierre Facquier – *67 r. du Don. ✆03 22 92 49 52.* Transforming them into traditional and invented wooden Picardy puppets, Monsieur Facquier carves life into pieces of wood before your eyes. Madame Facquier sews their clothes using fabric chosen with care.

Jean Trogneux – *1 r. Delambre, & 2nd branch at Parvis de la Cathédrale. ✆03 22 71 17 17. www.trogneux.fr.* The city's speciality since the 16C, the Amiens macaroon, a blend of almonds and honey, is ever popular.

Marché des Hortillons – The local market gardeners, who grow their produce in the *hortillonnages*, come to market Saturday mornings at **Place Parmentier**. On the third Sunday in June, a market is held as in years gone by: the gardeners, wearing traditional attire, come in flat-bottomed punts and unload their produce onto the docks.

Arras★★

Pas-de-Calais

The Abbey of St-Vaast formed the nucleus around which the capital of Artois grew in the Middle Ages. Between the 12C and 14C it gained privileges from the Counts of Artois encouraging an economy based on corn, banking and, especially, fabrics. The city prospered; poetic and literary societies thrived in which Arras' notables could enjoy hearing themselves lampooned by minstrels and entertainers. In the 15C, Artois passed into the hands of the Dukes of Burgundy, ensuring steady orders for its fine tapestries, which were notable for dealing realistically with secular themes.

▶ **Population:** 44 304
◉ **Michelin Map:** 301 J 5-6
▤ **Info:** pl. des Héros. ☏03 21 51 26 95. www.ot-arras.fr.
◗ **Location:** 62.5km/39mi NE of Amiens.
◷ **Timing:** Half a day to explore Arras leisurely.
◈ **Don't Miss:** The 45min Historama film shown at the tourist office makes an interesting introduction to the town.

A BIT OF HISTORY

The notorious **Maximilien Robespierre** was born in Arras in 1758 to a well-to-do legal family. He was called to the Bar before becoming a Deputy in 1789, a Republican in 1792, and a prominent member of the feared Committee of Public Safety in 1793. Determined and indifferent to favours, "Robespierre the Incorruptible" embodied the spirit of the Revolution. Backed by Saint-Just and Couthon, he harried plotters and crushed deviationists, going so far as to take part in the condemnation of his allies, the Girondins. Discredited in the end by the consequences of his extremist ideology, on 27 July 1794 he himself fell victim to the guillotine to which he had condemned so many others.

SIGHTS

Ancienne Abbaye St-Vaast★★

In 667, a small chapel found itself the site of the building of a new abbey intended for Benedictine monks.

The chapel had been erected by St Vaast (453–540), whose remains were moved from Arras cathedral into the new abbey. It was St Auburt who began the abbey's development, which was completed by his successor and richly endowed by King Theodoric. Independent until 1778, the abbey enjoyed huge importance in the surrounding area.

Grand'Place

Y. Tierny/ MICHELIN

After the Revolution the monastery was used as a hospital and later a barracks. In 1838, part of it was turned into a museum; the bishop held residence in the other part. In 1833, the abbey church was rebuilt and now serves as Arras Cathedral, replacing the former Gothic building destroyed during the Revolution.

The abbey houses the **Musée des Beaux-Arts★** (◷*open Wed–Mon 9.30am–noon, 2–5.30pm;* ◷*closed public holidays;* ☎*03 21 71 26 43).*

This museum displays a variety of medieval and archaeological artworks, paintings and ceramics.

Les Places★★ (Main Squares)

Dating from the 11C, the **Grand'Place**, **Place des Héros** and the **Rue de la Taillerie** linking them celebrate the city's status as an important regional market centre. Their present splendidly harmonious appearance is the fruit of the city fathers' purposeful civic design initiatives in the 17C and 18C.

The existing Spanish Plateresque buildings of the 16C and 17C (Arras was effectively under Spanish rule from 1492–1640) were given Flemish Baroque façades from 1635 onward.

To the north of the Grand'Place a brick building with a stone-built ground floor is topped by a stepped gable, the only one of its kind.

Arras' civic pride was symbolised by the construction of its Town Hall, **Hôtel de Ville★** *(pl. des Héros)* in 1572; its bell tower **(beffroi)** (◷*open mid Sept–mid-Mar Tue–Sat 9am–noon, 2–6pm, Mon 10am–noon, 2–6pm, Sun 10am–12.30pm, 2.30–6.30pm; Apr–mid-Sept Mon–Sat 9am–6.30pm, Sun 10am–1pm, 2.30–6.30pm;* ◷*closed 1 Jan, 25 Dec;* ⊜*€3;* ☎*03 21 51 26 95)* blends Flemish Gothic with Henri II-style ornamentation. It was destroyed in WW I but rebuilt using the original plans in 1919.

Circuit des souterrains

☁*Guided tours 45min; tour daily 10am–noon, 2–6pm (Sun and public holidays, 10am–12.30pm, 2.30–6.30pm.* ◷*Closed 1 Jan and 25 Dec.* ⊜*€5.50.*

The 10C galleries, or boves, cut into the limestone bank on which the town stands, served as a refuge in wartime (during WWI the British set up a field hospital here for 24 000 troops) and above all as an enormous wine cellar; the caves (boves) are at the ideal temperature for storing wine.

Cité Nature

◷*Open Tue–Fri 9am–7pm, Sat–Sun 2–6pm.* ⊜*7€.* ☎*03 21 21 59 59. www.citenature.com.*

An old warehouse renovated by Jean Nouvel in 2004 houses an interactive exposition on nature, ecology, and agriculture, with a green labyrinth in the gardens.

EXCURSIONS
Vimy Canadian Memorial★

▶ *10km/6.2mi N.*

A gripping sight that brings home some of the realities of WWI. The summit of this chalky ridge was taken by the Canadian Expeditionary Force, part of the British Third Army, in April 1917.

It is crowned by the Canadian Memorial. There are extensive views over a farmed landscape dotted with the conical tips of coal mines.

To the west are the cemetery and basilica of Notre-Dame-de-Lorette, and nearby, entrenchments and pitted landforms left by trench warfare, which can be visited.

ADDRESSES

🛏 STAY

⊜ **Le Clos Grincourt** – *18 r. du Château, 62161 Duisans. 9km/5.4mi W of Arras via N 39 then D 56.* ☎*03 21 48 68 33. www.leclosgrincourt.com.* ⊠ *3rms.*
A tree-lined lane leads to a lovely B&B.

🍽 EAT

⊜⊜ **Astoria** – *12 pl. Foch, Arras.* ☎*03 21 71 08 14.* Sit comfortably on the terrace or in the warm dining room of this brasserie-styl0e restaurant. Traditional breakfast dishes and regional specialities are served here.

Paris★★★

The brilliance and greatness of Paris – its evocative spirit, the imposing dignity of its avenues and squares, its vast cultural wealth and unique flair and style – are known the world over. The dominance of Paris in France's intellectual, artistic, scientific and political life can be traced back to the 12C when the Capetian kings made it their capital.

A BIT OF HISTORY
Origins

At the time of the fall of the Roman Empire towards the end of the 5C, Paris was a modest township founded seven centuries previously by Gallic fishermen. Following its occupation by the **Romans**, the settlement had been extended south of the river to where the remains of the Cluny Baths and a 2C amphitheatre now stand: the **Quartier Latin**. In the 3C, St Denis, Paris' first bishop, had met his martyrdom and the Barbarians had razed the place to the ground. This destruction, together with the threat posed by Attila's hordes (but supposedly averted by the intervention of St Geneviève, patron saint of the city), had caused the inhabitants to withdraw to the security of the Île de la Cité.

Clovis, King of **the Franks**, settled in Paris in 506. Two years later, he founded an abbey south of the Seine in honour of St Geneviève, just as 35 years previously a basilica had been erected over the tomb of St Denis.

In 885, for the fifth time in 40 years, the Norsemen sailed up the river and attacked Paris; Odo, son of Robert the Strong, bravely led the local resistance, and was elected king of "France" in 888; from then on, the town became the royal seat, albeit with some interruptions.

The Capetian Dynasty (987–1328)

In 1136, Abbot Suger rebuilt the abbey church of St-Denis in the revolutionary Gothic style, an example soon followed by Maurice de Sully at Notre-Dame.

▶ **Population:** 2 211 297
⊙ **Michelin Map:** 312 D 2
▯ **Info:** There are several branches of the tourist office in the city. The **main office** is at 25 r. des Pyramides. The other branches are located at pl. du 11 novembre 1918, **Gare de l'Est**; 20 bd Diderot, **Gare de Lyon**; 18 r. de Dunkerque, **Gare du Nord**; 72 bd Rochechouart, **Anvers**; 1 pl. de la Porte de Versailles, **Paris Expo**; corner of ave des Champs-Elysées and ave Marigny, **Clémenceau**; 99 r. de Rivoli, **Carrousel du Louvre**; and 21 pl. du Tertre, **Montmartre**. ℘0892 68 30 00. http://en.parisinfo.com.

▶ **Location:** Paris is France's capital and its largest city. It lies in the middle of the Île-de-France region, which sits between the Centre, Bougogne, Champagne-Ardennes, Picardie and Haute Normandie regions. Paris is 85.6km/53mi SW of Compiègne; 69km/42.8mi NW of Fontainebleau; 104km/64.6mi SE of Les Andelys.

▶ **Don't Miss:** Arc de Triomphe, Place de la Concorde, Eiffel Tower, Notre-Dame Cathedral, the Champs-Élysées, Quartier Latin, Montmartre, the Louvre and the Musée d'Orsay.

▶ **Kids:** La Villette encompasses the child-friendly Cité des Sciences et l'Industrie, the spherical cinema La Géode, Cité des Enfants, Jardin de Luxembourg, Palais de Découverte.

The Seine with a view towards the Île de la Cité with the Cathédral de Notre-Dame

GETTING AROUND PARIS

Seine River flows east–west across the city. Places north of the river are on the *rive droite*, while those to the south are on the *rive gauche*. Paris is divided into 20 **arrondissements** (districts or neighbourhoods), each one with its own local government and characteristics.

Each *arrondissement* is further divided into a number of neighbourhoods determined by history and the people who live there.

The métro is the easiest and most economical way of moving around the city. **Line 1**, which crosses **Paris east–west**, services many of the most famous attractions: the Louvre, the Champs-Élysées and the Arc de Triomphe. **Line 4** is useful for travelling across the **city from north–south**. The metro also services the immediate suburbs of Paris, but for those a bit farther out, use the **RER** suburban trains.

Between 1180 and 1210, **Philippe Auguste** surrounded the growing city with a continuous ring of fortifications anchored on the Louvre fortress. In 1215 France's first university was founded on the Ste-Geneviève hill.

The House of Valois (1328–1589)

On 22 February 1358, Étienne Marcel, the merchants' provost, succeeded in rousing the townsfolk to break into the Law Courts (Palais de Justice); entering the Dauphin's apartments, he slew two of the future Charles V's counsellors before his very eyes. On becoming king, **Charles V** quit this place of ill memory. In 1370, he built himself a stronghold in the eastern part of the city, the Bastille, which became the centrepiece of a new ring of fortifications.

Paris was taken by the English in 1418. **Joan of Arc** was wounded in front of Porte St-Honoré trying to retake the city in 1429. Paris was won back for France eight years later by Charles VII.

In 1492, the discovery of America marked the first beginnings of a new outlook and the modern age.

The Neapolitan artists brought back by **Charles VIII** from his campaigns in Italy were introducing new trends in taste and thought; the influence of the Renaissance became apparent in many new buildings. In the 1560s, the brothers Androuet Du Cerceau drew up the plans for the Flore Pavilion abutting the Louvre to the west, then set about the construction of the Pont Neuf (New Bridge), which today is the city's oldest surviving bridge.

On 24 August 1572, the bells rang out from the tower of St-Germain-l'Auxerrois to signal the start of the St Bartholomew's Day Massacre (of Protestants); Henry of Navarre, the future Henri IV, just married to Marguerite of Valois, barely escaped with his life. In 1589, Henri III was assassinated at St-Cloud in 1589 by the monk Jacques Clément. This violent act marked the end of the Valois line.

The Bourbons (1589–1789)

In 1594 Paris opened its gates to **Henri IV**, the new king who had renounced his Protestant faith and succeeded in pacifying the country. But on 14 May 1610, in the Rue de la Ferronnerie, this monarch too fell victim to an assassin.

Under **Louis XIII** (1610–43), Métezeau designed an imposing Classical west front for St-Gervais Church, the first of its kind in Paris; Salomon de Brosse built the Luxembourg Palace for Marie de' Medici; Jean Androuet Du Cerceau laid out the courtyards and gardens of the Hôtel de Béthune-Sully; as well as erecting a church for the Sorbonne with Classical columns on its courtyard side, Lemercier built the Palais-Royal for Richelieu. On the king's death in 1643, Anne of Austria became Regent, acting in concert with Mazarin and continuing the policies of Richelieu. Paris fell prey to the series of disturbances caused by unrest among the nobility and known as the Fronde; the young king came to the conclusion that it might be advantageous to separate Court from city.

The 23-year-old **Louis XIV** began his long and highly personal reign in 1661. Even more than the splendour of court life, it was the extraordinary advancement of the arts and literature at this time that gave Paris and France such prestige in Europe. Under the protection of a king keen to encourage artistic endeavour and promote creative confidence, writers, painters, sculptors and landscapers flourished as never before. In the space of 20 years, the great Le Nôtre redesigned the parterres of the Tuileries; Claude Perrault provided the Louvre with its fine colonnade and built the Observatory; Le Vau completed the greater part of both the Institut de France and the Louvre. France's "Century of Greatness" came to an end with Louis XIV's death in 1715.

The country now found itself, for the second time, under the rule of a five-year-old. The running of the country was therefore put into the hands of a regent, Philippe d'Orléans; the first action of the court was to pack its bags and quit the boredom of Versailles for the gaiety of the capital. A long period of peace accompanied the years of corruption; for 77 years France experienced no foreign incursions. Literary salons flourished, notably those of the Marquise de Lambert, Mme Du Deffand and Mme Geoffrin, all helping the spread of new ideas in what became known as the **Age of Enlightenment**. The Palais Bourbon (1722–28), which now houses the National Assembly, was erected at this time. The personal rule exercised by **Louis XV** was discredited by his favourites, but Paris nevertheless witnessed a number of great personalities and important advances; such as Charles de la Condamine, a surveyor and naturalist responsible for the discovery of rubber (1751); Jussieu, incumbent of the Chair in Botany at the Botanical Gardens, responsible for a systematic classification of plants (1759) and for many advances in pharmacology; Diderot, author, together with d'Alambert, of the great *Encyclopaedia*, a splendid summary of the technology of the age; Chardin, who had lodgings in the Louvre, devoted himself to working in pastel; Robert Pothier, who wrote the *Treatise of Obligations*; Ange-Jacques Gabriel, the last and most famous of a line of architects linked to Mansart and Robert de Cotte, who between them gave France a hundred years of architectural unity; it was he who designed the magnificent façades fronting the Place de la Concorde, the west front of St-Roch Church and the École Militaire (Military Academy). Finally there was Soufflot, creator of the dome which crowns the Panthéon.

Distinguished furniture-makers were at work too: Lardin with his cabinets and commodes with rosewood inlay, and Boudin with his virtuoso marquetry and secret compartments; they anticipated the masters who were to emerge in the following reign.

Revolution and Empire (1789–1814)

In 1788, King **Louis XVI (reigned 1774–92)** decided to convene the States-General. The delegates assembled at Versailles on 5 May 1789. As a result, on 17 June, the States-General transformed itself into a **National Assembly** which styled itself the Constituent Assembly on 9 July; the monarchy would eventually become a constitutional one.

On **14 July 1789**, in the space of less than an hour, the people of Paris took over the Bastille in the hope of finding arms there; the outline of the demolished fortress can still be traced in the paving on the west side of the Place de la Bastille (14 July became a day of national celebration in 1879). On 17 July, in the City Hall (Hôtel de Ville), Louis XVI kissed the recently adopted tricolour cockade. The feudal system was abolished on 4 August, and the Declaration of the Rights of Man adopted on 26 August; on 5 October, the Assembly moved into the riding-school of the Tuileries, and the royal family was brought from Versailles and installed in the Tuileries Palace.

On 12 July 1790 the Church became subject to the Civil Constitution for the Clergy. Two days later, a great crowd gathered on the Champ-de-Mars to celebrate the anniversary of the fall of the Bastille; Talleyrand, Bishop of Autun as well as statesman and diplomat, celebrated Mass on the altar of the nation and the king reaffirmed his oath of loyalty to the country.

After his attempt to join Bouillé's army at Metz had been foiled, Louis was brought back to Paris on 25 June 1791; on 30 September, he was forced to accept the constitution adopted by the Assembly, which then dissolved itself.

The Legislative Assembly – The new deputies met the following day in the Tuileries Riding School. On 20 June 1792, encouraged by the moderate revolutionary faction known as the Girondins, rioters invaded the Tuileries and made Louis put on the red bonnet of liberty. On 11 July, the Assembly declared France to be in danger, and during the night of 9 August the mob (sans-culottes) instituted a "revolutionary commune" with the status of an organ of government; the next day the Tuileries were sacked and 600 of the Swiss Guards massacred. The Assembly responded by depriving the king of his few remaining responsibilities and confining him with his family in the tower of the Templar Prison (Tour du Temple).

Soon after, the "September Massacres" began; 1 200 prisoners, some "politicals", but most of them common offenders, were hauled from the city's jails and arbitrarily executed on the Buci crossroads in a frenzy of fear and panic precipitated by fear of invasion. This grisly event marked the beginning of the Terror. On 21 September, the day after the French defeat at the Battle of Valmy, the Legislative Assembly gave way to the Convention.

The Convention – At its very first meeting, the new Assembly, now in the hands of the Girondins, formally abolished the monarchy and proclaimed the **Republic**. This day, 21 September 1792, became Day 1 of Year One in the new revolutionary calendar (which remained in force until 31 December 1805). At the end of May, beset by difficulties at home and abroad and bereft of popular support, the Girondins fell, to be replaced by the "Mountain" (the extreme Jacobin faction, so-called because they occupied the upper tiers of seating in the Assembly).

In one of its first acts, the monarch was guillotined on 21 January 1793 in Place de la Concorde. On 17 September, the Law of Suspects was passed, legalising **the Terror**. The first to be executed by the revolutionary tribunals were the Girondins, in October 1793.

On 8 June 1794, Robespierre the "Incorruptible" presided over the Festival of the Supreme Being. The event was orchestrated by the painter David, beginning in the Tuileries Gardens and proceeding to the Champ-de-Mars.

On 10 June (9 Prairial), the Great Terror began. Over a period of two months, the "national razor", as the guillotine was known, was to slice off 2 561 heads. Among those executed were Lavoisier, former Farmer-General and eminent chemist, responsible for the formulation of the theory of the conservation of mass on which much of modern chemistry rests, and André Chénier, the lyric poet who had condemned the excesses of the regime in his verse. The end of the Terror came with the fall and execution of Robespierre himself, on 27 July (9 Thermidor).

The Thermidorian Convention now attempted to put the sickening spectacle of the scaffold behind it with a policy calculated to promote stability. Among its most important achievements were measures designed to advance science and learning, including the founding of the École Polytechnique (School of Engineering); the creation of the Conservatoire des Arts et Métiers (National Technical Institution), and the setting up of the École Normale (the prestigious college).

In 1795, the metric system was adopted and the Office of Longitudes founded. Just before the Assembly's dissolution on 25 October, public education was instituted and the Institut de France founded, embracing the nation's learned academies (including the Académie Française).

The Directory and the Consulate – The period of the Directory was marked, in 1798, by the very first Universal Exhibition, but was brought to an end with the coup d'état of 9 November (18 Brumaire) 1799, when the Council of Elders persuaded the legislature to move to St-Cloud as a precautionary measure against Jacobin plots. On the following day, **Napoleon Bonaparte** entered the chamber to address the delegates, but was booed; he was saved by the presence of mind of his brother Lucien, who used the guard to disperse the members. By the same evening, power was in the hands of three consuls; it was the end of the Revolution. In less than five years, the Consulate allowed Napoleon to centralise power, opening the way to the realisation of his Imperial ambitions.

The Empire – Proclaimed Emperor of the French by the Senate on 18 May 1804, Napoleon I was anointed on 2 December by Pope Pius VII at Notre-Dame, though it was he himself who actually put the crown on his head in a ceremony immortalised by David. His reign was marked by the promulgation in 1804 of the Civil Code, which he had helped draft himself when he was still First Consul, and which, as the Code Napoleon, has since formed the legal basis of many other countries. In order to make Paris into a truly imperial capital, Napoleon ordered the erection of a great column in the Place Vendôme; cast from the melted-down metal of guns taken at the Battle of Austerlitz (Slavkov), it commemorated the victories of his Grande Armée.

Vignon was commissioned to design a temple which nearly became a railway station before ending up as the Madeleine Church; Chalgrin was put to work drawing up plans for a great triumphal arch (Arc de Triomphe); Brongniart built the Stock Exchange (Bourse); Percier and Fontaine, the promoters of the Empire style, constructed the north wing of the Louvre and the Carrousel Arch (Arc du Carrousel); Gros painted the battles and Géricault the cavalry of the Grande Armée. On 31 March 1814, despite the strong resistance offered by Daumesnil at Vincennes, the Allies occupied Paris. On 11 April, the Emperor, "the sole obstacle to peace in Europe", put his signature to the document of abdication at Fontainebleau.

The Restoration (May 1814–February 1848)
The reign of Louis XVIII – 1814–24
The period of rule of Louis XVI's brother was interrupted by the Hundred Days of Napoleon's attempt to re-establish himself between his sojourn on Elba and his final exile to St Helena. During the years of Louis XVIII's reign, Laënnec

invented the stethoscope, wrote his *Treatise on Mediate Auscultation* and founded the anatomo-clinical school together with Bayle and Dupuytren; Pinel studied mental illness at the Salpêtrière Hospital; Cuvier put biology on a sounder footing, formulated the principles of subordination of organs to their function and established a zoological classification; Bertholet studied the composition of acids, Sadi Carnot thermodynamics and temperature equilibrium, and Arago electromagnetism and the polarisation of light; Daguerre laid the foundations of his fame with his dioramas, and Lamartine conquered literary society with his *Méditations Poétiques* – its elegaic rhythms soothed Talleyrand's sleepless nights.

The reign of Charles X – 1824–30
Painting flourished with the brilliant sweep of Delacroix' great canvases and Corot's landscapes. At the same time, Laplace was establishing the fundamental laws of mathematical analysis and providing a firm basis for astronomical mechanics, and Berlioz was composing his *Symphonie Fantastique*, the key work of the Romantic Movement in music. On 21 February 1830, Victor Hugo's drama *Hernani* provoked a literary battle between "moderns" and "classicals" in which the latter were temporarily routed. In the summer, Charles' press ordinances provoked a crisis which led to his abdication; he was succeeded by Louis Philippe, a member of the cadet branch of the Bourbons.

Reign of Louis-Philippe – 1830–48
During the 1830s, the mathematician Evariste Galois put forward the theory of sets; Victor Hugo wrote *Notre-Dame de Paris* and Alfred de Musset *Caprices*. Chopin, the darling of Parisian society, composed scherzos, waltzes and his celebrated Polonaises. In 1838, while on holiday in Paris, Stendhal wrote *The Charterhouse of Parma*, a masterpiece of psychological observation which can be read on a number of levels. The first news agency was founded by Charles Havas. In 1839, a railway line was opened between Paris and St-Germain. The 1840s saw the publication of the *Mysteries of Paris* by Eugène Sue, the *Count of Monte Cristo* and The *Three Musketeers* by Dumas and many of the works of Balzac's prodigious Human Comedy as well as the *Treatise on Parasitology* by Raspail; the abuses of the July monarchy were satirised in the drawings of Daumier.

At the age of 79, Chateaubriand brought his finely chiselled *Memories from beyond the Tomb* to a triumphant conclusion. On 23 February in 1848, the barricades went up on the Boulevard des Capucines and the monarchy fell; the next day, at the City Hall, amid scenes of wild enthusiasm, Lamartine saluted the tricolour, "the flag which has spread the name of France, freedom and glory around the wide world".

Second Republic and Second Empire (1848–1870)

Second Republic
The abolition of the National Workshops in June 1848 led to rioting in the St-Antoine district, in which the archbishop of Paris was killed. In 1849, Léon Foucault proved the rotation and spherical nature of the earth by means of a pendulum (the experiment was repeated in 1855 from the dome of the Panthéon).

On 2 December 1851 the short life of the Second Republic was ended by a *coup d'état*.

Second Empire – 1852–70
Two great exhibitions (in 1855 and 1867) proclaimed the prosperity France enjoyed under the rule of Bonaparte's nephew, Napoleon III. **Baron Haussmann**, Prefect of the *département* of the Seine, was responsible for an ambitious programme of public works which transformed the capital, giving it many of the features which now seem quintessentially Parisian. Among them were the laying out of the Bois de Boulogne and the Bois de Vincennes, and the building of railway stations and the North Wing of the Louvre. But the Baron is remembered above all for the ruthless surgery he performed on the capital's ancient urban tissue, opening up new focal points (Place de l'Opéra) and linking them with great axial roadways (Grands

©UPPA/Photoshot

Paris Commune - the Vendome Column pulled down on 16th May 1871

Boulevards), splendid exercises in traffic engineering and crowd control.

In 1852, Alexandre Dumas wrote *The Lady of the Camellias* at the same time as Rudé was working on the memorial to Marshal Ney, which was to be placed on the spot where the great soldier had been executed in 1815; in Rodin's opinion, it was Paris' finest statue. In 1857 Baudelaire, the first poet of the teeming modern metropolis, published *Les Fleurs du Mal (The Flowers of Evil)*.

In 1859, Gounod presented *Faust* at the Opéra Lyrique. In 1860, Étienne Lenoir registered his first patent for the internal combustion engine.

The year 1863 was marked by the scandals caused by Manet's *Déjeuner sur l'herbe* and *Olympia*; Baltard masked the masterly iron structure of the St-Augustin Church with the stone cladding still obligatory in a religious building. In 1896 Pierre de Coubertin created the International Olympic Committee.

Republican Continuity (1870 to the present day)

On 4 September 1870, the mob which had invaded the National Assembly was led by Gambetta to the City Hall where the Republic was proclaimed. The new government busied itself in preparing to defend Paris against the advancing Prussians; the St-Cloud château was set on fire and a fierce battle took place at Le Bourget.

The ensuing siege subjected the population of Paris to terrible hardships; food ran out and the winter was exceptionally severe. The city surrendered on 28 January 1871.

The revolutionary **Commune** was ruthlessly suppressed by military force, not before the Communards had burnt down the City Hall, the Tuileries and the Audit Office (Cours des Comptes – on the site of what is now the Orsay Museum), pulled down the column in the Place Vendôme and shot their prisoners at the Hostages' Wall in the Rue Haxo. They made their last stand in the Père-Lachaise Cemetery, where those of their number who had survived the bitter fighting were summarily executed at the Federalists' Wall (Mur des Fédérés). But political institutions were re-established and the nation revived; the Republic was consolidated as France's political regime, notwithstanding Marshal Pétain's so-called French State (État Français), Nazi occupation and the provisional government following the end of WW II.

Third Republic – Carpeaux sculpted the Four Corners of the World for the Observatory Fountain, and Émile Littré completed the publication of his renowned *Dictionary of the French Language*. Bizet wrote *L'Arlésienne (the Woman of Arles)* for the Odéon theatre and followed it with *Carmen*, based on a short story by Mérimée.

In 1874, Degas painted *The Dancing Class* and Monet *Impression: Rising Sun*, which, when exhibited by his dealer Nadar, led to the coining of the initially derisive term Impressionism. Later, Renoir worked at the Moulin de la Galette, and Puvis de Chavannes decorated the walls of the Panthéon. The public applauded Delibes' innovatory *Coppélia* and *Lakmé*. Rodin created the *Thinker*, followed by figures of Balzac and Victor Hugo.

In 1879, Seulecq put forward the principle of sequential transmission on which television is based and Pasteur completed his vast body of work. Seurat's Grande Jatte heralded the establishment of the Pointillist school of painting. In the following year, 1887, Antoine founded the Free Theatre (Théâtre libre) based on spontaneous expression. The engineer Gustave Eiffel completed his great tower, centrepiece of the Universal Exhibition of 1889. In the century's final decade, Toulouse-Lautrec painted cabaret scenes and Pissarro Parisian townscapes, and Forain gained fame as a marvellous caricaturist. In the Catholic Institute, Édouard Branly discovered radio-conductors.

In 1891, René Panhard built the first petrol-engined motor car, which drove right across Paris.

In 1898, the 21-year-old Louis Renault built his first car, then founded his Billancourt factory; in 1902 he patented a turbocharger. The factory turned out cars, lorries, planes and, in 1917, light tanks which contributed to the German defeat in 1918. Nationalised at the end of WW II, the firm continued to produce vehicles in large numbers.

In October 1898 Pierre and Marie Curie succeeded in isolating radium and established the atomic character of radioactivity; their laboratory was a shed which has since disappeared, but its outline is shown in the paving pattern in the courtyard of the school at No 10 Rue Vauquelin. At the same time, Henri Bergson was teaching philosophy at the Collège de France and Langevin was conducting his investigations into ionised gases (in 1915, he was to use ultrasonic waves in the detection of sub-

marines); a combination of steel, stone and glass was employed by Girault in the construction of the exhibition halls (the Grand Palais and the Petit Palais) for the 1900 Exhibition; this occasion also saw the bridging of the Seine by the great flattened arch of the Pont Alexandre III. In 1900, Gustave Charpentier put on a musical romance *Louise*; with its lyrical realism and popular appeal it was a great "hit" of the time.

In 1902, Debussy's *Pelléas et Mélisande* was produced at the Salle Favart of the Comic Opera. In 1906, Santos-Dumont succeeded in taking off in a heavier-than-air machine, staying aloft for 21 seconds, and covering a distance of 220m/721.7ft.

Dalou's bronze group entitled *The Triumph of the Republic* graced the Place de la Nation, while at Montparnasse the re-erected Wine Pavilion from the 1900 Exhibition provided lodgings and studios for Soutine, Zadkine, Chagall, Modigliani and Léger; other innovative artists included the sculptor Maillol and the painter Utrillo, while Brancusi's work was evolving away from cubism towards abstraction *(The Sleeping Muse)*; the Perret brothers built the Théâtre des Champs-Élysées in reinforced concrete; its façade was adorned with eight relief panels by Bourdelle.

The theatre was opened in 1913 with a performance of Stravinsky's *Rite of Spring*; its music and choreography outraged an unprepared public.

In 1914 the construction of the Sacré-Cœur Church (begun in 1878 by the architect Abadie) on the Montmartre heights was completed. On the evening of 31 July, the eve of general mobilisation, Jean Jaurès was assassinated.

The World Wars

World War I (1914–18) put civilians as well as soldiers to the severest of tests; after three years of conflict, Clemenceau was made head of government, and, by restoring the country's confidence, earned the title of Father of Victory.

In 1920, the interment of an unknown soldier at the Arc de Triomphe marked France's recognition of the sacrifices made by her ordinary soldiers, the uns-haven *poilus* of the trenches.

In the course of the 1920s, Le Corbusier built La Roche Villa, and Bourdelle sculpted *France* at the Palais de Tokyo; Georges Rouault, with his predilection for religious themes, completed his *Miserere*, and Landowsky carved the figure of St Geneviève for the Tournelle Bridge; in the course of a fortnight, Maurice Ravel composed *Boléro* for the dancer Ida Rubinstein; with its subtle instrumentation and rhythmic precision it popularised the name of this aristocratic composer; Poulbot created the archetypal Montmartre urchin; Cocteau wrote *Les Enfants Terribles*; the dynamism of the theatrical scene was marked by many fine actors and producers, notably the Cartel of Four (Cartel des Quatre) consisting of Charles Dullin (at the Sarah Bernhardt Theatre), Gaston Baty (at the Montparnasse), Louis Jouvet (at the Champs-Élysées then the Athénée) and Georges Pitoëff (at the Mathurins).

At the end of the 19C, Émile Roux had studied the causes of and cure for diphtheria; he was now in charge of the Pasteur Institute, and brought to Paris the scientists Calmette and Guérin who had worked on vaccination against tuberculosis.

In 1934, André Citroën brought out the Traction Avant (Front-Wheel Drive) car; 15 years previously, his Type A had been Europe's first mass-produced car; 21 years later, he was to unveil the innovative DS 19.

In 1940, during **World War II**, Paris was bombed, then **occupied** by the German army. Between 16 and 17 July 1942, numerous French Jews, victims of the Nazi racial myth, were rounded up at the Vélodrome d'Hiver prior to their deportation eastwards for extermination; 4 500 members of the Resistance also met their deaths in the clearing on Mount Valérien where the National Memorial of Fighting France now stands. Finally, on 19 August 1944, Paris was **liberated**.

Fourth and Fifth Republics – In 1950, Alfred Kastler, working in the laboratories of the École Normale Supérieure,

succeeded in verifying the principle of "optical pumping", which has subsequently become the basis of one of the methods of producing a laser beam. The *Symphony for a Single Man* by Maurice Béjart, presented at the Étoile Theatre on 3 August 1955, was danced to *musique concrète* composed by Pierre Henry and Pierre Schaeffer, and led to many innovations in ballet throughout Europe. Since 1945 the influence of Le Corbusier (there are a few examples of his genius in Paris: Villa La Roche, Cité Universitaire pavilions) has given a new impetus to architecture: new forms (Maison de Radio-France), structures on piles (UNESCO), sweeping rooflines (CNIT building). The present trend is for glass buildings (GAN and Manhattan towers, Centre Georges-Pompidou, Institut du Monde Arabe).

The use of pre-stressed concrete led to technical advances (Palais des Congrès, Tour Montparnasse). But in the main architecture becomes an integral part of town planning: buildings are designed to fit into an overall plan: remodelling of an area (Maine-Montparnasse, les Halles, la Villette, Bercy) or new project (la Défense).

Grand new town-planning initiatives have also been implemented: the Opera house at la Bastille, the Ministry of Finance buildings at Bercy, the Grande Arche at la Défense and the Bibliothèque nationale de France François-Mitterrand at Tolbiac are distinctive modern landmarks.

THE CITY'S MONUMENTS
CIVIL ARCHITECTURE
Palais du Louvre★★★
See Musée du Louvre.

Neither the Merovingians nor the Carolingians, nor even the Capet kings lived in the old Louvre, which then lay beyond the city limits; instead, they preferred the Law Courts (Palais de Justice), their *hôtels* in the Marais, the manor at Vincennes, their own châteaux or those of their liegemen in the Loire Valley.

Contributions of the Heads of State
Floor plan below shows the evolution of the Louvre Palace.

453

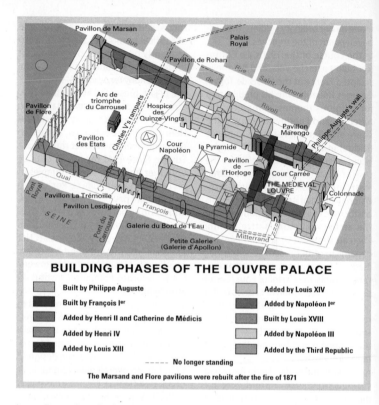

Pavillon de Marsan
Palais Royal
Pavillon de Rohan
Arc de triomphe du Carrousel
Hospice des Quinze-Vingts
Pavillon de Flore
Charles V's ramparts
Philippe-Auguste's wall
Pavillon des Etats
Pavillon Marengo
Cour Napoléon
la Pyramide
Pavillon de l'Horloge
Quai
Cour Carrée
THE MEDIEVAL LOUVRE
Colonnade
Pont Royal
Pavillon La Trémoille
Pavillon Lesdiguières
François
Galerie du Bord de l'Eau
SEINE
Pont du Carrousel
Petite Galerie (Galerie d'Apollon)
Mitterrand

BUILDING PHASES OF THE LOUVRE PALACE

- Built by Philippe Auguste
- Built by François Ier
- Added by Henri II and Catherine de Médicis
- Added by Henri IV
- Added by Louis XIII
- Added by Louis XIV
- Added by Napoléon Ier
- Built by Louis XVIII
- Added by Napoléon III
- Added by the Third Republic

----- No longer standing

The Marsand and Flore pavilions were rebuilt after the fire of 1871

It was **François I** who had the old Louvre pulled down, and, in 1546, commissioned Pierre Lescot to build the palace which was to become the residence of the kings of France. Lescot's work is regarded as the most prestigious part of the Louvre; it was he who brought the Italian Renaissance style, already flowering on the Loire, to the banks of the Seine; to the façade he built, sculptor Jean Goujon added the nymphs of the Fountain of the Innocents.

When Charles IX came to the throne at age ten, the Florentine **Catherine de' Medici** was made Regent. At first she lived in the Louvre on the floor since known as the Queens' Lodging (Logis des Reines), but ordered Philibert Delorme (succeeded by Jean Bullant) to build the Tuileries.

The site of this new palace was some 500m/550yd away, just beyond the fortifications built by Charles V, and, to link it with the Louvre, Catherine requested a covered way following the line of the Seine, with a smaller gallery at right angles.

Charles IX completed the southwestern part of the Cour Carrée, the courtyard which is the most impressive part of the Old Louvre to remain, embellishing it with his monogram (K = Carolus).

Henri III was responsible for the southeastern part of the Cour Carrée (which bears the monogram H). **Henri IV**, from 1595, had the work on the Great Gallery (Grande Galerie) continued by Louis Métezeau. He also had the Flora Pavilion (Pavillon de Flore) built by Jacques II Androuet Du Cerceau, completed the Small Gallery (Petite Galerie) (its first floor was occupied by Marie de' Medici and Anne of Austria, hence the monogram AA), and erected the upper part of the Henri III wing in the Cour Carrée, marked by his monogram.

Louis XIII continued with the construction of the Cour Carrée. At the same time as he was building the Sorbonne and the Palais-Royal, the architect Lemercier

Detail of the façade of Cour Napoléon

S. Sauvignier/MICHELIN

erected the Clock Pavilion (Pavillon de l'Horloge) together with the northwest corner of the courtyard, a Classical response to Lescot's work (the monogram LA = Louis and Anne). Anne of Austria lived in the Queens' Lodging; the bathroom designed for her by Lemercier now houses the Venus de Milo. In 1638, Charles V's rampart was razed and the moat filled in.

On the death of Louis XIII, Anne became Regent and moved to the Palais-Royal with the young **Louis XIV**. Nine years later, however, having been made aware of the palace's vulnerability by the uprising of the nobility (the Fronde), she took up residence in the Louvre again.

The young king, who had married Maria-Theresa, moved into the Tuileries in 1664 for three years. The architect Le Vau, working on the Louvre, his personal style evident in the Small Gallery, started again after a fire in 1661, and in the Apollo Gallery; he continued the enclosure of the Cour Carrée by adding a storey onto the western part of the north wing (monogram LMT = Louis, Maria-Theresa) and by building the Marengo Pavilion (Pavillon Marengo) (with the monogram LB = Louis XIV de Bourbon).

But the palace still needed a monumental façade facing the city; **Colbert** had refused permission for a number of projects designed with this in mind.

An appeal was made to the master-architect of the Italian Baroque, Bernini, already 67 years old. But his proposals were turned down too, since they would have either destroyed or clashed with Lescot's façade. In the end it fell to Claude Perrault, aided by Le Brun and Le Vau, to design an imposing colonnaded façade. In 1682, the king left Paris for Versailles. The Louvre now housed the Academy as well as a less desirable population. In 1715, the Court returned to Paris for a period of seven years; the young King Louis XV lived in the Tuileries and the Regent in the Palais-Royal. Coustou continued the work on the colonnade.

After the **Revolution**, the Convention used the Louvre theatre for its deliberations. The Committee of Public Safety (Comité du Salut public) convened in the state rooms of the Tuileries, which were subsequently appropriated for his own use by Napoleon.

Napoleon I took up residence in the Tuileries. Percier and Fontaine completed the Cour Carrée by adding a second floor to the north and south wings. They also provided a wing linking the Rohan and Marsan Pavilions and gave it a façade identical to Du Cerceau's Grande Galerie, as well as enlarging the Place du Carrousel to enable Napoleon to review his legions and embellishing it with a triumphal arch commemorating

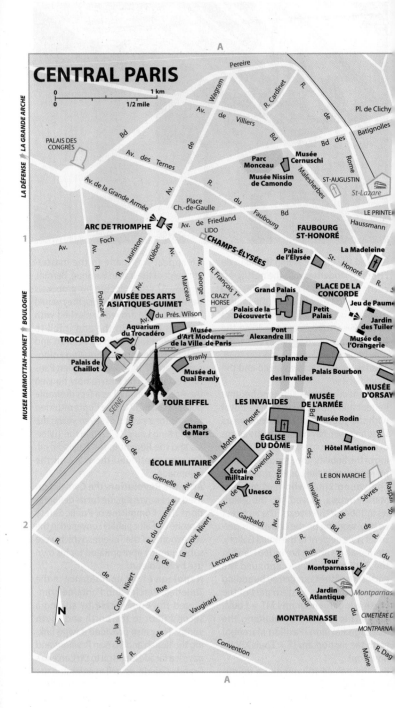

CENTRAL PARIS

0   1 km
0   1/2 mile

LA DÉFENSE ⬥ LA GRANDE ARCHE

MUSÉE MARMOTTAN-MONET ⬥ BOULOGNE

Pereire

Wagram

R. Cardinet

Av.   de   Villiers

Pl. de Clichy

Batignolles

Bd

Bd   des

Rome

PALAIS DES CONGRÈS

Av. des   Ternes

de

Av. de la Grande Armée

Parc Monceau

Musée Cernuschi

Musée Nissim de Camondo

Malesherbes

ST-AUGUSTIN

St-Lazare

LE PRINTE

Place Ch.-de-Gaulle

du   Faubourg

Bd

Haussmann

ARC DE TRIOMPHE

Av.   de   Friedland

LIDO

CHAMPS-ÉLYSÉES

FAUBOURG ST-HONORÉ

La Madeleine

Foch

Av.

Av.

R.

Lauriston

Kléber

R.

Av.

Poincaré

Marceau

George V

R. François 1er

Palais de l'Élysée

St-

Honoré

R.

MUSÉE DES ARTS ASIATIQUES-GUIMET

Av.   du   Prés. Wilson

CRAZY HORSE

Grand Palais

Palais de la Découverte

Petit Palais

PLACE DE LA CONCORDE

Jeu de Paume

Jardin des Tuiler

TROCADÉRO

Aquarium du Trocadéro

Musée d'Art Moderne de la Ville de Paris

Pont Alexandre III

Musée de l'Orangerie

Palais de Chaillot

Branly

Musée du Quai Branly

SEINE

Quai

Bd   de

Esplanade

Palais Bourbon

MUSÉE D'ORSAY

TOUR EIFFEL

Champ de Mars

des Invalides

LES INVALIDES

Piquet

MUSÉE DE L'ARMÉE

Bd

Musée Rodin

ÉCOLE MILITAIRE

Grenelle

Av.   de

Bd

École militaire

la Motte

Lowendal

ÉGLISE DU DÔME

Breteuil

des

Invalides

Av.

de

Hôtel Matignon

LE BON MARCHÉ

Sèvres

Raspail

⚜ Unesco

Garibaldi

Av.

de

Bd

de

R. du Commerce

R. de

R.

la Croix Nivert

Lecourbe

Bd

Rue

Av.

du

Tour Montparnasse

Montparnas

R.

Croix Nivert

Rue

la

de

Vaugirard

Pasteur

Jardin Atlantique

du

CIMETIÈRE D

MONTPARNA

R.   R.

de la

Convention

MONTPARNASSE

R. Dag

Maine

N

A

A

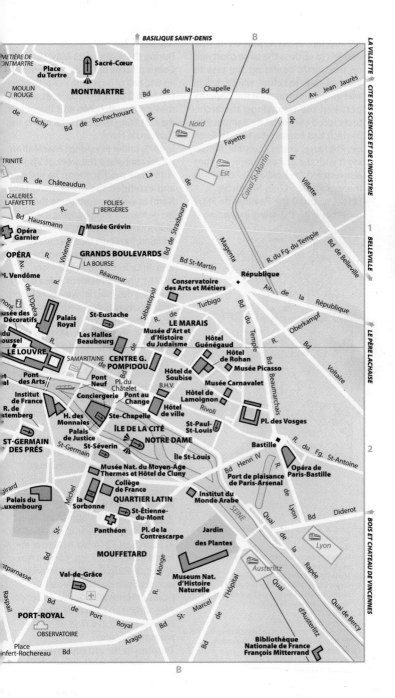

CIMETIÈRE DE
MONTMARTRE

Place
du Tertre

Sacré-Cœur

MOULIN
ROUGE

MONTMARTRE

BASILIQUE SAINT-DENIS

B

Bd   de   la   Chapelle   Bd

Av. Jean Jaurès

de   Clichy   Bd   de   Rochechouart   Bd   de

Nord

Fayette

Est

Canal St-Martin

Villette

TRINITÉ

R.   de   Châteaudun

La

de

GALERIES
LAFAYETTE

FOLIES-
BERGÈRES

Bd   Haussmann   R.

Musée Grévin

Bd de Strasbourg

Magenta

R. du Fg. du Temple   Bd de Belleville

Opéra
Garnier

OPÉRA   R.

Vivienne

GRANDS BOULEVARDS

LA BOURSE

Bd St-Martin

République

Av.   de   la   République

LA VILLETTE
CITÉ DES SCIENCES ET DE L'INDUSTRIE

BELLEVILLE

1

Pl. Vendôme

de

l'Opéra

R.

Réaumur

Conservatoire
des Arts et Métiers

Turbigo

Bd du Temple

Oberkampf

Bd

Voltaire

LE PÈRE LACHAISE

honoré

Musée des
Décoratifs

Roussel

LE LOUVRE

Palais
Royal

St-Eustache

Les Halles
Beaubourg

Sébastopol

R.   de

LE MARAIS

Musée d'Art et
d'Histoire
du Judaïsme

Hôtel
Guénégaud

Hôtel
de Rohan

Musée Picasso

SAMARITAINE

de

CENTRE G.
POMPIDOU

Hôtel de
Soubise

B.H.V.

Musée Carnavalet

Beaumarchais

Pont
des Arts

Pont
Neuf

Pl. du
Châtelet

Hôtel de
Lamoignon

Institut
de France

R. de
stemberg

Conciergerie

Pont au
Change

Hôtel
de ville

Rivoli

St-Paul-
St-Louis

Pl. des Vosges

ST-GERMAIN
DES PRÉS

H. des
Monnaies

Palais
de Justice

Ste-Chapelle

ÎLE DE LA CITÉ

NOTRE DAME

St-Germain   St-Séverin

Île St-Louis

Bastille

R.   du Fg. St-Antoine

2

Opéra de
Paris-Bastille

girard

Michel

Musée Nat. du Moyen-Age
Thermes et Hôtel de Cluny

Collège
de France

QUARTIER LATIN

Institut du
Monde Arabe

Bd Henri IV

Port de plaisance
de Paris-Arsenal

de   Lyon   Bd   Diderot

BOIS ET CHÂTEAU DE VINCENNES

Palais du
Luxembourg

la
Sorbonne

St-Étienne-
du-Mont

Panthéon

Pl. de la
Contrescarpe

Jardin
des Plantes

SEINE

Quai

de   la   Rapée

Lyon

Austerlitz

ntparnasse

Raspail

MOUFFETARD

Val-de-Grâce

R. Monge

Museum Nat.
d'Histoire
Naturelle

Quai

de l'Hôpital

St-   Marcel

Quai   d'Austerlitz

Quai de Bercy

PORT-ROYAL

OBSERVATOIRE

Bd   de   Port   Royal   Bd   St-   de

Arago   Bd

Bibliothèque
Nationale de France
François Mitterrand

Place
nfert-Rochereau   Bd

B

the Emperor's victories, its design based on the Arch of Septimus Severus.

All of the "restored" monarchs lived in the Tuileries, as did **Napoleon III**, who decided to enclose the large courtyard on the north, confiding the task to Visconti, then to Lefuel, whose design was intended to conceal the disparity between the two wings; the architects razed the Hôtel de Rambouillet 3 which had housed the literary *Salon des Précieuses* under Louis XIII, replacing it with the present pavilions. They also restored the Pavillon de Rohan (the monogram LN = Louis Napoleon).

Lefuel restored the Pavillon de Flore together with the wing extending it

ÉGLISE SAINT LOUIS DES INVALIDES

1) Tomb of Joseph Bonaparte, elder brother of Napoleon, King of Spain.
2) Monument to Vauban by Etex. The Emperor himself commanded that the military architect's heart be brought to the Invalides.
3) Marshal Foch's tomb by Landowsky.
4) Ornate high altar surrounded by twisted columns and covered by a baldaquin by Visconti. Vaulting decoration by Coypel.
5) General Duroc's tomb.
6) General Bertrand's tomb.
7) At the back – the heart of La Tour d'Auvergne, first grenadier of the Republic; in the centre, the tomb of Marshal Lyautey.
8) Marshal Turenne's tomb by Tuby.
9) St Jerome's Chapel (carvings by Nicolas Coustou). The tomb at the foot of the wall is Jerome Bonaparte's, Napoleon's younger brother and King of Westphalia.
10) The Emperor's tomb.

eastwards; his design is a not altogether successful copy of Métezeau's work; the gallery bears the monogram NE (= Napoleon, Eugénie).

During the night of 23 May 1871, the **Communards** burnt down the Tuileries and half of Napoleon I's North Wing (Aile Nord de Napoleon I), as well as the Pavillons Richelieu and Turgot and the East Wing (Aile Est) attached to the Pavillon de Flore.

In 1875, under **President MacMahon**, Lefuel continued the work of Visconti with some modifications; he restored and extended the North Wing (Aile Nord) as well as refurbishing the Pavillon de Marsan and providing it with the monogram RF (République Française); in addition, he rebuilt the Riverside Gallery (Galerie du Bord de l'Eau) and the Pavillons de La Trémoille and de Flore.

In 1883, under **President Jules Grévy**, the Palais des Tuileries was demolished; and the city was deprived of one of the key buildings in its history.

In 1984 **President Mitterrand** embarked on the "Grand Louvre and Pyramide" project. He commissioned the architect Ming Pei to expand the services and reception area of what had now become a world-famous art museum. Beneath the Cour Napoleon, a vast hall offering information and documentation services is lit up by the glass pyramid **(Pyramide★★)** which marks the main entrance to the museum.

Hôtel National des Invalides★★★

&♿🕐*Open daily Oct–Mar 10am–5pm (5.30pm Sun); Apr–Sept 10am–6pm (6.30pm Sun).* 🕐*Closed 1st Mon of the month in Oct–Jun, 1 Jan, 1 May, 1 Nov, 25 Dec.* ₪*€9 incl. audioguide (price includes Église du Dôme, Musée de l'Armée, l'Historial de Gaulle, Musée des Plans-Reliefs and Musée de l'Ordre de la Libération).* ☎*0810 11 33 99. www.invalides.org.*

The plans for the vast edifice were drawn up by Libéral Bruant between 1671 and 1676; their implementation was placed under the direction of Louvois. The main façade, nearly 200m/650ft long, is majestic without being monotonous; it is dominated by an attic storey decorated with masks and dormer windows in the form of trophies. Napoleon used to parade his troops in the main courtyard (Cour d'honneur); here the South Pavilion (Pavillon du Midi) forms the façade of the Église St-Louis, the resting-place of some of France's great soldiers; the interior is hung with flags taken from the enemy. It was here, in 1837, that Berlioz' *Requiem* was performed for the first time.

Église du Dôme★★★
🕐 *Same as Les Invalides*
The church of Les Invalides, designed by the master of proportion, **Jules-Hardouin Mansart**, was begun in 1677. With its beautiful gilded dome, it is one of the great works of the Louis XIV style, bringing to a peak of perfection the Classicism already introduced in the churches of the Sorbonne and the Val-de-Grâce, an ecclesiastical equivalent of the secular architecture of Versailles. In 1735, Robert de Cotte completed the building by replacing the planned south colonnade and portico with the splendid vista offered by the Avenue de Breteuil. On the far side he laid out the Esplanade, and set up the guns captured at Vienna in 1805 by Napoleon to defend the gardens and fire ceremonial salvoes on great national occasions.

The church became a military necropolis after Napoleon had Marshal Turenne (d. 1675) buried here. Note the memorial to Vauban, the great military architect, and the tomb of Marshal Foch.

In Visconti's crypt of green granite from the Vosges stands the "cloak of glory", the unmarked **Tombeau de Napoleon** completed in 1861 to receive the Emperor's mortal remains. In 1940, the body of Napoleon's son, King of Rome and Duke of Reichstadt, was brought here too. Also housed in Hôtel nacional des Invalides is the **Musée de l'Armée** (🕐 *same as Église du Dôme*).

Arc de Triomphe★★★
pl. Charles-de-Gaulle. 🕐 *Open daily Apr –Sept 10am–11pm; Oct–Mar 10am– 10.30pm.* 🕐 *Closed public holidays.* 💶 €9.50. 📞 01 55 37 73 77.
Together with the **Place Charles de Gaulle**★★★ and its 12 radiating avenues, the great triumphal arch makes up one of Paris' principal focal points, known as the **Étoile** (Star).

The façades of the buildings around were designed in a harmonious style by Hittorff as part of Haussmann's plans for the metropolis.

The Arc de Triomphe was the scene on 14 July 1919 of the great victory parade and, on 11 November 1920, of the burial of the Unknown Soldier. Three years later the flame of remembrance

Église du Dôme, Hôtel National des Invalides

Y. Kanazawa/Michelin

was kindled for the first time. The arch is ornamented with sculpture, notably Rude's masterpiece of 1836 known as the *Marseillaise*, depicting volunteers departing to defend France from the invading Prussians (1792).

Place de la Concorde★★★

A perfect expression of the Louis XV style, it was designed by Ange-Jacques Gabriel in 1755 and completed over a period of 20 years. On 21 January 1793, near where the statue of Brest now stands, the guillotine was set up for the execution of Louis XVI and other victims of the Terror.

The square owes its monumental character to the colonnaded buildings defining it to the north, to its octagonal plan, and to the massive pedestals intended for allegorical statues of French cities. Two great urban **axes**★★★ intersect here: one runs from the Église de la Madeleine to the Palais-Bourbon, the other from *Coysevox's Winged Horses (Chevaux ailés)*, which mark the entrance to the Tuileries, to the magnificent marble sculptures (copies) by Nicolas and Guillaume Coustou which flank the Champs-Élysées. The pink granite Luxor obelisk (Obélisque de Louksor), 3 300 years old, covered with hieroglyphics, was brought here from Egypt in 1836. The square's fountains adorned with statues are particularly fine.

Tour Eiffel★★★

7 r. de Belloy. Open daily: Lift: mid-Jun–Aug 9am–12.45am; Sept–mid-Jun 9.30am–11.45pm. €8.50 (children, €6.50 (elevator to 2nd floor), €13.50 and €12 (elevator to Top floor); Stairs 1st and 2nd floors only, €5 and €4.
01 44 11 23 23. www.tour-eiffel.fr.

The Eiffel Tower is Paris' most famous symbol. The first proposal for a tower was made in 1884; construction was completed in 26 months and the tower opened in March 1889 for the Universal Exhibition (Exposition universelle) of that year.

The structure is evidence of Eiffel's imagination and daring; in spite of its weight of 7 000 tonnes, height of 320.75m/ 1 051ft and the use of 2.5 million rivets, it is a masterpiece of lightness. It is difficult to believe that the tower actually weighs less than the volume of air surrounding it and that the pressure it exerts on the ground is that of a man sitting on a chair.

Palais de Justice and Conciergerie★★

2 bd du Palais. **Palais** *open daily 8.30am–6pm.* Closed public holidays.
01 44 32 52 52. **Conciergerie** Open daily 9.30am–6pm. Closed 1 Jan, 1 May, 25 Dec. €7.
01 53 40 60 80.

Known as the Palace (Palais), this is the principal seat of civil and judicial autho-

Place de la Concorde

S. Sauvignier/Michelin

rity. Before becoming the royal palace of the rulers of medieval France, it had been the residence of Roman governors, Merovingian kings and the children of Clovis, the mint of Dagobert and Duke Eudes' fortress.

The Capetian kings built a chapel and fortified the palace with a keep. Philippe le Bel (the Fair) entrusted Enguerrand de Marigny with the building of the Conciergerie as well as with the extension and embellishment of the palace; its Gothic halls of 1313 were widely admired. Later, Charles V built the Clock Tower (Tour de l'Horloge), the city's first public clock; he also installed Parliament here, the country's supreme court. Survivals from this period include the Great Hall (Salle des gens d'Armes) with its fine capitals, the Guard Room (Salle des Gardes) with its magnificent pillars, and the kitchens with their monumental corner fireplaces. The great hall on the first floor was restored by Salomon de Brosse after the fire of 1618; it was refurbished again in 1840 and once more after the fire of 1871.

The First Civil Court is in the former Parliamentary Grand Chamber (Grand'chambre du parlement), the place where the kings dispensed justice, where the 16-year-old Louis XIV dictated his orders to Parliament, where that body in its turn demanded the convocation of the States-General in 1788, and where the Revolutionary Tribunal was set up under the public prosecutor, Fouquier-Tinville.

The entrance to the royal palace was once guarded by the twin towers gracing the north front of the great complex; this is the oldest part of the building, albeit now hiding behind a 19C neo-Gothic façade.

The **Conciergerie** served as antechamber to the guillotine during the Terror, housing up to 1 200 detainees at any one time. The Galerie des Prisonniers (Prisoners' Gallery), Marie-Antoinette's cachot (cell) and the Chapelle des Girondins (Girondins' Chapel) are particularly moving.

☺ Where to Stay & Eat? ☺

Consult the red-cover *Michelin Guide Paris* and the *Michelin Green Guide Paris*.

Palais-Royal★★

6 r. de Montpensie.

In 1632, Richelieu ordered Lemercier to build the huge edifice which came to be known as the Palais Cardinal (Cardinal's Palace) when it was extended in 1639. It is remarkable for its impressive central façade, surmounted by allegorical statues and a curved pediment. On his deathbed, Richelieu bequeathed it to Louis XIII, whereupon its name was changed to the Palais-Royal. In 1783, Victor Louis laid out the charming formal gardens and the arcades which enclose them and which house a number of specialist shops and boutiques.

In 1986, Daniel Buren designed the arrangement of 260 columns, all of different height, which occupy the outer courtyard.

École Militaire★★

ave de Lowendal.

Though the original design could not be fully implemented because of lack of financial resources, the Military Academy by Jacques-Ange Gabriel is one of the outstanding examples of French 18C architecture. It was begun in 1752, financed in part by Mme de Pompadour, and completed in 1773. Under the Second Empire, cavalry and artillery buildings of nondescript design were added, together with the low-lying wings which frame the main building. True to its original function, it now houses the French Army's Staff College.

The superb main courtyard (**cour d'honneur**★), lined on either side by beautiful porticoes with paired columns, is approached via an exercise yard; the imposing central section and the projecting wings form a harmonious composition.

Panthéon★★

pl. du Panthéon. ⚫*Open daily Apr–Sept 10am–6.30pm; Oct–Mar 10am–6pm.* ⚫*Closed 1 Jan, 1 May, 25 Dec.* €8. ✆*01 44 32 18 00.* Guided tours *(1hr30min); reservations required.* ✆*01 44 54 19 30.*

In 1744, Louis XV had made a vow at Metz to replace the half-ruined church of St Geneviève's Abbey. Fourteen years later Soufflot began the construction of the new building on the highest point of the Left Bank. The scale of the building was such that its collapse was confidently predicted and the pretensions of its architect ridiculed. The present building has been much changed since Soufflot's day; its towers have gone, its pediments have been remodelled, its windows blocked up. In 1791, the Constituent Assembly closed the church to worshippers in order to convert it into the last resting place of the "great men of the epoch of French liberty".

Successively a church, a necropolis, headquarters of the Commune, and a lay temple, the Panthéon is representative of the time in which churches lost their dominant position in the urban landscape. Still crowned by Soufflot's dome, the great edifice is built in the shape of a Greek Cross. It has a fine portico with Corinthian columns and a pediment carved by David d'Angers in 1831. In the crypt are the tombs of the famous.

Opéra Garnier★★

1 pl. de l'Opéra. ⚫*Open daily 10am–5pm (mid Jul–Aug, 6pm).* €9. ⚫*Closed 1 Jan, 1 May and for special events.* ✆*0892 89 90 90. www.opera deparis.fr.*

This is the National Academy of Music, and was until 1990 France's premier home of opera. It opened in 1875 and it is the work of Charles Garnier, who had dreamed of creating an authentic Second Empire style. But the huge edifice, "more operatic than any opera" (Ian Nairn), magnificent though it was, lacked sufficient originality to inspire a new school of architecture. The interior, with its Great Staircase, foyer and auditorium, is of the utmost sumptuousness.

Garnier used marble from all the quarries of France, and there is a ceiling by Chagall.

Palais de Chaillot★★

pl. du Trocadéro.
This remarkable example of inter-war architecture was built for the 1937 Exhibition. Its twin pavilions are linked by a portico and extended by wings which curve to frame the wide terrace with its statues in gilded bronze.
From here there is a wonderful **view★★★** of Paris; in the foreground are the Trocadéro Gardens with their spectacular fountains, and beyond the curving river the Eiffel Tower, the Champ-de-Mars and the École Militaire. The Palais houses the **Théâtre de Chaillot** (✆*01 53 65 30 00. www.theatre-chaillot.fr)*, the **Musée de l'Homme★★**, (closed for renovation until 2012. ✆*01 44 05 72 72; www.mnhn.fr)*, **Musée de la Marine★★** (€9. ✆*01 53 65 69 69; www.musee-marine.fr)*, **Musée des Monuments Français★★** (€8. ✆*01 58 51 52 00. www.citechaillot.fr)* and **Musée du Cinéma Henri-Langlois★** (✆*45 53 21 86. www.paris.org/Musees/Cinema)*.

ECCLESIASTICAL ARCHITECTURE
Cathédrale Notre-Dame★★★

r. du cloître Notre-Dame. ⚫**Cathedral** *open Mon–Fri 8am–6.45pm, Sat–Sun 8am–7.15pm.* No charge. Guided *tours Wed & Thu 2pm, Sat 2.30pm.* **Towers** *open Apr–Sept 10am–6.30pm; Oct–Mar 10am–5.30pm.* €6. ✆*01 53 10 07 00. www.notredamedeparis.fr.*
People have worshipped here for 2000 years and the present building has witnessed the great events of French history.
Work on the cathedral was begun by Maurice de Sully in 1163. Notre-Dame is the last great galleried church building and one of the first with flying buttresses. In 1245 the bulk of the work was complete and St Louis held a ceremony for the knighting of his son and also placed the Crown of Thorns in the cathedral until the Sainte-Chapelle

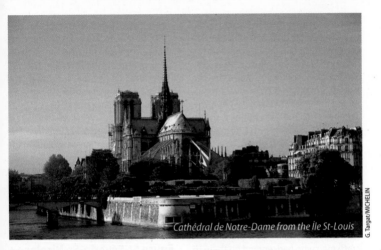

Cathédral de Notre-Dame from the Île St-Louis

G. Targat/MICHELIN

was ready to receive it. In 1250 the twin towers were finished.

In 1430, the cathedral was the setting for the coronation of the young Henry VI of England as King of France; in 1455, a ceremony was conducted to rehabilitate Joan of Arc; in 1558, Mary Stuart was crowned here on becoming Queen of France by her marriage to François II and, in 1572, the Huguenot Henri IV waited at the door as his bride, Marguerite of Valois, stood alone in the chancel; in 1594 the king converted to the Catholic faith.

The great building was not spared mutilations of various kinds; in 1699 the choir screen was demolished, and later some of the original stained glass was removed to let in more light, and the central portal demolished (18C) to allow processions to move more freely. During the Revolution statues were destroyed and the cathedral declared a Temple of Reason. It was in a much-dilapidated building that Napoleon Bonaparte crowned himself Emperor and the King of Rome was baptised.

In 1831, public opinion was alerted by Hugo's novel *Notre-Dame de Paris* to the state of the building, and in 1841 Louis-Philippe charged Viollet-le-Duc with its restoration. In the space of 24 years, he completed his work in accordance with his own, idealised, vision of the Gothic style; though open to criticism, it needs to be seen in the context of the

wholesale demolition of the medieval Île-de-la-Cité and its replacement with administrative buildings.

The magnificent Cloister Portal (Portail du Cloître – north transept) is 30 years older than the west front portals; with its richly carved gables and smiling figure of the Virgin – the only original large sculpture to have survived – it demonstrates clearly how far the art of sculpture had advanced over the period. At the beginning of the 14C, the bold array of flying buttresses was sent soaring over ambulatory and galleries to hold in place the high vaults of the east end.

Above the Kings' Gallery is the great rose window, still with its medieval glass. An enterprise of considerable daring – it was the largest such window of its time – its design is so accomplished that it shows no sign of distortion after 700 years and has often been imitated. Inside, the rose window has particularly fine stained glass of a deep bluish-mauve.

Sainte-Chapelle★★★

4 bd du Palais. ⚊ ⏱ *Open Mar–Oct 9.30am–6pm; Nov–Feb 9.30am–5pm.* ⏱ *Closed 1 Jan, 1 May, 1 and 25 Dec.* ⚊€8. ☎01 53 40 60 80. www.monum.fr. Only 80 years separate this definitive masterpiece of the High Gothic from the Transitional Gothic of Notre-Dame, but the difference is striking; in the lightness and clarity of its structure, the Sainte-Chapelle pushes Gothic ideas to the limit. The chapel was built on the orders of St Louis to house the recently acquired relics of the Passion within the precincts of the royal palace; it was completed in the record time of 33 months. The upper chapel resembles a shrine with walls made almost entirely of remarkable stained glass covering a total area of 618sqm/6 672sq ft; 1 134 different scenes are depicted, of which 720 are made of original glass. The windows rise to a height of 15m/49ft. By 1240, the stained glass at Chartres had been completed, and the king was thus able to call on the master-craftsmen who had worked on them to come to Paris; this explains the similarity between the glass of cathedral and of chapel, in terms of the scenes shown and the luminous colour which eclipses the simplicity of the design.

The theme is Christ's Passion, including its foretelling by the Prophets and by John the Baptist, together with the episodes which lead up to it. The original rose window is shown in a scene from the Très Riches Heures du Duc de Berry; the present rose window is a product of the Flamboyant Gothic, ordered by Charles VII, and showing the Apocalypse of St John. It is characteristic of its age in the design of its tracery and in the subtle variations of colour which had replaced the earlier method of juxtaposing a great number of small coloured panes. The glass of the Sainte-Chapelle has been much imitated, even in architecturally inappropriate situations.

Abbaye de St-Germain-des-Prés★★

pl. Saint-Germain des Prés.

This most venerable of the city's churches reveals more than visual delights to those who know something of the history of its ancient stones. With the exception of Clovis, the Merovingian kings were buried here. The church was subsequently destroyed by the Normans, but restored in the course of the 10C and 11C. Understandably, the tower rising above the west front

has a fortress-like character. Around 1160, the nave was enlarged and the chancel rebuilt in the new Gothic style. "Improvements" followed in the 17C (triforium and chancel windows), and in 1822 a somewhat over-zealous restoration took place.

But the church's years of glory were between 1631 and 1789, when the austere Congregation of St Maur made it a centre of learning and spirituality: the monks studied ancient inscriptions (epigraphy) and writing (paleography); the Church Fathers (Patristics), archaeology, cartography. Their library was confiscated at the time of the Revolution.

Église St-Séverin-St-Nicolas★★

3 r. Prêtres St Séverin.
www.saint-severin.com.

This much-loved Latin Quarter Church has features from a number of architectural styles. The lower part of the portal and the first three bays of the nave are High Gothic, while much of the rest of the building was remodelled in Flamboyant style (upper part of the tower, the remainder of the nave, the secondary aisle, the highly compartmentalised vaulting of the chancel and the famous spiral pillar in the ambulatory). In the 18C, the pillars in the chancel were clad in wood and marble.

Église St-Eustache★★

2 Impasse Saint-Eustache. ◷*Open Mon –Fri 9.30am–7pm, Sat 10am–7pm, Sun 9am–7pm. Audioguides available, suggested donation* ⊗€*3.* ✆*01 42 36 31 05. http://saint-eustache.org.*

This was once the richest church in Paris, centre of the parish which included the areas around the Palais-Royal and the Halles market; its layout was modelled on that of Notre-Dame when building began in 1532. But St-Eustache took over a hundred years to complete; tastes changed, and the Gothic skeleton of the great building is fleshed out with Renaissance finishes and detail.

The Flamboyant style is evident in the three-storey interior elevation, in the vaulting of the choir, crossing and nave, in the lofty side aisles and in the flying buttresses. The Renaissance is exemplified in the Corinthian columns and in the return to the use of semicircular arches, and Classicism in P. de Champaigne's choir windows and in Colbert's tomb, designed by Le Brun in collaboration with Coysevox and Tuby. In the Chapelle St-Joseph is the English sculptor Raymond Mason's colourful commemoration of the fruit and vegetable market's move out of Paris in 1969.

Église Notre-Dame-du-Val-de-Grâce★★

1 pl. Laveran. ⏱*Open Mon–Sat 2–6pm, Sun 9am–noon, 2–6pm.* ✆*01 43 29 12 31.*
After many childless years, Anne of Austria commissioned François Mansart to design a church in thanksgiving for the birth of Louis XIV in 1638. The work was completed by Lemercier and Le Muet. The church recalls the Renaissance architecture of Rome; the dome, rising above the two-tier west front with its double triangular pediment, is particularly ornate and obviously inspired by St Peter's.
Inside, the spirit of the Baroque prevails; there is polychrome paving, highly sculptured vaulting over the nave, massive crossing pillars and a monumental baldaquin with six wreathed columns. The **cupola**★★ was decorated by Mignard with a fresco featuring 200 figures.

URBAN DESIGN

Since the sweeping away of much of medieval Paris in the 19C, three central districts have come to typify particular stages in the city's evolution.

Le Marais★★★

Renaissance, Louis XIII and Louis XIV. Charles V's move to the Hôtel St-Paul in the Marais district in the 14C signalled the incorporation of a suburban area into Paris.
The area soon became fashionable, and Rue St-Antoine the city's finest street. It was here that that characteristic French town house, the hôtel, took on its definitive form with the collaboration of the finest architects and artists; it became the setting for that other distinctive

feature of Parisian life, the literary or philosophical salon.
The **Hôtel Lamoignon**★ *(24 r. Pavée)* of 1584 is a typical example of a mansion in the Henri III style. For the first time in Paris, its architect, Jean-Baptiste Androuet Du Cerceau, used the Giant Order with its flattened pilasters, Corinthian capitals and sculpted string-course.
The Henri IV style makes its appearance in the **Place des Vosges**★★★, designed by Louis Métezeau and completed in 1612. The 36 houses retain their original symmetrical appearance with arcades, two storeys with alternate brick and stone facings and steeply pitched slate roofs pierced with dormer windows. The King's Pavilion (Pavillon du Roi) is sited at the southern end of the square, balanced by the Queen's Pavilion (Pavillon de la Reine) at the sunnier northern end. Louis XIII's reign heralds the Classical style. In 1624, Jean Androuet Du Cerceau built the **Hôtel de Sully**★ *(62 r. Saint-Antoine)* with a gateway framed between massive pavilions and a main **courtyard**★★★ with triangular and curved pediments complemented by the scrolled dormer windows; beyond is an exquisite inner courtyard.
The early Louis XIV style is seen in Mansart's **Hôtel Guénégaud**★★ *(60 r. des Archives)* of 1648, where its plain harmonious lines, majestic staircase and small formal garden make it one of the finest houses of the Marais; in Le Pautre's **Hôtel de Beauvais**★ *(68 r. François Miron)* with its curved balcony on brackets and its ingenious internal layout; in the **Hôtel Carnavalet**★ *(23 r. de Sévigné)*, a Renaissance house rebuilt by Mansart in 1655; and in Cottard's **Hôtel Amelot-de-Bisseuil**★ *(47 r. Vieille-du-Temple)* of somewhat theatrical design with its cornice and curved pediment decorated with allegorical figures.
The later Louis XIV style features in two adjoining *hôtels* built by Delamair: the **Hôtel de Rohan**★★ *(87 r. Vieille-du-Temple)* with its wonderful sculpture of the *Horses of Apollo (Chevaux frémissants d'Apollon à l'abreuvoir)* by Robert Le Lorrain; and the **Hôtel de Soubise**★★ *(60 r.*

des Francs-Bourgeois) with its horseshoe-shaped courtyard and double colonnade. They are characterised by their raised ground floors, massive windows, roof balustrades and by the sculpture of their projecting central sections.

La Voie Triomphale (From the Tuileries to the Arc de Triomphe)★★★

A great axis leading from the courtyard of the Louvre to St Germain had been planned by Colbert, but today's "Triumphal Way" was laid out under Louis XVI, Napoleon III and during the years of the Third Republic.

Arc de Triomphe du Carrousel★
pl. du Carrousel.

This delightful pastiche of a Roman arch is decorated with statues of Napoleonic military men in full uniform. An observer standing in the Place du Carrousel commands an extraordinary perspective which runs from the Louvre, through the arch, to the obelisk in the Place de la Concorde, then onward and upward to the Grande Arche at the Défense.

Jardin des Tuileries★
r. de Rivoli.

The gardens were first laid out in the 1560s by Catherine de' Medici in the Italian style. A century later, they were remodelled by Le Nôtre, who here created the archetypal French garden, a formal setting for the elegant pleasures of outdoor life. The Riverside Terrace (Terrasse du Bord de l'Eau) became the playground of royal princes and of the sons of the two Napoleons, then of all the children of Paris.

Champs-Élysées★★★

In 1667, Le Nôtre extended the axis from the Tuileries to a new focal point, the Rond-Point, which he laid out himself. The avenue was then a service road for the houses facing the Rue du Faubourg-St-Honoré, but very soon refreshment stalls were set up and crowds flocked to the area. In 1724, the Duc d'Antin planted rows of elms to extend the "Elysian Fields" up to the Étoile. In 1729,

street lanterns lit the evening scene. Forty-eight years on, and the avenue had descended the gentle slope beyond the Étoile to reach the Seine at the Pont de Neuilly.

The buildings lining it included taverns and wine-shops, the later haunt of Robespierre and his friends. Finally, in 1836, the **Arc de Triomphe**★★★ was completed by Louis-Philippe.

The Champs-Élysées became fashionable during the reign of Louis-Napoleon, when high society flocked to the restaurants (like Ledoyen's), to the theatres (like the Folies Marigny and the Bouffes d'Été where Offenbach's operettas were performed), or to receptions in the grand houses (like No 25, today occupied by the Travellers' Club, with its doors of bronze and its onyx staircase). The avenue has undergone much change since 1914. Its character nowadays is determined by its luxury shops, expensive cafés, and motor showrooms; but it nevertheless remains the capital's rallying point at times of high national emotion (the Liberation, 30 May 1968, the funeral of De Gaulle in 1970, and annually on 14 July).

La Défense★★

An outstanding architectural achievement, La Défense has nothing in common with the traditional business districts found in most city centres.

A 1 200m/3 937ft terraced podium, pleasantly punctuated with gardens, fountains and shaded spots, runs from the Seine up to La Grande Arche. It is lined with an impressive ensemble of huge towers that compose a dazzling tableau of radiant light. It is also noted for many outdoor works by distinguished modern sculptors, which turn the district into an informal open-air museum.

La Grande Arche★★

◷*Open daily Sept–Mar 10am–7pm; Apr–Aug 10am–8pm.* ◉€10. ℘01 49 07 27 27. www.grandearche.com.

The Danish architect Johan Otto von Spreckelsen designed this vast hollow cube which stands at the end of the

La Défense seen from Arc de Triomphe, La Grande Arche in the middle

©naphtalina/iStockphoto.com

esplanade and houses private firms as well as several ministries.

The Cathédrale Notre-Dame with its spire could fit into the space between the walls of the arch. Each side of the cube is 110m/360ft long.

Towering 100m/328ft above the esplanade, the 1ha/2.4 acre terrace-roof is partly taken up by temporary exhibition rooms. From the belvedere visitors will also be able to admire Paris and its suburbs. At the foot of the arch lies the Palais de la Défense (CNIT): it was the first to be built (1958) and has been "rejuvenated". Now it is an important business centre focusing on three main areas of activity: technology, world trade and corporate communication.

Bercy

The modernised Bercy district boasts a Palais Omnisports by architects Andrault, Parat and Gavan; the **Cinémathèque Française** (51 r. de Bercy; www.cinematheque.fr), which hosts the largest archive of films in the world; the imposing buildings of the **Finance Ministry** designed by Chemetow and Huidobro – part of the structure rises above the Seine and the **Jardins de la Mémoire** with three planted areas.

Across the river, the **Bibliothèque nationale de France-François-Mitter-** rand★ (Quai François-Mauriac; www.bnf. fr) by Dominique Perrault – four tower blocks in the shape of open books – was the last of the "great projects" carried out under the former president.

La Villette★★

The **Parc de la Villette**★ is the largest architectural ensemble within the city. The 55ha/135-acre site houses an impressive urban complex featuring the **Cité des Sciences et de l'Industrie** and its cinema La Géode, the Zenith concert hall, the Paris-Villette Theatre, La Grande Halle and the Cité de la Musique.

THE INTELLECTUAL LIFE
POLITICAL AND INTELLECTUAL SIGHTS

In addition to the city's famous monuments, churches and modern structures, other buildings and districts have come to be identified with the political and intellectual aspects of Paris.

Hôtel de Ville★

pl. de l'Hôtel de Ville.

It is from here that central Paris is governed. Municipal government was introduced in the 13C, under the direction of leading members of the powerful watermen's guild appointed by Louis IX. The place has long been the epicentre of uprising and revolt.

Throughout the Revolution it was in the hands of the Commune, and in 1848 it was the seat of the Provisional Government. The Republic was proclaimed from here in 1870, and, on 24 March 1871, the Communards burnt it down. It was rebuilt from 1874.

Institut de France★★

quai Conti. ℘01 44 41 44 41.
www.institut-de-france.fr.

The Institute originated as the College of Four Nations founded by Mazarin for scholars from the provinces incorporated into France during his ministry (Piedmont, Alsace, Artois and Roussillon). Dating from 1662, its building was designed by Le Vau and stands on the far side of the river from the Louvre. The Institute is made up of five academies: Académie Française, founded 1635; Académie des Beaux-Arts, 1816; Académie des Inscriptions et Belles Lettres, 1663; Académie des Sciences, 1666; and Académie des Sciences morales et politiques, 1795.

Montmartre★★★

The "Martyrs' Hill" was a real village before becoming the haunt of artists and bohemians in the late 19C, and it still has something of the picturesque quality of a village in its steep and narrow lanes and precipitous stairways. The "Butte", or mound, rises abruptly from the city's sea of roofs; at its centre is the **Place du Tertre**★★ with the former town hall at No 3, still enjoying some semblance of local life, at least in the morning; by the afternoon, tourism has taken over, and the "art market" is in full swing.

Not far away from all this activity rises the exotic outline of the **Basilique du Sacré-Cœur**★★ *(r. du Chevalier-de-la-Barre; ⊜€5; ☎01 53 41 89 09; www.sacre-coeur-montmartre.com)*, a place of perpetual pilgrimage.

From here, particularly from the gallery of the dome, there is an incomparable **panorama**★★★ over the whole metropolitan area.

Palais de l'Élysée

55 r. du Faubourg Saint-Honoré.
The palace has been the Paris residence of the president of France since 1873. It was built in 1718 by Henri de La Tour d'Auvergne.

Palais Bourbon★

126 r. de l'Université.
The palace of 1722 has been the seat of the Lower House of France's parliament, the Assemblée Nationale, for more than 150 years.

Palais du Luxembourg★★

15 r. de Vaugirard.
This is the seat of the Senate, the French Upper House. The president of the Senate exercises the functions of Head of State if the presidency falls vacant.

It was constructed in the early 17C by the Regent, Marie de' Medici, who wished to have a palace of her own which would remind her of Florence's Pitti Palace.

Quartier Latin★★★

Lying on the left bank of the Seine, and on the slopes of the mount, **"Montagne" Ste-Geneviève**, and the surrounding area are concentrated many of the capital's most venerable institutions, notably the Sorbonne, the country's most illustrious university, founded in 1253. Around them is the ebb and flow of a perpetually youthful tide, the students and other young people who make up the population of the "Latin" Quarter (so-called because Latin was the language of instruction right up to the Revolution).

The area abounds in publishing houses, bookshops, and terrace cafés, including the legendary Flore *(172 bd St Germain)*, Deux-Magots *(6 pl. St Germain des Prés)* and Procope *(13 r. Ancienne Comédie)*.

Famous artists

On 19 December 1915, Édith Giovanna Gassion was born to abject poverty on the steps of 72 r. de Belleville. She later sang in the streets, before becoming a radio, gramophone and music-hall success in 1935 under the name of **Édith Piaf**. Beloved for the instinctive but deeply moving tones of her voice, she came to embody the spirit of France *(La vie en rose, Les cloches)*.

Another famous figure was **Maurice Chevalier** (1888–1972), film star, entertainer and cabaret singer *(chansonnier)*; he paired with Jeanne Mistinguett at the Folies Bergère (1911) and sang at the Casino de Paris between the wars.

Before attaining fame on Broadway in black tie and boater, he was known at home for songs that are rooted in Belleville: *Ma Pomme, Prosper* and *Un Gars de Ménilmontant*.

Quartier de St-Germain-des-Prés★★

Antique dealers, literary cafés, the night-life of side streets all combine to create the reputation of this former centre of international bohemian life.

MUSEUMS

The city has a total of 87 museums and over 100 art galleries. In addition, there are around 30 places where temporary exhibitions are held and a whole array of studios (particularly around the Rue St-Honoré, Avenue Matignon and the Rue de la Seine), as well as libraries and other institutions.

Between them, they offer the visitor a continuously changing view of past and present artistic achievement and aspiration. The most famous include the Grand Palais, the Palais de Tokyo, the Pavillon des Arts, the Petit Palais, the Pompidou Centre and the Grande Halle de la Villette.

Musée d'Orsay★★★

62 r. de Lille. &⃝*Open Tue–Sun 9.30am–6pm, Thu 9.30am–9.45pm.* ⃝*Closed 1 Jan, 1 May, 25 Dec.* ⊜*€8 for the permanent collection, €10 for access to the permanent and temporary collections (no charge 1st Sun of month).* ☏*01 40 49 48 14. www.musee-orsay.fr.*
The focus of the museum is the period 1848 to 1914. The upper floor is dedicated to the Impressionists, with one of the world's finest collections. There is a considerable collection of pre- and post-Impressionist works. Other sections include decorative arts and photography.

Highlights include:

La Source (The Spring) by Ingres – 1846
Un enterrement à Ornans (Burial at Ornans) by Courbet – c.1849–50
Des Glaneuses (Gleaners) and *L'Angélus (Angelus)* by Jean-François Millet
Le Déjeuner sur l'herbe and *Olympia* by Manet – 1863
La Danse (The Dance), sculpture by Jean-Baptiste Carpeaux – 1868
Le golfe de Marseille vu de L'Estaque (Marseille Bay from L'Estaque) by Cézanne – c.1878–79

Les Danseuses bleues (Blue Dancers) and *Dans un café (The Absinthe Drinker)* by Degas
L'Église d'Auvers-sur-Oise (The church at Auvers-sur-Oise) and *Autoportrait (Self-Portrait)* by Van Gogh
Aréarea joyeusetés (Women of Tahiti) by Gauguin – 1892
Jane Avril dansant (Jane Avril Dancing) by Toulouse-Lautrec – 1892
Balzac by Rodin – 1898
The Mediterranean by Maillol – 1902
Pendant and chain by René Lalique
Héraclès Archer (Hercules the Archer) in bronze by Antoine Bourdelle – 1909

♟♙Musée du Louvre★★★

&⃝*Open Wed–Mon 9am–6pm (Wed and Fri 10pm), 24 and 31 Dec 9am–5pm.* ⃝*Closed 1 Jan, 1 May, 11 Nov, 25 Dec.* **Hall Napoleon** *open Wed–Mon 9am–10pm.* ⊜*Permanent collections with Musée Delacroix included €10. Combined tickets: €14. www.louvre.fr.*
When the Grand Louvre was opened to the public in 1994, the different collections were divided into three large departments, **Sully**, **Denon** and **Richelieu**, which are located in the two wings and around the Cour Carrée.

Musée National d'Art Moderne (Centre Georges Pompidou)★★★

pl. Georges-Pompidou. &⃝*Open daily 11am–9pm.* **Atelier Brancusi** *Wed–Mon 2–6pm. Museum and exhibitions* ⊜*€12 (free 1st Sun in the month).* ☏*01 44 78 12 33.www.centrepompidou.fr.*
The Centre seeks to demonstrate that there is a close correlation between art and daily activities.

For both the specialists and the general public, this multipurpose cultural centre offers an astonishing variety of activities and modern communication techniques encouraging curiosity and participation. The Centre includes four departments: the **Bibliothèque Publique d'Information** (BPI), offering a wide variety of French and foreign books, slides, films, periodicals and reference catalogues; the **Musée National**

Musée du Louvre★★★

ROOM BY ROOM

Choose which section of the museum to visit:

Sully
- History of the Louvre: *Entresol.*
- Medieval Louvre: *Entresol.*
- Egyptian Antiquities: *Ground and 1st floors.*
- Greek Antiquities (Cariatides room, Hellenic period): *Ground floor.*
- Oriental Antiquities (Iran and art of the Levant): *Ground floor.*
- Greek Antiquities (Bronze room, Campana gallery): *1st floor.*
- 17–18C objets d'art: *1st floor.*
- 17–19C French painting, including Graphic arts: *2nd floor.*
- Beistegui collection (room A): *2nd floor.*

Denon
- Italian sculpture: *Entresol and ground floor.*
- Scandinavian sculpture: *Entresol.*
- Roman and Coptic Egypt: *Entresol (rooms A, B and C).*
- Greek Antiquities: *Ground and 1st floors.*
- Etruscan and Roman Antiquities: *Ground floor.*
- Italian painting: *1st floor.*
- Spanish painting: *1st floor.*
- 19C French painting (large sizes): *1st floor.*
- *Objets d'art* (Apollon gallery): *1st floor.*

Richelieu
- Exhibitions-documents: *Entresol.*
- Islamic art: *Entresol (closed until 2012; will reopen in Denon).*
- French sculpture (Marly and Puget rooms): *Ground floor.*
- Oriental Antiquities (Mesopotamia): *Ground floor.*
- *Objets d'art* (including Napoleon III's apartments): *1st floor.*
- 14–17C French painting: *2nd floor.*
- Scandinavian schools: *2nd floor.*

Select what to see within the chosen section:

Oriental Antiquities
- Statues of *Gudea* and *Ur-Ningirsu* – Mesopotamia: c.2150 BC
- *Code of Hammurabi* – Babylon: c.1750 BC
- *Frieze of the Archers* from Darius' palace – Susa: 6C BC
- Low-reliefs from Nineveh and Khorsabad – Assyria: 7C BC
- Vase from Amathus – Cyprus: early 5C BC

Egyptian Antiquities
- Gebel-el-Arak knife – Egypt: c.300–3200 BC
- *Sphinx* of the Crypt – Egypt: c.2600 BC
- Jewellery of Rameses II – middle of second millennium BC
- *Seated Scribe* from Sakkara – Egypt: Fifth Dynasty
- Funerary chapel of Akhout-Hetep – Fifth Dynasty
- Fragments from the Coptic monastery of Bawit – 5C

Classical Antiquities

- *Kore* from the Temple of Hera at Samos – Greece: archaic period
- *La Dame d'Auxerre (Lady of Auxerre)* – Greece: c.640–630 BC
- *Apollo of Piombino* – Greece: 1C BC
- *Venus de Milo* – Greece: Hellenistic period
- Parthenon fragments (metopes) – Greece: Classical period
- *Etruscan terracotta* sarcophagus from Cerveteri, Italy: 6C BC
- *Victoire de Samothrace (Winged Victory)* – Greece: Hellenistic period

Sculpture

- Limewood *Madonna* from the Church of the Antonites, Isenheim – late 15C
- *Diana the Huntress* (fountain) from Château d'Anet – French Renaissance
- *The Three Graces* (funerary monument for Henri II) by Germain Pilon
- *The Four Evangelists* by Jean Goujon
- *Madonna and Child* (terracotta) by Donatello – Florence c.1450
- Marble bust of *Voltaire* by Houdon: 1778
- *The Slaves* by Michelangelo – Florence: early 16C

Painting

- Malouel's circular *Pietà* – Dijon: c.1400
- St Denis Altarpiece by Henri Bellechose – Dijon: c.1415–16
- Avignon *Pietà* by Enguerrand Quarton – c.1455
- Portrait of *François I* by Jean Clouet – Loire Valley School
- *St Thomas* by Georges de La Tour – 17C; *Gilles* by Watteau – c.1718–19
- Portrait of *Mme Récamier* and *Sacre de Napoléon I*
  (The Coronation of Napoleon) by David
- *La Baigneuse de Valpinçon (The Turkish Bath)* and *Grande Odalisque* by Ingres
- *Scène des massacres de Scio (Scenes of the Massacres of Chios)* by Delacroix – 1824
- *Le Radeau de la Méduse (Raft of the Medusa)* by Géricault – 1819
- *Maestà (Virgin with Angels and Saints)* by Cimabue – Florence: c.1280
- *La Couronnement de la Vierge (Coronation of the Virgin)* by Fra Angelico –
  Florence: c.1430
- *La Joconde (The Gioconda – Mona Lisa)* by Leonardo da Vinci – Florence: c.1503–06
- *Les Noces de Cana (The Wedding at Cana)* by Veronese – Venice: 1563
- *La Mort de la Vierge (Death of the Virgin)* by Caravaggio – Naples: early 17C
- *Le Jeune Mendiant (Young Beggar)* by Murillo – Seville: c.1645–50
- *La Vierge du chancelier Rolin (The Rolin Madonna)* by Jan van Eyck – Dijon: c.1435
- *Charles I of England* by Van Dyck – England: 17C
- *Vie et règne de Marie de Médicis* – allegorical paintings of the *Life of Marie de'*
  Medici by Rubens
- *Les Pèlerins d'Emmaüs (Pilgrims at Emmaus)* by Rembrandt c.1660

Objets d'art

- The Regent Diamond and Crown Jewels of France
- Ivory figure of the Virgin Mary from the Sainte-Chapelle, Paris: middle of the 13C
- The *Hunts of Maximilian* tapestries – Brussels: 1537
- The study of the Elector of Bavaria by Boulle – early 18C
- Clock in ebony case inlaid with tortoiseshell by Boulle – early 18C
- Monkey commode (gilded bronze) by Charles Cressent – 1740
- The *Loves of the Gods* tapestries – Gobelins: mid-18C
- Writing desk, table and commode in the Oeben room – mid-18C
- Medici vase (Sèvres porcelain, bronzes by Thomire)

The Louvre and the pyramid

S. Sauvignier/MICHELIN

THE LOUVRE: GENERAL INFORMATION

ℹ Info: General information ℘01 40 20 51 51 (recorded message); ℘01 40 20 53 17 to speak to someone at the desk (six languages); *www.louvre.fr.* Some galleries are closed on certain days (or for restoration); check the schedule of open rooms online or call in advance. Fourteen video screens in the hall provide information about daily events at the museum. There is also a general activity programme (six languages) available at the main information desk, which comes out every three months. **Audioguides** can be hired (six languages) on the mezzanine level in the various wings.

▶ Location: The main entrance to the museum is at the **Pyramid.** There is also an entrance through the shopping mall of the **Carrousel du Louvre** (*metro stop Palais-Royal-Musée-du-Louvre (lines 1 and 7)*), on either side of the Arc du Carrousel, or at the Porte des Lions. You will find yourself in the well-lit **Napoleon Hall,** which leads you towards the three wings of the museum: **Denon,** **Richelieu** and **Sully.** There is a bookshop, restaurant and auditorium.

🅿 Parking: The closest underground car park (80 coaches, 620 cars) is **Parking Carrousel-Louvre,** located on avenue du Général Lemonnier.

Open daily 7am–11pm. After parking, enter the museum via the shopping mall of the Carrousel by the fortifications of Charles V.

⊛ Don't Miss: Of all the artworks inside the museum, probably the most famous are Leonardo's masterpiece, the *Mona Lisa* (here called La Joconde), and, among the classical works, the *Victoire de Samothrace* and the *Vénus de Milo.* All three are in the Denon section.

🕐 Timing: The Louvre cannot be enjoyed in its entirety even in several visits, let alone one. From the list of artworks on *p470–71,* decide what you would like to see and head for your selections. Cost notwithstanding, it is worth just concentrating on one or two sections per visit, and then keep coming back if time allows.

The information desks offer a variety of aids and amenities to enhance your visit. Audioguides are available, or choose one of the thematic trails (provided on leaflets) designed for all ages that allow you to discover both masterpieces and less well-known works while exploring a particular theme, such as the Da Vinci Code.

👥 Kids: Children aged 4 and up can take part in one of the many workshops for young people or follow a Children's Route through the museum. See website for details.

d'Art Moderne – **Centre de Création Industrielle** (MNAM – CCI), the former presenting collections of paintings, sculptures and drawings from 1905 to the present time, and the latter demonstrating the relationship between individuals and spaces, objects and signs through architecture, urbanism, industrial design and visual communication; the **Institut de Recherche et Coordination Acoustique/Musique** (IRCAM), bringing together musicians, composers and scientists for the purpose of sound experimentation.

Highlights include:

La Rue pavoisée (Street Bedecked with Bunting) by Dufy – Fauvism: 1906

Le Guéridon (Table) by Braque – Cubism: 1911

Nus de dos (Nudes) by Matisse – beginnings of Abstraction: 1916

Arlequin (Harlequin) by Picasso – mature Cubism: 1923

La Vache spectrale (Spectral Cow) by Dalí – beginnings of Hyperrealism: 1928

Le Phoque (Seal), sculpture by Brancusi – Surrealism in sculpture: c.1943–6

Hôtel de Cluny (Musée national du Moyen Âge)★★

Hôtel de Cluny, 6 pl. Paul Painlevé.
Open Wed–Mon 9.15am–5.45pm.
Closed 1 Jan, 1 May, 25 Dec. €8 (audioguide included) (free 1st Sun in month). 01 53 73 78 16. www.musee-moyenage.fr.

Highlights include:

Ivory casket – Constantinople: early 11C

Gilt altar-front made for Henri II – Basle cathedral: 11C

29 medallions from the stained glass of the Sainte-Chapelle – Paris: 13C

Limoges reliquaries in *champlevé* enamel – 13C

Golden rose given by Pope Clement V to the Prince-Bishop of Basle: early 14C

Eagle of St John (brass lectern) – Tournai cathedral: 1383

Life of St Stephen tapestry – Arras: mid-15C

Altarpiece from Limburg in painted and gilded wood – late 15C

Lady and the Unicorn tapestries – Brussels: late 15C

Mary Magdalene (probable likeness of Mary of Burgundy) – Flanders

Musée de l'Orangerie★★

Jardin des Tuileries.
Open Wed–Mon 9am–6pm.
Closed 1 May, 25 Dec. €7.50; €2 surcharge for temporary exhibitions (free 1st Sun in month). Guided tours (1hr30min) 8€. 01 44 77 80 07. www.musee-orangerie.fr.

Highlights include:

Portrait of Mme Cézanne by Cézanne

Baigneuse aux cheveux longs (Woman Bathing) and *Femme à la lettre (The Letter-Writer)* by Renoir

Nude on red background by Picasso – 1906

La Carriole du père Junier (Père Junier's Cart) by Douanier Rousseau – 1908

Maison de Berlioz (Berlioz' House) and *Église de Clignancourt* by Utrillo

Antonia by Modigliani

Nymphéas (Water-lilies) from Giverny by Claude Monet

Les Trois Soeurs (The Three Sisters) by Matisse

Le Petit Pâtissier (The Little Pastry-cook) and *Garçon d'étage (The Attendant)* by Soutine – 1922

Arlequin à la guitare (Harlequin with Guitar) and *Le Modèle blond (Blond Model)* by Derain

Musée de l'Armée (Hôtel National des Invalides)★★★

0810 11 33 99. www.invalides.org.

Highlights include:

Seussenhofer's suit of armour for François I – 1539

Model of the city of Perpignan (one of a series ordered by Vauban in 1696)

Napoleon's flag of farewell flown at Fontainebleau on 20 April 1814

The room where Napoleon died on St Helena (reconstruction)

The Armistice Bugle (which sounded the cease-fire at 9pm on 7 November 1918)

Cité des Sciences et de l'Industrie★★★

30 ave Corentin-Cariou. ⟨⟩Open Tue–Sat 10am–6pm, Sun 10am–7pm. ⟨⟩Closed 1 May and 25 Dec. €6–10.50. ℘01 40 05 70 00. www. cite-sciences.fr.

Built in response to the growing need of young and old alike to have a better understanding of the scientific and industrial world, this living museum encourages visitors to investigate, learn and have fun through a wide range of edifying and entertaining scenarios.

Highlights include:

L'Argonaute (a submarine formerly in use with the French Navy)
Le Nautile (full-size model of research submarine)
Voyager 2 space probe
Model of Ariane 5 rocket (scale 1:5)
Le Robot-mouche (a glimpse into the future development of bionics)

Cité des Enfants★

The ground floor of the Cité is designated especially for the young, encouraging scientific discovery through experimentation and play. It's cleverly divided into two sections: ages 2–7, and ages 5–12.

La Géode★★★

In the park just outside the museum. The most comfortable viewing is from the top of the hall. ⟨⟩Open Tue–Sun 10.30am–8.30pm (hourly sessions). €10.50 (children, €9). ℘01 44 84 44 84. www.lageode.fr.

The Cité's extraordinary reflective spherical cinema and its circular screen (diameter: 36m/118ft), which rests on a sheet of water, is a remarkable technical achievement, whose bold conception and perfect execution are the work of the engineer Chamayou.

Musée du Quai Branly★★

37 quai Branly. ⟨⟩Open Tue, Wed, Sun 11am–7pm, Thu–Sat 11am–9pm. €9. ℘ 01 56 61 70 00. www.quaibranly.fr.
Modern purpose-built museum opened in 2006, located on the left bank of the Seine near the Eiffel Tower, exhibiting indigenous art from Afric, Asia, Oceania and the Americas.

Palais de la Découverte★★

ave Franklin-D.-Roosevelt. ⟨⟩Open Tue–Sat 9.30am–6pm, Sun and public holidays 10am–7pm (last entrance 30min before closing). ⟨⟩Closed 1 Jan, 1 May, 14 Jul, 15 Aug, 25 Dec. €7 (children, €4.50); Planetarium €3.50. ℘01 56 43 20 20.

This children's museum is a marvel of ingenuity and interest, with clever animators to bring the exhibits to life.

Highlights include:

School of Rats
The Planetarium
Lunakhod (Soviet moon buggy) – 12 November 1970
Fragment of moon-rock – Apollo Mission XVII: 1972
The number Pi and the 703 prime numbers of the 16 000 000 decimals calculated

Musée des Arts et Métiers★★

60 r. Réaumur. ⟨⟩Open Tue–Sun 10am–6pm (Thu 9.30pm). ⟨⟩Closed 1 May, 25 Dec. €6.50. ℘01 53 01 82 00. www.arts-et-metiers.net.

Highlights include:

Microscope belonging to the Duke of Chaulnes – mid-18C
Cugnot's steam carriage of 1771
Marie-Antoinette's automaton "Dulcimer-Player" – 1784
Jacquard loom
Thimonnier's sewing machine – 1825
Foucault's pendulum (proving the rotation of the Earth)
L'Obéissante automobile by Amédée Bollée Snr – 1873
The Lumière brothers' cinematographic apparatus – 1895
Transmitting station from the Eiffel Tower
Blériot's No 9 aeroplane (in which he made the first cross-Channel flight)

ADDITIONAL MUSEUMS
Musée Picasso
⊶*Closed for renovations through 2012.*
℘*01 42 71 25 21.www.musee-picasso.fr.*

Musée Rodin
🕐*Open Apr–Sept Tue–Sun 9.30am–
5.45pm; Oct–Mar, Tue–Sun 9.30am–
4.45pm.* 🕐*Closed 1 Jan, 1 May, 25 Dec.*
👓*€6; €1 for garden only (free 1st Sun
of the month).* ℘*01 44 18 61 10.
www.musee-rodin.fr.*

A new visitors' entrance, gift shop, auditorium, library, research room, workshops, and a new temporary exposition
room: these now occupy the 5 000sq m/
5 980sq yd of space within the recently
renovated chapel of the Rodin Museum.
The architect in charge of the renovations, Pierre-Louis Faloci, wanted to turn
this already popular place into a "must-
see Parisian museum". Visitors enter via
the chapel. With its 12m/13yd-high glass
skylight, it's the perfect setting for temporary exhibitions.

Don't miss the superb gardens (and
pleasant little café), where some of
the artist's most important works are
displayed, including *The Thinker*, *The
Burghers of Calais* (made in 1884 with
the help of Camille Claudel), *The Gates
of Hell* and *Ugolino*.

Musée Carnavalet★★
🕐*Open Tue–Sun 10am–6pm.* 🕐*Some
public holidays.* 👓*Varying prices for
temporary exhibitions.* ℘*01 44 59 58
58. www.carnavalet.paris.fr.*

The museum illustrating the history of
Paris is housed in two separate mansions, the Hôtel Carnavalet and the Hôtel
Le Peletier de St-Fargeau: the variety of
its exhibits makes it one of the capital's
most attractive museums. Paris from its
tribal origins to the end of the Middle
Ages is vividly depicted by means of
archaeological finds such as the wooden
Neolithic canoes found in Bercy in 1999;
the oldest dates from 4 400 BC.

The museum also brings to life some of
the main events of the capital's history,
such as the Revolution and the Commune. It is particularly rich in decorative
arts: painted and carved wood panelling

and ceilings from other Parisian mansions have been reconstructed here
(drawing rooms from the Hôtel de la
Rivière painted by Lebrun, Belle-Époque
décor of the Fouquet jewellery shop).
Literary history is illustrated by many
portraits, pieces of furniture and souvenirs evoking famous writers (Marcel
Proust's bedroom).

Musée d'Art et Histoire
du Judaïsme
♿🕐*Open Mon–Fri 11am–6pm,
Sun and public holidays 10am–6pm.*
🕐*Closed 1 Jan, 1 May, 25 Dec, Jewish
holidays.* 👓*€7.* ℘*01 53 01 86 60.
www.mahj.org.*

An ultra-modern museum in a historic
setting, presenting ancient and contemporary exhibits. Accompanying explanatory notes provide the visitor with an
in-depth view of Jewish culture.

Musée de la Magie
🕐*Open Wed and Sat–Sun 2–7pm.
Call for information during school
holiday periods.* 👓*€9 (children, €7).*
℘*01 42 72 13 26. www.museede
lamagie.com.*

The collection of ingenious accessories
dispels some of the mystery from the
art of magic, conjuring, legerdemain,
prestidigitation and sleight-of-hand.
Midway through the museum, a stage,
a few seats and a number of tiers provide the setting for regular magic shows
(about 30min; included in the entry fee).

Musée Marmottan-Monet★★
🕐*Open Tue 11am–9pm. Wed–Sun
11am–6pm.* 🕐*Closed 1 Jan, 1 May,
25 Dec.* 👓*€9.* ℘*01 44 96 50 33.
www.marmottan.com.*

In 1932 the art historian Paul Marmottan
bequeathed his private house and collections of Renaissance tapestries and
sculpture, Consular and First Empire portraits (26 of Boilly), medallions, paintings
(Vernet) and furniture (Desmalter) to the
Académie des Beaux-Arts.

In 1950 Mme Donop de Monchy donated
a part of her father's collection, including
works by the Impressionists befriended
and treated by Dr de Bellio (*Impression*

– *Sunrise*, which gave the Impressionist movement its name).

In 1971, Michel Monet left 65 of his father's painted canvases to the museum, which has been further endowed by the Wildenstein legacy of 228 13C-16C illuminated manuscripts from various European schools.

The collection of Claude Monet paintings, probably the most important known body of work by the Master of Impressionism, is accommodated by a special purpose-built underground gallery; many of the works were painted at the artist's Normandy home at Giverny, depicting his beloved water-lilies, wisteria, iris, rose-garden, weeping willows and Japanese bridge. Other panels show the painter's preoccupation with light (The Houses of Parliament – London, The Europe Bridge, Rouen Cathedral).

Musée d'Art Moderne de la Ville de Paris

⊙*Open Tue–Sun 10am–6pm (10pm on Thu for temporary exhibitions).* ⊙*Closed public holidays.* ⊛*Free entry to the permanent collection.* ✆*01 53 67 40 00. www.mam.paris.fr.*

This municipal collection illustrates the main trends of 20C art, including some of the century's major works: *France* by Bourdelle (on a terrace), *Les Disques* by Léger (1918), *L'Équipe de Cardiff* by Robert Delaunay (1912–13), *Danse de Parisa* by Matisse (1932), *Évocation* by Picasso and *Rêve* by Chagall. Dufy's *Fée Électricitéa (The Good Fairy Electricity)* is the biggest picture in the world.

PARKS AND GARDENS

The city has as many as 450 parks, public gardens and green spaces, some perfect for a rest and some fresh air, or a place for children to play; other parks are prestigious and historic, and perhaps adorned with fine sculpture.

Highlights include:

Bois de Vincennes, 995ha/4 458 acres including the Parc Floral; **Bois de Boulogne,** 846ha/2 090 acres with the Bagatelle, iris and rose gardens; **Jardin des Plantes**, historic Botanic Gardens of Paris; **Jardin des Tuileries**, with

its ancient and modern statuary; 👫 **Jardin du Luxembourg**, very agreeable Latin Quarter park with a circular pond alongside a palace, popular with students and with big play areas for children; **Parc Montsouris and Square des Batignolles**, examples of "Jardins Anglais", with less formal layout; **Parc Paysager des Buttes-Chaumont**, without doubt the most picturesque; **Jardin du Palais-Royal**, a haven of silence and elegance in the very heart of Paris; **Jardin japonais de l'UNESCO**, in the grounds of the UNESCO headquarters, it is also known as "Garden of Peace"; **Jardin du Musée Rodin**, ideal spot to prolong the museum visit and discover the magnificent city view along its pathways; **Parc Monceau**, where it is enjoyable to encounter statues of Musset, Maupassant, Chopin and others; **Parc André-Citroën**, the most sophisticated; **Parc de La Villette**, the largest in Paris; **Parc de Belleville**, with views across the whole city; **Parc de Bercy**, recalling the wine-dealing past of this modernised district.

AROUND PARIS

▶*65km/40.3mi radius from Notre-Dame Cathedral (* 👣 *see Michelin Green Guide Northern France and the Paris Region).*

Barbizon★★

▶*61km/38mi S, along D637.*

The landscapes of the Forest of Fontainebleau and the Bière plateau inspired a group of landscape painters who worked directly from nature (1830–60) and came to be known as the Barbizon School. Together with their leader, Théodore Rousseau (1812–67), these forerunners of Impressionism favoured dark tones, soft light and stormy skies. The old **Auberge du Père Ganne★** where they used to stay is now the **Musée de l'École de Barbizon**; *92 Grande-Rue;* ✆*01 60 66 22 27.*

Château de Champs★★

An 18C mansion and landscape. The **park★★** was designed in typically French style, while the internal layout

Châteaux de Chantilly

© Nicolas Thibaut/Photononstop

Châteaux in the Île-de-France

Due to its proximity to the seat of royal power and its immense prestige, the Île-de-France was, for many centuries, a choice setting for architectural and artistic innovations. The quest for glory and love of art have inspired sovereigns and courtiers to build original and splendid mansions. Most of these are still extant and are a proud testimony to their past glory. For more châteaux, see the Châteaux of the Loire chapter in this guide or the *Michelin Green Guide Châteaux of the Loire*.

Highly recommended★★★

Palais de Versailles

Châteaux de Chantilly, Fontainebleau, Vaux-le-Vicomte

Recommended★★

Châteaux de Breteuil, Champs, Courances, Dampierre, Écouen, Malmaison, St-Germain-en-Laye, Sceaux, Thoiry

Interesting★

Châteaux de Ferrières, Fleury-en-Bière, Grosbois, Guermantes, Maintenon, Maisons-Laffitte, Marais, Rambouillet, La Roche-Guyon, Saussay

Also of Interest

Châteaux de Bourron, Blandy-les-Tours, Chevreuse, Courson, Malesherbes, St-Jean-de-Beauregard

of the **château** broke new ground in its time: the rooms are no longer directly connected with one another and each is provided with a closet and dressing room; a separate dining room makes its appearance. There is fine Rococo wainscoting (**boiseries**★) and a Chinese Room (**Salon chinois**★★).

Château d'Écouen ★★

◗ *21km/13mi N, off D 316.*

The château is a good example of the progress made in architecture between the Early and High Renaissance. It houses a **Musée de la Renaissance**★★ (○open Wed–Mon. ⊗€4.50. ℘01 34 38 38 50. www.musee-renaissance.fr) which has furniture, tapestries and embroidery, ceramics and enamels.

Château de Gros-Bois★

◗ *ave du Maréchal de Lattre de Tassigny, Boissy-St.-Léger. 23km/14.3mi SE, along N 19.* ℘*01 49 77 15 24.*

The early 17C château houses a fascinating **furniture collection**★★ of the

Classical and Empire periods; it includes a mahogany bed with gilded bronze decoration, porphyry candelabra and bronzes by Thomire, and furniture by Jacob.

Château de Maisons-Laffitte★

⟩ *ave Carnot. 20km/12.4mi NW.*
Ⓞ *Open Wed–Mon 10am–12.30pm, 2–5pm (6pm in summer).* Ⓞ *Closed public holidays.* ⊜€6.50.
www.maisonslaffitte.net.
Built 1642-51 by Mansart in early Louis XIV style, the château subordinates considerations of domestic well-being to the creation of grandiose effects (dominance of its site, majestic scale, use of columns and pilasters, lofty pediments).

Port-Royal-des-Champs★

⟩ *39km/24mi SW, off D 36.*
At the **Musée National des Granges de Port-Royal** *(rte des Granges;* Ⓞ *open year-round Wed–Mon (hours vary in summer);* ⊜€4.50; ℘01 39 30 72 72; www. port-royal-des-champs.eu), the spirit of Jansenism is captured in a magnificent painting by Philippe de Champaigne, *Ecce Homo*, whose power lies in its restraint and profound acceptance of suffering to come. The museum also has a copy of the Augustinus; an exposition of the doctrine of St Augustin. Below the museum there are remains of the famous abbey in the valley, scene of the struggle between Jesuits and Jansenists.

Abbaye de Royaumont★★

⟩ *33km/20.5mi N, off D 909.*
Founded by Louis IX in 1228. The extent of the original abbey church is indicated by the still-extant bases of its columns, while the splendid Gothic refectory and the 14C Madonna of Royaumont evoke the spirit of the Middle Ages.

Rueil-Malmaison★★

⟩ *15km/9.3mi NW, along D 913.*
Malmaison is a place of pilgrimage for all those fascinated by the figure of Napoleon. In 1799, three years after her marriage to Bonaparte, Josephine bought the château and its park from the actor Talma.

The First Consul spent much of his free time here with her; it was the happiest period of their life together and it was to Malmaison that Josephine returned after their divorce (1809). In June 1815, at the end of the Hundred Days (Josephine had been dead for more than a year), Napoleon fled here, staying with her daughter Hortense until his final departure from France.

Lemercier worked on the château around 1625; the building is interesting for its decoration by Percier and Fontaine and for its **collections★★**, which include busts of the Imperial family, Jacob furniture and many other ornamental objects.

The **Musée national du château de Bois-Préau★** (o– *closed for renovation;* ℘01 41 29 05 55) has many moving mementoes of Bonaparte's exile and of the return of his remains to France.

Cathédrale (or Basilique) St-Denis★★★

⟩ *2 r. de Strasbourg. 10km/6.2mi N.*
Ⓞ *Open Apr–Sept Mon–Sat 10am–6.15pm, Sun noon–6.15pm; Oct–Mar Mon–Sat 10am–5.15pm, Sun noon–5.15pm.* ⊜ *No charge.* ℘01 48 09 83 54.
St-Denis is an important manufacturing centre in the northern suburbs of Paris. It owes its name to the great mission-

Basilique St-Denis

Jacass/MICHELIN

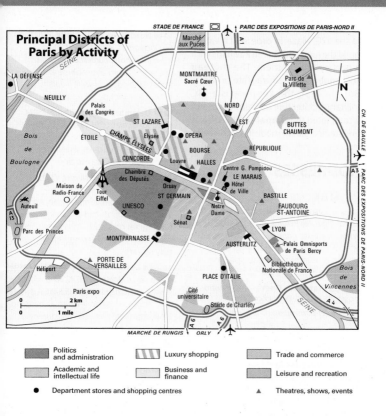

Principal Districts of Paris by Activity

Legend:
- Politics and administration
- Academic and intellectual life
- ● Department stores and shopping centres
- Luxury shopping
- Business and finance
- Trade and commerce
- Leisure and recreation
- ▲ Theatres, shows, events

ary who became the first bishop of Paris when it was still Roman Lutetia.

St Denis was beheaded at Montmartre around AD 250; legend has it that he walked all the way here with his head in his hands before finally expiring.

The basilica, begun in 1136 by Abbot Suger, is of central importance in the evolution of the Early Gothic style.

A century later, the upper parts of the chancel and transept, and the nave, were rebuilt by Pierre de Montreuil as masterpieces of High Gothic.

The many **royal tombs**★★ in chancel and pre-chancel make the cathedral a veritable museum of funerary art from the Middle Ages to the Renaissance.

Sèvres★★

🕑 *19km/11.8mi SW, along D 910.*

Sèvres owes its fame to the porcelain made here. In 1756, on the orders of Louis XV, the original factory at Vincennes was moved to Sèvres, halfway between Paris and Versailles; the government saw the

move as an opportunity to assuage the concerns that had arisen as a result of the beginnings of the development of industry. Sèvres products are featured in the **Musée National de Céramique**★★ *(pl. de la Manufacture; ⊙open Wed–Mon 10am–5pm; ⊙closed 1 Jan, 1 May, 25 Dec. ⊛€4.50. ℘01 41 14 04 20. www. musee-ceramique-sevres.fr)*, which also has examples of the work of other great porcelain makers.

Château de Vincennes★★

🕑 *ave de Paris. 10km/6.2mi E.*
⊙*Open daily Sept–Apr 10am–5pm; May–Aug 10am–6pm.* ⊙*Closed public holidays. ℘01 48 08 31 20. www.chateau-vincennes.fr.*

This "Versailles of the Middle Ages" originated in the manor house built by Philippe Auguste. Louis IX was wont to dispense justice here in the shade of an oak tree. The fortress, begun by Philippe VI, was completed by Charles V, whose place of birth it was.

In the 17C, Mazarin ordered Le Vau to build the King and Queen Pavilions with a portico linking them. The **château** subsequently became a state prison. Built in 1337, the **keep**★★ is a 14C military architecture masterpiece. Henri II completed the **chapel**★; the choir has fine stained glass★ made in 1556 in Paris.

ADDRESSES

🛏 STAY

🛏🛏 **Louvre Ste-Anne** – *32 r. Ste-Anne, 75001.* 🚇 *Pyramides.* ✆ *01 40 20 02 35. www.louvre-ste-anne.fr. 20rms.* In a street lined with Japanese restaurants, this hotel has small but well-equipped rooms decorated in pastel shades.

🛏🛏🛏 **Etats-Unis Opéra** – *16 r. d'Antin, 75002.* 🚇 *Opéra.* ✆ *01 42 65 05 05. www.hotel-paris-opera.com. 45rms.* Nestled by a quiet street, this hotel in a 1930s building offers modern, comfortable rooms.

🛏🛏🛏 **Hôtel des Archives** – *87 r. des Archives, 75003.* 🚇 *Temple.* ✆ *01 44 78 08 00. www.hoteldesarchives.com. 19rms.* Charming hotel near the National Archives, with small yet prettily decorated, comfortable rooms.

🛏🛏🛏 **Beaubourg** – *11 r. S. Le Franc, 75004.* 🚇 *Rambuteau.* ✆ *01 42 74 34 24. www.hotelbeaubourg.com. 28rms.* Nestled in a tiny street behind the Georges-Pompidou Centre.

🛏🛏 **Familia** – *11 r. des Ecoles, 75005.* 🚇 *Cardinal Lemoine.* ✆ *01 43 54 55 27. www.familiahotel.com. 30rms.* Notre-Dame and the Collège des Bernardins provide the backdrop for rustic rooms adorned with sepia frescoes.

🛏🛏🛏 **Eiffel Park Hôtel** – *17 bis, r. Amélie, 75007.* 🚇 *La Tour Maubourg.* ✆ *01 45 55 10 01. www.eiffelpark.com. 36rms.* From the Indian and Chinese artefacts to the ethnic fabrics, exoticism reigns through this elegant hotel.

🛏🛏🛏 **Elysées Mermoz** – *30 r. J. Mermoz, 75008.* 🚇 *Franklin D. Roosevelt.* ✆ *01 42 25 75 30. www.hotel-elyseesmermoz.com. 22rms.* This cosy hotel has rooms in sunny colours or shades of grey. Varnished wood panelling and blue stone in the bathrooms as well as a cane-furnished lounge.

🛏🛏 **Nord et Est** – *49 r. Malte, 75011.* 🚇 *Oberkampf.* ✆ *01 47 00 71 70. www.paris-hotel-nordest.com. 45rms.* The warm family atmosphere and reasonable prices draw regulars to this hotel near Place de la République.

🛏🛏 **Delambre** – *35 r. Delambre, 75014.* 🚇 *Edgar Quinet.* ✆ *01 43 20 66 31. 30rms.* French poet André Breton stayed in this hotel located in a quiet street close to Montparnasse railway station.

🛏🛏 **Aberotel** – *24 r. Blomet, 75015.* 🚇 *Volontaires.* ✆ *01 40 61 70 50. www.aberotel.com. 28rms.* A popular hotel with stylish rooms and an inner courtyard for summer breakfasts. It has a pleasant lounge adorned with paintings of playing cards.

🛏🛏🛏 **Le Hameau de Passy** – *48 r. Passy, 75016.* 🚇 *La Muette.* ✆ *01 42 88 47 55. www.hameaudepassy.com. 32rms.* A private lane leads to this hamlet with a charming inner courtyard overrun with greenery.

🛏🛏🛏 **7 Eiffel** – *17 bis r. Amélie, 75007.* 🚇 *La Tour Maubourg.* ✆ *01 45 55 10 01. www.hotel-7eiffel-paris.com. 32 rooms and junior suites.* Sleek contemporary design reigns in this elegant Left-Bank hotel. A rooftop summer terrace complete with bee hives affords great city views.

🍴 EAT

🍴🍴 **Pharamond** – *24 r. de la Grande-Truanderie, 75001.* 🚇 *Châtelet-Les-Halles.* ✆ *01 40 28 45 18. www.pharamond.fr.* An institution dating back to the heyday of Les Halles. The Pharamond still serves traditional dishes.

🍴🍴 **Vaudeville** – *29, r. Vivienne, 75002.* 🚇 *Bourse.* ✆ *01 40 20 04 62. www.vaudevilleparis.com.* This large brasserie with its sparkling Art Deco details in pure Parisian style is especially lively after theatre performances.

🍴🍴 **Le Carré des Vosges** – *15 r. St-Gilles, 75003.* 🚇 *Chemin Vert.* ✆ *01 42 71 22 21. www.lecarredesvosges.fr.* Friendly bistro a stone's throw from the Rue des Francs-Bourgeois and its trendy boutiques.

🍴🍴 **Bofinger** – *5 r. Bastille, 75004.* 🚇 *Bastille.* ✆ *01 42 72 87 82. www.bofingerparis.com.* The famous clients and remarkable décor have bestowed enduring renown on this brasserie created in 1864.

🍽🍽 **Atelier Maître Albert** – *1 r. Maître Albert, 75005.* 🚇 *Maubert Mutualité.* 🕾*01 56 81 30 01. www.ateliermaitrealbert.com.* A huge medieval fireplace and spits for roast meat take pride of place in this handsome interior. Guy Savoy is responsible for the mouth-watering menu.

🍽🍽 **Florimond** – *19 av. La Motte-Picquet, 75007.* 🚇 *Ecole Militaire.* 🕾*01 45 55 40 38.* Pocket-sized restaurant named after Monet's gardener in Giverny.

🍽🍽🍽 **La Maison de l'Aubrac** – *37 r. Marbeuf, 75008.* 🚇 *Franklin D. Roosevelt.* 🕾*01 43 59 05 14. www.maison-aubrac.com.* Aveyron farmhouse-style décor, generous portions of rustic cuisine (with an emphasis on Aubrac beef) and an excellent wine list. Close to Champs-Élysées.

🍽🍽 **Chardenoux** – *1 r. Jules Vallès, 75011.* 🚇 *Charonne.* 🕾*01 43 71 49 52.* Reopened under the chef Cyril Lignac on its 100th anniversary, this bistro is bringing back traditional cuisine.

🍽🍽🍽 **La Coupole** – *102 bd Montparnasse, 75014.* 🚇 *Vavin.* 🕾*01 43 20 14 20. www.flobrasseries.com.* The spirit of Montparnasse lives on in this huge Art Deco brasserie opened in 1927. The 24 pillars were decorated by artists of the period, while the cupola sports a contemporary fresco.

🍽🍽 **Le Troquet** – *21 r. François Bonvin, 75015.* 🚇 *Cambronne.* 🕾*01 45 66 89 00.* An authentic Parisian bar: single set menu shown on the blackboard, retro-style dining room, and tasty market-based cuisine.

🍽🍽 **Bistro de la Muette** – *10 chaussée de la Muette, 75016.* 🚇*Mo La Muette.* 🕾*01 45 03 14 84. www.bistrocie.fr.* The very attractive, all-inclusive formula of this elegant bistro explains part of its appeal in the neighbourhood.

🎭 ENTERTAINMENT

Consult *L'Officiel des Spectacles, Une Semaine à Paris* and *Pariscope*, and the daily press for details of time and place of exhibitions. The monthly booklet *Paris Selection*, edited by the Paris Tourist Office, lists exhibitions, shows and other events in the capital.

Paris may be said to be one huge "living stage", as it boasts a total of **100 theatres** and other venues devoted to the performing arts, representing altogether a seating capacity of 56 000. Most of these are located near the Opéra and the Madeleine, but from Montmartre to Montparnasse, from the Bastille to the **Latin Quarter**★★ and from Boulevard Haussmann to the Porte Maillot, state-funded theatres (**Opéra-Garnier**★★, Opéra-Bastille, Comédie Française, Odéon, Chaillot, La Colline) are to be found side by side with local and private theatres, singing cabarets and café-théâtres.

Cinemas, more than 400 in number, are to be found in every part of the city, with particular concentrations in the same areas as the theatres and on the Champs-Élysées. There are also two open-air cinema festivals in the city in the summer: one at **Parc de la Villette**★; the other, **Cinéma au Clair de Lune**, is held in parks and squares across Paris.

Music-hall, **variety shows** and **reviews** can be enjoyed at such places as the Alcazar de Paris, the Crazy Horse, the Lido, the Paradis Latin, the Casino de Paris, the Folies Bergère and the Moulin Rouge. As well as the **Opéra-Garnier**★★, the Opéra-Bastille and the Comic Opera (Opéra-Comique), there are a number of concert halls with resident orchestras like the Orchestre de Paris at the Salle Pleyel, the Ensemble Orchestral de Paris at the Salle Gaveau, and the orchestras of the French Radio at the Maison de Radio-France. In addition there are many other halls in which full-scale performances are put on.

There are also nightclubs, cabarets, dens where *chansonniers* can be heard, *café-théâtres*, television shows open to the public, concerts and recitals in churches, circuses, and other entertainment.

🛍 SHOPPING

SHOPPING DISTRICTS

Most major stores are concentrated in a few districts, whose names alone are suggestive of Parisian opulence.

Champs-Élysées

All along this celebrated avenue and in the surrounding streets (**avenue Montaigne, avenue Marceau**), visitors can admire dazzling window displays and covered shopping malls (**Galerie Élysée Rond-Point, Galerie Point-Show, Galerie Élysée 26, Galerie du Claridge, Arcades du Lido**) devoted to fashion, cosmetics and luxury cars.

Rue du Faubourg-St-Honoré
Here haute couture and ready-to-wear clothing are displayed alongside perfume, fine leather goods and furs.

Place Vendôme
Some of the most prestigious jewellery shops (**Cartier, Van Cleef & Arpels, Boucheron, Chaumet**) stand facing the Ritz Hotel and the Ministry of Justice.

Place de la Madeleine and r. Tronchet
An impressive showcase for shoes, ready-to-wear clothing, luggage, leather goods and fine tableware.

DEPARTMENT STORES 🔆 *See map p479*

For locals and visitors alike, the city's great department stores are the ideal way to find a vast choice of high-quality fashions and other goods under one roof. Most leading names are represented. Some have free fashion shows.

Department stores are usually open Monday–Saturday 9.30am–7pm.
Bazar de l'Hôtel de Ville (52 r. de Rivoli)
Galeries Lafayette (40 bd Haussmann)
Printemps (64 bd Haussmann)
Le Bon Marché (r. de Sèvres)

FAIRS AND EXHIBITIONS

Paris hosts a great number of trade fairs and exhibitions all year round. The following events are among the most important.

Paris – Expo, *pl. de la Porte de Versailles. www.viparis.com.* Over 200 exhibitions, conventions and events per year including the Paris Nautical Trade Show.

Parc International d'Expositions, *Paris-Nord Villepinte. www.viparis.com.* Trade Show for Crafts (SMAC) in March, the Maison & Objet home style expo, the International food industry exhibition (SIAL) and Japan Expo.

Parc des Expositions, *Le Bourget aerodrome. www.paris-air-show.com.* Paris Air Show (odd years: next, the 50th, is in 2013).

🏃 SPORT

Among the most popular sporting events held in and around Paris are the International Roland Garros Tennis Championships, the Paris Marathon, the legendary **Tour de France** with its triumphant arrival along the Champs-Élysées, and several prestigious horse races (Prix du Président de la République in Auteuil, Prix d'Amérique in Vincennes, Prix de l'Arc de Triomphe in Longchamp).

The **Parc des Princes stadium** *(24 r. Claude Farrère; www.leparcdesprinces.fr)* is host to the great football and rugby finals, attended by an enthusiastic crowd, and the **Palais Omnisport de Paris-Bercy** *(8 bd Bercy; www.bercy.fr)* organises the most unusual indoor competitions: indoor surfing, North American rodeos, ice figure-skating, tennis championships (Open de Paris), moto-cross races, martial arts, Six-day Paris Cycling Event, and also pop concerts by international stars.

Galeries Lafayette

© François Daburon/Galeries Lafayette

Château de Versailles★★★

Yvelines

Versailles is the creation of the French monarchy at the moment of its greatest splendour. Consisting of the **château**, the gardens, and the **Trianon**★★, it is a wonderfully harmonious composition of building and landscape, the definitive monument of French Classicism.

A BIT OF HISTORY

The birth of the Sun King's palace – The original château was a small hunting lodge around the present Marble Court, built in 1624 for Louis XIII, who had Philibert le Roy reconstruct it in brick and stone in 1631.

The young Louis XIV saw Versailles as the perfect place to build his own château far from the mobs of Paris, a magnificent palace of immense proportions and opulence never seen before. He wanted to demonstrate the glory of the French arts as well as establish the absolute power of the Sun King. He commissioned a renowned team to realise his dream: the architect Louis Le Vau, the landscape architect Le Nôtre and the decorator Le Brun.

Construction began – and continued to some extent for almost a century – in 1661 with the gardens, embellished for Louis XIV's splendid festivals.

In 1668 Le Vau constructed stone façades around the original château, creating an "envelope" which concealed the old façades.

Revolution and Restoration – Under Louis XV changes to the interior included the creation of the Petits Cabinets. He added the Petit Trianon and gardens in the château park next to the Grand Trianon, which was eventually given to Louis XVI's queen Marie-Antoinette, who would expand and embellish it with a private theatre and hamlet.

When the Revolution drove Louis XVI from Versailles, a century of royal occupation came to a close.

- **Michelin Map:** 311 I 3
- **Info:** 2 bis, ave de Paris. ℘01 39 24 88 88. www. versailles-tourisme.com.
- **Location:** Versailles is only 18km/11mi from Paris, easily reached by road or train (take line C of the RER to Versailles-Rive gauche, or SNCF rail link from St-Lazare to Versailles-Rive droite or from Montparnasse to Versailles-Chantiers). The château and park form one side of the town of Versailles. Place du Marché is the town's focal point, offering a variety of delightful restaurants, shops, cafés, brasseries and weekly markets.
- **Don't Miss:** The Grand Canal – rent a rowing boat and enjoy an impressive view of the palace and its gardens.
- **Timing:** A variety of guided tours for the interior of the palace is offered, ranging from 1–2hr. Allow 3hr for the gardens, and even more time if you wish to visit the Grand and Petit Trianons. The park is best seen when the Grands Eaux (fountains) are in operation (weekends and holidays in summer).
- **Kids:** Beyond the Petit Trianon is the Queen's Hamlet (Le Hameau de la Reine), where farm animals (ducks, black pigs, goats) roam about, serving as a great attraction for children.

The artworks were placed in the Louvre and the furnishings auctioned off. Today, the palace is listed as one of UNESCO's World Heritage Monuments following restoration work by the state and private patronage.

THE CHÂTEAU

The enjoyment of even the shortest of visits will be greatly enhanced if the **Michelin Green Guide Northern France and the Paris Region** *is used.*

A complete tour of the palace, gardens, park and Marie-Antoinette's Estate takes two days. If you have only one day begin with the interior of the château, where the most magnificent apartments are to be found. The park and gardens are best enjoyed at leisure.

HIGHLIGHTS

Full appreciation of Versailles demands a knowledge of Classical mythology and its symbols, the château and its gardens being in effect a temple dedicated to worship of the Sun God.

Grands Appartements★★★

Open Tue–Sun Apr–Oct 9am–6.30pm; Nov–Mar 9am–5.30pm. Closed 1 Jan, 1 May, 25 Dec. €18. 01 30 83 76 20. www.chateauversailles.fr.

These comprise the King's Suite on the north and the Queen's Suite to the south, facing the sun.

The six-room suite with decoration by Le Brun was the king's apartment from 1673 to 1682. Then Louis XIV took up residence definitively at Versailles and had a new apartment designed around the Marble Court.

Three times a week on mondays, Wednesdays and Thursdays from 6pm to 10pm the king held court in the Grands Appartements.

Cour de Marbre★★

Very much the heart of Louis XIII's chateau. Built in brick with stone dressings and reserved for the King's private use, it has fine raised paving in black and white marble, façades graced by 40 busts (some of them by Coysevox), mansard roofs decorated with urns, and a colonnaded portico supporting the wrought-iron balcony of the King's Bedchamber.

Galerie des Glaces (Hall of Mirrors)★★★

Jules Hardouin-Mansart completed this splendid reception room begun by Le Brun, and built over Le Vau's terrace. It lies between the War Salon and the

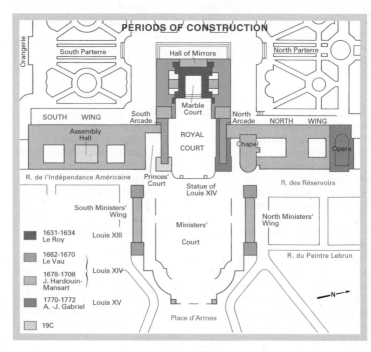

PERIODS OF CONSTRUCTION

Orangerie

South Parterre | Hall of Mirrors | North Parterre

Marble Court

SOUTH WING | South Arcade | North Arcade | NORTH WING

Assembly Hall | ROYAL COURT | Chapel | Opera

R. de l'Indépendance Américaine | Princes' Court | Statue of Louis XIV | R. des Réservoirs

South Ministers' Wing | Ministers' Court | North Ministers' Wing

R. du Peintre Lebrun

	1631–1634 Le Roy	Louis XIII
	1662–1670 Le Vau	
	1678–1708 J. Hardouin-Mansart	Louis XIV
	1770–1772 A. -J. Gabriel	Louis XV
	19C	

Place d'Armes

—N→

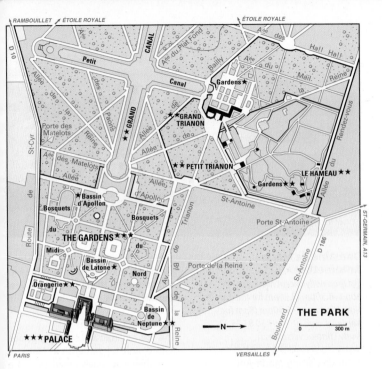

Peace Salon; its mirrors catch the rays of the setting sun. Its decoration was completed in 1687.

Appartement de la Reine★★

Entrance to the Queen's Suite is through the **Salon de la Paix**★, which is decorated with a canvas by Lemoyne of Louis XV presenting peace to Europe. The Queen's suite was constructed for Louis XIV's wife Queen Marie-Thérèse, who died here in 1683.

Chambre de la Reine

Le Brun's original decoration for Marie-Thérèse was redone for Queen Maria Leczczynska between 1729 and 1735. The white and gold woodwork, the greyish tones of the ceiling by Boucher, and the doors decorated by Natoire and De Troy demonstrate the inclination towards the Rococo under Louis XV. Marie-Antoinette had other renovations made in 1770; the two-headed eagle and the portraits of the house of Austria recall the queen's origins.

The floral wall hangings were rewoven to the original pattern in Lyon, matching exactly the original hanging of the queen's summer furnishings of 1786. In France, royal births were public events: in this room 19 children of France were born, among them Louis XV and Philip V of Spain.

The Gardens (Jardins)★★★

🕐 *Open daily 8am–8.30pm.*

Laid out by Le Nôtre, these are a masterpiece of the French landscape style, going beyond the evocation of the idea of majesty (as at Vaux-le-Vicomte) to celebrate the supreme authority of the monarch by the systematic use of Classical symbolism.

Among the 200 statues of this open-air sculpture museum are Keller's bronzes in the Water Gardens (Parterres d'eau), the Latona Basin (Bassin de Latone), Tuby's splendid Apollo in his chariot, and bas-reliefs by Girardon.

Hameau de la Reine

© S. Sauvignier/MICHELIN

Domaine de Marie-Antoinette★★

🕐*Open daily except Mon: Apr–Oct, noon–6.30pm (8.30pm for the gardens); Nov–Mar, noon–5.30pm (8pm for gardens).* ✆€10. ☏01 30 83 76 20. www.chateauversailles.fr.

No trip to Versailles would be complete without visiting Marie-Antoinette's Estate located on the northern edge of the Grand Park.

Formed by the **Petit Trianon** and its **gardens** and **hamlet**, the area has been returned to its former arrrangement. This is where Louis XVI's wife would retire, away from the Court's rigorous etiquette expected from a woman of her rank.

It started with the **Grand Trianon★★**, built as a personal retreat for Louis XIV in 1687, with its own gardens overlooking the Petit Canal and romantic groves. Next door is the **Petit Trianon★★** (1768), where Marie-Antoinette spent much of her time with her children. She had a private theatre, an English-style garden with lakes and follies, and a replica village, le **Hameau de la Reine★★**, complete with thatched-roof houses, animals and mill.

Château★★

This "pink marble and porphyry palace with delightful gardens", as Mansart described it, is widely regarded as the most refined set of buildings within the Versailles compound.

VILLE DE VERSAILLES★★

The town of Versailles was built as an annex to the château to house the numerous titled and untitled people who served the court. It has retained a certain austere charm. It was originally conceived in the symbol of the sun, with the château at the centre and the three main avenues radiating away like rays of light.

There are very few 17C houses left in Versailles; most of the old town dates from the 18C. The pedestrianised r. Satory, in the heart of old town, has become as lively as Quartier Notre-Dame, where antique dealers and outdoor cafés abound.

EXCURSION
Haras de Jardy

▶ *2km/1.2mi northeast along N 182. Leave Versailles by ave de St-Cloud towards Paris.*

This huge stud farm, a horse-lover's paradise, forms part of an important complex

😊 **Guided Tours** 😊

Take one of the tours offered by the tourist office to get better acquainted with both the château and its gardens, and with the town itself. There is a choice of guided tours at the château, each starting at a different entrance.

of leisure activities (tennis, golf, riding, show jumping). The vast park offers fine walks and is the site of numerous show-jumping competitions.

ADDRESSES

STAY

Ibis – *4 ave Gén. de Gaulle. ℘01 39 53 03 30. www.ibishotel.com. 85rms. ⌑ €8.* Near the château and town hall, offering the chain's latest standards of comfort. Poppy red rooms, which are functional and attractive.

Mercure – *19 r. Ph. de Dangeau. ℘01 39 50 44 10. www.mercure.com. 60rms. ⌑ €12.* In a quiet area, an establishment with particularly practical rooms. Well-furnished lobby giving on to a pleasant breakfast room.

Novotel Château de Versailles – *4 bd St-Antoine, 78152 Le Chesnay. ℘01 39 54 96 96. www.novotel.com. 105rms. ⌑ €14. Restaurant.* Hotel at the entrance to the town, on the place de la Loi. Functional rooms lead off an atrium made into a lounge (numerous green plants). Restaurant with modern, bistro-style interior and traditional menu.

Hôtel Le Versailles – *7 r. Ste-Anne. ℘01 39 50 64 65. www.hotel-le-versailles.fr. 46rms. ⌑ €14.* This hotel is situated in a quiet side street not far from the château. The Art Deco-style rooms are spacious, bright and elegant. Cosy bar-lounge and terrace where breakfast is served in summer.

Résidence du Berry – *14 r. d'Anjou. ℘01 39 49 07 07. www.hotel-berry.com. 38rms. ⌑ €14.* Located in the Saint-Louis quarter, this 18C edifice has been entirely restored by Les Bâtiments de France. Comfort and top-quality materials await you in rooms with time-worn beams overhead. In summer breakfast is taken on a veranda that opens onto the patio.

EAT

La Brasserie du Théâtre – *15 r. des Réservoirs. ℘01 39 50 03 21. www.flobrasseries.com. Closed 25 Dec, 1 May. Reservations advisable evenings.* The walls of this 1895 brasserie situated next to the theatre are covered with photos of artists who have frequented it over the years. 1930s-style décor, covered terrace and traditional cuisine.

Le Bœuf à la Mode – *pl. du Marché, 4 r. au Pain. ℘01 39 50 31 99. www.leboeufalamode-versailles.com.* A typical 1930s bistro with a convivial, relaxed atmosphere. The décor – red wall-seats, knick-knacks, posters, mirrors – is a hit and the regional specialities are delicious. Very busy on market days.

Le Potager du Roy – *1 Mar.-Joffre. ℘01 39 50 35 34. Closed Sun–Mon.* Delightfully retro setting and meat and fish dishes with vegetables in pride of place.

Au Chapeau Gris – *7 r. Hoche. ℘01 39 50 10 81. www.auchapeaugris.com. Closed Tue eve and Wed. Reservations required.* This restaurant, said to date back to the 18C, is a veritable institution hereabouts. Quintessential Versailles ambience and décor are the setting for appetising, traditional cuisine. Nothing too wild, just a reliable, very much sought-after establishment.

Valmont – *20 r. au Pain. ℘01 39 51 39 00. www.levalmont.com. Closed Sun eve and Mon.* This old house on the Place des Halles is bound to catch your eye. Venture inside and appreciate the first-rate reception, charming decoration, elegant tables and succulent cookery.

NIGHTLIFE

Fenêtres sur cour – *pas. de la Geôle, Quartier des Antiquaires. ℘ 01 39 51 97 77. Closed 3 weeks Aug.* A restaurant-salon de thé under a glass roof. The bric-a-brac décor - tile floor, carpets, lamps, chandeliers, plaster statues and paintings – is in perfect harmony with the neighbourhood antique shops.

SHOPPING

Shops – The principal shopping areas are: Rue de la Paroisse, Rue Royale, Rue du Général-Leclerc, Place du Marché and Les Manèges, opposite the Rive-Gauche station. You'll find many antique dealers in the Passage de la Geôle, near La Place du Marché.

Major stores – From the FNAC (books, CDs, cameras, etc.) to Printemps or BHV (department stores), the shopping complex Le Centre Commercial de Parly II, on your way out of Versailles towards St-Germain, has it all.

St-Germain-en-Laye★★

Yvelines

A residential suburb of Paris, and also a popular weekend resort, St-Germain's attractions are a château with delightful terraces and gardens, and a forest with pleasant walks.

A BIT OF HISTORY

Now a residential town forming part of the Paris suburbs, St-Germain's significance in the course of French history goes back hundreds, if not thousands, of years.

A strategic site 60m/197ft above a bend in the Seine persuaded Louis VI le Gros (the Fat) to build a stronghold here. Later, when the Hundred Years' War was at its height, the castle was restored by Charles V.

Three French kings were born here (Charles IX, Henri II, Louis XIV), as well as several princes, writers, historians and composers. Louis XIII died here. It was here that in 1641 Richelieu promulgated the edict limiting the rights of the French parliament.

On 28 February 1837, the first passenger railway in France was inaugurated, running to Paris.

SIGHT
Château★

Pl. Charles de Gaulle. ℰ01 39 10 13 00.
Its appearance is still much as it was when François I had it rebuilt by Pierre de Chambiges in the taste of the 16C. Louis XIV brought in Mansart to replace the corner turrets with pavilions, and Le Nôtre, who designed the park, laid out the very long terrace (**terrasse**★★) and replanted the forest.

The château houses the **Musée des Antiquités nationales**★★ (&⊙*Open Wed–Mon 10am–5.15pm.* ∞€6. ℰ01 39 10 13 00. www.musee-antiquites nationales.fr*); its priceless collection of archaeological exhibits traces French history from the Paleolithic to the Middle Ages.

▶ **Population:** 41 312
⚲ **Michelin Map:** 311 I 2
▯ **Info:** Maison Claude Debussy, 38 r. au Pain. ℰ01 34 51 05 12. www.ot-saintgermain enlaye.fr.
◗ **Location:** The town is 19km/11.8mi W of Paris and easily reached from the city on the RER (line A1).
◉ **Don't miss:** The main area of interest is the château.
◷ **Timing:** Allow an hour or so to visit the château.

EXCURSION
Auvers-Sur-Oise★★

◗ *32km/20mi NW of Paris, along the A 115.* ▯ *Manoir des Colombières, r. de la Sansonne, 95430 Auvers-sur-oise. ℰ01 30 36 10 06.*
www.auvers-sur-oise.com.

In the early 19C, this pleasant river village just outside Paris became the favoured stomping ground for a new generation of painters known as the "Impressionists" (& *see Introduction*), who came here to stay and paint, including Monet. Later, Van Gogh visited and subsequently committed some of the village sights to canvas, such as the church and town hall. An old walking trail, now a series of narrow streets, still carries the memory of the artists who brought it fame.

In Van Gogh's Footsteps

During his stay in Auvers, Vincent Van Gogh was extremely active. The restful countryside, where he hoped to find peace after his internment in Provence, encouraged his quest for freedom and his frantic need to work. He completed over 70 paintings in a very short time.

Auberge Ravoux★

◷ *Open Mar–Oct Wed–Sun 10am–6pm.* ∞€6. ℰ01 30 36 60 60. www.maison devangogh.fr.
Known as the **Maison de Van Gogh**, this is the inn where Van Gogh stayed for two

months before his tragic death. Feeling guilt towards his brother Theo, upon whom he was entirely dependent, Van Gogh shot himself in the chest while he was out in a field; he died two days later in his room. He was 37 years old.

The inn has been carefully restored and has retained its interior decoration and restaurant. Outside are panels describing the artist's eventful life. The small garret he occupied has remained unchanged and, despite the absence of furniture, gives an insight into the ascetic conditions in which he lived.

▶ *Follow rue des Colombières past the museum and studio of Charles-François Daubigny.*

A path to the right leads to a cemetery set among the corn fields that Van Gogh loved to paint.

Vincent and Theo Van Gogh's Graves

The famous Dutch painter's tomb stands against the left-hand wall. His brother Theo, who supported him and who died soon after him, rests by his side.

Musée de l'Absinthe

🕐*Open Mar–mid-Nov, Sat–Sun and public holidays 11am–6pm (mid-Jun–mid-Sept Wed–Sun 1.30–6pm).* €5. ☎01 30 36 83 26. www.musee-absinthe.com.

The famous green liqueur reached the peak of its popularity in the cafés of the 19C. It was often described as the **green fairy** and was closely linked to the life of the artists of the day who spent a great deal of time in cafés.

The documents, posters and objects displayed in the museum bring back to life the history of a drink which had a profound social influence until it was banned in 1915.

Musée Daubigny

🕐*Open daily except Mon–Tue: Apr–Oct 2–5.30pm (Sat–Sun and public holidays 10.30am–12.30pm, 2–6pm); Nov–Mar 2–5pm (Sat–Sun and public holidays 2–5.30pm).* €4. ☎01 30 36 80 20. www.musee-daubigny.com.

Housed in the Manoir des Colombières, this museum displays a collection of 19C paintings, watercolours, drawings and engravings illustrating the birth of Impressionism.

Maison-Atelier de Daubigny★

🕐*Open late Apr–Sept, except mid-Jul–mid-Aug: Thu–Sun and public holidays 2–6.30pm.* €6€. ☎01 34 48 03 03. www.atelier-daubigny.com.

Charles-François Daubigny (1817–78), a landscape painter, settled in Auvers on the advice of his friend, Camille Corot. He had a studio-house built in 1861 and asked his family and friends to take part in the interior decoration. Charles, his son Karl and his daughter Cécile, as well as Corot and Daumier, left their marks of artistic inspiration on the walls and doors.

👥 Château d'Auvers

🕐*Open Apr–Sept Tue–Sun 10.30am–6pm; Oct–Mar Tue–Sun 10.30am–4.30pm.* €13 (children, 6–18, €9). ☎01 34 48 48 40. www.chateau-auvers.fr.

This restored 17C château, laid out with extensive use of audiovisual presentations, offers visitors a chance to enjoy a **Journey Back to the Days of the Impressionists★** and gain some insight into the wonderful adventure that was art in the 19C.

Using reconstructions of interiors and the projection of some 600 works, it brings to life the Paris of the time, a city undergoing immense change thanks to the work of Baron Haussmann, and a city where the wealthy middle classes led a bustling, frivolous life with little appreciation of the new style of painting.

ADDRESSES

🍽 EAT

🍽🍽🍽 **Auberge Ravoux** – *Opposite the town hall.* ☎01 30 36 60 60. www.maisondevangogh.fr. *Closed Mon–Tue, Fri–Sat lunches, Nov–Feb. Reservations required.* This old artists' café, with its late 19C décor, was Van Gogh's last home. Very pleasant, history-rich atmosphere, a pretty serving counter and large tables of solid wood.

Compiègne★★★

Oise

The site of Compiègne had been appreciated by the Merovingians long before Charles the Bald built a château here in the 9C. A fortified town grew up around this nucleus. In 1429, Philippe le Bon (the Good), Duke of Burgundy, had designs on Picardy, which he hoped to incorporate into his realm by means of a joint operation with the English. The French line of defence along the Oise was reinforced on the orders of Joan of Arc; disgusted with the inertia prevailing at Sully-sur-Loire where the French Court had established itself, she had come to Compiègne on her own initiative. But on the evening of 23 May 1430, she was seized by the Burgundians. Wary of possible consequences, Philip the Good sold her on to the English; one year later she was burnt at the stake in Rouen.

- **Population:** 43 247
- **Michelin Map:** 305 H 4
- **Info:** pl. de l'Hôtel-de-Ville. 03 44 40 01 00. www.compiegne-tourisme.fr.
- **Location:** Hidden in the Forest of Compiègne, the town is 60km/37mi E of Beauvais, in southern Picardy.
- **Don't Miss:** The royal private apartments in the palace; the forest surrounding the town, one of the most beautiful of its type in France.
- **Timing:** The Palace will take about 2hr to visit.

Guided Tours

Compiègne offers themed discovery tours from mid-May–mid-Jul and mid-Aug–mid-Oct at weekends and on public holidays. Enquire at the tourist office.

SIGHTS

Le Château★★★

Open Wed–Mon 10am–6pm. Closed 1 Jan, 1 May, 25 Dec. €8.50 (free 1st Sun in the month). 03 44 38 47 02. www.musee-chateau-compiegne.fr.

Compiègne had been a royal residence since the time of the later Capetians, but Louis XV was dissatisfied with the ill-assorted and crumbling buildings inherited from his great-grandfather, and in 1738 he gave orders for the château to be reconstructed.

The architect was **Ange-Jacques Gabriel**, who succeeded in building one of the great monuments of the Louis XV style. Begun in 1751, the great edifice made use of the foundations of the previous structure, partly for reasons of economy, partly because the site was pitted with old quarries. Gabriel chose to emphasise the horizontality of his buildings, stretching them out and providing them with flattened roofs with balustrades, themes he took up again in the Place de la Concorde and École Militaire in Paris. The palace took 40 years to build; after Gabriel's retirement the work was carried on by his draughtsman, and a general movement in the direction of greater simplicity is very evident, with features like entablatures, ornamental window-brackets and attic floors tending to disappear. This evolution can be traced in the left wing of the main courtyard (1755), the principal façade facing the park, which was designed in 1775 and completed 10 years later (Napoleon's staircase of 1801 spoils the effect wished for by Gabriel), and the peristyle of 1783.

While the place was still a building site, it formed the background to the first meeting (1770) between Louis XVI and Marie-Antoinette. Later, in 1810, it was where Napoleon met Marie-Louise, Marie-Antoinette's great-niece.

During the Second Empire, Napoleon III made Compiègne his favourite residence, where he took muchpleasure in

Château de Compiègne

©Yann Guichaoua/age fotostock

the house-parties to which like-minded celebrities would be invited, some 80 at a time.

Inside, the palace is decorated and furnished in 18C and Empire style (chests of drawers, applied ornament, wall-cupboards, tapestries).

Musée de la Voiture et du Tourisme★★

Within the Château.

In addition to 18C and 19C coaches, the vehicles exhibited include: the **Mancelle** of 1898, a steam mail-coach designed by Amédée Bollée; a No 2 **Panhard**; a Type A **Renault** of 1899 with direct drive; the **Jamais Contente** ("Never Satisfied") of 1899, an electric car with tyres by Michelin, the first to reach 100kph/62mph; a Type C **Renault** of 1900, one of the first cars to have enclosed bodywork (by Labourdette); and a **Citroën** half-track of 1924.

ADDITIONAL SIGHTS

Hôtel de Ville★
Musée de la Figurine historique★
(pl. de l'Hôtel de Ville)
Musée Vivenel – Greek vases★★
(2 r. d'Austerlitz)

EXCURSIONS

Clairière de l'Armistice★★

▶ 8km/5mi E.

This is the place where, at 5.15am on 11 November 1918, the armistice was signed which put an end to WWI at 11am on the same day.

At the time the site was sheltered by forest trees. A restaurant-car identical to the carriage **(wagon-bureau)** (Oopen mid-Oct–Mar 9am–noon, 2–5pm; Apr–mid-Oct 10am–noon, 2–6pm. ⊛€4. ℘03 44 85 14 18) used by Marshal Foch displays the original objects handled by the delegates in 1918. **Ferdinand Foch** (1851–1929) is generally held to have been the architect of Allied victory in the Great War of 1914–18. He was born in Tarbes in the Pyrénées in an 18C middle-class home (now a museum). He taught strategy at the Military Academy (École de Guerre), then became its commandant. In 1914 he distinguished himself both in the Battle of the Frontiers in Lorraine and in the "Miracle of the Marne". After the German breakthrough in the Ludendorff offensive of early 1918, Foch was appointed supreme commander of the French and British armies. Promoted to marshal, it was he who launched the final Allied offensive on 8 August.

After the Battle of France in 1940, it was the turn of a French delegation to present itself here to the dignitaries of the Nazi regime in order to hear the victors' terms for an armistice. It was signed on the evening of 22 June.

The clearing and its historic monuments were then ransacked by the occupation forces; only the statue of Marshal Foch was spared.

Château de Pierrefonds

Château de Pierrefonds★★

▶ *14km/8.7mi SE.*

The stronghold seems to embody everything that a medieval castle should be as it looms over the village crouching at its feet. For the most part, however, it is a creation of the 19C. Pierrefonds was part of the Duchy of Valois, and its castle, whose origins go back as far as Carolingian times, was rebuilt in the middle of the Hundred Years' War by Louis d'Orléans, the brother of Charles VI, as part of a chain of defences between the rivers Oise and Ourcq. It was dismantled during the reign of Louis XIII.

The castle ruins were bought by Napoleon I. In 1857 Louis Napoleon, inspired by romantic ideals, commissioned **Viollet-le-Duc** (1814–79) to restore the keep; four years later he was entrusted with a complete rebuilding of the castle as an Imperial residence and a picturesque place for receptions given to entertain the emperor's guests at Compiègne. From the ramparts the view extends over the Vallée de Pierrefonds. Little of Louis d'Orléans' building is left save the base of the walls and the towers visible from the track leading to the castle.

Viollet-le-Duc's contributions, in the neo-Gothic style, are not without merit, but are notable more for originality than for strict historical accuracy, in terms of both architecture and decoration (arcading and gallery of the main façade in the courtyard, tribune in the chapel, roof of the Salle des Preuses). Nevertheless, it gives an excellent idea of a castle's defensive system prior to the age of cannon (north rampart walk).

Château de Blérancourt

▶ *31km/19mi NE.*

During WWI the château was taken over by Ann Morgan, who set up a temporary hospital here. Blérancourt subsequently became the headquarters for the organisation of relief for the civilian population.

When the war was over, Miss Morgan's efforts were directed towards the establishment of a museum of Franco-American history. In 1929, she presented the place to the French state, whereupon its name was changed to the **Musée National de la Coopération Franco-Américaine** (ⓘ*reopening 2012;* ℘*03 23 39 60 16; www.museefrancoamericain.fr*). About a dozen rooms in the left wing (at present closed for reconstruction) are devoted to the American War of Independence.

The exhibits on show in the right wing (Pavillon Florence Gould) illustrate aspects of the long and close relationship between the two countries; there are displays on the 1801 Treaty of Friendship, the Louisiana Purchase, emigration to the United States, the Gold Rush, etc. Other rooms evoke the two world wars, notably by means of relics of the

La Fayette Squadron and of the American Field Service.

Beauvais★★

◯ *Beauvais lies on the A 16 in southern Picardy.* 🏠 *1 r. Beauregard.* 📞 *03 44 15 30 30. www.beauvaistourisme.fr.*
An extraordinary Gothic cathedral stands at the centre of this fortified city.

Cathédrale St-Pierre★★★

◯ *Open daily: May–Oct 9am–12.30pm, 2–6.30pm (Jun–Sept 9am–6.30pm); Nov–Apr 9am–12.30pm, 2–5.30pm.* 📞 *03 44 48 11 60. www.cathedrale-beauvais.fr.*

The strange spireless building is the result of a long effort, technical and financial, which eventually ended in failure. In 1225 the Bishop of Beauvais decided to build the biggest and highest cathedral of the age in honour of St Peter. Its vaults were to top 48m/157.5ft. But in 1272, ten years after completion, the vault collapsed; it was rebuilt but fell again in 1284. Work had to start immediately on strengthening the walls, increasing the number of flying buttresses at the east end and using external struts at the base of the roof, 40m/131.2ft above ground, concealing the sheer daring of the original enterprise.

The interior was treated similarly. In the southern bays, additional pillars underpinned the structure above. The windows were given more lancets to subdivide and strengthen them, and glazing was added to the elevation, lightening it considerably.

After the Hundred Years' War, Martin Chambiges began the construction of the transepts and crossing. He designed the great gable and rose window of the south transept, then, instead of the nave, he built the crossing tower. It was completed in 1539, a century later, 11m/36ft higher than the tower of Strasbourg Cathedral. With no nave to buttress it, the great structure collapsed in 1573.

The dizzying height of the vaults is still most impressive and there is much decorative work to admire, from the Renaissance doors of the south portal, to the **stained-glass windows (vitraux)**★★

created by the Beauvais workshops founded by Ingrand Leprince. There's also the remarkable **astronomical clock** (horloge astronomique)★.

ADDRESSES

🛏 STAY

🍴🍽 **Auberge de la Vieille Ferme** – *58 r. de la République, Meux.* 📞 *03 44 41 58 54. 14rms.* 🛏 *9.50€. Restaurant* 🍴🍽. This old farmhouse built of Oise Valley brick offers rooms that are simple but well-kept and practical. The restaurant sports exposed beams, rustic furniture, a tile floor and gleaming copperware. The menu offers traditional and regional cuisine.

🍴🍽 **Hôtel des Beaux Arts** – *33 cours Guynemer.* 📞 *03 44 92 26 26. www.bestwestern.com. 50rms.* 🛏 *10€.* Located along the Oise waterfront, here's a contemporary hotel whose modern, well-soundproofed rooms have been furnished in teak or laminated wood. Some are larger and have a kitchenette.

🍽 EAT

🍴🍽 **Le Bistrot des Arts** – *33 cours Guynemer.* 📞 *03 44 20 10 10. Closed Sat lunch and Sun.* Located on the ground floor of the Hôtel des Beaux-Arts, an appealing, authentic bistro decorated with various objects and etchings. In the kitchen, the chef concocts appetising dishes using market-fresh produce.

🍴🍽 **Brasserie du Nord** – *pl. de la Gare.* 📞 *03 44 83 58 84. Closed Sun & public holidays.* This has become quite an institution locally for its seafood dishes. The dining room is modern and bright.

🍴🍽🍽 **Auberge du Buissonnet** – *825 r. Vineux, Choisy-au-Bac. 5km/3mi NE of Compiègne via N 31 and D 66.* 📞 *03 44 40 17 41. Closed Sun eve, Tue eve and Mon. Reservations recommended.* Ask for a table near the bay windows of the dining room or on the terrace, weather permitting, and watch ducks and swans glide peacefully over the pond, then shake themselves off and waddle proudly toward the garden.

🍴🍽🍽🍽 **Le Palais Gourmand** – *8 r. du Dahomey.* 📞 *03 44 40 13 13. http://le-palaisgourmand.com. Closed Sun eve and Mon .* This spruce-timbered house (1890) has a string of rooms and an attractive verandah where heaters, Moorish pictures and mosaics create an agreeable atmosphere. Traditional cuisine.

Laon★★

Aisne

This ancient town dominates the surrounding countryside from its magnificent **hilltop site★★**, a 100m/328ft-high limestone outlier rising abruptly from the plain. Its defensive potential was noted by the Carolingian kings who made it their capital for 150 years, from the reign of Charles le Chauve (the Bald) (840) to Louis V (987). It was only in the reign of Hugh Capet that the capital was moved to the Île-de-France.

SIGHT
Cathédrale Notre-Dame★★

🐾 *Guided tours available.*
€6. ☏03 23 20 26 54.

The present cathedral was begun in 1160 and completed towards 1230. It is in the early Gothic style, still caught up in the Romanesque idiom (as in its Norman-style lantern-tower).

The west front is a masterpiece, with its deep porches and stepped towers flanked by openwork turrets. The immensely long **nave★★★** shows the persistence of Carolingian traditions, but "nowhere else did the development of

▶ **Population:** 27 230
Ġ **Michelin Map:** 306 D 5
🛈 **Info:** pl. du Parvis Gautier de Mortagne. ☏03 23 20 28 62. www.tourisme-paysdelaon.com.
◐ **Location:** Laon lies 138km/86mi NE of Paris, mid-way between Reims and Saint-Quentin.
🅿 **Parking:** Driving and parking are difficult in the Upper Town. Parking is available at the foot of the cathedral and along Promenade de la Couloire.
🕐 **Timing:** The quickest and most enjoyable way to reach the Upper Town is on the cable railway, called Poma (Mon–Sat 7am–8pm. ☏03 23 23 52 01. www.tul-laon.net). The tourist office organises guided tours of local sights and sells Le Pass Enfant (€19), for reduced kids entry and activities around town.

Lantern tower of the cathedral
©Xiongmao/Fotolia.com

12C Gothic achieve such breadth and unity" (Henri Focillon). The elevation is four-storeyed, with great arches carried on circular columns, a gallery with bold double arches, a blind triforium and a clerestory. In the nave, transept and chancel the bays are marked – still in a less emphatic way than at either Sens (1140) or Senlis (1153) – by a pattern of major and minor clustered columns, the former with five, the latter with three engaged columns.

ADDITIONAL SIGHTS
Quartier de la Cathédrale★★ (Cathedral area)
Rempart du Midi★ (southern Ramparts) – **views★**
Musée Archéologique Municipal★ *(32 r. George-Ermant)*. **Chapelle des Templiers★** *(r. Paul Doumer)*. **Église St-Martin★** *(r. Eglise St Martin)*.
Porte de Soissons★

Senlis★★

Oise

A tributary of the Oise, the Nonette River runs through this picturesque medieval town surrounded by the rich cornfields of Valois and the wooded expanses of Ermenonville, Chantilly and Halatte forests. Strolling along the winding streets of the Old Quarter, paved with flagstones and lined with relics of its past, you may still feel the powerful presence of the Frankish rulers and cathedral builders who left behind an invaluable legacy for us to enjoy.

A BIT OF HISTORY

The election of Hugues Capet – The conquerors of Senlis built a massive stronghold over the first Gallo-Roman ramparts of the town. The kings of the first two **Frankish dynasties** would often take up residence here, lured by the game in the nearby forests.

The Carolingian line died out when Louis V suffered a fatal hunting accident. In 987, the Archbishop of Reims called a meeting at Senlis Castle in which he and the local lords decided that **Hugues Capet**, then Duke of France, would be the next king.

The last king of France to have stayed in Senlis was Henri IV. The city went out of fashion as a royal place of residence and was gradually replaced by Compiègne and Fontainebleau.

CATHÉDRALE NOTRE-DAME★★

🕐 *Open daily (except during religious office) 9am–7pm.* 📞 *03 44 53 01 59.*

The construction of Senlis cathedral started in 1153 – 16 years after St-Denis and 10 years before Notre-Dame in Paris – but progressed at a slow pace due to insufficient funds. The cathedral was not consecrated until 1191. It was only toward the mid-13C that the right tower was crowned with the magnificent **spire**★★ which was to have such a strong influence over religious architecture in the Valois area. The **main doorway**★★ is strongly reminiscent of the doorways at

▶ **Population:** 16 950

Michelin Local Map: 305 G 5 or map 106 folds 8, 9

Info: Office du tourisme de Senlis, pl. du Parvis-Notre-Dame, 60300. 📞 03 44 53 06 40. www.senlis-tourisme.fr.

Location: Access from Paris: by car, via the A 1 (51.5km/32mi); by train, from Gare du Nord to Chantilly, then bus link to Senlis.

P Parking: The car park near the cathedral fills early in the day. Try those off the rue de la République.

Don't Miss: Notre-Dame's magnificient spire; the view over the remains of the old ramparts from the Jardin du Roy; the Gallo-Roman and Merovingian collections of the Musée d'Art et d'Archéologie; St-Frambourg Royal Chapel and its stained-glass windows by Joan Miró.

Chartres, Notre-Dame in Paris, Amiens and Reims.

South front – Constructed by **Pierre Chambiges** (1509–44) in the 16C, the **transept façade**★★ contrasts sharply with the main façade. You can follow the evolution of Gothic architecture from the austere 12C to the 16C, when Late Flamboyant showed signs of Renaissance influence, introduced after the Italian wars.

North side – The cathedral's setting on this side is much less solemn. It features several patches of greenery and is extremely picturesque.

Skirt the little garden that follows the east façade of what was once the bishop's palace. The building rests on the ruins of the old Gallo-Roman ramparts; the base of one tower remains. Lovely **view** of the cathedral's east end.

Château de Chantilly★★★

Oise

A synonym for elegance, Chantilly is home to wonderful art collections, a great park and forest, and the cult of the horse as well as the château itself.

THE CHÂTEAU★★★

◷*Open Apr–Nov 10am–6pm; Nov–Mar 10.30am–5pm.* ∞*€13.* ✆⁂ *Guided tours (30min).* ✆*03 44 27 31 80. www.chateaudechantilly.com.*

Anne de Montmorency, the great Constable of France who served six monarchs (from Louis XII to Charles IX), had a Renaissance castle built here in 1528. The foundations of an earlier building (1386) were re-used. In 1560 the architect Jean Bullant designed a charming little château (Petit Château) to the south of the main building.

The Great Condé and his descendants later made the state rooms of the Petit Château into their living quarters; today, there is much to delight the eye, including Rococo woodwork, manuscripts, silver caskets and icons.

The greatest treasure is in the Library *(Cabinet des Livres.* ◷*Open daily 9.15am–5pm)*; this is the **Limbourg** brothers' sumptuously illuminated *Book of Hours for the Duke of Berry (Les Très Riches Heures du Duc de Berry)* of about 1415, completed 60 years later by Jean Colombe (on display in reproduction).

Under Louis II of Bourbon, known as the Great Condé, Le Nôtre laid out the park and gardens; François Mansart redesigned the principal façade and the layout of the rooms.

During the Revolution, the château was dismantled to first-floor level, the Petit Château was ruined and the park laid waste.

On the death of Louis-Joseph de Condé, the estate passed into the hands of the Duke of Aumale, who rebuilt the great edifice (1875–83) in a neo-Renaissance style.

⚐ **Michelin Map:** 305 F-G 6

🛈 **Info:** 60 ave du Maréchal Joffre. ✆03 44 67 37 37. www.chantilly-tourisme.com.

▶ **Location:** Chantilly is 50km/31mi N of Paris. When you arrive, the château is well signposted from here.

⏱ **Timing:** Allow at least 2hr for the château.

The château houses a **museum**★★ *(*◷ *open same hours as château;* ∞ *(park and gardens) €6;* ✆*03 44 62 62 62)* – manuscripts, furniture, paintings, sculpture – whose wealth would prove difficult to rival today.

The landscaped **English-style garden**★ *(*◷*22 Mar–Oct, 10am–8pm (last admission 6pm), 5 Nov–21 Mar, 10.30am–6pm (last admission 5pm);* ∞*€6 (under-18s free charge when with an adult);* ♿ ✆*03 44 27 31 80)* was laid out on the surviving relics of Le Nôtre's park in 1820.

Grandes Écuries★★

◷*Open Apr–Sept 10am–5pm.*

These stables were built in 1721 by Jean Aubert for Louis-Henri of Bourbon, the Great Condé's great-grandson. Much admired in its time, it is the finest example of 18C building at Chantilly to have come down to us.

The stables house the **Musée Vivant du Cheval et du Poney**★ *(*⚠*closed for restoration until 2014.* ✆*03 44 27 31 80; www.museevivantducheval.fr)*, which has stalls from the time of the Duke of Aumale, historic harnessing, costumes, and all kinds of objects associated with equitation. Riding displays take place in the central rotunda.

More than 3 000 horses are stabled and trained in and around Chantilly; race meetings and hunts both perpetuate the tradition begun on 15 May 1834 when France's first great official race meeting was held, and maintain Chantilly's reputation as the country's thoroughbred capital. The French Derby *(Prix du Jockey Club)* is held here every April.

Parc Astérix★★

Oise

Astérix the Gaul, comical hero of the famous cartoon strip by Goscinny and Uderzo known throughout the world and translated into several languages, provides the theme for this 50ha/123-acre fun park which opened in 1989. It is a fantasy world for all ages that offers a madcap journey into the past.

⚹ VISIT

🕐 Open early Apr–May daily except Mon–Tue, and Sat–Sun in Sept–Oct 10am–6pm; Jun–Aug 10am–7pm. ⚲€40 (under-11 €30). ℘08 26 30 10 40 (€0.15/min). www.parcasterix.fr.

The park is basically divided into five "historical" sections, complete with various attractions, shows, and a choice of snacks and meals. To explore this enchanting world, start at **Via Antiqua**, a "street" lined with stalls symbolising Asterix's journeys across Europe.

- 🖦 **Michelin Local Map:** 312: G-6 or map 106 fold 9. 30km/18.6mi north of Paris.
- ▷ **Location:** By **car**: 30min from central Paris on *autoroute* A 1; by **Métro**/RER train: line B3 from Châtelet or Gare du Nord stations (alight at Roissy-Charles de Gaulle 1 station); by **coach**: from Roissy coach station with Courriers Île-de-France (CIF; www.cif-bus.com).
- ⚹ **Kids:** Camp de Petitbonum, La Ronde des Rondins, Les Petits Drakkars, La Forêt des Druides, Au Pied du Grand Huit, La Petite Tempête, Les Petits Chars Tamponneurs.

Gaul

At the very heart of the park, Astérix's **Village Gaulois**★ consists of huts where visitors can meet the little hero and his fellow characters. Nearby, the atmosphere is much damper at the **Grand Splatch**★. But perhaps the most popular site is a Stone Age village built on piles, where an ingenious delivery system called **Menhir Express**★★ takes anybody who dares on a trip through a network of canals bristling with surprises! You will also love the ride known as the **Trace du Hourra**★★★ aboard a small train.

Roman Empire

In the arena, witness a charming young Gallic spy become the heroine of acrobatic fights in a show called **La Légion recrute**★★.

Join the **Espions de César**★ who have devised a very efficient surveillance system above ground level. And if you are really serious about a spy career, go through intensive spy training and meet the four challenges of the **Défi de César**.

Greece

The **Vol d'Icare** (Icarus' flight) takes you out of Daedalus' labyrinth, but you still have to defeat the terrible **Hydre de Lerne**. Once you are safe and sound, you may want to embark on a daring journey aboard a giant roller coaster called **Tonnerre de Zeus**★★, with the angry god watching you from atop Mount Olympus! After so much action, relax and enjoy a wonderful **spectacle of dolphins**★★ at the Theatre of Poséidon or a trip down the **Elis River**.

Vikings

The hiighlights of this section of the park include **Goudurix**★★, a gigantic roller coaster; **La Galère**, a funny swing in the shape of a boat; and for your little ones, **Les Petits Drakkars** (boats slipping on water) and **Les Petites Chaises Volantes** (flying chairs).

Across Time

A long journey in time takes place along **Avenue de Paris**★★. Ten centuries of history are illustrated here, each period represented by people in costume, typical shops and the avenue's own special atmosphere.

Disneyland Resort Paris★★★

Seine-et-Marne

Opened in 1992 under the name EuroDisney, **Disneyland Paris** is an enormous holiday resort outside Paris with hotels, a 27-hole golf course, Disney Village entertainment and shopping complex, and campsite. The Disney Studios opened in 2002, and other new developments are planned through to 2017.

A BIT OF HISTORY

Born in Chicago in 1901, Walt Disney showed great ability in drawing. After WWI, in which he served as an ambulance driver in France, he returned to the United States where he met a young Dutchman called Ub Iwerks, who was also passionate about drawing.

In 1923 the pair produced in Hollywood a series of short films called **Alice Comedies** and in 1928 Mickey Mouse was created.

There next followed the era of the Oscar-winning, full-length animated cartoon films: **Three Little Pigs** (1933), **Snow White and the Seven Dwarfs** (1937), **Dumbo** (1941).

Disney productions also developed to include films starring real people, such as **Treasure Island** (1950), and some mixing of the two, for instance **Mary Poppins** (1964), which won six Oscars.

DISNEYLAND PARK★★★

This theme park, like those in the United States and Japan, is a realisation of Walt Disney's dream of creating a small, enchanted park where children and adults can enjoy themselves together. The large Disneyland Paris site (over 55ha/136 acres) is surrounded by trees and comprises five territories or lands, each with a different theme.

Every day there's a **Disney Parade**★★, a procession of floats carrying all the favourite Disney cartoon characters. On some evenings and throughout the summer the **Main Street Electrical**

- ▷ **Location:** The resort is located 30km/18.6mi east of Paris in Chessy.
- ▣ **Parking:** Parking on-site, €15/car, €10/motorcycle, €20/camping-cars.
- ⊘ **Don't Miss:** The Disney Parade of characters down Main Street daily at 4pm.
- ◷ **Timing:** Allow two days to visit the entire resort.
- ⚇ **Kids:** "Meet & Greet" Disney characters at specific restaurants.

Parade★★ adds extra illuminations to the fairy-tale setting.

Main Street USA

Enter the park on to the main street of an American town at the turn of the 20C, bordered by shops with Victorian-style fronts. Horse-drawn street cars, double-decker buses, fire engines and Black Marias transport visitors from Town Square to Central Plaza while colourful musicians play favourite ragtime, jazz and Dixieland tunes. From Main Street station a small steam train, the **Euro Disneyland Railroad**★, travels across the park and through the **Grand Canyon Diorama**.

Frontierland

The conquest of the West, the gold trail and the Far West with its legends and folklore are brought together in Thunder Mesa, a typical western town. The waters here are plied by two handsome **steamboats**★, the *Mark Twain* and the *Molly Brown*.

In the bowels of **Big Thunder Mountain**★★★ lies an old gold mine which is visited via the mine train: this turns out to be a runaway train which hurtles out of control to provide a thrilling ride. A tour of the dilapidated **Phantom Manor**★★★ overlooking the rivers of the Far West is a spine-chilling house of hundreds of mischievous ghosts. The horseshoe-shaped **Lucky Nugget**

GETTING THERE

RER: (line A) Marne-la-Vallée–Chessy; by TGV from Lille, Lyon, Avignon, Marseille, Bordeaux, Nantes and Toulouse, by shuttle from Orly and Roissy-Charles de Gaulle Airports; **by car** via *autoroute'* A 4 direction Metz; **exit at junction 14** and follow signs to Disneyland.

GENERAL INFORMATION

Entry – Hours vary daily, these are general guidelines: mid-Jul–end Aug: 10am–11pm; Sept–mid-Apr: 10am–7pm, Sat–Sun and public holidays 10am–10pm; mid-Apr–mid-Jul: 10am–7pm, Sat 10am–10pm.

Disney Studios – High season and weekends 10am–pm; low season 10am–6pm. *01 60 30 60 30*. For **guided tours**, contact the City Hall (Disneyland Park) on Town Square in Main Street, USA. €10 (children, €6).

Disneyland Passport in high season: 1 day/1 park: 51€ (children, 3–11 years: €45); Park Hopper (Passepartout): 2 days €108 (children, €97); 3 days €134 (children, €115). Tickets allow total freedom of movement between both Parks. Ticket usually valid for one year.

Hotel reservations – *01 60 30 60 30*.

Internet – *www.disneylandparis.com*.

Booking a show – Entertainment programmes and booking facilities are available from City Hall, located in Town Square, inside Disneyland Park.

Currency exchange – Facilities are available at the parks' main entrance.

Disabled guests – A guide detailing special services available can be obtained from City Hall (Disneyland Park) or from the information desk inside Walt Disney Studios Park.

Lockers and storage – At the entrance and Main Street Station.

Rental – Guests can rent cameras and video cameras from Town Square Photography, pushchairs and wheelchairs in Town Square Terrace (Disneyland Park) and in Front Lot (Walt Disney Studios Park).

Animals – They are not allowed in the theme parks, in Disney Village or in the hotels. The Animal Care Center is located near the visitors' car park.

Baby Care Center, Meeting Place for Lost Children, First Aid – Near the Plaza Gardens Restaurant (Disneyland Park) or in Front Lot (Walt Disney Studios Park).

MAKING THE MOST OF IT

Tips – To avoid long queues at popular attractions, it is best to visit these attractions during the parade, at the end of the day, or get a **Fast Pass** issued by distributors outside the most popular attractions in both parks; this ticket bears a time slot of 1hr during which there is access to the attraction without waiting in line.

Disneyland Park – Indiana Jones (Adventureland); Space Mountain (Discoveryland); Buzz Lightyear Laser Blast (Discoveryland); Peter Pan's Flight (Fantasyland); Big Thunder Mountain (Frontierland); Star Tours (Discoveryland).

Walt Disney Studios Park – Rock'n Roller Coaster (Backlot); Flying Carpets (Animation Courtyard); The Twilight Zone Tower of Terror (Production Courtyard).

Where to eat – Park maps include a list of eating places, with symbols indicating those offering table service and vegetarian meals.

For quick meals go to **Bella Notte**, **Colonel Hathi's** or **Plaza Gardens** in Disneyland Park, or to the **Backlot Express Restaurant** in Disney Studios. Take time and go to one of the following table service restaurants to enjoy a fine meal enhanced by an original décor (booking recommended, *01 64 74 28 82* or call at City Hall): **Silver Spur Steakhouse**, **Blue Lagoon Restaurant**, **Walt's Restaurant** and **Auberge de Cendrillon** in Disneyland Park or **Café des Cascadeurs** in Walt Disney Studios Park.

Saloon★ – every western town had its saloon – presents the dinner show **Lilly's Follies**.

Adventureland

Access this land of exotic adventure from Central Plaza, through Adventureland Bazaar. In the tropical Caribbean seas, marauding pirates attack and loot a coastal fort and village in the famous action-packed encounter, **Pirates of the Caribbean**★★★.

Courageous archaeologists brave the ruined temple deep in the jungle in **Indiana Jones et le Temple du Péril… à l'envers**★★★, while the giant tree, **La Cabane des Robinson**★★ (27m/89ft high), offers panoramic views from the ingeniously furnished home of the ship-wrecked Swiss family Robinson from JD Wyss' novel.

Fantasyland

Based around Walt Disney's familiar trademark, Sleeping Beauty's castle, this land recalls favourite fairy tales by authors such as Charles Perrault, Lewis Carroll and the Brothers Grimm. **Le Château de la Belle au bois dormant**★★, with its blue and gold turrets crowned with pennants, is at the very heart of Disneyland. **It's a Small World**★★ is a delightful musical cruise in celebration of the innocence and joy of children throughout the world, while **Alice's Curious Labyrinth**★ is a maze leading to the Queen of Hearts' castle. Fly in a boat through the skies above London and in Never-Never Land on **Peter Pan's Flight**★★, or visit the lovable puppet Pinocchio and his friends on **Les Voyages de Pinocchio**★. Enjoyable tours lead through the mysterious forest in mining cars from the dwarfs' mine with **Blanche-Neige et les Sept Nains**★.

Discoveryland

This is the world of past discoveries and future dreams of great visionaries such as Leonardo da Vinci, Jules Verne and HG Wells and their wonderful inventions. **Space Mountain**★★★ – **Mission 2** is a fantastic journey through space, while **Star Tours**★★★ presents a breathtaking inter-planetary experience full of special effects inspired by the film *Star Wars*. Zap alien invaders in **Buzz Lightyear's Laser Blast**, or zoom around **Autopia**. Michael Jackson as **Captain EO** is back, mixing music and special effects.

WALT DISNEY STUDIOS PARK

This park is dedicated to the wonders of the cinema, and offers guests a chance to take a trip backstage and discover the secrets of filming, animation techniques and television. The park entrance is overlooked by a watertower, a traditional landmark in film studios. In the centre of the Spanish-style courtyard, planted with palm trees, is a fountain dedicated to Mickey.

Animagique★★★ celebrates Disney's full-length animation films; spectators find themselves at the centre of a 3D cartoon, next to Mickey, Donald Duck, Dumbo's pink elephants, and Pinocchio. The **Art of Disney Animation**★★ is an interactive discovery of the secrets of animation and **Flying Carpets**★★ is a film set where Aladdin's Genie guides guests on to flying carpets!

Cinémagique★★★ is where fiction meets reality, as spectators literally go through the screen and become the actors and heroes of the film. Sit back and enjoy the **Studio Tram Tour**★★ through amazing film sets until you reach **Catastrophe Canyon!**★★★.

Set on a meteorite-threatened space station, **Armageddon**★★ is a thrilling (and particularly loud) experience!

DISNEY VILLAGE★

Across from the theme parks is Disney Village. In the main street of this American town it's always party time. On summer evenings there is plenty going on in the shops, restaurants and bars. Night-birds can end the evening in the Sports Bar or Country Western Saloon. The famous adventures of pioneer William Frederick Cody (1846-1917), alias Buffalo Bill, are the inspiration for **La Légende de Buffalo Bill**★★, a cabaret dinner which evokes the story of the Wild West, complete with horses, bison, cowboys and Indians.

Château de Vaux-le-Vicomte★★★

Seine-et-Marne

This splendid château, one of the masterpieces of the 17C, lies at the heart of French Brie, a countryside of vast fields broken with occasional copses.

A BIT OF HISTORY

Nicolas Fouquet had been Superintendent of Finances since the days of Mazarin and built a vast personal fortune. In 1656, he decided to construct at Vaux a palace to symbolise his success. As architect, he chose Louis Le Vau, as interior decorator Charles Le Brun, as landscaper André Le Nôtre.

By 1661, Vaux looked as it does today. A connoisseur, a man of lavish tastes, but sadly lacking in political judgement, Fouquet had counted on being appointed in Mazarin's place right up to the moment when Louis XIV decided to take power into his own hands. Furthermore, he had alienated Colbert, and, even worse, had made advances to one of the king's favourites, Mlle de La Vallière.

By May, the decision to place him under arrest had already been taken. On 17 August, the unwitting Fouquet threw the most sumptuous of festivities among the Baroque splendors of Vaux. Hoping to impress the young Louis, he succeeded only in offending his monarch more deeply by the unparalleled extravagance of the proceedings. Dinner was presented on a solid gold service, at a time when the royal silverware had been melted down to repay the expenses of the Thirty Years' War! On 10 September, Fouquet was arrested at Nantes, his property confiscated, and his brilliant team of designers put to work on Versailles.

♣♣VISIT

Open mid-Mar–mid-Nov 10am–6pm. Day pass €16 (children, €13). ☎01 64 14 41 90. www.vaux-le-vicomte.com.

- **Michelin Map:** 312 F 4
- **Info:** Vaux-le-Vicomte. ☎01 64 14 41 90. www.vaux-le-vicomte.com.
- **Location:** Vaux-le-Vicomte is 60km/37mi SE of Paris.
- **Don't Miss:** A walk through the gardens.
- **Timing:** Plan to enjoy a candlit tour of the château (May–early Oct Sat 8pm–midnight) or a Fountains Show (every second and last Sat of the month, 29 Mar–25 Oct 3–6pm).
- **Kids:** There are Easter egg hunts, quizzes and treasure hunts throughout the year.

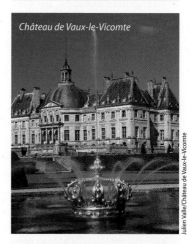

Château de Vaux-le-Vicomte

Julien Valle/Château de Vaux-le-Vicomte

Le Vau's château is the definitive masterpiece of the early Louis XIV style. It is majestic in its impact.

It is to be understood as the central feature of a grandiose designed landscape, an archetype of immense influence over the whole of Europe in the course of the following century and a half.

Le Brun's talent is here made manifest in all its richness and diversity.

His King's Bedroom anticipates the splendour of the Royal Apartments at Versailles.

In the **gardens** ★★★, Le Nôtre showed himself to be a master of perspective.

Fontainebleau★★★

Seine-et-Marne

As early as the 12C, the Capetian kings had built a hunting lodge here, drawn by the abundant game which thrived in the vast forest. It was to become an extraordinarily majestic palace and park listed as a World Heritage site.

A BIT OF HISTORY

The woodland covers 25 000ha/62 000 acres, much of it high forest of sessile oaks, Norway pines and beeches. It grows on the low east–west sandstone ridges, among the crags and boulders of stony wastelands, and in the sandy depressions between the ridges.

The forest is traversed by a network of well-signposted footpaths. Since the days of Colbert's Forestry Ordinance of 1669, "a masterpiece of forestry administration" (J L Reed), it has been carefully managed to ensure its long-term survival.

In spite of the forest's fame and popularity, it is the palace begun by François I which has made the reputation of Fontainebleau.

A taste for natural surroundings together with its role as a military base (notably for cavalry) led to the growth of the town of Fontainebleau in the 19C. Between 1947 and 1967 it was home to the headquarters of NATO.

CHÂTEAU★★★

77300 Fontainebleau. ⏱**Château** open Wed–Mon: Oct–Mar 9.30am–5pm; Apr–Sept 9.30am–6pm. ⏱Closed 1 Jan, 1 May, 25 Dec. ☞€10. ⏱**Gardens** open daily Nov–Feb 9am–5pm; Mar–Apr and Oct 9am–6pm; May–Sept 9am –7pm. ℘01 60 71 50 60. www.musee-chateau-fontainebleau.fr.

From the days of the Capetian kings to the time of Napoleon III, the Palace of Fontainebleau has been lived in, added to and altered by the sovereigns of France. Napoleon Bonaparte liked it; here, in contrast to Versailles, he was free of the overwhelming presence of Louis XIV, a formidable predecessor in

- ▶ **Population:** 15 945
- ⏱ **Michelin Map:** 312 F 5
- ▌ **Info:** 4 r. Royale. ℘01 60 74 99 99. www.fontainebleau-tourisme.com.
- ▷ **Location:** Fontainebleau and its château are in the midst of a large forest, 64km/39.7mi S of Paris.
- ⊘ **Don't Miss:** The Grand Apartments and famous horseshoe staircase.
- ⏱ **Timing:** The exterior of the Palace will take about an hour, the interior more than an hour.

the quest for glory. He called Fontainebleau "the house of Eternity", furnished it in Empire style and set about altering it for himself, for Josephine, and for Pope Pius VII.

In 1528, François I commissioned Gilles Le Breton to replace the existing medieval buildings with two structures linked by a gallery. Like his predecessor Charles VIII, while campaigning in Italy, François had acquired a taste for agreeable surroundings adorned with works of art. He brought in gifted and prolific artists who are known as the **First School of Fontainebleau**. They included Rosso (of Florence), Primaticcio (from Perugia), Niccolo dell'Abbate (from Parma), as well as architects, thinkers, cabinet-makers, goldsmiths and decorators.

He also acquired works of art including Leonardo's Mona Lisa and paintings by Raphael. France was thus permeated by Renaissance taste, by Renaissance mathematics and by an appreciation of the rules of proportion derived from the architecture of Greece and Rome. The pleasures of life were savoured anew, and painters and sculptors abandoned religious subjects in favour of older divinities. This era endowed the palace with many of its most splendid features: on the outside, the left wing and façade of the Court of the White Horse or Fare-

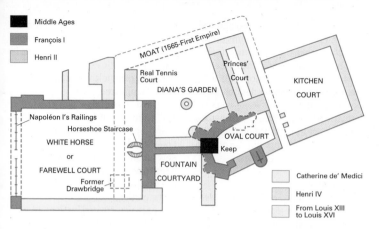

Legend:
- Middle Ages
- François I
- Henri II

MOAT (1565-First Empire)

Real Tennis Court
DIANA'S GARDEN
Princes' Court
KITCHEN COURT

Napoléon I's Railings
Horseshoe Staircase
WHITE HORSE
or
FAREWELL COURT
Former Drawbridge

OVAL COURT
Keep

FOUNTAIN COURTYARD

- Catherine de' Medici
- Henri IV
- From Louis XIII to Louis XVI

well Court (**Cour du Cheval-Blanc ou des Adieux★★**), the concave section of the Oval Court (**Cour Ovale★**), the Golden Gate (**Porte Dorée★**) with its loggia painted by Primaticcio; and on the inside, the François I Gallery (**Galerie François I★★★**) by Rosso, the first important French interior to mix frescoes and stucco work, and the Ballroom (**Salle de Bal★★★**) painted by Primaticcio and dell'Abbate and completed by Philibert Delorme in the reign of Henri II. Henri II, Catherine de' Medici and Charles IX carried on the work initiated during this most creative and productive period. Henri IV enlarged the palace further by building the real tennis court (Jeu de Paume), and the Diana Gallery (Galerie de Diane). He also completed the enclosure of the Oval Court. There

was a change of style; the Second School of Fontainebleau looked to Flanders for its inspiration and found its artists in the Île-de-France; oil was now the preferred medium for painting.

Louis XIII completed the Farewell Court. It was here, from the famous horseshoe staircase built by Du Cerceau, that Napoleon bade his men farewell on 20 April 1814, following his abdication.

Musée Napoléon I★

The **museum** is dedicated to the Emperor and his family; it occupies 15 rooms on the ground level and first floor of the Louis XV wing and is only accessible through the guided tour. Exhibits include portraits (paintings and sculptures), silverware, arms, medals, ceramics (Imperial service), clothing

Central façade of the Château de Fontainebleau

Ph. Gajic/MICHELIN

(coronation robes, uniforms) and personal memorabilia. The rooms on the first floor evoke the Coronation (paintings by François Gérard), the Emperor's various military campaigns, his daily life (remarkable folding desk by Jacob Desmalter), the Empress Marie-Louise in formal attire or painting the Emperor's portrait (picture by Alexandre Menjaud) and the birth of Napoleon's son, the future King of Rome (cradles).

Gardens★

⏱Open daily Nov–Feb 9am–5pm; Mar –Apr and Oct 9am–6pm; May–Sept 9am –7pm. ⏱Closed 25 Dec, 1 Jan. ✆01 60 71 50 70. www.musee-chateau-fontainebleau.fr.

Grotte du Jardin des Pins★

This rare ornamental composition carved in sandstone reveals the popular taste, copied from the Italians, for ponds, man-made features and bucolic landscapes in vogue toward the end of François I's reign. The rusticated arches are supported by giant telamones. The frescoes have disappeared.

The **Jardin anglais★** was created in 1812 on the site of former gardens (featuring a pine grove) redesigned under Louis XIV and abandoned during the Revolution. The Bliaut or Blaut fountain, which gave its name to the palace, plays in a small octagonal basin in the middle of the garden.

The **park** was created by Henri IV, who filled the canal (in 1609) and had the grounds planted with elms, pines and fruit trees. Sixty years before the installation of the Grand Canal at Versailles, this dazzling sight was a great novelty for the *Ancien Régime*, as were the aquatic displays.

ADDRESSES

🛏 STAY

🍽🍽 **Hôtel de la Chancellerie** – *1 r. de la Chancellerie.* ✆*01 64 22 21 70. www.hotel-chancellerie.com. 25rms.* ⌑ *€6.* This small hotel in the heart of the city is located in the former buildings of the chancellery. The small rooms are bright and practical.

🍽🍽🍽 **Hôtel Victoria** – *112–122 r. de France.* ✆*01 60 74 90 00. www.hotel victoria.com. 37rms.* ⌑ *€8.* This 19C building is a pleasant, relaxing place to stay only five minutes on foot from the Château and the centre of town. Most of the rooms on its three floors have been redecorated in shades of yellow and blue; five of them have a marble fireplace.

🍴 EAT

🍽🍽🍽 **Croquembouche** – *43 r. de France.* ✆*01 64 22 01 57. www.restaurant-croquem bouche.com. Closed Sat & Mon for lunch, Sun.* A plain and simple restaurant in the city centre frequented by regulars who appreciate the warm reception, the inviting dining room decorated in soothing colours, and the traditional food prepared from fresh produce.

🍽🍽 **L'Île aux Truites** – *6 chemin Basse-Varenne, Vulaines-sur-Seine. 7km/ 4.3mi E of Fontainebleau dir. Samoreau.* ✆*01 64 23 71 87. Closed Thu lunch and Wed. Reservations required.* A pretty thatched-roof country house on the banks of the Seine. Diners can savour trout and salmon from the restaurant's fish tank while enjoying an incomparable view of the river and forest. Summertime, meals are served outdoors.

🍸 NIGHTLIFE

Le Franklin-Roosevelt – *20 r. Grande.* ✆*01 64 22 28 73.* Wine bar with mahogany furniture and red leatherette wall seats, a library dedicated to the period between 1890 and 1920, and intimate ambience with jazz in the background and some fine vintages on offer. Heated terrace.

⛹ SPORT & LEISURE

Jeu de Paume de Fontainebleau – *Château de Fontainebleau.* ✆*01 60 71 5070. www.musee-chateau-fontainebleau.fr.* The *jeu de paume*, a sport whose descendants include tennis and squash, has been played since 1601 in this indoor court of the Château de Fontainebleau. Visitors can watch a match or try a game themselves.

Chartres★★★

Eure-et-Loir

Chartres' magnificent cathedral, the "Acropolis of France" (Rodin), still beckons to the pilgrim far off across the endless cornfields of the Beauce. The area was occupied by the Carnutes, and Druids once worshipped here; there is also evidence of the pagan cult of a holy spring, and possibly also of a mother-goddess, whom the first missionaries may have christianised as a forerunner of the Virgin Mary.

A BIT OF HISTORY

The picturesque old town **(le Vieux Chartres★)** lies at the point where the Eure cuts into the plain of the Beauce. Today, the old mill-races and laundry-houses have been restored, and a number of 17C houses have kept their embossed doorways topped by a bull's-eye. The most attractive townscape is to be found in the St-André quarter, by the riverbanks, and in Rue des Écuyers and Rue du Cygne. Loëns Granary (Grenier de Loëns) is a fine 12C building which once housed the tithes of grain and wine.

Chartres attracted pilgrims at an early date, first of all to Our Lady of the Underground Chapel *(Notre-Dame-de-Sous-Terre)*, then to the cathedral which Bishop Fulbert built in the 11C but which was burnt down in 1194.

▶ **Population:** 40 714
◉ **Michelin Map:** 311 E 5
▤ **Info:** pl. de la Cathédrale. ☎02 37 18 26 26. www.chartres-tourisme.com.
◗ **Location:** The cathedral dominates the old quarter, Quartier St-André.
◷ **Timing:** Allow at least 2hr for the cathedral.

SIGHT

Cathédrale Notre-Dame★★★

◷*Open daily 8.30am–7.30pm.* Guided tours Nov–Mar 2.45pm; Apr–Oct Sun–Mon 2.45pm, Tue–Sat noon and 2.45pm. ☎02 37 21 75 02.
◷ See *Introduction: Art – Architecture.* Reconstruction began immediately and was completed in the short space of 25 years. The north and south porches were added only 20 years later and the building consequently has a unity of style possessed by few other Gothic churches. Pilgrims have been coming here for eight centuries.

The new cathedral raised the Transitional Gothic style to new levels. The bays of the nave, previously square in plan, are now oblong and have sexpartite vaults; the arches of arcades and windows are more pointed; a round opening is inserted in the space above the highest windows; the structural functions of galleries are taken over by flying buttresses.

Cathédrale Notre-Dame

Jacass/MICHELIN

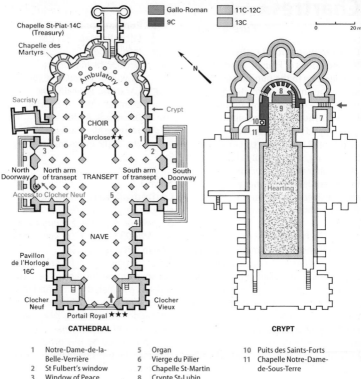

Gallo-Roman · 11C-12C
9C · 13C

0   20 m

CATHEDRAL

- Chapelle St-Piat-14C (Treasury)
- Chapelle des Martyrs
- Ambulatory
- Sacristy
- Crypt
- CHOIR
- Parclose ★★
- North Doorway
- North arm of transept
- TRANSEPT
- South arm of transept
- South Doorway
- Access to Clocher Neuf
- NAVE
- Pavillon de l'Horloge 16C
- Clocher Neuf
- Clocher Vieux
- Portail Royal ★★★

N

CRYPT

- Hearting

1	Notre-Dame-de-la-Belle-Verrière	5 Organ
2	St Fulbert's window	6 Vierge du Pilier
3	Window of Peace	7 Chapelle St-Martin
4	Chapelle Vendôme	8 Crypte St-Lubin
		9 Gallo-Roman wall
10	Puits des Saints-Forts	
11	Chapelle Notre-Dame-de-Sous-Terre	

Gothic verticality reigns outside, too, but the architect wisely kept two Romanesque masterworks, the Old Bell Tower (Clocher vieux) of 1145 and the Royal Doorway, **Portail Royal★★★**, of the west front, with its long-bodied but intensely expressive sculpted figures. The cathedral's interior is subtly lit by its superb stained glass (**vitraux★★★**) which covers a total area of 2 700sqm/25000sq ft and depicts 5 000 figures. Most of the windows date from the 12C and 13C and are the greatest achievement of this art form. "Chartres blue" is famous for the clarity and depth which can be seen in the wonderful Notre-Dame-de-la-Belle-Verrière Window *(first window on the south side of the ambulatory)*. In 1964, the American Society of Architects gave a window and in 1971 the German Friends of the Cathedral did likewise *(north transept)*.

ADDITIONAL SIGHTS
Musée des Beaux-Arts★
(29 cloître Notre Dame)
Église St-Pierre★ – stained glass★
(5 pl. St-Pierre)

EXCURSIONS
Rambouillet
▶ *53km/33mi SW of Paris, via the A 13 and A 12.* 🏛 *Hôtel de Ville, pl. de la Libération, 78120 Rambouillet. ℰ01 34 83 21 21. www.rambouillet-tourisme.fr.* 🅿 *Near the château or on the place Jeanne d'Arc (charge).*

The combination of an attractive château, park and forest makes Rambouillet one of the main sights in the Île-de-France. Since 1883 it has been the official summer residence of the President of the French Republic. Distinguished guests include Nelson Mandela (South Africa, July 1996), Boris Yeltsin (Russia,

October 1995), George Bush (United States, July 1991) and Mikhail Gorbachev (USSR, October 1990).

Château

Guided tours daily except Tue: Apr–Sept 10am, 11am, 2pm, 3pm, 4pm, 5pm; Oct–Mar 10am, 11am, 2pm, 3pm, 4pm. Closed 1 Jan, 1 May, 1 and 11 Nov, 25 Dec. €7. 01 34 83 00 25. www.monuments-nationaux.fr.
Leave from place de la Libération, the site of the town hall).

The château presents a triangular shape after Napoleon dismantled the left wing. The large round tower, where François I is believed to have died, belonged to the 14C fortress. It is difficult to distinguish because of the numerous additions made by the Comte de Toulouse. The façades are essentially 19C.

Mezzanine – The reception rooms commissioned by the Comte de Toulouse are embellished with superb Rococo **wainscoting★**. Note the charming boudoir designed for the Comte's wife.

The corridor adjoining the François I tower leads through to the Imperial bathroom suite, adorned with Pompeian frescoes. This opens onto the Emperor's Bedchamber, where he spent the night of 29 June 1815, and the study.

It was in the dining room – the former ballroom – that Charles X signed the abdication document. The view of the park is stunning.

Park★

Open daily May–Sept 8am–7pm (Jun–Aug 7.30pm); Feb–Apr 8am–6pm; Nov–Jan 8am–5pm. 01 34 94 28 79.
The château is set in a pleasant park, renowned for the variety of its gardens remodelled throughout the 17C and 18C, which reflect the evolution of taste during that period, from the formal parterres to the winding alleyways lined with exotic trees.

Jardin à la française

Walking back towards the château, one goes through the "petit bosquet" (small copse), the "miroir" (mirror) and the "grand bosquet" (large copse) forming a French-style garden.

Quinconce

This quincunx, situated to the east of the château and created in 1710, comprises a group of lime trees from Holland planted according to a chequered pattern known as a "quinconce".
In its centre stands *La Barque* solaire, a bronze sculpture by Karel, inaugurated in 1993.

Jardin à l'anglaise

In 1779, Hubert Robert designed an English-style garden beyond the green carpet of lawn. It is essentially planted with exotic species. The **Grotte des Amants** (Lovers' grotto) was named after a couple of lovers who took refuge inside during a thunderstorm. Canals crisscross the park, forming small islands: Île des Festins, Îles des Roches etc. 18C follies are scattered among the greenery.

Chaumière des Coquillages★

Open same hours as château. Guided tours only (45min). €3. 01 34 94 28 79.
The **landscape garden** in the park features a charming cottage built for the Princesse de Lamballe. The walls of the rooms are encrusted with a variety of seashells, chips of marble and mother-of-pearl. A small boudoir with painted panelling adjoins the main room.

Laiterie de la Reine★

Open same hours as château. Guided tours only (45min). €3. 01 34 94 28 79.
Louis XVI had the Dairy built in 1785 to amuse his wife Marie-Antoinette. The small sandstone pavilion resembling a Neoclassical temple consists of two rooms. The first – which houses the actual dairy – features marble paving and a marble table from the First Empire.
The room at the back was designed as an artificial grotto adorned with luxuriant vegetation. It includes a marble composition by Pierre Julien depicting a nymph and the she-goat Amalthea (1787).

Forêt de Rambouillet★

This vast forest has some delightful footpaths for those who enjoy walking, as well as 60km/37mi of cycle tracks, 20 or more lakes with picturesque banks, and a number of villages with old houses. The forest is home to a thriving game population.

Rambouillet is part of the ancient Yveline Forest, which in Gallo-Roman times stretched as far as the outskirts of Nogent-le-Roi, Houdan, Cernay-la-Ville and Etampes. A large part of it is now included in the Parc Naturel Régional de la Haute Vallée de Chevreuse.

Of the total 20 000ha/49 421 acres, 14 000ha/34 595 acres are State owned. They cover a clay plateau with an altitude of between 110m/358ft and 180m/585ft, crisscrossed by sandy valleys.

In the Middle Ages, wide-scale deforestation took place and the vast clearances now divide it into three main areas of woodland: St-Léger and Rambouillet itself, the most popular areas with tourists situated north of Rambouillet, and Yvelines to the south, which is rather more divided up into private estates.

Flora and fauna

The forest around Rambouillet is damper and has more rivers, lakes and ponds than the one at Fontainebleau. From time immemorial it has been particularly well stocked with game such as roe deer and wild boar – and it remains so today.

👫 Espace Rambouillet

🕐 Open Feb–Nov daily 10am–6pm (call ahead for demonstration schedule). 👓€12 (children, 3–12, €9). 📞01 34 83 05 00. www.onf.fr/espaceramb.

This 250ha/625-acre wildlife park has been divided into various areas (binoculars are recommended):

Forêt des Cerfs, where observation hides provide a view of deer and wild oxen. **Forêt Sauvage**, a 180ha/450-acre site in which the animals roam free. **Forêt des Aigles**, with more than 100 birds of prey in aviaries. Free flight shows. **Coin des Fourmis**, where young children can get acquainted with these industrious insects (ants).

🐾 WALKS AND TOURS

The **GR 1** trail runs through the forest from north to south between Montfort-l'Amaury and Rambouillet. The **GR 22** trail runs in a northwest/southwest direction from Gambaiseuil to St-Léger-en-Yvelines.

Rochers d'Angennes

▶ 8.5km/5.3mi from Rambouillet via D 936 then D 107. Leave from the parking area of the "Zone de Silence des Rabières'"

Walk 100m/110yd through the village up the steeper slope of the valley to find the right path leading to the summit.

🚶 Go past an arena-shaped shelf circled by boulders to reach the crest: **view** of the Guesle Valley and Angennes Lake, bordered by bulrushes, reeds and other aquatic plants.

Balcon du Haut Planet★

▶ 12km/7.4mi from Rambouillet along D 936 to Carrefour du Haut-Planet, then turn right onto the unsurfaced road which crosses rough, hilly ground and leave your vehicle in the car park at La Croix Pater.

🚶 After passing the Blue Fountain spring on the right, the lane reaches a shaded terrace on the edge of the plateau, unfolding the most spectacular panorama of the whole massif: to the north, the **view** extends across the Vesgre Valley and the Château du Planet.

Étangs de Hollande

▶ 8km/5mi from Rambouillet along N 10 then D 191 to St-Hubert; leave the car near the Étang de St-Hubert.

🚶 4hr there and back.

The ponds were part of one of Vauban's projects to create reservoirs for Versailles' water requirements. A series of six ponds separated by paths was laid out near the **Étangs de Hollande**. Only the two end basins are filled with water. In summer, the ponds offer **swimming** and **fishing** facilities. Head west out of St-Hubert, follow the Corbet forest track, cross the Villarceau alleyway, and walk to the Petites-Yvelines crossroads then the Malmaison crossroads. Turn left towards the Bourgneuf crossroads and, to the southeast, the Route des Étangs which skirts the north shore of the **Bourgneuf** pond. Follow D 60 to the south shore of the **Corbet** pond. Walk past the sluice-gate which separates it from the **Pourras** pond and skirt the Pourras woods to Croix Vaudin. A path on the left runs through the woods to the Pont Napoléon; on the right lies the **St-Hubert** pond. This leads back to the Corbet forest track.

Carrefour du Grand Baliveau

◗ *8km/5mi from Montfort-l'Amaury via D 138.* 🏃 *At the crossroads, follow the path to the right of the panel marked "Route forestière du Parc-d'en-Haut". 30min there and back.*

The path offers a charming walk through a lovely green glade. One of the clearings affords a good **view**★ of a secluded valley.

Étang de la Porte Baudet oudesMaurus

◗ *4km/2.5mi from Montfort by D 112 and D 13: go past the turning to Gambais (right) and turn left onto rue du Vert-Galant. Follow the plateau along the winding road.* 🏃 *Starting point: parking des Brûlins; 45min there and back.*

This is one of the finest sites in the forest; farther on, Route Belsédène then Route Goron lead (1km/0.6mi) to Chêne Baudet, a splendid 550-year-old oak tree.

ADDRESSES

🏠 STAY

⊖⊖ **Chambre d'hôte La Ferme du Château** – *Levesville, Bailleau-l'Évêque. 7km/4.3mi NW of Chartres via N 154 and D 134. ℘02 37 22 97 02. Closed 25 Dec, 1 Jan. 3rms.* This elegant Beauce farm offers comfortable rooms.

⊖⊖🗐🗐 **Le Grand Monarque** – *22 pl. des Épars. ℘02 37 18 15 15. www.bw-grand-monarque.com. 55rms.* ⌑ *€14. Le Georges restaurant*⊖⊖🗐🗐. A 16C coaching inn at the heart of the city. The comfortable rooms have a personal touch; some are embellished with cheerfully flowered patterns and canopies while others are more sober.

🍽 EAT

⊖⊖ **Le Café Serpente** – *2 r. du Cloître Notre-Dame. ℘02 37 21 68 81.* A bicycle on the ceiling, posters on the walls and enamelled plaques in the stairwell comprise the décor of this thoroughly genial old café opposite the cathedral.

⊖⊖🗐 **Le Pichet** – *19 r. du Cheval-Blanc. ℘02 37 21 08 35.* Just down the street from the cathedral, a very friendly little bistro that suits our tastes. Inside, there is a pleasant jumble of bric-a-brac: wooden chairs, a collection of coffeepots, pitchers, old street signs and other good stuff. The food is traditional French cuisine.

⊖⊖🗐 **Le Tripot** – *11 pl. Jean-Moulin. ℘02 37 36 60 11. Closed Sun–Mon & public holidays.* This house built in 1553 used to accommodate a *jeu de paume* (real tennis court) called "Le Tripot" whose Latin motto meaning "Belligerents: stay away" may still be seen above the front door.

🛒 SHOPPING

Marché aux légumes et volailles – *pl. Billard.* Each Saturday morning, the covered Vegetable and Poultry Market displays colourful stands featuring authentic Beauce produce. This carrousel of sights, tastes and fragrances is one of the most popular markets in the area.

VISIT

Atelier Loire – *16 r. d'Ouarville, 28300 Léves. Just N of Chartres on the way to Dreux. ℘02 37 21 20 71. http://vitrail-vitraux-chartres.ateliers-loire.fr. Closed Aug and public holidays.* A century-old, stately residence set amidst a park and adorned with stained-glass creations is the home of this atelier founded in 1946 by Gabriel Loire, and continued today by his grandchildren.

Brûlerie les Rois Mages – *6 r. des Changes. ℘02 37 36 30 52. Closed Mon for lunch.* Enter this "retro" coffee-roasting shop and choose among the wide variety of coffees roasted on site and the dozens of teas to enjoy in the *brûlerie* or to take home.

PROVENCE

The name Provence evokes an image of a magical land in the Midi, or south, of France where the sun always shines and Mediterranean influences are supreme: from the extensive remains of six centuries of Roman occupation to the traditional triumvirate of wheat, vine and olive, alternating with the remnants of the natural forest and the infertile but wonderfully aromatic *garrigues* (arid scrubland). Among the fertile Provençal plains stand the *mas*, shallow-roofed pantiled farmsteads protected from the fierce sun by stone walls with few window openings. Crops and buildings are shielded from the effects of the mistral, the strong regional wind, by serried ranks of cypresses.

Highlights

1. Wetland plain of the Rhône Delta: **La Camargue** (p526)
2. Classical Temple with columns at **Nîmes**: Maison Carrée (p531)
3. Palace built for the popes in **Avignon**: Palais des Papes (p534)
4. Roman Aqueduct and road bridge: **Le Pont du Gard** (p536)
5. Natural rock arch created by the river: **Pont d'Arc** (p538)

Geography – Beautiful Provence is synonymous with serene landscapes, from fine sandy beaches to plains of arable land with bountiful crops. These plains are flanked by ranges of limestone hills running east–west including the Alpilles, the rugged Luberon range and

the Vaucluse plateau with its chasms, gorges and great resurgent spring at Fontaine de Vaucluse. The River Rhône brings down 20 million cu m/706 293cu ft of sand, gravel and silt annually, creating the huge delta of the Camargue, now a nature reserve.

Further north the Gorges of the Ardèche cut through the rock to form one of the most impressive natural sights in France.

History – Provence has been occupied from the earliest times. From the 8C BC the Celts settled here, but were eventually subdued by the Romans who founded a settlement at Aix in 122 BC. The collapse of the Roman Empire led to incursions by Visigoths and later by the Franks.

Provence was annexed by the Holy Roman Empire in 1032, but the Counts of Provence retained a degree of independence. The region was incorporated into France in 1486, although the Parliament of Aix remained semi-independent until 1771.

The 18C was a golden age for agriculture and commerce, but during the 19C rural life was affected by phylloxera, which destroyed the vines.

Economy – In recent years Provence has seen much industrial expansion, especially around Marseille, and ever-increasing tourism has been facilitated by the construction of *autoroutes* and high-speed train lines. The climate is conducive to the production of wine, olive oil, fruit and vegetables.

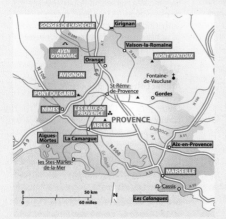

Marseille★★★

Bouches-du-Rhône

The 19C Romano-Byzantine Basilica of **Notre-Dame-de-la-Garde** stands in a commanding position overlooking this great Mediterranean seaport. The **view**★★★ from the church is immense, taking in the islands standing guard in the bay, the harbour, and the background of limestone hills as well as the sprawling city itself.

A BIT OF HISTORY

Marseille began life as a trading post set up by Greeks from Asia Minor around 600 BC. Its inhabitants soon established other commercial bases both in the interior and on the coast, at Nice, Antibes, the Lérins Islands, Agde, Glanum (St-Rémy) and Arles. By the 3C–2C BC the city they called Massilia covered an area of some 50ha/123.5 acres to the north of the Old Port, and the knolls rising above the busy streets were crowned with temples.

A cultural as well as a commercial centre, the city aroused the interest and envy of the Celto-Ligurians of Entremont, and in 123 BC Massilia found it prudent to conclude an alliance with Rome.

The Senate took the opportunity to begin its programme of expansion into Provence and subsequently Gaul.

Seventy years later, when Caesar and Pompey were engaged in civil war, Marseille was obliged to take sides and had the ill fortune to choose the loser. The victorious Caesar besieged the city and sacked it in 49 BC. Narbonne, Arles and Fréjus grew prosperous on the spoils, and Marseille went into decline.

Even after its sack by Caesar, Marseille remained a free city. Its life as a port carried on, with many ups and downs, based on the "Horn" (corne), the original basin sited to the northeast of today's Old Port, which itself came more and more into use as an outer harbour. Nevertheless, the decline of the city as a whole made it difficult to maintain the installations, and the original harbour

▶ **Population:** 859 543

◔ **Michelin Map:** 340 H 6

▯ **Info:** 4 La Canabière. ℰ04 91 13 89 00. www.marseille-tourisme.com.

◗ **Location:** Marseille is on the Mediterranean coast, 32km/20mi S of Aix-en-Provence.

🅿 **Parking:** There are several underground car parks around town.

◈ **Don't miss:** Bouillabaisse; this is arguably the best place in France to enjoy this hugely popular and filling fish dish.

👪 **Kids:** Hook up to the Count of Monte Cristo at Château d'If.

◴ **Timing:** Starting from the Vieux Port, it takes about 2hr to walk along the Canebière. Afterwards, return along the Canebière, but allow 1hr for the old Le Panier district.

gradually silted up, finally becoming completely blocked in the 11C.

The Crusades, together with the growth of the rivalry between Pisa and Genoa, led to a revival of the city's fortunes in the 12C. Further expansion followed, with the incorporation of Provence into the French kingdom in 1481 and even more with the construction of new quays under Louis XIII (a blow to its old rival Arles). In the 19C, the city's fortunes revived further with the expansion of French (and European) colonial activity in the Orient as well as in Africa.

◔ City Pass Marseille ◔

This is an all-inclusive pass giving free access to **museums, public transport, a boat trip** to the Château d'If and even a ride on the little tourist train. €22/1 day, €29/2 days. Enquire at the tourist office.

GETTING AROUND TOWN

METRO–THE RTM – This is the most convenient mode of transport; the two lines operate from 5am–9pm (12.30am Fri–Sun). From 10.30pm–12.35am during the week, the metro is substituted by the "fluobus". ℘04 91 36 58 11. www.le-tram.fr.

Tickets are sold in the form of magnetic cards and are valid for a single trip (€1.50), 1 day (*carte journée*: €5) or for several journeys (*carte liberté*: €6.30 for 5 journeys, €12.60 for 10). Network maps are given out at ticket offices. ℘04 91 91 92 10. www.rtm.fr.

FERRY BOAT – Trips from one side of the Vieux Port to the other (saving you about 800 paces!): place aux Huiles to the town hall. *Journeys daily 9am–7pm. No charge.*

SIGHTS
Basilique St-Victor★

A Christian quarter grew up opposite the old Greco-Roman city. It was here that St Victor is supposed to have met a martyr's death at the very beginning of the 4C, and here too that a fortified abbey is said to have been built in his memory around AD 420.

The basilica was rebuilt in 1040. Its crypt and nave were altered in the early Gothic period. In the **crypt★★** are a number of 4C sarcophagi, examples of the individualism that distinguishes Christian art from that of the Classical world.

Vieux-Port (Old Port and surrounding area)★★

On the south side of the Old Port is the bust of Vincent Scotto (1876–1952), the composer of much-loved popular melodies, surveying what is almost always a highly animated scene. To the east is the Canebière, the city's busy main artery, whose fame has been spread around the world by the mariners of Marseille. For a glimpse into the long history of the port, visit **Musée des Docks romains★** (*4 pl. Vivaux; open Tue–Sun Oct–May 10am–5pm; Jun–Sept 11am–6pm. Closed public holidays; €2; ℘04 91 91 24 62*), part of the **Musée d'Histoire de Marseille★**, known as the Garden of Ruins (Jardin des Vestiges).

The "horn" formed by the first harbour is dramatically visible, and inside there is a 3C boat excavated from the mud.

Centre de la Vieille Charité★★

Open: times vary with each exhibition. Closed public holidays. Each museum €2; major event exhibits €5. ℘04 91 14 58 38. www.vieille-charite-marseille.org.

The old workhouse and hospice (1671–1749) has been carefully restored. The

Vieux-Port

La Marseillaise

On 20 April 1792, Revolutionary France declared war against Austria. In Strasbourg, General Kellerman asked Claude Joseph Rouget de l'Isle, a captain in the engineering corps and a composer-songwriter in his spare time, to write a "new piece of music to mark the departure of the volunteers"; the *Chant de guerre pour l'Armée du Rhin (War Song for the Rhine Army)* was written during the night of 25–26 April. Soon adopted by a battalion from Rhône-et-Loire and carried south by commercial travellers, the Chant reached Montpellier on 17 June. On 20 June, a young patriot from Montpellier on assignment in Marseille, François Mineur, sang it at a banquet offered by the Marseille Jacobin club, located at r. Thubaneau. Enthusiasm was such that the words of the song were passed on to 500 national guards from Marseille, who had been called to arms for the defence of Paris. Renamed *Chant de guerre aux armées des Frontières (War song for the Border Armies),* the anthem was sung at each of the 28 stages of the journey towards the capital, with growing success and virtuosity.

On 30 July, the impassioned verses sung by the warm southern voices, ringing out across the St-Antoine district, was referred to by the electrified crowd as the *Chant des Marseillais (Song of the people of Marseille)*. A few days later, on the storming of the Tuileries, the new anthem was given its definitive name. *La Marseillaise* became the French national anthem on 26 Messidor an III (14 July 1795) of the Republican calendar, and again, after a long period of obscurity, on 14 July 1879.

chapel★ is a masterpiece by Pierre Puget, a Marseille man; it has a little ambulatory and recessed steps allowing the different categories of inmates to make their separate ways to the chapels and galleries, and a central, oval-shaped cupola resting on a drum and supported by Ionic columns and pilasters.

The second-floor gallery affords unusual views of the oblong chapel dome.

The rich and varied collections of the **Musée d'Archéologie de Marseille**, comprising some 900 artefacts from the Near East, Greece, Etruria and Rome, make this one of the few provincial museums able to offer a comprehensive survey of ancient Mediterranean civilisations.

ADDITIONAL SIGHTS

Corniche Président J.-F.-Kennedy★★

This Corniche runs for nearly 5km/3mi – almost entirely along the sea-front. It is dominated by elegant villas built at the end of the 19C. Level with the **Monument aux morts de l'armée d'Orient** (60 Corniche Kennedy), attractive views open out towards the coast and the islands.

Musée de la Faïence★

157 ave de Montredon. &⊙Open daily except Mon: Jun–Sept 11am–6pm; Oct–May 10am–5pm. ⊙Closed public holidays. ⊛€. ℘04 91 72 43 47.

Walk past the Parc Borély and proceed towards Pointe Rouge. The museum is situated at the far end of the Parc de Montredon. Set up in the Château Pastré, a fine 19C mansion built at the foot of the Marseilleveyre massif, this museum is devoted to the art of ceramics, from the early Neolithic Era up to the present day. A great many of the collections feature exhibits from Provence, and particularly Marseille, where the manufacturing of faïence pottery was considerable in the late 17C and 18C.

Musée Grobet Labadié★★

140 bd Longchamp. &⊙Open daily except Mon: Jun–Sept 11am–6pm; Oct–May 10am–5pm. ⊙Closed public holidays. ⊛€3. ℘04 91 62 21 82.

The bourgeois interior of this town house has been preserved, with its fine Flemish and French (16–18C) tapestries, furniture, 18C Marseille and Moustiers faïence ware, religious gold and silver plate, wrought-iron work and old musical instruments. Fine paintings hang on the walls: Flemish, German and Italian Primitives, French School covering the 17–19C.

Musée Cantini★

19 r. Grignan. ♿🕑*Open daily except Mon: Jun–Sept 11am–6pm; Oct–May 10am–5pm.* 🕑*Closed public holidays.* 👓€3. ℘04 91 54 77 75.

This museum specialises in 20C art after WWII until 1960, with particular attention to Fauvist, early Cubist, Expressionist and Abstract art, including works by Matisse, André Derain (*Pine Forest, Cassis*), Raoul Dufy (*Factory in the Estaque*), Alberto Magnelli (*Stones No 2*, 1932), Dubuffet (*Striking Woman*), Kandinsky, Chagall, Jean Hélion and Picasso.

EXCURSIONS
Îles du Frioul

⊙ *Sea crossing: leaves from quai des Belges, Vieux Port.* 👓*€10 return to If or Frioul, and* 👓*€15 to both. For times, see website.* ℘04 91 46 54 65. www.frioul-if-express.com.

👥👤 Château d'If★★

Accessible by boat from Embarcadère Frioul If Express, 1 quai de la Fraternité. 🕑*Open mid-May–mid-Sept, daily 9.30am–6.15pm; rest of year 9am–5.30pm.* 🕑*Closed Mon from 15 –ep-Mar, 1 Jan, 25 Dec.* 👓*€5 (child no charge).* ℘04 91 59 02 30. http://if.monuments-nationaux.fr.

Alexandre Dumas (1802–70), the popular 19C French author of *The Three Musketeers*, gave this castle literary fame by imprisoning three of his heroes here: the Man in the Iron Mask, the Count of Monte Cristo and Abbé Faria. Built rapidly from 1524 to 1528, Château d'If was an outpost destined to protect the port of Marseille. After falling into disuse, it became a state prison where Huguenots and various political prisoners were held; their cells can be visited.

The **panorama**★★★ from the old chapel terrace is remarkable, taking in the harbour, the city and the Ratonneau and **Pomègues** islands, linked by the new port of Frioul.

Massif des Calanques★★

The Massif des Calanques, with Mont Puget (565m/1 854ft) its highest peak, stretches almost 20km/12.4mi between Marseille and Cassis.

With its solid limestone, dazzling whiteness, and weather-worn pinnacles, it has long attracted nature lovers for its wild beauty. However, its unique character and exceptional charm stem above all from its deep and narrow indentations, the famous *calanques*, which have been chiselled out along its coastline, creating a majestic union of sea, sky and rocks.

🐾 There are no direct approach roads by car to the *calanques* with the exception of the less attractive coves of Goudes, Callelongue and Port-Miou. The only way to reach the others is on foot. Footpaths are often steep and rocky: it is advisable to get yourself the IGN map *Les Calanques de Marseille à Cassis* (www.ign.fr).

🐾 Make sure you are equipped with walking boots; carry water with you as there is none available. *Spring is probably the best time to visit.*

🐾 *No access either on foot or by car to the calanques between 1 July and the second Sunday in September, or on days when the mistral is blowing fiercely. Even when access to the calanques is permitted, restrictions may apply in bad weather conditions, particularly on weekends.*

🐾 *Some paths dangerous for children.*

What is a Calanque? – The word *calanque* (from the Provençal *cala*, meaning steep slope) describes a narrow and steep-sided coastal valley that has been bored into the solid rock by a river, whose course was usually guided by a fault, during the periods of the sea's retreat, and which has subsequently been submerged by the waves during cycles of flooding. Such fluctuations in sea level result from the alternation of glaciation and deglaciation on the earth's surface over the course of the past two million years. The most recent rise in the water level, an average of 100m/330ft, occurred 10 000 years ago, flooding caves inhabited by prehistoric man. The *calanques*, none of which is longer than 1.5km/0.9mi, extend towards the open sea via large underwater valleys.

A fragile, remarkable site – The absence of any form of surface water and the area's dryness can be explained by the permeability of the limestone, the proliferation of faults, and low levels of rainfall.

The temperature regulation of the sea, the sun's glare on the high, bare rocks and the area's sheltered position away from the *mistral* all combine to create an exceptionally hot microclimate on the southern slopes of this massif, conditions that occasionally result in winter temperatures 10°C higher than those on its northern side. Some typically tropical and extremely rare species of vegetation have been able to survive the periods of climatic cooling that occurred during the Quaternary period, creating today a botanical reserve of valuable scientific interest.

From the time of the first fire ordered by Julius Caesar in 49 BC to the catastrophic blaze on 21 August 1990 and further fires in July 2009, the forests of the Massif des Calanques have suffered indescribable damage over the centuries.

Increasing protective measures have been introduced in recent years: since 1975 the area has benefited from the protection granted natural monuments and sites. Following the 1990 disaster, measures restricting public access during the summer months were stepped up.

Flora and Fauna – 🖐 *It is strictly forbidden to pick any form of vegetation, stray from marked paths, smoke or light a fire at any time of the year.*

In this semi-arid environment, the best-adapted flora include copses or thickets of green oaks, viburnum, wild olive trees, myrtle and mastic. In addition to woods of Aleppo pine, stony scrub oak, rosemary, and heather-carpeted *garrigue* also predominate.

Samphire and sea lavender grow along the coast, replaced higher up the slopes by a thin cushion of plants including the rare Marseille Astragalus or "mother-in-law's cushion" with its fearsome thorns. Europe's largest lizard and longest snake

can also be found in the *calanques*: the ocellar lizard can grow to 60cm/1.96ft and the Montpellier grass snake can reach 2m/over 6.5ft in length.

Birds nest mainly on the coastal cliffs and outlying islands. The most common, the herring gull or *gabian*; the most rare, Bonelli's eagle, is a beautiful bird of prey with white, grey and dark brown plumage.

Goudes

▶ *Leave Marseille by the promenade de la Plage.*

An old fishing village, nestled amid grandiose rocky scenery. There is no beach, but there are a number of small local restaurants frequented by the local Marseillais. Lunch in the sun here is a delight.

▶ *Continue as far as Callelongue where the tarmac road ends.*

Callelongue

🚶 *(45min). From there you can get to the calanque of Marseilleveyre and its little pebble beach.*

This tiny cove has several *cabanons* (cabins) and provides shelter for a small flotilla of boats.

Sormiou★

🚶 *(45min) Leave Marseille on either ave de Hambourg or chemin de Sormiou. Park in the car park at the entrance to the tarmac road blocked off to vehicles. Walk down to the calanque.*

Considered by the local Marseillais population to be the best of all the *calanques*, there are numerous *cabanons*, a small port, a beach, and several fish restaurants.

Sormiou is separated from Morgiou by the **Cap Morgiou**, a viewpoint affording magnificent views of both *calanques* and the eastern side of the massif.

Morgiou★★

🚶 *(2hr) From Marseille take the same route initially as for Sormiou; turn left and follow the "calanque Morgiou" signs (you will pass the famous prison,*

Les Baumettes). Park near the "sens interdit" (no entry) sign; continue on foot along the paved road.

A wild setting with tiny creeks for swimming, crystal-clear water, *cabanons* clustered at the far end of the valley, restaurant, small port. Not to be missed!

Sugiton★★

🥾 (1hr30min) From Marseille take bd Michelet as far as Luminy; park in the car park near the École d'Art et d'Architecture and continue on foot along the forest track.

A small *calanque* with turquoise water, it is well sheltered by its surrounding high cliffs. It is popular with naturists.

En-Vau★★

🥾 (2hr 30min) Access via Col de la Gardiole (Route Gaston-Rebuffat beginning opposite the Carpiagne military camp); leave your car in the Gardiole car park.

🥾 (2hr) Or, from Cassis, walk past Port-Miou and Port-Pin calanques.

The best known of all the *calanques* with its white cliffs, emerald water and stony beach. It is encircled by a forest of rock pinnacles overlooked by the "Doigt de Dieu" (Finger of God).

Port-Pin★

🥾 Access via Col de la Gardiole (same directions as En-Vau – 3hr) or Cassis (skirting Port-Miou calanque).

A spacious *calanque* with a sandy beach surrounded by pine trees.

Cassis⌂

▶25km/15.5mi E of Marseille.

🛈Quai des Moulins, Cassis. ℰ08 92 25 98 92. www.cassis.fr. 🅿 Your best bet is to get the bus from Marseille (40min).

Cassis, a bustling fishing port, lies in an attractive **setting**★ at the end of a bay between the Puget heights and Cap Canaille. It is a popular summer resort with three beaches. Boat trips to the *calanques* are a popular excursion.

🚗▶ DRIVING TOUR

Corniche des Crêtes★★

▶ *From Cassis to La Ciotat 19km/12mi.*

The stretch of coast road between Cassis and La Ciotat skirts the crests of the Canaille, a limestone range that rises from the sea in white cliffs, some of the tallest in France.

▶ *Leave Cassis in an easterly direction, on the road to Toulon (D 559), and during the ascent take a signposted road to the right. At Pas de la Colle, turn left.*

Mont de la Saoupe

The **panorama**★★ from the television mast at the top includes Cassis, the Île de Riou and Chaîne St-Cyr to the west, the Chaîne de l'Étoile and Massif de la Ste-Baume to the north, La Ciotat and Cap de Sicié to the southeast.

▶ *Return to Pas de la Colle and continue uphill.*

Cap Canaille★★★

From the guard rail on the cape there is an outstanding **view**★★★ of the cliff face, Massif de Puget and the *calanques* and Massif de Marseilleveyre.

▶ *Beyond Grande Tête, turn right towards the coastguard station.*

From the **Coastguard station (semaphore)** the **view**★★★ embraces La Ciotat, Cap Sicié and Cap Canaille (telescope).

▶ *Return to the crest road; bear right for La Ciotat.*

The descent into town passes quarries, pinewoods, and the "pont naturel", a natural limestone arch.

ADDRESSES

⌂ STAY

⊜⊜ **Hôtel Benidorm** – *734 chemin du Littoral (Estaque), 12km/7.4mi NW.* ✆*04 91 46 12 91. 26rms.* ⌑*€6.* The only hotel in Estaque, the building is white and rooms are simple and practical.

⊜⊜ **Hôtel Relax** – *4 r. Corneille, Vieux Port.* ✆*04 91 33 15 87. www.hotelrelax.fr. 21rms. €*⌑*7.* Situated near Marseille's shopping area and a 2min walk from Vieux Port, the location is ideal. Rooms are neatly laid out with homely furnishings.

⊜⊜ **Hotel Le Richelieu** – *52 Corniche Kennedy.* ✆*04 91 31 01 92. www.lerichelieu-marseille.com. 17rms.* ⌑*€8.* Charming hotel near the Catalans beach.

⊜⊜ **Hôtel Edmond Rostand** – *31 r. du Dragon, Castellane.* ✆*04 91 37 74 95. www.hoteledmondrostand.com. 15rms.* ⌑*€9.* Clean, simple contemporary rooms with comfortable beds. Very reasonable price.

⊜⊜ **Hôtel Vertigo** – *42 r. des Petites Maries, Vieux Port.* ✆*04 91 91 07 11. www.hotelvertigo.fr.* Situated in the historic Belsunce neighbourhood, this place offers varying accommodation types from hostel-style sharing to twin or double rooms. Very nicely renovated.

⊜⊜⊜ **Hôtel Azur** – *24 cour Franklin Roosevelt, Réformés.* ✆*04 91 42 74 38. www.azur-hotel.fr. 18rms.* ⌑ *€8. Restaurant*⊜⊜. Very near the Canabière, this hotel is in typical Provençal style. Rooms are spread across four floors; some give onto the garden, where you can take breakfast. Friendly staff.

⊜⊜⊜ **Chambre d'hôte Villa Marie-Jeanne** – *4 r. Chicot, Cinq Avenue Long Champs.* ✆*04 91 85 51 31. 3rms.* ⌑ *€12.* A 19C building in a residential quarter of the city. Traditional, elegant Provençal touch, old-fashioned furniture with modern amenities.

⊜⊜⊜ **Hôtel Le Corbusier** – *280 bd Michelet.* ✆*04 91 16 78 00. www.hotellecorbusier.com. 21rms.* ⌑ *€9. Restaurant*⊜⊜. *Closed 1 week in Jan.* This unique hotel is located on three floors of Le Corbusier's Cité Radieuse, a short bus ride from the centre of town. Rooms all have original minimalist features and accessories and there's a 360-degree view from the roof. Great location for football fans as it's a 10min walk from the Stade Vélodrome.

⊜⊜⊜ **Chambre d'hote Villa Monticelli** – *96 r. du Cdt-Rolland, Rond-Point du Prado.* ✆*04 91 22 15 20. www.villamonticelli.com. 5rms.* ⌑. This Art Deco building near the centre has as an unusual, colourful interior. Modest, comfortable rooms.

⊜⊜⊜ **Hôtel les Cigales** – *rte Enco-de-Botte, 13190 Allauch, 15km/9.3mi NE.* ✆*04 91 68 17 07. www.hotel-lescigales.fr. Reservations advised. 6rms, 1 suite.* ⌑ *€7.* A recent building between Marseille and Allauch, rooms are tranquil and families welcome. Garden with pool.

⊜⊜⊜ **Hôtel Hermès** – *25 r. Bonneterie, Vieux Port.* ✆*04 96 11 63 63. www.hotelmarseille.com/hermes. 28rms.* ⌑*€9.* Unpretentious, centrally located hotel with small, well-kept rooms; those on the fifth floor have a terrace overlooking the quayside. Panoramic rooftop sundeck.

⊜⊜⊜⊜ **Hôtel Le Ryad** – *16 r. Sénac de Meilhan, Vieux Port.* ✆*04 91 47 74 54. www.leryad.fr. 9rms.* The Moroccan-inspired beautiful, stylish rooms are very inviting. Visit the colourful tea room in the afternoon or the hotel's little restaurant.

⊜⊜⊜⊜ **New Hôtel Vieux Port** – *3 bis, r. Reine-Elisabeth, Vieux Port.* ✆*04 91 90 76 24. www.new-hotel.com/vieuxport. 42rms.* ⌑*€11.* Well located in the centre of Marseille by the Vieux Port, this hotel's rooms are pretty and decorated in exotic themes: Pondichery, Rising sun, Arabian Nights, Vera Cruz or Tropical Africa. An invitation to relax and unwind!

⊜⊜⊜⊜ **Radisson SAS Hotel** – *38 quai de Rive Neuve, Vieux Port.* ✆*04 88 92 19 50. www.radissonblu.com. 189rms.* ⌑*€12. Restaurant*⊜⊜⊜. Right by Vieux Port, this plush establishment, between Fort St-Nicolas and Théâtre de la Criée, is furnished beautifully. Immaculate, bright rooms.

♔ EAT

⊜ **Le Salon Provençal** – *pl. Benjamin Chappe, 13190 Allauch, 15km/9mi NE.* ✆*04 91 68 39 92. Closed Thu.* An adorable small place in old Allauch. Amiable tea parlour, terrace and three small rooms where you can eat in peace.

⊜⊜ **Axis** – *8 r. Ste-Victoire, Castellane.* ✆*04 91 57 14 70. Closed Sat lunch, Sun, Mon eve.* The seasonal, contemporary-style cuisine makes this establishment worth a detour. Modern décor, with views of the chefs in action.

Le Café des Épices – *4 r. Lacydon, Vieux Port.* ℘*04 91 91 22 69. Reservations advised.* This tiny restaurant seats just 20, but the esplanade terrace and its olive grove in the background are delightful.

Le Charité Café – *2 r. de la Charité, Colbert.* ℘*04 91 91 08 41.* Very pleasant brasserie. Salads, sandwiches, desserts and drinks, etc. to eat in or take away.

Charles Livon – *89 bd Ch. Livon.* ℘*04 91 52 22 41. Closed Sat lunch, Sun, Mon lunch.* Opposite the Palais du Pharo, this restaurant has a minimalist décor adorned with orchids. Reinterpreted regional cuisine; fine selection of Provence and Rhône wines.

Chez Madie Les Galinettes – *138 quai du Port, Vieux Port.* ℘*04 91 90 40 87. Closed Sat lunch in Jul, Sun.* This Povençal restaurant with terrace gives onto the old port.

Cyprien – *56 ave de Toulon, La Timone.* ℘*04 91 25 50 00. Closed Mon eve, Sat lunch, Sun, public holidays.* This restaurant near the place Castellane offers classic, tasty cuisine and a décor to match. Interior adorned with floral touches and paintings.

Miramar – *12 quai du Port. Vieux Port.* ℘*04 91 91 10 40. www.bouillabaisse.com.* This restaurant, serving bouillabaisse and other fish specialities on the Vieux Port, has a 1960s style with varnished wood and red chairs.

La Part des Anges – *33 r. Sainte. Vieux Port.* ℘*04 91 33 55 70. www.lapart desanges.com.* This wine bar is fairly lively in the evening. Taste wine by the glass or bottle or take away. Cold cuts, cheese, etc. to accompany the wine. Rustic décor.

Le Resto Provençal – *64 cours Julien, Cours-Julien.* ℘*04 91 48 85 12. Closed Sun, Mon, Wed eve (except Mon and Wed in Aug), every afternoon in Aug.* A cosy place with Provençal specialities including sea bream soup and fig tart.

Une Table, au Sud – *2 quai du Port (1st floor). Vieux Port.* ℘*04 91 90 63 53. Closed Sun–Mon.* This colourful restaurant delights both the eye and the taste buds, thanks to its inventive cuisine with delicious southern accents, as well as views of the forts and hilltop basilica.

La Virgule – *27 r. de la Loge. Vieux Port.* ℘*04 91 90 91 11. Closed Sun-Mon.* Culinary surprises await you at this restaurant with black, white and steel décor.

Les Arcenaulx – *25 cours d'Estienne-d'Orves. Vieux Port.* ℘*04 91 59 80 30. www.jeanne-laffitte.com. Closed Aug, Sun.* Dine surrounded by books which cover the walls of this restaurant: it's combined with a bookshop and publishers, located in the orignal warehouses of the 17C Arsenal des Galères.

Bateau-Restaurant Le Marseillois – *quai du Port-Marine, just by the Town Hall. Vieux Port.* ℘*04 91 90 72 52. www.lemarseillois.com. Closed Sun–Mon, Feb.* A 19C building opposite the *mairie*. Provençal cuisine, particularly seafood.

Les Buvards – *34 Grand'Rue. Vieux Port.* ℘*04 91 90 69 98.* Friendly bistro with tasty, affordable cuisine and a decent wine list. Great place to meet in the evenings.

Chez Fonfon – *140 Vallon-des-Auffes.* ℘*04 91 52 14 38. www.chez-fonfon.com. Closed Mon lunch, Sun.* The dining room of this renowned restaurant dominates the Vallon des Auffes harbour. Every morning fresh fish and seafood are brought in by "pointus", the local fishing boats.

L'Épuisette – *quartier du Vallon des Auffes.* ℘*04 91 52 17 82. Closed Sun–Mon.* Set near the rocks in the picturesque Auffes Valley, this restaurant takes you on a pleasant culinary voyage in a light, warm and refined atmosphere. Attentive staff.

Le Moment – *5 pl. Sadi Carnot, Colbert.* ℘*04 91 52 47 49. www.lemoment-marseille.com.* Run by chef Christian Ernst, this new trendy restaurant near the old port offers a contemporary dining room, sitting rooms upstairs, workshops, wine library and takeaway dishes.

NIGHTLIFE

Bar de la Marine – *15 quai Rive-Neuve. Vieux Port.* ℘*04 91 54 95 42.* The setting for Marcel Pagnol's *Marius et Fanny* trilogy; you're likely to find the beautiful people having a drink here these days.

Café Parisien – *1 pl. Sadi-Carnot. Colbert.* ℘*04 91 90 05 77. Closed Sun.* At weekends this attractive Baroque-style café hosts musical events based on the themes presented in the monthly art exhibitions.

TOURS

Guided Tours – *By reservation at the tourist office. €6.50.* Guided tours (2hr) take place on various themes, in several languages, most days.

Le Grand Tour (bus) – *Leaves from quai du Port daily, on the hour from 10am.* 1€8 (€20 2 days). 04 91 91 05 82. *www.marseillelegrandtour.com.* Hop on-hop off bus tour (1hr 30min circuit) with audio commentary in several languages that takes you around all the major sights.

Tourist train – *Leaves from quai du Port. €7 (children, €4).* 04 91 25 24 69. *www.petit-train-marseille.com.* There are two itineraries: to Notre-Dame de la Garde going past the Basilica of St-Victor, and Le Panier, the old town.

EVENTS

Programmes are listed in local newspapers, and the tourist office also distributes a small monthly magazine, *In Situ*.

Festival de Marseille – *Jun–Jul.* 04 91 99 02 50. *www.festivaldemarseille.com.* Theatre, music and dance festival takes place in atmospheric venues in the city.

Fiesta des Suds – *www.dock-des-suds.org.* In late October, this world music festival brings 50 000 spectators to Marseille and vibrates with the music and traditions of the Mediterranean.

Folklore – International Folklore Festival at Château-Gombert takes place in early July *(www.roudelet-felibren.com).*

Pétanque World Championships – A very popular event frequented by celebrities who, after a few throws, let the champions take over. First week in July *(http://mediterranee.france3.fr/mondial-petanque).*

SHOPPING

BOOKS

Librairie-galerie-restaurant des Arcenaulx– *25 cours d'Estienne d'Orves. Vieux-Port.* 04 91 59 80 40. *www.les-arcenaulx.com.* Specialises in books on Marseille, Provence and food; old and rare books. Quality gifts; restaurant.

CLOTHES

The main shopping street is rue St-Ferréol, which has many individual and chain boutiques plus Galeries Lafayette. Adventurous dressers might like to visit Marseille's well-known designer, **Madame Zaza** *(73 cours Julien. Notre Dame du Mont.* 04 91 48 05 57. *www.madamezazaof marseille.com),* for colourful, daring outfits.

MARKETS

Fish market every morning on *quai des Belges.* **Food** markets are open Mon–Sat mornings in *cours Pierre Puget, place Jean-Jaurès* (la Plaine), *place du Marché-des-Capucins* and *avenue du Prado.* Boulevard *La Canebière* has a **flower** market every Tuesday and Saturday morning; this market is also set up on *avenue du Prado* every Friday morning.

OLIVE OIL

Lei Moulins – *4–6 bd Tellène. Estrangin Préfecture.* 04 91 59 49 78. *www.lei moulins.com. Closed Sun, Mon.* Cave-like shop in the St-Victor quarter. You'll find an interesting selection of olive oil from the Med and also a selection of jams made on the premises.

SANTONS

Santons Marcel Carbonel – *47–49 r. Neuve-Ste-Catherine. Vieux Port.* 04 91 13 61 36. *www.santonsmarcelcarbonel.com. Closed Sun.* Visit the workshop where the famous *santons* are made. Take a browse through the little museum before hitting the shop tp buy some of the traditional clay figurines – great souvenirs.

SOAP

La Compagnie de Provence – *18 r. Francis Davso. Vieux Port.* 04 91 33 04 17. *www.lcdpmarseille.com. Closed Sun.* Marseille soap and natural products make this shop smell wonderful.

Savonnerie de la Licorne – *34 cours Julien. Notre Dame du Mont.* 04 96 12 00 91. *www.savon-de-marseille-licorne.com. Mon–Fri 8am–5pm, Sat 10am–6pm.* The only artisan-made soap in the centre of town. Perfumes include rose, violet and pastis.

BOAT TRIPS

From Marseille – *ICARD Maritime, quai des Belges.* 04 91 33 03 29. *www.visite-des-calanques.com.* Trips in catamarans to Cassis along the coast. €10–25.

From Cassis – *Les Bateliers de Cassis.* 04 42 01 03 31. *www.calanques-cassis.com.* Departure from the port of Cassis visiting Port-Miou, Port-Pin and En-Vau, without landing. €14–23.

From La Ciotat – *Les Amis des Calanques, quai Ganteaume.* 06 09 35 25 68. *www.visite-calanques.fr.*

Aix-en-Provence★★

Bouches-du-Rhône

The old capital of Provence has kept much of its 17C and 18C character: the elegance of its mansions, the charm of its squares, the majesty of its avenues and the loveliness of its fountains. It is also a lively city whose large student population is much in evidence on the busy café terraces. The new part of town is rapidly expanding and attracting more residents; it has established itself as a city of the arts, a thermal spa and an important centre for industry and the tourist trade.

A BIT OF HISTORY

The Aix of today is the legacy of Good King René (1409–80). The Roman city Aquae Sextiae had long before destroyed by the Lombards (AD 574) and by Saracens; its deserted buildings served as a quarry for building materials for a good six centuries. Then in the 12C its fortunes were restored by the Counts of Provence who made it their place of residence.

The last and most illustrious of the line was René, Duke of Anjou, Lorraine and Bar, King of Naples, Count of Provence and Piedmont, and the ally of Charles VII of France against the English and Burgundians. This enlightened monarch supported literature and the arts and completed Aix cathedral. Though a benevolent ruler, he was also a strict administrator. Towards the end of his life he made Charles of Maine his heir; Charles however was to die childless, enabling Louis XI to incorporate Provence into France (1486). Harsh times intervened; invasion by Imperial troops, feuding, and religious conflict.

While the Aix Parliament was putting up a strong resistance to Richelieu's centralising policies, an administrative class grew and prospered.

Intellectual life continued to flourish and the roll-call of great men who were born or who lived in Aix is a long one.

▶ **Population:** 146 050

⊙ **Michelin Map:** 340 H-I 4

▮ **Info:** 2 pl. du Général-de-Gaulle. ℘04 42 16 11 61. www.aixenprovence tourism.com.

▷ **Location:** 32km/20mi N of Marseille and 35km/22mi SE of Salon-de-Provence.

☺ **Don't Miss:** Vieil Aix, the charming medieval heart of the city.

◷ **Timing:** The first thing to do in Aix is walk along the majestic Cours Mirabeau under its handsome plane trees, pause for a drink at one of the many cafés and then stroll through Vieil Aix. Allow at least 4hr in total. But, for an overview of the city, join a guided tour (the tourist office has details).

It includes the 17C astronomer Fabri de Peiresc who in 1636 drew the first map of the moon.

Finally, there is Paul Cézanne (1839–1906), one of the founders of modern painting; his many studies of Mount Ste-Victoire are justly renowned.

The room devoted to him in the Musée Granet houses among other paintings his *Still Life with Sugar-bowl*, *Nude at the Mirror* and the monumental *Bathers*.

SIGHTS

Vieux Aix★★

Elegant 17–19C mansions with corner statues, pleasant squares and charming fountains combine to give the old town its distinctive character.

Cours Mirabeau★★

Fountains splash under the canopy of fine plane trees shading this most pleasant of Provençal boulevards. It was laid out on the line of the 15C ramparts by Mazarin's brother (also responsible for building the district immediately to the south). Planned deliberately to give the mansions a formal façade to the north and a sunny garden to the south, the grand residences line the south side of the Cours, distinguished by sculptured doorways and balconies of wrought iron held up by caryatids and atlantes.

Musee Granet ★

🕐Open Tue–Sun Jun–Sept 11am–7pm; Oct–May noon–6pm. 🕐Closed 1 Jan, 1 May, 25 Dec. ᵍ€4. ℘04 42 52 88 32. www.museegranet-aixenprovence.fr.

In a 17C mansion, the town's principal art museum displays collections left by F M Granet (1775–1849), and rooms devoted to remnants of Roman Aix.

On view, French art from the 16–20C, Italian and Flemish schools, and works by Cézanne.

Place d'Albertas★

A fine mansion of 1724 and fountain of 1745 are complemented by other 18C buildings with soaring first-floor pilasters and graceful balconies contrasting with the more robust appearance of the ground floor which has semicircular arches and rusticated stonework.

Cathédrale St-Sauveur★

🕐Open daily 7.30am–noon, 2–6pm. 🕐Closed during services. ℘04 42 43 45 65. www.cathedrale-aix.net.

The **baptistery**★ dates to the Merovingian period (4C). Eight ancient columns, probably from a Roman basilica nearby, hold up the 18C octagonal cupola crowning the Gallo-Roman structure.

In the nave is the **Triptych of the Burning Bush**★★, painted around 1475 by Nicolas Froment, a masterpiece of the Second School of Avignon.

ADDITIONAL SIGHTS
Musée des Tapisseries★

28 pl. des Martyrs de la Résistance. 🕐Open Feb–mid-Apr daily 1.30–5pm; mid-Apr–mid-Oct 10am–6pm; mid-Oct–Dec 1.30–5pm. 🕐Closed Jan. ᵍ€3.50. ℘04 42 23 09 91.

Housed in the former bishop's palace, the Tapestry Museum presents the 19 magnificent tapestries made in Beauvais in the 17C and 18C, including nine panels illustrating the life of Don Quixote.

Cours Mirabeau

© Johnny Stockshooter/age fotostock

Fondation Vasarely★

1 ave Marcel Pagnol, Jas de Bouffan. ♿🕐Open Tue–Sat 10am–1pm, 2–6pm. ᵍ€9. ℘04 42 20 01 09. www.fondationvasarely.fr.

This foundation, created by Hungarian artist Victor Vasarely (1906–97), stanads on a hill to the west of Aix. The vast building, consisting of 16 hexagonal structures, has sober façades decorated with circles on alternately black and white squares. In 1955, the artist evolved into a field where by optical means he was able to produce visual illusion without the use of movement.

Atelier Paul Cézanne (Cézanne's Studio)

🕐Open Oct–Mar 10am–noon, 2–5pm (visit in English, 4pm); Apr–Jun and Sept 10am–noon, 2–6pm (in English at 5pm); Jul–Aug 10am–6pm (in English at 5pm). 🕐Closed 1–3 Jan, 1 May, 25 Dec, and Sun Jan–Feb and Dec. ᵍ€2.

🎫Guided tours (30min) daily Apr–Sept 5pm; Oct–Mar 4pm. ℘04 42 21 06 53. www.atelier-cezanne.com.

When his mother died in 1897, Cézanne had a traditional Provençal-style house built outside the ramparts. It was surrounded by a garden with colourful leafy plants growing right up to the windows of the artist's studio. The studio, called the *Lauves*, where he painted *The Bathers*, among other works, has been left as it was at his death in 1906.

ADDRESSES

🛏 STAY

😑😑🍽 **Hôtel Cardinal** – *24 r. Cardinale.* ✆*04 42 38 32 30. www.hotel-cardinal-aix.com. 29rms.* 🛏 *€8.* In an 18C mansion in the calm of the Mazarin quarter, tasteful, marrying old-fashioned style with modern comfort.

😑😑🍽 **Hôtel St-Christophe** – *2 ave Victor-Hugo.* ✆*04 42 26 01 24. www.hotel-saintchristophe.com. 60rms.* 🛏 *€11. Restaurant*😑😑🍽. This hotel is right in the centre of the city, near cours Mirabeau, and rooms are decorated in either a 1930s or Provençal style.

😑😑🍽 **La Manoir** – *8 r. d'Entrecasteaux.* ✆*04 42 26 27 20. www.hotelmanoir.com. Closed 5–25 Jan. 40rms.* 🛏 *€8.* A lovely old building, formerly a hat factory. Part of an adjoining 14C cloister has been converted into a summer terrace, creating a unique atmosphere.

😑😑😑🍽 **Hôtel des Augustins** – *3 r. de la Masse.* ✆*04 42 27 28 59. www.hotel-augustins.com. 29rms.* 🛏 *€8.* Stone vaulting and stained glass are reminders of the origins of this hotel, a stone's throw from cours Mirabeau, which was originally a 15C convent. The rooms, of which two have terraces with rooftop views, are decorated in a modern style.

🍽 EAT

😑😑 **Chez Charlotte** – *32 r. des Bernardines.* ✆*04 42 26 77 56. Closed Aug, 24, 25 & 31 Dec.* Upon entering you are greeted with a nostalgic atmosphere. The main eating area's décor is dedicated to the cinema.

😑😑 **Trattoria Chez Antoine Côté Cour** – *19 cours Mirabeau.* ✆*04 42 93 12 51. Closed Mon lunch and Sun.* This is a retreat with a luminous, verdant patio-veranda. All the flavours of Provence and Italy are at your fingertips.

😑😑😑 **Chez Féraud** – *8 r. du Puits-Juif.* ✆*04 42 63 07 27. Closed Aug, Sun & Mon.* Tucked away in an Old Quarter lane, an appealing place with typical local cuisine (pistou, daube) and grills.

🍷 NIGHTLIFE

Café des Deux Garçons – *53 bis cours Mirabeau.* ✆*04 42 26 00 51.* Bordered by plane trees, cours Mirabeau throngs with locals and visitors who come to relax at the outdoor tables of one of its many cafés. The Deux Garçons café, more familiarly known as "le 2 G", is the oldest and most famous of these cafés, dating from 1792. Cézanne and Zola were both regulars.

Château de la Pioline – *260 r. Guillaume-du-Vair.* ✆*04 42 52 27 27. www.chateaude lapioline.fr.* The bar of this hotel/restaurant, which dates from the 16C, is adorned with highly prestigious furnishings, such as those from the Medici hall (to commemorate the illustrious Catherine de' Medici) and the Louis XVI hall.

🛒 SHOPPING

Markets – Traditional market every morning in place Richelme and every Tue, Thu and Sat in place des Prêcheurs and place de la Madeleine. Flower market every Tue, Thu and Sat in place de l'Hôtel de Ville, and in place des Prêcheurs on other days.

Antiques – Antique market every Tue, Thu and Sat in place Verdun. Antiques fairs take place in the town hall square every 1st Sun of the month 9am–6pm.

Apparel – Clothes stalls spring around Cours Mirabeau on Tue and Thu and in the Palais de Justice on Sat.

Aperitifs – The definitive shop for Provençal liquers and aperitifs is **Liquoristerie de Venelles** – *36 ave de la Grand-Bégude, Venelles.* ✆*04 42 54 94 65. www.versinthe.net.* Free tour and tasting of the in-house absinthe distillery.

TOURS

Cézanne Tour – In the steps of Cézanne. Runs early May-early Oct Tue 2–7pm. €28. Tours in French and English (details from the tourist office). Visit all the sights associated with the artist.

🎭 EVENTS

International Opera and Music Festival – ✆*0820 92 29 23. www.festival-aix.com.* This prestigious festival takes place every July in the courtyard of the archiepiscopal palace. Concerts and recitals are held in the cathedral, the cloisters of St-Saveur and the Hôtel Maynier d'Oppède. The festival focuses on operas as well as contemporary music.

Wine Festival – Festival des Côteaux d'Aix en Provence – *cours Mirabeau. Last Sun in Jul.* An opportunity to sample the rich variety from the vineyards of Aix.

Arles★★★

Bouches-du-Rhône

Arles is one of the most important centres of Provençal culture, proud of its past and famed for an exceptional Roman and medieval heritage, yet vibrantly modern and forward-looking. Van Gogh produced many of his greatest works here; what he loved was not the culture or history, but the brilliance of the light. The town continues to play a role in artisitc life, hosting a renowned annual summer photography festival, Les Rencontres d'Arles.

A BIT OF HISTORY

The ancient Celtic-Ligurian town was colonised by the Greeks of Marseille as early as the 6C BC and was already a thriving town when the Romans conquered the region.

They built a canal linking it to the sea so that it could be supplied directly from Rome.

Growing into a prosperous port town, and well placed on the major Roman highways, it became an administrative and political capital of Roman Gaul, with many magnificent buildings.

SIGHTS
Théâtre Antique★★

🕐 *Open daily: Nov–Feb 10am–5pm; Mar–Apr and Oct 9am–6pm; May–Sept 9am–7pm.* 🕐*Closed public holidays and for concerts.* €6 *(includes Amphithéâtre).* 📞*04 90 49 38 20.*

This is among the most important surviving Roman theatres, and dates from the end of the 1C BC. All that remains of its stage wall are two elegant columns in African breccia and Italian marble.

The theatre began to be quarried for its stone as early as the 5C, and subsequently disappeared under houses and gardens. It was excavated in the 19C.

Amphithéâtre★★

🕐 *Open: same hours as for Théâtre Antique.* €6 *(includes Théâtre Antique).* 📞*04 90 49 59 05.*

▶ **Population:** 53 817
◔ **Michelin Map:** 340 C 3
▣ **Info:** 43 bd de Craponne. 📞04 90 18 41 20. www.tourisme.ville-arles.fr.
◑ **Location:** Arles stands on the edge of the Camargue wetlands and the Rhône delta, 80km/50mi W of Aix-en-Provence and 45km/28mi S of Avignon.
🅿 **Parking:** Park under the plane trees of bd Georges-Clemenceau.
◈ **Don't Miss:** Roman arena; the café on the Place de Forum as painted in September 1888 by Van Gogh.
🕐 **Timing:** Visitor passes are available at the tourist office or at any of the monuments and museums (except Museon Arlaten). The tourist office has information on walking tours. Expect to spend a couple of days if you want to see everything.

Here as many as 20 000 spectators enjoyed a variety of games pitting men against wild animals, and gladiatorial combat. Dating from about AD 75, this amphitheatre (or arena) is even larger than the one in Nîmes. Its good state of preservation is due to being maintained as a fortress in the 5C and 6C when the Empire was crumbling under the barbarian assault. The sturdy structure was later filled in with as many as 200 houses and two chapels! Excavataion and restoration began in 1825.

Église St-Trophime★

🕐*Open daily Nov–Feb 10am–5pm; Mar–Apr, Oct 9am–6pm; May–Sept 9am–7pm;* 🕐*Closed public holidays.* €3.50.

Standing on even more ancient ruins, the church was rebuilt from 1080 onwards. Its **porch**★★ is one of the

Arles by the Rhône

L. Campion/MICHELIN

masterpieces of late 12C Provençal Romanesque architecture. The arrangement of columns and design of the frieze hark back to Roman work like the **municipal arch**★ at Glanum and the 4C sarcophagi at nearby Alyscamps and Trinquetaille. The fact that the stone from which the church is built was taken from the Roman Theatre further strengthens a sense of continuity with the Classical past.

The **cloisters**★★ were built after 1150 and are renowned for their sculpture. Particularly fine are the corner pillars of the north gallery and the capitals, foliated or decorated with biblical scenes.

Musée d'Arles et de la Provence antique★★

Presqu'île-du-cirque-romain. ⊙ *Open daily except Tue 10am–6pm.* ⊙ *Closed public holidays.* ⊛€6 (free 1st Sun in month). ℘04 90 18 88 88. *www.arles-antique.cg13.fr.*
The town's extensive collection of ancient art is displayed here.

Museon Arlaten

29 r. de la République. ⊶*Closed for restoration until 2014.* ℘04 90 93 58 11. *www.museonarlaten.fr.*
Provençal culture and traditions.

Musée Réattu★

10 r. du grand Prieuré. ⊙ *Open Feb–Jun, and Oct–Dec 10am–12.30pm, 2–6.30pm; Jul–Sept 10am–7pm.* ⊙*Closed 1–22 Jan, 1 May, 1 Nov, 25 Dec.* ⊛€4. ℘04 90 49 37 58. *www.museereattu.arles.fr.*
Small musuem of contemporary art, showing paintings by Pablo Picasso, including **Picasso Bequest**★.

Thermes de Constantin★

r. Dominique Maïsto. ⊙ *Open daily Nov–Feb 10am–noon, 2–5pm; Mar–Oct 9am–noon, 2–6pm (May–Sept 7pm).* ⊙ *Closed 1 Jan, 1 May, 1 Nov, 25 Dec.* ⊛€3. ℘04 90 49 38 20. Here you'll find the largest baths in Provence.

Alyscamps★

Allow half a day. ⊙ *Open Nov–Feb 10am–noon, 2–5pm; Mar–Apr and Oct 9am–noon, 2–6pm; May–Sept 9am–7pm.* ⊛€3.50.
A famous Roman necropolis, located just outside the town walls of Old Arles.

EXCURSION
Les Alpilles★★

▶ *The area is divided between the Alpilles des Baux in the W and the Alpilles d'Eygalières in the E; in the middle is St-Rémy-de-Provence.*
The limestone chain of the Alpilles, a geological extension of the Luberon range, rises in the heart of Provence

between Avignon and Arles. From afar, these jagged crests rising 300–400m/985–1 313ft appear to be lofty mountains.

The arid, white peaks of these summits standing out against the blue sky are reminiscent of some Greek landscapes. At the mouths of the dry valleys that cross the mountain chain, olive and almond trees spread their foliage over the lower slopes.

Occasionally a dark line of cypress trees breaks the landscape. In the mountains, the gently sloping lower areas are planted with *Kermes* oaks and pines, but often the rock is bare and peppered with a few scraggy bushes covered by *maquis* or poor pasture suitable only for sheep.

⊛ *Due to the high risk of fire, access to the forested areas of the Alpilles is forbidden from July to 15 September.*

🚗 DRIVING TOURS

LES BAUX ALPILLES★★
Round trip starting from St-Rémy-de-Provence. 40km/25mi. Allow 4hr.

St-Rémy-de-Provence★
Ⓒ *See ST-RÉMY-DE-PROVENCE (p529)*

▷ *Leave St-Rémy-de-Provence going SW on chemin de la Combette; turn right into Vieux Chemin d'Arles. After 3.8km/2.3mi, turn left at a T-junction onto D 27 (signposted: Les Baux).*

Les Baux Panorama (Table d'Orientation)★★★
Just before reaching the top of the hill, on your left, you will see a road tracing the ledge where you can stop and gaze at the magnificent **panorama**★★★ of Les Baux (Ⓒ*see Les BAUX-DE-PROVENCE*).

▷ *Return to D 27; bear left on it.*

The road winds through Val d'Enfer (Ⓒ*see Les BAUX-DE-PROVENCE*).

Les Baux-de-Provence★★★
Ⓒ*See Les BAUX-DE-PROVENCE.*

▷ *Continue along D 27, then take a right before Maussane-les-Alpilles to connect to Paradou on D 17.*

▲▲ La Petite Provence du Paradou
75 ave de la Vallée des Baux, Le Paradou (towards Fontvieille (D 17) on the right). 🚻Ⓞ*Open daily 10am–6.30pm (Jul–Aug 7pm).* ⊛*No charge.* 𝒸*04 90 54 35 75. www.lapetiteprovenceduparadou.com.*
In a décor redolent of rural Provence, *santons* are produced here by *santon*-makers from Aubagne. They are dressed in the local costumes and some are even mobile.

They are arranged into evocative scenes of Provence past, with trades (fisherman, miller, shepherd), festivals, daily life (drinking holes, games of cards), and the like.

▷ *Return to the village, taking D 78 to the right through an olive grove.*

Aqueducs de Barbegal
▷ *5min round-trip on foot: follow the signposts for aqueduc romain.*

Note the impressive ruins, on the left in particular, of a pair of Gallo-Roman aqueducts. The aqueduct branching off to the west supplied Arles with water from Eygalières.

The other one cut through the rock and served a 4C hydraulic flour mill on the slope's south side, the ruins of which provide a rare example of Gallo-Roman mechanical engineering.

▷ *Go right on D 33.*

Fontvieille
🛈 𝒸*04 90 54 67 49. www.fontvieille-provence.com.*
For centuries, the main industry in this small town, where Alphonse Daudet is remembered for his *Lettres de mon Moulin* (1869), has been the quarrying of Arles limestone.

Moulin de Daudet (Daudet's Mill)
Ⓞ*Open daily: Feb–Dec 9am–7pm.* ⊛*€3.* 𝒸*04 90 54 60 78.*

Between Arles and Les Baux-de-Provence, the admirers of Alphonse Daudet's works can make a literary pilgrimage to his mill, the inspiration for his famous *Lettres de mon Moulin (Letters from my Mill)*, a charming and whimsical series of letters and tales from Provence. A lovely avenue of pines leads from Fontvieille to the mill.

Alphonse Daudet, the son of a silk manufacturer, was born in Nîmes on 13 May 1840 (d. 1897). An outstanding author of tales of Provençal life and member of the Académie Goncourt, he was also a contemporary of such important 19C literary figures as Zola and Mistral. The **view**★ from the mill is an inspiration, embracing the Alpilles, Beaucaire and Tarascon castles, the vast Rhône Valley, and the Abbaye de Montmajour.

⊳ *Take D 32 to return to St-Rémy-de-Provence.*

La Camargue★★

The main town in the Camargue is Les Saintes-Maries-de-la-Mer on the coast.
Try to catch sight of the three creatures that symbolise the Camargue – white horses, black bulls and pink flamingos.
The Rhône delta forms an immense wetland plain. Product of the interaction of the Rhône, the Mediterranean and the winds, this remarkable area has a culture and history all its own, as well as distinctive flora and fauna. It is divided into three distinct regions: a cultivated region north of the delta, salt marshes west of the Petit Rhône, and the watery nature reserve to the south.

Parc Naturel Régional de Camargue

Beware mosquitoes during summer.
The nature park includes the communes of Arles and Stes-Maries-de-la-Mer. Together with the nature reserve, **Réserve Nationale de Camargue**, aims to protect the fragile ecosystem of the region with its exceptional variety of flora and fauna – there are some 400 bird species. The traditional image of the Camargue is associated with the **herds (manades)** and the **horsemen (gardians)**. Many horse owners hire out their mounts for organised rides among the animals.
The *manade* designates livestock and all that relates to the upkeep of the herd: herdsmen, pastureland, horses, etc. The *gardian*, an experienced rider, is the symbol of the *manade* with his large felt hat and long three-pronged stick; he watches over the herd, cares for the sick animals and selects the bulls for the bullfights.

Les Stes-Maries-de-la-Mer

At the heart of the Camargue is situated Les Stes-Maries-de-la-Mer, clustered around its fortified church. The town, which is now at some distance from the coastline of medieval times, is protected by dikes to counter the encroachment of the sea.
A large, colourful **Gypsy Pilgrimage**★★ in honour of Sarah, whom they consider as their patron, takes place 24–25 May, attracting thousands of gypsies.

Musée Camarguais at Pont de Rousty

Located in Park Information Centre, Parc naturel régional de Camargue, Mas du Pont de Rousty, 13200 Arles. ♿ ○ *Open Apr–Sept daily 9am–6pm; Oct–Mar Wed–Mon 10am–5pm.* ○*Closed 1 Jan, 1 May, 25 Dec.* ⊜€5. *℘04 90 97 10 82. www.parc-camargue.fr.*
Occupying a former sheep farm deep in the Camargue, the Museum traces the the history of human activity in the delta. Much of the exhibition is devoted to life in a *mas* or traditional farmhouse during the 19C, but also features the economic activities of the present time: wine production, rice growing, sea salt.

ADDRESSES

STAY

⊜⊜**Hôtel Muette** – *15 r. des Suisses.* *℘04 90 96 15 39. www.hotel-muette.com. Closed Feb. 18rms.* ⊑8€. A beautiful building (originally 15C and 17C) in the heart of historic Arles. Solid stone walls in authentic Provençal rooms guarantees they are soundproof.

Hôtel du Musée – *11 r. du Grand-Prieuré.* *04 90 93 88 88. www.hoteldu musee.com.fr. Closed Jan. 28rms.* €8. Facing the Musée Réattu, this hotel was built in the 17C. It's a charming labyrinth of green pathways through intimate courtyards, with tranquil rooms.

Le Relais de Poste – *2 r. Molière.* *04 90 52 05 76. 16rms.* €6. This centrally based hotel was once the 18C postal relay. The restaurant evokes its era, with beams and frescoes.

Hôtel d'Arlatan – *26 r. Sauvage.* *04 90 93 56 66. www.hotel-arlatan.fr. 41rms.* €15. Fall under the spell of this old mansion dating from the 15C, a stone's throw from place du Forum. Admire the underground Roman fragments through the glass floor of the bar and the drawing room. Rooms furnished with antiques and pretty fabrics.

Hôtel Mireille – *Rive droite, Trinquetaille.* *04 90 93 70 74. www.hotel-mireille.com. 34rms.* €13. Dive into the swimming pool at this peaceful hotel outside the city centre. Good size, colourful rooms with Provençal furniture.

Hôtel Calendal – *5 r. Porte-de-Laure.* *04 90 96 11 89. www.lecalendal.com. 38rms.* €12. This hotel has all the stylishness of Provençal interiors with its colourful façade, pretty inner shaded garden and cosy sitting room. Blue and yellow make up the colour scheme of furniture, fabrics and ceramics.

EAT

Le Criquet – *21 r. Porte-de-Laure.* *04 90 96 80 51. Closed Wed.* Go for the charming dining room with its beams and exposed stonework rather than the terrace in this little restaurant near the amphitheatre.

Jardin de Manon – *14 ave des Alyscamps.* *04 90 93 38 68. Closed public holidays.* Situated just outside the city centre, this place's interior courtyard terrace, full of trees and flowers, will appeal to lovers of alfresco dining. There are two dining rooms, and the local cooking, which uses seasonal market produce, offers good value for money.

Lou Calèu – *27 r. Porte-de-Laure.* *04 90 49 71 77. www.loucaleu.com. Closed Sun, Mon.* A real classic: fresh salads, *taureau* stew, lamb with rosemary. All Arle's delights are at your fingertips. An excellent wine list. The place for gourmets.

ON THE TOWN

Bar de l'Hôtel Nord Pinus – *pl. du Forum.* *04 90 93 44 44. www.nord-pinus.com.* An essential stop in Arles, the small bar of the 17C Hotel Nord Pinu has entertained artists, writers, film stars, and bullfighters, including Picasso, Jean Cocteau and Yves Montand. There's great charm in details such as its boat-shaped lamps, bullfighting bar, squat armchairs and a background of flamenco music.

Café Van Gogh – *11 pl. du Forum.* *04 90 96 44 56.* This bright, popular café with its large terrace was the subject of Vincent Van Gogh's *The Cafe Terrace on the Place du Forum.*

L'Entrevue – *pl. Nina Berberova.* *04 90 93 37 28.* Arles is the birthplace of the flourishing Actes Sud publishing house, who also run this arty café-restaurant, a cultural hub of the town.

Le Méjan – *23 quai Marx-Dormoy.* *04 90 93 33 56.* Enjoy evening and afternoon musical performances, jazz concerts, lectures, conferences, and exhibitions in the chapel Saint-Martin-du-Méjan.

SHOPPING

Markets – Browse traditional markets every Wed in *bd Émile-Combes* and every Sat in *bd des Lices* and *boulevard Clemenceau.* **Antique market** first Wed of the month in *bd des Lices.*

Les Étoffes de Romane – *10 bd des Lices.* *04 90 93 53 70.* Choose from wonderful **Provençal fabrics** in an array of colours.

Olive Oil – Best quality Provençal olive oil is found (together with other olive specialities) at *Fad'ola (46 r. des Arènes; *04 90 49 70 73).*

EVENTS

Festival Les Suds – *mid-Jul. www.suds-arles.com.* World music festival.

Fête des Gardians – *1 May.* *04 90 18 41 20.* Mass is held in Provençal dialect, with the blessing of horses, typical Camargue games, local folk music and dances.

Les Rencontres d'Arles – *10 rond-point-des Arènes.* *04 90 96 76 06. www.rencontres-arles.com.* This photography festival is a feast of exhibitions, talks and activities in locations throughout the town, including the Roman Theatre.

Les Baux-de-Provence★★★

Bouches-du-Rhône

With its ruined castle and deserted houses capping an arid rocky spur plunging abruptly to steep ravines on either side, the old village of Baux has the most spectacular of sites. Baux has also given its name to bauxite, a mineral first discovered here in 1822 that led to the development of aluminium.

A BIT OF HISTORY

The lords of Baux were renowned in the Middle Ages, described by Mistral as "warriors all – vassals never". They traced their ancestry back to the Magi king Balthazar and boldly placed the Star of Bethlehem on their coat of arms.

SIGHTS

Town

The original entrance into the town is guarded by a gate (Porte Eyguières). Go through the fortified gateway into the town, and simply wander in the old streets.

The **Place St-Vincent★**, pleasantly shaded by elms and lotus-trees, has a terrace giving views of the small Fontaine Valley and Val d'Enfer. The 17C former Town Hall (Hôtel de Ville) has rooms with ribbed vaulting.

The church (Église St-Vincent) dates from the 12C; dressed in their long capes, the shepherds from the Alpilles hills come here for their **Christmas festival★★**, celebrated at Midnight Mass. The **Rue du Trencat★** was carved into the solid rock which has subsequently been pitted and eroded by wind and rain.

Château des Baux

Open Spring 9am–6.30pm; Summer 9am–8.30pm; Autumn 9.30am–6pm; Winter 9.30am–5pm. €7.50–9 according to season. 04 90 54 55 56. www.chateau-baux-provence.com.
By the 11C the lords of Baux, "that race of eagles", were among the most powerful rulers in the south of France.

▶ **Population:** 417
Michelin Map: 340 D 3
Info: Maison du Roy, r. Porte-Mage. 04 90 54 34 39. www.lesbauxde provence.com.

Location: Les Baux is 30km/18.6mi S of Avignon and 9.5km/6mi SW of St-Rémy-de-Provence, in the midst of the beautiful rocky hills of the Chaîne des Alpilles. The D 78 approaches from Fontvielle and the first few houses of the old village clinging to the hillsides come into view suddenly in a bend.

Parking: Park the car in one of the car parks (€4) at the foot of the escarpment, before the road up to the village (where cars are not usually allowed). In high season the car parks can be full, so you may need to park by the roadside some way down from the village.

Timing: A walk through the streets of Les Baux is a magical experience. Take 1hr to see the village and the same for the château.

Their turbulent ways, together with their support for the Reformation, were a great irritant to Louis XIII who in 1632 ordered the castle and ramparts to be dismantled; this was the town's death-blow.

From the remains of the 13C keep a fine **panorama★★** unfolds over the Alpilles with the windmills of Fontvieille to the west. One of them is Daudet's Mill (Moulin de Daudet).

It was here that **Alphonse Daudet**, the Nîmes-born author very popular in France (and available in English translation), is supposed to have written his delightful *Letters from My Mill*, creating the characters of the Woman of Arles

Les Baux-de-Provence

© Pierre Jacques/hemis.fr

(*L'Arlésienne*), Monsieur Seguin's goat, the Pope's grumpy mule and Dom Balaguère the gourmand.

Musée Yves-Brayer★

pl. François-de-Hénain. ⏲*Open Apr– Sept daily 10am–12.30pm, 2–6.30pm; Oct–Dec and mid Feb–Mar Wed–Mon 10am–12.30pm, 2–5.30pm.* ✆€5. 𝄞*04 90 54 36 99. www.yvesbrayer.com.* The museum houses works by Yves Brayer (1907–90), a figurative painter deeply attached to Les Baux (he is buried in the village cemetery).

It is the glowing landscapes of Provence which inspired some of his best paintings, such as *Les Baux* and *Field of Almond Trees.*

EXCURSION
St-Rémy-de-Provence★

▷ *The little town is just north of Les-Baux-de-Provence.*
🛈*pl. Jean-Jaurès.* 𝄞*04 90 92 38 52. www.saintremy-de-provence.com.* Just to the north of the jagged peaks of the Alpilles, St-Rémy encapsulates the character of inland Provence; plane trees shade its boulevards from the intense light and there are charming old alleyways.

The Place de la République is Renaissance in style. Check out with the tourist office the dates for the annual bull running through the streets – it's quite an exciting tradition.

Les Antiques★★

▷ *1km/0.6mi S of the town.*
These fascinating remains mark the site of the prosperous Roman city of Glanum. The **mausoleum**★★ of the 1C BC is the best preserved of its kind in the Roman world; it was erected in memory of the Emperor Augustus' grandsons Gaius and Lucius, whose early death deprived them of their Imperial inheritance.

The **triumphal arch**★, which is much damaged, dates from the beginning of Augustus' reign and is one of the oldest such structures in the south of the country. Its decorative sculpture (garlands of flowers, groups of prisoners and symbols of victory) demonstrates the continued existence of Greek art in Provence.

The ruined site of **ruines de Glanum**★ (⏲*open daily except Mon: Apr–Sept 10am–6.30pm; Oct–Mar 10am–5pm;* ✆€7; 𝄞*04 90 92 23 79*) have revealed the city's history. The original settlement here was founded by the Celts because of the existence of a spring. Later, in the 6C BC, it was extended by Greek merchants, and fine houses in Hellenic style were erected in the following centuries. The place was destroyed by the Teutons, probably not long before their defeat by Marius near Aix in 125 BC; it was restored by Caesar, but laid to waste by Germanic tribes in the 3C AD. From this time on, the city was more or less abandoned, and its streets and canals slowly filled up with material washed down from the Alpilles.

Nîmes★★★

Gard

Nîmes lies between the limestone hills of the Garrigue to the north and the alluvial plain of the Costière du Gard to the south. Its elegant and bustling boulevards are shaded by lotus-trees. The quality of its Roman remains is outstanding.

A BIT OF HISTORY

Emperor Augustus heaped privileges on Nîmes and allowed the building of fortifications.

The town, situated on the Domitian Way, then proceeded to erect splendid buildings: the Maison Carrée along the south side of the forum, an amphitheatre able to hold 24 000 people, a circus, baths fed by an imposing aqueduct, the Pont du Gard. In the 2C the town won favour with Emperors Hadrian and Antoninus Pius (whose wife's family came from Nîmes); it continued to flourish and build and reached the peak of its glory. In 1873, a Bavarian emigrant to the United States called Lévy-Strauss called his new trousers, made from the blue serge manufactured locally, "Denims", meaning literally "from Nîmes".

SIGHTS
Arènes★★★

○ Open daily Jan–Feb, Nov–Dec 9.30am–5pm; Mar, Oct 9am–6pm; Apr–May and Sept 9am–6.30pm; Jun 9am–7pm; Jul–Aug 9am–8pm. ○Closed to visitors during events. ☞€10. ℘04 66 21 82 56. www.arenes-nimes.com.

This superb structure was built in the reign of Augustus, possibly some 80 years before the amphitheatre at Arles. The scale of the great structure is extraordinarily impressive, as is the achievement in cutting, transporting and placing stonework of such dimensions with such precision. The big, crowded bullfights still held here give a flavour of the original arena.

▶ **Population:** 143 199
◌ **Michelin Map:** 339 L 5
▯ **Info:** 6 r. Auguste. ℘04 66 58 38 00. www.ot-nimes.fr.
◑ **Location:** Nîmes is 32km/ 19.8mi NW of Arles. The main shopping street is Rue de la Madeleine.
▣ **Parking:** Entering the city along the canal de la Fontaine and boulevard Victor-Hugo, go around the amphitheatre to get to the underground car park beneath the Esplanade.
◔ **Timing:** Those who can't stand the heat should avoid the city in August. Visitors who object to bull-fighting or crowds are advised not to come during Pentecost.

Maison Carrée★★★

○ Open daily Jan–Feb, Nov–Dec 10am –1pm, 2–4.30pm; Mar 10am–6pm; Oct 10am–1pm, 2–6pm; Apr–May and Sept 10am–6.30pm; Jun 10am–7pm; Jul– Aug 10am–8pm. ○Closed to visitors during events. ☞€4.50. ℘04 66 58 38 00. www.arenes-nimes.com.

Heading northwest along boulevard Victor-Hugo, the Maison Carrée sits in the centre of an elegant paved square separated from the Carré d'art by the boulevard. This house, built in the reign of Augustus (1C BC), is the purest and best preserved of all Roman temples; it is not known which cult was observed here.

Jardin de la Fontaine★★

In Roman times this site was occupied by a spring, a theatre, a temple and baths. Today's shady gardens exemplify the subtle use of water in the landscapes of Languedoc: laid out in characteristic 18C manner, with pools leading into a canal, balustraded walks and porticoes.

Arènes

© Florian Villesèche/Fotolia.com

ADDITIONAL SIGHTS
Musée Archéologique★

○Open Tue–Sun 10am–6pm. ○Closed 1 Jan, 1 May, 1 Nov, 25 Dec. ☜No charge for permanent exhibitions; otherwise ☜€5. ♪04 66 76 74 80.

In the ground-floor gallery, pre-Roman carvings and Roman inscriptions are displayed. Upstairs are Gallo-Roman coins, utensils, headdresses, funerary stelae, oil lamps, glassware and pottery (Archaic Greek, Etruscan and Punic). There is also a collection of cork models of the city's ancient monuments.

Musée des Beaux-Arts★

r. Cité-Foulc. &○Open Tue–Sun 10am–6pm. ○Closed 1 Jan, 1 May, 1 Nov, 25 Dec. ☜No charge for permanent exhibitions; otherwise ☜€5. ♪04 66 67 38 21.

On the ground floor there is a large Roman mosaic depicting the marriage of Admetus; it was discovered in Nîmes in the 19C. The museum displays works of art from the French, Italian, Flemish and Dutch Schools (15–19C) including paintings by Bassano, Rubens, Jean-François de Troy, Delaroche, Andrea della Robia, Nicolas Largillière and Hyacinthe Rigaud. Local works are represented by the portraits of Xavier Sigalon (1787–1837) from Uzès, a seascape by Joseph Vernet, historical paintings by Natoire, a native of Nîmes, and *Landscape near Nîmes*, by J.-B. Lavastre.

Musée du Vieux Nîmes

○Open Tue–Sun 10am–6pm. ○Closed 1 Jan, 1 May, 1 Nov, 25 Dec. ☜No charge for permanent exhibitions; otherwise ☜€5. ♪04 66 76 73 70.

This museum, housed in the former episcopal palace (17C), was founded in 1920 by Henri Bauquier, a rival of Frédéric Mistral, and contains numerous local exhibits in a well-restored historical setting. The city of Nîmes reflects characteristics of both Languedoc and Provence, and there are some pieces of furniture typical of both these regions on display here. There's also an interesting display of denim.

Carré d'Art★

pl. de la Maison Carrée. ○Open Tue–Sun 10am–6pm. ○Closed 1 Jan, 1 May, 1 Nov, 25 Dec. ☜No charge for permanent exhibitions; otherwise ☜€5. ♪04 66 76 35 70.

Designed by the British architect **Norman Foster** to house both the city's Museum of Contemporary Art and its media library, the Carré d'Art stands opposite the Maison Carrée, from which it has copied several of its architectural features. Its collection includes paintings, sculptures and drawings from 1960 onwards, with three main themes: French art from 1960 to the present day, Anglo-Saxon and Germanic artists, and Mediterranean identity.

The museum gives precedence to certain key movements in contemporary art such as New Realism, Supports/Surfaces, the BMPT group, Figuration Libre and New Figuration. Some famous names in the museum's collection include Jean Tinguely, Sigmar Polke, Christian Boltanski, Gérard Garouste, Martial Raysse, Julian Schnabel, Miquel Barceló, Annette Messager, Thomas Struth and local artist Claude Viallat.

There is a good restaurant on the top floor, with sweeping views over the city from the terrace.

EXCURSION
Aigues-Mortes★★
◗ *Aigues-Mortes is 46.6km/29mi SW of Arles.* 🏠*pl. St-Louis.* ✆*04 66 53 73 00. www.ot-aiguesmortes.fr.* 🅿*Parking is available around the exterior of the ramparts.* ⊚*Climb to the the Tour de Constance (53 steps) for an impressive panorama over the town and surrounding flatlands.*

Few places evoke the spirit of the Middle Ages as vividly as Aigues-Mortes sheltering behind its ramparts in a landscape of marshland, lakes and saltpans. A tourist train runs around Aigues-Mortes, offering an overview of the main attractions and entertainment options. Shops, restaurants and hotels lie within the city walls, and a traditional market can be found on Avenue Frédéric-Mistral.

A Bit of History – In 1240, Louis IX (St Louis), then 26 years old, was troubled by the lack of French involvement in the kind of commerce undertaken by the merchant fleets of Pisa and Genoa. He was also taken by the idea of a Crusade, but lacked a Mediterranean port.

A French king could not countenance sailing from a foreign harbour (at this time Provence was part of the Holy Roman Empire, Sète did not exist, and Narbonne was silting up). Louis' solution was to buy a site from a priory and grant a charter to the township which began to develop on what up to then had been virtually an island. The new settlement was laid out on the geometrical lines of a bastide and linked to the sea by an artificial channel.

On 28 August 1248, Louis IX set sail from here on the 7th Crusade, which was a failure. On 1 July 1270 he left from here again, on the 8th Crusade, which only reached Tunis, where Louis died.

By the 14C Aigues-Mortes' population totalled 15 000, but its waterways had begun to silt up; the Tour de Constance lost its military significance and instead became a prison.

For more than a century after the revocation of the Edict of Nantes in 1665, Protestant rebels were held here, from 1715–68 the Tour de Constance being reserved for women prisoners.

The silting up of the port and the incorporation of Marseille into the French kingdom in 1481 pushed Aigues-Mortes into decline and the coup de grâce was the founding (17C) and subsequent development of Sète.

Tour de Constance★★
♿⊙*Open daily May–Aug 10am–7pm; Sept–Apr 10am–5.30pm.* ⊙*Closed public holidays.* ⊚€7. ✆*04 66 53 61 55. http://aigues-mortes.monuments-nationaux.fr.*

The tower (1241–49) rests on wooden piles and was intended to be a symbol of royal power as much as a purely military installation. The layout of its elaborate internal defences (staircases, winding passageways, portcullises) is typical of the Capetian dynasty, and its fine walls of Beaucaire limestone stand out boldly against the surrounding sandy landscape. Its turret originally served as a lighthouse, the sea being only 3km/1.8mi away at the time.

Remparts★★
⊙*Same hours as Tour de Constance.*
The ramparts were never seen by St Louis. They were begun in 1272 on the orders of Philippe le Hardi (the Bold) and their completion led to Aigues-Mortes becoming the Capetian kingdom's principal Mediterranean harbour.

At the end of the 13C Philippe le Bel (the Fair) improved the port and completed the defences, adding 20 massive towers to protect the gateways and provide enfilading fire along the walls themselves.

ADDRESSES

🛏 STAY

🛏–🛏🛏 **Hôtel Côté Patio** – *31 r. de Beaucaire.* ℘*04 66 67 60 17. www.hotel-cote-patio.com. 17rms.* 🚪 €*10.* Charming hotel with a lively feel to it. Very near old Nîmes and the Arènes. Advance reservations around Feria.

🛏🛏 **Hôtel l'Orangerie** – *755 r. de la Tour-de-l'Évêque.* ℘*04 66 84 50 57. www.orangerie.fr. 37rms.* 🚪 €*9. Restaurant*🛏🛏. A new building with the air of an old *mas*, 1km/0.6mi from the town centre. Spacious and individual bedrooms; some have terraces, some jacuzzis. Provençal theme throughout.

🛏🛏 **Chambre d'hôte La Mazade** – *12 r. de la Mazade, 30730 St-Mamert-du-Gard, 14km/9.3mi W via D 999 and D 1.* ℘*04 66 81 17 56. www.bbfrance.com/couston.html. 4rms, 1 gîte.* 🚪. Modern equipment combines with antique furniture in the well fitted-out, bright rooms of this B&B in a quiet, rural location.

🛏🛏 **Hôtel Royal** – *3 bd Alphonse Daudet.* ℘*04 66 58 28 27. www.royalhotel-nimes.com. 22rms.* 🚪 €*9.* Stylish boutique hotel next to the Carré d'Art. Original features and fittings complement minimalist colour and design. Loved by bullfighting superstars, there's an excellent tapas bar, La Bodeguita, downstairs. Can get lively and noisy at weekends.

🛏🛏🛏 **New Hôtel La Baume** – *21 r. Nationale.* ℘*04 66 76 28 42. www.new-hotel.com. 34rms.* 🚪 €*12.* This 17C mansion successfully blends contemporary and antique styles. An interior stone staircase leads to the simple bedrooms, a few of which have pretty, French-style painted ceilings.

🍴 EAT

🍴 **Bistrot des Arènes** – *11 r. Bigot.* ℘*04 66 21 40 18. Closed Aug, Sat lunch and Sun.* Lyon specialities in a delightful setting crammed with objects including Lyonnais Guignol puppets.

🍴🍴 **Le Bouchon et L'Assiette** – *5 bis, r. Sauve.* ℘*04 66 62 02 93. Closed Tue, Wed.* A carefully chosen décor, warm welcome, and tasty seasonal cooking.

🍴🍴 **Le Chapon Fin** – *3 pl. du Château-Fadaise.* ℘*04 66 67 34 73. www.chaponfin-restaurant-nimes.com. Closed Sat, Sun.* Quirky bistro with feria and film posters.

🍴🍴🍴 **Aux Plaisirs des Halles** – *4 r. Littré.* ℘*04 66 36 01 02. www.auxplaisirs deshalles.com. Closed Sun, Mon.* Behind a discreet façade is an elegant room with armchairs draped in fabric, a pretty patio terrace, and good food and wine.

🍸 NIGHTLIFE

Nîmes has a huge number and variety of cafés, including café-concerts, bodegas, Irish pubs or the great fin-de-siècle establishments: each has its own following.

La Grand Bourse – *2 bd des Arènes.* ℘*04 66 67 68 69. www.la-grande-bourse.com.* With its Napoleon III-style coffered ceiling, a terrace facing the amphitheatre and deep, comfortable rattan armchairs, this is the most prestigious café in Nîmes. Excellent, professional service.

🛍 SHOPPING

Maison Villaret – *13 r. de la Madeleine.* ℘*04 66 67 41 79.* Crunchy almond biscuits known as *croquants*.

Wine – *La Vinothèque, 18 r. Jean-Reboul.* ℘*04 66 67 20 44.* Local wines.

Markets – **Large market** on Mon on *bd Gambetta.* **Organic** market Fri mornings on *ave Jean-Jaurès.* **Flea** market Sun mornings in the *Costières* stadium car park. **Evening market** Jul–Aug Thu 6–10pm *(les jeudis de Nîmes).*

🎭 ENTERTAINMENT

Programmes – See the daily newspaper *Midi-Libre*, the weekly publications *La Semaine de Nîmes* or its rival, the *Gazette de Nîmes*, or *Le César* (from the tourist office).

Ferias and bullfighting – There are three major annual ferias: the "spring" feria in Feb: *novilladas* take place throughout the weekend; the Pentecost feria across the Whitsun long weekend, includes a *pégoulade* along the boulevards, *abrivados*, *novilladas* and *corridas* throughout the day and evening, as well as other entertainments all over the city; the harvest feria takes place in mid-September.

Le Printemps du jazz – (3rd week in March) Jazz concerts in a variety of venues around town.

Avignon★★★

Vaucluse

Protected by a ring of imposing ramparts, the historic core of Avignon is a lively centre of art and culture. For 68 years it was the residence first of seven French popes, then of three others once Pope Gregory XI had returned to Rome in 1377; the Papal Legates remained until the city was united with France in 1791.

A BIT OF HISTORY

Very little remains of the Roman settlement of Avenio which fell into ruin after the Barbarian invasions of the 5C.

At the beginning of the 14C the popes felt the need to escape from the turbulent political life of Rome. Avignon formed part of the papal territories, and occupied a central position in the Europe of the time. The case for moving there was put by Philippe le Bel (the Fair), possibly with a view to involving the papacy in his own political manœuvrings. In 1309 Pope Clement V took the plunge, and Avignon became for most of a century the capital of Western Christendom. When Pope Clement VI succeeded him in 1342, he greatly enlarged the Papal Palace, and brought to Avignon his love of the arts.

Avignon remains an influential cultural centre. It owes much to Jean Vilar, who in 1947 founded the prestigious annual event, **Festival d'Avignon**. This led to a blossoming of the arts: it now hosts various cultural events each week.

SIGHTS
Palais des Papes★★★

◷*Open daily 1–mid-Mar 9am–6.30pm; mid-Mar–Jun and mid-Sept–Oct 9am–7pm; Jul and 1–mid-Sept 9am–8pm; Aug 9am–9pm; Nov–Feb 9.30am–5.45pm.* ⊜€10.50 (mid-Mar–mid-Nov); €8.50 (mid-Nov–mid Mar); €11 combined ticket with pont St-Bénézet. ✆04 90 27 50 00.
www.palais-des-papes.com.
The huge feudal structure, fortress as well as palace, conveys an overwhelm-

▸ **Population:** 92 339
◔ **Michelin Map:** 32 B-C 10
▯ **Info:** 41 cours Jean-Jaurès. ✆04 32 74 32 74. www.ot-avignon.fr.
◑ **Location:** Avignon is located 37km/23mi N of Arles.
▯ **Parking:** Parking is available in the Palais des Papes underground and at numerous other car parks, and at various parking areas along the riverfront.
⊛ **Don't Miss:** The Palais des Papes, and the Pont St-Bénézet. The Rocher des Doms gives an excellent view of the surrounding countryside.
◔ **Timing:** With so much to do in Avignon, allow a leisurely full day. Start at the southern end of the city, and walk up the main street to the Palais des Papes, and then visit the ramparts to gain access to the city's famous bridge.
⚌ **Kids:** There's a lovely old-fashioned carousel in Place de l'Horloge. A fun way to see the sights is via "Le Petit Train d'Avignon", several times a day from Place du Palais des Papes – 40min, every half-hour from 10am–7pm. ⊜€7 (children, 4–9, €4); commentary in 8 languages.

ing impression of defensive strength with its high bare walls, its massive corbelled crenellations and stalwart buttresses. Inside, a maze of galleries, chambers, chapels and passages contains almost no furnishings. While the popes were in residence the palace was extremely luxuriously equipped.

Palais des Papes

S. Sauvignier/MICHELIN

Pont St-Bénézet★★

Accessed via ramparts. r. Ferruce.
&⃝ *Open daily 1–mid-Mar 9am–6.30pm; mid-Mar–Jun and mid-Sept–Oct 9am–7pm; Jul and 1–mid-Sept 9am–8pm; Aug 9am–9pm; Nov–Feb 9.30am–5.45pm; 25 Dec–1 Jan 10.30am–5.45pm.* ✆€4.50 (mid-Mar–mid-Nov); €4 (mid-Nov–mid-Mar); €11 combined ticket with Palais des Papes).*
☎04 32 74 32 74.

Stepping out into the swirling Rhône, and coming to an abrupt end in midstream, this beautiful bridge was first built in 1177, according to legend, by a shepherd-boy called Bénézet.

Until the Bridge Brotherhood (Frères Pontifes) built Pont-St-Esprit more than a century later this was the only stone bridge over the Rhône. It helped the economic development of Avignon long before becoming a useful link with Villeneuve when the Cardinals built their villas there. Eighteen of its arches were carried away by the floodwaters of the river in the 17C.

ADDITIONAL SIGHTS

Petit Palais

pl. du Palais des Papes.

This was formerly Cardinal Arnaud de Via's residence (livrée) before being bought by the pope in 1335 to house the bishopric. The building deteriorated during the different sieges imposed upon the Palais des Papes, and had to be repaired and transformed in the late 15C, especially by Cardinal della Rovere, who subsequently became Pope Julius II.

Rocher des Doms★★

There is a well laid-out garden planted with different species on this bluff. From the terraces you will encounter superb **views**★★ of the Rhône and Pont St-Bénézet, Villeneuve-lez-Avignon with Tour Phillipe-le-Bel and Fort St-André, the Dentelles de Montmirail, Mont Ventoux, Vaucluse plateau, the Luberon hills and the Alpilles.

Musée Calvet★

65 r. Joseph Vernet. ⃝ *Open Wed–Mon 10am–1pm, 2–6pm.* ⃝ *Closed 1 Jan, 1 May, 25 Dec.* ✆€6 (€7 with Musée Lapidaire).* *☎04 90 86 33 84. www.musee-calvet.org.*

This celebrated museum is named after its creator, the physician Esprit Calvet. Highlights include a range of sculptures, a collection of silverware and faïence, and French, Italian and Flemish painting from the 16C to the 19C.

Musée Lapidaire★

65 r. de la République. &⃝ *Open Wed–Mon 10am–6pm.* ⃝ *Closed 1 Jan, 1 May, 25 Dec.* ✆€6 (€7 with Musée Calvet).* *☎04 90 85 75 38. www.musee-lapidaire.org.*

Located in the former chapel of the 17C Jesuit College, this building has a unique nave and is flanked by side galleries where you will find displays of sculpture and stone carvings that together represent the different civilisations that left their mark on the region.

EXCURSIONS
Villeneuve-lès-Avignon★
▶ *2km/1.2mi W, on the west bank of the river.*

At the point where St Bénézet's bridge originally touched French territory Philippe le Bel built a small fort (only a tower remains).

Half a century later, feeling hemmed in at Avignon, the Cardinals crossed the river and built themselves 15 fine houses (*livrées*) here. At the same time, Jean le Bon (John the Good) erected the St-André fortress on the hill which was already crowned by an abbey. Protected by its walls and with a splendid twin-towered gatehouse, this vast building complex offers (from its Romanesque Chapel of Notre-Dame de Belvézet) one of the finest views over the Rhône Valley. In the foreground is the gateway, Porte St-André, and beyond, on the far bank, the Palace of the Popes.

In 1352 the General of the Carthusian Order had been elected pope but humbly refused the throne. Pope Innocent VI, elected in his stead, founded a charterhouse, **Chartreuse du Val de Bénédiction**★ (🕐 *open daily Apr–Sept 9am–6.30pm; Oct–Mar 9.30am–5.30pm;* 🕐*closed 1 Jan, 1 May, 1, 11 Nov, 25 Dec;* 📞*04 90 15 24 24)* to commemorate the gesture. It soon became the greatest charterhouse in France. It has a monumental 17C gateway, small cloisters and graveyard cloisters, the latter fringed by the cells of the Fathers.

Le Pont du Gard★★★
🔢 *Pont du Gard site, rte du Pont du Gard* 📞*0820 90 33 30. www.pontdugard.fr.* 🅿 *Both banks of the river have a large car park, open 7–1am (€5).*

This superb aqueduct and road bridge was built between AD 40 and 60. It formed part of a water-supply system with a total length of 49km/30mi, stretching from its source near Uzès via a whole series of cuttings, trenches, bridges and tunnels to supply the Roman city of Nîmes with fresh water.

The three great rows of arches of the aqueduct rise 49m/160.7ft above the valley of the Gardon: imagine the effect such a structure must have had on the imagination of the local Gauls, impressing with the power and prestige of Roman achievement.

A slight curve in the upstream direction increases its ability to withstand seasonal high waters, while the independent construction of the arches lends a certain flexibility to the whole. Careful calculation of the dimensions of the huge blocks of stone meant that they could be put in place without the use

Pont du Gard

Parc Naturel Régional du Luberon

Founded in 1977, the park incorporates 60 communes covering 185 145ha/457 503 acres including the *départements* of Vaucluse and Alpes-de-Haute-Provence (that is, from Manosque to Cavaillon and the Coulon – or Calavon – Valley to the Durance). Its goal is to preserve the natural balance of the region with the aim of improving the living conditions of villagers, the promotion of agricultural activity through irrigation, mechanisation and the reorganisation of the holdings. The main developments in the tourist industry are the opening of tourist information offices and museums at Apt, Buoux and La Tour-d'Aigues, and the creation of nature trails through the cedar forest at Bonnieux, the ochre cliffs of Roussillon, the Viens *bories* and the cultivation terraces at Goult, as well as thematic tourist routes such as the "Route de Vaudois". It also produces attractive publications.

of mortar. The channel on the topmost level was faced with stone in order to maintain water quality and alongside it ran the carriageway of a Roman road. The Pont du Gard fulfilled its function until the 9C, when lack of maintenance and blocking by deposits of lime finally put it out of use.

Le Luberon★★★

🛈 *La Maison du Parc, 60 pl. Jean Jaurès, Apt. ℘04 90 04 42 00. www.parcduluberon.fr.*

Midway between the Alps and the Mediterranean lies the mountainous Luberon range. This region is full of charm: striking solitary woods and rocky countryside plus picturesque hilltop villages and dry-stone huts. The diversity of the vegetation is a delight to nature lovers: oak forests, Atlas cedar (planted in 1862) on the heights of the Petit Luberon, beech, Scots pine, moors of broom and boxwood, *garrigues*, an extraordinary variety of aromatic plants (herbs of Provence) clinging here and there to the rocky slopes.

The Luberon has been inhabited by humans since prehistoric times. Villages appeared during the Middle Ages, clinging to the rock face near a waterhole.

Fontaine de Vaucluse

▷ *The village of Fontaine de Vaucluse is at the end of a 7km/4.3mi-long country road from the town of L'Isle sur la Sorgue.* 🛈 *chemin de la Fontaine. ℘04 90 20 32 22.* ☺*The fountain is much more impressive in spring than in autumn.*

This impressive resurgent spring was famous enough to figure in Strabo's *Geography* 2 000 years ago.

The humanist poet Petrarch retired here in 1337 to write his "Sonnets to Laura" inspired by the beautiful Laura de Noves with whom Petrarch had fallen in love whilst living in Avignon.

Gushing forth at the foot of a cliff among trees in an enclosed valley, this is one of the most spectacular phenomena of its kind. Fed by rain falling on the Vaucluse hills, the water penetrates the limestone uplands and collects in a vast cavern from which it is forced out under pressure. In late winter, the flow can amount to 100cu m/3 531.4cu ft per second.

At such times the waters foam and spray against the rocks, a magnificent natural spectacle.

Gordes★

▷ *The village is in scenic back-country 40km/25mi E.* 🛈 *Le Château. ℘04 90 72 02 75. www.gordes-village.com.*

The **site**★ is outstanding, the charming village rising in tiers up rocky slopes.

Château

🕙*Open daily 10am–noon, 2–6pm.*
🕙*Closed 1 Jan, 25 Dec.* ⬤€4.

The imposing Renaissance château stands dramatically on the village's highest point, facing Old Gordes.

Today it houses the the **Musée Pol Mara**, displaying the work of this Flemish artist who lives in the village.

Village des Bories★

▶ *3.5km/2mi SW.*

Curious dry-stone structures of this kind exist from Iceland to the Middle East. In Vaucluse they were built between the 14C and the 19C. The village consists of a number of dwellings as well as structures for threshing, baking, oil pressing, and housing animals.

Gorges de l'Ardèche★★★

The Ardèche gorge runs most of the way from Vallon Pont d'Arc to St Martin-d'Ardèche. 🄸 *Vallon-Pont d'Arc.* 🖉*04 75 88 04 01. www.vallon-pont-darc-07.com.*
The Ardèche rises in hills to the north of the Col de la Chavade and flows 119km/74mi before joining the Rhône. It is notorious for spring floods and sudden spates which can increase its flow by as much as 3 000 percent, causing immense damage. Vertical cliffs, dramatic meanders and rapids, alternating with calm stretches, are a lesson in the geography of river formation. Prehistoric people settled here very early, and dolmens and cave-dwellings in the area date from the Bronze Age.

Aven d'Orgnac★★★

▶ *South bank.*
♿ *See Aven d'ORGNAC.*

Aven de Marzal★

▶ *North bank.*

At the bottom of this deep swallowhole the Gallery of Diamonds glitters with calcite crystals. A museum presents a display of equipment used by the great explorers of these caverns. Nearby, the popular **Prehistoric Zoo** features reproductions of prehistoric animals.

Gorges: From Vallon Pont d'Arc to Pont-St-Esprit

▶ *47km/29.2mi.*

The meanders of the river mark the course it originally followed on the ancient surface of the plateau before cutting down through the rocks as they were uplifted during the Alpine-building period. Great sweeps of vertical cliffs with dramatic meanders cut deep into the rock and rapids alternating with calm stretches of water combine to form a very impressive natural site.

Pont-d'Arc★★

Spanning the full width of the river, the arch of this gigantic natural bridge is 34m/111.5ft high and 59m/193.5ft wide. In geological terms it is a recent phenomenon, caused by the action of the river, which, helped by the presence of fissures and cavities in the limestone, has succeeded in eroding away the base of a meander.

Haute Corniche (Scenic route)★★★

The road links a number of splendid viewpoints. From the Serre de Tourre can be seen the Pas du Mousse meander where the river has still to cut through the wooded isthmus; the view from the Morsanne Needles (Aiguilles de Morsanne) gives a good idea of the structure of the plateau as it dips down to the south. Limestone ridges can be viewed from Gournier, while the rock spires of the Rocher de la Cathédrale lend this natural monument the appearance of a ruined cathedral.

Aven d'Orgnac★★★

🕐*Open daily* ⬥*guided tours (1hr): Feb–Mar 10am–noon, 2–5pm; Apr–Jun and Sept 9.30am–5.30pm; Jul–Aug 9.30am–6pm; Oct–mid-Nov 9.30am–noon, 2–4.30pm; Dec (public holidays only) 2–5pm.* ⬥€*10 (includes museum)* 🖉*04 75 38 65 10. www.orgnac.com.*
This extraordinary chasm, Aven d'Orgnac, lies among the woods covering the Ardèche plateau. It was first explored by Robert de Joly (1887–1968) on 19 August 1935. Joly was an electrical engineer, fascinated by cars and planes but above all by spelaeology.
Of the four caverns at Orgnac, only **Orgnac I** has so far been opened up to the public. Orgnac III is known to have been inhabited 300 000 years ago; the **museum** has displays on the culture which flourished in the region before the Bronze Age.

ADDRESSES

⌂ STAY

⊜⊜ **La Ferme** – *110 chemin des Bois, Île de la Barthelasse, 5km/3mi N.* ℘*04 90 27 15 47. 20rms. Closed Mon lunch, Wed lunch.* Country-style dining room with beams, fireplace and old stone can be found at this haven of peace.

⊜⊜–⊜⊜⊜ **Bagatelle**– *25 allées Antoine Pinay, Île de la Barthelasse.* ℘*4 90 86 30 39. www.campingbagatelle.com. 10rms for 2–4 people at the hotel, 230 placements at the campsite.* Large campground with a separate hotel. Great setting on an island near Pont St-Bénezet.

⊜⊜–⊜⊜⊜ **Boquier** – *6 r. du Portail Boquier.* ℘*04 90 82 94 11. www.hotel-boquier.com. 12rms.* ⊑*€8.* Each room is individually and tastefully decorated.

⊜⊜–⊜⊜⊜ **Hôtel Bristol** – *44 cours J.-Jaurès.* ℘*04 90 16 48 48. www.bristol-hotel-avignon.com. 11rms.* ⊑ *€12. Closed 15 Dec–14 Jan.* Situated on the main avenue of the walled city. Spacious and sensibly functional rooms, most overlook the inside courtyards.

⊜⊜⊜ **Chambre d'hôte Villa Agapè** – *13 r. Agricol.* ℘*04 90 85 21 92. 3rms. Closed 1–15 May, Jul, Feb.* It's easy to forget the town-centre location of this attractive villa, with its verdant terrace and swimming pool.

⊜⊜⊜ **Colbert** – *7 r. Agricol Perdiguier.* ℘*04 90 86 20 20. www.avignon-hotel-colbert.com. Closed Nov–Feb. 15rms.* ⊑ *€10.* Simplicity and family home atmosphere in this discreet hotel. Bedrooms are decorated with Provençal colours, antiques and billboards.

⊜⊜⊜ **Hôtel de Blauvac** – *11 r. de la Bancasse.* ℘*04 90 86 34 11. www.hotel-blauvac.com. 16rms.* ⊑*€8.* The former home of the Marquis de Tonduly, Lord of Blauvac, in the 17C, is one of the best value-for-money hotels in town.

⊜⊜⊜ **Mignon** – *12 r. Joseph Vernet.* ℘*04 90 82 17 30. www.hotel-mignon.com. 16rms.* ⊑*€12.* A small hotel in the heart of Avignon's historic centre. All rooms are soundproofed.

⊜⊜⊜⊜ **Banasterie** – *11 r. de la Banasterie.* ℘*04 32 76 30 78. www.la-banasterie.com. 5rms.* A Virgin with Child adorns the listed façade of this 16C edifice. A cosy, romantic interior.

⊜⊜⊜⊜ **Hôtel Cloître St-Louis** – *20 r. Portail Boquier.* ℘*04 90 27 55 55. www.cloitre-saint-louis.com. 77rms.* ⊑*€16. Restaurant*⊜⊜⊜⊜. Situated in 16C cloisters, part of this hotel was designed by Jean Nouvel. The building uses a variety of materials including glass, steel and stone.

⊜⊜⊜⊜ **Hôtel du Palais des Papes** – *1 r. Gérard Philipe.* ℘*4 90 86 04 13. www.hotel-avignon.com. 27rms.* ⊑*€8.* Beautiful rooms and beautiful views at this luxurious, reasonably priced hotel in the old centre.

⊜⊜⊜⊜ **Maison d'hôte Lumani** – *37 r. du Rempart St-Lazare.* ℘*04 90 82 94 11. http://hoteldanieli-avignon.com. 5rms.* Artists are particularly welcome in this fine 19C manor house, which has an attractive courtyard shaded by a couple of hundred-year-old plane trees.

⊉/ EAT

⊜ **Ginette et Marcel** – *25 pl. des Corps Saints.* ℘*04 90 85 58 70.* More a bisto/caféteria than a restaurant, you can grab a decent sandwich or salad here.

⊜⊜ **Entrée des Artistes** – *1 pl. des Carmes.* ℘*04 90 82 46 90. Closed Sat–Sun.* The dining room of this restaurant is decorated in the style of a Parisian bistro, with old posters and movie memorabilia. Tables are placed close together and the cooking is traditional.

⊜⊜ **L'Ami Voyage... en compagnie** – *5 r. Prevot.* ℘*04 90 82 41 51.* French cuisine is served at this cute place set in an old library. An air of elegance reigns here.

⊜⊜ **Le Jardin de la Tour** – *9 r. de la Tour.* ℘*04 90 85 66 50. www.jardindelatour.fr. Closed Sun–Mon.* Situated near the ramparts, this restaurant has a lovely garden. Provençal cuisine.

⊜⊜ **L'Isle Sonnante** – *7 r. Racine.* ℘*04 90 82 56 01. Closed lunch in Aug, Sun, Mon.* This restaurant near the town hall is proud of its Rabelaisian name. Cosy interior combines rustic style with warm tones.

⊜⊜ **Piedoie** – *26 r. 3-Faucons.* ℘*04 90 85 17 32. Closed last week Aug, last week Nov, Feb school holidays, Mon off season, Wed.* Beams, parquet flooring and white walls hung with contemporary paintings for the décor and creative cuisine based on market produce. A family atmosphere.

⊜⊜🍽 **Christian Étienne** – *10 r. Mons.* *☎04 90 86 16 50. www.christian-etienne.fr.* Historically charged setting in 13C and 14C buildings adjoining the Palais des Papes. Here the chef produces fine cuisine that pays tribute to the Provence of his birth.

⊜⊜🍽 **Le Grand Café** – *La Manutention, r. des Escaliers Ste Anne.* *☎04 90 86 86 77. Closed Sun and Mon.* Backing onto the buttresses of the Palais des Papes, these old barracks have become an essential part of local life.

⊜⊜🍽 **Le Moutardier du Pape** – *15 pl. du Palais-des-Papes.* *☎04 90 85 34 76. www.restaurant-moutardier.fr. Closed Wed from Oct–Mar.* This 18C building, listed in France's National Heritage, makes an exceptional setting for a simple, fresh meal.

⊜⊜🍽🍽 **L'Essentiel** – *2 r. Petite-Fusterie.* *☎04 90 85 87 12. www.restaurantlessentiel. com. Closed Sun.* Thie restaurant focuses on the "essential", delighting guests with its generous cuisine, full of sunny French and Italian flavours. Modern décor.

⊜⊜🍽🍽 **La Mirande** – *4 pl. Amirande.* *☎04 90 85 93 93. www.la-mirande.fr. Closed Tue–Wed.* An 18C Provençal décor, antiques, ornaments and a profusion of refined detail set the stunning scene here.

🍷 NIGHTLIFE

La Cave Breysse – *41 r. des Teinturiers.* *☎04 32 74 25 86. Closed Sun.* A very popular wine bar, this is a nice place to enjoy a well-priced glass of wine or an apéritif, and to take in the night, the ambience and the festivities.

Café In et Off – *pl. du Palais-des-Papes.* *☎04 90 85 48 95. Closed mid-Nov–late Feb.* Don't miss the only café that enjoys unbeatable views of the Palais des Papes.

Cloître des Arts – *83 r. Joseph-Vernet.* *☎04 90 85 99 04. Open Mon–Sat 7am– 1.30am (during the festival 7am–3am). Closed the first fortnight of Jan.* Sixty varieties of beer from all over the world and a relaxed atmosphere attract beer enthusiasts of all ages, whether among friends or with family.

😋 SHOWTIME

Le Rouge Gorge – *10 bis, r. Peyrolerie.* *☎04 90 14 02 54. Closed Sun, Jul–Aug.* The only cabaret in Avignon, the Rouge Gorge, modestly sheltered by the Palais des Papes, unveils the sensual charms of its show every Friday and Saturday, while two Sundays a month there is an operetta lunch.

🛒 SHOPPING

Markets – **Les Halles Centrales**, *pl. Pie*, traditional covered market Tue–Sun. **Flower market** Sat in *pl. des Carmes.* **Fair** Sat and Sun, *rempart St-Michel.* **Flea market** Sun in *pl. des Carmes.*

Honey – **Miellerie des Butineuses**, *189 r. de la Source, St-Saturnin-lès-Avignon.* *☎04 90 22 47 52. www.miellerie.fr.* Honey, pollen, and royal jelly, as well as honey-based products.

🏃 LEISURE ACTIVITIES

👥 **Avignon by boat** – *CroisiEurope.* *☎03 88 76 44 44. www.croisieurope.com.* Audioguide tours from 1hr30 to 4hr of Avignon and along the Rhône.

Coach excursion – **Provence Vision (Cars Lieutaud)** – *36 bd St-Roch.* *☎04 90 86 36 75. www.cars-lieutaud.fr.* Offers half- and full-day excursions from Avignon to the Camargue, Pont du Gard, Fontaine-de-Vaucluse, the Alpilles, a lavender tour and a wine tour to Châteauneuf-du-Pape.

Trips on the Rhône – "Grands Bateaux de Provence" (*☎04 90 85 62 25. www.avignon-et-provence.com/mireio)* organises several full-day round-trip boat outings from Avignon along the Rhône.

🗓 EVENTS

Festival d'Avignon – *Every July.* It promotes France's cultural life through theatre, dance, lectures, exhibitions and concerts in and around Avignon. *Information:* *☎04 90 27 66 50. Reservations* *☎04 90 14 14 14. www.festival-avignon.com*

Booking "Festival Off" – The programme for Avignon's Fringe Festival, on at the same time, is available mid-June. *☎04 90 85 13 08. www.avignonleoff.com.*

Hivernales d'Avignon – This contemporary dance festival takes place during two weeks in July. *☎04 90 82 33 12. www.hivernales-avignon.com.*

Animo Nature – *Early Oct at Parc des Expositions d'Avignon.* *☎04 90 84 02 04. www.animo-nature.com.* The largest animal show in France.

Orange★★

Vaucluse

Gateway to the Midi, Orange is famous for its remarkable Roman remains, including the triumphal arch and the Roman Theatre, as well as for its prestigious international music festival, **Chorégies d'Orange**.

A BIT OF HISTORY

Orange flourished in the days of the Pax Romana as an important staging post on the great highway between Arles and Lyon. In the 16C, it came into the possession of William the Silent, ruler of the German principality of Nassau, then Stadtholder of the United Provinces. He took the title of Prince of Orange and founded the Orange-Nassau line. Orange is still proud of its association with the royal house of the Netherlands, whose preferred title is Prince (or Princess) of Orange. In 1678 under the Treaty of Nijmegen, the town became French territory.

SIGHTS

Théâtre Antique★★★

r. Madeleine Roch. ⊙*Open Jan–Feb, Nov–Dec 9.30am–4.30pm; Mar, Oct 9.30am–5.30pm; Apr–May, Sept 9am–6pm; Jun–Aug 9am–7pm.* ⊙*Closed on event days.* ⊛€8. ℘04 90 51 17 60. www.theatre-antique.com.

Dating from the reign of Roman **Emperor Augustus**, this theatre is the best-preserved structure of its type in the whole of the Roman world. The stage wall measures 103x36m/ 338x118ft; Louis XIV called it "the finest wall in all the kingdom". Its outer face is of striking simplicity, interrupted only by the mounts for the poles supporting the awnings shading the audience from the sun. On the auditorium side, the wall has lost its marble facing and mosaic decoration, its columns and its statues.

The great statue of Augustus has been replaced in its central niche; together with some remaining hammer-finished granite blocks, it gives some idea of how the theatre must have appeared originally.

▶ **Population:** 30 228

⚙ **Michelin Map:** 332 B 9

🛈 **Info:** 5 cours Aristide Briand. ℘04 90 34 70 88. www.otorange.fr.

◉ **Location:** Orange, on the River Meyne, close to the Rhône, is at the meeting of *autoroutes* and other highways, 32km/20mi N of Avignon.

⊘ **Don't miss:** The stunning Théâtre Antique, and, if you have time, go to Vaison-la-Romaine for the Tuesday market.

Théâtre Antique

Grégoire Saint Martin © Office de Tourisme Orange

Arc de Triomphe★★

A UNESCO World Heritage Site, Orange's Arc de Triomphe was built between the years AD 21 and 26 as a tribute to Emperor Augustus. It is a remarkable piece of architecture covered with beautiful sculptures. On its north and east sides are reliefs depicting the exploits of the Second Legion in Gaul (weapons both of Gauls and of Amazons), the triumph of Rome (captured Gauls in chains) and Roman domination of the seas following the naval battle of Actium (anchors, oars, warships).

EXCURSIONS
Vaison-la-Romaine★★
▶ *The town is on the N slopes of the Dentelles de Montmirail hills, some 30km/18.6mi E of the Rhône Valley and the town of Orange.*

🛈 *pl. du Chanoine Sautel.* ☎*04 90 36 02 11. www.vaison-la-romaine.com.*

This charming and picturesque old market town in the hills near Mont Ventoux has outstanding and extensive ruins of the original Gallo-Roman town, as well as a Romanesque cathedral and cloisters.

Founded 60 years before Caesar's conquest of Gaul, Vaison was the capital of a Celtic tribe, the Vocontii. Under Roman rule it became the seat of great landed proprietors, a flourishing city possibly as large as Arles or Fréjus, one of the centres of Transalpine Gaul and subsequently of Narbonensis. It fell into ruin at the time of the barbarian invasions, and was covered in debris.

In the Middle Ages the town grew again, but around the castle of the Counts of Toulouse on the other side of the river. In the 17C and 18C, new dwellings were built on the right bank, on top of the Roman site. Its ruins were discovered in the 19C, and began to be excavated in the early 20C.

In 1992, torrential rains caused a disastrous flood in and around Vaison. The Ouvèze rose to the point where it flowed over the top of the Roman bridge (which was undamaged, although the 16C parapet had to be replaced). The Roman and medieval sites were virtually undamaged but a campsite and modern houses and commercial premises by the river were entirely swept away. Thirty-seven people lost their lives.

Ruines Romaines★★
The layout of modern Vaison has allowed two parts of the Roman city to be excavated. The La Villasse quarter **(quartier de la Villasse)** lies to the southwest of the Avenue Général-de-Gaulle on either side of a paved central street; there are shops, houses and a basilica.

The Dolphin House (Maison du Dauphin) dating from 30 BC is particularly interesting, as is the House of the Silve Bust (Maison du Buste-d'argent). The **quartier de Puymin** lies to the east o the avenue. Here there is the House o the Messii (Maison des Messii) with it atrium, peristyle and baths, as well as the Roman Theatre.

The latter structure *(approached via a tunnel)* dates from the time of the Emperor Augustus; the pits containing the machinery and curtain have been well preserved and the tiers of seating were reconstructed in 1932.

Musée Archéologique Théo-Desplans★
♿🕐*Open daily Nov–Feb 10am–noon, 2–5pm; Mar and Oct 10am–12.30pm, 2–5.30pm; Apr–May 9.30am–6pm; Jun–Sept 9.30am–6.30pm.* ⊛€8 *(including Roman Ruins).* ☎*04 90 36 50 05.*

This fascinating archaeological museum displays the finds excavated at Vaison Different aspects of Gallo-Roman civilisation are presented thematically: religion, living quarters, pottery, glassware arms, tools, ornaments, toiletries and imperial coins. The statues are remarkable. They are all in white marble; in chronological order: Claudius (dating from 43) wearing a heavy oak crown Domitian in armour; naked Hadrian (dating from 121) in a majestic pose in the Hellenistic manner; Sabina, his wife, represented more conventionally as a great lady in state dress. Two other pieces are worthy of interest: the 2C marble head of Apollo crowned with laurel leaves and a 3C silver bust of a patrician and mosaics from the Peacock Villa.

Château de Grignan★★
▶ *Grignan is SE of Montélimar, E of the Rhône.*

🕐*Open daily 9.30am–noon, 2–6pm.* 🕐*Closed Tue from Nov–Mar, 25 Dec, 1 Jan.* ⊛€5.50. ☎*04 75 91 83 55.* 🛈 *Place Sévigné, Grignan.* ☎*04 75 46 56 75. www.ville-grignan.fr.*

The old town of Grignan is dominated by its medieval château, which owes its fame to the delightful letters written over a twenty-year period in the 17C by

Aerial view of Mont Ventoux

© Camille Moirenc/hemis.fr

Mme de **Sévigné** to her daughter Mme de Grignan.

The medieval castle was remodelled in the 16C. In 1669, the Count of Grignan married the daughter of Mme de Sévigné, who became a frequent visitor. The letters written by mother to daughter over a period of 27 years were to create a new literary genre; they are full of keen observation, wit and spontaneity. The Renaissance south front of the château was restored early in the 20C following a fire. With its superimposed columns, moulded pilasters, mullioned windows and shell-decorated niches, it marks the arrival of the Renaissance in Provence.

The original courtyard is flanked by a Gothic pavilion and opens out onto the terrace with a **view**★★ over the Tricastin area and Mont Ventoux. Inside are evocative furnishings (**mobilier**★) of many periods and Aubusson tapestries.

Mont Ventoux★★★

▶ *The massif is served by a scenic route 67km/41.6mi long between Vaison and Carpentras. The road was used for motor racing until 1973, and the ascent is a major challenge in those years when it features as part of the Tour de France. The mountain's upper section is blocked by snow from mid-Nov–mid-March.*

Mount Ventoux enjoys an isolated position far from any rival summit, making it a commanding presence in northwestern Provence, visible over vast distances especially when topped in winter with a sparkling coat of snow.

Summit★★★

1 909m/6 263ft.

The top of the mountain consists of a vast field of white shingle from which protrude numerous masts and instruments, radar equipment, a TV transmitter and a weather station.

Mont Ventoux, the Windy Mountain, is so named because of the mistral which blasts it with a force unequalled elsewhere. On average, the temperature here is 11°C lower than in the valley.

The flora even includes polar vegetation. In the early morning and late afternoon, as well as in autumn, the vast **panorama**★★★ extends from the Écrins Massif to the northeast to the Cévennes and the shore of the Mediterranean.

Below the resort of Chalet-Reynard on the descent southward are fine stands of Aleppo and Austrian black pine and Atlantic cedar, as well as beeches and oaks. Finally, beyond St-Estève, vines and fruit trees make an appearance.

INDEX

A

Abbaye de Fontenay................ 229
Abbaye de Fontfroide 393
Abbaye de Jumièges 402
Abbaye de Noirlac................. 290
Abbaye de Royaumont 478
Abbaye de St-Benoît-sur-Loire 277
Abbaye de St-Martin-du-Canigou ... 396
Abbaye d'Hambye................. 417
Abbaye du Bec-Hellouin 401
Abbaye du Thoronet 356
Accessibility...................... 34
Aigues-Mortes 532
Aiguille des Grands-Montets........ 320
Aiguille du Midi 319
Aiguilles de Bavella............... 280
Aix-en-Provence................. 520
   Cézanne's Studio.................. 521
   Cours Mirabeau 520
   Eat 522
   Shopping........................ 522
   Stay 522
   Tours 522
   Vieux Aix 520
Aix-les-Bains 315
   Roman Town..................... 315
   Spa Town 315
Ajaccio......................... 279
   Excursions 280
Albi............................ 370
   Cathédrale Ste-Cécile 370
   Eat 373
   Excursions 371
   Leisure Activities................. 373
   Musée Toulouse-Lautrec 371
   Shopping........................ 373
   Stay 372
   Tours 373
Albigensian Crusade............ 370, 374
Alençon......................... 420
   Excursions 421
   Musée des Beaux-Arts et de la
     Dentelle (lace) 420
   Walking Tour.................... 421
Alsace 94
Amboise 265
Amiens 438
   Cathédrale Notre-Dame 438
   City Pass (sightseeing)............. 438
   Eat 442
   Entertainment 442
   Excursion 440

   Guided Tours 442
   Musée de Picardie................ 440
   Nightlife........................ 442
   Puppet Shows 439
   Shopping........................ 442
   Stay 441
Andelys, Les 402
Andorra........................ 396
   Port d'Envallra 396
Angers......................... 253
   Cathédrale St-Maurice............. 254
   Château 253
   Eat 259
   Excursions 255
   Musée Jean-Lurçat et de la Tapisserie
     contemporaine 254
   Outdoor activities................ 259
   Shopping........................ 259
   Stay 258
Angoulême 147
   Excursion 148
Annecy 312
   Excursions 314
   Le Lac (The Lake) 312
   Vieil Annecy (Old Annecy) 312
Aquitaine 138
Arcachon 146
   Dune du Pilat 146
Arc de Campanus................. 315
Arc-et-Senans 246
Ardennes 94
Argentière 319
Arles.......................... 523
   Amphithéâtre.................... 523
   Driving Tour 525
   Eat 527
   Events 527
   Excursion 524
   Musée d'Arles et de la Provence antique. 524
   Roman period.................... 523
   Shopping........................ 527
   Stay 526
   Théâtre Antique.................. 523
Arras 443
   Ancienne Abbaye St-Vaast.......... 443
   Eat 444
   Les Places....................... 444
   Stay 444
Artenay......................... 276
Art Nouveau 288
Atlantic Coast 138
Auch........................... 377

Aulnay.................................154
Autun 236
Auvergne.......................... 168
Auvers-Sur-Oise................... 488
Auxerre........................240
  Cathédrale St-Étienne.................. 240
  Excursions........................... 240
Avant-Garde.........................89
Aven d'Orgnac..................... 538
Avignon 534
  Eat 539
  Events.............................. 540
  Excursions.......................... 536
  Leisure Activities.................... 540
  Nightlife............................ 540
  Palais des Papes..................... 534
  Papacy 534
  Pont St-Bénézet..................... 535
  Rocher des Doms..................... 535
  Shopping........................... 540
  Stay 539

B

Bagnoles-de-l'Orne 422
Banks................................45
Barbizon............................476
Basic Information 44
Bastia..........................284
  Excursions.......................... 284
Bastides 286
Battle of Hastings 415
Bauxite 528
Bayeux 414
  Bayeux Tapestry 414
  Cathédrale Notre-Dame................ 414
  Eat 416
  Musée-Mémorial de la Bataille
    de Normandie 415
  Nightlife............................ 416
  Shopping........................... 416
  Stay 416
Bayonne 161
  Musée Basque 161
  Musée Bonnat 161
Béarn 166
Beaulieu-Sur-Dordogne 305
Beaune 233
  Beaune for wine lovers............... 239
  Collégiale Notre-Dame, tapestries,...... 234
  Eat 238
  Excursions.......................... 235
  Hôtel-Dieu.......................... 233

Les Trois Glorieuses (wine auction)...... 233
  On the town 239
  Stay 238
  Taking a break 239
  Walking tours....................... 234
Beaune, Montagne de 235
Beauvais........................... 493
Bed and Breakfast...................40
Belle-Île 222
  Côte Sauvage 222
Béout mountain.................... 381
Bergerac........................301
  Musée d'anthropologie du Tabac 302
Bernard, Émile 89
Berry 286
Besançon 244
  Citadel and Museums 244
  Eat 247
  Excursions.......................... 245
  Musée des Beaux-Arts et d'Archéologie . 244
  Stay 247
Beynac-et-Cazenac................. 300
Biarritz 160
  Entertainment 163
  Excursions.......................... 161
  Hotels 162
  Restaurants......................... 162
  Shopping........................... 163
  Sport and leisure.................... 163
Blois............................270
  Château 270
  Eat 274
  Excursions.......................... 271
  Shopping........................... 274
  Son et lumière 274
  Stay 274
Bocage 198
Bonaguil, Château de.............. 305
Bonaparte, Napoleon...63, 279, 349, 449
Bonifacio 282
  Excursions.......................... 282
  Parc Marin International des
    Bouches de Bonifacio 282
Bonnard, Pierre 89
Bontemps, Pierre.....................77
Books...............................24
Bordeaux 140
  Château de Roquetaillade 144
  Entertainment 145
  Excursions.......................... 143
  Grand-Théâtre 141
  Hotels 144

INDEX

Musée d'Aquitaine 142
Musée des Beaux-Arts 142
Place de la Bourse 141
Restaurants 145
Shopping 145
Vineyards 143
Boucher, François .84
Bouguereau, Adolphe William 88
Boulogne-sur-Mer 436
Excursions 437
Nausicaä 436
Roman period 436
Ville haute 436
Bourbons 59
Bourg-en-Bresse 249
Excursions 250
Monastère royal de Brou 249
Bourgeois, Louise 90
Bourges 288
Cathédrale St-Étienne 288
Eat 292
Entertainment 292
Excursions 290
Leisure activities 292
Palais Jacques Cœur 289
Shopping 292
Stay 291
Brantôme 297
Braque, Georges 89
Brest 209
Excursions 210
Océanopolis 209
Breton 198
Briançon 324, 332
Ville Haute (Upper Town) 332
Brittany 198
le Brun, Charles .83
Burghers of Calais, the 431
Burgundy 226
Business Hours 44

C

Cabanel, Alexandre 88
Caen 409
Abbaye-aux-Dames 409
Caen Stone 409
Eat 412
Excursions 410
L'Abbaye-aux-Hommes 409
Leisure Activities 412
Le Mémorial 410
Musée de Normandie 410

Musée des Beaux-Arts 410
Shopping 412
Stay 412
Cahors 306
Eat 309
Excursions 308
Pont Valentré 306
Shopping 309
Stay 309
Walking tour 306
Calais 431
Calais Lace 432
Excursions 433
Monument des Bourgeois de Calais 432
Calanches de Piana 281
Calanques, walks 514
Calvaire de Plougastel-Daoula 210
Camping 40
Canal du Midi 376
Cannes 352
Boulevard de la Croisette 352
Cannes International Film Festival 352
Eat 355
Events 355
Excursions 353
Leisure Activities 355
Musée de la Castre 353
Nightlife 355
Resorts 354
Shopping 355
Stay 354
Tours and Transport 352
Canoeing 20
Cap Corse 284
Cap d'Antibes 349
Capetians 57
Cap Fréhel 205
Cars/Driving 35, 36
Carcassonne 387
Eat 391
Excursions 389
La Cité Walk 387
Stay 391
Carnac 221
Megaliths 221
Musée de Préhistoire J.-Miln-Z.-Le-Rouzic 221
Carolingians 56
Car rental 39
Cartier, Jacques 201
Cascade du Hérisson 248
Catharism 370, 374, 390
Cathédrale (Basilique) St-Denis 478

Causses............................ 286
Cell/Mobile phones.................46
Cévennes mountain range......... 360
Cézanne, Paul................... 89, 520
Chablis wines 242
Châlons-en-Champagne 132
　Cathédrale St-Étienne................ 132
　Excursion............................ 132
Chalon-sur-Saône 237
　Musée Nicéphore Niépce............... 238
Chambéry 314
Chamonix-Mont Blanc 318
　Excursions 319
　Viewpoints, by cable car............... 320
Champagne........................128
Champagne region...................94
Channel Tunnel 431
Chaos de Montpellier-le-Vieux 368
Chapelle de Ronchamp 247
Chardin, Jean Baptiste Simeon 84
Charlemagne 56
Charlet, Armand....................319
Chartres 505
　Cathédrale Notre-Dame............... 505
　Eat 509
　Excursions 506
　Shopping........................... 509
　Stay 509
　Visit 509
Château d'Ancy-le-Franc.............242
Château d'Azay-le-Rideau 267
Château de Bonaguil 305
Château de Brissac 255
Château de Carrouges 423
Château de Chambord.............. 272
Château de Champs 476
Château de Chantilly............496
　Grandes Écuries (stables) 496
Château de Châteaudun 277
Château de Chenonceau............. 266
Château de Cheverny............... 273
Château d'Écouen 477
Château de Grignan 542
Château de Hautefort............... 297
Château de Josselin 220
Château de Langeais 263
Château de Lapalisse 196
Château de La Rochefoucauld....... 148
Château de Meillant 290
Château de Montségur 390
Château de Peyrepertuse 396
Château de Pierrefonds............. 492

Château de Serrant.................. 255
Château de Tournoël 195
Château de Valençay 274
Château de Vaux-le-Vicomte....... 501
Château de Versailles 483
　Appartement de la Reine.............. 485
　Cour de Marbre..................... 484
　Domaine de Marie-Antoinette.......... 486
　Eat 487
　Excursion 486
　Galerie des Glaces (Hall of Mirrors) 484
　Grands Appartements................. 484
　Guided Tours 486
　Louis XIV, Sun King 483
　Nightlife........................... 487
　Shopping........................... 487
　Stay 487
　The Gardens (Jardins) 485
　Ville de Versailles................... 486
Château de Vincennes.............. 479
Château d'If.......................514
Château du Haut-Koenigsbourg......120
Châteaudun.......................277
Châteaux, Île-de-France 477
Châteaux of the Loire.............. 252
Châtillon-sur-Seine 228
　Le Trésor de Vix 229
Cheese............................53
Chevalier, Maurice................. 468
Chinon........................... 263
Cirque de Baume 248
Cirque de Navacelles 364
Citadel, Sisteron................... 335
Clermont-Ferrand 185
　Basilique Notre-Dame du Port 186
　Cathédrale Notre-Dame-de-
　　l'Assomption....................... 186
　Excursions 188
　Musée d'Art Roger-Quilliot 187
　Old Montferrand 186
Climate 18, 91
Climbing..........................20
Clouet, François....................77
Clouet, Jean.......................77
Cluny 250
　Abbaye Bénédictine de Cluny........... 251
Coach/Bus travel 35
Coeur, Jacques 289
Cognac 149
Cognac, production 149
Col d'Aubisque 167
Col de Balme....................... 320

INDEX

Col de la Cayolle. 325
Col d'Izoard 324
Col du Galibier 323
Collonges-la-Rouge 305
Colmar. 118
   Excursions 120
   Hotels 120
   Musée Unterlinden. 118
   Nightlife. 121
   Restaurants. 121
   Retable d'Issenheim. 118
   Shopping. 121
   Ville Ancienne 119
Colonne de la Grande Armée   437
Compiègne 490
   Clairière de l'Armistice. 491
   Eat 493
   Excursions 491
   Le Château. 490
   Musée de la Voiture et du Tourisme 491
   Musée Vivenel 491
   Stay 493
Concarneau. 214
Conques 369
   Église St-Foy 369
   Excursion 369
Cordes-sur-Ciel. 369
Corneille de Lyon. 77
Corniche basque 164
Corniches de la Riviera. 340
Corsica. 278
   Walking 281
Corte 285
   Église San Michele de Murato. 285
Côte d'Albâtre (Alabaster Coast). 408
Côte de la Lumière, ...151
Côte d'Émeraude. 202
Côte d'Opale 435
Côte Sauvage .210
Cottage rental 40
Council of Europe 94
Courbet, Gustave. 88
Courchevel. 327
   Excursions 327
   Resorts 327
   Visits from 328
Courchevel 1550 327
Courchevel 1850 327
Coutances. 417
   Cathédrale Notre-Dame de Coutances . . 417
   Eat 419
   Excursions 417
   Stay 419

Coysevox, Antoine. 83
Credit cards 45
Crozon Peninsula. 210
Crusades, the 511
Cubism 89
Cuisine 53
Currency. 45
Currency exchange. 45
Customs regulations. 33
Cycling Holidays. 21

D

Daumier, Honore 88
David, Jean Louis 86
Dax. 165
D-Day Landings 398, 413
Deauville 410
de Berry, Jean 288
de Champaigne, Philippe 82
Degas, Edgar. 89
Delacroix, Eugene 88
Delaune, Étienne 79
de Maupassant, Guy. 356
de Montfort, Simon 370, 387
Denis, Maurice 89
De Stijl. 89
Dieppe 408
Dijon 227
   Driving Tour 229
   Eat 231
   Excursions 228
   Musée des Beaux-Arts. 228
   On the town 231
   Palais des ducs et des États de Bourgogne. 228
   Salle des Gardes. 228
   Shopping 231
   Stay 231
   Taking a break 231
Dinan. 202
Dinard 202
Disneyland Resort Paris. 498
   General Information. 499
   Walt Disney Studios Park 500
Domme. 300
Dorat, Le. 294
Dordogne. 286
Dreux. 403
Driving 36
Driving Tours
   Corniche des Crêtes 516
   Corniches de la Riviera 340

Dijon: Côte de Nuits 229
Golfe-Juan to Grenoble. 349
Les Baux Alpilles 525
Route des Grandes Alpes 321
Dubois, Ambroise .79
Dubreuil, Toussaint. 79
Duchy of Brittany. 198
Du Guesclin, Bertrand 199
Dukes of Burgundy 227
Dumas, Alexandre. 514
Dunkerque. 433

E
Ecomusée d'Alsace 126
Economy. 52
Edict of Nantes 223
Église de St-Nectaire. 190
Electricity 44
Embassies and Consulates 32
Emergencies 44
Ensemble Mégalithique de
    Locmariaquer 219
Entry Requirements 33
Errard, Jean 335
Étretat. 407
Eurotunnel. 35
Events calendar 26
Évian-les-Bains. 316
    Excursions 317
Évreux. 402
Èze 340

F
Fauvism. 89
Fécamp. 407
    Palais Bénédictine. 408
Ferries 34
Figeac 308
Filitosa. 282
Films 25
Fishing 19
Flanders 424
Flaubert, Gustave 399
Foch, Ferdinand. 491
Fontainebleau 502
    Château 502
    Eat 504
    Nightlife 504
    Sport and Leisure 504
    Stay 504
Fontainebleau, First School of. 77
Fontainebleau, Second School of. 78

Fontevraud l'Abbaye 262
Food and Drink. 53
Food Glossary. 54
Forêt de Tronçais 197
Fort de Salses 395
Fougères 200
Fragonard, Jean-Honoré. 84, 350
Fréminet, Martin 79
French Alps 310
French Revolution. 61
French Riviera (Côte d'Azur) 336
    Tourism. 336
Futuroscope 158

G
Gaffori, Jean-Pierre 285
Gallé, Emile 89
Garrigues 510
Gauguin, Paul 89
Geology 91
Getting Around 36
Getting There 34
Girardon, François. 83
Gobelins. 83
Golf 20
Golfe de Porto 281
Golfe du Morbihan 219
Gorges de Daluis 325
Gorges de l'Ardèche 538
    Pont-d'Arc 538
Gorges du Tarn (Tarn Gorges). 366
    Shopping. 368
    Sports and Recreation. 368
    Stay 368
Gothic Art. 70
Gouffre de Padirac 304
Goujon, Jean. 77
Government 52
Grand Ballon. 127
Grand Canyon du Verdon. 333
    Excursion 335
    La Corniche Sublime 333
    La route des Crêtes. 333
    Walking tours 333, 334, 335
Grand Colombier. 251
Grenoble. 329
    Excursions 330
    Fort de la Bastille. 329
    Musée de Grenoble 329
Greuze, J B 86
Grimaldi family. 343
    Prince Rainier III. 343

INDEX

Grotte de Clamouse 365
Grotte de Lascaux 301
Grotte de l'Aven Armand 367
Grotte des Demoiselles 364
Grotte du Mas-d'Azil 390
Grotte du Pech-Merle 309
Grottes de Bétharram 382
Guimard, Hector .88

H

Hardouin-Mansart, Jules 83
Haussmann,
    Baron Georges-Eugene 87, 450
Hautefort, Château de 297
Haute Soule, La 167
Hauts-Massifs 197
Health 33
Henri IV 59
Héré, Emmanuel 101
Highway code 38
History 56
Hohneck 127
Honfleur 406
Hostels 40
Hotels **40**
Houdon, J A 86
Hundred Years' War 58
Hunspach 115

I

Île-de-France **424**
    Tourism 425
Île de Ré 151
Île d'Ouessant 210
Impressionism 89
Impressionists 405
India Company 215
Industrialisation .88
Ingres, Jean Auguste Dominique 88
International Visitors 32
Islands 22
Issoire 188

J

Jardins et Château de Villandry 268
Joan of Arc 275, 490
Jura Mountains 226

K

Kallisté (Corsica) 278
Kaysersberg 120
Kernascléden 217

Kids
    Activities 21
    Useful Websites 22
Klein, Yves 90
Know Before You Go 30

L

La Baule 225
La Camargue 526
Lac du Bourget .314
Lace 182
La Chaise-Dieu .183
La Clusaz 322
La Cornouaille 213
La Côte de Granit Rose 206
La Côte Vermeille 395
La Couvertoirade 365
La Dombes 177
La Haute Soule .167
La Marseillaise (national anthem) 513
Lamour, Jean 101
Langue d'Oc 374
Languedoc-Roussillon **360**
    Tourism 361
Lannion 206
Laon **494**
    Cathédrale Notre-Dame 494
    Quartier de la Cathédrale 494
La Rhune 164
La Rochelle **150**
    Excursions 151
    Hotels 153
    Restaurants 153
    Vieux Port 151
    Vieux Ville 151
La Saulire 327
La Suisse Normande 411
La Ville Ducale (Dijon) 228
Le Dorat 294
Le Havre **405**
    Excursions 406
    Ste-Adresse 405
Leisure Activities 19
Le Mans **257**
    Motor-racing circuits 257
    Musée de l'Automobile de la Sarthe . . . 258
Lemercier, Jacques 81
Le Nain, Antoine 82
Le Nain, Loius 82
Le Nain, Mathieu 82
Le Nôtre, Andre .83
Le Pont du Gard 536

Le Praz (Courchevel 1300)........... 327
Le Puy de Dôme.................... 189
Le Puy de Sancy 189
Le Puy du Fou 159
  Cinéscénie 160
  Market............................... 159
Le Puy-en-Velay 181
  Cathédrale Notre-Dame............... 182
  Chapelle St-Michel-d'Aiguilhe 182
  Excursions 183
  Religious Art Treasury 182
  Walks................................ 183
Le Puy Mary 191
  Activities 191
  Panorama 191
Les Alpilles........................ 524
Les Andelys 402
  Château Gaillard 402
Les Baux-de-Provence 528
  Excursion 529
Les Corbières (wine) 395
Les Détroits (The Straits)........... 367
Les Eyzies-de-Tayac 300
Les Îles de Lérins 353
Les Monts Dore 190
Les Sables-d'Olonne................151
Lessay 418
le Téméraire, Charles 227
Le Touquet........................437
Le Vieux Honfleur 406
Lifestyle 52
Lille 426
  Eat 430
  Entertainment 430
  Excursion 429
  Guided Tours 426
  Les fêtes des Gayants................. 429
  Le Vieux Lille........................ 426
  Musée d'Art Moderne 429
  Musée des Beaux-Arts................. 427
  Nightlife............................. 430
  Shopping............................. 430
  Stay 430
  Vieille Bourse 426
Limoges 293
  Eat 295
  Enamel 293
  Excursions 294
  Musée Adrien-Dubouché.............. 293
  Shopping............................. 295
  Stay 295
Limosin, Léonard....................81

Limousin........................... 286
Lisieux............................ 406
Loches............................ 267
Locronan 213
  The Troménies 213
Loire Valley 252
L'Oisans 330
Lons-le-Saunier 248
  Excursions 248
  Walking tour......................... 248
Lorient.........................215
  Excursions 217
Loti, Pierre 155
Louis XIV 60
Louis XV 61
Lourdes.........................381
  Eat 386
  Excursions 382
  Leisure Activities..................... 386
  Pilgrimage........................... 381
  Stay 386
Luberon mountain range 537
Lyon 170
  Entertainment 178
  Festival of Lights 172
  Hotels 178
  Le Vieux Lyon (Old Lyon).............. 173
  Musée de l'Imprimerie 174
  Musée des Beaux-Arts................. 175
  Musée des Tissus et Musée des
    Arts Décoratifs 175
  Musée gallo-romain de Fourvière....... 173
  Quartier St-Jean...................... 173
  Restaurants.......................... 178
  Shopping 171
  Town tours........................... 171

M

Magritte, René 90
Mail/Post 45
Maison de Roaldès, Cahors.......... 307
Maison des Vins -
  Cloître des Récollets, Bergerac ... 302
Majorelle, Louis 89
Manet, Edouard 89
Mansart, François 81
Margaret of Austria................. 249
Maritime Alps 336
Markets............................24
Marseille........................511
  Boat trips 519
  Centre de la Vieille Charité............ 512

INDEX

City Pass (sightseeing)................ 511
Corniche Président J.-F.-Kennedy 513
Driving tour.......................... 516
Eat 517
Events 519
Excursions 514
Getting around 512
Musée Grobet Labadi 513
Nightlife 518
Notre-Dame-de-la-Garde 511
Shopping............................ 519
Stay 517
Vieux-Port 512
Walking tours........................ 514
Martel, Edouard A 304
Massif Central 168
Massif de l'Aigoual 364
Massif de la Vanoise 328
Massif de l'Esterel 353
Massif des Calanques................514
Massif des Maures.................. 356
Massif Du Ézenc....................183
Massif du Vercors..................331
Master of Moulins 76
Matisse, Henri.......................89
Media and internet..................52
Meillant, Château de............... 290
Menton **326**
Excursions 348
Lemon Festival...................... 347
Promenade du Soleil 348
Seafront and Beaches 347
Vieille Ville......................... 347
Mercantour National Park.......... 341
Mer de Glace........................319
Metz............................**96**
Cathédrale St-Étienne 97
Centre Pompidou-Metz 97
Hotels 98
Musées de Metz Métropole-La Cour d'Or. 97
Restaurants........................... 98
La Meuse Ardennaise................133
Michelin, André 185
Michelin, Édouard 185
Midi-Pyrénées 360
Millau Viaduct/Millau Bridge........ 368
Millet, Jean-François................88
mistral (wind).......................510
Mobile/Cell phones..................46
Moissac............................. 378
Monaco **343**
Boat Trips............................346

Eat 345
Events 346
Jardin Exotique 344
Le Rocher (The Rock) 343
Monte-Carlo 344
Musée Océanographique.............. 344
Nice School, paintings............... 344
Nightlife............................. 346
Shopping............................. 346
Stay 345
Monet, Claude 89
Money.............................45
Mont Bégo, prehistoric engravings .. 341
Monthermé **133**
Excursions 133
Montpellier **362**
Excursions 363
Musée Fabre 363
Promenade du Peyrou................ 362
Mont-St-Michel 418
Mont Ventoux....................... 543
Mont Vinaigre....................... 354
Moriond (Courchevel 1650) 327
Morzine.............................321
Motor boating 20
Motor-car industry, birthplace 256
Motor tyres 185
Moulins........................**196**
Excursion 197
Moustiers-Ste-Marie................ 333
Mulhouse **125**
Excursion 126
Hôtel de Ville 125
Musée de l'Automobile – Collection
Schlumpf 125
Musée français du Chemin de fer........ 125
Musée
de la Cloche........................ 313
Faure 315
Musée de Tautavel
(Centre européen de préhistoire).. 395
Musée du Tabac, Bergerac 302
Musée National de l'Automate,
Souillac 305

N
Nabis 89
Nancy...........................**101**
Entertainment 106
Hotels 106
Musée de l'École de Nancy........... 104
Musée des Beaux-Arts............... 105

Musée Lorrain............................ 105
Nightlife.................................. 106
Palais ducal 104
Place Stanislas 101
Restaurants.............................. 106
Walking tours............................ 101
Nantes..........................223
Château des Ducs de Bretagne......... 223
Excursions 225
Musée des Beaux-Arts.................. 224
Muséum d'Histoire Naturelle 224
Napoleon 62, 279, 349, 449
Narbonne.......................392
Archaeological Museum................ 393
Cathédrale St-Just..................... 392
Excursion 393
Roman period........................... 392
National Parks.......................... 311
Nature................................... 91
New Realism 90
Nice 337
Carnival 338
Eat 341
Events 342
Excursions 340
Le Vieux Nice (old quarter)............. 337
Musée d'Art Moderne et
    d'Art Contemporain................. 339
Musée des Beaux-Arts.................. 339
Musée Marc-Chagall................... 339
Musée Matisse 339
Nightlife............................... 342
Promenade des Anglais 339
Riviera Pass (sightseeing).............. 337
Shopping............................... 342
Stay 341
Nîmes 530
Arènes 530
Denims................................. 530
Eat 533
Entertainment 533
Excursion 532
Jardin de la Fontaine 530
Maison Carrée 530
Nightlife............................... 533
Roman period.......................... 530
Shopping............................... 533
Stay 533
Noirlac, Abbaye de 290
Norman Conquest..................... 415
Normandy 398
Normandy invasion 413

O
Obernai................................ 115
Opening hours 23
Oradour-sur-Glane 294
Orange 541
Arc de Triomphe 541
Excursions 542
Roman period.......................... 541
Théâtre Antique........................ 541
Oratoire du Chazelet 323
Orcival................................. 189
Orléans 275, 277
Cathédrale Ste-Croix 275
Excursions 276
Musée des Beaux-Arts................. 275
Out and about 19

P
Palissy, Bernard 79
Paoli, Pascal.......................... 285
Parc Astérix 497
Parc des Oiseaux 177
Parc du Marquenterre 440
Visitor information 441
Parc floral de la Source.............. 276
Parc National des Pyrénées 382
Leisure and Recreation 383
Useful Addresses...................... 383
Walking 384
Parc Naturel Régional de Camargue . 526
Parc Naturel Régional du Luberon....537
Parc Pyrénéen de l'Art Préhistorique
    (Tarascon-sur-Ariège) 390
Paris...........................445
Eat 461, 480
Ecclesiastical Architecture
    Abbaye de St-Germain-des-Prés 464
    Cathédrale Notre-Dame.............. 462
    Église Notre-Dame-du-Val-
        de-Grâce 465
    Église St-Eustache................... 464
    Église St-Séverin-St-Nicolas.......... 464
    Sainte-Chapelle..................... 463
    Entertainment 481
    Excursions 476
    Fairs and Exhibitions 482
    Getting around 446
    History 445
Monuments
    Arc de Triomphe 459
    École Militaire...................... 461
    Hôtel National des Invalides 458

INDEX

Opéra Garnier 462
Palais de Chaillot 462
Palais de Justice and Conciergerie 460
Palais du Louvre 453
Palais-Royal 461
Panthéon 462
Place de la Concorde 460
Tour Eiffel 460
Museums
Cité des Sciences et de l'Industrie 474
Hôtel de Cluny (Musée national
    du Moyen Âge) 473
Musée Carnavalet 475
Musée de l'Armée
    (Hôtel National des Invalides) 473
Musée de l'Orangerie 473
Musée des Arts et Métiers 474
Musée d'Orsay 469
Musée du Louvre 469, 470
Musée du Quai Branly 474
Musée Marmottan-Monet 475
Musée National d'Art Moderne
    (Centre Georges Pompidou) 469
Palais de la Découverte 474
Parks and Gardens 476
Political and Intellectual Sights
Institut de France 467
Montmartre 468
Palais du Luxembourg 468
Quartier Latin 468
Revolution, The 448
Shopping 481
Sport 482
Stay 461, 480
Urban Design
Champs-Élysées 466
La Défense 466
La Grande Arche 466
La Villette 467
La Voie Triomphale 466
Le Marais 465
Parking regulations 38
Pau **166**
Château 167
Pays de Loire 138
Pays noir 424
Périgueux **296**
Eat 298
Excursions 297
Shopping 298
Stay 298
St-Front District 296

Pérouges 176
Perpignan **394**
Excursions 395
Perret, Auguste 405
Petrol/Gasoline 36
Piaf, Édith 468
Picardy 425
Picasso, Pablo 89
Pic de Pibeste 382
Pic du Midi de Bigorre 383
Pigalle, J B 86
Pilon, Germain 77
Pissarro, Camille 89
Plane travel 34
Planète Sauvage 225
Pointe du Raz 214
Poitiers **155**
Église Notre-Dame-la-Grande 156
Excursions 158
Hotels 158
Musée Ste-Croix 157
Restaurants 159
Poitou-Charentes .138
Pontarlier 246
Pont-Aven School 89
Population 52
Prieuré de Serrabone 397
Primaticcio 77
Provence 510
Provins **137**
Excursion 137
Ville Haute 137
Public holidays 46
Puget, Pierre 83
Pyrénées mountain range 360, 382

Q
Quarton, Enguerrand 76
Quercy 306
Quimper **212**
Cathédrale St-Corentin 212
Excursions 213
Musée des Beaux-Arts 212

R
Rail Europe 35
Rambouillet **506**
Forêt de Rambouillet 508
Walks and Tours 508
Regional Parks 311
Reims **128**
Basilique St-Rémi 130

Cathédrale Notre-Dame 129
Champagne Houses 131
Chocolatiers 131
Events 131
Hotels 130
Nightlife 131
Restaurants 130
Religion 52
Renaissance 76
René, Duke of Anjou 520
Rennes 199
Excursions 200
Palais du Parlement de Bretagne 199
Renoir, Auguste 293
Renoir, Pierre Auguste 89
Réserve Naturelle de Scandola 281
Résistance 330
Restaurants 41
Rhône Valley 168
Riding and pony trekking 20
Riding Tours 21
Parc du Marquenterre 441
Riom 193
Riquewihr 122
Hotels 124
Restaurants 124
Walking tour 122
River and canal cruising 19
River Loire 252
River Var, Upper Valley 325
Robespierre, Maximilien 443
Rocamadour 303
Excursions 304
Rochefort 154
Excursions 154
Rock climbing 20
Rodez 371
Rodin, Auguste 89, 432
Roman Empire 510
Romanesque Art 66
Roquebrune-Cap Martin 348
Roscoff 207
Rosso 77
Rouen 399
Aître St-Maclou 400
Cathédrale Notre-Dame 399
Eat 404
Église St-Maclou 400
Église St-Ouen 400
Entertainment 404
Excursions 401
Musée de la Céramique 401

Musée des Beaux-Arts 400
Musée Le Secq des Tournelles 401
Nightlife 404
Palais de Justice 401
Shopping 404
Stay 404
Vieux Rouen 399
Route des Crêtes .127
Route des Grandes Alpes 321
Driving tour 321
Route des Vins 122
Route Napoléon 349
Antibes 349
Barrage de Sautet 351
Ceramics 351
Eat 351
Events 351
Grasse 350
Route planning 38
Royan 152
Rueil-Malmaison 478

S

Sailing 19
Saintes 154
Saint-Véran 324
Salers 192
Sancerre 291
Wine 291
Saône Valley 226
Saorge 348
Sarlat-la-Canéda 299
Excursions 300
Old Sarlat 299
Sarrazin, Jacques .82
Sartène 283
Saumur 260
Château 261
Excursions 262
Saut du Doubs 245
Scuba-diving 20
Seasons 18
Senlis 495
Cathédrale Notre-Dame 495
Sens 241
Cathédrale St-Étienne 241
Sérusier, Paul 89
Sète 363
Seurat, Georges 89
Sèvres 479
Shopping 23
Signac, Paul 89

INDEX

Sisteron. 335
Skiing. 20
Smoking. 46
Solignac 294
Sommet de la Saulire 328
Soubirous, Bernadette (of Lourdes). . 381
Spas and well-being. 20
Sport 52
St-Bertrand-de-Comminges 378
St-Brieuc. **204**
   Excursions 205
St-Étienne 180
St-Flour. 192
St Francis of Sales 312
St-Germain-en-Laye **488**
   Eat 489
   Excursion 488
   Musée des Antiquités nationales. 488
St-Guilhem-le-Désert 365
St-Jean-de-Luz **164**
   Église St-Jean Baptiste. 164
   Excursions 164
St-Malo **201**
   Excursions 202
   Le Grand Aquarium 201
   Old Town and Ramparts 201
St-Omer 434
St-Pol-de-Léon **207**
   Enclos Paroissial de St-Thégonnec 208
   Excursions 207
Strasbourg. **108**
   Cathédrale Notre-Dame. 109
   Excursion 115
   Hotels 116
   La Petite France 113
   Musée d'Art Moderne et Contemporain . 114
   Musée de l'Œuvre Notre-Dame 111
   On the town 117
   Restaurants. 116
   Rue du Bain-aux-Plantes. 113
   Walking tours 112
St-Rémy-de-Provence 529
St-Savin. 158
St-Tropez **356**
   Eat 357
   Excursions 356
   Musée de l'Annonciade. 356
   Nightlife 357
   Shopping. 357
   Stay 357

St-Tropez Peninsula. 356
Sueur, Eustache le 82
Surrealism 90

T

Tax refunds 46
Telephones 46
Temperature chart 48
Temple de Diane, Aix-les-Bains. 315
Thonon-les-Bains 321
Time. 47
Tipping 48
Tolls 39
Topography. 91
Toulon **358**
   Excursions 359
   La Rade 358
   Mont Faron 358
Toulouse **374**
   Basilique St-Sernin 374
   Eat 379
   Église des Jacobins 375
   Events 380
   Excursions 376
   Hôtel d'Assezat 376
   Leisure Activities. 380
   Musée des Augustins. 376
   Musée St-Raymond 376
   Muséum d'Histoire Naturelle 376
   Nightlife 380
   Shopping 380
   Stay 379
   Toulouse City Pass (sightseeing) 374
de la Tour, Georges 82
Tourist Offices. 30
Tournier, Nicolas 82
Tours **21, 264**
   Cathédrale St-Gatien 264
   Eat 269
   Excursions 265
   Musée des Beaux-Arts. 264
   Musée du Compagnonnage 265
   Shopping 269
   Stay 269
Train travel. 35, 36
Tréguier 205
Troyes **134**
   Cathédrale St-Pierre et St-Paul. 135
   Entertainment 136
   Hotels 135

Maison de l'Outil et de la
  Pensée ouvrière..................... 134
Musée d'Art Moderne 135
Nightlife............................... 136
Old Town 134
Shopping............................. 136

U

UNESCO World Heritage Sites 49
Useful Websites 30
Useful Words and Phrases 41

V

Vaison-la-Romaine 542
Val d'Isère......................... 323
Vallée des Merveilles 340
Valois, House of 58
Van Gogh, Vincent.............. 89, 488
Vannes 218
  Excursions 219
  Vieille Ville (Old Town)................. 218
VAT..................................24
le Vau, Louis..........................81
Vauban, Marquis de 428
Vendée...............................61
Vendée Globe........................152
Vendôme 273
Veneti 218
Vercors Regional Natural Park.......331
Verdun 99
Verdun, Champ de Bataille
  de (Battlefield) 100
Vesunna - Musée Gallo-Romain
  de Périgueux 297
Vézelay 243
Vichy 193
  Excursions 193
  Springs 194
Vieil-Armand........................127
Vienne..........................179
  Cathédrale St-Maurice................. 179
  Temple d'Auguste et de Livie 179
Viollet-le-Duc.......................87
Vitré...............................200
Vuillard, Edouard....................89

W

Walking...............................19
Walking Tours
  Abbaye de Cluny 250
  Alençon Old Town..................... 421
  Beaune ramparts...................... 235
  Beaune town centre................... 234
  Belvédère de Rancoumas
    (Grand Canyon du Verdon) 335
  Cahors............................... 306
  Gorges du Tarn........................ 368
  Marseille calanques 514
  Massif de Néouvielle 385
  Nancy: Lorraine's Capital City.......... 101
  Nancy Old Town and New Town 104
  Parc du Marquenterre 441
  Rambouillet 508
  Riquewihr 122
  Sentier de Découverte des Lézards
    (Grand Canyon du Verdon) 334
  Sentier des Cascades 248
  Sentier Martel (Grand Canyon du Verdon). 333
  Strasbourg Old Town................... 112
  Strasbourg Old Town via Place Broglie .. 114
  Vallée de Gavarnie 384
  Vallée des Merveilles 341
  Vallées des Cauterets.................. 384
Wars of Religion......................59
Water-skiing 20
Watteau, Antoine 84
Weather Forecast 18
What to See and Do 19
When and Where to Go...............18
Where to Eat 41
Where to Stay 39
William, Duke of Normandy
  ('The Conqueror').........57, 409, 415
Wine Tours...........................21
Winterhalter, Franz Zaver 88

Y

Yvoire 317

Z

Zoo de la Palmyre 153

INDEX

🏨 STAY

Aix-en-Provence 522
Albi 372
Amiens 441
Angers 258
Arles 526
Arras 444
Avignon 539
Bayeux 416
Beaune 238
Besançon 247
Biarritz 162
Blois 274
Bordeaux 144
Bourges 291
Caen 412
Cahors 309
Cannes 354
Carcassonne 391
Chartres 509
Château de Versailles 487
Colmar 120
Compiègne 493
Coutances 419
Dijon 231
Fontainebleau 504

Gorges du Tarn 368
La Rochelle 153
Le Puy Mary 192
Lille 430
Limoges 295
Lourdes 386
Lyon 178
Marseille 517
Metz 98
Monaco 345
Nancy 106
Nice 341
Nîmes 533
Paris 461, 480
Périgueux 298
Poitiers 158
Reims 130
Riquewihr 124
Rouen 404
Strasbourg 116
St-Tropez 357
Toulouse 379
Tours 269
Troyes 135

🍴 EAT

Aix-en-Provence 522
Albi 373
Amiens 442
Angers 259
Arles 527
Arras 444
Avignon 539
Bayeux 416
Beaune 238
Besançon 247
Biarritz 162
Blois 274
Bordeaux 145
Bourges 292
Caen 412
Cahors 309
Cannes 355
Carcassonne 391
Chartres 509
Château de Versailles 487
Colmar 121
Compiègne 493
Coutances 419
Dijon 231

Fontainebleau 504
La Rochelle 153
Lille 430
Limoges 295
Lourdes 386
Lyon 178
Marseille 517
Metz 98
Monaco 345
Nancy 106
Nice 341
Nîmes 533
Paris 461, 480
Périgueux 298
Poitiers 159
Reims 130
Riquewihr 124
Rouen 404
Route Napoléon 351
St-Germain-en-Laye 489
Strasbourg 116
St-Tropez 357
Toulouse 379
Tours 269

MAPS AND PLANS

THEMATIC MAPS

Relief Map . . . . Inside front cover
Paris Métro and
    Arrondissements . . . Inside back cover
Principal Sights. .8-15
The Growth of France. 57

MAPS AND PLANS

Alsace Lorraine Champagne
Alsace Lorraine Champagne 94-95
Nancy 103
Strasbourg 110-111
Route des Vins. 123

Atlantic Coast
Atlantic Coast 139

Auvergne Rhône Valley
Auvergne Rhône Valley. 169

Brittany
Brittany. 198

Burgundy Jura
Burgundy Jura 226
Cluny Abbey, Bourg-en-Bresse. 250

Châteaux of the Loire
Châteaux of the Loire. 252

Corsica
Corsica 278
Ajaccio. 279
Bonifacio 282
Bastia. 284

Dordogne Berry Limousin
Dordogne Berry Limousin 287

French Alps
French Alps 311

French Riviera
French Riviera. 336

Languedoc-Roussillon Tarn Gorges
Languedoc-Roussillon Tarn Gorges. 361
Carcassonne: La Cité. 388

Normandy
Normandy 398

Northern France and Paris
Northern France and Paris 425
Louvre Palace, Paris. 454
Central Paris 456-457
Les Invalides Church, Paris 458
Principal Districts of Paris by Activity . . . 479
Château de Versailles Palace 484
Château de Versailles: The Park 485
Château de Fontainebleau. 503
Chartres Cathedral 506

Provence
Provence 510

MAP LEGEND

★★★ **Highly recommended**

★★ **Recommended**

★ **Interesting**

Tourism

	Sightseeing route with departure point indicated	AZ B	Map co-ordinates locating sights
	Ecclesiastical building		Tourist information
	Synagogue – Mosque		Historic house, castle – Ruins
	Building (with main entrance)		Dam – Factory or power station
	Statue, small building		Fort – Cave
	Wayside cross		Prehistoric site
	Fountain		Viewing table – View
	Fortified walls – Tower – Gate		Miscellaneous sight

Recreation

	Racecourse		Waymarked footpath
	Skating rink		Outdoor leisure park/centre
	Outdoor, indoor swimming pool		Theme/Amusement park
	Marina, moorings		Wildlife/Safari park, zoo
	Mountain refuge hut		Gardens, park, arboretum
	Overhead cable-car		Aviary, bird sanctuary
	Tourist or steam railway		

Additional symbols

	Motorway (unclassified)		Post office – Telephone centre
	Junction: complete, limited		Covered market
	Pedestrian street		Barracks
	Unsuitable for traffic, street subject to restrictions		Swing bridge
	Steps – Footpath		Quarry – Mine
	Railway – Coach station		Ferry (river and lake crossings)
	Funicular – Rack-railway		Ferry services: Passengers and cars
	Tram – Metro, underground		Foot passengers only
Bert (R.)...	Main shopping street		Access route number common to MICHELIN maps and town plans

Abbreviations and special symbols

A	Agricultural office (Chambre d'agriculture)	P	Local authority offices (Préfecture, sous-préfecture)
C	Chamber of commerce (Chambre de commerce)	POL.	Police station (Police)
H	Town hall (Hôtel de ville)		Police station (Gendarmerie)
J	Law courts (Palais de justice)	T	Theatre (Théâtre)
M	Museum (Musée)	U	University (Université)
			Hotel
			Park and Ride

Some town plans are extracts from plans used in the Green Guides to the regions of France.

COMPANION PUBLICATIONS

LOCAL MAPS

For each site in this guide, you will find map references which correspond to **local maps (nos 301 to 345)** of France.

MAPS OF FRANCE

For all of France, there are 5 formats at a 1:1 000 000 scale to choose from: **France no 721**, **the whole country** on a single sheet with an index of place names; **no 722**, **reversible, divided north/south**; **no 724, northern France**; **no 725 southern France**; and the collection of atlases. Atlases to France are published in several formats for your convenience: spiral, paperback and hardback all include the Paris region, town plans and an index of place names. Now available in a mini format as well. You may also wish to consult **no 728 France Administrative**, showing regions, departments, main roads, distance tables, universities.

MOTORWAYS

Other useful maps include **no 726 Route Planning**, with motorways, alternative routes, journey times and 24-hour service stations.

INTERNET

Michelin is pleased to offer a route-planning service on the Internet: **www.viamichelin.com** **www.travel.viamichelin.com** Choose the shortest route, a route without tolls, or the Michelin recommended route to your destination; you can also access information about hotels and restaurants from *The Michelin Guide*, and tourist sites from *The Green Guide*.

YOU ALREADY KNOW THE GREEN GUIDE, NOW FIND OUT ABOUT THE MICHELIN GROUP

The Michelin Adventure

It all started with rubber balls! This was the product made by a small company based in Clermont-Ferrand that André and Edouard Michelin inherited, back in 1880. The brothers quickly saw the potential for a new means of transport and their first success was the invention of detachable pneumatic tires for bicycles. However, the automobile was to provide the greatest scope for their creative talents. Throughout the 20th century, Michelin never ceased developing and creating ever more reliable and high-performance tires, not only for vehicles ranging from trucks to F1 but also for underground transit systems and airplanes.

From early on, Michelin provided its customers with tools and services to facilitate mobility and make traveling a more pleasurable and more frequent experience. As early as 1900, the Michelin Guide supplied motorists with a host of useful information related to vehicle maintenance, accommodation and restaurants, and was to become a benchmark for good food. At the same time, the Travel Information Bureau offered travelers personalised tips and itineraries.

The publication of the first collection of roadmaps, in 1910, was an instant hit! In 1926, the first regional guide to France was published, devoted to the principal sites of Brittany, and before long each region of France had its own Green Guide. The collection was later extended to more far-flung destinations, including New York in 1968 and Taiwan in 2011.

In the 21st century, with the growth of digital technology, the challenge for Michelin maps and guides is to continue to develop alongside the company's tire activities. Now, as before, Michelin is committed to improving the mobility of travelers.

MICHELIN TODAY

WORLD NUMBER ONE TIRE MANUFACTURER

- 70 production sites in 18 countries
- 111,000 employees from all cultures and on every continent
- 6,000 people employed in research and development

Moving
for a world

Moving forward means developing tires with better road grip and shorter braking distances, whatever the state of the road.

CORRECT TIRE PRESSURE

RIGHT PRESSURE

- Safety
- Longevity
- Optimum fuel consumption

-0,5 bar

- Durability reduced by 20% (- 8,000 km)

-1 bar

- Risk of blowouts
- Increased fuel consumption
- Longer braking distances on wet surfaces

forward together
where mobility is safer

It also involves helping motorists take care of their safety and their tires. To do so, Michelin organises "Fill Up With Air" campaigns all over the world to remind us that correct tire pressure is vital.

WEAR

DETECTING TIRE WEAR

The legal minimum depth of tire tread is 1.6mm. Tire manufacturers equip their tires with tread wear indicators, which are small blocks of rubber moulded into the base of the main grooves at a depth of 1.6mm.

Tires are the only point of contact between the vehicle and road.

The photo below shows the actual contact zone.

NEW TIRE

WORN TIRE
(1,6 mm tread)

If the tread depth is less than 1.6mm, tires are considered to be worn and dangerous on wet surfaces.

Moving forward
means sustainable mobility

By 2050, Michelin aims to cut the quantity of raw materials used in its tire manufacturing process by half and to have developed renewable energy in its facilities. The design of MICHELIN tires has already saved billions of litres of fuel and, by extension, billions of tons of CO2.

Similarly, Michelin prints its maps and guides on paper produced from sustainably managed forests and is diversifying its publishing media by offering digital solutions to make traveling easier, more fuel efficient and more enjoyable!

The group's whole-hearted commitment to eco-design on a daily basis is demonstrated by ISO 14001 certification.

Like you, Michelin is committed to preserving our planet.

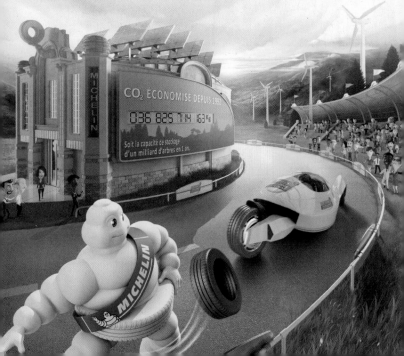